PEARSON

my World
GEOGRAPHY
PART 2

D1203651

PEARSON

Taken from:

My World Geography
Copyright © 2012 by Pearson Education, Inc.
Published by Prentice Hall
Upper Saddle River, New Jersey 07458

This special edition published in cooperation with Pearson Learning Solutions.

Pearson Learning Solutions, 501 Boylston Street, Suite 900
Boston, MA 02116
A Pearson Education Company
www.pearsoned.com

Printed in the United States of America

6 7 8 9 10 V0UD 20 19 18 17 16

000200010271276446

EG

PEARSON

ISBN-10: 1-256-33195-3
ISBN-13: 978-1-256-33195-7

Program Authors

Gregory H. Chu, a native of Hong Kong, is Professor and Chair of Geography at the University of Wisconsin-La Crosse and Editor of *FOCUS on Geography*, a journal published by the American Geographical Society. He earned his Ph.D. degree in geography from the University of Hawaii and has served as Program Director of Geography and Regional Science at the National Science Foundation, on the Editorial Board of *Cartographic Perspectives*, and Board of Directors of the North American Cartographic Information Society.

Susan Hardwick is a geography professor at the University of Oregon. She is an expert in the human geography of North America and is the past president of the National Council for Geographic Education. She is best known as the co-host of *The Power of Place*, an Annenberg geography series produced for public television. Professor Hardwick was awarded the Association of America's Gilbert Grosvenor Award in Geographic Education, the National Council for Geographic Education's Outstanding Mentor Award, and the statewide California Outstanding Professor Award when she taught at California State University, Chico, before moving to Oregon. She is the parent of four grown sons who all live on a west coast.

Don Holtgrieve received his Ph.D. degree in geography from the University of Oregon and was a professor of geography and environmental studies in the California State University system for 30 years. He now teaches geography and environmental planning at the University of Oregon. His attraction to geography was the interdisciplinary nature of the field and the opportunity to do research out-of-doors. Dr. Holtgrieve enjoys bringing his "real-world" experiences as a high school teacher, community planner, police officer, and consultant to government agencies into his writing and teaching.

Program Consultant

Grant Wiggins is the President of Authentic Education in Hopewell, New Jersey. He earned his Ed.D. degree from Harvard University and his B.A. from St. John's College in Annapolis, Maryland. Wiggins consults with schools, districts, and state education departments on a variety of reform matters; organizes conferences and workshops; and develops print materials and Web resources on curricular change. Over the past 20 years, Wiggins has worked on some of the most influential reform initiatives in the country, including Vermont's portfolio system and Ted Sizer's Coalition of Essential Schools. He is the coauthor, with Jay McTighe, of *Understanding by Design* and *The Understanding by Design Handbook*, the award-winning and highly successful materials on curriculum published by ASCD. He is also the author of *Educative Assessment* and *Assessing Student Performance*, both published by Jossey-Bass.

Academic Reviewers

Africa
Benjamin Ofori-Amoah
Department of Geography
Western Michigan University
Kalamazoo, Michigan

Australia and the Pacific
Christine Drake, Ph.D.
Department of Political Science
  and Geography
Old Dominion University
Norfolk, Virginia

Peter N. D. Pirie
Department of Geography
University of Hawaii at Manoa
Honolulu, Hawaii

East and Southeast Asia
Jessie P. H. Poon
Department of Geography
University of Buffalo
State University of New York
Buffalo, New York

Susan M. Walcott
Department of Geography
University of North Carolina
  at Greensboro
Greensboro, North Carolina

Europe
William H. Berentsen
Department of Geography
University of Connecticut
Storrs, Connecticut

Nancy Partner
Department of History
McGill University
Montreal, Quebec, Canada

Charles Rearick
Department of History
University of Massachusetts
Amherst, Massachusetts

Middle and South America
Connie Weil
Department of Geography
University of Minnesota
Minneapolis, Minnesota

North America
Mark Drayse
Department of Geography
California State University
Fullerton, California

South and Central Asia
Dr. Reuel R. Hanks
Department of Geography
Oklahoma State University
Stillwater, Oklahoma

Pradyumna P. Karan
Department of Geography
University of Kentucky
Lexington, Kentucky

Southwest Asia
Michael E. Bonine
School of Geography and
  Development
Department of Near Eastern
  Studies
University of Arizona
Tucson, Arizona

Shaul Cohen
Department of Geography
University of Oregon
Eugene, Oregon

Religion
Brent Isbell
Department of Religious Studies
University of Houston
Houston, Texas

Shabbir Mansuri
Munir Shaikh
Institute on Religion and
  Civic Values
Fountain Valley, California

Gordon Newby
Department of Middle Eastern
  and South Asian Studies
Emory University
Atlanta, Georgia

Robert Platzner, Ph.D.
Emeritus Professor of
Humanities and Religious
Studies
California State University
Sacramento, California

Master Teachers and Contributing Authors

George F. Sabato
Past President, California Council for
   the Social Studies
Placerville Union School District
Placerville, California

Michael Yell
President, National Council for
   the Social Studies
Hudson Middle School
Hudson, Wisconsin

Teacher Consultants

James F. Dowd IV
Pasadena, California

Susan M. Keane
Rochester Memorial School
Rochester, Massachusetts

Timothy T. Sprain
Lincoln Middle School
LaCrosse, Wisconsin

Marilyn Weiser
North Dakota Geographic
   Alliance Coordinator
Minot State University
Minot, North Dakota

Reviewers

Carol Bacak-Egbo
Waterford Schools
Waterford, Michigan

John Brill
Bellevue School District
Bellevue, Washington

Helene Brown
Gwinnett County Public Schools
Lawrenceville, Georgia

Sherry Echols
Hartselle Junior High School
Hartselle, Alabama

MaryLynne Fillmon
George N. Smith Junior High
Mesa, Arizona

Douglas Fillmore
Bloomington Junior High School
Bloomington, Illinois

Chad Hayes
Beadle Middle School
Omaha, Nebraska

Bill Huser
Prairie Catholic Middle School
Prairie du Chien, Wisconsin

Steve Missal
Saint Peter's College
Jersey City, New Jersey

James Reed
Caledonia High School
Caledonia, Mississippi

Gina S. Rikard
Greenwood Middle School
Goldsboro, North Carolina

Chuck Schierloh
Lima City Schools
Lima, Ohio

Welcome to
my World Geography!

We hope you enjoy learning more about your world and its people. One of the most difficult parts of studying world geography is that there are nearly 7 billion people in the world. It's very difficult to think about such a large number. To make it easier, the map on these pages shows the world divided into regions. Page numbers on the map indicate where in the book you can read about each region.

This map also shows how many people would live in each region if there were only 100 people in the entire world.

We hope you enjoy your exploration of your world.

The myWorld authors

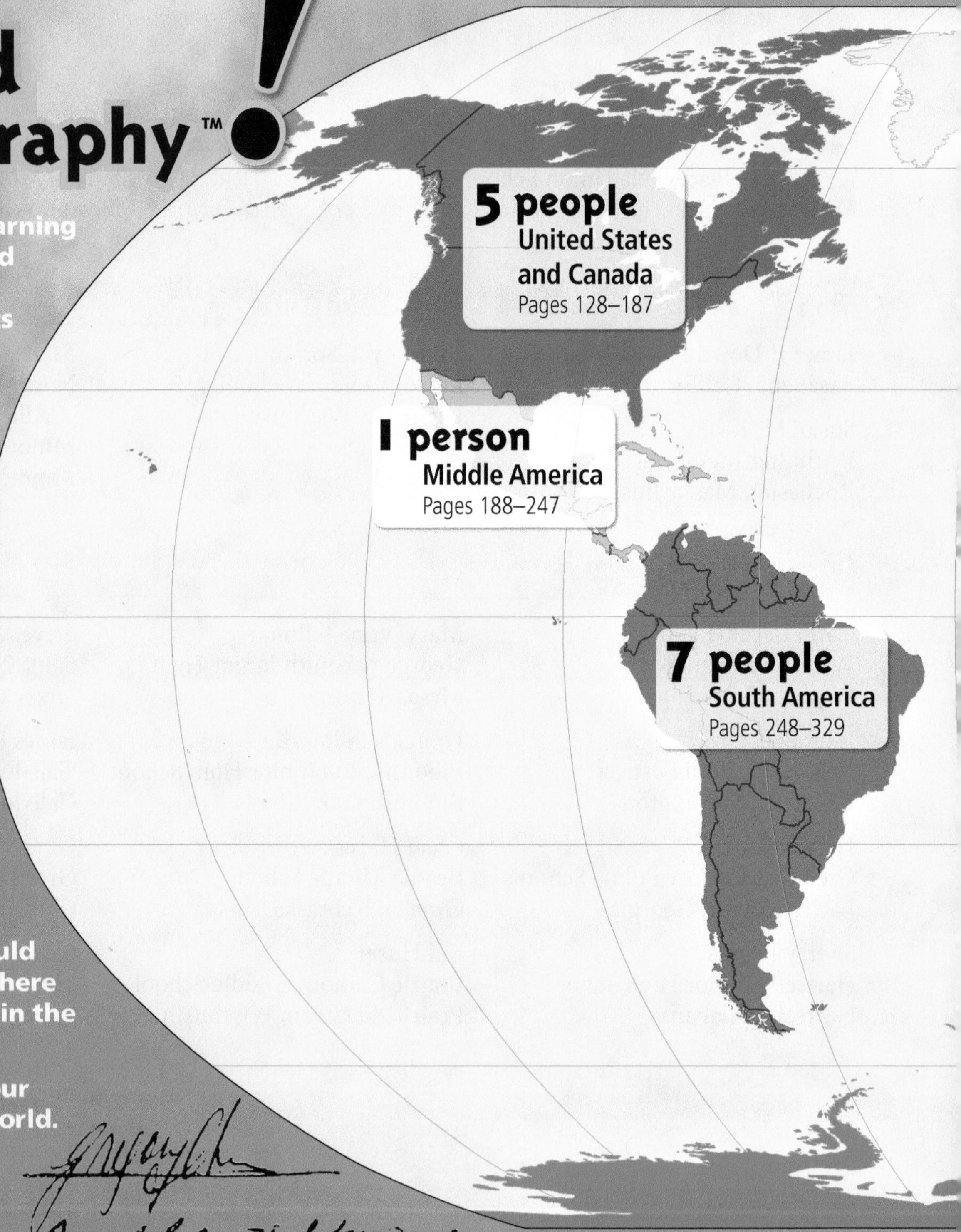

5 people
United States and Canada
Pages 128–187

1 person
Middle America
Pages 188–247

7 people
South America
Pages 248–329

11 people
Europe and Russia
Pages 330–493

32 people
East and Southeast Asia
Pages 736–823

4 people
Southwest Asia
Pages 580–673

15 people
Africa
Pages 494–579

24 people
South and
Central Asia
Pages 674–735

1 person
Australia and
the Pacific
Pages 824–859

If there were **100 people** in the world,
where would they *live?*

Contents

Core Concepts Handbook

Core Concepts Handbook

Unit 6 Southwest Asia

Unit 7 South and Central Asia

myWorld **Geography** Contents

Unit 8 East and Southeast Asia

Unit 9 Australia and the Pacific

my Story

Connect to stories of real teens from around the world.

21st Century Learning

Learn new skills through interactive activities.

Closer Look

Photographs, maps, charts, illustrations, and text help you take a closer look at the world.

Case Studies

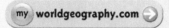 my worldgeography.com ➔

Go online to explore and investigate important global topics.

Primary Sources

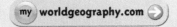

Go online to compare viewpoints through eyewitness accounts and documents.

Charts, Graphs, and Diagrams

Diagrams and data help you visually access important information.

Charts, Graphs, and Diagrams (continued)

Maps

Interactive Maps help you actively learn and understand your world.

Maps (continued)

CONNECT  EXPERIE

Welcome to a new and exciting way to learn about world geography. The *myWorld Geography* program is a blend of technology, hands-on activities, and student books that will take you on a one-of-a-kind journey around the globe and through history. Get ready to connect, experience, and build an understanding of the world in a whole new way.

CONNECT
to Different Cultures and People

Develop a deeper understanding of your world by making personal connections to the people and places in *myWorld Geography*.

myStory videos introduce you to the stories, families, hopes, and challenges of 23 real teens from around the world.

my Story

Xiao
Age: 18
Home: Wutang village, China
Chapter 21

Regional Overview

East and
Southeast

East and Southeast Asia are regions mountains, vast plains, dense forests crowded coastlines. These regions are populated. The largest country in these is China, which has more inhabitants tha other country on Earth.

The Unit Ahead
- Chapter 21 China and Its Neighbors
- Chapter 22 Japan and the Koreas
- Chapter 23 Southeast Asia

my worldgeography.com
Plan your trip online by doing a Data Discovery Activity and watching the myStory Videos of the region's teens.

my Story
Xiao
Age: 18
Home: Wutang village, China
Chapter 21

my Story
Asuka
Age: 18
Home: Yokohama, Japan
Chapter 22

my Story
Ridwan
Age: 19
Home: Bukittinggi, Indonesia
Chapter 23

Rice fields in Bali, Indonesia

See for yourself at myWorldPearson.com/learnmore

UNDERSTAND

EXPERIENCE
the World in New Ways

Travel across regions and through time—without a passport. *myWorld Geography's* interactive approach using technology, student books, and classroom activities will make learning geography fun and exciting.

Take a virtual and interactive trip around the world with myWorldGeography.com.

UNDERSTAND
and "Own" Your Learning

myWorld Geography isn't just about reading content—it's about providing you with the tools so you really "get it."

Finding answers to the Essential Questions—found throughout the print, digital, and hands-on activities—helps you understand the key ideas of world geography.

China and Its Neighbors: Population Density

KEY
Population Density

Persons per sq. mile		Persons per sq. kilometer
500		195
300		115
150		60
25		10
1		1

Urban Areas
- ☐ More than 10,000,000
- △ 5,000,000–10,000,000
- ○ Less than 5,000,000

0 ——— 400 mi
0 ——— 400 km
Lambert Conformal Conic Projection

Ulaanbaatar
Harbin
MONGOLIA
Changchun Jilin
Ürümqi
Shenyang
Kashgar
Beijing
Tianjin
Zibo
Yellow Sea
Xi'an
CHINA
Wuxi Shangh
Plateau of Tibet
Wuhan
Chengdu
East China Sea
Lhasa
Chongqing
Taipei
TAIWAN
Guangzhou Shenzhen
Hong Kong
South China Sea
Bay of Bengal
Hainan
TROPIC OF CANCER

Name _____ Class _____ Date _____

? Essential Question

How can you measure success?

Preview Before you begin this chapter, think about the Essential Question. Understanding how the Essential Question connects to your life will help you understand the chapter you are about to read.

Connect to Your Life

1. Think of some ways to measure success in the categories shown in the chart below. List at least one way in each column. For example, under school you could list grades.

Measures of Personal Success

Family	Friends	School	Other (Sports, Arts, Chores)

Core Concepts Handbook

Part 1

Tools of Geography

Learn about the study of Earth.

page 2

Part 2

Our Planet, Earth

Examine the forces that affect Earth.

page 16

Part 3

Climates and Ecosystems

Learn about how climate and weather affect the world and its lifeforms.

page 30

Part 4

Human– Environment Interaction

Explore the ways in which people use resources and affect the environment.

page 46

Part 5

Economics and Geography

Study how people make economic decisions.

page 56

Part

6

Population and Movement

Learn how and why people live in certain places.

page 72

Part

7

Culture and Geography

Understand how the practices of a people make up their culture, and how culture can change over time.

page 84

Part

8

Government and Citizenship

Learn about how people organize governments and what governments do.

page 102

Part

9

Tools of History

Examine the ways in which people study history.

page 116

Tools of Geography

Several Maijuna people study a map.

A Peruvian toucan overlooks mountains and rain forest. The Maijuna live in a rain forest area.

2

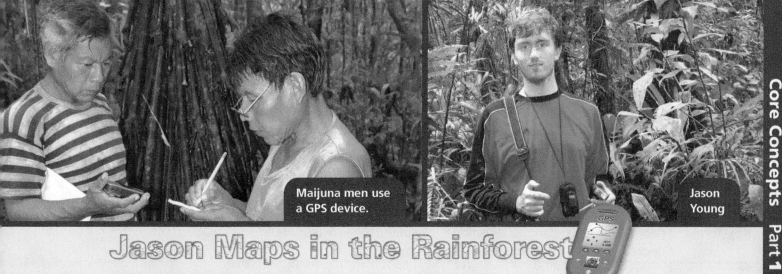

Maijuna men use a GPS device.

Jason Young

Jason Maps in the Rainforest

Story by Miles Lemaire for myWorld

There were a number of things that took some getting used to for Jason Young when he first traveled to Peru. There was no electricity in the village where he was living, which meant that there was no place to charge his cell phone. The same was true for his computer, which he could not use much since there was no Internet connection.

He was alone in a foreign country, eating food that the hunters of the village provided for him. He ate toucan and piranha. "It is an entirely different world," Jason says. "The people there are living off the rainforest, so they go hunting and whatever they catch is what I eat."

Nothing about this place on the edge of the Amazon jungle felt like home to Jason. However, it was home to the people of the Maijuna (mai HU na) tribe and he was going to help them prove it.

According to Jason, the Maijuna "do not own the land where they live, and it is being threatened by things like logging. The Peruvian government wants to construct a road right through some of their traditional territory."

Fortunately, there is a way for the Maijuna to keep their land if they can prove their ownership of it. To do this, they need accurate maps of the area.

That is where Jason comes in. Jason studies geography, which deals with the human and nonhuman features of Earth. Using his geography skills, he has created maps to help the Maijuna prove their case. He used a GPS device, which uses satellites to locate places on Earth's surface.

Jason says, "I went down there and worked with them for four months over different field seasons. I worked with them to do what is called participatory mapping. It is where you have them draw what they believe is their territory on their traditional land. You use that to go out with a GPS unit and collect [data] points from each of the different spots. I actually took video interviews of them talking about the history of the spots that we went to."

Maijuna people took pictures of the spots, and Jason is working on putting them online in an interactive map. Eventually, users will be able to click on traditional sites to view videos or pictures.

"We are hoping to use that mostly as a teaching tool for safeguarding the Maijuna's traditions, as well as using it as a tool with which to speak to the government."

Jason's involvement with the Maijuna came to an end in 2009. Still, his bond with the Maijuna is so strong that he wants to revisit his new friends as often as he can. He feels that he has learned a lot from his experience.

"The level of poverty opened my eyes to how privileged I have been and how much potential I have to give back to the world," Jason says.

3

Geography: The Study of Earth

Key Ideas
- Geographers use directions to help locate points on Earth's surface.
- Geographers have drawn imaginary lines around Earth, dividing it into parts to help pinpoint locations.

Key Terms
- geography
- degree
- cardinal direction
- hemisphere
- sphere
- longitude
- latitude

→ **Visual Glossary**

Geography is the study of the human and nonhuman features of Earth, our home. Geographers try to answer two basic questions: Where are things located? Why are they there? To answer these questions, geographers study oceans, plant life, landforms, countries, and cities. Geographers also study how Earth and its people affect each other.

Directions

In order to study Earth, geographers need to measure it and locate points on its surface. One way to do this is with directions. Geographers use both cardinal and intermediate directions. The **cardinal directions** are north, east, south, and west. Intermediate directions lie between the cardinal directions. For example, northwest is halfway between north and west.

Latitude

Earth is an almost perfect **sphere** (sfeer), or round-shaped body. Geographers have drawn imaginary lines around Earth to help locate places on its surface. One of these is the Equator, a line drawn around Earth halfway between the North and South Poles. The Equator is also known as the 0-degree (0°) latitude line. **Latitude** is the distance north or south of the Equator. It is measured in degrees. **Degrees** are units that measure angles. Minutes (') measure smaller units. On this map, lines are drawn every 20° of latitude.

Lines of latitude form east-west circles around the globe. Lines of latitude are also called parallels, because they are parallel to one another. That means they never cross.

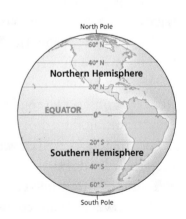

North Pole
60° N
40° N
Northern Hemisphere
20° N
EQUATOR 0°
20° S
Southern Hemisphere
40° S
60° S
South Pole

The Equator divides Earth in half. Each half of Earth is called a **hemisphere.** The half of Earth north of the Equator is known as the Northern Hemisphere. The half of Earth south of the Equator is the Southern Hemisphere.

Longitude

Geographers have also drawn imaginary north-south lines that run between the North Pole and the South Pole on Earth's surface. One of these lines is the Prime Meridian, which passes through Greenwich, England. The Prime Meridian and the other north-south lines measure **longitude,** or the distance in degrees east or west of the Prime Meridian. Lines of longitude are also called meridians.

The half of Earth east of the Prime Meridian is known as the Eastern Hemisphere. The half of Earth west of the Prime Meridian is the Western Hemisphere.

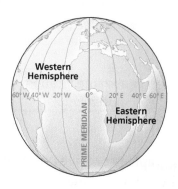

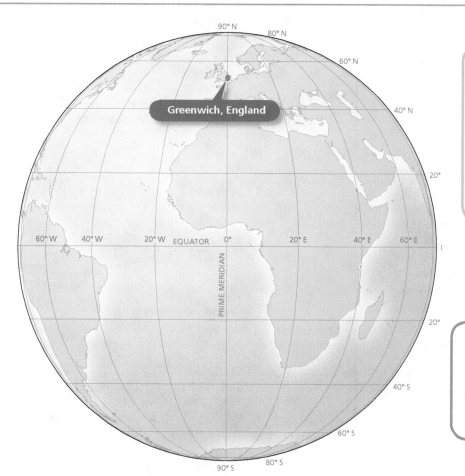

The Global Grid

Latitude and longitude form a global grid. You can describe the location of any point on Earth's surface using degrees of longitude and latitude. For example, Greenwich, England, is located at 0° longitude and about 51°29′ north latitude.

Assessment

1. What do geographers study?

2. Based on the diagrams shown here, in which two hemispheres do you live?

5

Geography's Five Themes

Key Ideas
- Using five themes can help you make sense of geography.
- The theme of location is used to describe where a place is found, while the other themes describe features of a place.

Key Terms • absolute location • relative location • place • region • movement • human-environment interaction

Visual Glossary

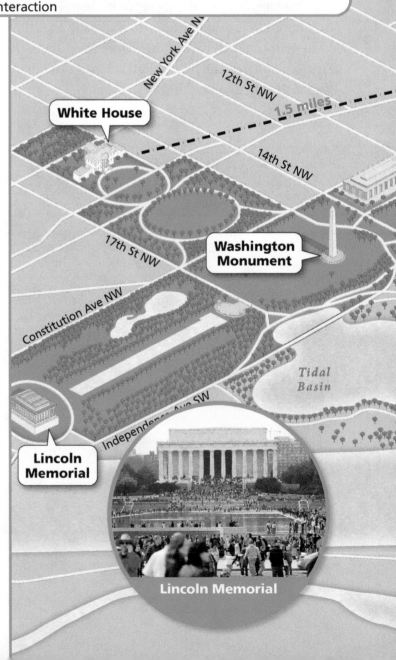

White House

1st St NW

New York Ave N

12th St NW

1.5 miles

14th St NW

Washington Monument

17th St NW

Constitution Ave NW

Tidal Basin

Independence Ave SW

Lincoln Memorial

Lincoln Memorial

Geographers use five different themes, or ways of thinking. These themes are location, place, region, movement, and human-environment interaction. They can help answer the geographer's two basic questions: Where are things located? Why are they there? You can see how the five themes work by looking at the example of our nation's capital, Washington, D.C.

Location

Geographers begin to study a place by finding where it is, or its location. There are two ways to talk about location. **Absolute location** describes a place's exact position on Earth in terms of longitude and latitude. Using degrees of longitude and latitude, you can pinpoint any spot on Earth. For example, the absolute location of the center of Washington, D.C., is at the intersection of the 38°54' north latitude line and the 77°2' west longitude line. **Relative location,** or the location of a place relative to another place, is another way to describe location. For example, you can say that Washington, D.C, is about 200 miles southwest of New York City.

Place

Geographers also study place. **Place** refers to the mix of human and nonhuman features at a given location. For example, you might talk about how many people live in a place and the kinds of work they do. You might mention that a place is hilly or that it has a wet climate. As a place, Washington, D.C., is on the Potomac River. It has a humid climate with cool winters and hot summers. It is a major city and the center of government for the United States.

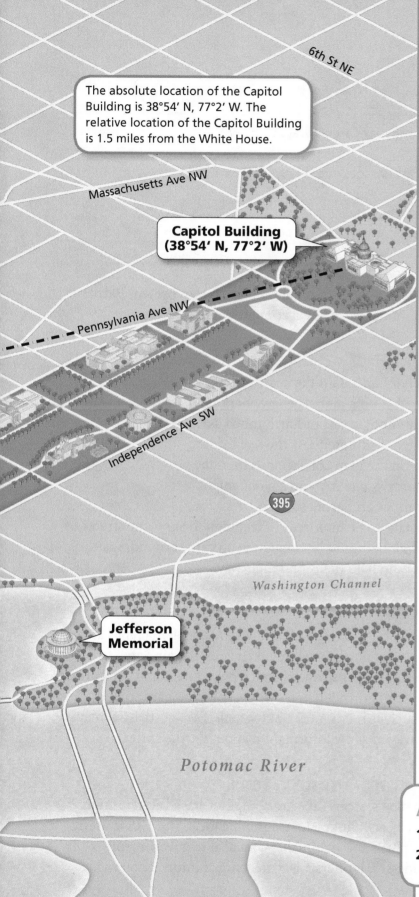

The absolute location of the Capitol Building is 38°54' N, 77°2' W. The relative location of the Capitol Building is 1.5 miles from the White House.

6th St NE

Massachusetts Ave NW

Capitol Building (38°54' N, 77°2' W)

Pennsylvania Ave NW

Independence Ave SW

395

Washington Channel

Jefferson Memorial

Potomac River

Region

Geographers use the theme of region to group places that have something in common. A **region** is an area with at least one unifying physical or human feature such as climate, landforms, population, or history. Washington, D.C., is part of a region called the Washington Metropolitan Area, which includes the city of Washington and its suburbs. This region shares a job market and a road and rail network. New technology, such as high-speed railroads, may give places new unifying features and connections. This can change the way people see regions.

Movement

The theme of **movement** explores how people, goods, and ideas get from one place to another. A daily movement of trucks and trains supplies the people of Washington with food, fuel, and other basic goods.

Human-Environment Interaction

The theme of **human-environment interaction** considers how people affect their environment, or their natural surroundings, and how their environment affects them. The movement of water from the Potomac River into Washington's water system is an example of human-environment interaction.

Assessment

1. What are the five themes of geography?

2. What is the difference between your hometown's location and your hometown as a place?

7

Ways to Show Earth's Surface

Key Ideas	• Globes, photographs, computer images, and maps are all ways to show and view Earth's surface.
	• Each way of showing Earth's surface has advantages and disadvantages.

Key Terms
• scale   • aerial photograph   • satellite image
• geographic information system (GIS)   • distortion   • projection

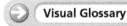
Visual Glossary

Geographers use a number of different models to represent Earth's surface. Each model has its own strengths and weaknesses.

Globes

A globe is a model of Earth with the same round shape as Earth itself. With a globe, geographers can show the continents and oceans of Earth much as they really are. The only difference is the **scale,** or the area a given space on the map corresponds to in the real world. For example, one inch on a globe might corespond to 600 miles on Earth's surface.

A globe would have to be hundreds of feet high to show the streets of your town. Such a globe would be impossible to carry around. Instead, people use flat maps to help them find their way.

Photographs

Geographers use photographs as well as maps. **Aerial photographs** are photographic images of Earth's surface taken from the air. **Satellite images** are pictures of Earth's surface taken from a satellite in orbit. They show Earth's surface in great detail. However, it can be hard to find specific features, such as roads, on a photograph. For this reason, maps are still the main way to show information about Earth's surface.

Geographic Information Systems

Geographic information systems (GIS) are computer-based systems that store and use information linked to geographic locations. GIS is useful not only to geographers and mapmakers but also to government agencies and businesses. It offers a way to connect information to places.

▲ An aerial photo taken in Antactica (top) and a satellite image of Antarctica (above).

Map Projections

Flat maps and photos have one major problem. Earth is round. A map or photo is flat. Can you flatten an orange peel without stretching or tearing it? There will be sections that are stretched or bent out of shape.

Showing Earth on a flat surface always brings some **distortion,** or loss of accuracy in the size or position of objects on a map. Something is going to look too large, too small, or out of place.

To show a flat image of Earth's round surface, mapmakers have come up with different **projections,** or ways to map Earth on a flat surface. A few examples show how they differ.

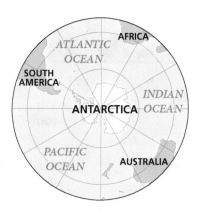

▲ This projection shows the size and shape of Antarctica nearly correctly.

HOW TO SHOW OUR ROUND EARTH ON A FLAT MAP

The Equal-Area Projection

An equal-area map shows the correct size of landmasses. However, their shapes are distorted.

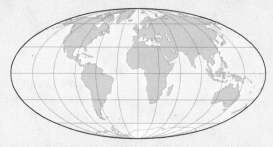

The Mercator Projection

The Mercator (mur KAYT ur) projection shows correct shapes and directions but not true distances or sizes. Mercator maps make areas near the poles look bigger than they are.

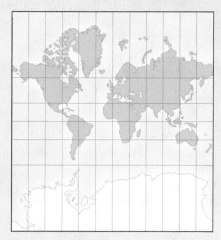

The Robinson Projection

The Robinson projection shows nearly the correct size and shape of most land areas. However, even a Robinson projection has distortions, especially in areas around the edges of the map.

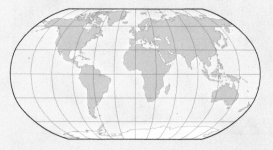

Assessment

1. How are maps different from globes?
2. What are the strengths and weaknesses of each of the three projections in showing Antarctica?

Understanding Maps

Key Ideas
- Maps have parts that help you read them.
- Though different maps show different things about a place, you can use the same tools to help understand them.

Key Terms • key • locator map • scale bar • compass rose

Visual Glossary

Look at the maps on these two pages. One is a physical map of the state of Colorado. The other is a road map of Colorado. These maps cover the same area but show different kinds of information. Despite their differences, both maps have all of the basic parts that you should find on any map.

The map has a title that tells you the subject of the map.

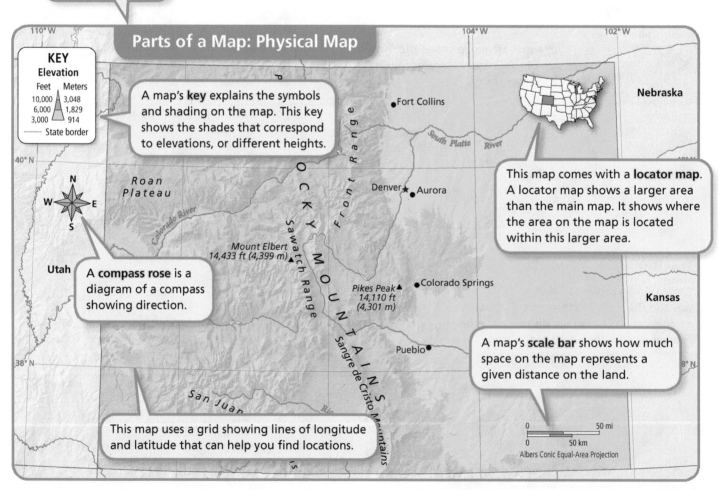

Parts of a Map: Physical Map

KEY
Elevation
Feet	Meters
10,000	3,048
6,000	1,829
3,000	914
— State border

A map's **key** explains the symbols and shading on the map. This key shows the shades that correspond to elevations, or different heights.

This map comes with a **locator map**. A locator map shows a larger area than the main map. It shows where the area on the map is located within this larger area.

A **compass rose** is a diagram of a compass showing direction.

A map's **scale bar** shows how much space on the map represents a given distance on the land.

This map uses a grid showing lines of longitude and latitude that can help you find locations.

Albers Conic Equal-Area Projection

Reading a Map

Look at the map below. It is a highway map of the state of Colorado. This map looks different from the physical map of Colorado that you have just studied. However, it has the same parts that can help you read it. In fact, you can read most maps using the key, scale bar, and other map tools that you have learned about.

Find the key on this map. Using the key, can you find the route number of the Interstate highway that connects Denver and Colorado Springs, Colorado? Using the scale bar, estimate the number of miles between these two cities. Using the compass rose, find the direction that you would need to travel from Denver to Colorado Springs. Now you have learned to read a highway map!

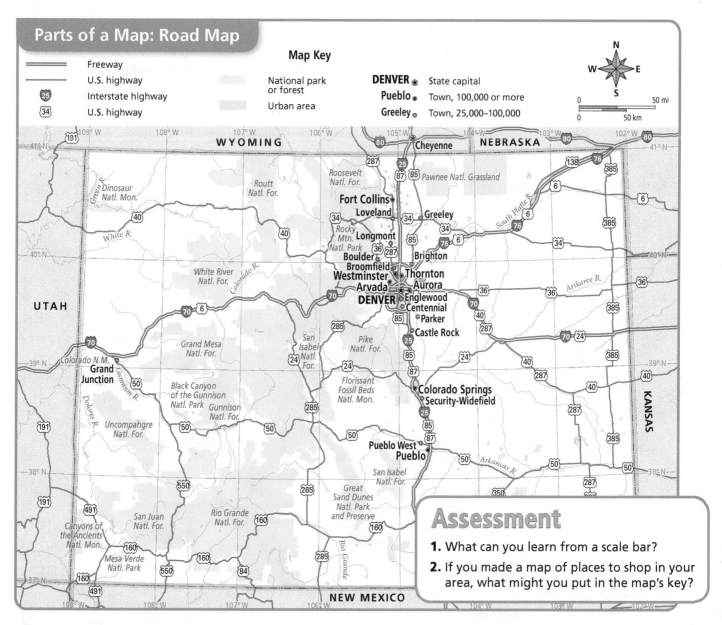

Parts of a Map: Road Map

Freeway
U.S. highway
Interstate highway
U.S. highway

Map Key

National park or forest
Urban area

DENVER — State capital
Pueblo — Town, 100,000 or more
Greeley — Town, 25,000–100,000

Assessment

1. What can you learn from a scale bar?
2. If you made a map of places to shop in your area, what might you put in the map's key?

11

Types of Maps

Key Ideas

- Maps can show many different kinds of information.
- Political, physical, and special-purpose maps are the main types of maps.

Key Terms • physical map • elevation • political map • special-purpose map  **Visual Glossary**

The map projections, or ways to represent Earth's surface, that you have studied can be used to show different things about the area they cover. For example, they might represent the physical landscape, political boundaries, ecosystem zones, or almost any other feature of a place. People use different kinds of maps in different situations.

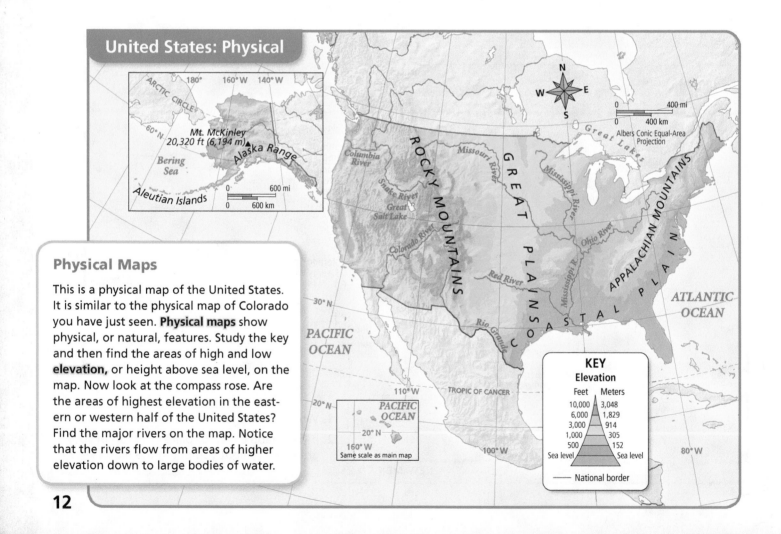

United States: Physical

Physical Maps

This is a physical map of the United States. It is similar to the physical map of Colorado you have just seen. **Physical maps** show physical, or natural, features. Study the key and then find the areas of high and low **elevation,** or height above sea level, on the map. Now look at the compass rose. Are the areas of highest elevation in the eastern or western half of the United States? Find the major rivers on the map. Notice that the rivers flow from areas of higher elevation down to large bodies of water.

KEY
Elevation

Feet	Meters
10,000	3,048
6,000	1,829
3,000	914
1,000	305
500	152
Sea level	Sea level

— National border

United States: Political

Political Maps

This is a political map of the United States. **Political maps** show political units, such as countries or states. They may also show capitals of countries, or centers of government, and other major cities. Study the key and compass rose of this map. Now look at the map. Which state is directly west of Georgia? How many states border Canada?

United States: Election 2008

KEY
- McCain
- Obama

0   200 mi
0   200 km
Albers Conic Equal-Area Projection

Special-purpose Maps

Maps can show many different kinds of information. **Special-purpose maps** show the location or distribution of human or physical features. This map shows the results of the 2008 presidential election. A highway map is another kind of special-purpose map. Other special-purpose maps may show a region's weather patterns or other features. Study this map's key. Which presidential candidate won your home state in the 2008 election?

Assessment

1. What are the elements of a physical map?

2. What are the elements of a political map?

13

Part 1 Assessment

Key Terms and Ideas

1. **Compare and Contrast** What is the difference between **latitude** and **longitude**?

2. **Describe** What are some features of **place** and **region**?

3. **Analyze Cause and Effect** Why do map **projections** lead to **distortion**? Give a specific example.

4. **Discuss** What does the **scale bar** of a map show?

5. **Compare and Contrast** How do **aerial photographs** and **satellite images** show Earth's surface? What differences do you find between these types of images?

6. **Recall** What are the basic parts of a map, and what does each part show to readers?

7. **Categorize** What kind of map shows elevation?

8. **Summarize** What does a **political map** show?

Think Critically

9. **Problem Solving** Which kinds of maps could you use to choose a new city as your home? How would you use them?

10. **Decision Making** Which kinds of projections would best show the distance between your hometown and Washington, D.C., on a map of the United States? Explain.

11. **Synthesize** What can you learn from the latitude and longitude lines on a map?

12. **Categorize** Match each feature to the correct theme of geography: very flat landscape, four trains in and out of town every day, factory waste enters a local river, large Hispanic population across three states, and 42° S 147° E.

Identify

For each part of a map, write the letter from the map that shows its location.

13. title
14. compass rose
15. latitude line
16. longitude line
17. scale bar
18. key
19. What type of map is this?

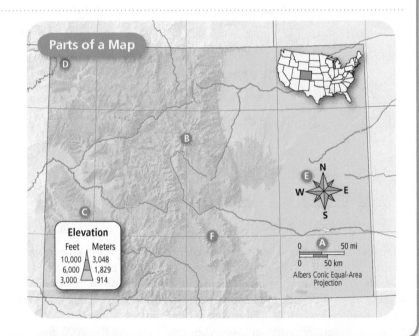

Parts of a Map

Elevation

Feet	Meters
10,000	3,048
6,000	1,829
3,000	914

0   50 mi
0   50 km
Albers Conic Equal-Area Projection

Journal Activity

Fill in the graphic organizers in your student journal.

Demonstrate Understanding Complete the Sum-It-Up activity in your journal to demonstrate your understanding of the Tools of Geography. After you complete the activity, discuss your map with a partner. Be sure to support your completed map with information from the lesson.

Document-Based Questions

Success Tracker™
Online at myworldgeography.com

Use your knowledge of the tools of geography and Documents A and B to answer Questions 1–3.

Document A

Document B

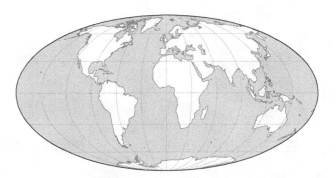

1. Which of the five themes of geography is best represented by this map?

   A location

   B place

   C region

   D human-environment interaction

2. What kind of projection does Document B show?

   A Mercator

   B equal-area

   C Robinson

   D global grid

3. **Writing Task** What are the advantages and disadvantages of the map shown in Document B? Explain your answer.

my worldgeography.com   Self-Test

Our Planet, Earth

The volcano
Kilauea erupting

▲ Looking down into
the crater of an active
volcano, you can almost
glimpse the interior of
our planet, Earth.

A road destroyed by an earthquake in Indonesia

Lava flowing into the sea (left)
Tamsen Burlak (right)

Tamsen Studies a Volcano

Story by Miles Lemaire for myWorld

As 21-year-old Tamsen Burlak watched the volcano Kilauea, in Hawaii, blow lava and ash into the sky she had only one thought: "This is pretty cool."

When she was a young girl, Tamsen didn't know much about what makes up our planet, Earth, only that she loved to collect rocks during nature hikes with her parents.

"I would always pick up rocks from everywhere that we went—anything that looked cool," she says. "It was probably around middle school or high school while I was looking at the rocks that I realized I wanted to know what they were called and how they formed. So I went out and bought a bunch of those field guides, geology dictionaries for rocks. That's when I found out the field name was geology." Tamsen knew what she wanted to study.

When she went to college, Tamsen studied geology, the field of science that deals with the structure of Earth. She concentrated on volcanoes and fault lines, places where earthquakes are likely to happen. Geologists like Tamsen investigate earthquake zones to find out how likely another earthquake is, and how destructive it will be. Earthquakes sometimes occur where volcanoes are erupting.

Tamsen was able to go to Hawaii to study. The islands that make up the state of Hawaii were formed by volcanoes. Lava flowed out of volcanoes, cooled, and formed new land over millions of years. Some of the islands still have active volcanoes. Tamsen visited Kilauea, where lava has been flowing since 1983.

"The active area I went to was part of a summer course I took on the big island of Hawaii. At that time Kilauea had just started erupting, so we were there for the first days of it," Tamsen said.

"It was really exciting," she added, but not always easy, "because of the volcanic gasses in the air. That sort of stuff can itch the throat and cause irritation, but I loved every second of it!"

Tamsen, who now has a degree in geology, says that she has been studying dormant, or inactive, volcanoes and earthquake zones for years. Her experience in Hawaii is something that she and her fellow geologists dream of.

"We'd all be really excited if there was an actual earthquake that we all got to study," says Tamsen, "but we just look at faults in the area, offsets, and the different rock types, and measure how much displacement has gone on and how big a threat we think it might be."

As Tamsen learned firsthand, studying the structure of Earth can be very exciting. Geologists face down erupting volcanoes in order to learn how to predict earthquakes and save lives. Understanding Earth may someday make that possible.

Earth in Space

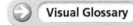

Key Ideas
- Planet Earth moves around the sun.
- This movement causes places on Earth's surface to receive varying amounts of sunlight from one season to the next.

Key Terms
- orbit
- axis
- solstice
- revolution
- equinox

[→ Visual Glossary]

Earth, the sun, the planets, and the stars in the sky are all part of our galaxy, or cluster of stars. We call our galaxy the Milky Way because its stars look like a trail of spilled milk across a dark night sky. Our sun is one of its billions of stars.

Earth, the Sun, and the Seasons

Even though the sun is about 93 million miles (150 million km) away, it provides Earth with heat and light. To understand how far Earth is from the sun, consider that this distance is nearly 4,000 times the distance around Earth at the Equator.

Earth travels around the sun in an oval-shaped **orbit,** which is the path one object makes as it revolves around another. Earth takes 365 1/4 days, or one year, to make one **revolution,** or complete journey, around the sun.

Earth's **axis,** an imaginary line between the North and South Poles, is tilted relative to its orbit. Therefore, as Earth makes its revolution, the sun shines most directly on different places at different times. That is why seasons occur.

March Equinox

About March 21, the sun is directly overhead at noon on the Equator. At this point in Earth's orbit, its axis is tilted neither toward nor away from the sun. An **equinox** (EE kwih nahks) is a point at which, everywhere on Earth, days and nights are nearly equal in length. This is the spring equinox in the Northern Hemisphere and the fall equinox in the Southern Hemisphere.

June Solstice

About June 21, the North Pole is tilted closest to the sun. This brings the heat of summer to the Northern Hemisphere. This is the summer **solstice** in the Northern Hemisphere and the winter solstice in the Southern Hemisphere. A solstice (SOHL stis) is a point at which days are longest in one hemisphere and shortest in the other.

December Solstice

About December 21, the South Pole is tilted closest to the sun. The area north of the Arctic Circle is in constant darkness, while the area south of the Antarctic Circle has constant daylight. This is the winter solstice in the Northern Hemisphere and the summer solstice in the Southern Hemisphere. The lack of sunlight in the Northern Hemisphere brings the cold of winter.

September Equinox

About September 23, the sun is again directly overhead at noon on the Equator, and all of Earth has days and nights of equal length. This is the fall equinox in the Northern Hemisphere and the spring equinox in the Southern Hemisphere. Less-direct sunlight in the Northern Hemisphere brings the chill of fall.

Assessment

1. If it is summer in the Northern Hemisphere, what season is it in the Southern Hemisphere?

2. How can days be short and cold in one hemisphere when they are long and hot in another?

19

Time and Earth's Rotation

Key Ideas
- Earth's spinning movement causes day and night.
- This spinning also causes it to be different times in different places on Earth's surface.

Key Terms • rotation • time zone

 **Visual Glossary**

You have learned that Earth revolves around the sun in an oval-shaped orbit. Earth also moves in another way. This motion explains why day and night occur.

Rotation of Earth

As Earth revolves around the sun, it is also rotating, or spinning, in space. Earth rotates around its axis. Each complete turn, or **rotation,** takes about 24 hours. At any one time, it is night on the side of Earth facing away from the sun. As Earth rotates, that side of Earth turns to face the sun, and the sun appears to rise. The sun's light shines on that side of Earth. It is daytime. Then, as that side of Earth turns away from the sun, the sun appears to set. No sunlight reaches that side of Earth. It is nighttime.

Time Zones

Because Earth rotates toward the east, the day starts earlier in the east than it does farther west. Over short distances, the time difference is small. For example, the sun rises about four minutes earlier in Beaumont, Texas, than it does in Houston, 70 miles to the west. But if every town had its own local time, people would have a hard time keeping track. So governments have agreed to divide the world into standard **time zones,** or areas sharing the same time. Times in neighboring zones are one hour apart.

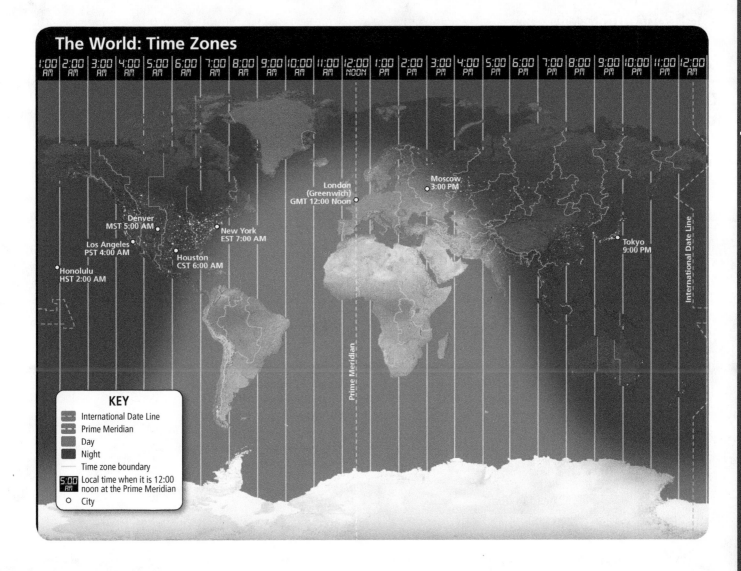

The World: Time Zones

1:00 AM 2:00 AM 3:00 AM 4:00 AM 5:00 AM 6:00 AM 7:00 AM 8:00 AM 9:00 AM 10:00 AM 11:00 AM 12:00 NOON 1:00 PM 2:00 PM 3:00 PM 4:00 PM 5:00 PM 6:00 PM 7:00 PM 8:00 PM 9:00 PM 10:00 PM 11:00 PM 12:00 AM

Moscow 3:00 PM

London (Greenwich) GMT 12:00 Noon

Denver MST 5:00 AM

New York EST 7:00 AM

Los Angeles PST 4:00 AM

Houston CST 6:00 AM

Honolulu HST 2:00 AM

Tokyo 9:00 PM

International Date Line

Prime Meridian

KEY

- International Date Line
- Prime Meridian
- Day
- Night
- Time zone boundary
- 5:00 AM Local time when it is 12:00 noon at the Prime Meridian
- ○ City

The Prime Meridian

The Prime Meridian, in Greenwich, England, is at the center of one of these zones. The time in that zone is sometimes known as Greenwich Mean Time or Universal Time (UT). Other time zones are sometimes described in terms of how many hours they are behind or ahead of UT. (For example, Central Standard Time in the United States is UT – 6, or six hours behind UT.)

Assessment

1. What is the rotation of Earth?

2. If it is 8 P.M. in New York, what time is it in Los Angeles?

Earth's Structure

Key Ideas
- Earth is made up of different parts, above and below its surface.

Key Terms
- core
- mantle
- crust
- atmosphere
- landform

 Visual Glossary

The diagram to the right reveals Earth's interior, or the parts beneath its surface. It also shows some of the parts above its surface. Understanding Earth's inner and outer structure will help you to understand the forces that shape the world we live in.

Earth's Core

A sphere of very hot metal at the center of Earth is called the **core**. Despite temperatures greater than 5,000°F (3,000°C), the inner core is solid because of the great pressure of the layers above it. The outer core is hot liquid metal.

Mantle

The **mantle** is a thick, rocky layer around the core. The mantle is also hot, with temperatures greater than 3,300°F (1,800°C). The mantle is solid, but its temperature makes it fluid, or able to flow. If you warm a stick of butter, you can move the top in one direction and the bottom in another. Even though the mantle is rock, its high temperature allows it to move something like a stick of warm butter.

Crust

The thin layer of rocks and minerals that surrounds the mantle is called the **crust**. The surface of the crust includes the land areas where people live as well as the ocean floor. The crust is thinnest beneath the ocean floor. It is thickest beneath high mountain ranges, such as the Himalayas, in Asia. In effect, it floats on top of the mantle. The great heat deep inside Earth and movements within the mantle help to shape Earth's crust.

Atmosphere

Above Earth's surface is the **atmosphere,** a thick layer of gases or air. It includes life-giving oxygen. Earth's atmosphere acts like a blanket. It holds in heat from the sun, which makes life possible.

Landforms

Only 25 percent of Earth's surface is land. There are many different **landforms,** or shapes and types of land. Two kinds of processes shape these landforms: processes beneath Earth's surface that push Earth's crust up, and processes on Earth's surface that wear it down.

Water

Water covers about 75 percent of Earth's surface. This water forms a layer above Earth's crust. The oceans hold about 97 percent of Earth's water. This water is salty. Most fresh water, or water without salt, is frozen in ice sheets around the North and South Poles. Only a tiny portion of Earth's water is unfrozen fresh water. People need this water for many things. Fresh water comes from lakes, rivers, and ground water, which are fed by rain and snow.

Assessment

1. What are Earth's three main layers?

2. What part of Earth's structure are oceans located on?

Forces on Earth's Surface

Key Ideas
- Forces such as wind, water, and ice shape Earth's surface.
- These forces produce a variety of different landforms.

Key Terms
- weathering
- valley
- erosion
- deposition
- plateau
- plain
- delta

Visual Glossary

Forces on Earth's surface wear down and reshape the land. Along with forces inside Earth, which you will read about later, forces on Earth's surface help create the landforms we see around us.

An eroded landscape in the southwestern United States. ▼

Wearing Away Earth's Surface

Weathering is a process that breaks rocks down into tiny pieces. There are two kinds of weathering: chemical weathering and mechanical weathering. In chemical weathering, rainwater or acids carried by rainwater dissolve rocks. In mechanical weathering, moving water, ice, or sometimes wind breaks rocks into little pieces. Mechanical weathering can happen after chemical weathering has weakened rocks.

Weathering helps create soil. Tiny pieces of rock combine with decayed animal and plant material to form soil. Soil and pieces of rock may undergo **erosion,** a process in which water, ice, or wind remove small pieces of rock. Soil is required to sustain plant and animal life, and for agriculture. Because of this, weathering is very important to human settlement patterns.

Shaping Landforms

Weathering and erosion have shaped many of Earth's landforms. These landforms include mountains and hills. Mountains are wide at the bottom and rise steeply to a narrow peak or ridge. Hills are lower than mountains and often have rounded tops. While forces within Earth create mountains, forces on Earth's surface wear them down. An area in which a certain type of landform is dominant is called a landform region.

The parts of mountains and hills that are left standing are the rocks that are hardest to wear away. Millions of years ago, the Appalachian Mountains in the eastern United States were as high as the Rocky Mountains of the western United States. Rain, snow, and wind wore the Appalachians down into much lower peaks.

Rebuilding Earth's Surface

When water, ice, and wind remove material, they deposit it farther downstream or downwind to create new landforms. **Deposition** is the process of depositing material eroded and carried by water, ice, or wind. Deposition creates landforms such as sandy beaches. **Plains,** or large areas of flat or gently rolling land, are often formed by the deposition of material carried downstream by rivers. Through deposition on the floor of the sea, rivers can create new land.

A **plateau** is a large, mostly flat area that rises above the surrounding land. At least one side of a plateau has a steep slope. At the top of this slope is usually a layer of rock that is hard to wear down.

Valleys are stretches of low land between mountains or hills. Rivers often form valleys where there are rocks that are easy to wear away.

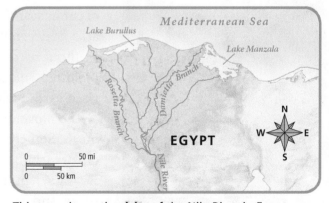

This map shows the **delta** of the Nile River in Egypt. Deltas are flat plains built on the seabed where a river fans out and deposits material over many years.

Assessment

1. How is erosion different from weathering?
2. How do plains form from the tops of worn-down mountains?

Forces Inside Earth

Key Ideas	• Movements of hot, soft rock in Earth's mantle affect Earth's surface, forming volcanoes and pushing continents together or apart.

Key Terms
- plate tectonics
- magma
- plate
- fault

Visual Glossary

The volcano Kilauea in Hawaii spews molten rock. ▼

Forces deep inside Earth are constantly reshaping its surface. The theory of **plate tectonics** states that Earth's crust is made up of huge blocks called **plates.** Plates include continents or parts of continents, along with parts of the ocean floor. Earth's continental plates sit on streams of molten, nearly melted, rock called **magma.** Some scientists believe magma acts as a conveyor belt, moving the plates in different directions. Plates may move only an inch or two (a few centimeters) a year.

This movement slowly builds mountains. When two plates of crust push against each other, the pressure makes the crust bend to form steep mountains.

Earthquakes and Volcanoes

Earthquakes occur when plates slide against each other. They often occur at seams in Earth's crust called **faults**, often near the boundaries between plates. Earthquakes cause the ground to shake. Some earthquakes are too small for people to feel. But others can destroy buildings and cause great harm. For example, the 1906 San Francisco earthquake killed more than 3000 people.

The movement of continental plates creates great pressure inside Earth. Sometimes this pressure forces magma up through Earth's crust, forming volcanoes. Volcanoes spew magma from inside Earth. When magma erupts out of a volcano, it is called lava. Ash, rocks, and poisonous gasses also explode out of volcanoes during an eruption. Volcanic eruptions can be very dangerous for people. But volcanoes also serve an important purpose. When lava cools, new land forms. Undersea volcanoes even grow into islands after thousands of years of eruptions.

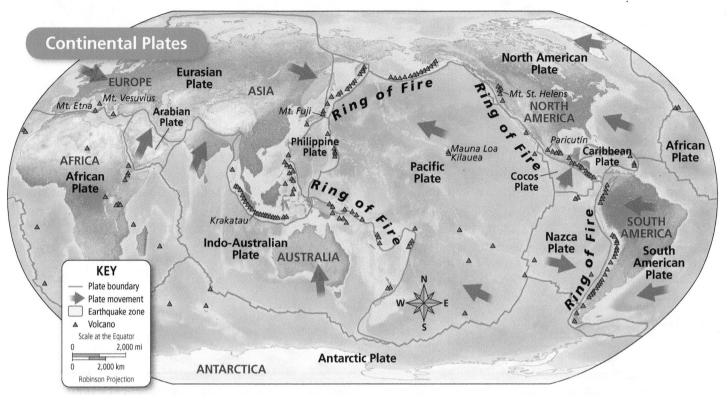

Continental Plates

EUROPE
Eurasian Plate
Mt. Etna
Mt. Vesuvius
Arabian Plate
ASIA
Mt. Fuji
Ring of Fire
North American Plate
Mt. St. Helens
NORTH AMERICA
Ring of Fire
AFRICA
African Plate
Philippine Plate
Paricutín
Caribbean Plate
African Plate
Pacific Plate
Mauna Loa
Kilauea
Cocos Plate
Ring of Fire
Krakatau
Indo-Australian Plate
AUSTRALIA
Nazca Plate
SOUTH AMERICA
South American Plate
Ring of Fire

KEY
— Plate boundary
➤ Plate movement
☐ Earthquake zone
△ Volcano

Scale at the Equator
0   2,000 mi
0   2,000 km
Robinson Projection

N E S W

Antarctic Plate
ANTARCTICA

The Plates of Earth's Crust The map above shows how Earth's plates fit together today. It also shows the directions in which plates are moving. As you can see on the map, earthquakes and volcanoes occur along plate edges.

Natural Hazards

Volcanoes and earthquakes are examples of natural disasters. They are also called natural hazards, meaning dangers. Other natural hazards include hurricanes, tornados, landslides, and floods.

These events threaten lives and property. But people can take steps to prepare for natural disasters, so that damage will not be as severe when they strike. For example, architects can design buildings that will not collapse when the ground shakes. Local governments can set routes for people to leave affected areas during a hurricane. Citizens can practice what to do during an earthquake, and keep emergency supplies at home.

Preparing for a Natural Hazard
Above: Damage caused by an earthquake
Right: Students hide under their desks for an earthquake drill

Assessment

1. How do forces inside Earth shape Earth's surface?
2. What are some ways people prepare for natural hazards?

27

Part 2 Assessment

Key Terms and Ideas

1. **Compare and Contrast** What is the difference between an **equinox** and a **solstice**?

2. **Analyze Cause and Effect** How does Earth's **orbit** influence climate on Earth?

3. **Describe** How is Earth's **axis** part of its **rotation**?

4. **Identify Main Ideas and Details** What is sunrise? In which part of the United States does sunrise occur earliest?

5. **Categorize** Which part of Earth's structure is the thinnest? Where is this part?

6. **Summarize** How do **weathering** and **erosion** shape Earth's surface?

7. **Sequence** Describe the process that causes movement of the continents.

Think Critically

8. **Draw Inferences** How would our lives change if Earth's atmosphere were damaged? Explain.

9. **Draw Conclusions** Which parts of Earth's orbit are best for warm-weather activities in the Northern Hemisphere? For cold-weather activities? Explain using the terms *equinox* and *solstice*.

10. **Ask Questions** To choose a safe location for a new town, what questions about Earth's structure and movement would you ask? Explain.

11. **Categorize** Consider three different landforms. For each, list the main process that formed it. Was that process on the interior or exterior of Earth? How are the different processes related?

Identify

Identify the time in each location if it is noon GMT.

12. **New York, New York**

13. **Houston, Texas**

14. **Denver, Colorado**

15. **Los Angeles, California**

16. **Anchorage, Alaska**

17. **Honolulu, Hawaii**

18. Compare the time of sunrise in New York, New York, with that in Houston, Texas. Which is earlier and which is later? Are these cities in the same time zone?

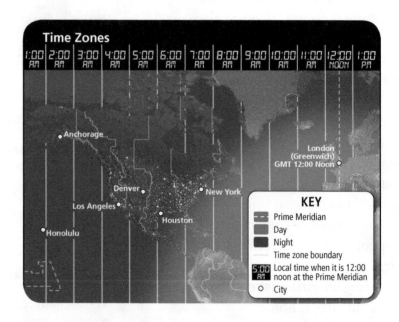

Journal Activity

Fill in the graphic organizer in your Student Journal.

Demonstrate Understanding Complete the Sum-It-Up activity in your journal to demonstrate your understanding of Our Planet, Earth. After you complete the activity, discuss your diagram with your class. Be sure to support your diagram with information from the lessons.

Make a Difference

Think about earthquake or volcano safety in your community or a community like yours in an earthquake or volcano danger area. Develop ideas to raise community awareness of the dangers and the ways people can avoid them. Share your ideas on a Web page, poster, or handout.

Document-Based Questions

Success Tracker™
Online at myworldgeography.com

Use your knowledge of our planet Earth and Documents A and B to answer Questions 1–3.

Document A

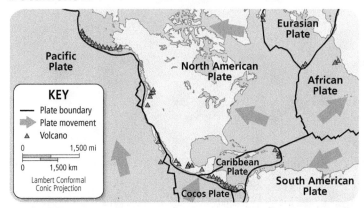

KEY
— Plate boundary
➡ Plate movement
▲ Volcano
0   1,500 mi
0   1,500 km
Lambert Conformal Conic Projection

Pacific Plate
North American Plate
Eurasian Plate
African Plate
Caribbean Plate
Cocos Plate
South American Plate

Document B

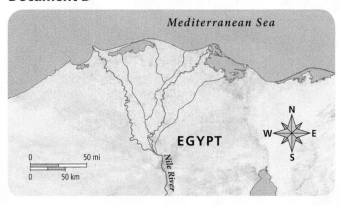

Mediterranean Sea
EGYPT
Nile River
0   50 mi
0   50 km

1. Why are there volcanoes where the North American Plate meets the Pacific Plate?

   A Erosion breaks down the land where plates meet.

   B Magma is forced through Earth's surface at plate boundaries.

   C Earth's rotation causes the sun to shine directly on this area.

   D Land in this area has been shaped by chemical weather.

2. How is the natural feature depicted on this map formed?

   A Tectonic plates push land upward.

   B A river flows into the ocean, depositing material on the seabed.

   C Wind and rain wear down mountains.

   D A river carves out a valley.

3. **Writing Task** Suppose a volcano forms on the ocean floor and grows thousands of feet upwards. Use that information and Document A to explain the many islands between Asia and Australia.

Climates and Ecosystems

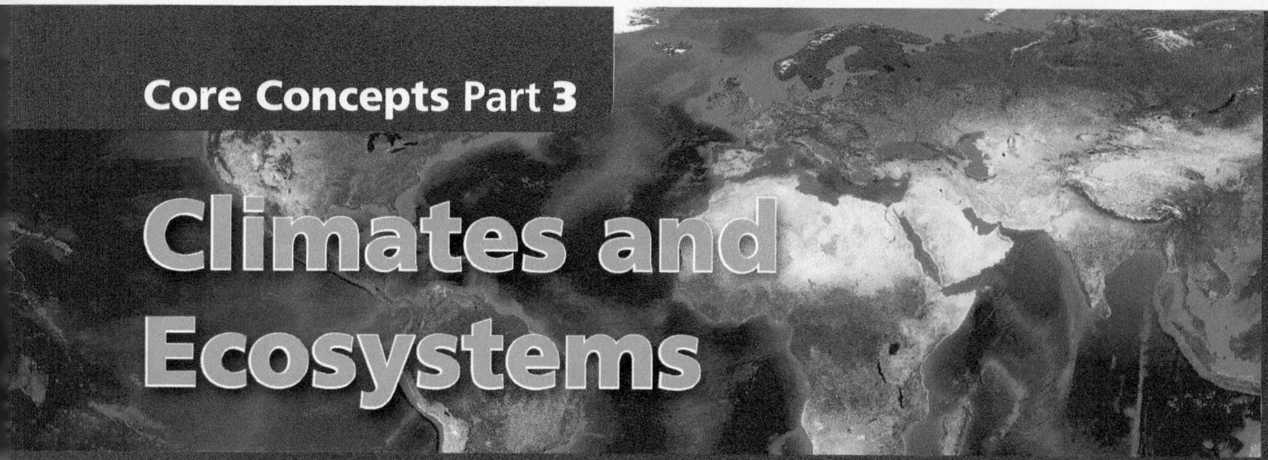

Hurricane Katrina spins toward New Orleans.

New Orleans residents trapped by floodwaters wave for help. ▲

Katrina caused severe destruction.

Airin McGhee

HURRICANE KATRINA STRIKES

Story by Miles Lemaire for myWorld Geography

Powerful tropical storms sweep across the southeastern United States and the Gulf Coast nearly every year. At first, teenager Airin McGhee thought that Hurricane Katrina would be just like any other storm. She was wrong. Instead, Katrina was so powerful that it flooded much of Airin's city, New Orleans, Louisiana.

When weather forecasters and government officials first started warning New Orleans residents about Hurricane Katrina in late August 2005, Airin was not worried. "Every year we would get the warning and up until that point it just never happened," she said. "Nobody expected Katrina to be like it was."

Fortunately, Airin and her mother and sister decided to leave New Orleans before the storm arrived. They drove through heavy traffic to Jackson, Mississippi, a city about 190 miles north of New Orleans. While they waited for the storm to pass, they feared the worst for their home, their city, and the friends and neighbors they had left behind.

Hurricane Katrina hit New Orleans on August 29. Its powerful winds ripped buildings apart and tore trees out of the ground. Worse, Katrina's winds and rain broke the levees, or raised flood barriers, that had protected much of the area. Millions of gallons of water poured through the broken levees into the city.

After Katrina ended, Airin's family tried to get news from friends in New Orleans. "I was really devastated for a while," Airin says, "because the cell phones were really bad and I just had all these thoughts of, 'Is this person okay? Is this person okay?' For weeks all … numbers had a busy signal and it was hard to get in touch with people."

When Airin's family was finally able to return to New Orleans, they saw the results of Katrina's destructive power in person. Years later, Airin's memories of what they saw are still strong. "We had six feet of water in our house," Airin said. "We lost everything. We lost my mom's car and my car, our entire house, including all the furniture and clothes … I pretty much lost everything."

It wasn't long before Airin's family was able to find another place to live, but they still feel the effects of the storm years later.

"I'll just never forget Katrina," Airin says. "It wiped away all my memories. I lost my high school diploma, all my pictures and things that you might take for granted. I collected things like my baby teeth and blanket. All those things are just gone."

When Airin thinks about how the storm affected her, she says, "It really taught me to value sentimental things. It changed how I do certain things, because now I want to capture every moment, and I find myself taking pictures of everything."

31

Climate and Weather

Key Ideas	• Different areas of the world have different weather patterns.
	• Weather and climate are described using precipitation and temperature.

Key Terms • weather • climate • precipitation • temperature

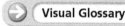 Visual Glossary

You have learned about the powerful forces that shape Earth, including global movements, water, and sunlight. These forces also shape Earth's weather patterns. Weather patterns can vary widely from one region to another.

The climate of Iquitos (ee KEE tohs), Peru, is hot and wet year-round. ▼

Weather or Climate?

Do you look outside before you choose your clothing in the morning? If so, you are checking the weather. **Weather** is the condition of the air and sky at a certain time. Or do you choose your clothing based on the normal weather for the time of year in the place where you live? If so, you dress according to your local climate. **Climate** is the average weather of a place over many years.

How you feel about today's weather may depend on your local climate. If you live in a place with a wet climate, you may be unhappy to see rainy weather, because your climate means that you get rain frequently. On the other hand, if you live in a dry climate where water is scarce, you might be very happy to see rainy weather.

Rain is a form of **precipitation,** which is water that falls to the ground as rain, snow, sleet, or hail. **Temperature** is a measure of how hot or cold the air is. Precipitation and temperature are the main ways to describe both daily weather and long-term climate.

Comparing Climates

One way to understand and compare climates is to use climate graphs. Climate graphs show the average climate for a place for each month of a year. A climate graph has a curved line that shows average temperatures. It has bars that show average monthly precipitation. The next page has two examples of climate graphs.

Chicago, Illinois

This is a climate graph of Chicago, Illinois, a city in the north central United States. It shows that Chicago has cold winters, hot summers, and moderate precipitation year-round. Notice that the line for temperature is much higher in July than it is in January. However, the heights of the bars for precipitation do not change much.

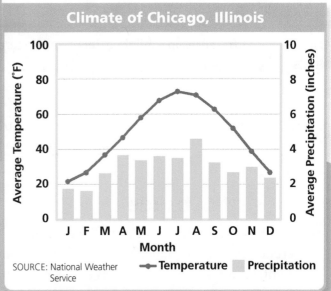

Climate of Chicago, Illinois

SOURCE: National Weather Service

—•— Temperature   ▪ Precipitation

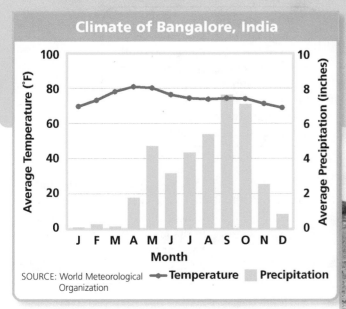

Climate of Bangalore, India

SOURCE: World Meteorological Organization   —•— Temperature   ▪ Precipitation

Bangalore, India

In some parts of the world, precipitation changes greatly from season to season. This is a climate graph of Bangalore, India. It shows that most of Bangalore's rain falls during a rainy season that lasts from May to October. Almost no precipitation falls from January to March.

Assessment

1. How is climate different from weather?
2. How would you describe your region's climate?

Temperature

Key Ideas
- Differences in sunlight affect temperatures at different latitudes.
- Earth's temperature patterns change from season to season.

Key Terms
- polar zone
- high latitudes
- tropics
- low latitudes
- temperate zone
- middle latitudes
- altitude

 Visual Glossary

Zones of Latitude

Energy from the sun heats Earth. Because of the tilt of Earth's axis, different areas of the planet receive different amounts of direct sunlight. As a result, some regions are warmer than others.

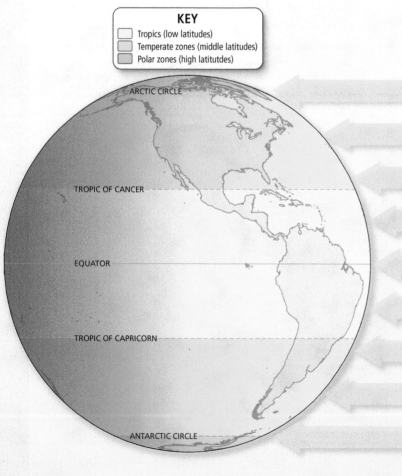

KEY
- Tropics (low latitudes)
- Temperate zones (middle latitudes)
- Polar zones (high latitutdes)

ARCTIC CIRCLE
TROPIC OF CANCER
EQUATOR
TROPIC OF CAPRICORN
ANTARCTIC CIRCLE

The **polar zones,** also known as the **high latitudes,** are the areas north of the Arctic Circle and south of the Antarctic Circle. In the polar zones, the sun is below the horizon for part of the year and near the horizon the rest of the year. Temperatures stay cool to bitterly cold.

The **tropics,** or the **low latitudes,** are the areas between the Tropic of Cancer and the Tropic of Capricorn. In the low latitudes, the sun is overhead or nearly overhead all year long. In this region, it is usually hot.

The **temperate zones,** or the **middle latitudes,** are the areas between the high and low latitudes. These areas lie between the Tropic of Cancer and the Arctic Circle in the Northern Hemisphere and between the Tropic of Capricorn and the Antarctic Circle in the Southern Hemisphere. They have a hot summer, a cold winter, and a moderate spring and fall.

Seasonal Changes in Temperature

Because of the tilt of Earth's axis, temperature patterns change from season to season. The maps below show the world's average monthly temperatures in January and July.

In January, it is winter in the Northern Hemisphere and summer in the Southern Hemisphere. In July, the seasons are reversed. Notice that temperatures are cooler year-round over western South America and other areas. The lower temperatures are due to the high altitude of these regions. **Altitude** is height above sea level. As altitude increases, temperature drops.

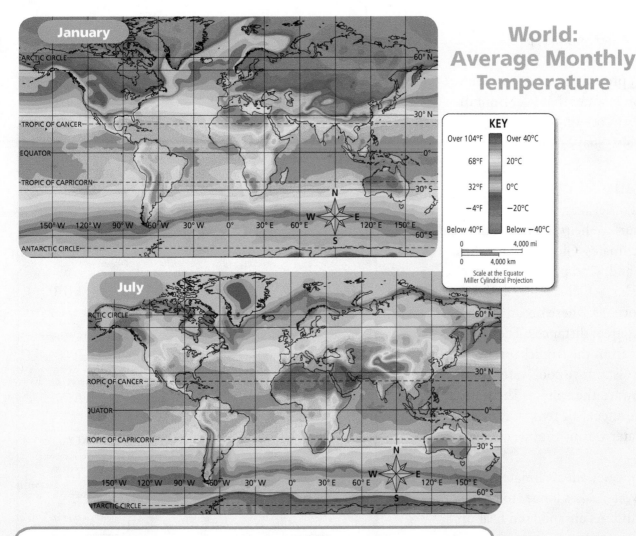

World:
Average Monthly
Temperature

KEY	
Over 104°F	Over 40°C
68°F	20°C
32°F	0°C
−4°F	−20°C
Below 40°F	Below −40°C

0   4,000 mi

0   4,000 km

Scale at the Equator
Miller Cylindrical Projection

Assessment

1. Why are most of the tropics, or the low latitudes, warm all year?

2. How does the tilt of Earth's axis explain changes in temperature from one season to another in the temperate zones?

Water and Climate

Key Ideas
- Water affects climate and weather.
- Water is always moving in the process called the water cycle.

Key Terms • water cycle • evaporation

 Visual Glossary

Like plants and animals, people need fresh water to live. All fresh water comes from precipitation. As you know, precipitation is water that falls from the sky in the form of rain, snow, sleet, or hail. Water also shapes climates.

Oceans and Climate

Oceans and other large bodies of water on Earth's surface help spread Earth's heat and shape climates. Global temperature differences and wind patterns create ocean currents, which act like large rivers within the oceans. These ocean currents move across great distances. They move warm water from the tropics toward the poles. They also move cool water from the poles toward the tropics. The water's temperature affects air temperature near it. Warm water warms the air; cool water chills it.

Bodies of water affect climate in other ways, too. Water takes longer to heat or cool than land. As air and land heat up in summer, water remains cooler. Wind blowing over the cool water helps cool land nearby. So in summer, areas near an ocean or lake will be cooler than inland

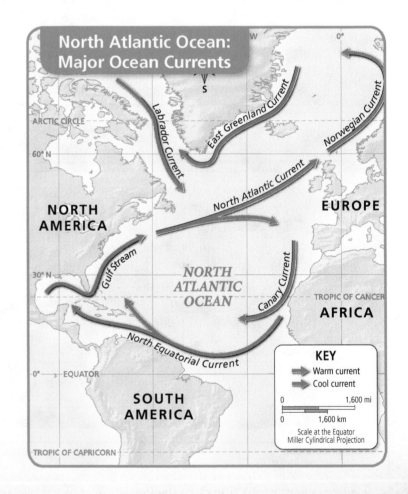

North Atlantic Ocean: Major Ocean Currents

Labrador Current
East Greenland Current
Norwegian Current
North Atlantic Current
Gulf Stream
Canary Current
North Equatorial Current

NORTH AMERICA
EUROPE
AFRICA
SOUTH AMERICA
NORTH ATLANTIC OCEAN

ARCTIC CIRCLE
60° N
30° N
0° EQUATOR
TROPIC OF CANCER
TROPIC OF CAPRICORN

KEY
Warm current
Cool current

0   1,600 mi
0   1,600 km
Scale at the Equator
Miller Cylindrical Projection

areas at the same latitude and altitude. In the winter, on the other hand, water remains warmer than land. So in winter, areas near oceans or lakes are warmer than inland areas.

For example, in the Atlantic Ocean, the Gulf Stream, a warm current, travels northeast from the tropics. The Gulf Stream and the North Atlantic Current carry warm water all the way to Western Europe. That warm water helps give Western Europe a much milder climate than other regions at the same latitude.

The Water Cycle

Earth's water is always moving in a process called the water cycle, shown in the illustration below. The **water cycle** is the movement of water from Earth's surface into the atmosphere and back. As water heats up, it moves from rivers, oceans, and lakes up into the air. As it cools, it falls to Earth's surface and flows back to rivers, oceans and lakes. The water cycle includes precipitation and evaporation. **Evaporation** is the process in which a liquid changes to a gas.

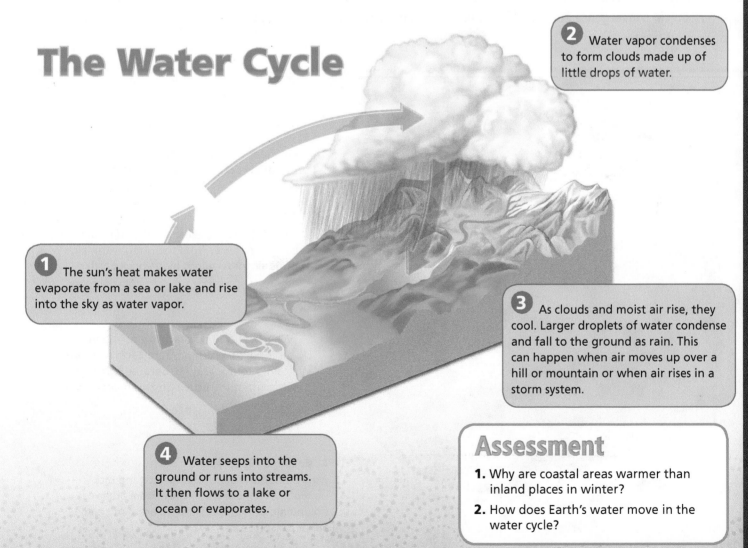

The Water Cycle

2 Water vapor condenses to form clouds made up of little drops of water.

1 The sun's heat makes water evaporate from a sea or lake and rise into the sky as water vapor.

3 As clouds and moist air rise, they cool. Larger droplets of water condense and fall to the ground as rain. This can happen when air moves up over a hill or mountain or when air rises in a storm system.

4 Water seeps into the ground or runs into streams. It then flows to a lake or ocean or evaporates.

Assessment

1. Why are coastal areas warmer than inland places in winter?

2. How does Earth's water move in the water cycle?

Air Circulation and Precipitation

Key Ideas
- Wind and air currents move heat and moisture between different parts of Earth.
- Air movement leads to precipitation and intense storms.

Key Terms
- intertropical convergence zone
- tropical cyclone
- hurricane
- tornado

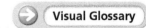 Visual Glossary

Belts of rising and sinking air form a pattern around Earth. Air rises near the Equator, sinks at the edge of the tropics, rises in the temperate zones, and sinks over the poles. The **intertropical convergence zone,** or ITCZ, is the area of rising air near the Equator.

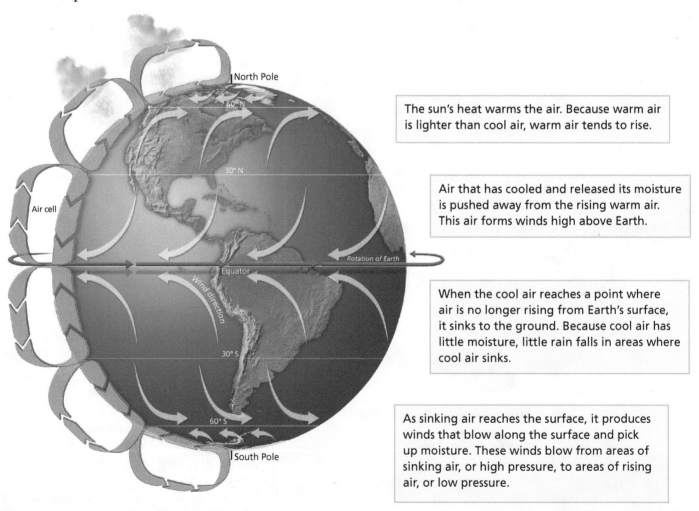

The sun's heat warms the air. Because warm air is lighter than cool air, warm air tends to rise.

Air that has cooled and released its moisture is pushed away from the rising warm air. This air forms winds high above Earth.

When the cool air reaches a point where air is no longer rising from Earth's surface, it sinks to the ground. Because cool air has little moisture, little rain falls in areas where cool air sinks.

As sinking air reaches the surface, it produces winds that blow along the surface and pick up moisture. These winds blow from areas of sinking air, or high pressure, to areas of rising air, or low pressure.

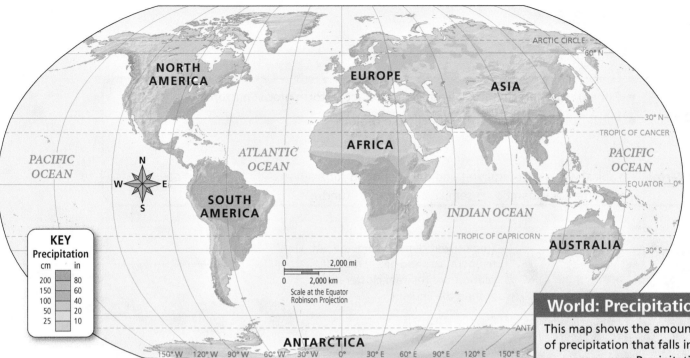

KEY
Precipitation
cm	in
200	80
150	60
100	40
50	20
25	10

0   2,000 mi
0   2,000 km
Scale at the Equator
Robinson Projection

World: Precipitation

This map shows the amount of precipitation that falls in an average year. Precipitation is heaviest near the Equator, where air usually rises. It is also heavy along coastlines, where moist air blows onshore and is forced to rise. Precipitation is lightest where cool air sinks near the poles and at the edges of the tropics, where deserts are normally found.

Raging Storms

Most storms occur when two air masses of different temperatures or moisture contents come together. Some storms bring small amounts of rain or snow, while others bring heavy wind and rain, causing great destruction.

A **tropical cyclone** is an intense rainstorm with strong winds that forms over oceans in the tropics. A **hurricane** is a cyclone that forms over the Atlantic Ocean. These storms can cause much damage. A **tornado** is a swirling funnel of wind that can reach 200 miles (320 km) per hour. Tornadoes can be more dangerous than hurricanes, but they affect smaller areas.

Most other storms are less dangerous. In winter, blizzards dump snow on parts of North America. Severe rainstorms and thunderstorms strike North America most often in spring and summer.

Assessment

1. Why is precipitation heaviest near the Equator?

2. How do physical processes such as air circulation and precipitation affect humans?

Tornadoes can cause severe damage.

Types of Climate

Key Ideas
- Temperature, precipitation, and wind interact to form global patterns.
- Earth has a number of different climate regions.

Key Terms
- tropical wet
- tropical wet and dry
- humid subtropical
- maritime
- subarctic
- semiarid
- arid
- tundra

→ **Visual Glossary**

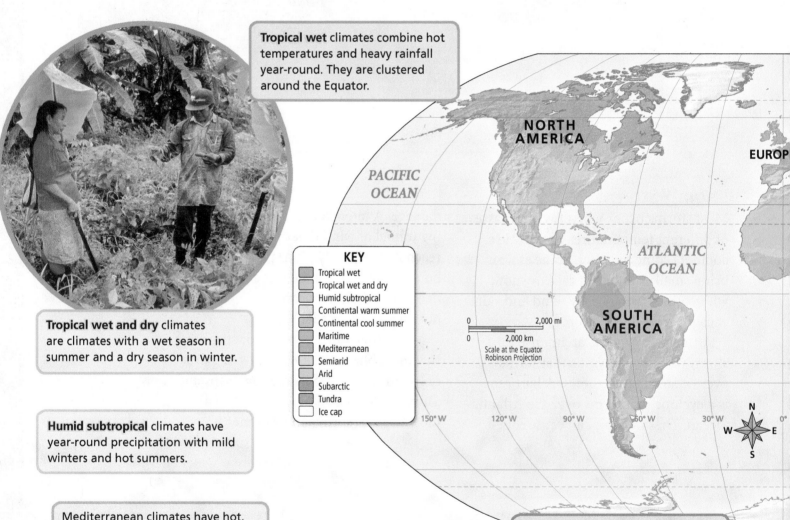

Tropical wet climates combine hot temperatures and heavy rainfall year-round. They are clustered around the Equator.

Tropical wet and dry climates are climates with a wet season in summer and a dry season in winter.

Humid subtropical climates have year-round precipitation with mild winters and hot summers.

Mediterranean climates have hot, dry weather in the summer and a rainy season in the winter.

Maritime climates are wet year-round, with mild winters and cool summers. They exist where moist winds blow onshore.

Continental warm summer climates have year-round precipitation, warm summers, and cold, snowy winters. Continental cool summer climates are similar, but they have generally lower temperatures.

KEY
- Tropical wet
- Tropical wet and dry
- Humid subtropical
- Continental warm summer
- Continental cool summer
- Maritime
- Mediterranean
- Semiarid
- Arid
- Subarctic
- Tundra
- Ice cap

NORTH AMERICA

EUROP

PACIFIC OCEAN

ATLANTIC OCEAN

SOUTH AMERICA

0   2,000 mi
0   2,000 km
Scale at the Equator
Robinson Projection

150° W   120° W   90° W   60° W   30° W   0°

N
W   E
S

You have already learned about the most important shapers of climate: temperature, precipitation, and wind. These factors form global patterns. For example, temperatures are warmest in and around the tropics and are coolest close to the poles. Precipitation is greatest near the Equator. These patterns of temperature and precipitation create world climate regions. Climate regions are areas that share a similar climate.

Subarctic climates have limited precipitation, cool summers, and very cold winters.

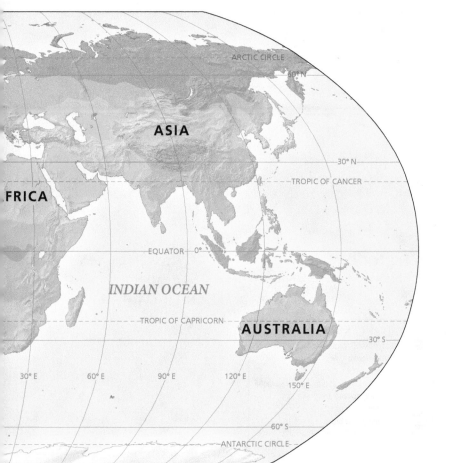

Semiarid, or dry, climates and **arid**, or very dry, desert climates occur where there is steadily sinking air.

Tundra climates have cool summers and bitterly cold, dry winters. Close to the poles, ice caps, or permanent sheets of ice covering land or sea, have bitter cold and dry climates year-round.

Assessment

1. In the winter, what kind of weather would you expect in a continental warm summer climate?

2. What factors explain the locations of Earth's tropical wet and tropical wet and dry climates?

Tropical or Subtropical Forest

Steady hot temperatures and moist air support the rich ecosystems known as tropical rain forests.

Temperate Forest

Moist temperate climates support thick forests of **deciduous trees,** or trees that lose their leaves in the fall. Some temperate forests include a mix of deciduous and evergreen trees.

Subarctic Forest

Coniferous trees are trees that produce cones to carry seeds. They also have needles. These features protect trees through the cold, dry winters of subarctic climates.

Tropical or Subtropical Grassland or Savanna

A **savanna** is a park-like landscape of grasslands with scattered trees that can survive dry spells. Savannas are found in tropical areas with dry seasons.

Temperate Grassland and Brush

Vast grasslands cover regions that get more rain than deserts but too little to support forests.

Core Concepts 3.6

Ecosystems

Key Idea

- An ecosystem is a network of living things that depend on one another and their environment for survival.

Key Terms

- deciduous tree
- coniferous tree
- savanna
- ecosystem

Visual Glossary

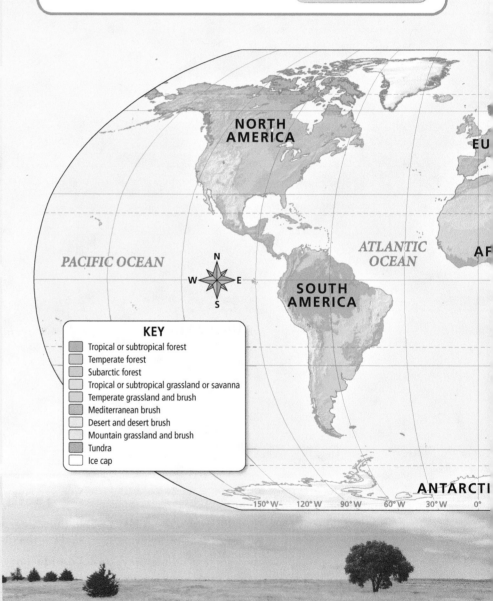

NORTH AMERICA

EU

PACIFIC OCEAN

ATLANTIC OCEAN

AF

SOUTH AMERICA

N
W E
S

ANTARCTI

150° W 120° W 90° W 60° W 30° W 0°

KEY
- Tropical or subtropical forest
- Temperate forest
- Subarctic forest
- Tropical or subtropical grassland or savanna
- Temperate grassland and brush
- Mediterranean brush
- Desert and desert brush
- Mountain grassland and brush
- Tundra
- Ice cap

The connections between living things and the environment form ecosystems. An **ecosystem** is a group of plants and animals that depend on each other and their environment for survival. Ecosystems can be small or large. The map below shows Earth's major types of ecosystems.

Ecosystems can change over time due to physical processes or human activities. For example, a lack of rain in a temperate forest ecosystem might kill off many plants and animals. The building of a city is an example of a human activity that changes an original ecosystem.

Mediterranean Brush

Shrubs and other low plants in Mediterranean climates have to hold water from winter rains to survive hot, dry summers.

Desert and Desert Brush

Dry semiarid areas and deserts with some rain support animals and low-lying desert plants. These plants need little water and can live in extreme temperatures. The driest desert areas have little or no plant life.

Mountain Grassland and Brush

In mountain grassland and brush regions, vegetation depends on elevation, since temperatures drop as altitude increases.

Tundra

The tundra is an area of cold climate and low-lying plants. Here, grasses grow and low shrubs bloom during brief, cool summers. Animals of the tundra are able to live with cold temperatures and scarce food.

Ice Cap

Thick ice caps form around the poles, with their year-round climates of extreme cold. No plants can live on this ice.

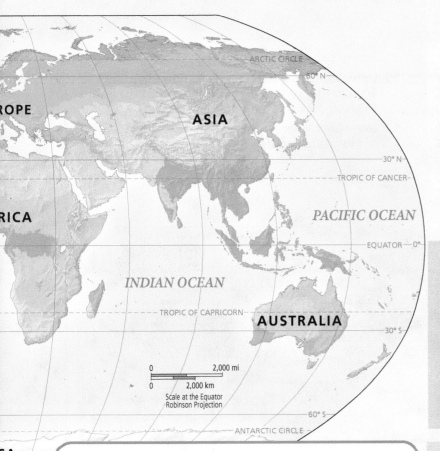

EUROPE
ASIA
AFRICA
PACIFIC OCEAN
INDIAN OCEAN
AUSTRALIA
ANTARCTICA

ARCTIC CIRCLE
60° N
30° N
TROPIC OF CANCER
EQUATOR — 0°
TROPIC OF CAPRICORN
30° S
60° S
ANTARCTIC CIRCLE
30° E

0   2,000 mi
0   2,000 km
Scale at the Equator
Robinson Projection

Assessment

1. How do climate differences affect plant and animal life?

2. What features of the plants and animals in your own region let them live in your region's climate?

Part 3 Assessment

Key Terms and Ideas

1. **Summarize** What is a region's **weather**? What is a region's **climate**?

2. **Identify** What are the three most important factors of climate?

3. **Compare and Contrast** How do temperatures in the **low latitudes** differ from temperatures in the **middle latitudes**?

4. **Sequence** Rank these climates in terms of amount of precipitation, from most precipitation to least precipitation: **subarctic, arid, tropical wet.**

5. **Compare and Contrast** How are **deciduous trees** different from **coniferous trees**?

6. **Connect** What is the role of air temperature in the **water cycle**?

7. **Describe** How does the physical environment affect humans?

Think Critically

8. **Categorize** Explain in one sentence how today's weather is related to your region's climate.

9. **Predict** How would winter temperatures differ between two cities on the same continent at the same latitude, one on the coast and one inland?

10. **Draw Inferences** Use what you know about the amount of moisture in cool air to predict the level of precipitation in a tundra climate.

11. **Draw Conclusions** How does altitude affect temperature in different latitudes?

Identify

Answer the following questions based on the map.

12. What do the arrows on this map show?

13. In which zone of latitude is the West Wind Drift?

14. Is the North Atlantic Current warm or cool?

15. Is the California Current warm or cool?

16. Is the Brazil Current located in the Northern Hemisphere or the Southern Hemisphere?

17. Does the Benguela Current bring cool water to the polar zones or to the tropics?

18. What important parallel of latitude does the Kuroshio Current cross?

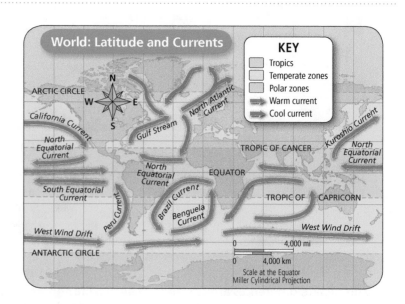

Journal Activity

Fill in the graphic organizer in your Student Journal.

Demonstrate Your Understanding Complete the Sum-It-Up activity in your journal to demonstrate your understanding of climates and ecosystems. After you complete the activity, discuss your predictions with a partner. Be sure to support your predictions with information from the lessons.

21st Century Learning

Give an Effective Presentation

Research and deliver an illustrated oral presentation on the features of one of the ecosystems described in Lesson 6. Be sure to address the following topics:
- Climate characteristics
- Effect of climate on animal and plant life
- Effect of climate on human life, including the economy

Document-Based Questions

Success Tracker™
Online at myworldgeography.com

Use your knowledge of climates and ecosystems and Documents A and B to answer Questions 1–3.

Document A

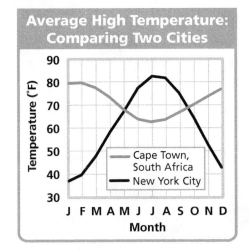

Document B

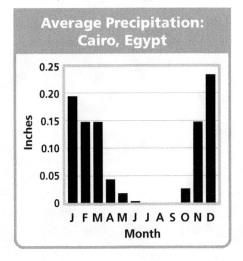

1. Examine Document A. Which of the following statements is true?

A New York City and Cape Town are located in the same hemisphere.

B New York City is in the Southern Hemisphere, while Cape Town is in the Northern Hemisphere.

C New York City is in the Northern Hemisphere, while Cape Town is in the Southern Hemisphere.

D none of the above

2. Examine Document B. Judging from the average precipitation Cairo receives, in which of the following climates is it most likely to be located?

A tropical wet

B maritime

C arid

D humid subtropical

3. Writing Task Using information from Document A as evidence, describe how a location's hemisphere affects its seasons.

Human–Environment Interaction

Young people support clean energy sources.

Oil leaks from an abandoned oil barrel in Alaska. ▲

Environmental workers clean up an oil spill.

Lauren Hexilon

MAKING A DIFFERENCE

Story by Miles Lemaire for myWorld Geography

Lauren Hexilon wants to save the world. Lauren has wanted to protect the environment for as long as she can remember. After she graduated from college recently, Lauren decided to go to work for the U.S. Environmental Protection Agency (EPA).

The EPA was an obvious choice for Lauren. After all, the organization's main focus is to protect human health and the environment. Today Lauren works with people who help protect public health and the environment in many ways. Some of their work deals with hazardous waste spills around the country. Hazardous waste includes chemicals, radioactive materials, and other waste dangerous to humans, wildlife, and the environment.

Cleaning up hazardous waste can be "a very long process," Lauren says. To dispose of waste safely, she explains, "you have to follow certain rules and procedures, so it takes a while to see a project from its beginning to its end."

Lauren doesn't clean up pollution and hazardous waste herself. Still, she helps protect the environment at her job each day. She spends much of her time working with young people to teach them about environmental issues. Raising public awareness is important, she says.

Right now Lauren is working with the University of North Texas on projects that help people understand threats to the environment. She is also helping to create an environmental video conference. This conference will connect young people from countries around the world. Lauren likes these projects because they teach people to protect the environment. Plus, she says, she gets to see the results of her work quickly.

But you don't have to work for the EPA to help prevent pollution and protect the environment. Lauren says that each of us makes choices every day that have an impact on the environment, whether we realize it or not. Take conserving energy, for example. "Flipping on a light switch, that's an environmental impact," says Lauren. "If you leave the light on, you're wasting electricity."

So what does Lauren think that young people should know about human interaction with the environment? Simply this: She would like each of us to think about how our actions affect the environment. Whenever possible, Lauren says, try to make good choices about your actions. For example, consider riding a bicycle or taking public transportation instead of driving in a car.

In fact, everyone can take small steps to improve the way they interact with the environment. We should think about "all the little things" we do each day, says Lauren. As she points out, "The little things add up."

47

Environment and Resources

Key Ideas
- People depend on the environment for food, water, energy, and other natural resources.
- Some resources are replaced by Earth over time, but others are not.

Key Terms
- natural resource
- renewable resource
- nonrenewable resource
- fossil fuel

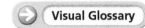

Visual Glossary

People use many natural resources in their daily lives. Above, a young woman in Chad uses soil to build a shelter. Below, German workers use metals to build an automobile.

Humans depend on their natural environment to survive. We need the environment to provide energy, water, food, and other materials. In prehistoric times, people lived in areas where they could hunt, gather food, and find fresh water. Later, people settled where they found pasture for their livestock or fertile soils and sufficient water for farming. Today, rapid transportation and other technologies allow people to be less dependent on their immediate environment. However, people still need access to resources.

Natural Resources

Water is just one example of a **natural resource,** or a useful material found in the environment. People depend on many kinds of natural resources. These resources can be divided into two types: renewable and nonrenewable resources.

Major Natural Resources

Resource		Type	Formation	Major Uses
Soil		Renewable	Formed from rocks and organic material broken down by natural processes	Agriculture
Water		Renewable	Renewed through the water cycle	Drinking, agriculture, washing, transportation
Plants		Renewable	Usually grow from seeds; require water and sunlight	Food, lumber, clothing, paper
Animals		Renewable	Formed through natural reproduction; require water and food	Food, agricultural labor, transportation, clothing
Fossil fuels		Nonrenewable	Formed over millions of years from plant and animal material	Energy, plastics, chemicals
Minerals		Nonrenewable	Formed through a variety of natural geologic processes	Automobile parts, electronics, and many other human-made products

A **renewable resource** is a resource that Earth or people can replace. Examples of renewable resources include water, plants, and animals. All of these resources can be replaced over time if they are used wisely. For example, if you cut down a tree, another one can grow in its place. When dead plants decay, their nutrients increase soil fertility.

A **nonrenewable resource** is a resource that cannot be replaced in a relatively short period of time. Nonrenewable resources include nonliving things such as minerals, metal ores, and fossil fuels. **Fossil fuels** are nonrenewable resources formed over millions of years from the remains of plants and animals. Coal, natural gas, and petroleum are important fossil fuels. When nonrenewable resources such as fossil fuels are used up, they are gone.

Energy Resources

Sources of energy are important for human activity. Some sources, such as wind and sunlight, are renewable. Today, we mostly rely on nonrenewable energy resources such as coal and petroleum. Because these sources are nonrenewable, Earth will eventually run out of them.

Some countries have large supplies of petroleum and are able to export it, or sell it to other countries. Most countries, however, must buy petroleum and other energy resources from other countries.

Assessment

1. What do people need from the physical environment?
2. How are renewable and nonrenewable natural resources formed?

49

Core Concepts 4.2

Land Use

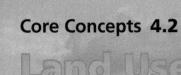

Key Ideas
- People use land in different ways.
- Land use can change over time.

Key Terms • colonization • industrialization • suburb

→ **Visual Glossary**

The ways people use land are affected by both the natural environment and culture. In many regions, land use has changed over time.

Reasons for Land Use

How people use land depends partly on the environment. For example, people living in temperate climates with fertile soil may use land mainly for farming. People in arctic areas may use land mainly for hunting. Even in similar environments, however, people may use land differently because they have different customs and ways of life.

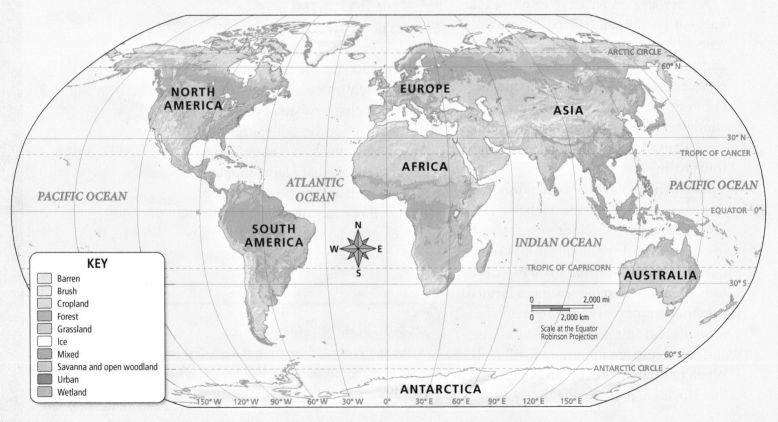

KEY
- Barren
- Brush
- Cropland
- Forest
- Grassland
- Ice
- Mixed
- Savanna and open woodland
- Urban
- Wetland

Changes in Land Use

Land use can change over time. For example, colonization has led to many changes in land use. **Colonization** is a movement of new settlers and their culture to an area. Settlers may change a region's landscape. For example, European colonists brought new crops and new ways of farming to the Americas, Africa, and Australia. These new ways led to dramatic changes in land use as Europeans cleared large areas of land for cropland and livestock pasture.

Since the 1800s, industrialization has changed landscapes in many countries. **Industrialization** is the development of machine-powered production and manufacturing. Large cities have grown around factories. Technology such as machines for clearing land and building roads has made it easier for people to change their environment. This environmental change has allowed the growth of suburbs. A **suburb** is a residential area on the edge of a city or large town.

In the United States and some other countries, most people live in cities or suburban areas. Although cities and suburbs cover a relatively small area, they are an important use of land. Land uses covering large areas include cropland, forests, and grassland.

Land use varies around the world. Above, Tokyo, Japan, is a large city with millions of residents. Below, these people from the Dominican Republic use land for agriculture.

A large portion of Rio de Janeiro, Brazil, is built on steep hills along the Atlantic Ocean. ▼

Assessment

1. How does land use vary from place to place and over time?

2. How have people adapted to and changed the environment?

People's Impact on the Environment

Key Ideas
- People affect the environment in many ways.
- People try to decrease the negative effects of using resources.

Key Terms • deforestation • biodiversity • pollution • spillover

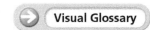
Visual Glossary

A ll people need food, water, clothing, and shelter. To meet these needs, people have to use materials from their environment. As a result, people have impacts on the environment in their daily lives.

Extracting Resources

People extract, or remove, many kinds of natural resources from the environment. For example, to get wood for building houses, people cut down trees. Advances in technology have allowed people to extract some resources more easily. For example, to get petroleum for fuel, people drill deep wells, sometimes far into the ocean floor.

Extracting resources can harm ecosystems and the environment. For example, cutting down too many trees can cause deforestation. **Deforestation** is the loss of forest cover in a region. Animals that live in the forest may suffer as a result. Drilling oil wells and transporting oil can lead to oil spills, which harm the land and water. Deforestation and producing oil can also reduce biodiversity. **Biodiversity** is the variety of living things in a region or ecosystem.

A bird is covered in oil from an oil spill in Spain. Oil spills and other pollution can affect land, water, and animals. ▼

Other Impacts

People also affect the environment by growing food or producing other goods and services. For example, new technology has allowed farmers to plow more land for crops. But when land is cleared, soil is loosened and can erode, or wash away.

People's activities can also produce **pollution,** or waste that makes the air, soil, or water less clean. For example, many farmers use chemicals called fertilizers and pesticides to help plants grow and to kill pests. These chemicals can help farmers produce more food. They can also harm the environment by causing pollution.

Pollution is a **spillover,** which is an effect on someone or something not involved in an activity. For example, air pollution affects everyone who breathes the polluted air, even people who did not cause the pollution.

Finding the Best Solution

People try to increase the positive and decrease the negative effects of using resources. For example, using a resource might lead to economic growth but also create pollution that needs to be reduced. Working together, people, governments, and businesses can try to use resources wisely. In some cases, governments limit land use to preserve the environment.

▲ These wind turbines in Canada convert wind energy into electricity.

Advances in technology can also help protect resources and the environment. One way of protecting the environment is for people to use vehicles that burn less fuel, such as hybrid cars. Vehicles that burn less fuel create less air pollution. People can also use clean energy sources, such as solar power and wind power. They are considered clean energy sources because they do not pollute the air.

Assessment

1. How have new technologies affected people's ability to change the environment?

2. How might future uses of technology affect Earth?

Part 4 Assessment

Key Terms and Ideas

1. **Identify** List two **fossil fuels.**
2. **Recall** What is an example of a **natural resource**?
3. **Discuss** How might **colonization** affect a region?
4. **Paraphrase** In your own words, describe the causes and effects of **deforestation.**

5. **Sequence** Explain how **suburbs** develop.
6. **Summarize** How do people use natural resources?
7. **Cause and Effect** If a company pollutes a river, what is one possible **spillover**?

Think Critically

8. **Draw Inferences** Give two examples of ways technology has made people less dependent on the environment around them.
9. **Analyze Cause and Effect** Imagine that your state's supply of fossil fuels was suddenly cut in half. How might this affect daily life in your state?

10. **Solve Problems** Explain what the following statement means: *While trees are a renewable resource, it often takes human effort to make them renewable.*
11. **Synthesize** Imagine that a large factory is about to be constructed on the edge of a rain forest. How might this factory affect the region's biodiversity?

Identify

Answer the following questions based on the map.

12. India is a former British colony. Why do you think it was a valuable colony for Britain?
13. What natural resources are found in India?
14. What geographic features could also be natural resources?
15. How do you think land might be used in the Himalayas?
16. How do you think land might be used along the coast?
17. What environmental problems might use of India's natural resources cause?
18. How might altitude affect where people live in India?

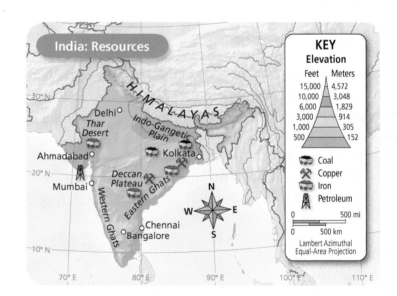

Journal Activity

Answer the questions in your Student Journal.

Demonstrate Your Understanding Complete the Sum-It-Up activity in your journal to demonstrate your understanding of human–environment interaction. After you complete the activity, discuss your answers in a small group. Be sure to support your answers with information from the lessons.

21st Century Learning

Search for Information on the Internet

Pollution can cause many harmful effects. Use online resources to research some of the effects of pollution and present your findings in a poster. When researching, remember the following:
- Use reputable Web sites, particularly those with addresses ending in *.gov* or *.edu*.
- Identify the site's author and check for bias.

Document-Based Questions

Success ⭐ Tracker™
Online at myworldgeography.com

Use your knowledge of human–environment interaction and Documents A and B to answer Questions 1–3.

Document A

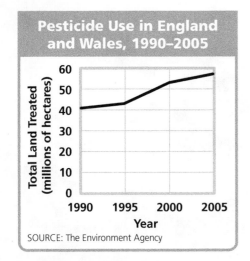

Pesticide Use in England and Wales, 1990–2005

SOURCE: The Environment Agency

Document B

1. **Examine** Document A. How has pesticide use changed in England and Wales in recent years?

   A It has increased.

   B It has decreased.

   C It has stopped completely.

   D It has not changed.

2. **Examine** Document B. Which of the following statements is true?

   A Major cities are spread out evenly across Massachusetts.

   B Most major cities are located far from Boston.

   C Most major cities are near Boston.

   D The location of Boston does not appear to have affected the locations of other cities.

3. **Writing Task** How might settlement and land use in Massachusetts be different if Boston were not its largest city? Explain your answer.

Economics and Geography

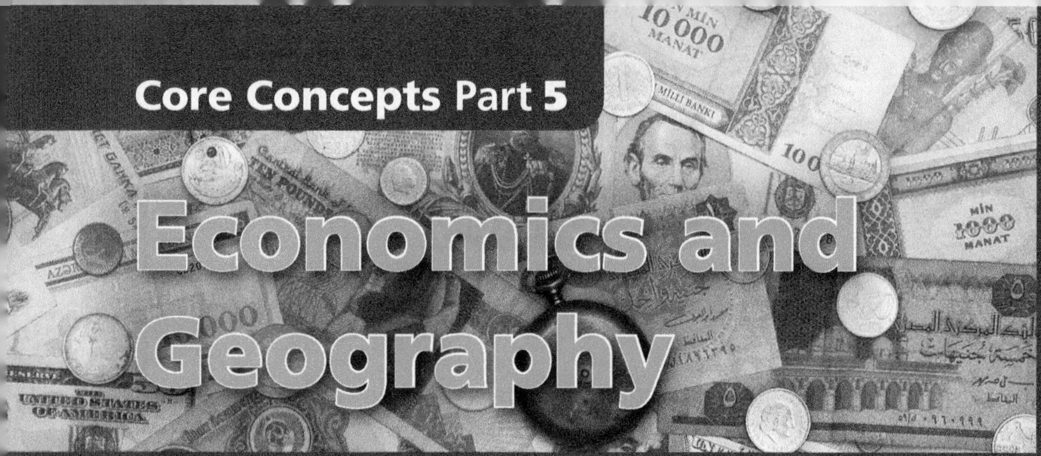

Surf shops are common in southern California.

Chris's childhood love of surfing helped inspire his first business.

Chris's business specializes in Web site design.

Chris Kerstner

An Extraordinary Entrepreneur

Story by Miles Lemaire for myWorld Geography

Chris Kerstner is still in his early twenties, but he has already created and successfully run four companies. In fact, Chris started his first business when he was still in middle school.

Chris is an entrepreneur, or a person who starts new businesses. "I surfed when I was a kid," Chris says, "so I'd repair surfboards for friends, and that kind of blossomed to the point where I was the main repair guy for all the local surf shops in Newport Beach [California]."

By the time he was old enough to drive, Chris had started a second business, this time on dry land: working on car stereos. This business grew quickly, Chris says. "It was like I had [an auto parts store] running out of my garage!"

Then, one night at a friend's party, Chris had an experience that led to his most successful company yet. "One of my friend's parents was talking to me about his small business and the Web designers that he had to deal with," Chris says. "He was telling me that they did great work but that they were never on time, and that he would pay anything for a Web designer who could get the work done on time. All I heard, as an entrepreneur, was 'I'll pay anything,' so immediately I turned around and said, 'Oh, yeah, I can do that. No problem!'"

The only problem was that Chris did not know anything about Web design. In fact, he did not even own a computer! But he did not let those obstacles stop him. Within a few weeks, Chris had taught himself how to design Web sites and had produced a Web site for his client.

It was this job that gave Chris the idea for his next company, which specializes in Web design and marketing. Chris created the company while attending business school at the University of Southern California. The company earned nearly $2 million during his first year of school alone. Today, Chris's business has offices in three countries. It has designed Web sites and marketing plans for many major companies.

Chris thinks that the business has been successful because of his belief in providing customers with fast, reliable service. That's the only way a company can survive in the fast-paced modern economy, he says.

So what advice would Chris give to someone else starting a business? Chris says that he loved his professors at business school, but that there was one thing he wished he had been taught in class: "Keep the customers happy. That's it! It's not complicated. … Just keep your customers happy, and that's it."

57

Economic Basics

Key Ideas
- People make choices about how to meet their wants and needs.
- Economies bring together people and businesses that make, sell, and buy goods and services.

Key Terms
- economics
- scarcity
- opportunity cost
- demand
- supply
- producer
- consumer
- incentive

Visual Glossary →

Economics is the study of how people meet their wants and needs. People must answer three basic economic questions:

1. What goods and services should be produced?
2. How should goods and services be produced?
3. Who uses or consumes those goods and services?

The resources people use to make goods and services are called factors of production. The three main factors are land, labor, and capital. Geographers study where the factors of production are located.

Making Choices

There is no limit to the things that people want, but there are limits to what can be created. This difference between wants and reality creates **scarcity,** or having a limited quantity of resources to meet unlimited wants. Since people have limited money and time, they have to choose

Factors of Production

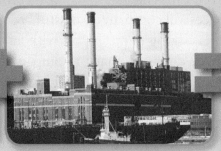

Entrepreneur
A person known as an entrepreneur combines resources to create new businesses.

Land, Labor, Capital
The three main factors of production are land and resources; human labor; and capital, or human-made goods like tools and buildings.

Goods and Services
Entrepreneurs use the factors of production to produce goods and services.

what they want most. Making a choice involves an **opportunity cost,** or the cost of what you have to give up.

Economics also involves demand and supply. **Demand** is the desire for a certain good or service. **Supply** is the amount of a good or service that is available for use. Demand and supply are connected to price. As the price of a product increases, people will buy less of it. That is, demand will decrease. If the price of the product decreases, demand will increase.

Supply functions in a similar way. If the price of a product increases, companies will make more of it. If the price of the product decreases, companies will make less of it. The price at which demand equals supply is the market price, or the market-clearing price.

Basic economic choices have influenced world events. For example, high demand for resources such as gold or oil has led to exploration and colonization.

Making Goods and Services

Economies bring together producers and consumers. **Producers** are people or businesses that make and sell products. **Consumers** are people or businesses that buy, or consume, products. Producers try to win consumers' business by offering better products for lower prices than other producers. If they sell more products, they

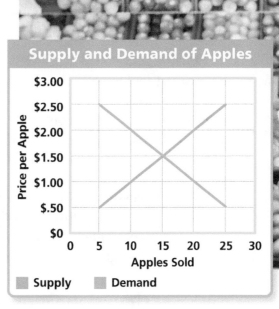

Supply and Demand of Apples

Supply   Demand

usually increase production. But producers will not make more products if the sale price is less than the marginal cost. Marginal cost is the cost of making one more unit of the product. Therefore, the marginal cost for the producer sets a minimum price for the product.

Businesses make products because of economic incentives. An **incentive** is a factor that encourages people to act in a certain way. Money is an incentive. The desire to earn money gives most producers an incentive to make and sell products. The incentive to save money leads most consumers to look for lower prices.

Assessment

1. On the line graph on this page, what is the market-clearing price?

2. How might a change in the price of one good or service lead to changes in prices of other goods or services?

Economic Process

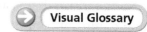
The economic process is complicated, but its basic idea is simple: Producers and consumers exchange goods and services in a market. A **market** is an organized way for producers and consumers to trade goods and services.

Exchanging Goods and Services

Throughout history, people have often engaged in barter, the trading of goods and services for other goods and services. Today, the means of exchange in a market is usually money. Modern governments issue money in the form of currency, or paper bills and metal coins. Different countries use different currencies. As a result, countries must establish the relative values of their currencies in order to trade. They must also establish a system for exchanging different currencies.

Businesses and the Economic Process

Businesses want to make a profit. **Profit** is the money a company has left after subtracting the costs of doing business. To make a profit, companies try to reduce expenses and increase revenue. **Revenue** is the money earned by selling goods and services. The price of resources affects revenue and profit. If resources become more expensive, the cost of making goods with them will also increase. Businesses' profits will drop.

Companies can increase profit and revenue through **specialization,** the act of concentrating on a limited number of goods or activities. Specialization allows people and companies to use resources more efficiently and to increase production and consumption.

Companies' profits are affected by **competition,** which is the struggle among producers for consumers' money. If one company raises the price of its products, another company may sell similar goods

Economists divide economic activity into four levels, as you can see in this table. ▼

Levels of Economic Activity	
Primary Industry	Collects resources from nature. Examples: farming, mining
Secondary Industry	Uses raw materials to create new products. Example: manufacturing
Tertiary Industry	Provides services to people and secondary industries. Examples: banking, restaurants
Quaternary Industry	Focuses on research and information. Example: education

Competition in the Market

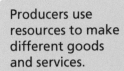

Producers use resources to make different goods and services.

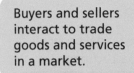

Buyers and sellers interact to trade goods and services in a market.

Competition between buyers and between sellers affects product price, quality, and marketing.

for a lower price to win more business. Companies use advertising to help increase demand for their products and to compete with other companies.

Nonprofit organizations are business-like institutions that do not seek to make a profit. Nonprofit organizations can include churches, museums, hospitals, and other bodies.

A healthy economy grows as companies produce and sell more goods and services. In a growing economy, prices may increase over time. This general increase in prices is called **inflation.**

Economies do not keep growing forever. Eventually, economic activity falls as production slows and consumers buy fewer goods and services. This lack of demand for goods and services can lead to increased unemployment. A decline in economic growth for six or more months in a row is known as a **recession.**

Assessment

1. Does a person always need money to obtain goods or services?

2. How does competition affect producers and consumers?

Economic Systems

Key Ideas
- Different societies have different types of economic systems.
- Most societies have economic systems with some element of government control.

Key Terms
- traditional economy
- market economy
- command economy
- mixed economy

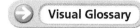
Visual Glossary

Every society has an economic system in which people make and distribute goods and services. There are four basic economic systems: traditional, market, command, and mixed. The roles of individuals, businesses, and government vary in each system. Economic goals, incentives, and government regulations can also vary.

Traditional Economies

A **traditional economy** is an economy in which people make economic decisions based on their customs and habits. They usually satisfy their needs and wants through hunting or farming, as their ancestors did. People in traditional economies usually do not want to change their basic way of life. Today, traditional economies are not common.

The Fulani people in Niger are livestock herders. ▶

Market Economies

A **market economy** is an economy in which individual consumers and producers make economic decisions. This type of economy is also called capitalism, or a free market. Market economies encourage entrepreneurs to establish new businesses by giving them economic freedom.

A consumer makes a purchase at a grocery store. ▶

◀ In North Korea, government leaders make most economic decisions.

Command Economies

A **command economy** is an economy in which the central government makes all economic decisions. This kind of system is also called a centrally planned economy. In a command economy, individual consumers and producers do not make basic economic decisions.

Circular Flow in a Mixed Economy

- Resources
- Payments

- Goods and services
- Wages

Businesses

Households

- Goods and services
- Taxes

- Resources
- Taxes

- Services
- Payments

- Services
- Wages

Governments

Mixed Economies

In reality, pure market or command economies do not exist. Most societies have mixed economies with varying levels of government control. A **mixed economy** is an economy that combines elements of traditional, market, and command economic systems. The diagram at left shows the circular flow of economic activity in a mixed economy.

Countries such as the United States and Australia have mixed economies that are close to pure market economies. In these countries, government makes some economic decisions. For example, government passes laws to protect consumers' rights. Government spending and taxation provide jobs and services and influence economic growth.

Countries such as North Korea and Cuba have mixed economies that are close to pure command economies. In these countries, government owns and controls most businesses.

Assessment

1. What are the differences among traditional, command, and market economies?

2. What are some possible advantages of the free-market system used in the United States and other countries?

63

Core Concepts 5.4

Economic Development

> **Key Ideas**
> - The level of a country's development has direct effects on the lives of its people.
> - There are many ways for a country to increase economic development.
>
> **Key Terms** • development • developed country • developing country
> • gross domestic product (GDP) • productivity • technology
>
> ⊙ **Visual Glossary**

Economists use the concept of development to talk about a country's economic well-being. **Development** is economic growth or an increase in living standards.

Measuring Economic Development

When we study development, we look at factors like people's education, literacy, and life expectancy. We also examine their individual purchasing power, or their ability to buy goods and services.

A **developed country** is a country with a strong economy and a high standard of living, such as the United States or Japan. Only about 20 percent of the world's countries are developed. The remaining 80 percent are **developing countries,** or countries with less-productive economies and lower standards of living, such as Haiti or Ethiopia.

Economists use gross domestic product to measure a country's economy. **Gross domestic product (GDP)** is the total value of all goods and services produced in a country in a year.

World Population, 2008

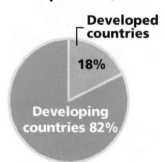

Developed countries
18%

Developing countries 82%

SOURCE: UN Population Division

People in developed countries such as Japan often work in offices. Most have access to education and healthcare.

Developing countries such as Guatemala have fewer industries. People often have lower life expectancies and literacy rates.

64

World: Human Development

KEY
Human Development
High
Medium
Low
No data

Increasing Development

A country can increase economic development in many ways. It can find more resources to use in creating products. It can invest in capital goods such as factories and equipment. It can improve education and training to increase human capital. Human capital is workers' skill and knowledge.

Highly skilled workers usually earn higher wages, or money paid for work. Wages are also affected by supply and demand. If there is a high demand for workers and a limited supply of applicants, companies must pay higher wages to attract workers.

A country can improve development by increasing **productivity,** or the amount of goods and services produced given the amount of resources used. A business that increases productivity can produce goods and services more efficiently. More productive workers often earn higher wages.

Improved technology can lead to economic growth. **Technology** is the practical application of knowledge to accomplish a task. Technological advances can create new products, such as computers. They can make it easier for people to communicate and do business. However, it can be difficult for poor countries to afford new technology.

Assessment

1. What factors do economists use to study development?

2. How might economic factors affect the use of technology in various places, cultures, and societies?

Trade

Key Ideas
- Individuals and countries trade with one another to get the things they need and want.
- Many countries are working toward the removal of trade barriers.

Key Terms • trade • export • import • tariff • trade barrier • free trade

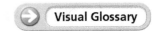 Visual Glossary

In the past, most people grew or hunted their own food. They made their own clothing. They built their own homes. In short, people did nearly everything for themselves. Today, however, most people depend on others to supply the goods and services they need. Our world is interdependent. That is, people and countries depend on one another for goods and services.

Trade and Geography

To get the products we need and want, we engage in trade. **Trade** is the exchange of goods and services in a market. When individuals engage in trade, they do so because they gain from that trade. In other words, trade benefits both the buyer and the seller.

Geographic location can give a country or region advantages in trade. For example, a region that is close to an ocean can more easily ship goods overseas. On the other hand, a manufacturing plant located far away from a market will need to add transportation costs to its products, making them higher in price.

Container ships, such as the ones in this photo, carry most of the world's goods from one port to another. ▼

Types of Trade

All of the buying and selling that takes place within a country is known as domestic trade. Domestic trade involves producers and consumers located inside the same country.

Domestic producers and consumers can also engage in international trade, or trade with foreign producers and consumers. International trade involves exports and imports. **Exports** are goods and services produced within a country and sold outside the country's borders. **Imports** are goods and services sold in a country that are produced in other countries. International trade requires a system for exchanging types of currency.

Trade Barriers and Free Trade

If imported goods are cheaper than domestic goods, consumers will usually buy more of them. These lower prices can harm domestic producers by reducing their sales. Governments sometimes try to protect domestic producers through tariffs. A **tariff** is a tax on imports or exports. Tariffs are an example of trade barriers. A **trade barrier** is a government policy or restriction that limits international trade.

Today, many countries are working toward **free trade,** or the removal of trade barriers. Free trade gives consumers lower prices and more choices. However, domestic producers can suffer if consumers prefer cheaper imported goods.

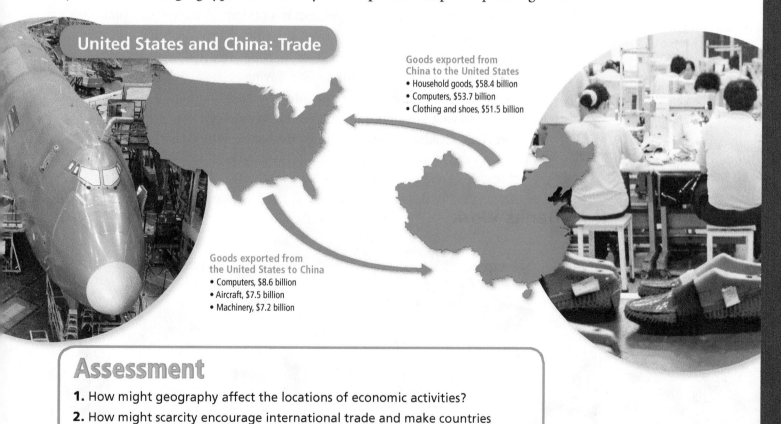

United States and China: Trade

Goods exported from China to the United States
• Household goods, $58.4 billion
• Computers, $53.7 billion
• Clothing and shoes, $51.5 billion

Goods exported from the United States to China
• Computers, $8.6 billion
• Aircraft, $7.5 billion
• Machinery, $7.2 billion

Assessment

1. How might geography affect the locations of economic activities?
2. How might scarcity encourage international trade and make countries interdependent?

Money Management

Key Ideas
- People must manage money to have enough for their needs and wants.
- Many people save and invest money.

Key Terms • budget • saving • interest • credit • investing • stock • bond → **Visual Glossary**

Money is anything that is generally accepted as payment for goods and services. Money is a scarce resource that people must manage to have enough for their needs and wants. Because people's needs, wants, and incomes can change, it is important to plan ahead.

Budgeting, Saving, and Lending

A key tool in money management is a budget. A **budget** is a plan that shows income and expenses over a period of time. A budget's income should be equal to or greater than its expenses. A budget should also include money reserved for saving. **Saving** is the act of setting aside money for future use. Many people save by using banks. A bank is a business that keeps money, makes loans, and offers other financial services. Credit unions are nonprofit banks owned by their members.

A man uses an automated teller machine (ATM) to access his bank account. ▼

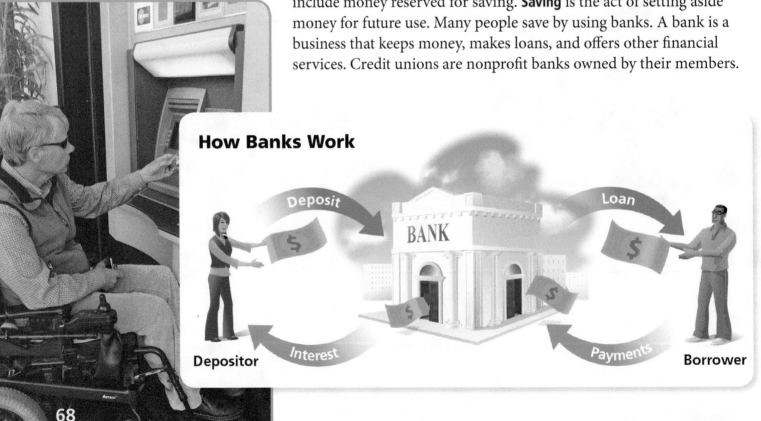

How Banks Work

Deposit

BANK

Loan

Depositor

Interest

Payments

Borrower

Many people who save money in banks do so using checking or savings accounts. Banks may pay interest on money deposited in these accounts. **Interest** is the price paid for borrowing money. Interest is an incentive for people to save money.

Banks use deposits to make loans to people and businesses around the world. These loans help people buy houses or make other large purchases. They help businesses get started or grow. As a result, banks are a big part of economic growth.

Loans are a form of credit. **Credit** is an arrangement in which a buyer can borrow to purchase something and pay for it over time, such as by using a credit card. Banks and other lending organizations charge borrowers interest on loans. As a result, it costs more for a borrower to purchase a good using credit than to pay cash for the good at the time of purchase.

Investing

Investing is the act of using money in the hope of making a future profit. Some people invest in stocks, bonds, or mutual funds. A **stock** is a share of ownership in a company. A **bond** is a certificate issued by a company or government promising to pay back borrowed money with interest. A mutual fund is a company that invests members' money in stocks, bonds, and other investments.

▲ Stockbrokers buy and sell stocks and bonds for investors at places such as the New York Stock Exchange.

Investments offer different levels of risk and return—the amount of money an investor might earn. In general, the safest investments offer the lowest rates of return. For example, a savings account is very safe, but it pays a relatively low rate of interest. Stocks are riskier but can earn a great deal of money for an investor if they increase in value. On the other hand, stocks can decline in value and become worth less than the stockholder paid. Bonds are less risky than stocks, but they usually offer a lower rate of return.

Assessment

1. How do banks function?

2. Why do people invest money in stocks, bonds, and mutual funds?

69

Economics and Geography

Part 5 Assessment

Key Terms and Ideas

1. **Recall** What is the most common type of economy today?

2. **Define** What is a **tariff** and why do governments sometimes use them?

3. **Paraphrase** Explain the relationship among **revenue, profit,** and the costs of doing business.

4. **Sequence** How does increased **productivity** affect business owners, employees, **consumers,** and entire nations?

5. **Explain** What is **opportunity cost**?

6. **Identify Cause and Effect** What role does risk play in investment?

7. **Identify** What level of economic activity includes mining? What level includes medical care?

Think Critically

8. **Draw Conclusions** What problems or issues might a company face if it has a shortage of one or more factors of production?

9. **Decision Making** How do societies organize and make decisions about the production of goods and services?

10. **Draw Inferences** How do factors such as location, physical features, and distribution of natural resources influence the economic development of societies?

11. **Summarize** How do government policies affect free market economies such as the U.S. economy?

Identify

Answer the following questions based on the map.

12. What kind of trade is shown on this map?

13. What is a major U.S. export?

14. What is a major U.S. import?

15. What are three goods that the United States produces?

16. What are three goods that Mexico produces?

17. What possible area of competition is shown on this map?

18. The United States and Mexico participate in free trade. What U.S. industries might free trade help or hurt?

United States and Mexico: Trade

UNITED STATES

MEXICO

U.S. exports to Mexico:
Petroleum products
Plastics
Chemicals
Automobile parts
Electronics

Mexican exports to the United States:
Petroleum
Fruits and vegetables
Electronics
Computers
Automobiles

Journal Activity

Fill in the graphic organizer in your Student Journal.

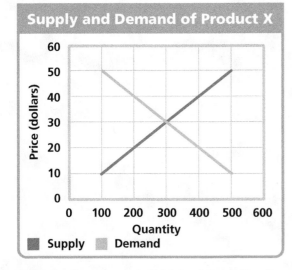 **Demonstrate Your Understanding** Complete the Sum-It-Up activity in your journal to demonstrate your understanding of economics and geography. After you complete the activity, discuss your answers with the class. Be sure to support your answers with information from the lessons.

21st Century Learning

Search for Information on the Internet

China had a command economy for many years, but since the 1970s the government has reduced its control over the economy. Use the Internet to research China's changing economy. Create a timeline to share your findings. Use a variety of online sources, including

- encyclopedias
- national and international newspapers
- magazines and journals

Document-Based Questions

Success Tracker™
Online at myworldgeography.com

Use your knowledge of economics and geography and Documents A and B to answer Questions 1–3.

Document A

Supply and Demand of Product X

- ■ Supply   ■ Demand

Document B

UN Human Development Index (HDI) Values, 2005	
Nation	**HDI Value**
Iceland	0.968
Samoa	0.785
Sierra Leone	0.336

SOURCE: *CIA World Factbook*

1. Examine Document A. Which of the following statements is true?

    A As the price of Product X increases, demand for it decreases.

    B As the price of Product X decreases, its supply increases.

    C As the price of Product X increases, demand for it increases.

    D As the price of Product X decreases, its supply does not change.

2. Examine Document B. The Human Development Index is a UN measure of levels of economic development and well-being in a country. Countries with higher HDI values have higher levels of development. Which of the following statements is true?

    A Samoa is less developed than Sierra Leone.

    B Samoa is more developed than Iceland.

    C Sierra Leone and Iceland are very different in terms of development level.

    D Sierra Leone is more developed than Iceland.

3. **Writing Task** A nation's rating in the UN Human Development Index is influenced by GDP per capita and people's education, literacy, and life expectancy. Why are these factors important to a country's development?

my worldgeography.com   Self-Test

Population and Movement

U.S. and Mexican flags

MEXICO

NADA QUE DECLARAR NOTHING TO DECLARE

CARRIL PARA DECLARAR DECLARATION LANE

Automobiles line up to cross the busy U.S.– Mexican border. ▲

U.S. students in a classroom

Ludwig Barragan

Searching for a New Home

Story by Miles Lemaire for myWorld Geography

Anyone who has ever moved to a new place knows that it can be hard to make friends and adjust to a new school. Moving to a different country can be even more challenging. You can ask Ludwig Barragan, who moved to the United States from Mexico a few years ago.

Like many other people, Ludwig and his mother decided to move in search of more opportunities and a better life. "My position in Mexico was fine economically," says Ludwig, "but I wanted to receive an education that I knew I wouldn't be able to get in Mexico. I love my country, yet the [school] system there was not what I wanted."

Ludwig and his mother moved to McAllen, Texas, a city on the U.S.–Mexican border. He looked forward to learning more about American culture and society.

Life in McAllen was an adjustment for Ludwig and his mother. "I would say that when you live so close to the border you live in a different world," Ludwig says. "You live in a place that is neither the U.S. nor Mexico."

Ludwig found that there were a number of different cultural groups in McAllen. "The number of immigrants [in] McAllen was huge," Ludwig says, "and there was a large community in my high school that spoke only Spanish. There was a second group there that were bilingual, and they were mainly people who were born in the U.S. but had parents that were from Mexico or spoke Spanish. It was hard to relate to them because … they didn't know the Mexican culture or values that I knew, yet they were not completely incorporated into the American culture."

At first, Ludwig felt that he didn't fit in. "I knew that I had to learn the language and the values even more. I tried to get in contact with the students that spoke mostly English. That's what I did and that's what helped me a lot."

Ludwig looked for ways that he could learn about the customs of his adopted country. He eventually joined the Junior Reserve Officers Training Corps (JROTC). The JROTC is a citizenship and military program supported by the U.S. armed forces. Ludwig says that the JROTC taught him much about life in the United States.

"My friends in Mexico made fun of me because here I was, a Mexican, carrying the U.S. flag with the JROTC," remembers Ludwig. "At first I said, 'Yeah, it's kind of weird,' but then later I realized that I don't have to feel bad about it. I chose this country because I love it and it doesn't mean that I love Mexico any less. I think … the beauty of immigration is that you can learn to love both cultures. I feel honored that I had a chance to carry the U.S. flag."

Population Growth

Key Ideas	• Earth's population has grown quickly in recent years.
	• Population growth can affect economic development and the environment.

Key Terms • demographer • birth rate • death rate • infant mortality rate

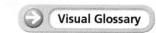 Visual Glossary

Today, the world's population is around 7 billion. When people first began farming around 12,000 years ago, it was fewer than 10 million. Earth's population grew slowly, eventually reaching 1 billion by 1800. Since then, better food production and healthcare have caused a population boom.

Measuring Growth

Demographers are scientists who study human populations. They measure the rate at which a population is growing. To do this, demographers compare birth rates and death rates. The **birth rate** is the number of live births per 1,000 people in a year. The **death rate** is the number of deaths per 1,000 people in a year. When the birth rate is higher than the death rate, a population tends to grow. Population can also change when people move into or out of a region.

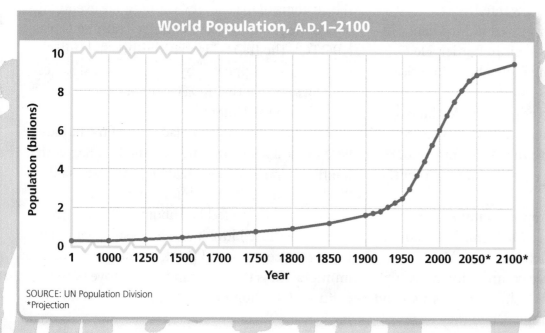

World Population, A.D. 1–2100

SOURCE: UN Population Division
*Projection

Causes and Effects of Population Growth

Improvements in hygiene, such as this water purifier in Uganda, can lead to population growth.

Causes of Growth

Until about two hundred years ago, the global birth rate was only slightly higher than the death rate. As a result, the population grew slowly. Then came the Industrial Revolution, which brought many changes.

Better medical care saved many lives. Improvements in food production increased the food supply and made food healthier. Living conditions improved. These and other changes led to a much lower death rate in most regions. By 1950, the world's population had begun to soar.

In Haiti, population growth has led to to overcrowding and poor living conditions. ▼

Effects of Growth

Population growth can have positive effects. For example, a growing population can produce and consume more goods and services. This can improve a country's standard of living. However, rapid population growth can also cause problems. The population can grow faster than the supply of food, water, medicine, and other resources.

The problems caused by rapid population growth are greatest in poor developing countries. A lack of clean food and water can lead to widespread starvation and disease. In these places, the **infant mortality rate**—the number of infant deaths per 1,000 births—is high.

The environment often suffers as well, as people use up resources to survive. Pollution is common. People cut down forests for firewood or clear land for farming. This can lead to desertification, or the spread of dry desert-like conditions. A lack of fertile soil makes it even harder to grow enough food.

Assessment

1. How are the birth rate and death rate used to measure population growth?
2. If the population of your town suddenly doubled, how might your daily life change?

75

Population Distribution

Key Ideas
- The distribution of a population can vary greatly within an area.
- Population density has important effects on an area.

Key Terms • population distribution • population density

 Visual Glossary

A country's population is the total number of people living within its borders. That number can be large or small. Geographers study a country's population to learn more about life in that country.

Population Distribution

Population distribution is the spreading of people over an area of land. The world's population is distributed unevenly on Earth's surface. Some places have many people. Other places are almost empty. What factors lead people to live where they do?

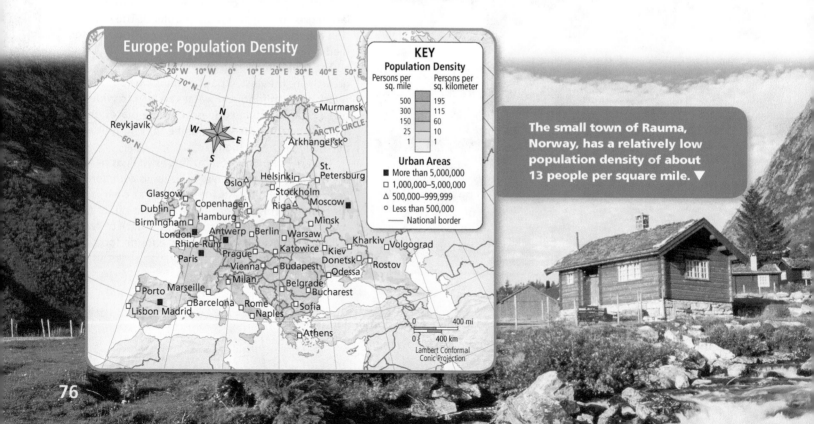

Europe: Population Density

KEY
Population Density

Persons per sq. mile	Persons per sq. kilometer
500	195
300	115
150	60
25	10
1	1

Urban Areas
- ■ More than 5,000,000
- □ 1,000,000–5,000,000
- △ 500,000–999,999
- ○ Less than 500,000
- — National border

0   400 mi
0   400 km
Lambert Conformal Conic Projection

The small town of Rauma, Norway, has a relatively low population density of about 13 people per square mile. ▼

People try to live in places that meet their basic needs. Natural obstacles such as oceans, mountains, and extremely cold or hot weather limit the areas where people can live easily. Throughout human history, most people have lived in areas with fertile soil, fresh water, and mild climates. Regions with good soil and plenty of water became crowded. Places that were too cold or dry for farming never developed large populations.

After about 1800, improved transportation and new ways of making a living changed things. As factories and industries grew, the ability to farm became less important. Industrial centers and large cities could develop in regions that were less suited for farming. Today, population tends to be highest in areas that were centers of early farming, industry, or trade.

Population Density

Population density is the number of people per unit of land area. It is expressed as the number of people per square mile or square kilometer. Population density gives us a way to describe how thickly settled an area is. It also lets us compare places of different sizes and populations. The density figure for any country is an average. Population density can vary greatly from one part of a country to another.

Population density has some important effects on a region. The more people there are per square mile, the more crowded a place is. Cities with high population densities tend to have crowded roads and living conditions. These places require many resources to meet people's needs. Places with low population densities tend to have more undeveloped land.

London, in the United Kingdom, has a very high population density, about 13,000 people per square mile. ▼

Assessment

1. How are population distribution and population density different?

2. How might a rapid increase in a region's population density change the region?

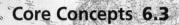

Core Concepts 6.3

Migration

Key Ideas	• People move from one place to another for a number of reasons.
	• People may move within a country or from one country to another.

Key Terms • migration • emigrate • immigrate • push factor • pull factor

 Visual Glossary

For thousands of years, people have migrated to new places. **Migration** is the movement of people from one place to another. Scientists believe that more than 50,000 years ago, a group of early humans migrated from Africa to Asia. Over many years, their descendants spread slowly across Asia and Europe. Some crossed from Asia to the Americas.

Forms of Migration

People often migrate within a country. In modern times, this internal migration has largely been movement to cities from the countryside. People generally migrate to cities to find jobs.

In the 1800s, many people migrated from Europe to the United States in search of a better life.

People also move from one country to another. When people leave their home country, they **emigrate,** which means to migrate out of a place. To enter a new country is to **immigrate,** or to migrate into a place. Moving to another country can lead to big changes in a person's life. For example, people moving to a new country may have to learn a new language and new customs. Mass migration can greatly change a region's culture and society. Migration can also affect a region's government, economy, and environment.

Reasons for Migration

People who migrate are often looking for a better life. They may move to escape poverty, a lack of jobs, or a harsh climate. In some countries, war or other conflict forces people to migrate. These reasons for migration are known as push factors. **Push factors** are causes of migration that push people to leave their home country.

Other reasons for migration are known as pull factors. **Pull factors** pull, or attract, people to new countries. One example of a pull factor is a supply of good jobs.

People generally migrate because they choose to do so. For example, millions of Europeans chose to migrate to the United States during the 1800s and early 1900s. Some of these people were Irish, fleeing a shortage of food. Others were Jews

These immigrants to the United States become U.S. citizens at a naturalization ceremony.

escaping persecution, or mistreatment. Millions more have come from Asia and Latin America since then.

History is also full of involuntary migrations. For the most part, these involved the forced movement of enslaved people. In the late 1400s European slave traders began buying and selling captured Africans. They shipped most of these enslaved people to the Americas. As many as 10 million enslaved Africans were forced to migrate to the Americas.

Assessment

1. Why did Europeans migrate to the United States in the 1800s and early 1900s?

2. Suppose your family migrated after a flood destroyed your home. Would the flood be considered a push factor or a pull factor? Explain.

Urbanization

Key Ideas
- Cities around the world have grown quickly over the last two hundred years.
- The growth of cities has created many challenges.

Key Terms • urban   • rural   • urbanization   • slum   • suburban sprawl

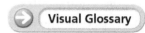 Visual Glossary

Panama City, Panama, had a population of 171,000 in 1950. By 2025, it is expected to grow to 2.4 million.

1950s

Panama City, Panama

Today

In many parts of the world, people are migrating to urban areas from rural areas. **Urban** areas are cities. **Rural** areas are settlements in the country. In China, for example, many new jobs have been created in cities in recent years. As a result, many rural Chinese workers have moved to cities in search of jobs. This process is known as urbanization. **Urbanization** is the movement of people from rural areas to urban areas.

The Shift from Rural to Urban

Over the last two hundred years or so, billions of people around the world have left rural agricultural areas to move to cities. In 2008, for the first time in history, more than half of the world's population lived in cities and towns.

In Europe and North America, urbanization began in the 1800s as modern industry developed. As a result, people moved to cities in search of jobs in factories and other businesses. Today, urbanization is happening most quickly in Asia and Africa. In those places, people move to cities in search of jobs, education, and better lives for their children.

Challenges of Urbanization

Rapid urbanization has created challenges for growing cities, especially those in poor countries. In some cases, cities simply have more people than they can handle. These cities cannot provide the housing, jobs, schools, hospitals, and other services that people need. One result is the spread of **slums,** or poor, overcrowded urban neighborhoods. Slums exist in cities around the world. Most people in slums live in run-down buildings or shacks. They are unable to meet their basic needs, such as enough food and clean water.

Urbanization can also create challenges in wealthy countries. Today, most large urban areas have a central core city. The core city has stores, office buildings, government buildings, and some housing. In wealthier countries, most people live in the suburbs surrounding the core city. As the population of a wealthy urban area grows, so does suburban sprawl. **Suburban sprawl** is the spread of suburbs away from the core city.

As suburbs spread, they replace farmland and other open spaces. New sewer lines, water lines, and roads must be built and maintained by the government. Because most people in suburbs use cars for transportation, suburban sprawl can increase pollution and energy use. Today, many towns and cities are working to limit sprawl.

1950s

Mumbai, India, had a population of 2.9 million in 1950. By 2025, it is expected to grow to 26.4 million.

Mumbai, India

Today

World Urbanization

30%
70%
1950

53% 47%
2000

30%
70%
2050*

■ **Rural population**　　■ **Urban population**

SOURCE: UN Population Division
　　*Projected

Assessment

1. What are some causes of urbanization?

2. Think about living in a suburb versus living in the center of a city or town. List a few things you might like or dislike about each.

Part 6 Assessment

Key Terms and Ideas

1. **Identify** Define the terms **birth rate** and **death rate.**

2. **Summarize** Describe the process of **urbanization**.

3. **Recall** Name three negative effects of rapid population growth.

4. **Define** What is **migration**?

5. **Compare and Contrast** What is the difference between a **pull factor** and a **push factor**?

6. **Recall** What is **population density**?

7. **Explain** What factors affect **population distribution**?

Think Critically

8. **Draw Inferences** How do you think world population patterns might change in the future?

9. **Compare Viewpoints** What arguments could be made for living in an area that has a high population density or in one with a low population density? Explain your views.

10. **Synthesize** During the 1800s, millions of Europeans migrated to the United States. Identify at least one possible push factor and one possible pull factor behind this mass migration.

11. **Solve Problems** Imagine that you are a member of a city government that is trying to limit urban growth. What steps might you suggest?

Identify

Answer the following questions based on the map.

12. Describe London's population.

13. Which cities have populations between 500,000 and 1,000,000?

14. Which city is located at 0° longitude?

15. In general, where are the areas in the United Kingdom with the highest population density?

16. Describe Cardiff's population.

17. Which city is closest to 50° N latitude?

18. Which is the westernmost city shown on the map?

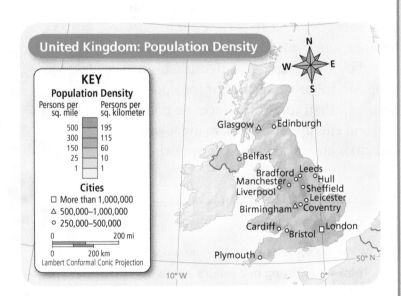

Journal Activity

Fill in the graphic organizer in your Student Journal.

Demonstrate Your Understanding Complete the Sum-It-Up activity in your journal to demonstrate your understanding of population and movement. After you complete the activity, discuss your predictions as a class. Be sure to support your predictions with information from the lessons.

21st Century Learning

Analyze Media Content

Find examples of recent articles about immigration to the United States. Then create a table to compare and contrast these articles. Ask yourself the following questions when reading:
- What is the main idea of each article?
- Does the author support every statement?
- Does the author show any bias?

Document-Based Questions

Success ⭐ Tracker™
Online at myworldgeography.com

Use your knowledge of population and movement and Documents A and B to answer Questions 1–3.

Document A

Annual Birth & Death Rates in Selected Countries		
Country	Birth Rate (per 1,000 people)	Death Rate (per 1,000 people)
Austria	8.7	9.9
Chad	41.6	16.4
Pakistan	28.4	7.9
Sri Lanka	16.6	6.1
United States	14.2	8.3

SOURCE: *CIA World Factbook*

Document B

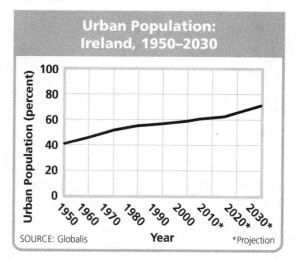

Urban Population: Ireland, 1950–2030

SOURCE: Globalis   Year   *Projection

1. Examine Document A. How does population growth in the United States most likely compare with that in Pakistan and Chad?

   A It is much faster.

   B It is much slower.

   C It is much faster than growth in Pakistan but slower than growth in Chad.

   D It is much faster than growth in Chad but slower than growth in Pakistan.

2. Examine Document B. What might be one cause for Ireland's changing rate of urbanization?

   A more dependence on agriculture

   B a higher death rate

   C growth in industry

   D housing shortages

3. **Writing Task** How do you think a graph showing urban population in Asia since 1950 might compare to Document B? Explain your answer.

my worldgeography.com   Self-Test

Culture and Geography

Tepees at a Native American powwow

Native American dancers

Joanna Baca (at right) dances at a powwow.

Joanna Baca

EXPLORING CULTURE THROUGH DANCE

Story by Miles Lemaire for myWorld Geography

When Joanna Baca and her family moved to Las Vegas, Nevada, from the Native American Navajo reservation in Shiprock, New Mexico, she looked for things that reminded her of home—and her Navajo culture.

"Most of our family stayed back home," Joanna says. "After we first moved here [Las Vegas], we didn't think there was anyone out here that was Native American, and it actually took us a while to find someone we knew."

In an effort to make their new city feel like home, Joanna and her family looked for community organizations that promoted Native American culture. Joanna eventually discovered the Las Vegas Indian Center. Among other things, this organization helps Native American high school students apply to and get accepted at colleges.

"[The Center helps] Native American kids find out what colleges are good for them," Joanna says. "They teach us that college is possible for Native American kids, not just for the kids that live on the reservation, but for kids who live in the city, too."

The more time Joanna spent with the organization, the closer she felt to her Navajo culture. She decided that she wanted to get involved in more aspects of Native American culture, especially traditional forms of dance.

Joanna had grown up going to powwows with her family. A powwow is a gathering where Native American people dance, sing, and honor Native American cultures. "I'd just see all the dancers there and how beautiful they were," Joanna remembers. She decided that she wanted to learn more about Native American dance. "I did ballet, jazz, and hip-hop before, and I thought they were fun," she says, "but I wanted to do something cultural, because dancing is a big part of my culture."

It has been several years since Joanna first started studying and performing Native American dances. She loves how these traditional forms of dance help her connect to her culture. But she also thinks dance is a wonderful way for non-Native American people to learn more about native culture.

"We go to events where they have dancers from all over the world, and they'll have a bit of everyone's culture in this one little get-together," Joanna says. "So we shared food, we were part of the dancing there, and a lot of people were like, 'Oh that's nice, I've never seen that type of dance before, what kind is that?' We'd tell them that it's Navajo, or native and … it got them very interested. Some of those people would come to the show again just to see our part of the performance and to see what it was all about."

85

What Is Culture?

Key Ideas
- Every culture has a distinctive set of cultural traits.
- Earth has thousands of different cultures.

Key Terms • culture • cultural trait • norm • culture region • cultural landscape

 Visual Glossary

A ll people have the same basic needs and wants, such as food, clothing, and shelter. But different cultures respond to those needs and wants in different ways. **Culture** is the beliefs, customs, practices, and behaviors of a particular nation or group of people.

Where Culture Comes From

The features that make up a culture are known as cultural traits. A **cultural trait** is an idea or way of doing things that is common in a certain culture. Cultural traits include language, laws, religion, values, food, clothing, and many other customs. Children learn cultural traits from their parents and other adults. People also learn cultural traits from the mass media and from organizations such as schools, social clubs, and religious groups. Common cultural traits are called norms. A **norm** is a behavior that is considered normal in a particular society.

French Quebec Culture Region

CANADA Quebec

UNITED STATES

0   500 mi
0   500 km

Lambert Azimuthal
Equal-Area Projection

120° W 110° W 100° W 90° W 80° W 70° W

Culture Regions

A **culture region** is an area in which a single culture or cultural trait is dominant. In Canada, French Canadian culture dominates much of the province of Quebec. The people of Quebec who have this culture identify themselves as French Canadian or Québécois (kay bek WAH).

Cultural Landscapes

Human activities create **cultural landscapes**, or geographic areas that have been shaped by people.

◄ Bolivia

Left, Egypt; below, Ukraine

Some cultural traits remain constant over many years. But culture can change over time as people adopt new cultural traits. For example, the way Americans dress today is very different from the way Americans dressed 100 years ago.

The environment can also affect culture. For example, the environment of a region influences how people live and how they earn their living. Humans can also shape their environment by creating cultural landscapes. The cultural landscape of a place reflects how its people meet their basic needs for food, clothing, and shelter. These landscapes differ from one culture to another.

Culture and Geography

Earth has thousands of different cultures and culture regions. In a specific culture region, people share cultural traits such as religion or language.

Culture regions are often different from political units. Occasionally, a culture region may cover an entire country. In Japan, for example, nearly everyone speaks the same language, eats the same food, and follows the same customs. A country may also include more than one culture region. For example, the French Canadian culture region of Quebec is one of several culture regions in Canada.

Culture regions can also extend beyond political boundaries. For example, many of the people who live in Southwest Asia and northern Africa are Arab Muslims. That is, they practice the religion of Islam. They also share other cultural traits, such as the Arabic language, foods, and other ways of life. This region of Arab Muslim culture covers several countries.

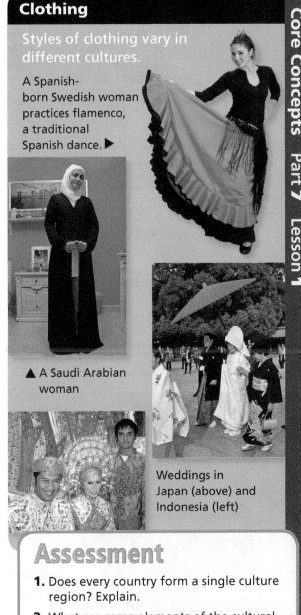

Clothing

Styles of clothing vary in different cultures.

A Spanish-born Swedish woman practices flamenco, a traditional Spanish dance. ▶

▲ A Saudi Arabian woman

Weddings in Japan (above) and Indonesia (left)

Assessment

1. Does every country form a single culture region? Explain.

2. What are some elements of the cultural landscape in the area where your school is located?

Food

People in different cultures eat different types of food.

◀ A man in Saudi Arabia sells vegetables.

Women in Ukraine selling potatoes and other produce

87

Families and Societies

Key Ideas
- The most basic unit of any society is the family.
- Family structures vary in different cultures, but every society has organized relationships among groups of people.

Key Terms • society • family • nuclear family • extended family • social structure • social class

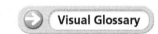
Visual Glossary

Culture, society, and family are all related. A **society** is a group of humans with a shared culture who have organized themselves to meet their basic needs. Societies can be large or small. A group of a few dozen hunter-gatherers is a society. So is a country of more than a billion people, such as India or China.

Nuclear and extended families are two kinds of family unit.

Nuclear Family

Kinds of Families

The most basic unit of any society is the family. A **family** is two or more people who are closely related by birth, marriage, or adoption. Traditionally, one person heads a family. A man has been the head of the family in many societies throughout history. Today, however, men and women often share this responsibility.

Family structures vary in different cultures. Two common family units are the nuclear family and the extended family. A **nuclear family** is a family that consists of parents and their children. An **extended family** is a family that includes parents, children, and other family members, such as grandparents, aunts, uncles, and cousins. Extended families are more common in developing countries. In some places, extended families work together on farms. In other places, relatives work separately but live together in order to share resources.

Extended Family

Kinds of Societies

Every society has a social structure. A **social structure** is a pattern of organized relationships among groups of people within a society. People interact with one another, with groups, and with institutions. For example, you have ties to friends and family members. You probably attend a school. You may also take part in a sports team or some other group. Adults have ties to coworkers and to economic institutions such as businesses and banks. Families may also have ties to religious institutions, such as a church, a synagogue, or a mosque.

Societies vary around the world and can change over time. All societies have some common institutions. These include government, religious, economic, and educational institutions.

Societies also have differences. One basic difference has to do with a society's economy. Some societies rely mainly on farming. Others depend on industry.

Industrial societies often organize members according to their social class. A **social class** is a group of people living in similar economic conditions. In modern societies, the main groupings are upper class, middle class, and lower (or working) class. The size of the world's middle class has increased greatly in recent years.

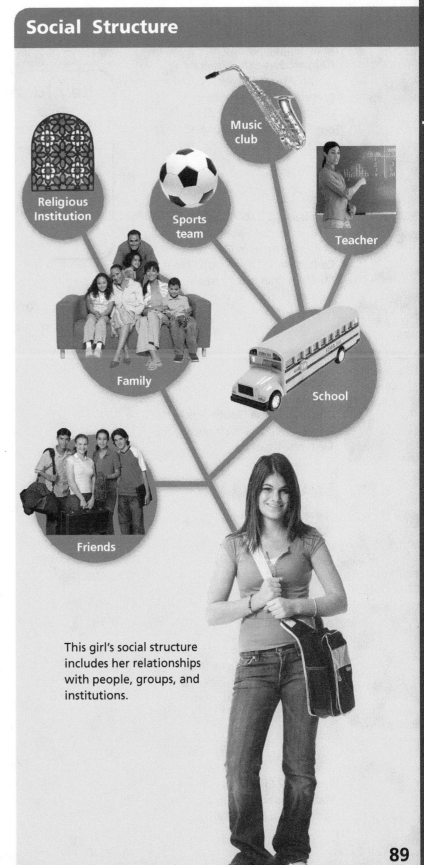

Social Structure

Religious Institution

Music club

Sports team

Teacher

Family

School

Friends

This girl's social structure includes her relationships with people, groups, and institutions.

Assessment

1. What aspects of culture do all societies share?

2. What aspects of culture differ among societies?

Indo-European

Speakers 2.722 billion
Main languages English, German, Swedish, Afrikaans (South Africa), French, Spanish, Portuguese, Italian, Russian, Polish, Farsi (Iran), Hindi (northern India), Bengali (Bangladesh, India), Greek

Sino-Tibetan

Speakers 1.259 billion
Main languages Mandarin Chinese (northern China), Cantonese (southeastern China), Min Nan Chinese (Taiwan), Tibetan (Tibet), Burmese (Myanmar)

Niger-Congo

Speakers 382 million
Main languages Ibo and Yoruba (Nigeria), Xhosa (South Africa), Twi (Ghana), Swahili (Kenya, Tanzania, Uganda)

Afro-Asiatic

Speakers 359 million
Main languages Arabic (Southwest Asia, North Africa), Hebrew (Israel), Hausa (West Africa)

Austronesian

Speakers 354 million
Main languages Malay (Malaysia), Javanese (Indonesia), Tagalog (Philippines), Maori (New Zealand)

Dravidian

Speakers 223 million
Main languages Telugu (India), Tamil (India, Sri Lanka)

Core Concepts 7.3

Language

Key Ideas

- Language provides the basis for culture.
- Language can unify people or keep them apart.

Key Term

- language

 Visual Glossary

Cultures could not exist without language. **Language** is a set of spoken sounds, written symbols, or hand gestures that make it possible for people to communicate.

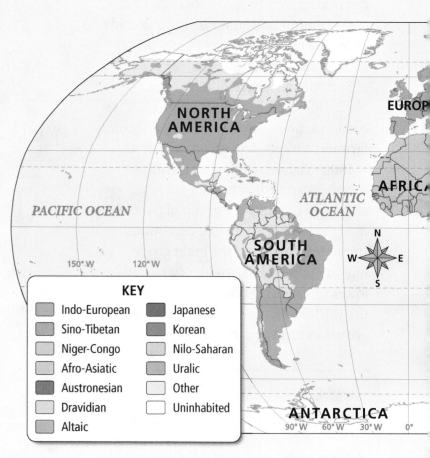

KEY

- Indo-European
- Sino-Tibetan
- Niger-Congo
- Afro-Asiatic
- Austronesian
- Dravidian
- Altaic
- Japanese
- Korean
- Nilo-Saharan
- Uralic
- Other
- Uninhabited

Core Concepts Part 7 Lesson 3

Without language, people would not be able to share information or ideas. They could not pass on cultural traits to their children.

Languages often vary from one culture to another. Within a country, differences in language can keep cultures apart and make it harder to unify the country. Language differences can also keep countries apart by preventing communication.

People who speak different languages sometimes turn to a third language in order to communicate with each other. In modern times, English has often served as the world's common language.

The map below shows the locations of the world's major language groups. Languages in each of these groups share a common ancestor. This ancestor was a language spoken so long ago that it gradually changed to become several related languages.

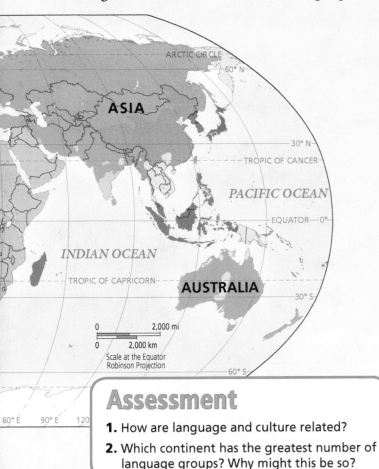

Altaic

Speakers 140 million
Main languages Turkish, Kazakh (Kazakhstan), Bashkir (Russia), Tatar (Russia), Uighur (China), Mongolian (Mongolia)

Japanese

Speakers 123 million
Spoken mainly in Japan.

Korean

Speakers 66 million
Spoken mainly in North Korea and South Korea.

Nilo-Saharan

Speakers 38 million
Main languages Luo (Kenya), Maasai (Tanzania), Kanuri (Niger)

Uralic

Speakers 21 million
Main languages Hungarian, Finnish, Estonian, Sami (Norway, Sweden, Finland), Samoyed (Russia)

Other

Speakers 394 million
These include Native American languages (North and South America), Paleosiberian languages (eastern Russia), Aboriginal languages (Australia), and languages spoken in Southeast Asia.

Assessment

1. How are language and culture related?

2. Which continent has the greatest number of language groups? Why might this be so?

Core Concepts 7.4

Religion

Key Ideas
- Religious beliefs play an important role in shaping cultures.
- The world has many different religions.

Key Terms • religion • ethics

Visual Glossary

Judaism

Judaism is based on a belief in one God, whose spiritual and ethical teachings are recorded in the Hebrew Bible. It began in the Middle East around 2000 B.C. By A.D. 100, Jews lived in Europe, Southwest Asia, and North Africa. The Jewish state of Israel was established in 1948. There are about 14 million Jews.

Christianity

Christianity is based on the teachings of Jesus, who Christians believe was the son of God. The Christian Bible is their sacred text. Christianity began in Southwest Asia around A.D. 30 and spread to Europe and Africa. It later spread to the rest of the world. There are about 2.07 billion Christians.

Islam

Islam is based on the Quran, a sacred text. The Quran contains what Muslims believe is the word of God as revealed to Muhammad beginning in A.D. 610. Islam spread quickly across Southwest Asia and North Africa, then to the rest of the world. There are about 1.25 billion Muslims.

An important part of every culture is religion. **Religion** is a system of worship and belief, including belief about the nature of a god or gods. Religion can help people answer questions about the meaning of life. It can also guide people in matters of **ethics**, or standards of acceptable behavior. Religious beliefs and values help shape cultures.

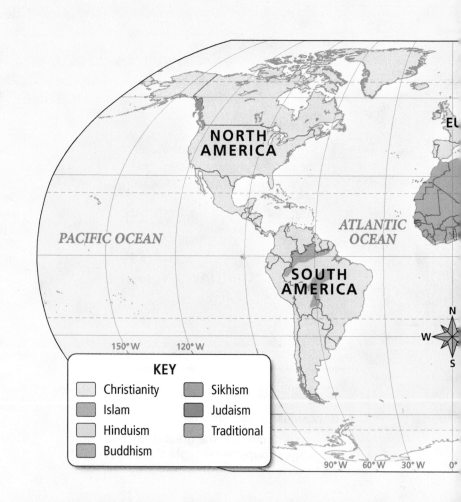

KEY
- Christianity
- Islam
- Hinduism
- Buddhism
- Sikhism
- Judaism
- Traditional

The world has many religions. Jews, Christians, and Muslims believe in one God. Members of other religions may believe in several gods.

All religions have prayers and rituals. Followers also observe religious holidays. For example, Jews celebrate the world's creation on Rosh Hashanah and their escape from slavery in Egypt on Passover. On Yom Kippur, Jews make up for their sins. Christians celebrate Jesus' birth on Christmas and his return to life on Easter. For Muslims, the holy month of Ramadan is a time to avoid food during daytime, to pray, and to read the Quran.

The world's major religions began in Asia. Hinduism, Buddhism, and Sikhism first developed in India. Judaism, Christianity, and Islam began in Southwest Asia before spreading throughout the world.

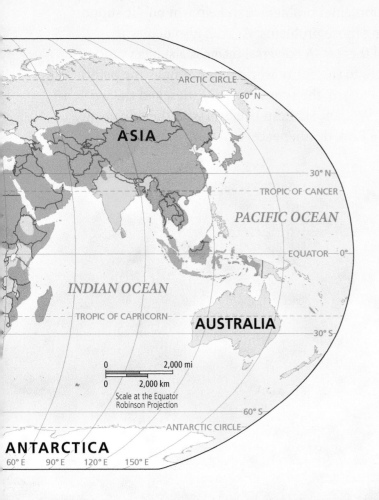

Hinduism

Hinduism evolved gradually over thousands of years in South Asia. It has several sacred texts. Hindus believe that everyone in the universe is part of a continuing cycle of birth, death, and rebirth. There are about 837 million Hindus.

Buddhism

Buddhism is based on the teachings of Siddhartha Gautama, known as the Buddha, who was born in India about 563 B.C. The Buddha's teachings include the search for enlightenment, or a true understanding of the nature of reality. There are about 373 million Buddhists.

Sikhism

Sikhism is based on the writings of several gurus, or prophets. Guru Nanak founded Sikhism about A.D. 1500 in South Asia. Sikhism's teachings include the cycle of rebirth and the search for enlightenment. There are about 24 million Sikhs.

Traditional Religions

Traditional religions include thousands of distinct religions. These religions tend to be passed down by word of mouth instead of through sacred texts. Each has its own set of beliefs. Examples include many African religions.

Assessment

1. How does religion help shape a culture?

2. What does the map tell you about the major religion where you live?

93

A print of a fish by Japanese artist Katsushika Taito, 1848

The Arts

Key Ideas
- Art is an important part of culture.
- Works of art can reveal much about society.

Key Terms
- universal theme
- visual arts
- architecture
- architect
- music
- literature

 Visual Glossary

The arts are an important aspect of culture. Works of art can reflect a society by dealing with topics or issues that are important to that society. Art can even shape society. For example, books that describe poverty or environmental problems can help win public support for solving those problems. Art can also deal with universal themes. A **universal theme** is a subject or idea that relates to the entire world. For example, the paintings of Pablo Picasso, the songs of the Beatles, and the written works of William Shakespeare deal with the universal themes of love, death, peace, and war.

Visual Arts

Art forms meant to be seen, such as painting, sculpture, and photography, are known as the **visual arts.** The visual arts can express emotions and spiritual ideas. They can also show us what life is like in other cultures and how people lived in the past. For example, a painting created in Italy in 1600 can show us how Italian people lived during this period.

Architecture

Architecture is the design and construction of buildings. A person who designs buildings is an **architect**. Architecture can show us what a society values and how it uses its resources. For example, are a society's most impressive buildings its religious buildings or its government buildings? Architectural works can be important cultural symbols.

This art museum in Bilbao, Spain, was designed by architect Frank Gehry.

Music

Music is an art form that uses sound, usually produced by instruments or voices. Music varies widely in different societies and cultures. It also changes over time as our tastes change. What one person considers beautiful music might be unpleasant noise to someone from a different place or time period. As a result, music can tell us about a society's tastes.

A Peruvian man plays a flute near the Inca ruins at Machu Picchu, Peru.

Literature

Literature is written work such as fiction, poetry, or drama. Literature can tell us what ideas a society considers important. By describing harmful things in society, literature can push for change.

A performance of Shakespeare's *A Midsummer Night's Dream*

Assessment

1. What are two ways in which the arts are related to society?

2. What might a painting of a main street in your area tell a stranger about your society?

Cultural Diffusion and Change

Key Ideas
- Cultures change over time.
- Cultural traits can spread from one culture to another.

Key Terms
- cultural hearth
- cultural diffusion
- diversity

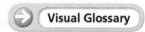
Visual Glossary

Chinese people in France celebrate the Chinese New Year.

All cultures change over time. That is, their cultural traits change. In general, for a new cultural trait to be adopted by a culture, it must offer some benefit or improvement over an existing trait.

How Cultural Traits Spread

A **cultural hearth** is a place where cultural traits develop. Traits from cultural hearths spread to surrounding cultures and regions. Customs and ideas can spread in many ways, including settlement, trade, migration, and communication. **Cultural diffusion** is the spread of cultural traits from one culture to another.

In the 1500s, Spanish explorers and settlers brought horses to the Americas. Many native peoples saw the advantages of using horses for moving quickly and for hunting. Horses soon became part of some Native American cultures.

Cultural traits can also spread through trade. Traders can move among different cultures. As they travel, they carry with them elements of their own culture, such as food or religious beliefs. Traders expose people to these new traits. If people find that an unfamiliar religion or other cultural trait improves their lives, they may make it a part of their own daily lives. For example, hundreds of years ago, Muslim traders helped spread Islam from Arabia to other cultures in Asia and Africa.

In a similar way, migrants spread cultural traits. Migrants bring cultural traditions with them to their new homelands. Over time, many migrants, or immigrants, have come to the United States. Immigrants have brought with them foods, languages, music, ideas, and other cultural traits. Some of these new ways of doing things have become part of American culture.

Technology and Culture

Technology also helps spread culture. The Internet, for example, has made instant communication common. Today, Americans can find out instantly what people in places such as Peru, India, or Japan are wearing, eating, or creating. If we like some of these traits, we may borrow them and make them a part of our culture.

Rapid transportation technologies, such as airplanes, make it easier for people to move all over the world. As they travel, people may bring new cultural traits to different regions.

Cultural change has both benefits and drawbacks. If customs change too quickly, people may feel that their culture is threatened. Some people worry that rapid communication is creating a new global culture that threatens diversity. **Diversity** is cultural variety. These people fear that the things that make people and cultures unique and interesting might disappear. They worry that we might end up with only a single worldwide culture.

Assessment

1. Why do cultures change?
2. What cultural traits have you borrowed in the last few years?

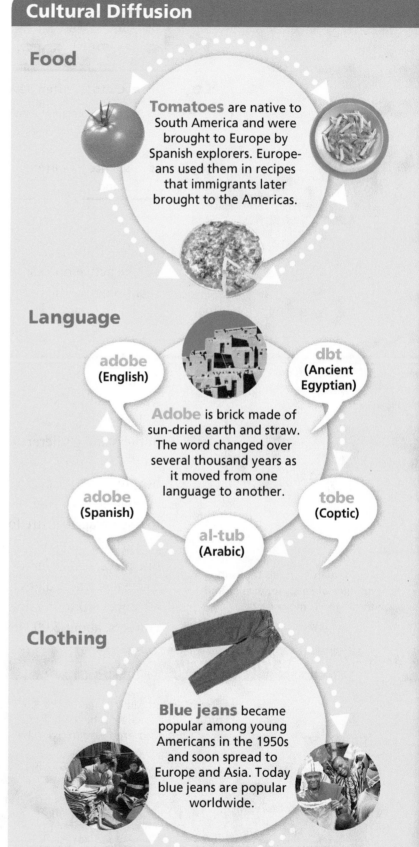

Cultural Diffusion

Food

Tomatoes are native to South America and were brought to Europe by Spanish explorers. Europeans used them in recipes that immigrants later brought to the Americas.

Language

adobe (English)

dbt (Ancient Egyptian)

Adobe is brick made of sun-dried earth and straw. The word changed over several thousand years as it moved from one language to another.

adobe (Spanish)

al-tub (Arabic)

tobe (Coptic)

Clothing

Blue jeans became popular among young Americans in the 1950s and soon spread to Europe and Asia. Today blue jeans are popular worldwide.

Core Concepts 7.7

Science and Technology

Key Ideas
- Cultures often develop along with science and technology.
- Technological advances have greatly changed human life.

Key Terms
- science
- irrigate
- standard of living

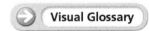 Visual Glossary

The Roman empire's thousands of miles of roads let armies and trade goods move easily.

Science and technology are important parts of culture. **Science** is the active process of acquiring knowledge of the natural world. Technology is the way in which people use tools and machines.

Technology and Progress

Early humans made gradual advances in technology. About 3 million years ago, people first learned how to make tools and weapons out of stone. They later discovered how to control fire.

Technological advances changed cultures. Early humans were hunters and gatherers who traveled from place to place to find food. Later, people discovered how to grow crops. They learned how to adapt plants to make them more useful. They tamed wild animals for farming or used them as food. Over time, people began to rely on agriculture for most of their food.

Agriculture provided a steady food supply and let people settle in one place. As settlements grew and turned into cities, people began to create laws and governments. They developed writing. These advances led to the first civilizations, or societies with complex cultures, about 5,000 years ago.

Evolution of the Wheel

The wheel transformed culture. Below, the Sumerian Standard of Ur, about 2600 B.C., showing chariots pulled by donkeys; at right, a covered wagon from the 1800s

98

Early civilizations developed new technologies that allowed people to grow more crops. People invented tools such as the plow to help increase food production. They built canals and ditches to **irrigate,** or supply water to, crops. Cultures that lacked writing developed more slowly. Over time, agriculture and civilization spread across the world.

Modern Technology

Beginning around 1800, people developed new technologies that used power-driven machinery. This was the Industrial Revolution. It led to the growth of cities, science, and many new businesses. Eventually, people developed even more advanced technologies such as automobiles, airplanes, computers, and space travel.

All of these advances in science and technology have greatly changed people's lives and raised their standard of living. **Standard of living** is the level of comfort enjoyed by a person or a society. Modern technology also helps to connect people, products, and ideas.

Political decisions and belief systems can affect the use of technology. For example, the Chinese government has limited Chinese citizens' use of the Internet. This is an attempt to control discussion of government policies and other issues. Many religions have used technology as part of their practices. For example, religious groups have used the printing press to print the Hebrew Bible, the Christian Bible, the Quran, and other holy writings. Today, some religious organizations use radio, television, and the Internet to broadcast their beliefs.

Technology and Culture	
Technological Advances	**Effects on Culture**
Control of fire	Allowed humans to cook food, have light, protect themselves from animals
Irrigation	Increased food production; allowed people to do jobs other than farming; led to growth of cities
Wheel	Led to improved transportation in the form of carts and carriages; eventually led to trains, cars, and other vehicles
Printing press	Allowed the mass production of books; spread knowledge and ideas, increasing the number of educated people
Steam engine	Steam-powered machines performed work once done by hand; people moved to cities to find work in factories.
Refrigeration	Kept food fresh and safe longer; allowed food to be shipped over long distances from farms to cities

Assessment

1. What are science and technology?

2. How do you think technology might change culture in the future?

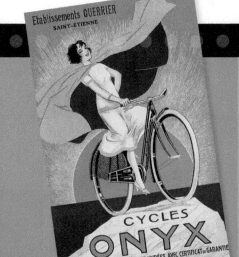

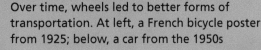

Over time, wheels led to better forms of transportation. At left, a French bicycle poster from 1925; below, a car from the 1950s

99

Part 7 Assessment

Key Terms and Ideas

1. **Define** What is **culture**?

2. **Recall** What is **religion**?

3. **Summarize** Does migration cause **cultural diffusion**? Explain why or why not.

4. **Connect** Are all **cultural traits** also **norms**? Explain.

5. **Draw Conclusions** How can **language** both unify and divide cultures?

6. **Compare and Contrast** What is the difference between a **nuclear family** and an **extended family**?

7. **Explain** Explain the relationship between technology and a **standard of living**.

Think Critically

8. **Draw Inferences** As technology makes it easier for people to travel to different countries, how might world culture regions change?

9. **Make Decisions** What other aspects of culture might link people in a country who speak different languages?

10. **Identify Evidence** Give two examples of ways in which today's cultures are influenced by past cultures.

11. **Draw Conclusions** How do you think ethics guide a country's laws?

Identify

Answer the following questions based on the map.

12. What does this map show?

13. What is the most widely spoken dialect in China?

14. What do the two purple and pink colors represent on the map?

15. What does the color orange represent on the map?

16. Across from which island do Chinese speakers of the Min dialect live?

17. Which dialect is spoken just to the north of the largest area of the Min dialect?

18. Not including the areas shown on the map as "other dialects or languages," in what part of China are most non-Mandarin dialects spoken?

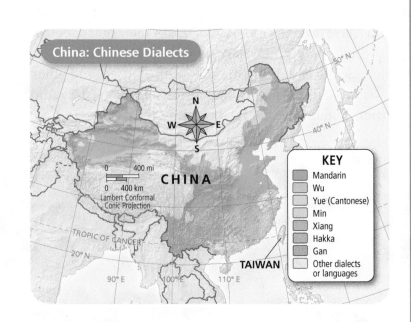

China: Chinese Dialects

KEY
Mandarin
Wu
Yue (Cantonese)
Min
Xiang
Hakka
Gan
Other dialects or languages

Journal Activity

Fill in the graphic organizer in your Student Journal.

Demonstrate Your Understanding Complete the Sum-It-Up activity in your journal to demonstrate your understanding of culture and geography. After you complete the activity, discuss your drawing with a partner. Be sure to support your answers to the questions with information from the lessons.

Work in Teams

Working with your partners, choose a country that is not familiar to anyone in your group. Then research and create an illustrated informational brochure about the country's culture. Be sure to

- provide examples of the country's art
- identify and describe the country's major religions and languages

Document-Based Questions

Success ☆ Tracker™
Online at myworldgeography.com

Use your knowledge of culture and geography and Documents A and B to answer Questions 1–3.

Document A

Main Language Spoken in U.S. Homes, 1980–2000

Percentage / Year

SOURCE: U.S. Census Bureau   ■ English   ■ Other

Document B

" What a society [judges] important is [preserved] in its art."

—Harry Broudy

1. Examine Document A. Which of the following statements is probably true?

   A Migration to and cultural diffusion to the United States are likely decreasing.

   B Migration to and cultural diffusion to the United States are likely increasing.

   C Migration and cultural diffusion are unrelated to the changes shown in the graph.

   D Migration and cultural diffusion are no longer taking place in the United States.

2. Read Document B. Which of the following statements might Harry Broudy agree with?

   A Art does not reveal clues about past societies.

   B Art does not show the artist's beliefs.

   C Paintings reflect culture better than music does.

   D Looking at art is a good way to learn more about a society.

3. **Writing Task** Think of a favorite piece of art, such as a painting, a song, or a book. Then write one paragraph about what that piece of art reveals about your culture and beliefs.

my worldgeography.com   Self-Test

Government and Citizenship

Supporters hold campaign signs.

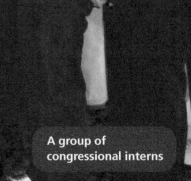

A group of congressional interns

Voters in the 2008 presidential election

Anne Marie Sutherland

Serving Her Country

Story by Miles Lemaire for myWorld Geography

Anne Marie Sutherland has been trying to get people to vote since before she was old enough to join them at the polls.

Anne Marie is the daughter of a high school government teacher. She became interested in politics as a child. Her first experience with a political campaign was the U.S. presidential election in 1996, when she was just nine years old. "[M]y friends and I made some signs and walked up and down the street with them before the election," Anne Marie says. "We started talking to people, and we stayed up all night to see who would win."

As Anne Marie grew older, her interest in the political process increased. In 2000 and 2004, she worked as a volunteer on George W. Bush's presidential campaigns. In the 2008 presidential primaries, she helped manage candidate Mitt Romney's campaign in Atlanta, Georgia.

"We did lots of grassroots work," Anne Marie says about her work with the Romney campaign. "We were talking to different folks, getting signs out, working on some strategies for the area."

When Romney failed to win the Republican nomination for president, Anne Marie worked for 2008 Republican nominee John McCain. She looks back on her work with the Romney and McCain campaigns as a great learning experience. Most of all, she loved discussing political issues with people.

"What I took away from that opportunity was working directly with voters," Anne Marie says. "That's not something that you get to do for very long in politics [before] you move up and start taking on larger roles."

Anne Marie soon began taking on larger roles herself, winning an internship with U.S. Senator Saxby Chambliss. As part of her internship, Anne Marie helped other young people achieve their own goals. As she explains, "Every year a senator appoints a certain number of graduating [high school] seniors to the United States military academies. … so I put most of my energy into working on that process.

"I love doing that," she says, "because what I'm able to do is [to help] prepare our future military leaders at such a young age. … [S]ometimes when I'm working with them, I honestly think, 'This young student could really be our future president, or could be leading us in a major war, or could be the leader of any one of the branches of the military.' You never know."

Now 22 years old, Anne Marie is about to graduate from college with a degree in political science. She isn't content with helping other people achieve their dreams. "Maybe there is a campaign of my own in the future," she says. "I'd do anything I can to serve my country."

103

Core Concepts 8.1

Foundations of Government

Key Ideas
- Governments are created to keep order in a society and provide for the people's common needs.
- A government's powers are either limited or unlimited.

Key Terms • government • constitution • limited government
• unlimited government • tyranny

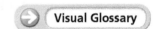
Visual Glossary

A **government** is a group of people who have the power to make and enforce laws for a country or area. The basic purpose of government is to keep order, to provide services, and to protect the common good, or the well-being of the people. Governments make and enforce laws to keep order. Protecting the common good can include building roads and schools or defending the country from attack. Governments also collect taxes, or required payments, from people and businesses. Governments use these taxes to pay for the goods and services they provide. The purpose of government has not changed much throughout history.

Origins of Government

Long before modern governments existed, people lived together in groups. These groups often had leaders who kept order and made decisions for the group. This was a simple form of government.

More complex governments first appeared in Southwest Asia more than 5,000 years ago. By that time, groups of people had begun to settle down. Villages grew into cities. People found that they needed an organized way to resolve problems and oversee tasks such as repairing irrigation canals and distributing food. They formed governments to manage those tasks.

Hammurabi's Code is a set of laws created in ancient Babylon—now Iraq—around 1760 B.C. The code was carved onto a large stone slab, below. The photo at the bottom of the page shows the ruins of ancient Babylon. ▼

Powers of Government

Today, most governments have a constitution. A **constitution** is a system of basic rules and principles by which a government is organized. A constitution also identifies the powers a government has. A government's powers are either limited or unlimited.

Limited Government

People gather in front of the U.S. Capitol.

Today, most constitutions call for limited government. **Limited government** is a government structure in which government actions are limited by law. Limited governments work to protect the common good and provide for people's needs.

In the United States, government actions are limited in order to protect people's individual freedoms. Generally, people in a limited government may gather freely to express their opinions and work to change government policies.

Unlimited Government

Chinese police arrest a protester.

Unlimited government is a government structure in which there are no effective limits on government actions. In an unlimited government such as China, a ruler or a small ruling group has the power to make all decisions for a country or society. This much power can lead to **tyranny**, which is the unjust use of power.

Unlimited governments often do not protect citizens' basic rights. They may censor, or restrict, citizens' access to the Internet and other forms of communication technology.

Assessment

1. How do constitutions limit the powers of government?
2. How do limited and unlimited governments differ?

Political Systems

Key Ideas
- Types of states have varied throughout history.
- There are many different kinds of government.

Key Terms
- state
- city-state
- empire
- democracy
- nation-state
- monarchy
- authoritarian
- communism

 Visual Glossary

A **state** is a region that shares a common government. The first real states—called city-states—developed in Southwest Asia more than 5,000 years ago. A **city-state** is an independent state consisting of a city and its surrounding territory. Later, some military leaders conquered large areas and ruled them as empires. An **empire** is a state containing several countries. Geographic features such as rivers and mountains sometimes helped governments control territory by protecting against invasion.

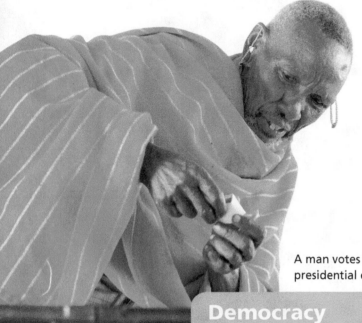

A man votes in Kenya's 2007 presidential election.

Democracy

Examples Direct democracy: ancient Athens; representative democracy: United States

- **Democracy** is a form of government in which citizens hold political power; citizens are the ultimate source of government power and authority.

- In a direct democracy, citizens come together to pass laws and select leaders.

- In a representative democracy, citizens elect representatives to make government decisions.

- The powers of a democratic government are usually limited.

Queen Elizabeth II of the United Kingdom

Nation-States

Today, most states are nation-states. A **nation-state** is a state that is independent of other states. The United States is an example of a nation-state. We often use the general words *nation* or *country* to refer to nation-states.

All nation-states have some common features. For example, nation-states have specific territory with clearly defined borders. Nation-states have governments, laws, and authority over citizens. Most are divided into smaller states or provinces that contain cities and towns.

Forms of Government

Each state has a government, but there are many different kinds of government. Throughout history, most states were autocracies (ruled by a single person) or oligarchies (ruled by a small group of people). Today, however, many states have some form of democracy in which citizens hold political power.

A large statue of former leader Kim Il-Sung stands above people in communist North Korea.

Monarchy

Examples Absolute monarchy: Saudi Arabia; Constitutional monarchy: United Kingdom

- A **monarchy** is a form of government in which the state is ruled by a monarch.
- A monarch is usually a king or queen.
- Power is inherited by family members.
- Absolute monarchs have unlimited power.
- Monarchs in constitutional monarchies are limited by law and share power with other branches of government.
- The powers of a monarchy can be limited or unlimited.

Authoritarian Government

Examples Nazi Germany, Cuba, North Korea

- An **authoritarian** government is one in which all power is held by a single person or a small group.
- Government may control all aspects of life.
- One of the common forms of authoritarian government is **communism**, a political and economic system in which government owns all property and makes all economic decisions.
- The powers of an authoritarian government are unlimited.

Assessment

1. What are states, city-states, and nation-states?
2. Which form of government relies most on its citizens? Explain your answer.

Political Structures

Key Ideas
- Political structures help governments operate in an organized way.
- The U.S. government follows basic democratic principles.

Key Terms • unitary system   • federal system

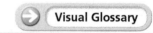 Visual Glossary

Central Government

Central governments are responsible for national affairs.

U.S. Capitol

Regional Government

Regional governments include state or provincial governments.

Texas State Capitol

Local Government

Local governments include county, city, and town governments.

Trumbull, Connecticut, town hall

Countries distribute power between the central government and smaller units of government. We can learn more about how a government functions by examining its structure and principles.

Systems of Government

Governments can distribute power in three basic ways: the unitary system, the federal system, and the confederal system. In a **unitary system,** a central government makes all laws for the entire country. In a **federal system,** power is divided among central, regional, and local governments. In a confederal system, a group of independent states join together and give limited powers to a common government. Most countries have a unitary system. The United States and some other countries have a federal system. The confederal system is rare.

Principles of Government

Every government has basic principles that affect the way it serves its people. Authoritarian governments may seek to control all aspects of society, even people's actions and beliefs. For example, some authoritarian governments limit citizens' use of communications technology such as the Internet. Most democratic governments act to protect individual rights and the common good.

In the United States, government follows basic democratic principles. For example, government follows the rule of law. That is, government powers are defined by laws that limit its actions. Also, government decides issues by majority rule. A law cannot pass unless the majority—most—representatives vote for it. At the same time, the majority may not take away the basic rights and freedoms of minority groups or individuals. In other words, government must balance majority rule with minority rights.

Branches of Government

Under the U.S. Constitution, power is divided among the three branches of government: the legislative, executive, and judicial branches. This division is called separation of powers. The Constitution also establishes a system of checks and balances that limits each branch's power. Each branch has some power to change or cancel the actions of the other branches.

Legislative Branch

The legislative branch establishes laws. In a representative democracy like the United States, citizens elect legislative representatives to make decisions for them. The legislative branch also imposes taxes, or required payments. Taxes are used to pay for government services and public goods such as roads, parks, fire departments, and national defense. Public goods are owned by everyone in the country.

U.S. Congress

Executive Branch

The executive branch carries out, or enforces, the laws. It also provides for the country's defense, conducts foreign policy, and manages day-to-day affairs. The United States and some other countries have a presidential system with an elected president as the head of the executive branch. Other democracies, such as the United Kingdom, have a parliamentary system. In this system, the parliament, or legislative branch, chooses a prime minister as chief executive.

U.S. President Barack Obama

Judicial Branch

The judicial branch makes decisions about disputes. It does this through courts of law. These courts can range from local criminal courts to the highest court in the land. In the United States that court is called the Supreme Court. Among other things, the Supreme Court interprets the law. That is, it judges how a law should be applied and whether the law violates the Constitution.

U.S. Supreme Court

Assessment

1. What are the three branches of government?
2. What are three key democratic principles?

109

Conflict and Cooperation

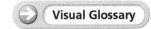
Every nation-state, or country, has clearly defined territory and sovereignty over that territory. **Sovereignty** is supreme authority, or power. Every country also has a central government. The central government takes care of matters that affect the whole country. This includes dealing with other countries' governments. Interactions between governments can take the form of conflict or cooperation.

Conflict

Most countries have a **foreign policy,** a set of goals describing how a country's government plans to interact with other countries' governments. A country's foreign policy reflects its values and intentions. Geographic factors such as location, physical features, and distribution of natural resources can influence foreign policy.

A country's foreign policy can lead to conflict with other countries. Wars and fighting begin for many reasons. Some wars begin as conflicts over control of land or resources. Others result from religious disagreements, political revolutions, or conflict between ethnic groups. Wars can lead to widespread death and destruction.

Food being distributed in Angola. ▼

Public Health Organizations

International Red Cross and Red Crescent Movement Provides medical aid, food, and other relief services to victims of war or natural disasters

World Health Organization Fights disease, especially among the world's poor, by providing health information, medical training, and medicine

Cooperation

Many people view the world as a global community in which people should cooperate to avoid conflict and help others. This cooperation may take the form of a **treaty,** a formal agreement between two or more countries. Some treaties are agreements to help defend other countries. Other treaties are agreements to limit the harmful effects of war. For example, the Geneva Conventions list rules for the proper treatment of wounded soldiers, prisoners, and civilians.

The United Nations (UN) is the largest international organization that works for peace. Nearly every country in the world belongs to the UN. Governments send representatives to the UN to engage in diplomacy. **Diplomacy** is managing communication and relationships between countries. The UN Declaration of Human Rights lists the rights that all people should have, including life, liberty, and security. The UN works to protect these rights around the world.

Governments also cooperate for reasons other than avoiding conflict. For example, governments often work with one another to improve their countries' economies through trade. International trade can provide new goods and markets. Trade agreements involving multiple countries have become common in recent years.

This water pump in South Africa was funded by the World Bank.

Economic Organizations

World Bank Provides loans for projects aimed at promoting economic development

International Monetary Fund (IMF) Seeks to prevent and resolve economic crises by offering advice, information, technical training, and loans

Humanitarian Organizations

United Nations (UN) Seeks to encourage international cooperation and achieve world peace but sometimes faces criticism

CARE International Seeks to end world poverty through development and self-help

◀ UN peacekeeping troops in Bosnia

Assessment

1. What are some of the functions of international organizations?
2. How do governments resolve conflict and cooperate?

111

Citizenship

The United States is a representative democracy. In a democracy, all political power comes from citizens. A **citizen** is a legal member of a country. In the United States, most people become citizens by being born on U.S. territory. Immigrants to the United States can become citizens through a legal process known as naturalization.

Rights and Responsibilities

Citizens' rights and responsibilities can come from a number of sources. These sources include constitutions, cultural traditions, and religious laws.

Americans' basic rights are protected by the Bill of Rights, a part of the U.S. Constitution. The Bill of Rights and other laws protect rights such as freedom of speech and freedom of religion. If the government violates these rights, citizens can fight the injustice in court. For the most part, these rights are also guaranteed to noncitizens.

Immigrants to the United States become citizens at a naturalization ceremony. ▼

Americans also have responsibilities. For example, we have the right to speak freely, but we also have the responsibility to allow others to say things we may not agree with. Our responsibilities include a duty to participate in government and **civic life,** or activities having to do with one's society and community. Voting is both a right and a responsibility for U.S. citizens.

Rights and responsibilities can vary widely in different countries and societies. Although most democratic governments protect basic human rights, nondemocratic governments often do not. Citizens who live in autocracies or oligarchies usually cannot take part in government or express their views openly.

Citizenship Worldwide

Ideas about rights and responsibilities can change over time. Many countries have become democracies over the past 200 years. These democracies now protect basic human rights such as freedom of expression and freedom from unfair imprisonment. Some of these countries did not protect these rights in the past or did not protect these rights for all people.

Today, international trade, transportation, and communication have linked the world's people. As a result, some people think that we should consider ourselves to be citizens of a global community. They believe that we are responsible for supporting human rights and equality for all people around the world.

Assessment

1. What is the main source of American citizens' basic rights?

2. How do the roles and responsibilities of citizens vary between democratic and nondemocratic countries?

Civic Participation

Voting is one type of **civic participation,** or taking part in government. Here are some others:

- Keeping informed about local, state, and national issues
- Contacting an elected representative, such as a state legislator or member of Congress
- Voicing opinions at town meetings
- Taking part in public gatherings, protests, or demonstrations
- Signing a petition, a formal request for government to do something
- Running for public office
- Getting involved in a political party—a group that supports candidates for public offices
- Joining an interest group—a group that seeks to influence public policy on certain issues

113

Part 8 Assessment

Key Terms and Ideas

1. **Recall** There are two types of democracy: direct and representative. Which kind of **democracy** is the United States?

2. **Identify** Describe the powers of an **unlimited government.**

3. **Connect** Why did **governments** first develop thousands of years ago?

4. **Describe** How does the U.S. government balance legislative, executive, and judicial power?

5. **Compare and Contrast** How are the **unitary system** and the **federal system** similar and different?

6. **Paraphrase** Explain **diplomacy** in your own words.

7. **Identify** Name two ways American **citizens** can participate in the political process.

Think Critically

8. **Draw Inferences** Consider that you can freely read about your government's actions and policies on the Internet. How might Internet access differ in a country with an authoritarian government?

9. **Make Decisions** Do you think that people who live in a democracy should be required to fulfill their civic responsibilities?

10. **Synthesize** Imagine that a country shares its borders with three others. How do you think its geography might relate to its foreign policy?

11. **Draw Conclusions** Who do you think is more likely to speak out against the government: a citizen in a limited government or a citizen in an unlimited government? Explain.

Identify

Answer the following questions based on the map.

12. Which country is the westernmost member of the European Union?

13. Which EU members border Latvia?

14. List the EU members with territory located to the north of 60° N latitude and to the east of 0° longitude.

15. Which EU members border Slovenia?

16. How many members made up the European Union in 2009?

17. What sea do Spain and Greece border?

18. How would you describe EU membership?

European Union, 2009

KEY
European Union member states

0   400 mi
0   400 km
Lambert Conformal Conic Projection

Journal Activity

Fill in the graphic organizer in your Student Journal.

Demonstrate Your Understanding Complete the Sum-It-Up activity in your journal to demonstrate your understanding of government and citizenship. After you complete the activity, discuss your If-Then statements with a small group. Be sure to support your statements with information from the lessons.

Document-Based Questions

Success Tracker™
Online at myworldgeography.com

Use your knowledge of government and citizenship and Documents A and B to answer Questions 1–3.

Document A

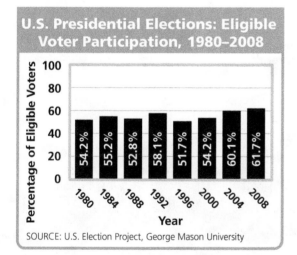

U.S. Presidential Elections: Eligible Voter Participation, 1980–2008

(Percentage of Eligible Voters by Year)
- 1980: 54.2%
- 1984: 55.2%
- 1988: 52.8%
- 1992: 58.1%
- 1996: 51.7%
- 2000: 54.2%
- 2004: 60.1%
- 2008: 61.7%

SOURCE: U.S. Election Project, George Mason University

Document B

" The accumulation of all powers, legislative, executive, and judiciary, in the same hands, whether of one, a few, or many … may justly be pronounced the very definition of tyranny."

—James Madison, *The Federalist,* No. 48

1. Examine Document A. How has eligible voter participation changed in the time period shown?

   A It has declined steadily.

   B It has increased steadily.

   C It has declined since 1996.

   D It has increased since 1996.

2. Read Document B. Which of the following statements would James Madison agree with?

   A Separate branches of government are unnecessary.

   B Unlimited government is not a form of tyranny.

   C Separate branches of government are essential.

   D A unitary system of government is ideal.

3. **Writing Task** Do you agree or disagree with James Madison? Write a short essay in which you respond to Madison's quotation. Be sure to explain your position clearly, supporting it with information from the lessons.

my worldgeography.com   Self-Test

Tools of History

Inca ruins in Peru

An archaeologist sketches a
dig in Lima, Peru.

Archaeologists at a dig

Brian McCray

Digging for Clues

Story by Miles Lemaire for myWorld Geography

Brian McCray likes to dig in the dirt. But Brian isn't just playing around. He's an archaeologist who has traveled around the world to dig up objects from the past and learn more about the people who made them.

Carrying out an archaeological dig isn't as simple as picking a location, grabbing a shovel, and starting to dig, Brian says. He spends weeks or months researching the history of the dig's location before a shovel goes into the ground. Brian will study maps, look at photographs, and read written descriptions of the area. He wants to know as much as possible about the site before he begins to explore it.

Once an archaeological dig begins, archaeologists like Brian carefully examine all the objects found at the site. Then they record and save the objects for future research. Keeping good records is very important. All archaeological sites are drawn and mapped carefully, with detailed information about where each object was found. It can take months or years to fully examine all of the artifacts, or objects made by people, found at an archaeological site.

"The things that are deeper in the ground are, in most cases, older than the things closer to the surface," says Brian. "We keep track of every layer of soil and what we find there."

Brian's research has allowed him to travel throughout the Americas. He has studied sites in the northern United States, the Caribbean, and western South America. Brian has worked with the Digital Archaeological Archive of Contemporary Slavery. This research has helped historians learn more about the lives of enslaved Africans in North America and the Caribbean. But his most interesting discovery was in the Andes Mountains in South America. In the Andes, Brian studied something that researchers still don't fully understand.

"It was actually what appears to be a swimming pool," Brian says. "It was constructed by the Incas at the very end of the Incan Empire." That was almost 500 years ago.

What was the "pool" used for? "Who knows?" Brian says. "It was a big sunken court with really amazing cut-stone masonry and five or six canals bringing water down into it from up the hill … It's way too cold up there for anyone to want to swim all that often."

But although Brian and his fellow archaeologists don't yet know why the Incas built this pool, you can be sure that they'll keep digging to find out the answer. Who knows? Maybe Brian will be the one to finally uncover the truth.

Measuring Time

Key Ideas

- Throughout history, societies and cultures have organized time in different ways.
- People have used a number of different calendars to measure time.

Key Terms • historian • timeline • chronology • period • prehistory

 Visual Glossary

It can be hard to describe the concept of time. But **historians**—people who study events in the past—know that organizing time is important if we want to understand past events.

Using a Timeline

Historians use timelines as a tool. A **timeline** is a line marked off with a series of events and dates. Historians use timelines to put events in a **chronology,** a list of events in the order in which they occurred.

A timeline is flexible. It can cover a day, a year, a decade (ten years), a century (one hundred years), a millennium (one thousand years), or any other period in history. A **period** is a length of time singled out because of a specific event or development that happened during that time. A period is also known as an era or an epoch. Historians use periods and eras to organize and describe human activities.

The timeline on this page shows watershed events—important points in history. The period 1940–1949 is an example of a decade, or a period of ten years. Below, a Sumerian writing tablet. ▼

A.D. 1945 World War II ends.

| 1940 | 1941 | 1942 | 1943 | 1944 | 1945 | 1946 | 1947 | 1948 | 1949 |

3200 B.C. Sumerians develop the earliest known form of writing.

| 3000 B.C. | 2000 B.C. | 1000 B.C. | A.D. 1 | A.D. 1000 | A.D. 2000 |

1766 B.C. China's Shang dynasty begins.

A.D. 250 Maya Classic period begins in Mexico and Central America.

A.D. 1492 Christopher Columbus sails to the Americas.

Organizing Time

The past is often split into two parts, prehistory and history. **Prehistory** is the time before humans invented writing. *History* refers to written history, which began about 5,200 years ago.

We can also organize history by beginning with a key event from the past. Today much of the world uses the believed birthdate of Jesus as a key event. Years before that event are labeled B.C., for "before Christ," or B.C.E., for "before common era." Years after Jesus's birth are labeled A.D., meaning *anno Domini,* Latin for "in the year of our Lord." These years are also known as C.E., for "common era."

The Jewish calendar counts the years since the creation of the world, according to Jewish tradition. The Islamic calendar is dated from the year that the prophet Muhammad moved to the city of Medina.

Throughout history, societies have used different calendars. Maya and Aztec priests made calendars for farming and religious purposes. Today much of the world uses the Gregorian calendar, which has a 365- or 366-day year. It is based on the movement of Earth around the sun. The Jewish year, based on both sun and moon, varies from 353 to 385 days to adjust to the solar year. The Islamic year, however, is based on the cycles of the moon and lasts about 354 days.

Calendar Systems

Calendars are based on the movements of Earth, the moon, the stars, or a combination. Throughout history, people have used different methods to create calendars. The objects shown here were all different ways of measuring the passage of time.

Astrolabe This astrolabe was used by Muslim astronomers to calculate the positions of the sun, moon, planets, and stars. ▶

◀ **Aztec Calendar Stone** The Aztecs had two calendars: a 365-day agricultural calendar and a 260-day religious calendar.

Roman Calendar Early Roman calendars were based on the movements of the moon and had 10 months and 304 days. Later, the calendar had 12 months and 355 days. ▶

Assessment

1. How do people organize time?

2. If you created a timeline of everything you did yesterday, what would you choose to be the first event? What would be the last event? How would you decide which events are important enough to include on the timeline?

Historical Sources

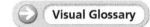
Historians try to accurately understand and describe the past. To understand past events, historians study historical sources.

Primary and Secondary Sources

A **primary source** is information that comes directly from a person who experienced an event. It consists of what the person writes, says, or creates about the event. Primary sources include letters, diaries, speeches, and photographs. Artifacts are also primary sources. An **artifact** is an object made by a human being, such as a tool or a weapon. We use primary sources to understand events from the points of view of people who lived at the time in which they happened.

Books, articles, movies, and other sources that describe or make sense of the past are secondary sources. A **secondary source** is information about an event that does not come from a person who experienced that event.

This U.S. poster created during World War II is an example of a primary source. ▼

We Can Do It!

WAR PRODUCTION CO-ORDINATING COMMITTEE

Letters written by soldiers are primary sources.

Primary Sources

❝ Yesterday, December 7, 1941—a date which will live in infamy—the United States of America was suddenly and deliberately attacked by naval and air forces of the empire of Japan . . . No matter how long it may take us to overcome this premeditated [planned] invasion, the American people in their righteous might will win through to absolute victory. ❞

—President Franklin D. Roosevelt, December 8, 1941

Evaluating Historical Sources

Historical sources do not always give a true account of events. Even primary sources can be wrong or misleading. An author's personal opinions may have influenced what he or she recorded. Sometimes the author may not remember the event accurately. A historian must decide what, if anything, to trust in a primary source.

A historian must also be cautious when using secondary sources. Not all secondary sources are equally reliable. For example, the Internet includes millions of well-researched articles, books, and other reliable secondary sources. However, any Internet search will also find many inaccurate Web sites.

Historians and students of history—like you—must evaluate a source to determine its reliability. When you examine primary and secondary sources, ask yourself questions like these:

- Who created the source material? A witness to an event may be more trustworthy than someone looking back at the event from a later time. However, a scholar or publication with a good reputation is also a reliable source. For example, a college professor who specializes in Chinese history would be a reliable source on China.

- Is the information fact or opinion? A fact is something that can be proved true or false. An opinion is a personal belief. Opinions are valuable not as a source of facts but as a clue to the author's judgments or feelings.

- Does the material seem to have a bias? A **bias** is an unfair preference for or dislike of something. Biased material often leaves out facts that do not support the author's point of view.

The painting and article below are secondary sources. ▼

Secondary Sources

❝ Japanese planes attacked the U.S. naval base at Pearl Harbor, Hawaii, on December 7, 1941.... This disaster caused the American public to support an immediate American entry into the war. ❞

—*History of Our World*, Prentice Hall, 2008

Assessment

1. What is a primary source?
2. Which online source will likely be more accurate, an encyclopedia or a personal journal such as a blog? Explain.

Archaeology and Other Sources

Key Idea

- Archaeology and other historical sources offer clues to what life was like in the distant past.

Key Terms
- archaeology
- anthropology
- oral tradition

→ Visual Glossary

Machu Picchu, Peru, is an Incan city abandoned in the 1500s and largely forgotten until the 1800s.

The Temple of Inscriptions in Palenque, Mexico, contains the tomb of the Maya ruler Pakal, who died in A.D. 683. ▼

Archaeologists Louis and Mary Leakey found many fossil remains of human ancestors in Africa's Olduvai Gorge.

Over time, much of the ancient world has disappeared. Large cities have collapsed into ruins. Buildings are buried under layers of soil and sand or covered by thick forests. The artifacts that show what life was like in ancient times are often buried or hidden. The science of archaeology aims to uncover this hidden history. **Archaeology** is the scientific study of ancient cultures through the examination of artifacts and other evidence.

Archaeologists and Anthropologists

Archaeologists are part treasure hunters and part detectives. They explore the places where people once lived and worked, searching for artifacts such as tools, weapons, and pottery. Archaeologists study the objects they find to learn more about the past.

Artifacts can help us identify the resources available to ancient people. They can help us understand how these people used technology and how they adapted to their environment.

Anthropology also helps historians understand the past. **Anthropology** is the study of humankind in all aspects, especially development and culture. Anthropologists seek to understand the origins of humans and the ways humans developed physically. This field often involves studying fossils—bones and other remains that have been preserved in rock.

Anthropologists also try to determine how human cultures formed and grew. Clues to the past can come from a culture's oral traditions. **Oral tradition** is a community's cultural and historical background, passed down in spoken stories and songs.

New Zealand's Maori people have passed down many aspects of their culture through oral tradition. ▼

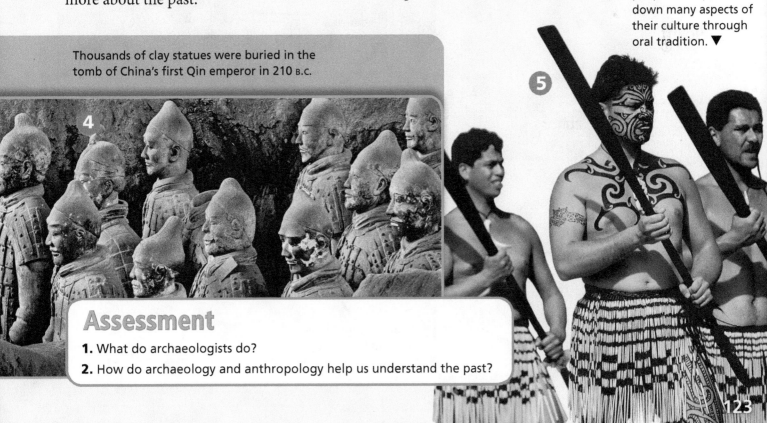

Thousands of clay statues were buried in the tomb of China's first Qin emperor in 210 B.C.

4

5

Assessment

1. What do archaeologists do?

2. How do archaeology and anthropology help us understand the past?

123

Core Concepts 9.4

Historical Maps

Key Ideas
- Historical maps offer visual representations of historical information.
- Historical maps show information about places at certain times.

Key Term • historical map

Visual Glossary

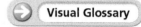

When you read about a historical event like an important battle, it can be hard to get a clear picture of what really happened. You may have to understand how landforms like rivers and hills affected the battle. Or perhaps the location of a nearby town, railroad, or road influenced the fighting. Sometimes the best way to learn about a historical event or period is by examining a historical map.

The title identifies the map's subject and time period.

The Roman Empire, about A.D. 117

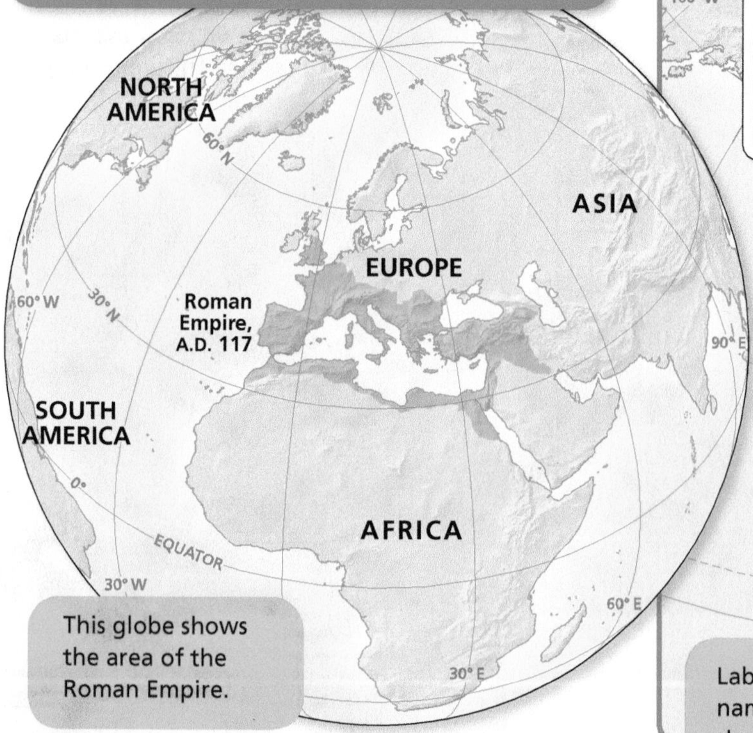

NORTH AMERICA
60° N
ASIA
EUROPE
60° W
30° N
Roman Empire, A.D. 117
90° E
SOUTH AMERICA
0°
EQUATOR
AFRICA
30° W
60° E
30° E

This globe shows the area of the Roman Empire.

North America, 1783

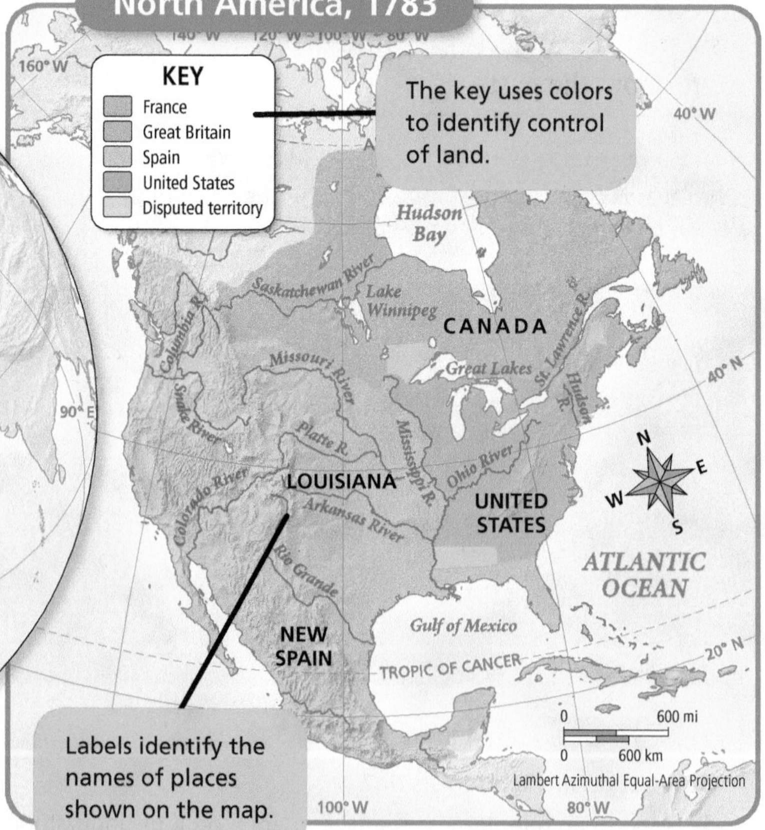

160° W
KEY
France
Great Britain
Spain
United States
Disputed territory
40° W
Hudson Bay
Saskatchewan River
Lake Winnipeg
CANADA
Columbia R.
Missouri River
Great Lakes
St. Lawrence R.
Hudson R.
40° N
Snake River
Platte R.
Mississippi R.
Ohio River
LOUISIANA
Colorado River
Arkansas River
UNITED STATES
N
E
W
S
ATLANTIC OCEAN
Rio Grande
Gulf of Mexico
NEW SPAIN
TROPIC OF CANCER
20° N
0
600 mi
0
600 km
Lambert Azimuthal Equal-Area Projection
100° W
80° W

The key uses colors to identify control of land.

Labels identify the names of places shown on the map.

A **historical map** is a special-purpose map that provides information about a place at a certain time in history. Historical maps can show information such as migration, trade patterns, or other facts.

Historical maps have similar features. Most have a title and a key. Most use colors and symbols to show resources, movement, locations of people, or other features. Use the following four steps to become familiar with historical maps.

1. Read the title. Note the date, the time span, or other information about the subject of the map. If the map includes a locator map, examine it to see what region is shown.

2. Study the map quickly to get a general idea of what it shows. Read any place names and other labels. Note any landforms.

3. Examine the map's key. Pick out the first symbol or other entry, read what it stands for, and find an example on the map. Repeat this process for the remaining key entries until you understand them all.

4. Study the map more thoroughly. Make sure you have a clear understanding of the picture the map presents. If you need help, reread the related section of your textbook or examine the map again.

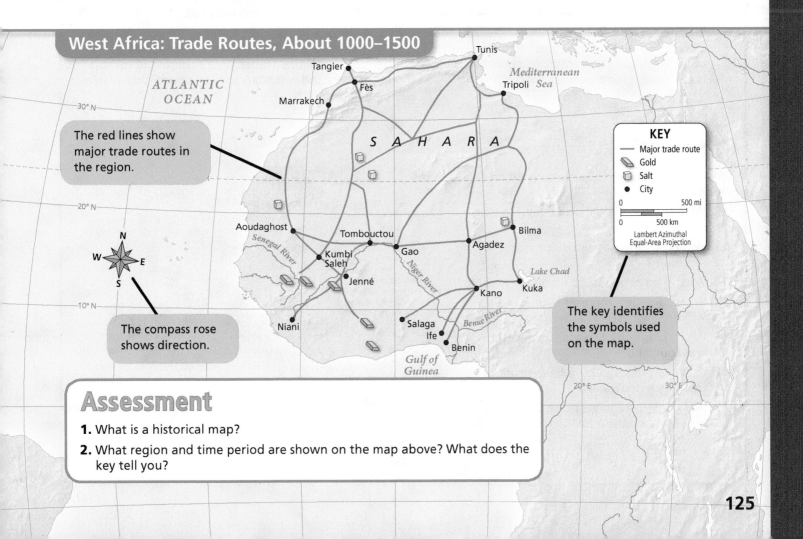

West Africa: Trade Routes, About 1000–1500

The red lines show major trade routes in the region.

The compass rose shows direction.

KEY
— Major trade route
Gold
Salt
• City

0   500 mi
0   500 km
Lambert Azimuthal
Equal-Area Projection

The key identifies the symbols used on the map.

Assessment

1. What is a historical map?

2. What region and time period are shown on the map above? What does the key tell you?

Part 9 Assessment

Key Terms and Ideas

1. **Summarize** What is **archaeology**?

2. **Identify** When a person who did not experience an event describes the event, is the description a **primary source** or a **secondary source**?

3. **Compare and Contrast** Explain the difference between history and **prehistory.**

4. **Identify Cause and Effect** What do archaeologists do with **artifacts**?

5. **Synthesize** How do **timelines** show historical events or periods?

6. **Identify** What do **historical maps** show?

7. **Recall** What three questions should you ask when evaluating a source?

Think Critically

8. **Make Decisions** Imagine that you are creating a map that will show ancient trade routes. Name three things you might include in the map's key.

9. **Draw Conclusions** How do you think the work of archaeologists and anthropologists can help present and future generations?

10. **Draw Inferences** Why do you think so many different calendars still exist today?

11. **Analyze Primary and Secondary Sources** Imagine that you are writing a biographical profile of a famous political leader. Give examples of reliable primary and secondary sources you might use in your research.

Identify

Answer the following questions based on the map.

12. What area of the United States is shown on the map?

13. What do the light yellow dots represent?

14. What time period is shown on the map?

15. What color dots represent hurricanes with the highest wind speeds?

16. What large body of water borders Texas and Louisiana?

17. List two states that have been struck by category 4 hurricanes.

18. How many category 5 hurricane strikes are shown on the map?

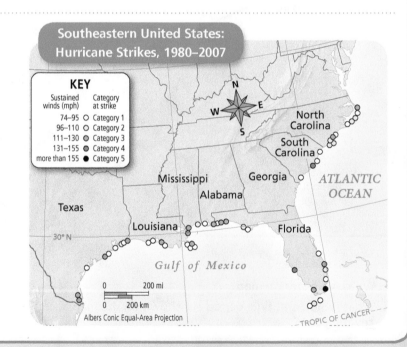

Southeastern United States: Hurricane Strikes, 1980–2007

KEY

Sustained winds (mph)	Category at strike
74–95	○ Category 1
96–110	○ Category 2
111–130	◉ Category 3
131–155	● Category 4
more than 155	● Category 5

North Carolina
South Carolina
Georgia
Mississippi
Alabama
Texas
Louisiana
Florida
ATLANTIC OCEAN
Gulf of Mexico
30° N
0   200 mi
0   200 km
Albers Conic Equal-Area Projection
TROPIC OF CANCER

Journal Activity

Fill in the graphic organizer in your Student Journal.

 **Demonstrate Your Understanding** Complete the Sum-It-Up activity in your journal to demonstrate your understanding of the tools of history. After you complete the activity, discuss your plan for using historical resources with a small group. Be sure to support your plan with information from the lessons.

21st Century Learning

Develop Cultural Awareness

Oral tradition remains an important part of many cultures. Research a song or story still passed on by oral tradition today, either in your own culture or in another. Then share the song or story with the class. Be sure to address the following topics:

- Origins of the song or story
- Cultural significance of the song or story

Document-Based Questions

Success ⭐ Tracker™
Online at myworldgeography.com

Use your knowledge of the tools of history and Documents A and B to answer Questions 1–3.

Document A

```
        KEY
☐  Allies, 1918
☐  Central Powers, 1918
☐  Neutral nations
••••  Front line 1914
▬ ▬  Front line 1915–1916
──  Front line 1917
▬▬  Front line 1918
✳  Battle site
```

Document B

" [Alexander] was only twenty years old when he succeeded to the crown, and he found the kingdom torn into pieces by dangerous [groups of people]."

— Plutarch, *Life of Alexander,* about A.D. 100

1. Document A is a key to a historical map showing Europe during World War I. What information does this map not give you?

   A location of front line in 1917

   B locations of battles

   C members of the Central Powers in 1918

   D outcome of World War I

2. Document B is an excerpt about the ancient Greek leader Alexander the Great, written by a historian about 400 years after Alexander's death. Which of the following best describes this excerpt?

   A primary source

   B secondary source

   C artifact

   D prehistoric

3. **Writing Task** Using information from Documents A and B and your knowledge of the tools of history, describe how historians use sources to understand and explain historical events.

my worldgeography.com   Self-Test

Regional Overview

Southwest Asia

Southwest Asia is a region of towering mountains in the north and vast deserts in the south. It is a continental crossroads that connects Asia to Europe and Africa. The region includes the world's most important oil producer, Saudi Arabia, and several other oil-rich nations. Southwest Asia is also the birthplace of three great world religions: Judaism, Christianity, and Islam.

What time is it there?

Washington, D.C.	Jidda, Saudi Arabia
9 A.M. Monday	5 P.M. Monday

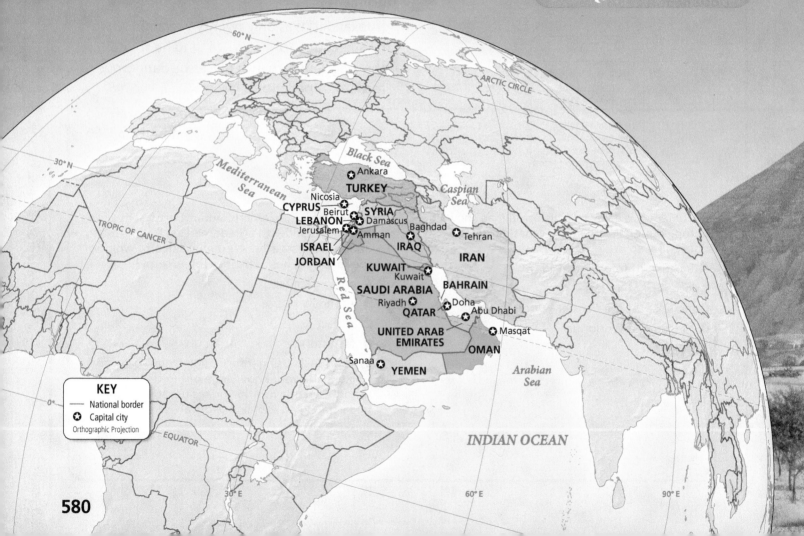

Black Sea

Mediterranean Sea

⊗ Ankara
TURKEY

CYPRUS Nicosia ⊗
Beirut ⊗ **SYRIA**
LEBANON ⊗ Damascus
Jerusalem ⊗⊗ Baghdad ⊗ Tehran
Amman

ISRAEL
JORDAN **IRAQ** **IRAN**

KUWAIT
Kuwait ⊗ **BAHRAIN**
SAUDI ARABIA
Riyadh ⊗ ⊗ Doha
QATAR ⊗ Abu Dhabi
UNITED ARAB EMIRATES ⊗ Masqat
OMAN

Sanaa ⊗ **YEMEN**

Caspian Sea

Red Sea

Arabian Sea

ARCTIC CIRCLE

60° N

30° N

TROPIC OF CANCER

0°

EQUATOR

30° E

60° E

90° E

INDIAN OCEAN

KEY
— National border
⊗ Capital city
Orthographic Projection

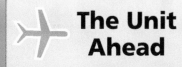

The Unit Ahead

➜ **Chapter 16** Arabia and Iraq

➜ **Chapter 17** Israel and Its Neighbors

➜ **Chapter 18** Iran, Turkey, and Cyprus

my worldgeography.com

Plan your trip online with a Data Discovery Activity and the myStory Videos of the region's young people.

my Story

Hanan
Age: 20
Home: Jidda, Saudi Arabia

Chapter 16

my Story

Maayan
Age: 18
Home: Adi, Israel

Chapter 17

my Story

Muhammad
Age: 15
Home: Jerusalem, Israel

Chapter 17

my Story

Bilal
Age: 18
Home: Urfa, Turkey

Chapter 18

Dry mountains rise above fertile plains in eastern Turkey.

Regional Overview
Physical Geography

Black Sea

Caspian Sea

Anatolia

Taurus Mountains

Tigris River

Zagros Mountains

Elburz Mountains

Mesopotamia

Euphrates River

Iranian Plateau

Mediterranean Sea

Syrian Desert

Persian Gulf

Hejaz

Red Sea

Arabian Peninsula

Rub' al-Khali

Asir

Green mountains and fertile valleys run through Turkey, Syria, Lebanon, Israel, Jordan, northern Iraq, and western Iran.

The Tigris and Euphrates rivers bring life to the dry lowlands of Iraq.

Arabian Sea

Not much grows in the vast deserts of the Arabian Peninsula.

I N D I A N   O C E A N

Regional Flyover

Suppose that you are in an airplane flying toward Southwest Asia. Flying east from Europe, you come to Turkey, whose mountains and plains lie between the Black Sea and the Mediterranean Sea. To its south is the Mediterranean island country of Cyprus.

Along the eastern shore of the Mediterranean lies a range of hills that runs through Syria, Lebanon, Jordan, and Israel. Next, you come to the flat valley of the Tigris and Euphrates rivers in Iraq. Farther east, you come to the high plateaus and mountains of Iran.

Turning south from Iran, you fly across the Persian Gulf, surrounded by oil wells and refineries. Across the Persian Gulf lies the Arabian Peninsula. Vast deserts stretch across this peninsula. Small countries line the coast of the peninsula. These are Kuwait, Bahrain, Qatar, the United Arab Emirates, Oman, and Yemen. You fly across Saudi Arabia, which covers most of the peninsula. In Saudi Arabia, your plane lands in Jidda.

➔ **In-Flight Movie**

Take flight over Southwest Asia and explore the region from the air.

my worldgeography.com **In-Flight Movie**

583

Regional Geography
Human Geography

A Diverse Region

Southwest Asia is home to different peoples and religions. Arabs are the main ethnic group in most countries. However, Turks are the dominant group in Turkey, Persians are the dominant group in Iran, and Jews are the dominant group in Israel. A people called the Kurds are spread across several countries. Most people in the region are Muslims, or people who follow the religion of Islam. However, the region's Muslims belong to different branches of Islam. Most follow either Sunni or Shia Islam. There are also Christians and other religious minorities and a Jewish majority in Israel.

Judaism
This Jewish man is worshiping at the Western Wall in Jerusalem.

Christianity
This Christian man is worshiping at a shrine in Lebanon.

Islam
This Muslim man is reading from the Quran, Islam's holy book.

my World IN NUMBERS

Southwest Asia has a rich variety of ethnic groups and religions. Arab Muslims dominate most countries in the region, but they follow different branches of Islam. Turkish Muslims dominate Turkey, Persian Muslims dominate Iran, and Israeli Jews dominate Israel. Each country has many minority groups.

Southwest Asia: Religion

KEY
- Christianity
- Druze
- Ibadism
- Judaism
- Shiism
- Sunnism
- Yezidi
- Zoroastrianism
- Sparsely populated

Lambert Conformal Conic Projection

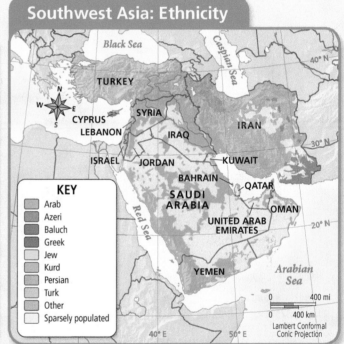

Southwest Asia: Ethnicity

KEY
- Arab
- Azeri
- Baluch
- Greek
- Jew
- Kurd
- Persian
- Turk
- Other
- Sparsely populated

Lambert Conformal Conic Projection

Put It Together

1. What physical features cause parts of this region to be sparsely populated?

2. In which country do most of the region's Jewish people live?

3. In which countries do the Kurds live?

Find your own data to make a regional data table.

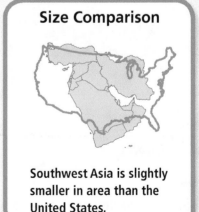

Size Comparison

Southwest Asia is slightly smaller in area than the United States.

my worldgeography.com Data Discovery

585

Chapter 16

Arabia and Iraq

? Essential Question

How much does geography shape a country?

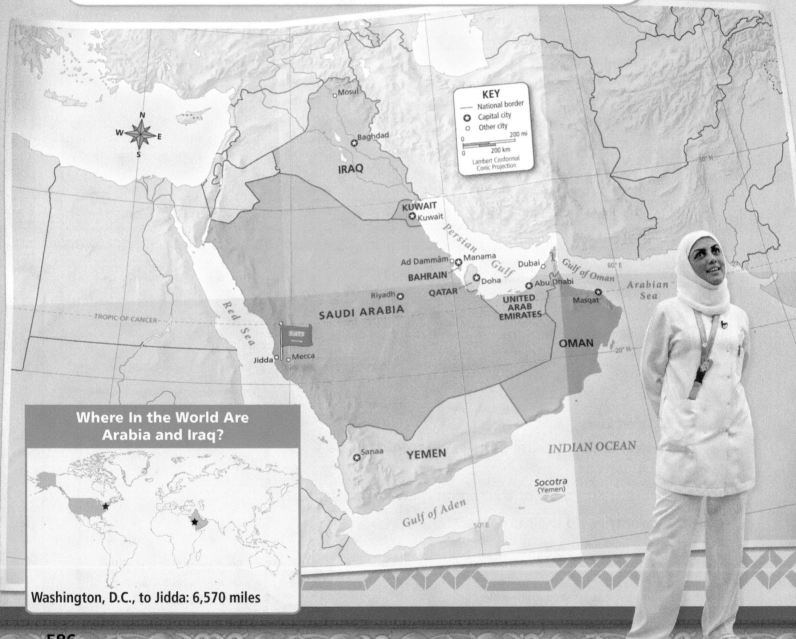

KEY
- National border
- ⊛ Capital city
- ○ Other city

0   200 mi
0   200 km

Lambert Conformal
Conic Projection

Mosul
Baghdad
IRAQ
KUWAIT
Kuwait
Persian Gulf
Ad Dammām Manama Dubai Gulf of Oman
BAHRAIN Doha Abu Dhabi Arabian Sea
Riyadh **QATAR**
SAUDI ARABIA **UNITED ARAB EMIRATES** Masqat
TROPIC OF CANCER
Red Sea
OMAN
Jidda Mecca
Sanaa **YEMEN** **INDIAN OCEAN**
Socotra (Yemen)
Gulf of Aden

30° N
60° E
20° N
50° E

Where In the World Are Arabia and Iraq?

Washington, D.C., to Jidda: 6,570 miles

my Story

Hanan's Call to Care

In this section, you'll read about Hanan, a young Saudi woman who has become a professional in a country where women face many difficulties. **What does Hanan's story tell you about life in Arabia and Iraq today?**

Explore the Essential Question

- at **my worldgeography.com**
- using the **my World Chapter Activity**
- with the **Student Journal**

Story by Danya M. Alhamrani for myWorld Geography Online

In the darkness of the early morning, Hanan awakes to the sound of adhan. This is the Islamic call to prayer, sung out by a muezzin, often from the minaret, or high tower, of an Islamic house of worship called a mosque. The adhan call tells the faithful that it is time to begin their daily prayer rituals. They will perform these rituals five times over the course of the day.

As the muezzin's voice drifts through the warm stillness remaining from the night, it is joined by another, then another, and yet another voice calling out the prayer, in Arabic: "Allahu akbar. Hayya alal sala. Hayya alal falah." That is Arabic for "God is most great. Come to prayer. Come to success."

The calling continues as Hanan walks to the bathroom to make her wudu, her ritual washing before beginning prayer. She covers herself from head to toe with her sharshaf, a long, traditional robe, and joins her mother for the first prayer of the day.

my worldgeography.com On Assignment

587

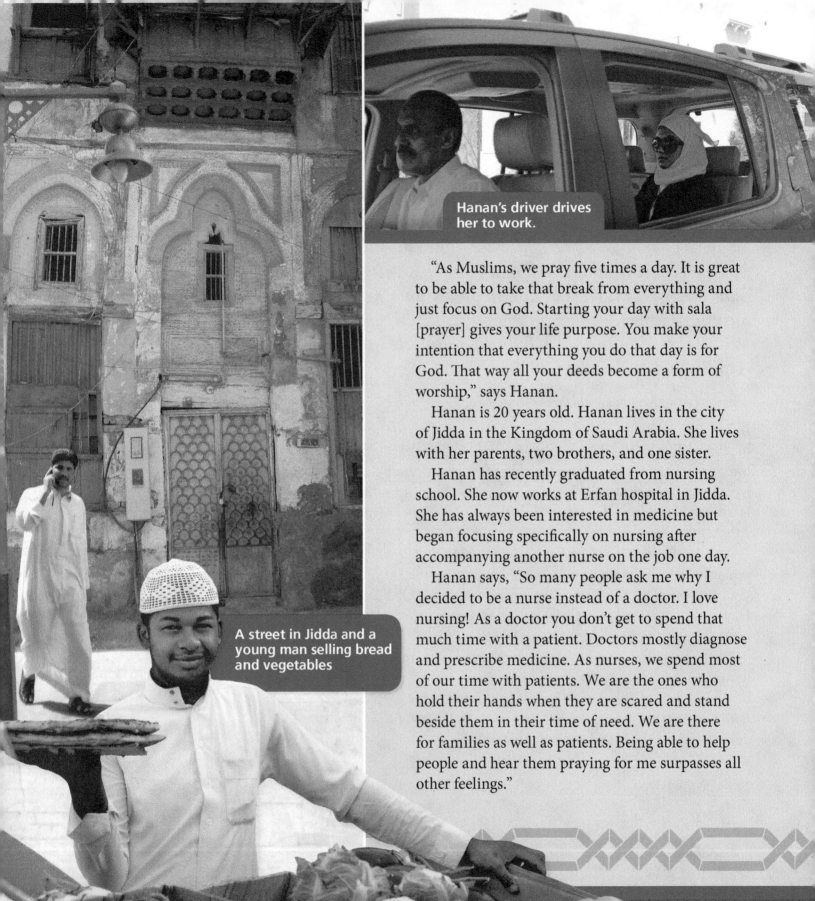

Hanan's driver drives her to work.

A street in Jidda and a young man selling bread and vegetables

"As Muslims, we pray five times a day. It is great to be able to take that break from everything and just focus on God. Starting your day with sala [prayer] gives your life purpose. You make your intention that everything you do that day is for God. That way all your deeds become a form of worship," says Hanan.

Hanan is 20 years old. Hanan lives in the city of Jidda in the Kingdom of Saudi Arabia. She lives with her parents, two brothers, and one sister.

Hanan has recently graduated from nursing school. She now works at Erfan hospital in Jidda. She has always been interested in medicine but began focusing specifically on nursing after accompanying another nurse on the job one day.

Hanan says, "So many people ask me why I decided to be a nurse instead of a doctor. I love nursing! As a doctor you don't get to spend that much time with a patient. Doctors mostly diagnose and prescribe medicine. As nurses, we spend most of our time with patients. We are the ones who hold their hands when they are scared and stand beside them in their time of need. We are there for families as well as patients. Being able to help people and hear them praying for me surpasses all other feelings."

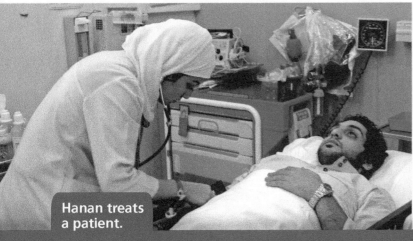

Hanan treats a patient.

Hanan's family in their living room

Many nurses in Saudi Arabia come from other countries, but the number of Saudi nurses is growing. Nursing, however, is not a typical profession for Saudi women.

In fact, few Saudi women work outside the home. Saudi law and culture place many restrictions on the lives of women. For example, Saudi women are not legally allowed to drive cars. They may not travel abroad without the permission of their husband or a male relative.

Saudi culture strongly encourages women to stay home and take care of their families rather than work. Because of these cultural and legal restrictions it is difficult for them to hold jobs. Still, 20 percent of Saudi women work outside their homes.

Restrictions aside, Hanan's biggest headache is her hectic schedule. The necessity of working around-the-clock in shifts takes a toll on family life.

"Nursing is a tough profession," Hanan says. "People who want to go into this line of work need to have patience and endurance. I end up missing a lot of family gatherings due to long working hours. I sometimes stay at home on my days off just to get some rest."

Despite the hardships she sometimes faces, Hanan loves her job and looks forward to a long career in her chosen field of nursing.

 myStory Video

Join Hanan as she shows you more about life in her city.

Meet the Journalist

Name Camilo Moreno
Favorite Moment Watching families pray together at the beach

Hanan and her mother praying together

Chapter Atlas

Key Ideas
- Physical geography has made much of this region rich in oil and natural gas.
- The climate of Arabia and Iraq makes water scarce.
- The region is home to different ethnic and religious groups.

Key Terms
- plate
- fossil fuel
- desalination
- urbanized
- majority

 Visual Glossary

 Reading Skill: Label an Outline Map Take notes using the outline map in your journal.

◄ A Yemeni woman. Her hands are painted with henna.
Behind her is the Rub' al-Khali desert in Oman. Its name means "the empty quarter" in Arabic.

Physical Features

Arabia, or the Arabian Peninsula, is surrounded on three sides by water. To the west, the Red Sea separates the peninsula from Africa. To the south are the Gulf of Aden and the Arabian Sea. The Persian Gulf and the Gulf of Oman to the east separate the peninsula from the rest of Asia. All of these bodies of water are arms of the Indian Ocean.

North of the Arabian Peninsula are the nation of Iraq and other parts of Southwest Asia. Arabia and Iraq are part of the continent of Asia.

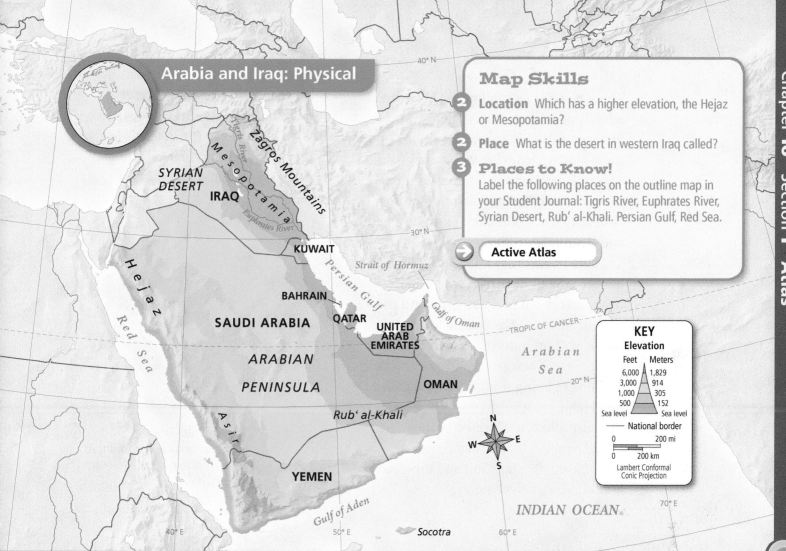

Arabia and Iraq: Physical

Zagros Mountains

Tigris River

SYRIAN DESERT

Mesopotamia

IRAQ

Euphrates River

KUWAIT

Persian Gulf

Strait of Hormuz

BAHRAIN

Hejaz

QATAR

SAUDI ARABIA

UNITED ARAB EMIRATES

Gulf of Oman

Red Sea

ARABIAN PENINSULA

Asir

OMAN

TROPIC OF CANCER

Arabian Sea

20° N

Rub' al-Khali

YEMEN

Gulf of Aden

Socotra

INDIAN OCEAN

40° E   50° E   60° E   70° E

30° N

40° N

Map Skills

2 **Location** Which has a higher elevation, the Hejaz or Mesopotamia?

2 **Place** What is the desert in western Iraq called?

3 **Places to Know!**
Label the following places on the outline map in your Student Journal: Tigris River, Euphrates River, Syrian Desert, Rub' al-Khali. Persian Gulf, Red Sea.

→ **Active Atlas**

KEY
Elevation

Feet		Meters
6,000		1,829
3,000		914
1,000		305
500		152
Sea level		Sea level

— National border

0   200 mi
0   200 km
Lambert Conformal Conic Projection

As you read in the Core Concepts Handbook, Earth's crust consists of separate **plates,** or blocks of rock and soil. Most of Arabia and Iraq are on the Arabian Plate. Mountains rise sharply from the Red Sea and Gulf of Aden to form the plate's southeastern and western edges. The Arabian Plate is, in effect, a plateau, or raised flat area, that slopes gradually toward the east.

Near the eastern edge of the Arabian Plate, the plate's rocks bend downward to form a long, broad depression, or dip. In the south, the Persian Gulf also lies within this depression.

The Tigris (TY gris) and Euphrates (you FRAY teez) river valleys also lie within this depression. These rivers provide fresh water to a region that is mostly desert. They are the only major rivers in the region.

The eastern edge of the Arabian Plate presses against the Eurasian Plate. The pressure has pushed up rocks to form mountains in northeastern Iraq and in the southeastern corner of the Arabian Peninsula, in the nation of Oman.

Reading Check **Which major rivers flow through Iraq?**

Oil and Gas Riches

There was once a shallow sea between what is now the Arabian Peninsula and the rest of Asia. When living things in the sea died, their decayed bodies formed a thick layer of muck on the sea floor. Forces within Earth slowly pushed the Arabian Plate against the Eurasian Plate and bent it downward into folds.

These pockets are known as fold traps because the undersea layer of muck became trapped in them. Heat and pressure from inside Earth transformed the muck over millions of years into oil and natural gas. Because oil and gas are the remains of living things, they are called **fossil fuels.**

Many fold traps formed in the rock of the Arabian Plate. They lie mainly beneath the Persian Gulf and the Tigris and Euphrates river valleys.

These fold traps have given Saudi Arabia the world's largest oil reserves and output. Iraq, Kuwait, Qatar, Oman, and the United Arab Emirates have also grown rich by selling their oil and gas.

Reading Check **Where are the largest oil reserves?**

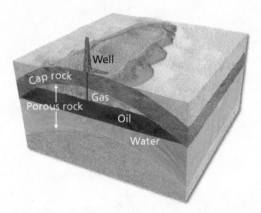

Oil and Gas Field in a Fold Trap
A hard cap rock traps gas and oil in a fold trap. Wells are drilled through the cap rock to reach the gas and oil beneath it.

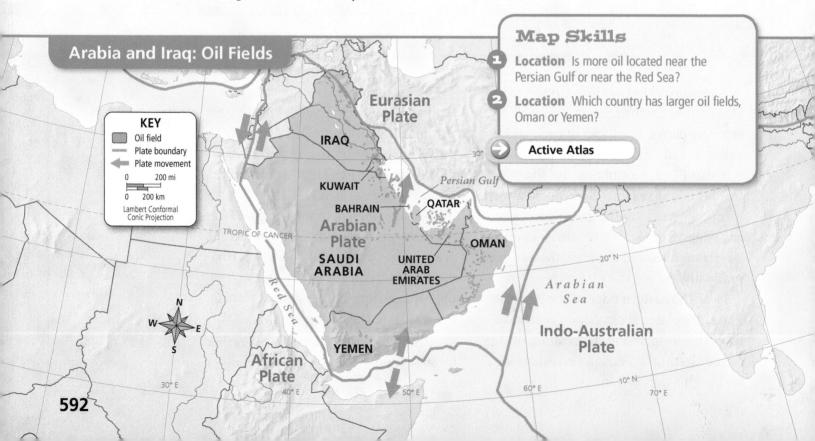

Arabia and Iraq: Oil Fields

KEY
- Oil field
- Plate boundary
- Plate movement

0   200 mi
0   200 km

Lambert Conformal
Conic Projection

Eurasian Plate

IRAQ

KUWAIT

BAHRAIN

QATAR

Persian Gulf

Arabian Plate

SAUDI ARABIA

UNITED ARAB EMIRATES

OMAN

TROPIC OF CANCER

Red Sea

YEMEN

African Plate

Arabian Sea

Indo-Australian Plate

30° E   40° E   50° E   60° E   70° E

10° N   20° N   30°

Map Skills

1. **Location** Is more oil located near the Persian Gulf or near the Red Sea?

2. **Location** Which country has larger oil fields, Oman or Yemen?

→ **Active Atlas**

Living on Oil

Iraq and most countries in Arabia rely on oil and natural gas to pay for nearly all of their needs.

The Importance of Oil Because these countries lack water, they use money from oil and gas sales to build water facilities. Even so, most countries in the region do not have enough water to grow their own food. They use money from oil and gas sales to pay for food grown in other regions.

The countries of Arabia also rely on millions of foreign workers, paid with oil money, to keep their economies running.

Arabia and Iraq produce more than one fourth of the world's oil. People in other parts of the world use oil to power their cars, to heat their homes, and for other purposes. As a result, the rest of the world is very dependent on this region's oil supplies. Any disruption of oil exports from this region creates shortages of oil and sends oil prices soaring.

In the long run, prospects are uncertain for the nations rich in oil and gas. These nations are slowly using up their oil and gas reserves, and it will take millions of years for more oil and gas to form.

Oil and the Environment Oil production has sometimes harmed the region's environment. Oil spills in the Persian Gulf have killed sea life and polluted shorelines. Oil production and processing create toxic chemicals that have polluted the soil, and the rivers of Iraq.

Reading Check **Why is oil so important to Arabia and Iraq?**

An oil refinery in southern Iraq

Oil Production: Selected Countries

SOURCE: CIA World Factbook Online, 2009

Chart Skills

1 Which country produces the most oil?

2 Which country produces the least oil?

→ **Data Discovery**

my **worldgeography.com** Data Discovery

Vast Deserts and Scarce Water

Most of Arabia and Iraq is desert, or an area that receives very little rainfall or snowfall. You read in the Core Concepts Handbook that a belt of deserts circles the subtropical latitudes. Most of the region lies in this subtropical desert belt.

The main ecosystems across the region are desert and desert scrub. Deserts have few plants and animals. Desert scrub has some plants. Camels, which can live without much water, live in the desert and were used by people to cross it.

The region's deserts are dry, but the hills and mountains of northern and eastern Iraq are slightly <u>moister.</u> They get some rainfall. Moist air comes from the Mediterranean Sea in the west. In the summer, moist air from the Indian Ocean drops rain in the mountains of Yemen.

moist, *adj.,* slightly wet

Farming is possible only where there is enough water. The mountains of Yemen and Iraq receive enough rainfall to support some farming. Elsewhere, farming depends on water taken from rivers or oases in the desert. The most important rivers in the region are the Tigris and the Euphrates in Iraq. The water from these rivers nurtured one of the world's first civilizations thousands of years ago. Most people in Iraq live in the valleys around these rivers. Their water is crucial to the country. It supports Iraq's population, which is by far the largest in the region.

The driest countries in the region, such as Saudi Arabia, Kuwait, and the United Arab Emirates, depend on **desalination,** or the removal of salt from seawater. These countries have large desalination plants.

Reading Check **Which parts of Arabia and Iraq get seasonal precipitation?**

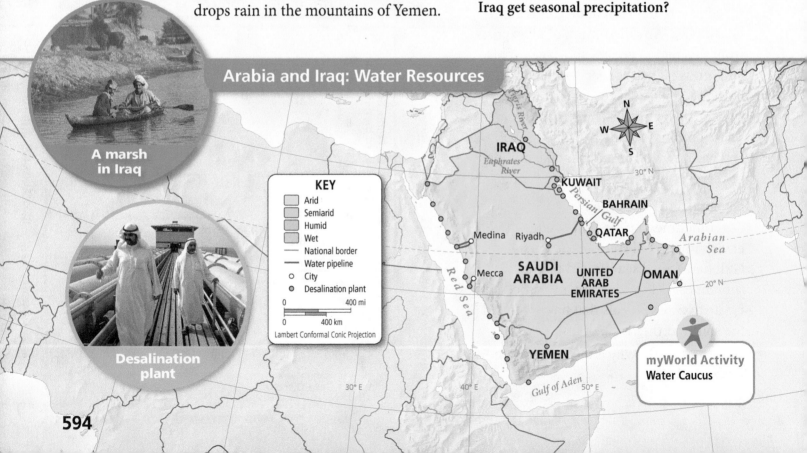

A marsh in Iraq

Desalination plant

Arabia and Iraq: Water Resources

KEY
- Arid
- Semiarid
- Humid
- Wet
- National border
- Water pipeline
- ○ City
- ● Desalination plant

0   400 mi
0   400 km
Lambert Conformal Conic Projection

IRAQ
Euphrates River
Tigris River
KUWAIT
30° N
Persian Gulf
BAHRAIN
Medina   Riyadh   QATAR
Arabian Sea
Mecca   SAUDI ARABIA   UNITED ARAB EMIRATES   OMAN
20° N
Red Sea

YEMEN
Gulf of Aden

30° E   40° E   50° E

myWorld Activity
Water Caucus

Population Patterns

People cannot live without water. Because water is very scarce in most of the region, its people cluster where there is water for drinking and cleaning.

As a result, the region's population has clustered for centuries in the places with the most water. These places include the mountains of Iraq and Yemen, near the Tigris and Euphrates rivers of Iraq, and desert oases on the Arabian Peninsula.

As you just read, some nations in the region have used money from oil and gas sales to to build desalination plants. These plants provide fresh water for growing populations. As a result, people in these countries depend on water from desalination. Countries usually build desalination plants near their cities.

Except for Yemen, the countries of the region are heavily **urbanized.** This means that most of their people live in cities.

Money from oil and natural gas sales has helped these countries develop jobs in construction and services. These kinds of jobs are usually found in cities. Many people from outside the region have also moved to oil-producing areas in search of jobs. They generally settle in the cities.

Arabia and Iraq have some of the highest rates of population growth in the world. These high rates of growth result from both migration and high birth rates. Local customs and religious traditions practiced in many parts of the region favor large families. When most women have many children, populations grow quickly. This high rate of population growth poses challenges for the region. The growing population will need more jobs, water, education, and other services.

Reading Check **Why are populations growing in this region?**

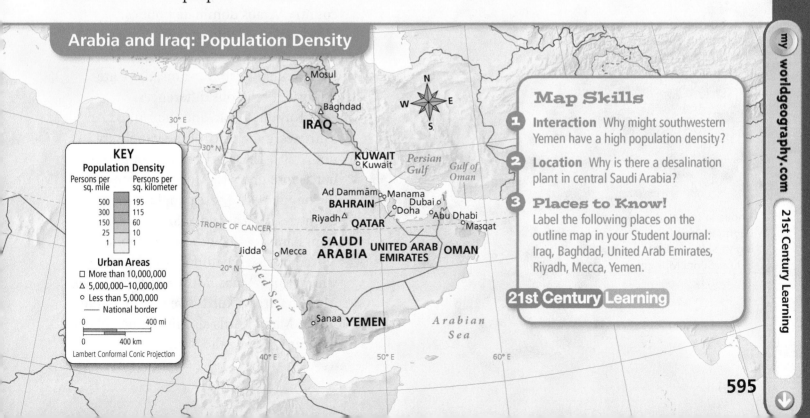

Arabia and Iraq: Population Density

KEY

Population Density

Persons per sq. mile	Persons per sq. kilometer
500	195
300	115
150	60
25	10
1	1

Urban Areas
- ☐ More than 10,000,000
- △ 5,000,000–10,000,000
- ○ Less than 5,000,000
- —— National border

0 ___ 400 mi
0 ___ 400 km
Lambert Conformal Conic Projection

Map Skills

1 **Interaction** Why might southwestern Yemen have a high population density?

2 **Location** Why is there a desalination plant in central Saudi Arabia?

3 **Places to Know!** Label the following places on the outline map in your Student Journal: Iraq, Baghdad, United Arab Emirates, Riyadh, Mecca, Yemen.

21st Century Learning

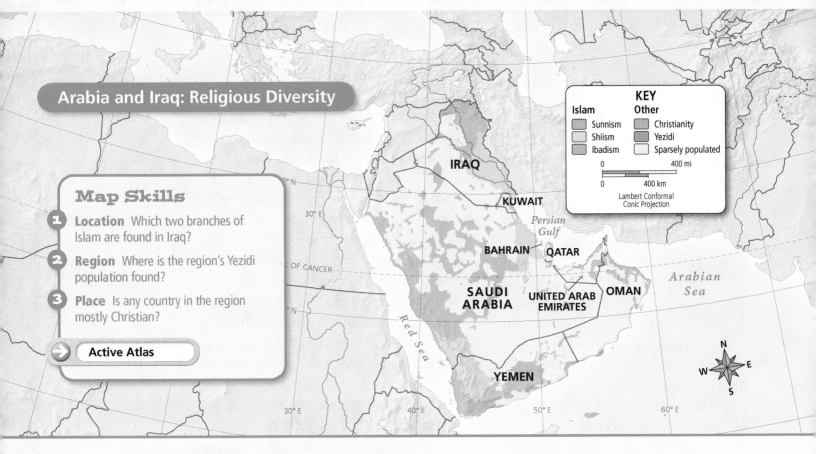

Arabia and Iraq: Religious Diversity

KEY

Islam
- Sunnism
- Shiism
- Ibadism

Other
- Christianity
- Yezidi
- Sparsely populated

0   400 mi
0   400 km

Lambert Conformal
Conic Projection

IRAQ
KUWAIT
BAHRAIN   QATAR
SAUDI ARABIA   UNITED ARAB EMIRATES   OMAN
YEMEN
Persian Gulf
Red Sea
Arabian Sea

Map Skills

1 Location Which two branches of Islam are found in Iraq?

2 Region Where is the region's Yezidi population found?

3 Place Is any country in the region mostly Christian?

→ **Active Atlas**

Above: a crowded market in Baghdad, Iraq
Right: Shia Muslims
Below: Sunni Muslims

A Diverse Region

In most countries of Arabia and Iraq, Arab Muslims form a **majority,** or more than half, of the population. In every country, Arabs dominate politics. However, most countries in Arabia and Iraq have large non-Arab minorities. Even among Arab Muslims, there are important religious differences.

In Kuwait, Qatar, and the United Arab Emirates, a majority of the people are not Arabs. These people are not citizens, but as foreigners they make up most of the population. These people come from countries such as India, Sri Lanka, Pakistan, Bangladesh, and the Philippines.

Iraq has a large minority of Kurds, who are not Arabs. Most Kurds are Sunni Muslims. Iraq's Kurds live mainly in the north. Many Kurds also live in neighboring Iran, Turkey, and Syria.

Iraqi Kurds suffered brutal treatment under Saddam Hussein. In recent years, they have <u>created</u> a self-governing area in northern Iraq.

The vast majority of the people of Arabia and Iraq follow Islam. However, there are important differences within Islam. Long ago, the religion split into two main groups—the Sunnis and the Shias. Most people in Oman follow a third branch of Islam, called Ibadism.

The majority of the region's people are Sunnis, even though Shias are the majority in some places. Most Iraqis are Shia Arabs. Since the elections of 2005, Shias took power in Iraq for the first time.

Most of the citizens of Bahrain are Shia, but their ruler is a Sunni. Sunnis rule Kuwait, Saudi Arabia, and Yemen. However, large Shia minorities live in all three of these countries.

In Iraq, a three-way civil conflict developed among Sunni Arabs, Shia Arabs, and Kurds after U.S.-led forces overthrew Iraq's secular, Sunni-led dictatorship in 2003. Tensions among these groups could lead to conflict in the future.

The region also has small non-Muslim religious minorities. Iraq's Christians are an ancient community. Most practice eastern forms of Christianity that are different from Eastern Orthodox, Roman Catholic, or Protestant Christianity.

From ancient times to the recent past, Iraq and Yemen had important Jewish communities. However, 180,000 Jews fled, mostly to Israel, because of discrimination in the mid-1900s. Only a few hundred Jewish people remain in the region today.

Iraq's Yezidis are Kurdish speakers who practice a religion that combines Islam with more ancient religions. Finally, while most foreign workers in the Persian Gulf countries are Muslims, there are also Christians, Hindus, and Buddhists.

create, *v.,* form, cause to exist

Reading Check **What are some differences among Muslims in this region?**

Section 1 Assessment

Key Terms

1. What are fossil fuels?

2. Use the word desalination in a sentence.

Key Ideas

3. Describe the fossil fuel resources of Arabia and Iraq.

4. What are some natural sources of water in Arabia and Iraq, and where are they located?

5. Describe the region's religious diversity.

Think Critically

6. **Draw Conclusions** What might happen to Arabia and Iraq if they began to use up their oil reserves?

7. **Compare and Contrast** In what ways has the urban population in the region changed in recent years? Give reasons for the changes.

Essential Question

How much does geography shape a country?

8. What features of Arabia and Iraq depend on the region's geography? What features do not depend on its geography? Go to your Student Journal to record your answers.

Section 2

History of Arabia and Iraq

Key Ideas

- Civilization developed along the rivers of Mesopotamia.
- Islam arose in Arabia and spread to other regions in the early Middle Ages.

- Britain controlled parts of the region and redrew borders in the early 1900s.

- The region gained independence and oil wealth, but some countries faced dictatorship and war.

Key Terms • civilization • monotheism • Quran • caliph • mosque
• minority • dictator

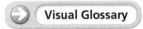 Visual Glossary

Reading Skill: Summarize Take notes using the graphic organizer in your journal.

Reconstructed gates of the ancient city of Babylon ▼

Arabia and Iraq have played a key role in world history. This region was one of the places where **civilization** began. A civilization is a culture that has a written language and in which people have many different kinds of jobs. Writing first developed in this region. The world's first known empires also developed in what is now Iraq. Later, Arabia was the birthplace of Islam, one of the world's major religions. Over the centuries, foreign powers controlled much of this region. In modern times, Arabia and Iraq became the world's most important source of oil, a fuel that every country in the world needs.

3000 B.C. The Sumerians

The figure at the left shows a Sumerian man. The Sumerians invented cuneiform. This kind of writing uses wedge-shaped marks on clay tablets. The name comes from the Latin word for wedge.

Early Civilizations and Empires

Mesopotamia means "between the rivers" in Greek. It refers to the valley of the Tigris and Euphrates rivers. This region is mainly in present-day Iraq.

In Mesopotamia, people developed a new way of life. For thousands of years, people lived by hunting, fishing, and gathering wild plants. About 10,000 years ago, people in Southwest Asia began to plant crops and raise animals. These farmers produced plenty of food for everyone. Some people were now free to do other work. They became potters and weavers and merchants.

Farmers and others had to pay taxes. These taxes supported priests and government officials. Populations grew. By 4000 B.C., the first cities appeared.

A Birthplace of Civilization Sumer was a region in southern Mesopotamia. Sumerians developed a civilization. Around 3000 B.C. they created the world's first writing system, which is called cuneiform (kyoo NEE uh form). They built irrigation canals and invented mathematics and the potter's wheel.

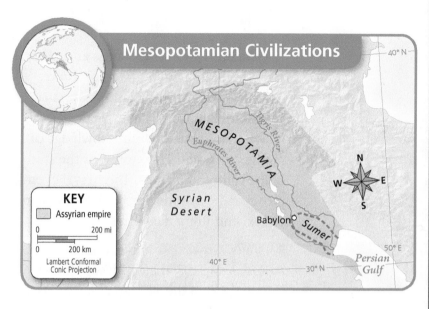

Mesopotamian Civilizations

KEY

Assyrian empire

0   200 mi
0   200 km
Lambert Conformal
Conic Projection

MESOPOTAMIA

Tigris River

Euphrates River

Syrian Desert

Babylon   Sumer

Persian Gulf

We can learn about the Sumerians from the Epic of Gilgamesh. This is one of the world's oldest written stories. The story is based on a real Sumerian king, Gilgamesh, who lived around 2700 B.C.

> 66 Surpassing all kings, powerful and tall
> beyond all others, violent, splendid,
> a wild bull of a man . . .
> huge, handsome, radiant, perfect. 99
> —The Epic of Gilgamesh

The most complete version of this story appears on cuneiform tablets.

The First Empires Sumerian cities grew into the first city-states. Each was a small country, focused on a single city. Around 2270 B.C., King Sargon from the city of Akkad conquered Sumer and other parts of Mesopotamia to found the first known empire. Later, around 1700 B.C., the city-state of Babylon built an empire that included all of Mesopotamia.

The Assyrian people built an even larger empire. Assyria was an area in northern Mesopotamia. By around 900 B.C., Assyria had defeated Babylon.

331–129 B.C. Greek Rule

After Alexander conquered Mesopotamia in 331 B.C., Greeks ruled the region for 200 years. Later, Romans and Persians fought over the region.

599

Assyria brought Mesopotamia and other areas, including Egypt, into its empire.

Both the Babylonians and Assyrians contributed to world civilization. The Babylonians added to our knowledge of mathematics and astronomy, or the study of the stars and planets. The Assyrian empire became a model for the later Persian, Greek, and Roman empires.

Persians, Greeks, Romans, and Arabs Around 550 B.C., Mesopotamia became part of the Persian empire, based in modern Iran. The Persian empire stretched from North Africa to India.

Alexander the Great defeated the Persian Empire in 331 B.C. When he died, his Greek empire split apart. But Alexander's influence <u>persisted.</u> He had founded dozens of new cities and spread Greek culture far and wide. Mesopotamia remained under Greek rule for 200 years.

The Roman Empire eventually took over the western parts of Alexander's empire. After 235 B.C., Persians regained power in the east. Persians fought with the Roman Empire for control of the fertile lands of Mesopotamia. For several centuries they continued to fight with the Eastern Roman empire, which was also called the Byzantine empire.

Through trade, Greeks, Romans, and Persians met the Arab tribes of the Arabian Peninsula. Many Arabs were nomads. They had no permanent homes. They herded sheep, goats, and camels. Nomads visited oases for food and water. Oases were centers for trade.

Reading Check **Which civilization first developed writing?**

persist, *v.,* to continue, often in spite of setbacks

▲ A copy of the Quran, the holy book of Islam

A New Religion

One important oasis was the city of Mecca. It was a trading and religious center. People throughout the Arabian Peninsula traveled to Mecca. They went to worship at a shrine called the Kaaba. Many worshiped more than one god. In the A.D. 600s, however, this changed.

A man named Muhammad made Mecca a center for the new religion of Islam. Its believers are called Muslims. Like Jews and Christians, Muslims worship only one god, whom they consider the Creator, or God. Worshiping only one god is called **monotheism.**

The Birth of Islam Muhammad was born in Mecca. One day, he was meditating in a cave. There, Muslims believe, he saw the angel Gabriel, who brought him a message from God. Muhammad later received more messages.

Muhammad shared these messages with the people of Mecca. Some people began to follow the ideas Muhammad spread. They believed that Muhammad was bringing messages from the God recognized by Jews and Christians. These messages were collected and preserved in the **Quran,** the holy book of Islam.

The wealthy people of Mecca wanted visitors to keep coming to the Kaaba. They knew that most of these visitors worshiped many gods. They opposed Muhammad's teachings. Muhammad and his followers had to leave Mecca.

In A.D. 622 they moved to the city of Medina. When Mecca attacked the Muslims in Medina, the Muslims won.

Muhammad returned to Mecca in 632. He made the Kaaba a place of worship for Islam before dying later that year.

Muhammad's followers argued over how to choose leaders to follow him. One group believed that Muhammad had chosen his son-in-law, Ali, and his heirs, as leaders. This group became known as the Shia. Another group, known as the Sunnis, wanted Muhammad's father-in-law, Abu Bakr, as the next leader.

Muhammad's Sunni followers chose Abu Bakr to be the new leader. He became their first **caliph.** The caliph was the Muslims' political and religious leader.

Over time, differences in belief grew between Sunni and Shia Muslims. Today, about 15 percent of all Muslims are Shia. In some parts of Arabia and Iraq, however, most Muslims are Shia.

The Beliefs of Islam The word *Islam* means "submission" in Arabic. This term comes from the idea of submitting one's will to God. Muslims believe that the will of God lies in the words of the Quran.

Like Judaism and Christianity, Islam stresses the importance of family, community, and social justice. Many Muslims turn to the Quran and Muhammad's teachings to help them make good choices. The Quran, Muhammad's teachings, and the traditions of the Muslim community form the basis for Islamic law.

Reading Check Why did Sunni and Shia Muslims split?

myWorld Activity
Comparing Religions

Muslims circle around the Kaaba, in Mecca, as part of their pilgrimage to that city. ▶

The Five Pillars of Islam

The Quran says that Muslims have five religious duties. These are the Five Pillars of Islam.

1 The Declaration of Faith
Muslims must recognize a single God and Muhammad as his messenger.

2 Prayer
Muslims must pray five times each day while facing toward Mecca.

3 Giving Alms
Muslims must give part of their income to care for the poor.

4 Fasting During Ramadan
Muslims must fast from dawn to sunset during this holy month in the Islamic calendar.

5 Pilgrimage
Muslims must travel to worship in the holy city of Mecca at least once in their life if they can.

⊙ Culture Close-up

Muslim Civilization

Within 10 years of Muhammad's death, Muslims under the first caliphs had conquered all of Arabia and Iraq. Within 100 years of Muhammad's death, the caliphs ruled a vast empire, stretching from India to Spain. Arabia and Iraq were at the center of a rich civilization. Muslim civilization made great advances in science, mathematics, and the arts.

A Muslim Empire During the 600s and 700s, the Muslims conquered all of the Persian Empire, much of the Byzantine Empire, North Africa, Spain, and parts of India and Central Asia. In 762, the caliphs founded Baghdad, in present-day Iraq, as the capital of their empire.

The Muslim Empire controlled key trade routes between Asia, Africa, and Europe. One of these was the Silk Road to China. Sea routes from Eastern Africa brought goods, as well as many enslaved Africans, to Arabia and Iraq.

The caliph's control allowed merchants to travel more safely. The empire grew prosperous from trade. Cities grew along busy trade routes. Baghdad became the largest and one of the richest cities in the world. In the empire's cities, people from distant lands came together to trade.

A Center of Learning Travel and trade brought the Muslim Empire into contact with ideas from around the world. Muslim scholars learned about Greek science and philosophy through contact with the Byzantine Empire. They learned about advances in mathematics and astronomy made in India.

Map Skills

1. **Location** In which region did the Muslim empire get its start?

2. **Interaction** Which regions did the Muslims expand their empire to include?

→ Active Atlas

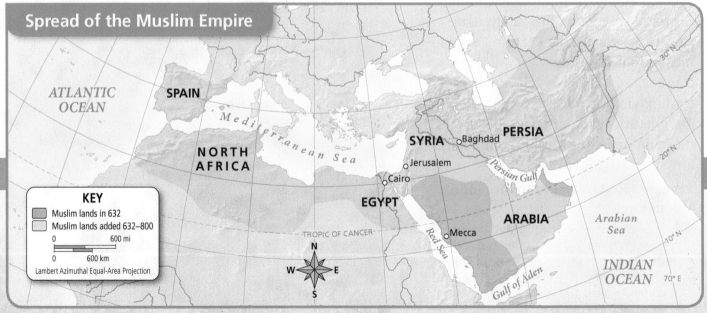

Spread of the Muslim Empire

KEY
- Muslim lands in 632
- Muslim lands added 632–800

0   600 mi
0   600 km
Lambert Azimuthal Equal-Area Projection

ATLANTIC OCEAN · SPAIN · Mediterranean Sea · NORTH AFRICA · SYRIA · Baghdad · PERSIA · Jerusalem · Cairo · EGYPT · TROPIC OF CANCER · Red Sea · Mecca · ARABIA · Persian Gulf · Arabian Sea · Gulf of Aden · INDIAN OCEAN

Baghdad became more than a center of Muslim culture and trade. It became a center of learning. Literature and other arts blossomed. Muslim architects built beautiful **mosques,** or Islamic houses of worship. Muslim scientists and mathematicians built on the work of the Greeks and Indians. Their work formed a basis for modern chemistry, physics, and medicine. They also developed algebra. Our own system of numerals came to us from India by way of Arab Muslims.

The Ottoman Empire After the 900s, the Muslim Empire fell apart into several states. These states were partly independent. The last caliph in Baghdad was defeated by Mongol invaders in 1258. In the 1500s, Ottoman Turks conquered much of the region. The Ottoman Empire, centered in Turkey, included Iraq and much of the Arabian Peninsula. At its height it included most of Southwest Asia outside of Persia. The Ottomans remained in control until World War I ended in 1918.

Reading Check **How did trade advance Muslim learning?**

The Persian Gulf in Modern Times

World War I brought much of the region under European control. The region's countries gained independence later in the 1900s. Still, foreign powers continued to play a role.

British Domination By World War I, the British dominated several countries on the Arabian Peninsula. These countries were Bahrain, the United Arab Emirates, Oman, Qatar, Kuwait, and part of Yemen.

Britain defeated the Ottoman Empire in World War I. After the war, Britain and the League of Nations created Iraq from part of the Ottoman empire, ignoring divisions in the new country.

Within Iraq's borders were Shia Arabs in the south, Sunni Arabs in the west, and non-Arab Kurds in the north. There were also Turks, Assyrian Christians, and Jews. Until 2003, the Sunni Arab **minority**—a group with less than half of the population—dominated the country. Their rule led to conflicts with the other groups.

my worldgeography.com Timeline

Timeline

622 Muhammad and his followers establish the first Islamic community in Medina.

1258 Mongol invaders conquer Iraq and destroy Baghdad.

1918 Britain defeats Ottoman Turks and occupies Iraq and parts of Arabia.

500	750	1000	1250	1500	1750	2000

762 Caliphs make Baghdad the center of a vast Muslim Empire.

1500s Ottoman Turks make Iraq and much of Arabia part of their empire.

vital, *adj.,* extremely important, needed for survival

Oil was discovered in Iraq in 1927 and in Saudi Arabia and Kuwait in 1938. The region became a <u>vital</u> source of fuel for the world's growing energy needs.

In 1930, Saudi Arabia, Oman, and northern Yemen were the only independent countries in the region. Saudi Arabia controlled much of the Arabian Peninsula, including Mecca. Saudi Arabia is an absolute monarchy. This means that its king has total control over the country. There is no elected government.

Independent Iraq Britain controlled Iraq and Kuwait. However, Iraqis fought to end British rule. In 1921, Britain put King Faisal, an Arab, into power. Iraq gained independence in 1932. Still, King Faisal kept close ties with Britain. He let a British company take control of Iraq's oil.

In 1958, Iraqi army officers forced King Faisal out of power. This caused a period of disorder during which Iraq's Kurds rebelled. In 1963, the Baath Party took power. It took over the oil industry. It used oil income to improve people's lives, but became oppressive. Baath leader Saddam Hussein took control in 1979.

◄ Ibn Saud, king of Saudi Arabia 1932-1963

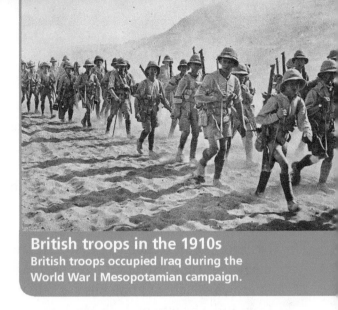

British troops in the 1910s
British troops occupied Iraq during the World War I Mesopotamian campaign.

Under Baath rule, Iraq became a one-party government. When elections were held, Iraqis had no choice of parties. The Baath leader had total control over the country. Under Saddam Hussein, Iraq became a dictatorship, a country under the control of a dictator. A **dictator** is a leader who seizes power undemocratically and has complete control over a country.

The Gulf Monarchies The smaller Persian Gulf states—Kuwait, Bahrain, Qatar, the United Arab Emirates, and Oman—are all monarchies like Saudi Arabia. These smaller countries gained full independence from Britain only in the 1960s and 1970s. Some monarchs have complete control, but others have more limited power.

In 1960, Saudi Arabia, Iraq, and Kuwait joined Iran and Venezuela to form OPEC, the Organization of the Petroleum Exporting Countries. Qatar and the United Arab Emirates joined OPEC later. This organization helps members agree on a shared oil policy. Often members agree to limit oil production. This keeps the price of oil high and increases their income.

American troops in the 1990s
American troops in Saudi Arabia in 1991 prepare to free Kuwait from Iraqi control.

Persian Gulf Conflicts In 1980, under Saddam Hussein, Iraq invaded Iran's oil-rich lands. Iraq had the open support of Saudi Arabia, Kuwait, and other Arab states. The United States also quietly supported Iraq. The Iran–Iraq War dragged on for eight years at a high cost. It ended without a clear winner in 1988.

Then Iraq invaded Kuwait in 1990. The United States and other nations went to war with Iraq. The United States and its allies wanted to defend Kuwait's independence. They also wanted to protect the world's oil supplies. These countries quickly defeated Iraq in 1991. They drove Iraqi troops out of Kuwait.

In 2003, U.S. President George W. Bush claimed that Iraq was a threat to the region and the world. He claimed that Iraq had weapons of mass destruction.

Later that year, the United States and some allies again went to war with Iraq. U.S.-led forces quickly removed Saddam Hussein from power. No weapons of mass destruction were found.

Some Iraqis resisted U.S.-led forces. Fighting also broke out among Iraq's Kurds, Sunni Arabs, and Shia Arabs. The United States and its allies supported the creation of a democratic Iraqi government in 2005. Additional US troops were sent to Iraq in 2007 to support the Iraqi government. US and other foreign troops were still in Iraq in 2009.

Reading Check **What form of government does Saudi Arabia have?**

Section 2 Assessment

Key Terms

1. Use the following terms to describe religion in Arabia and Iraq: monotheism, Quran, mosque, caliph.

Key Ideas

2. Describe the importance of the Sumerians to world history.

3. What are the main beliefs of Muslims?

4. What role did the United States play in the history of Arabia and Iraq?

Think Critically

5. Draw Conclusions Use what you know about history in Arabia and Iraq to explain how trade contributed to the region's rich cultural heritage. Give examples.

6. Categorize Identify different groups within Islam and explain their role in modern Iraq.

Essential Question

How much does geography shape a country?

7. How has geography shaped the history of Arabia and Iraq? Are there parts of its history that did not depend on its geography? Go to your Student Journal to record your answers.

Arabia and Iraq Today

Key Ideas
- Regional traditions and modern global culture have shaped the region's culture.
- Many oil-rich countries in the region have worked to make their economies less dependent on oil.

Key Terms • fundamentalism • Islamism • jihad • terrorism • entrepreneurship • hijab

Visual Glossary

Reading Skill: Analyze Cause and Effect Take notes using the graphic organizer in your journal.

▼ A luxury hotel in Dubai, United Arab Emirates

Islam and other traditions have shaped the cultures of Arabia and Iraq. So have the rich oil and natural gas reserves that come with the region's geography. Oil has brought wealth and contact with outside cultures. The region's people have worked to balance tradition and modern culture.

Religious Traditions

The people of Arabia and Iraq value their cultural traditions. Islam is a very important source of tradition. Most people in the region are Muslims who follow the five pillars of Islam. Islam shapes many parts of daily life.

Although most people in the region share a religion, they have different ideas about politics and cultural activities. For example, some Muslims believe that women should not mix with men in public. Others believe that Islam allows unrelated men and women to work together. There are many cultural traditions as well. Some traditions concern the foods that people like to eat, or the importance of tribal membership. Others concern how to welcome guests, treat elders with respect, or give gifts.

Fundamentalism One powerful <u>tradition</u> in the region is a branch of Sunni Islam called Wahhabism, which was founded in the 1700s. Wahhabis believe in returning to the original teachings of Islam, interpreting the Quran literally, and rejecting all modern interpretations of Islamic scripture. Wahhabism is a form of **fundamentalism,** or the belief that holy books should be taken literally, or word for word. Fundamentalist Muslims believe the Quran provides clear meanings that do not need to be debated.

Wahhabis also believe that government should be based on the original teachings of Islam. It is a form of **Islamism,** or the belief that politics and society should follow Islamic teachings. The rulers of Saudi Arabia are Wahhabis. Wahhabism determines much of the kingdom's politics. Most Muslims in the region are neither Wahhabis nor Islamists.

While Wahhabis are both fundamentalist and Islamist, the two beliefs do not always coincide. Many fundamentalists are Islamists, because they believe that Islamic scripture calls for Islamic government. However, not all Islamists are fundamentalists. Some Islamists, like other Muslims, accept less literal interpretations of Islam.

Islamism and Jihad A small number of Muslims in the region see European and American influence as a threat. They have adopted a form of Islamism that draws on the tradition of **jihad.** The word *jihad* in Arabic simply means "struggle." It can refer to the struggle to be a better person.

However, some groups use the word to mean violent struggle. Some of the region's Islamists believe in violent jihad. This small minority supports the use of violence to attack Westerners or Muslims with different approaches to Islam. Those calling for violence include groups such as al Qaeda. Al Qaeda is a group of radical Islamists led by Osama bin Laden, who came from Saudi Arabia. Al Qaeda practices **terrorism.** Terrorism is the use of violence against innocent civilians to create fear for political reasons. In fact, the holy writings of Islam call on Muslims to avoid violence toward innocent people. Most Muslims reject violent jihad and terrorism.

Reading Check **Are all Islamists fundamentalists?**

tradition, *n.,* practices handed down from one generation to the next

Students study the Quran at an Islamic school in Medina, Saudi Arabia. ▶

Arabia and Iraq have a little more

than **1%** of the world's population but nearly **50%** of the world's oil.

A Region Built on Oil

The world today depends on oil to power cars, trucks, and other vehicles; as a fuel for industries; for heating homes; and as a raw material for plastics and other products. Oil is one of the world's most important products. It is also a vital source of income for this oil-rich region.

One-Track Economies Oil and natural gas were found in the region in the 1920s and 1930s. Every country in the region but oil-poor Yemen had an oil boom, or rapid growth in jobs, construction, and income due to oil production. From then on, the economies of the oil-rich countries specialized in oil production. Specialization led to trade. The region sold oil to other countries. It bought many basic goods, such as food, from other countries. Income from oil allows the region to buy goods that it cannot grow or make.

Oil sales have made some governments in the region wealthy. Many give cash or free services directly to citizens, even if they do not work. As a result, the region's businesses can hire millions of foreign workers. These workers do jobs that citizens are unwilling or unable to do.

Economic growth depends on four conditions: natural resources, educated workers, investment in local businesses, and **entrepreneurship** (ahn truh pruh NUR ship). Entrepreneurship is the willingness to take the risks of starting a business.

The region's oil and gas are great natural resources. However, money from oil sales lets the region get by without meeting the other three conditions for economic growth. Until recently, education in the region has failed to prepare its people—especially its women—for many available jobs. There has been little investment outside the oil industry. There has also been little entrepreneurship. As a result, the region has depended largely on oil sales.

Foreign workers
Like these construction workers, foreign workers hold lower-paying jobs.

Saudi workers
Like these investment bankers, Saudis usually hold higher-paying jobs.

Trying to Diversify In recent years, leaders in the region have seen the need to diversify their economies. To diversify is to go from just one or two sources of income, such as oil and gas, to many sources. To help diversify, many countries in the region have improved education for the whole population, including women. They have encouraged investment and entrepreneurship.

Two parts of the region have built economies that depend less on oil. Bahrain, and Dubai, a state in the United Arab Emirates, have become regional financial centers. Their economies have diversified away from reliance on oil. They now rely more on services.

Banks from Bahrain, Dubai, and elsewhere have provided finance to other parts of the region. The region's banks keep the savings of people in the region who have made money from oil. The banks invest this money in new businesses that help diversify the region's economy. The countries' governments have also used government money saved from oil earnings. They have invested these savings in construction projects. Some of these have strengthened the region's economy.

These projects include desalination plants that provide water to many parts of the region. According to a Saudi prince,

> 66 Currently, Saudi Arabia is the largest producer of desalinated water in the world, and the kingdom continues to invest in research and development to make access to fresh water more affordable. 99
> —Prince Dr. Turki Al Saud Al Faisal, from ibm.com

Governments have also invested in education, so that their people can compete in the global economy in areas other than the oil industry.

Reading Check Why are there so many foreign workers in Arabia?

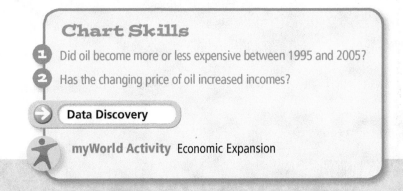

Chart Skills

1 Did oil become more or less expensive between 1995 and 2005?

2 Has the changing price of oil increased incomes?

→ **Data Discovery**

myWorld Activity Economic Expansion

Oil, Population, and Income

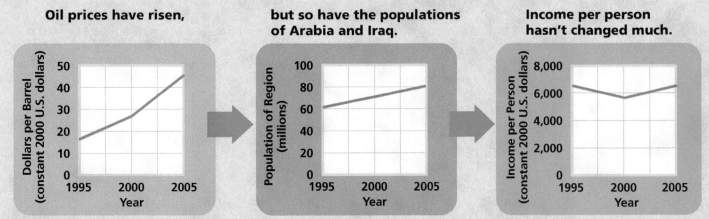

Oil prices have risen,

but so have the populations of Arabia and Iraq.

Income per person hasn't changed much.

SOURCE: *CIA World FactBook, BP Statistical Review*

my **worldgeography.com**   (Data Discovery)

Arab Culture, Old and New

Culture in Arabia and Iraq today is a mix of modern and traditional elements. One traditional art form is Arabic calligraphy, or decorative writing. Most Muslims believe that depicting humans or animals in art is forbidden by Islam. Because of this, art forms that show letters and geometric designs are highly developed in the Islamic world.

Contemporary music of the region uses more modern elements as well as traditional styles. Arabia has long been famous for its poetry. Many modern Arabic songs use traditional poems, but back them up with synthesizers instead of the instruments that would have been used in the past.

Think Critically Why is calligraphy an important art form in Islamic societies?

Below is modern Iraqi singer Shatha Hassoun.

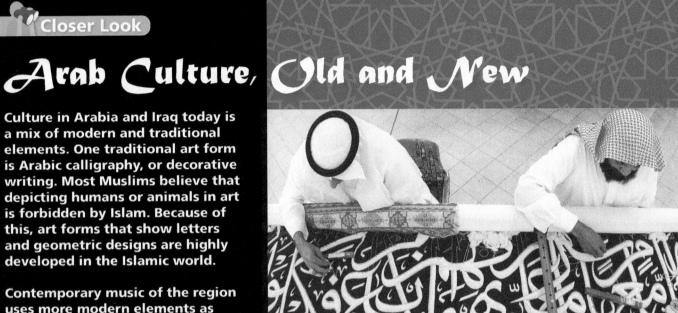

Tradition These artists are decorating the covering that will go over the Kaaba in Mecca. They are using Arabic calligraphy.

Cultural Change A piece of calligraphy used as a background for modern dance. ▼

Arabia and Iraq in the Modern World

Income from oil changed society in the region. From the mid-1900s, elite people in the region met Westerners working in the oil industry. They bought televisions and computers. They traveled to foreign countries and sent their children to study there. They were <u>exposed</u> to Western and global culture.

The Pull of Global Culture Modern, foreign culture appealed to many people in the region. They have adopted some aspects of modern global culture. Some of the region's people work for Western firms. Others work for local firms using Western business practices. The region has become part of the modern world. However, not all people in the region are comfortable with this change.

The Place of Women Traditionally, women in the Arab world have had to obey men. In much of Arabia, they cannot travel without the permission of a father, husband, or other male relative.

In most of the region, women are expected to cover their faces and hair. They are expected to wear concealing, baggy garments known as **hijab.**

Despite the pull of global culture, tradition still shapes the lives of men and especially women in this region. In most countries, women face more restrictions than in the United States or other Western countries. The most restricted country is Saudi Arabia, where women are forbidden to drive cars or ride bicycles. They cannot legally meet with unrelated men in public. Many Saudi women cannot pursue certain careers, since that would mean working with unrelated men.

However, attitudes are changing. In some countries, such as Iraq, women are free to work outside the home. Some can dress as they wish. Even in Saudi Arabia, women like Hanan are finding ways to pursue careers.

Reading Check How is life changing for women in Arabia and Iraq?

expose, *v.,* to show, make aware of, uncover

▲ Hanan at work

Section 3 Assessment

Key Terms

1. Explain the different meanings of the word jihad.

2. What is entrepreneurship, and why is it important?

Key Ideas

3. How are some Islamic traditions regarding women different from those in modern Western culture?

4. Why do leaders in Arabia and Iraq want to diversify their countries' economies?

Think Critically

5. **Analyze Cause and Effect** How have Islamic traditions shaped lives in this region?

6. **Categorize** What benefits and problems have resulted from Western involvement in Arabia and Iraq?

? Essential Question

How much does geography shape a country?

7. What are some challenges the region's nations could face if oil and gas reserves run out? Go to your Student Journal to record your answer.

Chapter Assessment

Key Terms and Ideas

1. **Draw Conclusions** How do the physical features of Arabia and Iraq, such as desert oases, affect where people live in the region?

2. **Summarize** Why are **fossil fuels** important to Arabia and Iraq?

3. **Recall** What are some important accomplishments of early **civilizations** in Arabia and Iraq?

4. **Categorize** What are some features of the religion of Islam? Make sure you include the Five Pillars of Islam.

5. **Analyze Cause and Effect** How did British control change Arabia and Iraq after World War I?

6. **Compare and Contrast** Compare and contrast **Islamism** and **fundamentalism** in their beliefs and their influence on modern society in Arabia and Iraq. Is there any overlap between the two? Give examples in your explanation.

7. **Synthesize** Why do many countries in Arabia and Iraq want to boost **entrepreneurship** to lessen their dependence on oil?

Think Critically

8. **Problem Solving** Water and oil are both important to Arabia and Iraq. How are the region's supplies of these two resources related? How can the region use a wealth of one resource to take care of a shortage of the other?

9. **Make Inferences** Since World War I, Iraq has overthrown its king and fought several wars. What role did oil play in these conflicts? How might oil and instability be linked? Explain.

10. **Compare Viewpoints** How do traditional Islamic cultures in the region view the role of women in society? How do these views differ from those held in most Western nations?

11. **Core Concepts: Culture and Geography** What role has religion, especially religious differences, played in the history of Arabia and Iraq?

Places to Know

For each place, write the letter from the map that shows the place's location.

12. Persian Gulf

13. Mecca

14. Euphrates River

15. United Arab Emirates

16. Yemen

17. Iraq

18. **Draw Inferences** Which of these countries does not have a coastline on the Persian Gulf?

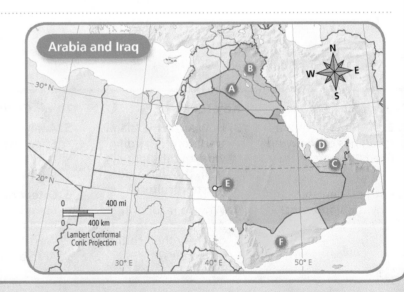

Arabia and Iraq

Essential Question

How much does geography shape a country?

Water for Arabia and Iraq Follow your teacher's instructions to participate in a regional meeting on water scarcity and oil dependency in Arabia and Iraq. Remember to consider how one nation's needs interact with the needs of other nations in the region.

21st Century Learning

Develop Cultural Awareness

Using reliable sources in the library or online, research an ethnic group in the region. Create a Venn diagram that includes the regional ethnic group's culture and your own culture. List information such as the following:
- main religious views
- foods
- language

Document-Based Questions

Success Tracker™
Online at myworldgeography.com

Use your knowledge of Arabia and Iraq, as well as Documents A and B, to answer Questions 1–3.

Document A

" Brother Osama: How much blood has been spilled? How many innocent children, women, and old people have been killed, maimed, and expelled from their homes in the name of "al-Qaeda"? …
This religion of ours comes to defense of the life of a sparrow. It can never accept the murder of innocent people, regardless of what supposed justification is given for it."

—Sheikh Salman al-Oadah, Islamic religious leader from Saudi Arabia

Document B

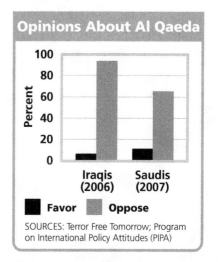

SOURCES: Terror Free Tomorrow; Program on International Policy Attitudes (PIPA)

1. Which of the following sums up the main idea of Document A?
   A Islam calls for violent jihad.
   B Al Qaeda's killings are justified
   C Islam opposes the killing of innocent people.
   D This leader sees Osama bin Laden as his brother.

2. Which of the following can you conclude from Document B?
   A Saudis support only 10% of al Qaeda's actions.
   B Large majorities in Iraq and Saudi Arabia oppose al Qaeda.
   C Only 10% of Iraqis support al Qaeda.
   D Al Qaeda is most popular in Iraq.

3. **Writing Task** Based on what you have learned from the chapter and the documents above, explain the information presented in Document B.

Chapter 17

Israel and Its Neighbors

? Essential Question

Is conflict unavoidable?

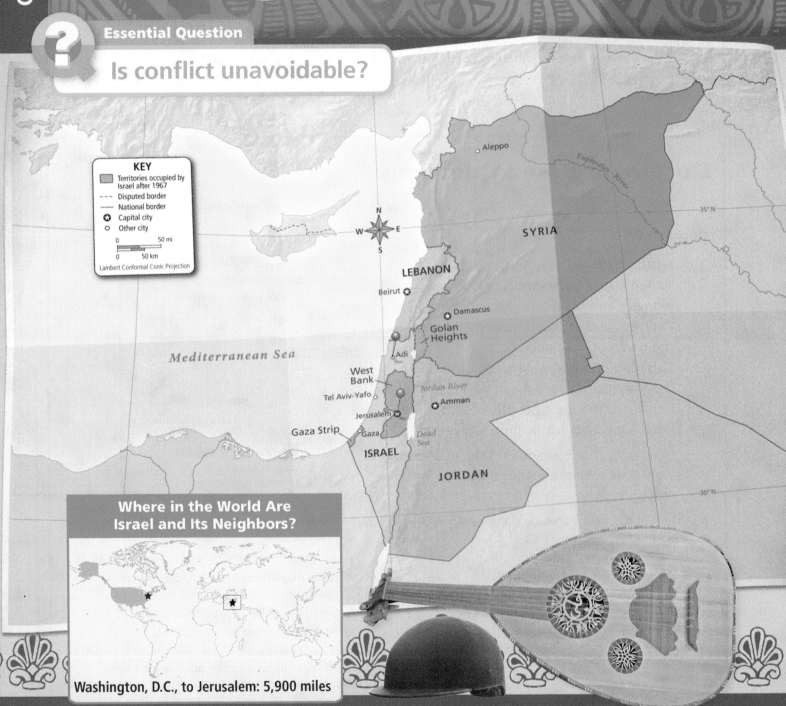

KEY
- Territories occupied by Israel after 1967
- - - - Disputed border
- ——— National border
- ✪ Capital city
- ○ Other city

0 ——— 50 mi
0 ——— 50 km
Lambert Conformal Conic Projection

Aleppo

Euphrates River

35° N

SYRIA

LEBANON

Beirut ✪

Damascus ○

Golan Heights

Mediterranean Sea

○ Adi

West Bank

Tel Aviv-Yafo ○

Jordan River

Jerusalem ✪

✪ Amman

Gaza Strip

Gaza

Dead Sea

ISRAEL

JORDAN

30° N

Where in the World Are Israel and Its Neighbors?

Washington, D.C., to Jerusalem: 5,900 miles

my **Story**

Maayan and Muhammad

In this section, you'll read about Maayan, a young Jewish Israeli woman, and Muhammad, an Israeli Arab boy. What do Maayan's and Muhammad's stories tell you about life in this region today?

Explore the Essential Question
- at **worldgeography.com**
- using the **myWorld Chapter Activity**
- with the **Student Journal**

Story by Hila Baroz for myWorld Geography Online

Maayan is an 18-year-old Israeli woman from Adi, a small community in northern Israel. She decided to put off her required military service in order to volunteer in Magen David Adom (MDA). MDA is Israel's equivalent to the Red Cross. Maayan is a paramedic giving first-aid treatment to injured and sick patients.

Maayan studied in an agricultural school near her home. The school has a dairy barn and a horse ranch. Maayan completed the school's horse care program and she enjoys riding horses. She loves the landscapes of her childhood, and does not think she would like to live in the city. Still, not everything is peaceful and quiet in the region where she grew up. Israel faces the threat of terrorist attacks.

"MDA is a reflection of the country we live in. At any given moment, something might happen, and you must always be prepared. I've learned to save lives in a place where life is not taken for granted."

Maayan practices first aid at MDA.

Maayan's family eating together

Talking about her first-aid work, Maayan says, "The first few seconds are the most critical. Whatever mistake you make during those seconds, even the most sophisticated hospital equipment could not put right. It gives you a sense of mission."

"I remember how we once [revived] a 48-year-old woman. It took us an hour and a half. Eventually, we managed to bring her back to life. . . . After this case, I felt tremendous pride and satisfaction."

When Maayan returns home from MDA, she drives past Arab villages. "My ignorance is so great. I see these houses, but I don't know anything about the people who live in them. There's this huge cultural gap, and there's also fear. Sometimes when I take the bus and I see an Arab sitting inside I'm afraid the bus might blow up. I wish we didn't live in a conflict, but you have to learn a lot about the other side and get to know it."

Fifteen-year-old Muhammad likes to walk the narrow streets of the Old City of Jerusalem where he was born. Muhammad lives in a Jerusalem neighborhood called Beit Safafa. His family has been living here for many generations. It was built by two large families, or clans, and Muhammad's is one of them. Like Maayan, Muhammad enjoys horseback riding. "I particularly like to ride my cousins' horses. . . . I am sure I'd like to spend the rest of my life in Beit Safafa."

Muhammad is a Muslim living in Israel as part of its Arab minority. Both he and his family have many Arab Palestinian friends and acquaintances living in the Israeli-controlled West Bank.

Seven years ago, Israel built a wall near Muhammad's home—part of the West Bank security barrier—to try to prevent terrorist attacks on Israel.

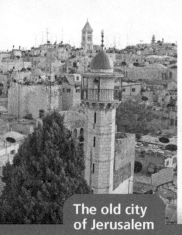
The old city of Jerusalem

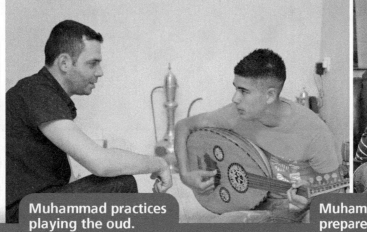
Muhammad practices playing the oud.

Muhammad's father prepares coffee.

Muhammad doesn't like the barrier, because security restrictions make it difficult or impossible to cross. Those who do cross may have difficulty returning. Muhammad says, "I still remember how we used to walk to Bethlehem, which is only two miles away. . . . Some people in my neighborhood are Israeli Arabs whose partners are Palestinian. Because of the barrier, they cannot meet now."

Muhammad is learning to play the oud (ood), a traditional pear-shaped wooden stringed instrument, in a music school not far from the Old City. Both Arabs and Jews attend this school. Muhammad plays traditional Arab music. In the school, he joined a Jewish-Arab youth orchestra, with 25 musicians. They play original adaptations of traditional Arab music and combinations of eastern and western musical styles.

"I don't really care about the conflict. Only human beings are important to me. In music, there are no Arabs or Jews, only people playing together and getting to know each other. In our music school, there are both Jewish and Arab teachers. This orchestra is proof we can coexist."

→ **myStory Video**

Join Maayan and Muhammad as they show you more about life in their hometowns.

Meet the Journalist

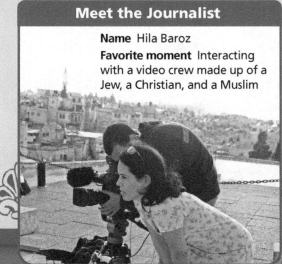

Name Hila Baroz
Favorite moment Interacting with a video crew made up of a Jew, a Christian, and a Muslim

Chapter Atlas

Key Ideas
- Israel and its neighbors are a continental crossroads, near the points where Europe, Asia, and Africa meet.
- Water is a scarce but vital resource for Israel and its neighbors.
- The region has a complex pattern of ethnic and religious differences.

Key Terms
- Fertile Crescent
- Druze
- rain shadow
- Alawite
- aquifer

 Visual Glossary

 Reading Skill: Label an Outline Map Take notes using the outline map in your journal.

Mountains along the coast of Lebanon ▼

▲ A boy from coastal Lebanon

A Continental Junction

Israel and its neighbors—Lebanon, Syria, Jordan, the Golan Heights, West Bank, and Gaza Strip—are in Southwest Asia. The West Bank and Gaza Strip together are sometimes called the Palestinian Territories.

These countries and territories lie on or near the coast of the Mediterranean Sea where the continents of Asia and Africa meet. This region is a continental cross-roads, and it also borders Turkey, where Asia and Europe meet.

Four geographic zones make up this region. On its western edge, a narrow

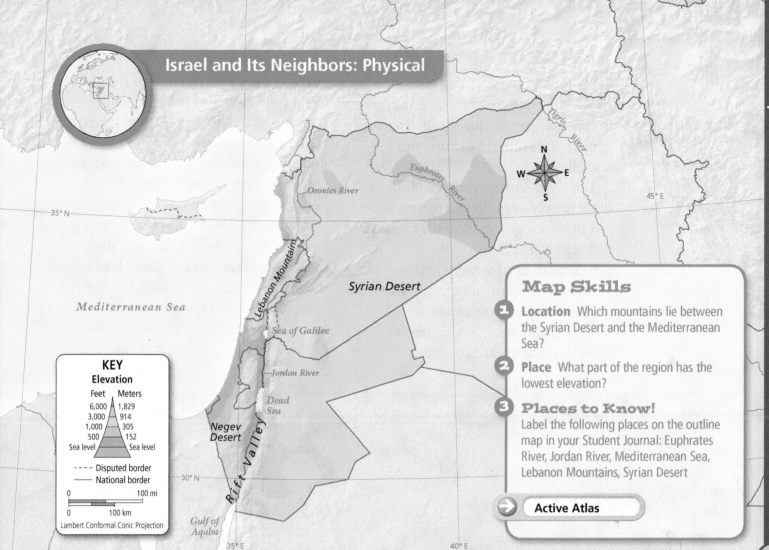

Israel and Its Neighbors: Physical

Tigris River

Euphrates River

Orontes River

35° N

Mediterranean Sea

Lebanon Mountains

Syrian Desert

Sea of Galilee

45° E

KEY
Elevation

Feet	Meters
6,000	1,829
3,000	914
1,000	305
500	152
Sea level	Sea level

- - - - Disputed border
——— National border

0   100 mi
0   100 km
Lambert Conformal Conic Projection

Jordan River

Dead Sea

Negev Desert

Rift Valley

30° N

Gulf of Aqaba

35° E   40° E

Map Skills

1 **Location** Which mountains lie between the Syrian Desert and the Mediterranean Sea?

2 **Place** What part of the region has the lowest elevation?

3 **Places to Know!**
Label the following places on the outline map in your Student Journal: Euphrates River, Jordan River, Mediterranean Sea, Lebanon Mountains, Syrian Desert

→ **Active Atlas**

coastal plain runs along the Mediterranean Sea. Just east of this plain is a chain of hills and mountains. Farther east is a branch of the Great African Rift Valleys. This chain of valleys runs from Africa through the Red Sea into Israel and its neighbors. Above these valleys to the east is a vast desert plateau. The Syrian Desert covers much of this plateau.

Flowing through one of the rift valleys is the Jordan River. Its water flows from Syria and Lebanon into the freshwater Sea of Galilee. It then flows south from this lake to the Dead Sea, also in this rift valley. The Dead Sea shoreline is the lowest land on Earth, at 1,378 feet (420 meters) below sea level.

The Euphrates River flows from the rainy mountains of Turkey, through eastern Syria, and across the Syrian Desert into Iraq. These river valleys and the relatively rainy Mediterranean coast and highlands are part of the Fertile Crescent. The **Fertile Crescent** is a region that stretches from the Mediterranean coast east through Mesopotamia (modern Iraq) to the Persian Gulf. It has good conditions for growing crops.

Reading Check **Which three continents meet in or near this region?**

Wet and Dry Climates

Israel and its neighbors have three types of climate. They are the Mediterranean climate, the semiarid climate, and the arid climate.

condense, v., to become denser, change from a gas to a liquid

The Mediterranean coast and the chain of highlands—or hills and mountains—just to its east gets most of the rainfall in this region. The rainy coast and highlands run through northwestern Syria, all of Lebanon, northern and central Israel, and the West Bank. These areas have a Mediterranean climate. In a Mediterranean climate, summers are hot and dry. Moist air flows over this region from the Mediterranean Sea during the mild winter months. As it rises over the highlands, it cools. When it cools, most of the moisture <u>condenses</u> and falls as rain or snow.

Farther east, the rift valleys and the desert plateau lie behind the rain shadow cast by the highlands. A **rain shadow** is a dry area that forms behind a highland that captures rainfall and snow. East of the highlands, dry air flows over the rift valley and Syrian Desert.

In northwestern Syria, the low hills do not cast a strong rain shadow. So most

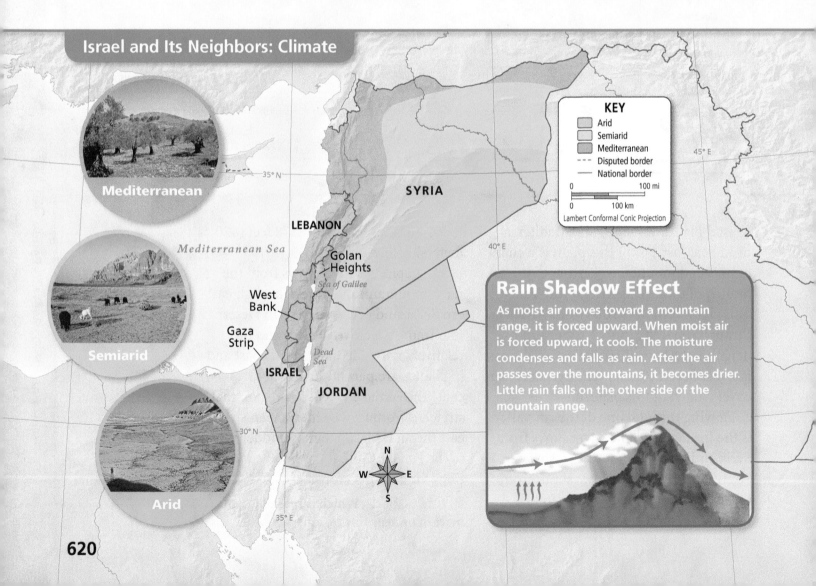

Israel and Its Neighbors: Climate

Mediterranean

Semiarid

Arid

Mediterranean Sea

SYRIA

LEBANON

Golan Heights

Sea of Galilee

West Bank

Gaza Strip

Dead Sea

ISRAEL

JORDAN

35° N

40° E

45° E

30° N

35° E

KEY
Arid
Semiarid
Mediterranean
--- Disputed border
— National border

0   100 mi
0   100 km
Lambert Conformal Conic Projection

N
W   E
S

Rain Shadow Effect

As moist air moves toward a mountain range, it is forced upward. When moist air is forced upward, it cools. The moisture condenses and falls as rain. After the air passes over the mountains, it becomes drier. Little rain falls on the other side of the mountain range.

of northern Syria has a semiarid climate. This is a dry climate, but with enough rainfall for some animals and plants, such as wheat. The semiarid climate stretches through central Syria to western Jordan.

Southeastern Syria and eastern Jordan have an arid, or desert, climate. This area is behind the rain shadow cast by the hills around the rift valleys. Very little moisture reaches the plateau. Few plants or animals can live in the desert.

Southern Israel and Jordan also have an arid climate, with a belt of semiarid climate just to its north. In the semiarid zone, low hills cause the air to lose some moisture during winter.

The desert to the south is part of the belt of subtropical deserts that stretches around the world. These deserts include the Sahara and the deserts of Arabia. As you learned in the Core Concepts Handbook, cool, dry air tends to sink over this belt of deserts. This sinking air keeps moist air from flowing in from the Mediterranean Sea. It also keeps air from rising and dropping rain or snow.

Reading Check Why is the climate of eastern Jordan so dry?

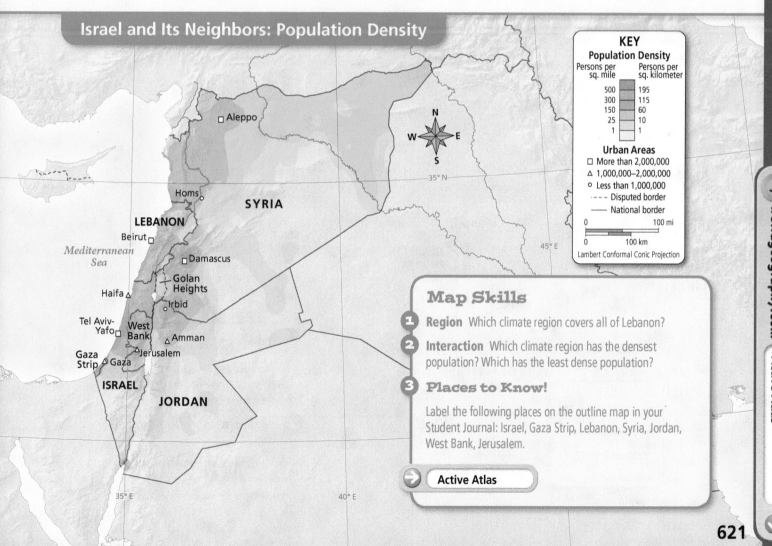

Israel and Its Neighbors: Population Density

KEY

Population Density

Persons per sq. mile	Persons per sq. kilometer
500	195
300	115
150	60
25	10
1	1

Urban Areas

☐ More than 2,000,000
△ 1,000,000–2,000,000
○ Less than 1,000,000
--- Disputed border
— National border

0   100 mi
0   100 km

Lambert Conformal Conic Projection

Map Skills

1. **Region** Which climate region covers all of Lebanon?

2. **Interaction** Which climate region has the densest population? Which has the least dense population?

3. **Places to Know!**

   Label the following places on the outline map in your Student Journal: Israel, Gaza Strip, Lebanon, Syria, Jordan, West Bank, Jerusalem.

➡ **Active Atlas**

Water for a Thirsty Region

Israel and its neighbors get little rain outside the winter rainy season. Fresh water is a scarce resource here.

Many of the region's streams run only during the rainy winter or shrink to a trickle in the summer. People need year-round sources of fresh water.

Main Water Sources Some of the most important sources of water for Israel and its neighbors are their aquifers. **Aquifers** are underground layers of rock where water collects. Wells and pumps can bring this water to the surface for use. However, the region's population and water use have grown faster than these aquifers can refill. Some are slowly running out of water. This makes wells run dry. Desalination plants are another possible source of fresh water for this region. However, they are expensive.

Lebanon is the only country in the region with plenty of fresh water. Syria, on the other hand, has a water shortage. Few rivers run year-round. An exception is the Euphrates River, which flows across eastern Syria. The Euphrates is a major

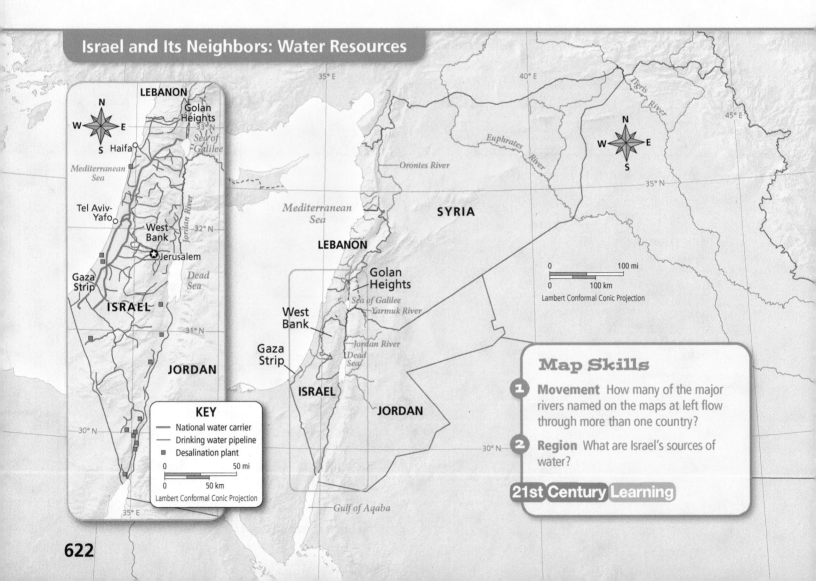

Israel and Its Neighbors: Water Resources

KEY
— National water carrier
— Drinking water pipeline
■ Desalination plant

0   50 mi
0   50 km
Lambert Conformal Conic Projection

0   100 mi
0   100 km
Lambert Conformal Conic Projection

Map Skills

1 Movement How many of the major rivers named on the maps at left flow through more than one country?

2 Region What are Israel's sources of water?

21st Century Learning

source of water for Syria. Syria also uses water from aquifers, but some wells have run dry.

Conflicts Over Water Competition over the Euphrates has brought tensions. The river flows from Turkey through Syria to Iraq. Turkey takes water from the Euphrates. This reduces the supply for Syria and Iraq.

Jordan has the region's most serious shortage of water. It shares the Jordan and Yarmuk rivers with Israel and Syria. Jordan has had disagreements with its neighbors over these rivers.

Israel depends on two main water sources. It gets surface water from the Jordan River and the Sea of Galilee. The Sea of Galilee is the largest body of fresh water in the region. Israel also takes water from underground aquifers.

Israel also has had tensions with its neighbors over water. The Jordan River flows from the Golan Heights, an area that Syria claims and that Israel has occupied since 1967. Water also flows into the Jordan River from southern Lebanon and from the country of Jordan.

Israel also uses aquifers that lie partly under the West Bank, which is home to many Palestinians. Some Palestinians complain about Israel's use of these aquifers. Because the aquifers are limited, both sides fear a loss of their water. However, Israel has made agreements with Jordan and with the Palestinians over water use.

An Israeli water expert has warned that disagreements over water with other countries in the region could lead to war:

> 66 I can promise that if there is not sufficient water in our region, if there is scarcity of water, if people remain thirsty for water, then we shall doubtless face war. 99

—Meir Ben Meir, Israel's former Water Commissioner

Reading Check **What river does Israel share with three other countries?**

occupy, *v.,* to take or hold, especially by military force

myWorld Activity
Water Rules

An Israeli farmer watering crops

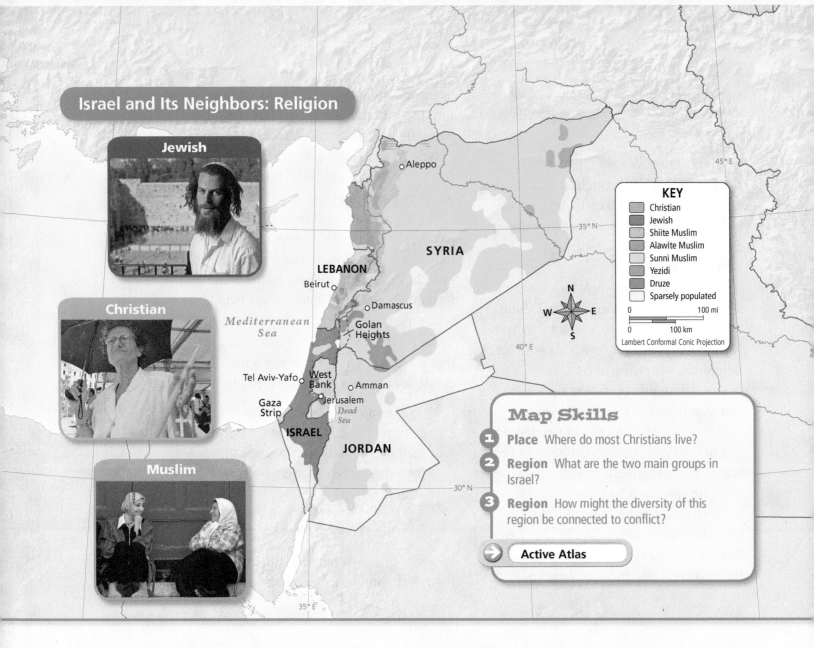

Israel and Its Neighbors: Religion

Jewish

Christian

Muslim

Aleppo

SYRIA

LEBANON
Beirut

Mediterranean Sea

Damascus

Golan Heights

Tel Aviv-Yafo
West Bank

Gaza Strip

Jerusalem
Dead Sea

Amman

ISRAEL

JORDAN

45° E

35° N

40° E

30° N

35° E

KEY
- Christian
- Jewish
- Shiite Muslim
- Alawite Muslim
- Sunni Muslim
- Yezidi
- Druze
- Sparsely populated

0   100 mi
0   100 km

Lambert Conformal Conic Projection

Map Skills

1 **Place** Where do most Christians live?

2 **Region** What are the two main groups in Israel?

3 **Region** How might the diversity of this region be connected to conflict?

→ Active Atlas

A Region of Many Peoples and Religions

Most of the people of Israel and its neighbors fall into two broad ethnic groups, or groups sharing a language and an identity. These groups are the Jews and the Arabs. Most of Israel's people are Jews. Most Israeli Jews speak Hebrew.

Arabs speak Arabic. Arabs make up a large majority of the people in the Palestinian Territories, Jordan, Lebanon, and Syria. Arabs also make up a minority of the population of Israel. Syria has an important Kurdish minority in the northeast. Syria also has much smaller Turkish and Armenian minorities.

Differences Among Jews Most people in Israel are Jewish. Some Israeli Jews strictly follow the rules of Judaism, while others are less strict. Most Israeli Jews, even if they are not religious, identify with the culture and history of Judaism. This is a cornerstone of their identity.

Israel's Jews have ancestors from many parts of the world. Some families have lived in the area for thousands of years. Other families immigrated from neighboring countries or other areas in Southwest Asia and North Africa. Still others came from Europe, Russia, North America, Ethiopia, and elsewhere. These immigrants have brought different customs from their former homes.

Differences Among Arabs The Arabs of the region share an ethnic identity, but they follow several different religions. Most Arabs here are Sunni Muslims, but some are Shia Muslim, Alawite Muslim, Christian, or Druze. The **Druze** follow a religion that combines Islam with other teachings. The **Alawites** follow a form of Islam similar to Shia Islam.

Most Arabs of Israel, the West Bank, and the Gaza Strip are Sunni Muslim. Some are Christian. Many Israeli Arabs consider themselves Palestinian, like the Arabs of the West Bank and Gaza Strip.

In Lebanon, almost all of the people are Arabs, but no one religious group has a majority. The two largest groups of Lebanese are the Shia Muslims and Christians. There are also Sunni Muslims and Druze in Lebanon.

Most Syrians, including Syria's Kurds, are Sunni Muslims. However, some are Christians. Others are Shia or Alawite Muslims. Smaller numbers are Druze. Syria's rulers for the past 40 years belong to a family of Alawites.

A large majority of Jordanians are Sunni Muslim Arabs. Jordan has a small Christian population and smaller groups of Shia Muslims and Druze.

Tensions among ethnic and religious groups in this region have led to conflicts within and between its countries. For example, Israel and its Arab neighbors have fought several wars. Lebanon suffered through years of war among its Christian, Druze, and Muslim groups.

Reading Check Which ethnic group lives in every country of this region?

my World IN NUMBERS

This region's population is **13%** Jewish, **10%** Christian, **73%** Muslim, and **4%** Druze or another religion.

Section 1 Assessment

Key Terms

1. Use the terms *rain shadow* and *aquifers* to describe where water can be found in Israel and its neighbors.

2. What is the Fertile Crescent?

Key Ideas

3. How does the climate change from the coast to inland areas?

4. What is the most important resource for Israel and its neighbors? Explain.

5. How would you describe ethnic and religious patterns in this region?

Think Critically

6. **Draw Inferences** How might religious patterns in the region contribute to conflict?

7. **Analyze Cause and Effect** How has water affected the relationships among Israel and its neighbors?

Essential Question

Is conflict unavoidable?

8. Describe steps that Israel and its neighbors have taken to reduce conflict over water resources. Go to your Student Journal to record your answer.

myworldgeography.com Active Atlas

History of Israel and Its Neighbors

| **Key Ideas** | • Judaism is the oldest monotheistic religion, and its idea of justice remains important around the world. | • Nearly 2,000 years ago, the religion of Christianity developed in this region.

 • During the Middle Ages, the region became mainly Muslim and Arabic-speaking. | • Seeking safety from persecution, Jews founded the state of Israel in 1948, but conflict between Jews and Arabs continues. |

Key Terms • agriculture • prophet • ethics • messiah
• Trinity • Crusades • anti-Semitism • Zionism

 Visual Glossary

Reading Skill: Compare and Contrast Take notes using the graphic organizer in your journal.

A jar made in Canaan around 1500 B.C. ▼

Israel and its neighbors are part of the Fertile Crescent. The first people in the Fertile Crescent were hunters and gatherers. Then, about 10,000 years ago, they began to practice **agriculture,** or the raising of plants and animals. These early farmers built permanent villages. They developed new tools for farming, such as plows.

A Cradle of Civilization

Villages grew into towns. One of the world's oldest towns, Jericho, still exists today in what is now the West Bank. It was settled about 9,000 years ago.

Present-day Israel and the Palestinian Territories were once called Canaan. North of Canaan, in modern Lebanon and Syria, was a region called Phoenicia. The Phoenicians invented an alphabet. Through trade, the Phoenicians spread their alphabet, which is the basis for our own. The Canaanites—the people of Canaan—and the Phoenicians were pagan. That is, they worshiped more than one god.

After 2000 B.C., a people known as Israelites moved into the region. Unlike the Canaanites, the Israelites worshiped only one God. Their religion came to be known as Judaism.

Reading Check **When was Jericho settled?**

The Origins of Judaism

The Israelites practiced monotheism, the belief in a single God. They rejected the gods of the Canaanites.

Abraham's Covenant According to the Hebrew, or Jewish, Bible, Abraham was the father of the Jewish people. According to the Bible, God promised that Abraham would found a great nation in Canaan. In return, Abraham and his people had to obey God. God's agreement with Abraham is called a covenant. Abraham's grandson Jacob, later called Israel, had twelve sons. Their families grew to form the people known as the Israelites.

Escape From Slavery Famine drove the Israelites to Egypt, where the Egyptians enslaved them. According to the Bible, God chose an Israelite named Moses to lead his people out of Egypt. Moses was later known as a **prophet,** a messenger of God. The pharaoh, or Egyptian king, refused to let the Israelites go. God then caused Egypt to suffer until the pharaoh freed the Israelites. Moses then led his people out of Egypt to the edge of Canaan. The Jewish holiday of Passover commemorates this event.

During this time, according to the Bible, God gave Moses a law code including the Ten Commandments. The Ten Commandments are ten rules for good behavior. The Israelites took control in Canaan and established first the kingdom of Israel and later the kingdom of Judah. In 587 B.C., however, the Babylonian empire conquered the Israelite kingdom of Judah.

Captivity, Return, and Diaspora The Babylonians destroyed the great Temple of Jerusalem and carried away many people from Judah as captives. However, the people of Judah preserved their religion. They came to be known as Jews, a name derived from *Judah*. Captivity in Babylonia was the start of the Jewish Diaspora, or scattering. After the Persians conquered Babylonia, the Persian king allowed Jews to return to Judah. The Jews rebuilt their Temple in Jerusalem.

The region eventually came under Roman rule as the province of Judea. The Romans demanded heavy taxes and outlawed parts of the Jewish religion. Jews rebelled against Rome twice. The Romans destroyed the Temple in A.D. 70 and later killed thousands of Jews. Many Jews fled the region, and the Romans banned Jews from Jerusalem.

Reading Check What was the Diaspora?

Moses leading his people out of Egypt in a scene from the Hebrew Bible ▼

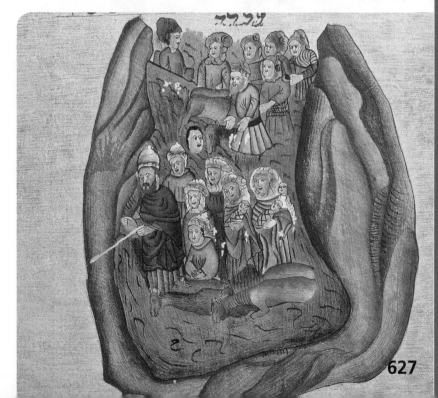

The Beliefs of Judaism

Judaism developed a system of **ethics**— or beliefs about what is right and wrong. Judaism also developed a tradition of acting responsibly within a community. These traditions are guidelines for living a just and righteous life.

Faith in One God At the core of Judaism lies the belief that there is a single God who created the universe and has always existed. This God does not take a physical form. Most Jews refer to God as *He*. However, for Jews, God is neither male nor female. God knows the thoughts and actions of people. He rewards the good and punishes the evil. Jews believe that they carry on the Israelites' covenant with God. They believe that God chose them to bear the responsibility of upholding his laws and serving as an example of justice to other peoples.

The Holy Scriptures The scriptures, or religious writings, of Judaism include the Hebrew Bible, known as the Tanakh. The Tanakh has three parts: the Torah, the Nevi'im, and the Ketuvim. The Torah, or Law, tells the story of the Israelites from God's creation of the world until the death of Moses. It provides the basis for Jewish ethics and religious practice. The Nevi'im, or Prophets, contains the teachings of the many prophets of Judaism. The Ketuvim, or Writings, includes psalms (sacred poems or songs) and proverbs (writings of wisdom). Another Jewish religious text, not part of the Tanakh, is the Talmud. This text explains and interprets the Torah.

The Ten Commandments and Justice Jews' covenant with God includes rules that form a system of ethics. According to the Bible, God gave rules to Moses on the journey from Egypt to Canaan. They include the Ten Commandments. These are guidelines for acting justly and fairly that are meant to create a stable and peaceful society. Judaism calls on people to follow the righteous example of God. Jewish ideas of justice form a basis for democracies, legal systems, and ethics in many parts of the modern world.

Reading Check **Why is justice important to Jews?**

▼ A jeweled Torah cover, with wrapped Torah scrolls below and to the right

▲ Israeli Jewish worshipers

The Birth of Christianity

Around A.D. 35, a new religion arose in the Roman province of Judea. This religion, based on Jewish traditions, was Christianity.

Jewish Roots Judaism included a belief in a **messiah**—a leader chosen by God. This messiah would restore the Jewish nation and help create God's kingdom in the world. For Christians, this messiah was Jesus.

As with Abraham, what we know of Jesus comes mainly from scripture. According to the Christian Bible, Jesus was a Jew born in Judea. He grew up in the town of Nazareth. As an adult, Jesus began to preach about Jewish beliefs and ethics. He preached forgiveness, compassion for the poor, and trust in God. He attracted many followers.

According to scripture, the Roman governor of Judea put Jesus to death by crucifixion, or nailing to a cross. The cross became an important Christian symbol.

The Story of the Resurrection According to the Christian Bible, two days after Jesus' death, some of his followers went to his tomb and found it empty. Jesus then appeared to many followers. God, they believed, had raised Jesus from the dead, or resurrected him.

Unlike other Jews, Jesus' followers believed that his resurrection proved that he was the messiah. Jesus' followers called him "Christ," which was a Greek translation of the word *messiah*. His followers became known as Christians.

The Early Church and Its Spread At first, most Christians came from a Jewish background. However, one of Jesus' followers, Paul—known to Christians as Saint Paul—began preaching Christian beliefs to non-Jews. Gradually, non-Jewish Christians began to outnumber Christians with a Jewish background. For hundreds of years, Christians faced harsh treatment in the Roman Empire.

In 312, however, Roman Emperor Constantine became a Christian, and the religion spread throughout the Roman world. Today it is the most practiced religion in the world. There are more than 2 billion Christians today.

Reading Check **Why is the resurrection important to Christians?**

▼ An early Christian painting of Jesus

Beliefs of Christianity

The beliefs of Christianity are based on the life and teachings of Jesus, as described in the Christian Bible. Christians believe that Jesus was more than a wise man, like Abraham or Moses. They believe that he was God in human form. They see Jesus' death as proof of his humanity and his resurrection as proof that he is the son of God.

concept, *n.,* an idea about how something is or should be

For Christians, the resurrection is also God's promise of eternal life. The resurrection shows that God controls life and death. For Christians, belief in Jesus can lead to a rewarding life after death. Christians believe that Jesus died on the cross because of people's sins, or evil actions. They believe that Jesus' resurrection, with its promise of eternal life, is proof of God's forgiveness.

The Christian Bible The Tanakh, or Hebrew Bible, makes up most of the Christian Bible. Christians refer to the writings from the Tanakh as the Old Testament. In addition to the Old Testament, the Christian Bible contains the New Testament. The New Testament contains writings about the life and teachings of Jesus and the writings of early Christian leaders.

The Trinity The **Trinity** is one of the most complex concepts of Christianity. Most Christians believe that God exists in three forms, or persons. Together, these three persons form the Trinity. These three persons are God the Father, the creator; God the Son, or Jesus; and the Holy Spirit. The Holy Spirit (also known as the Holy Ghost) is sometimes described as the power of God as experienced on Earth. The idea of the Trinity separates Christianity from the other two monotheistic religions. Judaism and Islam do not recognize the Trinity.

Reading Check **What are the two main parts of the Christian Bible?**

A Christian religious procession in Lebanon ▼

A Crossroads of Empires and New Religions

Over the centuries, armies from different empires conquered the region that is now Israel and its neighbors. Some of these conquests brought new religions to the region or re-established old religions.

Life Under the Romans and Byzantines

After the Jewish revolt of A.D. 135, the Romans changed the name of the region from Judea (or land of the Jews) to Palestine as punishment for the revolt.

After his conversion in 312, Roman Emperor Constantine made the region a center of Christian worship. Palestine and Syria were part of the Eastern Roman, or Byzantine, empire. In Byzantine times, most people in the region were Christian.

Arab Conquest and Islam

Between 614 and 629, the Byzantine empire lost control of Syria and Palestine to the Persian empire. The weakened Byzantine empire recovered the province in 629. However, Muslim Arabs attacked the region just five years later. The Byzantines were too weak to hold back the Arabs.

By 640, the Arabs had conquered the entire region. In 661, Damascus became the capital of a Muslim empire. Muslims recognize Abraham and Jesus as prophets. However, they believe that Muhammad was God's last and most important prophet. Muslims believe that Muhammad traveled to heaven from Jerusalem.

Because of its importance to Muhammad and earlier prophets, Muslims consider Jerusalem a holy city. There they built an important mosque in 705.

Islamic law favored Muslims but tolerated Christians and Jews. By the 800s, most people in the region had converted to Islam, and Arabic was the main language.

myWorld Activity
Diversity Mosaic

Crusaders and Muslim Rule

Beginning in the late 1000s, Christian soldiers from western Europe attacked Palestine in religious wars called the **Crusades.** They aimed to stop the spread of Islam and to take control of Palestine from the Muslims.

Around 1100, Crusaders established Christian kingdoms in Palestine. Muslims and Jews suffered brutal treatment under the Crusaders. In 1187, however, Muslim forces reconquered Jerusalem.

In 1517, the Muslim Ottoman Turks conquered the entire region. The Ottoman Turks ruled until the early 1900s.

Reading Check **Why is Jerusalem a holy city for Muslims?**

The Dome of the Rock, a Muslim shrine built in Jerusalem in 691 ▼

Culture Close-up

my worldgeography.com | Culture Close-up

Independence and Conflict

Britain, France, and other European nations defeated the Ottoman empire in 1918, at the end of World War I. This defeat ended Ottoman rule.

European Mandates After World War I, most of the world's nations joined to form the League of Nations. The League of Nations created mandates for areas conquered during the war. Mandates were territories placed under the control of powerful nations with a promise of future independence. Syria (including modern Lebanon) became a French mandate. Palestine (modern Israel and Jordan) became a British mandate.

Zionism and Jewish Settlement In Europe, Jews faced cruel and sometimes violent anti-Semitism. **Anti-Semitism** is <u>discrimination</u> against Jews. In the late 1800s, Jews in Europe formed a movement called Zionism. **Zionism** aimed to create a Jewish state in Palestine because of Jews' historic connection to the region. A Jewish state would allow Jews to create a safe homeland. Jews from the Diaspora began to move to Palestine, where an ancient Jewish community already existed.

discrimination, *n.,* unfair treatment of a person or group

Independence Anti-Semitism in Europe grew and led to the Holocaust during World War II. This pushed more Jews to migrate to the Palestine Mandate.

Meanwhile, the mandates gained independence: Lebanon in 1943 and Syria and Jordan in 1946. Thousands of Jews migrated from Europe to Palestine after the end of World War II in 1945. Tensions mounted between the Arab majority and Jews over the future of Palestine.

In 1947, the United Nations created a plan to partition, or divide, Palestine into two separate states—an Arab state and a Jewish state. Arabs rejected the UN plan, which Jews accepted. Israel declared independence as a Jewish state in 1948.

Arab-Israeli Conflicts Tensions erupted into violence. Neighboring Arab states attacked Israel. During the Arab-Israeli War of 1948, half of the Arab people in the land that came under Israeli control fled as refugees. Israel gained more territory than under the UN plan. Arab states took control of the West Bank and Gaza Strip. Many Jewish refugees from Arab countries came to Israel. Israel and Egypt fought a second war in 1956.

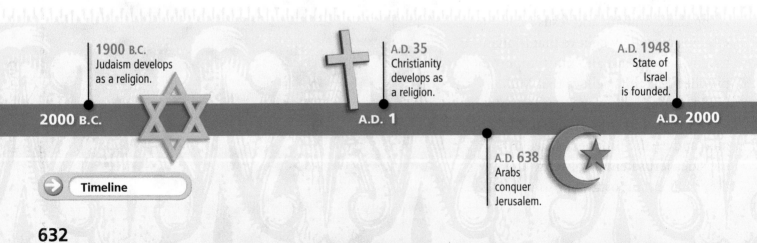

1900 B.C. Judaism develops as a religion.

A.D. 35 Christianity develops as a religion.

A.D. 1948 State of Israel is founded.

2000 B.C. A.D. 1 A.D. 2000

A.D. 638 Arabs conquer Jerusalem.

→ Timeline

In 1967, Syria, Jordan and Egypt massed troops on Israel's border and threatened to attack. Israel then attacked Syrian, Jordanian, and Egyptian territory. After six days, Israel controlled the West Bank of the Jordan River and East Jerusalem—both of which Jordan had controlled. Israel also gained control of the Sinai Peninsula and the Gaza Strip from Egypt and the Golan Heights from Syria. Egypt and Syria attacked Israel in 1973, hoping to regain their lost territories. However, Israel defeated them.

In 1979, the United States helped Egypt and Israel reach a peace agreement. Under this agreement, Israel returned the Sinai Peninsula to Egypt. Israel and Jordan signed a peace treaty in 1994.

War in Lebanon When Lebanon gained independence, Christians were the largest group and held the most power. After Palestinian Arabs fled Palestine, Muslims

▲ Israeli artillery in the Syrian Desert in 1973

became the largest group and demanded more power. In 1975, civil war broke out between Muslims and Christians. Syrian troops invaded Lebanon in response. In 1982, Israel invaded to stop terrorist attacks from Lebanon. War continued until 1990. Peace during the 1990s allowed Lebanon to rebuild. Israeli and Syrian troops had left by 2005. However, tensions among Lebanese groups remained.

Reading Check What are some reasons for the conflict between Jews and Arabs?

Section 2 Assessment

Key Terms

1. Use the term *ethics* to describe Jewish beliefs.

2. Explain the meaning of the term *Trinity* in Christianity.

3. Describe how anti-Semitism and Zionism affected the founding of Israel.

Key Ideas

4. In what historical order did religions influence the region of Israel and its neighbors?

5. How do the scriptures of Judaism and Christianity show that these religions have common roots?

6. What conflict between Arabs and Jews followed the United Nations plan to divide the Palestine Mandate?

Think Critically

7. **Compare Viewpoints** Why are ethics so important to Judaism and Christianity?

8. **Analyze Cause and Effect** How did conquest bring a new religion and culture to the region of Israel and its neighbors?

Essential Question

Is conflict unavoidable?

9. Give an example of a conflict in the region. Could it be avoided? If so, explain how. Go to your Student Journal to record your answers.

Israel and Its Neighbors Today

Key Ideas

- Political systems in the region include democracy, autocracy, and monarchy.

- Standards of living vary widely across the region.
- Israelis and Palestinian Arabs have been fighting over land and security.

- The region is important to the world because it is sacred to Judaism, Christianity, and Islam and is located at a crossroads for trade.

Key Terms
- parliamentary democracy
- capital
- hereditary monarch
- Israeli settlement
- autocracy
- Intifada

 Visual Glossary

Reading Skill: Summarize Take notes using the graphic organizer in your journal.

This Israeli man is voting in an election, a key feature of a democracy. ▼

As you have learned, the region of Israel and its neighbors contains sites sacred to three great religions: Judaism, Christianity, and Islam. Followers of each of these religions live in the region. Tensions among religious groups have led to conflict here. However, there are many differences among the region's countries besides religion.

Different Political Systems

There are great differences among the political systems of Israel and its neighbors. These systems range from Israel's strong democracy to Syria's autocracy.

Democratic Footholds Israel has a **parliamentary democracy,** or a democracy in which parliament chooses the government. Its parliament is called the Knesset. The Knesset elects the prime minister, who runs the government. Like Britain, the nation has no written constitution. Instead, its basic laws and practices function as an unwritten constitution. All citizens 18 and older—including both Jews and Arabs—may vote in elections to choose Knesset members.

The Palestinian Authority (PA) was established to govern the Gaza Strip and West Bank, which remain subject to Israeli control. According to its constitution, the PA is also a democracy. Since 2006, however, a conflict between the two main Palestinian parties—Hamas and Fatah—has divided the PA. In 2007, armed fighters from Hamas seized control of the Gaza Strip. At the same time, Fatah took control in the parts of the West Bank governed by the PA.

Lebanon also has a democracy. However, its constitution requires that its leaders belong to specific religious groups. For example, the president must be a Christian and the prime minister must be a Sunni Muslim.

Seats in Lebanon's parliament are reserved for religious groups in a way that no longer reflects their populations. Tensions among the religious groups have made it hard for them to govern together.

A Constitutional Monarchy Jordan's King Abdullah II is a **hereditary monarch,** a ruler who is the son or younger relative of the previous ruler. The king is more powerful than most presidents, but a constitution limits his power somewhat. A two-chamber legislature passes laws. The king appoints members of one chamber. Citizens freely elect members of the other.

A Family Autocracy Syria has an autocracy. An **autocracy** is a government controlled by one person who has not won a free election. In Syria, that person is President Bashar al-Assad. He took office when his father died, so power stayed in the family. His family controls the only legal party, the Ba'ath Party. Syria has been under a state of emergency since 1963. The state of emergency <u>suspends</u> protections for Syria's people and most of the powers of parliament.

suspend, *n.,* to call off, cancel, or remove

Reading Check What is the Knesset?

Political Systems

Parliamentary Democracy
Lebanon's elected parliament, shown below, makes laws for the country.

Monarchy
The king of Jordan and his sister, shown below, are both members of the royal family.

Autocracy
Bashar al-Assad is the president of Syria, an autocracy. He relies on the support of the army to hold power.

Different Standards of Living

Standards of living vary throughout the region. Israel has a higher standard of living than its neighbors. Israel's neighbors are poor by comparison.

A Land of Opportunity Israelis enjoy a high standard of living, even though Israel has few resources and faces ongoing conflict. Most Israelis are employed in the service sector. Israel also has a large industrial sector.

Israel's success is partly due to its strong schools and universities. Israel offers its citizens more educational opportunities than its neighbors. As a result, it has highly skilled workers. These skilled workers produce valuable products that allow them to earn high incomes.

Israel's skilled workforce has also attracted capital from other countries. **Capital** is money or goods that are used to make products. Israel's large supply of capital has created a strong economy. Foreign aid from the United States also helps boost Israel's economy.

Because Israel has few natural resources of its own, it benefits from trade. Israel trades its people's skill for resources by selling its goods and services and buying natural resources.

Barriers to Success Israel's neighbors lack these strengths. Some earn money from limited supplies of mineral resources. However, most have relatively poor schools and universities. In many Arab countries, women have fewer opportunities for education. Ongoing tension and conflict in Lebanon and the Palestinian Territories have also discouraged the creation of capital and jobs. Corruption has also weakened the economies of some Arab countries.

Different Outcomes Because Israel's Arab neighbors have weak economies, most people in these countries are relatively poor. The middle class is small compared to Israel's. However, a small number are rich. In Lebanon, the rich often belong to families that have been wealthy for many years. In other Arab countries, wealthy people often have government connections and benefit from corruption. In these economies, the poor earn little.

Reading Check **How has education helped Israel?**

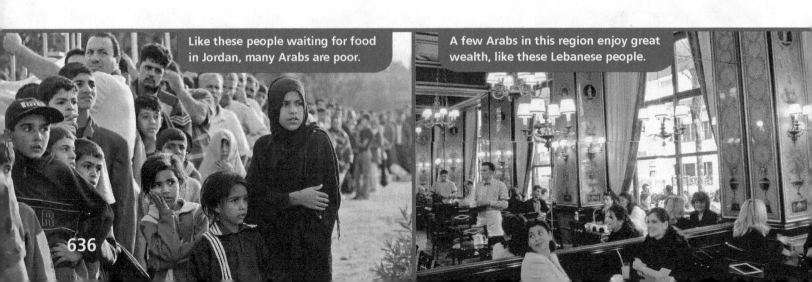

Like these people waiting for food in Jordan, many Arabs are poor.

A few Arabs in this region enjoy great wealth, like these Lebanese people.

636

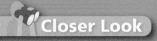
Closer Look

THE ECONOMIES
of Israel and Its Neighbors

Israel's economy is different from those of its neighbors. Israel's workers make products that require advanced skills and technology. Neighboring economies depend mainly on activities that require less skill and technology. As a result, Israelis tend to have higher incomes than their neighbors.

THINK CRITICALLY If education improved in countries neighboring Israel, how might that affect their economies?

Workers preparing medicines in Israel

Per Capita GDP, 2007

Israel $23,383; Jordan $2,654; Lebanon $6,011; Palestinian Territories $1,359; Syria $1,883

SOURCE: UN Data — Country (Dollars)

Farmers delivering wheat in Syria

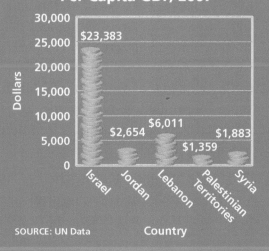
College Enrollment

Israel 58%; Jordan 39%; Lebanon 48%; Palestinian Territories 48%

SOURCE: UN Data — Country (Percentage)

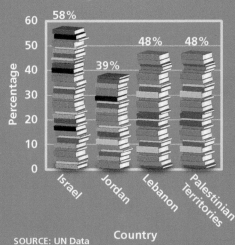

Shoppers at an outdoor market in Jordan

637

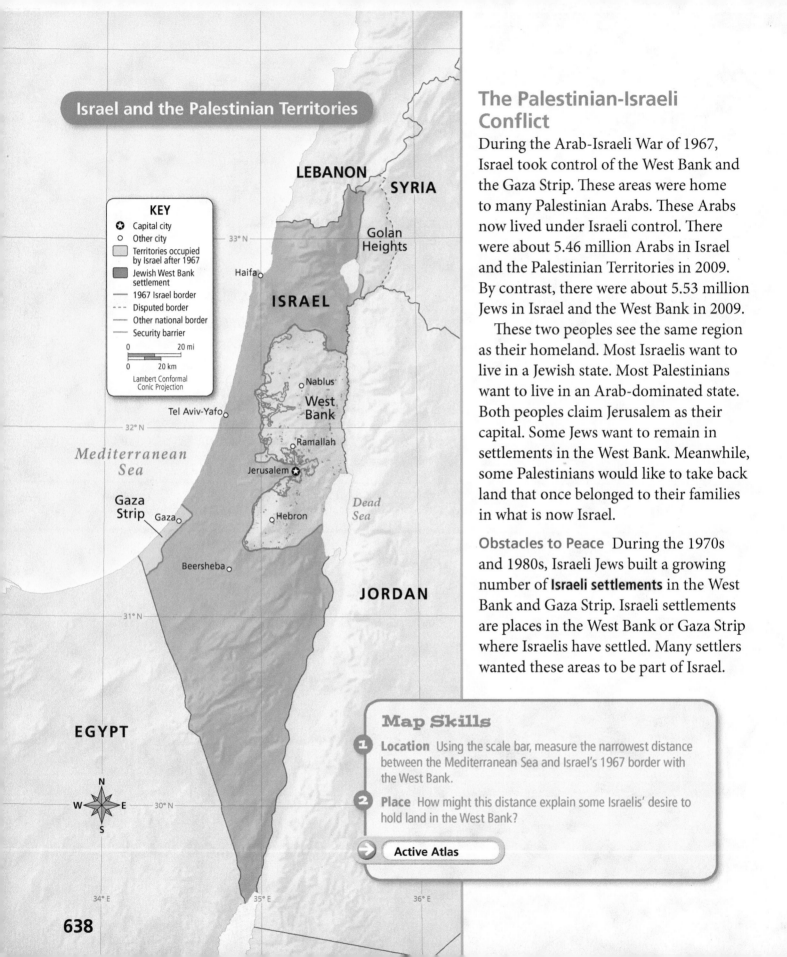

Israel and the Palestinian Territories

KEY
- ⊛ Capital city
- ○ Other city
- ☐ Territories occupied by Israel after 1967
- ▨ Jewish West Bank settlement
- —— 1967 Israel border
- - - - Disputed border
- —— Other national border
- —— Security barrier

0   20 mi
0   20 km

Lambert Conformal Conic Projection

LEBANON

SYRIA

Golan Heights

Haifa

ISRAEL

Nablus

West Bank

Tel Aviv-Yafo

Ramallah

Jerusalem ⊛

Mediterranean Sea

Gaza Strip

Gaza

Hebron

Dead Sea

Beersheba

JORDAN

EGYPT

33° N

32° N

31° N

30° N

34° E   35° E   36° E

N W E S

The Palestinian-Israeli Conflict

During the Arab-Israeli War of 1967, Israel took control of the West Bank and the Gaza Strip. These areas were home to many Palestinian Arabs. These Arabs now lived under Israeli control. There were about 5.46 million Arabs in Israel and the Palestinian Territories in 2009. By contrast, there were about 5.53 million Jews in Israel and the West Bank in 2009.

These two peoples see the same region as their homeland. Most Israelis want to live in a Jewish state. Most Palestinians want to live in an Arab-dominated state. Both peoples claim Jerusalem as their capital. Some Jews want to remain in settlements in the West Bank. Meanwhile, some Palestinians would like to take back land that once belonged to their families in what is now Israel.

Obstacles to Peace During the 1970s and 1980s, Israeli Jews built a growing number of **Israeli settlements** in the West Bank and Gaza Strip. Israeli settlements are places in the West Bank or Gaza Strip where Israelis have settled. Many settlers wanted these areas to be part of Israel.

Map Skills

1 **Location** Using the scale bar, measure the narrowest distance between the Mediterranean Sea and Israel's 1967 border with the West Bank.

2 **Place** How might this distance explain some Israelis' desire to hold land in the West Bank?

→ Active Atlas

By 1988, Israel controlled more than half of the land in the West Bank, although Israelis made up less than one tenth of the West Bank's population. Some Israelis think it was wrong to build the Israeli settlements. Most other nations have opposed the settlements.

During this time, Palestinians living in Arab countries had launched repeated terrorist attacks against Israel. Many attacks <u>targeted</u> Israeli civilians. Civilians are people other than soldiers.

In the late 1980s, some Palestinians began the Intifada. The **Intifada** was a campaign of violent resistance against Israeli control. Israeli troops fought the Intifada. More than 1,000 people died, mainly young Palestinians.

A Peace Plan Frustrated In 1994, Israel agreed to a peace plan with the Palestine Liberation Organization, or PLO, which represented Palestinians. This plan created the Palestinian Authority to rule the parts of the West Bank and Gaza Strip not controlled by Israel. Israel agreed to remove settlers from the Gaza Strip and parts of the West Bank. The PLO recognized Israel's right to exist and agreed to end terrorist attacks on Israel.

However, each side accused the other of violating the peace plan, and the plan failed. In 2000, Palestinians launched a second Intifada. Terrorists also attacked civilians inside Israel. These attacks brought the peace process to a halt, and Israel again fought back. The fighting died down around 2005 when Israel removed its settlers from the Gaza Strip.

Israel built security barriers around the Gaza Strip and the West Bank in the 1990s and 2000s. The West Bank barrier separated Arab from Jewish areas to prevent attacks on Israel. It also separated some Palestinian villages from each other and blocked some Palestinians' access to their farmland. The barriers succeeded in reducing attacks on Israel but made life more difficult for Palestinians.

target, *v.,* to aim for, make a target

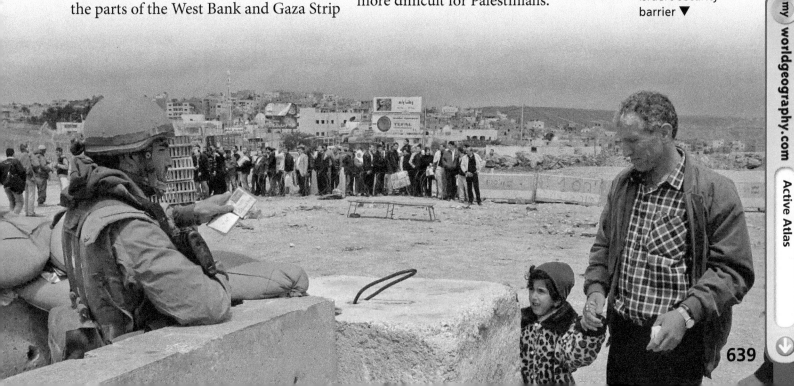

Palestinians at a checkpoint along Israel's security barrier ▼

my worldgeography.com Active Atlas

myWorld Activity
Peace Conference

Ongoing Conflict and Hopes for Peace
In 2006, a Palestinian political party called Hamas won the most seats in the Palestinian parliament. Hamas has stated that it wants to eliminate the state of Israel. Hamas fighters took control of the Gaza Strip in 2007. Israel then imposed a blockade on the Gaza Strip, blocking all traffic by air, sea, or land. Hamas began shooting rockets into Israel. These rockets killed more than a dozen Israeli civilians.

In response, Israel bombed the Gaza Strip in 2008 and 2009 and sent troops to kill or capture Hamas fighters. Hundreds of Palestinian civilians were killed, as were hundreds of Hamas fighters.

Most Palestinians and Israelis want peace. Many support creating an independent Palestinian state in the Palestinian Territories alongside Israel. However, violence from both sides will need to end for this solution to work.

Reading Check Which city do both Israelis and Palestinians claim as their capital?

A Region of Worldwide Importance

Israel contains sites holy to three major world religions. The region lies along key trade routes linking three continents.

A Region Sacred to Three Religions
Jews, Christians, and Muslims all believe that they worship the God who made a covenant with Abraham. This region is the Jewish Holy Land and the land where Jesus lived and died. According to Islamic tradition, Jerusalem is the place where the prophet Muhammad rose to heaven. Jews, Christians, and Muslims retain an intense interest in this region.

At the Intersection of Three Continents Israel and its neighbors sit at a continental crossroads. Throughout history, many peoples passed through the region. Ancient trade routes through the region connect Africa, Europe, and Asia.

Bombing in Israel
A bus in Israel blown up by Palestinian suicide bombers

Bombing in the Palestinian Territories
A neighborhood in the Gaza Strip damaged by Israeli bombing

A Gateway to Vital Oil Supplies

Southwest Asia has the world's largest oil reserves. Most of these reserves surround the Persian Gulf to the east of Israel and its neighbors. Israel, Jordan, and Lebanon have almost no oil reserves, while Syria has only small reserves.

Still, Europe and other parts of the world depend on oil that must pass through or past Israel and its neighbors. It is difficult to reach the Persian Gulf by air from the United States or Europe without flying over this region.

For this reason, Israel and its neighbors have great economic and military importance. Regional conflicts could disrupt the flow of oil from the Persian Gulf. Thus, tensions within the region can drive up oil prices. For military as well as cultural reasons, the United States and other nations have a strong interest in Israel and its neighbors.

Reading Check **Why is this region so important for trade?**

my **Story** 📷 **Photo**

Jerusalem is a city sacred to three religions: Judaism, Christianity, and Islam. In this photograph, Jews worship at Jerusalem's Western Wall, a sacred Jewish site and a remnant of the Jewish Temple. Both Christian and Muslim holy sites lie close by.

Section 3 Assessment

Key Terms

1. Use the terms *parliamentary democracy* and *autocracy* to describe governments in the region.

2. Define the terms *Intifada* and *Israeli settlement*.

3. Describe the role of capital in Israel's economy.

Key Ideas

4. Describe differences in standards of living in the region.

5. What are the main reasons for the conflict beween the Israelis and the Palestinians?

6. How does the location of oil make Israel and its neighbors important to the rest of the world?

Think Critically

7. **Draw Inferences** Israelis and Palestinians agreed to a peace plan in 1994. Why do you think both sides accused the other of breaking its promises?

8. **Compare and Contrast** How are the democracies in the region the same and different?

? Essential Question

Is conflict unavoidable?

9. What evidence from this chapter—including the myStory in the chapter opener—shows how Arabs and Jews might avoid conflict? Go to your Student Journal to record your answers.

Chapter Assessment

Key Terms and Ideas

1. **Analyze Cause and Effect** How does the region's location help explain the many conflicts it has suffered?

2. **Summarize** Why did Palestinians begin the **Intifada?**

3. **Synthesize** How do **rain shadows** create deserts?

4. **Draw Conclusions** How are **ethics** important to the religion of Judaism?

5. **Categorize** What are the core beliefs of Christianity, including the **Trinity**?

6. **Compare and Contrast** What is life like for most Arabs in the region? Most Israelis? All people in the region?

7. **Draw Inferences** Why is the future of **aquifers** so important to the people of the region?

Think Critically

8. **Analyze Cause and Effect** How are Arabs in the region different from one another? How are they all different from most Israelis? How have differences within the groups led to greater conflict in the region?

9. **Identify Evidence** Defend the statement that if the region had more water, there would be less conflict. Use evidence from this chapter.

10. **Compare and Contrast** How are the conflicts within Lebanon similar to and different from the Palestinian-Israeli conflict?

11. **Core Concepts: Culture and Geography** What role has religion played in the history of Israel and its neighbors?

Places to Know

For each place, write the letter from the map that shows its location.

12. Syria
13. Jordan River
14. Euphrates River
15. Jerusalem
16. Lebanon
17. Gaza Strip
18. **Estimate** Using the scale, estimate the distance between Jerusalem and the Gaza Strip.

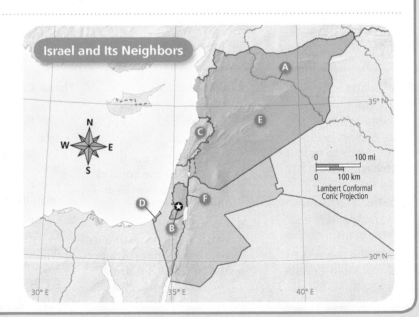

Israel and Its Neighbors

Essential Question

myWorld Chapter Activity

History Museum Tour You want to teach other people about the history of Israel and its neighbors. Develop a stop on a history museum tour to tell about one time period. Present your tour stop and view other tour stops, then join a discussion about the entire tour.

21st Century Learning

Analyze Media Content

Find three articles about conflicts between Israelis and Palestinians. Using what you know from the chapter, analyze the articles. How accurate are the facts? Is there evidence of bias, or a favoring of one view over another? Does the article clearly explain the current conflict and connect it to the larger conflicts in the region?

Document-Based Questions

Success Tracker™
Online at myworldgeography.com

Use your knowledge of Israel and its neighbors, as well as Documents A and B, to answer questions 1–3.

Document A

Peace and Prosperity in Israel and the Palestinian Territories

How important is peace to economic prosperity?

- ■ % very
- ■ % somewhat
- ■ % not very

	Israel	Palestinian Territories
% very	78%	83%
% somewhat	12%	12%
% not very	8%	4%

SOURCE: Gallup Poll, December, 2007

1. In 2007, what percentage of Israelis felt that peace was very important to their country's economic future?

A 70%

B 77%

C 78%

D 83%

Document B

"Today, many policy makers [call for] a total separation between Israel and the Palestinians. But the [Palestinians] cannot develop a prosperous economy . . . in economic isolation. Separation will result in economic ruin. . . . The fates of Israelis and Palestinians are economically intertwined."

—Daniel Doron, "Mideast Peace Can Start with Economic Growth," Wall Street Journal, March 12, 2009

2. According to Document B, what must Israeli and Palestinian economies do?

A The Israeli economy must control the Palestinian economy.

B The Palestinian economy must control that of Israel.

C The two economies should work together.

D The two economies should separate entirely.

3. **Writing Task** Do you think the views expressed in Document A support the views expressed in Document B? Explain.

Chapter 18

Iran, Turkey, and Cyprus

Essential Question

What are the challenges of diversity?

KEY
National border
Disputed border
⊛ Capital city
○ Other city

0   200 mi
0   200 km
Lambert Conformal Conic Projection

Black Sea

Istanbul

Ankara

TURKEY

Izmir

Urfa

Tabriz

Caspian Sea

Mashhad

Tehran

IRAN

Esfahan

CYPRUS   Nicosia

Mediterranean Sea

Shiraz

Persian Gulf

Gulf of Oman

TROPIC OF CANCER

Arabian Sea

Where in the World Are Iran, Turkey, and Cyprus?

Washington, D.C., to Urfa: 5,780 miles

← Belediye

↑ Eyyüp Peygamber

↑ Harran

↑ Havaalanı ✈

Akçakale ↗

my Story

Bilal Looks Forward

In this section, you'll read about Bilal, a young Kurdish man from Turkey who lives in Urfa. **What does Bilal's story tell you about life in Iran, Turkey, and Cyprus today?**

? Explore the Essential Question
- at **my worldgeography.com**
- using the **myWorld Chapter Activity**
- with the **Student Journal**

Story by Can Ertür for myWorld Geography Online

Looking out over the rooftops of Urfa, 18-year-old Bilal is proud of his town. This town, located in southeastern Turkey, has been home to Bilal and his family for most of his life.

"Urfa has a very rich history. I want people to come to see Urfa. It is a beautiful place," says Bilal.

The city of Urfa is several thousand years old. It was once called Edessa, and was one of the most important cities in the area in ancient times. Like most of Urfa's people, Bilal is a member of the Kurdish ethnic group. He is proud to be both a Kurd and a citizen of the Republic of Turkey.

Kurdish people are a minority in Turkey. For many years, the Turkish government tried to suppress Kurdish culture. Kurds were not allowed to speak the Kurdish language or even give their children Kurdish names. Many Kurds fought the Turkish government because of this. Some still do, although today the government treats Kurdish people better.

Bilal believes that Turks and Kurds are getting along well in Turkey today. "Kurds have been living here for many years. Turks and Kurds have fought in wars together side by side. There are no

my worldgeography.com On Assignment

Feeding the fish in the courtyard of a famous mosque in Urfa.

Bilal hard at work serving tea

problems between the Kurds and Turks."

Bilal speaks Kurdish with his parents and Turkish with his four brothers and two sisters.

"Turkish has become so widespread," he explains. "Older Kurds did not speak much Turkish, but today we speak more Turkish than Kurdish. Turkish is much more useful."

Bilal has been working since he was nine years old. He goes to school as well. "I work and go to school because it is necessary. In the morning I work in the tea house of a hospital. I serve tea. I go to school in the afternoon."

Bilal's father works day jobs during the winter and grows pistachios in the summer. "There are a lot of pistachios grown in this part of Turkey," Bilal adds with a smile. "I work on the farm all summer when I am not at school."

Bilal's family has only a small plot of land, so they mainly work in his uncle's field. Lack of water is a constant problem on the farm and across Turkey.

"Turkey is surrounded by sea, but salt water is useless," Bilal notes. "Drinking water is scarce. There will be conflict over water.

A statue of the founder of modern Turkey in Bilal's hometown

HAYATTA
EN HAKİKİ MÜRŞİT
İLİMDİR

K. ATATÜRK

Bilal in class

Bilal and his family at dinner

Something must be done about that."

Bilal is concerned about some of the things that lie ahead for his country. He follows current events closely by reading newspapers on the Internet.

"I read the Internet every day," he says. "If we want to see ahead, we have to learn from mistakes and try not repeat them."

Though Bilal worries about the future, he is encouraged by the progress he has already seen. Urfa's new mayor has brought about many changes to the city, according to Bilal.

"The roads here were awful. My younger brothers and sisters always would come home covered in mud. The mayor fixed the roads. He built new green parks and gardens. I believe he will win again next time around."

Bilal really looks forward to his weekends. "I spend most of my time playing soccer. Like everyone else, everywhere, we like to listen to music and play football." A few years ago, Bilal even made plans to move to Istanbul and become a professional soccer player.

"Back then I thought I wanted to be a soccer player," he laughs. "But as time goes by people change. At one time I wanted to become an engineer, but it was not possible. Now I would like to be a historian. As you investigate the distant past, eventually you come to the recent past. When you study the recent past, you can use it to see ahead."

myStory Video

Join Bilal as he shows you more about his life in Turkey.

Meet the Journalist

Name Can Ertür
Favorite Moment Bilal's description of the peaceful world he hopes to live in

A group of young children from Urfa ▼

Section 1

Chapter Atlas

Key Ideas

- Mountains cover much of this region and have a major effect on rainfall patterns and climate.

- The location of water resources is important to land use and settlement patterns.

- Oil and natural gas are important to Iran's economy.

- A variety of ethnic and religious groups call this region home.

Key Terms • strait • shamal • qanat • Zoroastrianism

 Visual Glossary

 Reading Skill: Label an Outline Map Take notes using the outline map in your journal.

▲ Mount Ericyes, in central Turkey

A young Turkish woman ▶

Physical Features

Iran and Turkey form a broad band stretching from the Mediterranean Sea to Afghanistan. South of Turkey, in the Mediterranean, lies the island of Cyprus. Much of this region is mountainous.

Mountains and Seas Turkey is located on two continents, Europe and Asia. Most of Turkey is made up of the peninsula of Anatolia, in Asia. Anatolia is bordered by the Black Sea to the north, the Mediterranean to the south, and a narrow waterway connecting the two seas.

Iran, Turkey, and Cyprus: Physical

Black Sea

Bosporus

Pontic Mts.

ANATOLIAN

PLATEAU

Euphrates River

Taurus Mts.

Aegean Sea

20° E

Mediterranean Sea

Cyprus

40° N

Caspian Sea

Tigris River

Elburz Mts.

IRANIAN

PLATEAU

Kavir Desert

Zagros Mountains

30° N

Strait of Hormuz

Persian Gulf

Gulf of Oman

Arabian Sea

TROPIC OF CANCER

20° N

30° E

40° E

N W E S

Map Skills

Location Which has a higher elevation, the Elburz mountains or the Kavir desert?

Places to Know!
Label the following places on the outline map in your Student Journal: Black Sea, Zagros Mountains, Taurus Moutains, Anatolian Plateau, Cyprus.

→ **Active Atlas**

0   400 mi
0   400 km
Lambert Conformal Conic Projection

KEY
Elevation

Feet	Meters
6,000	1,829
3,000	914
1,000	305
500	152
Sea level	Sea level

—— National border
---- Disputed border

myWorld Activity
Trade Talk for Turkey

my worldgeography.com Active Atlas

A smaller part of Turkey is in Europe. It is divided from Asia by water. The city of Istanbul is split between the two continents. It guards a part of the waterway between the Mediterranean Sea and the Black Sea, a strait called the Bosporus. A **strait** is a narrow body of water that cuts through land, connecting two larger bodies of water. Because of its location on the Bosporus strait, Istanbul has been a major port and trading center for nearly two thousand years.

Two bands of mountains extend across Turkey from east to west along the northern and southern edges of the country. These mountains join in eastern Turkey, where they form a rugged a landscape. The mountains surround the high Anatolian plateau. Narrow plains lie along the coasts.

Like Turkey, Iran is ringed by mountains. They surround a central plateau. Iran's plateau is larger and flatter than Turkey's. It is mostly covered by desert. Iran also has lowlands in the northwest, along the shores of the Caspian Sea, and to the south, along the Persian Gulf.

Similarly, two bands of mountains run across the north and south of Cyprus. Between them lies a highland plateau.

649

vary, *v.,* to be different

A Natural Hazard Earthquakes occur frequently in this region. In recent decades, both Iran and Turkey have been shaken by severe quakes that have killed thousands. After these earthquakes, people have rebuilt buildings or added wall supports. Most do not move away, though. Hundreds of thousands of people live in quake-prone cities, including Istanbul. Some regions that earthquakes often strike have good farmland. Turkey's government has passed laws requiring builders to construct buildings that can withstand earthquakes.

Reading Check Why is Istanbul's location so important?

Climate and Rainfall

Climates <u>vary</u> across Iran and Turkey. Both temperatures and rainfall differ from one area to another. This variation is in large part because of the mountains and the mix of inland and coastal areas.

Iran In northwestern Iran, summers are warm but winters are generally below freezing. People to the south and east have much longer, hotter summers and milder winters. In some areas of Iran, summer temperatures can reach as high as 110°F. Adding to the summer heat are dry winds that blow across the far

Map Skills

1. **Place** Why might central Turkey have a semiarid climate?

2. **Region** Where can the humid subtropical climate zone be found?

→ **Active Atlas**

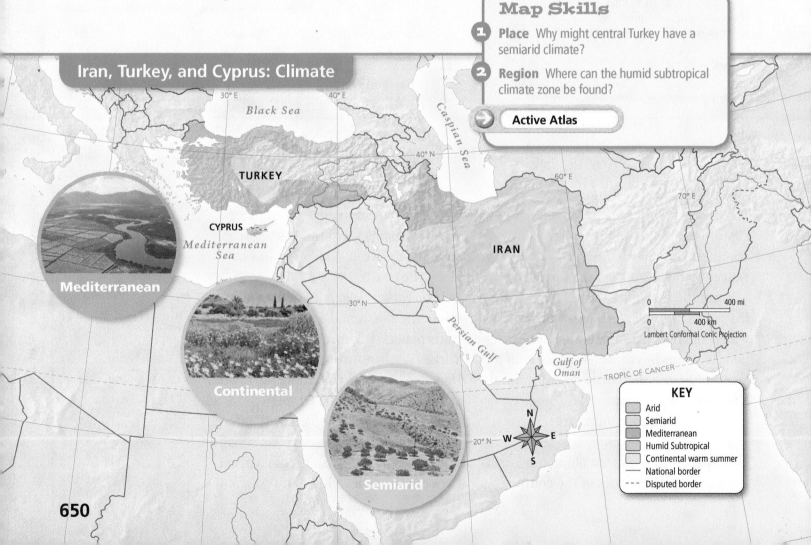

Iran, Turkey, and Cyprus: Climate

Mediterranean

Continental

Semiarid

Black Sea

Caspian Sea

TURKEY

CYPRUS

Mediterranean Sea

IRAN

Persian Gulf

Gulf of Oman

TROPIC OF CANCER

0   400 mi
0   400 km
Lambert Conformal Conic Projection

KEY
- Arid
- Semiarid
- Mediterranean
- Humid Subtropical
- Continental warm summer
- — National border
- --- Disputed border

western part of Iran from northwest to southeast. These winds are called the **shamal.** The shamal and other winds blow almost constantly during the summer. They can start powerful dust storms.

Rainfall in different parts of Iran varies. The wettest area is along the shore of the Caspian Sea. There, moist winds blowing over the sea strike the Elburz Mountains. As the air rises, it cools and drops its moisture on the coastal plain. Areas on the other side of the mountains are a desert that receives little or no rain.

Cyprus and Turkey Cyprus has a Mediterranean climate. Hot, dry summers are followed by milder, rainier winters. Farmers depend on the autumn and winter rains for their crops.

Parts of Turkey also have a typical Mediterranean climate like that of Greece or Lebanon. But seas on three sides and high mountains change climate patterns. Coastal areas tend to have milder winters than interior regions. Winter temperatures can remain around freezing in the central plateau and plunge well below freezing in the eastern mountains.

Coastal areas in Turkey receive more rain than the central plateau or the mountains—32 or more inches a year on the shores of the Black Sea and 24 to 32 inches along the western coast. As in Iran, the mountains create a rain shadow. As a result, the central plateau receives only about 16 inches a year.

Reading Check Why does the central plateau in Turkey receive little rain?

A salt flat in Iran's Kavir desert ▶

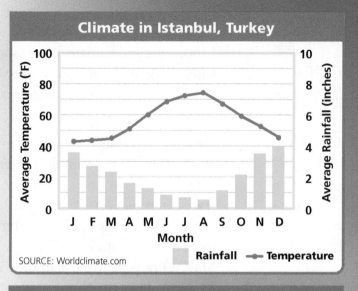

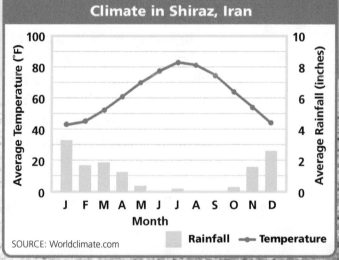

Chart Skills

1 What is the average temperature in Istanbul in November?

2 Do you think Shiraz is located in a semiarid or in a continental climate zone?

Data Discovery

my worldgeography.com Data Discovery

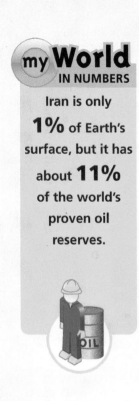
Land Use and Energy

Landforms and climate patterns affect where people live in Iran, Turkey, and Cyprus. Rainfall is especially important.

Settlement Patterns Few people live in the high mountains or in the driest areas of this region. For example, settlements are sparse in Iran's desert interior. Those few people who do live in the desert cluster around oases, where water comes from below the ground to the surface. Most of Iran's people live in the rainier western and northern parts of the country, including the capital Tehran.

In Turkey, more than half of the people live along the narrow coastal plains, especially in the milder and wetter north. The hotter southern coast has fewer people, as does the interior. Similarly, most people in Cyprus live along the coastal plains.

Iran, Turkey, and Cyprus receive more rainfall than most other countries in Southwest Asia, but water is still scarce. In ancient times, the people of Iran developed a clever method for bringing water to their homes and fields. First, they looked in the foothills of mountains for aquifers, or underground sources of water. Then they built tunnels from the aquifers to their villages. These tunnels, called **qanats,** channeled water to their villages. They used the water to irrigate their fields.

The qanat system has an advantage over irrigation channels on the surface. Because most of the channel is below the ground, the water does not dry up, or evaporate, even in Iran's hot climate.

Although qanats are still used today, wells and above-ground irrigation are also widely practiced in Iran. They account for most of the country's water usage. But some people argue that this change has been a mistake. According to one Iranian urban planner and architect,

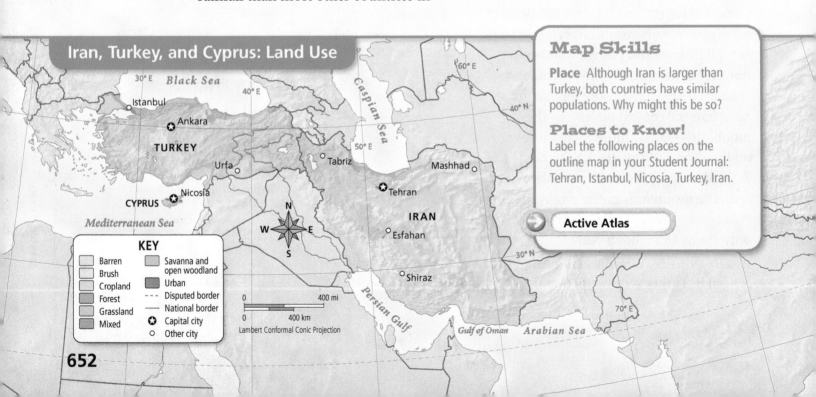

Iran, Turkey, and Cyprus: Land Use

KEY
- Barren
- Brush
- Cropland
- Forest
- Grassland
- Mixed
- Savanna and open woodland
- Urban
- --- Disputed border
- — National border
- ✪ Capital city
- ○ Other city

Lambert Conformal Conic Projection

Map Skills

Place Although Iran is larger than Turkey, both countries have similar populations. Why might this be so?

Places to Know!
Label the following places on the outline map in your Student Journal: Tehran, Istanbul, Nicosia, Turkey, Iran.

Active Atlas

> " in comparison to qanats, wells have a shorter life span (that is between 20–50 years), whereas qanats hold good for centuries. Excavation of such wells in the past half a century has further led to the drying up of wells and qanats both, contributing to drought and increasing water shortages "
>
> —Mohammad Reza Haeri

Oil and Natural Gas In today's world, oil and natural gas are also precious resources. Iran has large deposits of both fuels. It has more oil than all but four countries, and has 10 percent of the world's natural gas. Iran's oil is a vital source of national income. Oil sales provide more than 85 percent of the government's income.

Turkey has very little oil and must import most of its fuel. It does have coal and generates hydroelectric power from mountain rivers. Cyprus has few energy resources but uses its sunny climate to make solar power.

Reading Check What important resources are plentiful in Iran?

An oil refinery in Iran. Oil is by far Iran's most important export.

Iran's Exports

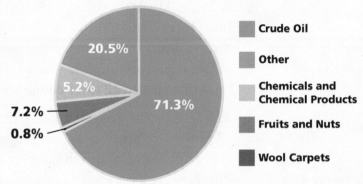

- Crude Oil
- Other
- Chemicals and Chemical Products
- Fruits and Nuts
- Wool Carpets

71.3%
20.5%
5.2%
7.2%
0.8%

SOURCE: *Time Alamanac*, 2009

Chart Skills

What percentage of Iran's exports does crude oil make up?

Data Discovery

◀ A rose farm in Iran

my worldgeography.com Active Atlas

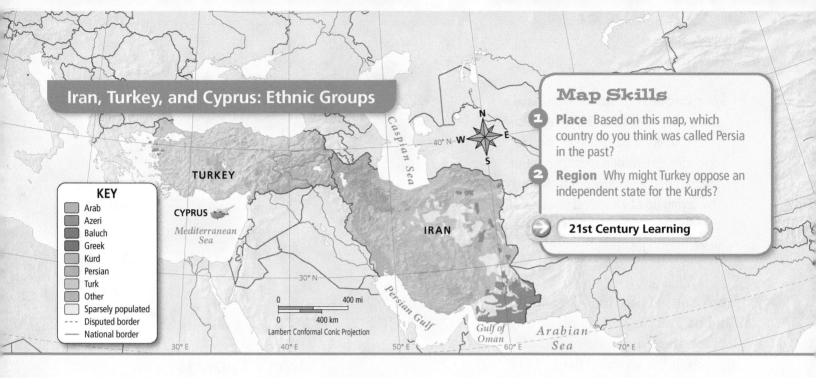

Iran, Turkey, and Cyprus: Ethnic Groups

KEY
- Arab
- Azeri
- Baluch
- Greek
- Kurd
- Persian
- Turk
- Other
- Sparsely populated
- - - - Disputed border
- —— National border

TURKEY

CYPRUS

Mediterranean Sea

Caspian Sea

IRAN

Persian Gulf

Gulf of Oman

Arabian Sea

0   400 mi
0   400 km
Lambert Conformal Conic Projection

Map Skills

1 **Place** Based on this map, which country do you think was called Persia in the past?

2 **Region** Why might Turkey oppose an independent state for the Kurds?

→ **21st Century Learning**

Ethnicity and Religion

Iran, Turkey, and Cyprus are ethnically diverse. More than 97 percent of people in this region are Muslims, but religious minorities live in all three countries.

Turkey The Turkish government defi es all people in Turkey as Turks. It does not recognize separate ethnic groups. But there are large ethnic minorities in Turkey. About 80 percent of the people in Turkey are ethnic Turks, while about 20 percent are Kurds. Small numbers of people from other ethnic groups, such as Arabs and Greeks, also live in Turkey.

The Kurdish people live in a region that is split among Iran, Turkey, Iraq, and Syria. Many Kurds in these countries seek independence or self-government.

A Christian priest in Cyprus ▼

Muslim worshipers in Turkey ▼

654

In the past, Turkey banned all expressions of Kurdish culture. The government fought Kurdish rebels who wanted their own independent country. Recently, Turkey has given the Kurds more rights and the situation has improved.

Most people in Turkey are Sunni Muslims. About a quarter are Alevis, who practice a form of Shia Islam. Smaller groups include Christian Greeks and Armenians, along with Jews.

Iran In the past Iran was called Persia. Today just over half of Iranians are ethnic Persians. About a quarter of people in Iran are Azeris. They live mainly near neighboring Azerbaijan, a mostly Azeri country. Several million Kurds also live in Iran.

Nearly all people in Iran are Muslims. Almost 9 in 10 practice Shia Islam. Sunnis are a minority. Jews and Christians, who have lived in Iran since ancient times, form much smaller minorities. Today, more Jews live in Iran and Turkey

◀ A Zoroastrian fire temple in Iran

than in any other Muslim countries.

A very small number of Iranians practice **Zoroastrianism,** an Iranian religion that dates back to ancient times. Many more practice the Baha'i faith, which was founded in Iran in the 1800s.

Cyprus People who live in Cyprus are called Cypriots. About three quarters of Cypriots are Greek-speaking Christians. The rest are Turkish-speaking Muslims. Confl ct between these groups has occurred in recent <u>decades</u>.

Reading Check **Which large minority group is found in both Iran and Turkey?**

decade, *n.,* period of ten years

Section **1** Assessment

? Essential Question

What are the challenges of diversity?

Key Terms

1. How does the rain shadow affect climate in Iran and Turkey?

2. What are qanats, and why are they important?

Key Ideas

3. How do people in Turkey adapt to living in an earthquake-prone area?

4. How have landforms and climate influenced where people live in these countries?

5. How does the religious makeup of Iran show the long history of this region?

Think Critically

6. Compare and Contrast How are the landforms of Turkey and Iran similar? How are they different?

7. Analyze Cause and Effect Why do these countries have ethnic diversity?

8. What political issues have arisen from the ethnic diversity of these countries? Go to your Student Journal to record your answer.

Section 2
History of Iran, Turkey, and Cyprus

Key Ideas

- The countries in this region are at a cultural crossroads, blending influences from many different regions and peoples.

- Civilizations of this region have made important contributions to world culture.

- In the 1900s, empires in this region fell and were replaced by modern nations.

Key Terms
- satrap
- millet
- shah
- Armenian genocide
- Ataturk
- Ayatollah

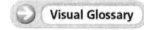 Visual Glossary

Reading Skill: Sequence Take notes using the graphic organizer in your journal.

◀ The Persian emperor Darius

As you have read, Iran used to be called Persia. Ancient Persia was influenced by Mesopotamian civilization, in modern-day Iraq.

The Persian Empire

Around 550 b.c., the Persian king Cyrus the Great conquered the Babylonian empire, in Mesopotamia, and many other lands. He created the Persian empire.

Cyrus and the rulers who followed him spread Persian control from modern Pakistan and Afghanistan in the east to modern Turkey, Cyprus, and Egypt in the west. Th s empire lasted about two hundred years. A Persian ruler was called the King of Kings, or the Great King.

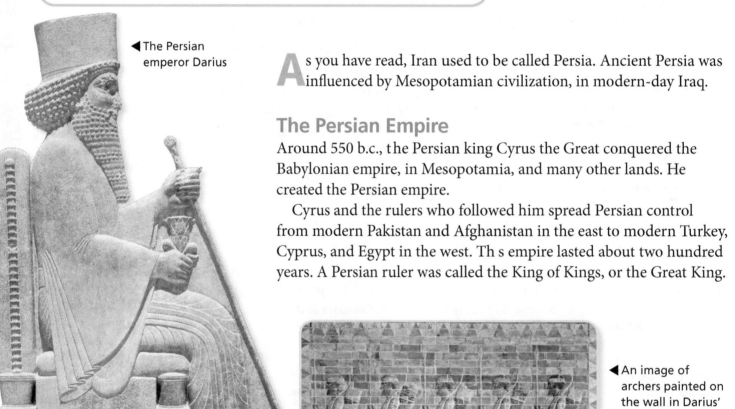

◀ An image of archers painted on the wall in Darius' palace at Susa

Government and Trade To control their empire, Persian rulers sent a governor, called a **satrap,** to run each province. A general commanded the army in each area. A third official collected taxes. By splitting power, rulers made sure no satrap grew too powerful. They also regularly sent inspectors to observe these officials and report back to the king.

The Persians built a system of roads to improve communication across their empire. The roads made travel faster for soldiers and messengers sent by the government. They also made it easier for merchants to carry goods.

To help people from far-away regions trade fairly with one another, the Persians created a system of weights and measures. They also minted, or produced, coins that could be used across the empire.

Life in the Persian Empire Although they were feared conquerors, the Persians were not overly harsh rulers. They respected local traditions, though at the same time they were willing to crush revolts brutally.

Art flourished under Persian rule. Kings brought artists and craft people to their capital. They built large palaces decorated with sculptures and jewels.

Conquest by Alexander the Great The Persian empire met its match in Alexander the Great. In the 330s b.c., Alexander led armies from Greece into Persia. He conquered the Persian empire.

Alexander adopted some customs of Persian rulers. For example, he wore Persian-style clothing. Alexander planned to

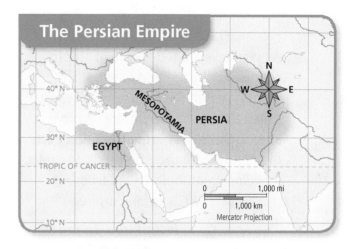

The Persian Empire

rule with Persian help. However, after his sudden death, his empire broke up into smaller kingdoms ruled by Greek kings.

These kingdoms spread Greek culture in the region. Much of modern-day Turkey became Greek-speaking. Eventually these Greek kingdoms fell too.

A new Persian empire, called the Sassanian empire, took their place. That empire dominated Iran for four hundred years. The Sassanian rulers made Zoroastrianism their official religion, though many Jews and Christians lived under their rule.

Reading Check **How did the Persians govern their empire?**

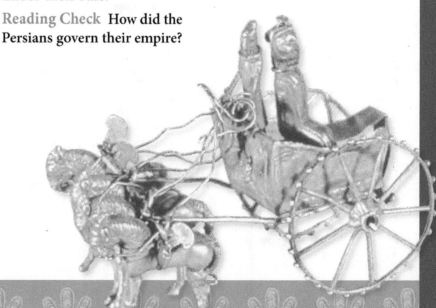

A gold model of a chariot from the Persian empire ▼

Romans, Arabs, and Turks

As you have read, the Roman empire conquered Turkey and Cyprus. The eastern part of the Roman empire, usually called the Byzantine empire, survived after the western part fell. It ruled parts of the region until the A.D 1400s. Is capital was Constantinople, called Istanbul today. It was a Christian empire.

establish, v., to found or build

The Arab Conquest of Iran
In the 600s, Muhammad began to preach Islam in Arabia. His followers spread Islam in many regions. They defeated the Sassanian empire and conquered Iran.

Over time, most Iranians converted to Islam. Iran became a vital part of Muslim economic and cultural life. The fi st madrassas, or Islamic religious schools, were founded there in the 900s before spreading to other areas. However, ethnic pride remained strong in Iran. Its native language and culture survived.

The Ottoman Empire
In the 1000s, Muslim Turks from Central Asia migrated into Turkey and Iran and began to gain power. They spread their language and culture. They gave the country of Turkey its name.

The Turks established kingdoms in the region. By the 1400s, the kingdom of the Turkish Ottoman family became the most powerful. The Ottomans claimed to be caliphs, or religious leaders of all Muslims. They captured Constantinople, and ended the Byzantine empire, in 1453. The Ottomans made Constantinople, now called Istanbul, their capital. They built an

---

Map Skills

1. **Place** Which empire ruled the Islamic holy cities of Mecca and Medina?

2. **Region** Which empire was based in Persia?

→ **Active Atlas**

The Ottoman and Safavid Empires

KEY
- Ottoman empire, 1566
- Safavid empire, 1629
- ○ City

0   400 mi
0   400 km
Miller Cylindrical Projection

empire that spread over three continents.

The Muslim Ottomans ruled over many Jews and Christians. They allowed their subjects to practice their own religions. Some Jews and Christians rose to high positions in the government. Religious groups were organized into **millets,** or self-governing religious communities. Millets had their own laws and leaders.

Perhaps the greatest Ottoman ruler was Suleiman the Magnifice t, who conquered much of southeastern Europe. In the 1500s, Suleiman was probably the richest ruler in the world, and one of the most powerful. He built mosques, schools, and libraries. His court was a center of art and culture.

The Safavids In the 1500s, the Safavid empire rose in Iran. It fought several large wars with the Ottomans. The Safavid ruler was called a **shah,** the Persian word for king. The Safavids made Shia Islam the offi al religion of Iran. Th s set Iran apart from its Sunni neighbors.

Iranian art and architecture reached new heights under Safavid rule. The Safavids built a magnifice t capital in Esfahan. It was famous for its dazzling mosques and beautiful fl wer gardens.

Reading Check **What religion did the Ottomans practice?**

Hagia Sophia

For centuries, Hagia Sophia was the most famous church of the Byzantine empire. It was built in Constantinople, which is today called Istanbul. It became a model for many other churches. After the Ottomans captured the city, they turned the Church into a mosque called Ayasofya. Today the building is a museum. You can see the influences of both faiths in its decoration.

Christian Influence
Mosaics showing scenes from the Christian Bible, such as the painting of Mary and Jesus at the left

Muslim Influence
Panels painted with verses from the Quran written in Arabic calligraphy

myWorld Activity
History Detectives

my worldgeography.com Active Atlas

Empires Collapse in the Modern Age

By the 1800s, old empires in Turkey and Iran were losing power rapidly. European countries began to influence affairs in the region. But nationalists in Turkey and Iran opposed them.

Last Days of the Ottoman Empire In the early 1900s, a group of army officers called the Young Turks took power in the Ottoman empire. They wanted to create a secular nation, like those of Europe. They sided with Germany in World War I.

Though the Ottoman empire was mostly tolerant of minorities, Armenian Christians faced persecution before World War I. During the war, when some Armenians sided with Russia, the empire's enemy, Turkish soldiers forced large numbers of Armenian civilians from their homes onto long marches. The soldiers killed many, and caused the death of others from starvation and disease. Between 600,000 and 1,500,000 Armenians died. The killing of Armenians by Turkish leaders from 1915 to 1918 is called the **Armenian genocide.** The leaders of modern Turkey do not use this term. They deny the Turkish government's responsibility for the killings.

Turkey Forms After the Ottoman empire and its allies lost World War I, the empire collapsed. European powers took control of some of its lands. They tried to take control of Turkey itself, too. But a Turkish army officer named Mustafa Kemal led forces to save Turkey's independence.

Under Kemal's rule, Turkey became a republic. Kemal tried to modernize Turkey and to westernize it, or to make it more European. Kemal made Turkey a secular state. That is, government was strictly separated from religion. Women were given more rights. People were encouraged to wear European clothes. Language and writing were reformed.

Kemal ruled using undemocratic methods. Still, many of his reforms won great respect from the Turkish people. He called himself **Ataturk,** which means "Father of the Turks." Most Turks today consider him a national hero.

A New Iran Around the beginning of the 1900s, the dynasty that ruled Iran was in trouble. It had run out of money. Russia and Britain controlled Iran's oil resources and influenced the government. Many Iranians resented this situation.

In the 1920s, a military leader named Reza Pahlavi overthrew the government

A Turkish Republic Day parade ▼

Mustafa Kemal Ataturk ▼

of Iran. He made himself shah. He tried to modernize and westernize Iran.

After 1941, his son, Mohammad Reza Pahlavi, continued this work. He became a close ally of the United States. In 1953, an elected government threw out the shah, but he returned with American help. The shah became a more oppressive ruler. He created a powerful secret police force that arrested or killed critics of his rule.

Revolution in Iran The shah's repressive policies created opposition. One leading critic of the shah was a Shia religious leader named Ayatollah Ruhollah Khomeini. **Ayatollah** is a title for high-ranking Shia leaders in Iran. Khomeini opposed the shah's efforts to make Iran more like western countries. He wanted Iran to follow Islamic law and traditions. The shah forced Khomeini to leave Iran, but the Ayatollah's attacks continued.

In 1978, a revolution broke out. Iranians took to the streets to protest the shah's rule. When the shah ordered troops to attack the protestors, this

Protesters hold a poster of Khomeini during the Iranian Revolution.

provoked even more protests. Eventually, the shah and his family fled, and his government collapsed. In February 1979, Khomeini returned and took power.

Reading Check What happened to the shah's government?

Section 2 Assessment

Key Terms
1. What is a satrap? What function did satraps perform?
2. What is a secular state?

Key Ideas
3. How did the rulers of the Persian empire encourage trade?
4. How did Iran contribute to Muslim cultural life?
5. What were the goals of Mustafa Kemal Ataturk's reforms?

Think Critically
6. **Analyze Cause and Effect** What effect did Alexander's conquest have on the culture of the region?
7. **Compare and Contrast** How were the new governments formed in Turkey and Iran in the early 1900s similar? How were they different?

Essential Question
What are the challenges of diversity?
8. What role did national feeling play in the creation of modern Turkey and Iran? Go to your Student Journal to record your answer.

Iran, Turkey, and Cyprus Today

Key Ideas	• Iran's government is a theocracy, while Turkey and Cyprus are democracies.	between tradition and modernity while it seeks greater economic ties with Europe.	• The island of Cyprus has been divided by conflict between Greeks and Turks.
	• Turkey's culture is split		

Key Terms • Majlis • cleric • brain drain • coup

 Visual Glossary

Reading Skill: Identify Main Ideas Take notes using the graphic organizer in your journal.

▼ Ayatollah Ali Khamenei, Supreme Leader of Iran

662

After the 1979 Iranian revolution, a government that was dedicated to following Islamic law took power. The people of Iran have some say in their government, but lack many important rights.

The Islamic Republic of Iran

Iran's government is a theocracy in which religious leaders hold great power. Laws must follow Islam as it is interpreted by these leaders.

Structure of Iran's Theocracy The head of Iran's government is a religious figu e called the Supreme Leader. He must approve all major government policies. He is the head of the military. Revolutionary leader Ayatollah Ruhollah Khomeini was the fi st Supreme Leader.

Iran's voters elect a president and a legislature, called the **Majlis.** The Majlis passes the laws for the president to carry out. The president is sometimes better known outside Iran than the Supreme Leader, but the Supreme Leader is more powerful.

The Supreme Leader names six of the twelve members of a body called the Guardian Council. All members of the council are **clerics,** or religious leaders. The Council reviews all laws passed by the Majlis. It vetoes any that it believes violate Islamic law. The Guardian Council also decides who can run for offi . It uses this power to block candidates who want to change the system of government.

Rights and Restrictions on Citizens

Iranians have the right to vote. The constitution guarantees other rights as well. However, Iran's government places many limits on people's freedom. It restricts freedom of speech and freedom of the press, or newspapers and other media. The government can close newspapers and imprison journalists. It also sometimes imprisons or executes people who oppose the government.

As well, Iranian women and men do not have fully equal rights. Harsh punishments can be applied to people who violate certain moral codes established by the government.

Reform and Opposition

Many Iranians are unhappy with their government. Even some clerics oppose government policies. They work within the current system to reform it. One reformist cleric, Mohammed Khatami, was elected president by a large majority in 1997. He carried out some changes, but many of his reforms were stopped by the Supreme Leader and Guardian Council. Iranians who supported reform were disappointed.

> 66 We thought that Mr. Khatami's victory was a victory for us as well. The election of a more democratic government seemed to be a bright new beginning . . . But within less than a year of the election, the journalists, reformists and intellectuals began to be persecuted by hard-liners in the judiciary and Intelligence Ministry . . . 99
>
> —Camella Entekhabifard, "Tehran's Eternal Youth," *The New York Times*

Some Iranians hold public protests, risking imprisonment or death. In 1999 and 2003, many students protested. In 2009, reformists claimed that an election had been rigged against their candidate. They held the largest street protests since the revolution. The government used violence against the protesters, killing many.

Reading Check **Does the Supreme Leader or the president of Iran have more power?**

◄ Iranian students protest against their government's restriction of the press.

Iran and the United States

Iran has had difficult relations with the United States. After the revolution, many Iranians were angry with the United States for supporting the shah. Iranian students attacked the American embassy and held Americans inside hostage for 444 days. Relations between the two countries have been tense ever since.

Another issue has been Iran's nuclear program. Iran says it needs nuclear energy. But the United States and other countries fear it is trying to develop nuclear weapons. The United States has tried to convince other countries to stop trading with Iran until it shows that it is not building nuclear weapons.

The United States government also accuses Iran of supporting groups that have attacked both Israel and United States troops in Iraq.

Reading Check **Why do some countries object to Iran's nuclear energy program?**

The Economy of Iran

Iran's economy is dominated by oil. Money from oil sales brings in most of the government's income. But the economy is still weak.

Economic Problems Unemployment is a major problem in Iran. In 2008, one in every eight workers was out of work. High rates of population growth contribute to unemployment. The economy has not grown fast enough to provide jobs for all of Iran's people.

In recent years, inflation, or the rise in prices from year to year, has been another problem. Rising prices mean that people can buy fewer goods with their money.

The lack of freedom and economic opportunity in Iran have a cost. Perhaps as many as 1.5 million Iranians have left their country since the 1979 revolution. Many of them are highly educated. Educated people leaving a place is called a **brain drain**. These migrants hope to fi d more opportunity and freedom in other places. Iranian immigrants have built prosperous communities in other countries, including the United States.

Industries A major industry in Iran is the petrochemical industry, which turns crude oil into different products. Iran also makes automobiles, appliances, steel, paper and rubber, medicines, and textiles. For centuries, craft orkers in Iran have been famous for their skill in making beautiful hand-woven rugs. Weavers carry on that traditional work today.

Reading Check **Why do many educated Iranians leave their country?**

A poor neighborhood on the outskirts of Tehran, Iran.

Closer Look

Iranian Art and Architecture

A scene from the Iranian movie
Children of Heaven

The Imam Mosque in Esfahan ▼

Iranians today are proud of the beautiful art Iran has produced throughout the ages. Iranian culture has had a large influence on the cultures of neighboring countries. For example, Iranian architecture has been widely imitated in Central and South Asia, while Iranian painting influenced Ottoman art. Today, Iranian movies receive international praise and win prestigious awards, as do movies made by Iranians living abroad.

THINK CRITICALLY **How did Iranian culture influence the cultures of other countries?**

A man painting in a traditional style ▼

Turkey: Connections to Europe and the Middle East

Turkey bridges Southwest Asia and Europe. It is a mostly Muslim country with strong connections to Europe.

Turkey's Democracy Turkey is a democracy led by a president and prime minister. Its constitution forbids discrimination and guarantees important human rights for all Turkish citizens.

Voters elect the 550 members of the legislature, which passes laws. The president can challenge laws. He or she can also send laws to the constitutional court for review. If the judges of that court believe a law <u>violates</u> the constitution, they can strike down the law.

One issue in Turkish democracy is the power of the military. The army is a very important institution in Turkish society. It has overthrown four civilian governments since the Turkish Republic was founded in 1923. When the military uses force to overthrow a government, it is called a **coup.**

Another issue is a law that makes it a crime to "insult the Turkish nation." This law is opposed by human rights activists.

Some people who write about subjects that offend the government have been put on trial under this law. Turkish nationalism remains a very strong force in society.

A Secular State Turkey's constitution separates the nation's government from Islam. The military is strongly in favor of secularism, or nonreligious government. It helped force out a government it did not consider secular enough in 1997.

In recent years, a political party that embraces Islam more closely has grown popular. It is called the Justice and Development Party. Its initials are AKP in Turkish. In 2003, an AKP member became prime minister. Some feared that the military would overthrow the AKP government.

AKP leaders have promised they will keep Turkey a secular state. Some Turks are not convinced. In 2008, the party passed a controversial law that allowed women who wear traditional headscarves to attend universities, which the government runs. In the past the scarves had been banned at universities because they were thought to violate the government's secular character.

violate, *v.,* to break a rule or law

Istanbul Today
With more than twelve million people, Istanbul is Turkey's largest city. Istanbul and its suburbs span two continents. ▼

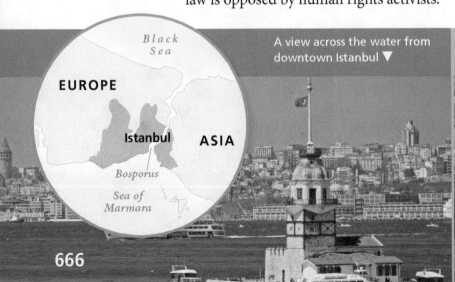

A view across the water from downtown Istanbul ▼

Hagia Sophia, Istanbul's most famous landmark ▼

Some Turks strongly opposed the law. One opposition leader even challenged the AKP in Turkey's constitutional court. He said that the party should be banned because it is not secular. The court disagreed and the AKP continued to govern.

Turkey's Culture Today Turkey's culture shows European and Asian influences. Most urban men and women, and most rural men, for instance, wear Western-style clothing. Rural women often wear traditional Middle Eastern clothes.

Women's roles in Turkish society show similar differences. In rural areas women generally do not work outside of their homes. In cities, women can be found in many occupations. A woman was Turkey's prime minister in the 1990s.

Life in Istanbul is very different from life in rural Turkey. Istanbul today is a modern city with skyscrapers and a busy port, though there are also traditional areas. Many people have moved to Istanbul from the countryside in search of jobs and a higher standard of living.

Reading Check What role does Turkey's military play in its government?

Turkey's Economy

Unlike Iran, Turkey does not have large deposits of oil that it can sell to bring in money. It has a more mixed economy, with agriculture, industry, and services all playing important roles.

Development For many decades, Turkey has lagged behind European nations economically. One reason is that agriculture has been a large sector in the economy, and farming does not usually lead to high incomes. In addition, the government used to run many industries. These industries were not very productive. Turkey also set up barriers to trade with other nations. These barriers prevented Turks from importing low-cost goods to improve their standard of living.

Starting in the 1980s, Turkey made changes. It removed trade barriers and became more active in importing and exporting goods. It cut the government's role in the economy and made it easier for private companies to form. As a result, the economy has grown rapidly in most recent years. People are more productive and enjoy higher incomes.

occupation, *n.,* job or profession

my worldgeography.com   Culture Close-up

Culture Close-up

A traditional crafts market in Istanbul ▼

Modern Istanbul's business district ▼

Turkey's Trade Partners

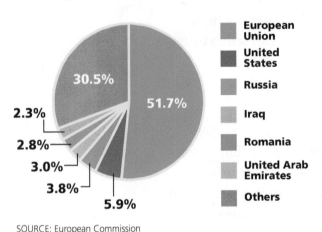

- European Union — 51.7%
- United States — 30.5%
- Russia
- Iraq
- Romania
- United Arab Emirates
- Others

- 51.7%
- 30.5%
- 2.3%
- 2.8%
- 3.0%
- 3.8%
- 5.9%

SOURCE: European Commission

A woman weaving a decorated textile in Turkey. Textiles are one of Turkey's major exports.

Chart Skills

1. Does Turkey trade more with Russia or the United Arab Emirates?
2. Based on this graph, do you think Turkey's economy is more closely tied to Europe or to Southwest Asia?

Data Discovery

myWorld Activity
To Join or Not
To Join

The European Union Turkey's government has attempted to join the European Union (EU). Turks who support this argue that it will improve the economy by allowing Turkey to trade more freely with Europe. But not all members of the EU are willing to admit Turkey. Some criticize Turkey's record on human rights, especially its treatment of Kurds and its role in Cyprus. Many Turks resent this criticism. Some fear that joining the EU will force Turkey to change its policies. Still, Turkey continues to move slowly towards EU membership.

Reading Check **Why do some EU nations object to admitting Turkey?**

Divided Cyprus

Confli t between Greeks and Turks has been a problem on Cyprus for decades.

Violence and Invasion Cyprus gained its independence from Great Britain in 1960. The new republic faced difficulties from the start. Many people in the Greek majority wanted Cyprus to become a part of Greece. Turkish Cypriots feared Greece would not protect their rights. They opposed unifi ation. They also resented Greek domination of the government of Cyprus. Greeks and Turks fought bitterly.

Events came to a boil in 1974. At that time a dictatorship held power in Greece. It sponsored an attempt to overthrow the government of Cyprus so that the island would join with Greece.

In response, Turkey invaded the island and soon controlled its northern third. The Greek-dominated Republic of Cyprus held the rest. During and after the invasion, tens of thousands of Greek and Turkish Cypriots were forced from their

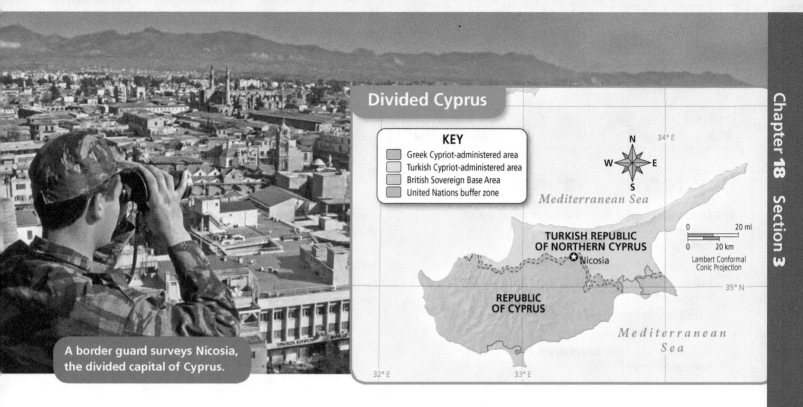

Divided Cyprus

KEY
Greek Cypriot-administered area
Turkish Cypriot-administered area
British Sovereign Base Area
United Nations buffer zone

Mediterranean Sea

TURKISH REPUBLIC OF NORTHERN CYPRUS
⊗ Nicosia

REPUBLIC OF CYPRUS

Mediterranean Sea

0   20 mi
0   20 km
Lambert Conformal
Conic Projection

A border guard surveys Nicosia, the divided capital of Cyprus.

homes. About one third of all people in Cyprus were displaced.

Continuing Divisions In 1983, Turkish Cypriots declared independence. They formed the Turkish Republic of Northern Cyprus. Turkey is the only nation in the world that recognizes this government.

Turkish troops remain in the northern part of the island. UN peacekeepers patrol a buffer zone that separates the two parts of the island. Movement between them was closed off u til 2003.

Many efforts have been made to reunite the island. These have not yet succeeded. In 2004, Turkish Cypriots voted in favor of a reunifi ation plan, but Greek Cypriots voted against it. Cyprus joined the EU without the Turkish north.

Reading Check How is Cyprus divided?

Section 3 Assessment

Key Terms

1. What is the role of clerics in Iran's government?

2. What happens during a military coup?

Key Ideas

3. Is Iran's government an example of rule by many, by few, or a combination? Explain your answer.

4. Why was the AKP challenged in court, and what was the result?

5. What new economic policies did Turkey adopt in the 1980s?

Think Critically

6. **Analyze Cause and Effect** What has caused Iran's brain drain?

7. **Compare and Contrast** How do women's rights compare in Iran and Turkey?

Essential Question

What are the challenges of diversity?

8. What political conflict has arisen in Turkey as a result of different views about religion? Go to your Student Journal to record your answer.

Chapter Assessment

Key Terms and Ideas

1. **Summarize** How does the location of water resources affect settlement patterns in Iran, Turkey, and Cyprus?

2. **Compare and Contrast** How is Iran's government today different than the government before the Revolution of 1979?

3. **Recall** What resources are most important to Iran's economy?

4. **Describe** Has Iran's **brain drain** been good or bad for the country?

5. **Recall** List the majority ethnic and religious group in each of Iran, Turkey, and Cyprus.

6. **Describe** How did the founding of modern Turkey affect that country's laws and culture?

7. **Explain** Why is Cyprus divided and how did the division happen?

Think Critically

8. **Compare and Contrast** What are some aspects of Turkey's government that could be considered more democratic and less democratic?

9. **Make Inferences** Why might the United States and other countries be worried by Iran seeking nuclear weapons?

10. **Solve Problems** What did the Turkish government do in the 1980s to improve its economy?

11. **Core Concepts: Cultural Diffusion and Change** How did the ancient Persians and later Arab Muslims change the region's culture?

Places to Know

For each place, write the letter from the map that shows its location.

12. Cyprus
13. Istanbul
14. Turkey
15. Iran
16. Tehran
17. Black Sea
18. **Estimate** Using the scale, estimate the distance between Istanbul and Tehran.

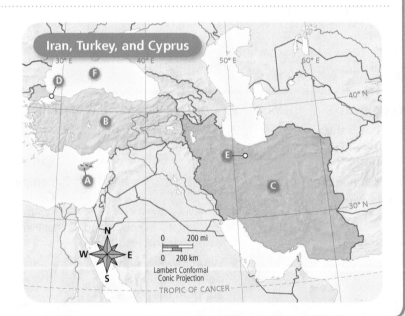

Iran, Turkey, and Cyprus

Essential Question

What are the challenges of diversity?

Regional Ethnic Cooperation Conference
Suppose you represent either an ethnic group or a government in Turkey, Iran, or Cyprus. You will attend a United Nations conference to exchange ideas and present a plan of action for addressing common problems.

21st Century Learning

Solve Problems

Suppose you are working to help people in Cyprus end their conflict. Develop a list of questions you could ask people you meet in Cyprus. Focus your questions on helping those you interview to identify actions or changes in attitude that they feel would lead Greek and Turkish Cypriots to more effective efforts at peace.

Document-Based Questions

Success Tracker™
Online at myworldgeography.com

Use your knowledge of Iran, Turkey, and Cyprus, as well as Documents A and B to answer Questions 1–3.

Document A

Individual Freedom		
Country	Individual Freedom Rank*	Government Type
Israel	29	Democracy
Turkey	61	Democracy
Iran	125	Theocracy
Saudi Arabia	130	Absolute monarchy

SOURCE: The State of World Liberty Project
* The freest country in the world is ranked 1.
  The least free is ranked 159.

Document B

" There are two countries in the Middle East that offer models for the future: the democratic Republic of Turkey and the Islamic Republic of Iran."

—Bernard Lewis,
Middle East historian

1. According to the table, which country provides its citizens with the least individual freedom?

   A Saudi Arabia

   B Iran

   C Turkey

   D Israel

2. Which statement best restates the views in Document B?

   A Turkey and Iran have similar governments.

   B Turkey is a theocracy and Iran is a monarchy.

   C Turkish democracy and Iranian theocracy are two paths other countries might follow.

   D Iran gives citizens more freedom than Turkey.

3. **Writing Task** Write a paragraph comparing the governments of Iran, Turkey, and one other country in Southwest Asia that you have studied.

Sharing the Wealth:
How the Oil Rich Can Help the Oil Poor

Your Mission Divide into at least two groups. Research and develop a proposal for ways that oil-rich countries can help oil-poor countries. Each group should listen to the other groups' proposals. Together, the groups then develop one proposal that everyone can accept.

Imagine a group of friends in which half the people receive very large allowances and the other half receive hardly any allowance at all. The friends who have money would be able to do activities and buy things that the others can't afford. Resentments might build up over time. Keeping friendships intact in such a group might be difficult.

Southwest Asia faces a similar situation. Several of the nations earn enormous wealth from exporting oil, while other nations in the region have much lower incomes. Because of this economic gap, the nations of this region develop at different rates. Such a situation could lead to instability in the region.

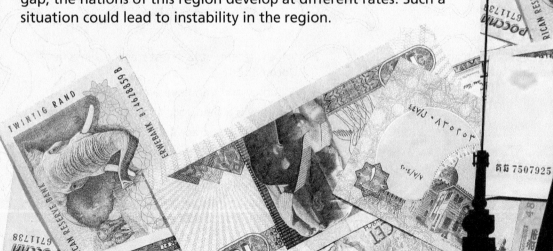

Oil Production: Jordan and Saudi Arabia

9.2 million

Oil Production (barrels per day)

0

Jordan   Saudi Arabia

SOURCE: *CIA World Factbook*

An oil refinery in Saudi Arabia ▼

STEP 1

Research the Problem.

Identify which countries in Southwest Asia are oil-poor (OP) and which are oil-rich (OR). If your group represents an OP country, research the economic and social conditions there. Consider how an OP nation might expand existing resources or attract foreign investment. If your group represents an OR country, research how you might use your nation's advantages to help a neighbor with fewer resources. Discuss ways in which helping your neighbor will also benefit you.

STEP 2

Make a Decision.

After both groups have made their presentations, discuss the two sets of ideas. The research and the proposals from the two groups may not agree. However, before you reject a proposal entirely, think about how you might use certain elements and work them into a new solution that benefits both OP and OR nations. Remember that part of your task as a combined group is to come up with a compromise plan that both sides can accept. Discuss how to present the new proposal.

STEP 3

Present Your Ideas.

After you have finished your research and discussion, prepare a presentation with the new plan. Your presentation should explain your group's ideas about how OR countries can help OP countries. Use graphs, charts, photographs, maps, diagrams, and quotations to support your proposal. When you are ready to make your presentation, your teacher will pair OP representatives with OR representatives. The paired groups should then make their presentations to each other.

my worldgeography.com 21st Century Learning

Regional Overview

South and Central Asia

South and Central Asia are regions of grasslands, deserts, huge lakes, and mountains. The mountainous Himalayas dominate the area. Extremes of climate characterize these regions, with heavy monsoon rains in South Asia and desert climates in Central Asia.

What time is it there?

Washington, D.C.	Palampur, India
9 A.M. Monday	7:30 P.M. Monday

GEORGIA
Tbilisi
ARMENIA
Yerevan
Caspian Sea
Baku
AZERBAIJAN
Ashgabat
TURKMENISTAN
UZBEKISTAN
Tashkent
Astana
KAZAKHSTAN
Bishkek
KYRGYZSTAN
Dushanbe
TAJIKISTAN
AFGHANISTAN
Kabul
Islamabad
PAKISTAN
New Delhi
NEPAL
Kathmandu
BHUTAN
Thimphu
Dhaka
INDIA
BANGLADESH
Arabian Sea
Bay of Bengal
Colombo
SRI LANKA
Male
MALDIVES
INDIAN OCEAN

60° N
ARCTIC CIRCLE
30° N
TROPIC OF CANCER
EQUATOR
60° E
90° E
120° E

KEY
- - - Disputed border
— National border
✪ Capital city
Orthographic Projection

The Unit Ahead

my worldgeography.com

Plan your trip online by doing a Data Discovery Activity and watching the myStory Videos of the region's teens.

my Story

Askar

Age: 15

Home: Naryn, Kyrgyzstan

Chapter 12

my Story

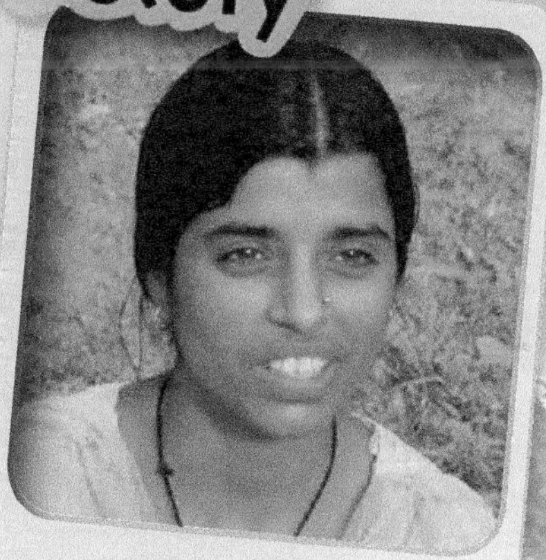

Nancy

Age: 18

Home: Palampur, India

Chapter 13

View of the Himalayas

675

The Caspian Sea is the largest landlocked body of water in the world.

Kirghiz Steppe

Syr Dar'ya

Aral Sea

Amu Dar'ya

Caspian Sea

Kara-Kum Desert

Himalayas

Indus River

Persian Gulf

The Kara-Kum Desert occupies most of Turkmenistan.

Arabian Sea

676

The Himalayas are the highest mountains on Earth.

Himalayas

Ganges River

Indo-Gangetic Plain

The Indo-Gangetic Plain stretches from the Ganges River delta to the Indus River valley.

Regional Flyover

Buckle your seatbelt for a quick flight around South and Central Asia. As your plane lifts off from Calcutta, India, look down to see the waters of the huge Ganges-Brahmaputra delta, the largest delta in the world. Traveling northwest you follow the curve of the mountains known as the Himalayas. After you've crossed the Hindu Kush mountain range, you eventually see the Syr Dar'ya River in Kazakhstan.

Now you're flying west over a vast desert that stretches to the Caspian Sea. When you reach the Caucasus on the west bank of the Caspian, your plane turns and heads back east to cross the Kara-Kum Desert in Turkmenistan. Notice how the ground rises again as you approach Afghanistan. Eventually you see this mountainous area plunging down to the lowlands of the Indus River in Pakistan and the Thar Desert. As you cross India's Deccan Plateau, see if you can glimpse the island of Sri Lanka off India's southeast coast. After your plane lands back in Calcutta, make a list of the 16 countries you have seen.

 In-Flight Movie

Take flight over South and Central Asia and explore the regions from the air.

my **worldgeography.com** In-Flight Movie

Human Geography

Economic Systems

South and Central Asia are two of the poorest regions in the world. The Central Asian nations that were once part of the communist economic system of the Soviet Union all suffer from shaky economies. In South Asia, economies are so weak that millions live in poverty and do not have enough food to eat. Despite this, in India a small minority enjoys great wealth.

However, there are signs of hope in these regions. In Central Asia, Kazakhstan has a healthier economy than its neighbors. Azerbaijan is developing its oil industry. In South Asia, India has a growing middle class and an economy that has been expanding since the 1950s.

Relief workers distribute food.

Weddings in India allow families to display their wealth.

Homelessness and poverty are widespread in these regions.

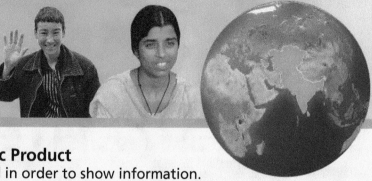

Cartogram of Regional Gross Domestic Product

A cartogram is a map that has been distorted in order to show information. In this map, the size of the country is related to its GDP, or total economic output. The map below the cartogram shows the region without distortion.

GEORGIA
ARMENIA
AZERBAIJAN
KAZAKHSTAN
UZBEKISTAN
KYRGYZSTAN
TAJIKISTAN
TURKMENISTAN
AFGHANISTAN
PAKISTAN
NEPAL
BHUTAN
INDIA
BANGLADESH
MALDIVES
SRI LANKA

Each square represents $1 billion in GDP.

South and Central Asia GDP

Country	GDP per Person*
Afghanistan	$800
Armenia	$6,600
Bangladesh	$1,500
Georgia	$5,000
India	$2,900
Pakistan	$2,600
Turkmenistan	$5,800
Uzbekistan	$2,700
United States (*for comparison*)	$48,000

SOURCE: *CIA World Factbook* *2008 Estimate

Put It Together

1. Why do you think that countries that were once part of the Soviet Union are having so many economic problems?

2. Which are the poorest countries in these regions?

3. What does the cartogram tell you about these regions?

 Data Discovery

Find your own data to make a regional data table.

Size Comparison

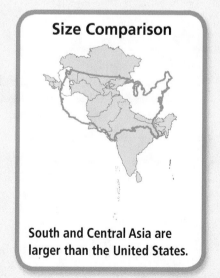

South and Central Asia are larger than the United States.

my worldgeography.com Data Discovery

Chapter 19

Central Asia and the Caucasus

What should governments do?

KEY
— National border
✪ Capital city
○ Other city

0   200 mi
0   200 km
Lambert Conformal
Conic Projection

RUSSIA

Astana

KAZAKHSTAN

CENTRAL

Aral Sea

Lake Balkhash

THE CAUCASUS

Black Sea

GEORGIA
Tbilisi

ARMENIA
Yerevan

TURKEY

Baku

Caspian Sea

ASIA

UZBEKISTAN

Tashkent

Almaty

CHINA

Bishkek

KYRGYZSTAN

Naryn

Samarqand

TURKMENISTAN

Ashgabat

Dushanbe

TAJIKISTAN

AZERBAIJAN

AFGHANISTAN

PAKISTAN

INDIA

Where in the World Are Central Asia and the Caucasus?

Washington, D.C., to Naryn: 6,630 miles

my Story

Askar Serves His People

In this section, you'll read about Askar, a young man who lives in the mountains of Kyrgyzstan. What does Askar's story tell you about the people of Kyrgyzstan and their government?

? Explore the Essential Question
- at **my worldgeography.com**
- using the **myWorld Chapter Activity**
- with the **Student Journal**

Story by Can Ertur for myWorld Geography Online

Askar lives in the mountains of Kyrgyzstan. This morning he eats two raw eggs, drinks a glass of milk, and puts on his ceremonial clothes and begins to chant lines from the Epic of Manas. This ancient poem tells the story of a legendary hero called Manas, who fought to save the Kyrgyz people and their homeland.

Like his brothers before him, Askar is trying to memorize what may be the world's longest poem. The Epic of Manas has about half a million lines and would take anywhere from 36 hours to 3 weeks to recite. It seems like an impossible task, but this hasn't stopped Askar from trying. Kyrgyz men take part every year in competitions reciting the poem.

A family document

Askar recites the Epic of Manas.

Askar plays keyboard.

Askar's grandparents and extended family

Askar collects water from a spring.

Askar explains, "If it hadn't been for our ancestor Manas, we would have been enslaved as a nation." Today, Manas is a symbol of Kyrgyz pride.

Besides memorizing the Manas poem, Askar has a number of other interests. Like most Kyrgyz boys, horseback riding is at the top of the list. He also likes fishing, skiing, playing an electric keyboard, and singing and dancing the waltz at school. In the winter, he helps his father to feed the livestock, and in the summer he goes to stay with a relative and helps pick apples and apricots.

It is a tradition among the Kyrgyz people for the youngest son to look after and live with his grandparents—on his father's side— when he grows up. As the youngest of 5 brothers, this duty falls on Askar's shoulders. When his uncle is not at home to take care of his grandparents, Askar goes and helps. He cleans the house, brings in water and firewood, and takes care of anything else.

Askar's town is located in the Central Tian Shan Mountains. It is the coldest part of the country, with temperatures falling as low as -40°F. Askar likes living there but is disturbed by the problems he and his neighbors face.

Askar and his mother take the bus.

Celebrations for the last day of school

He believes that water is the most pressing problem. "In the villages there is no clean water to drink," he says. Furthermore, in winter, the water pipes freeze and the villagers have no running water in their homes. They have no choice but to carry water to their homes from a nearby spring. Given the extremely cold weather, some villagers must depend on their neighbors to bring them their drinking water.

But water is not the only problem these mountain people have to deal with. Despite the country's many hydropower plants, Askar was unable to attend school for 2 months last year because there wasn't enough electricity to keep the schools warm and lighted. Askar says the government told them that they couldn't provide all of Kyrgyzstan with electricity because there was a shortage of water at the power plants. Given Kyrgyzstan's plentiful water supply, Askar believes that the government should do a better job of providing a steady supply of electricity.

After graduating from high school, Askar wants to go to medical school and become a doctor. He would like to work in a big city like Bishkek, the capital of Kyrgyzstan, for a year or two. Then he plans on returning home, or to one of the mountain villages, to serve his community as a skilled doctor.

myStory Online

Join Askar as he shows you more about his life in Kyrgyzstan.

Meet the Journalist

Name Can Ertur
Favorite Moment Sharing a meal with Askar's family

Chapter Atlas

Key Ideas

- Deserts and mountains shape farming and trade patterns.
- Herders have long grazed animals on the grasslands of Central Asia.
- Natural resources, such as oil and natural gas, are important to countries in these regions.

Key Terms • landlocked • steppe • irrigate • overgrazing • temperate • riot

> **Visual Glossary**

 **Reading Skill: Label and Outline Map** Take notes using the outline map in your journal.

A woman in front of her home in Tajikistan

Physical Features

Central Asia is **landlocked,** that is, cut off rom direct contact with any ocean. Traveling across the region's mountains and deserts is a challenge. Yet, for thousands of years, farmers have survived in the rich mountain valleys. Nomads have grazed their herds on the vast, mostly flat grasslands.

The Caucasus (KAW kuh sus) region is the area near the Caucasus Mountains. This mountain range runs between the Black Sea and the Caspian Sea. Three countries make up this region: Georgia, Armenia, and Azerbaijan.

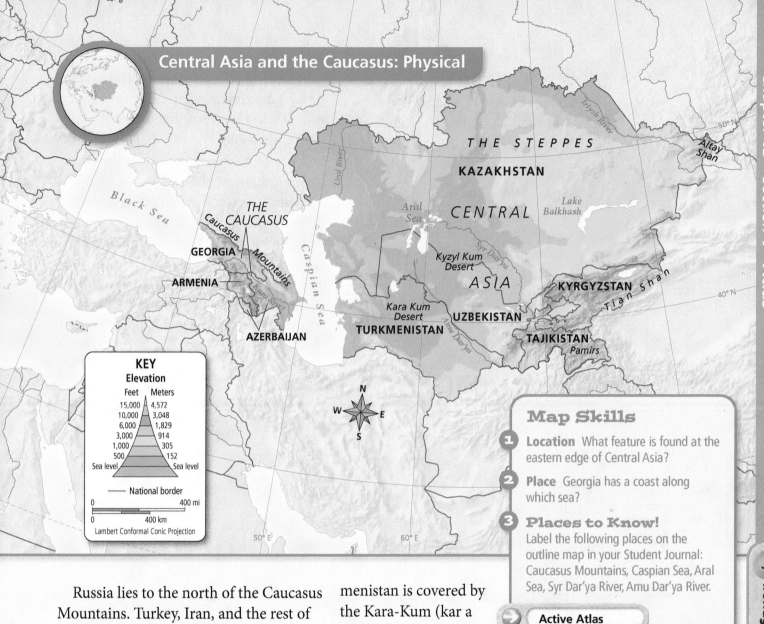

Central Asia and the Caucasus: Physical

THE STEPPES

KAZAKHSTAN

Black Sea

THE CAUCASUS

Caucasus Mountains

GEORGIA

ARMENIA

AZERBAIJAN

Aral Sea

CENTRAL

Lake Balkhash

ASIA

Kyzyl Kum Desert

Kara Kum Desert

TURKMENISTAN

UZBEKISTAN

KYRGYZSTAN

Tian Shan

TAJIKISTAN

Pamirs

Altay Shan

Irtysh River

Ural River

Caspian Sea

Kura River

Syr Dar'ya

Amu Dar'ya

50° N

40° N

50° E

60° E

KEY
Elevation

Feet	Meters
15,000	4,572
10,000	3,048
6,000	1,829
3,000	914
1,000	305
500	152
Sea level	Sea level

—— National border

0   400 mi
0   400 km
Lambert Conformal Conic Projection

N W E S

Map Skills

1 Location What feature is found at the eastern edge of Central Asia?

2 Place Georgia has a coast along which sea?

3 Places to Know!
Label the following places on the outline map in your Student Journal: Caucasus Mountains, Caspian Sea, Aral Sea, Syr Dar'ya River, Amu Dar'ya River.

Active Atlas

Russia lies to the north of the Caucasus Mountains. Turkey, Iran, and the rest of southwest Asia stretch to the south.

Central Asia, unlike the Caucasus, is a broad expanse of land at the heart of Asia. At its eastern edge, the towering mountains of Kyrgyzstan and Tajikistan separate this region from East and South Asia.

The **steppe,** or mostly flat grasslands, of Kazakhstan lie to the northwest of the mountains. The deserts and plains of Uzbekistan and Turkmenistan spread west from these mountains to the Caspian Sea. The climate of Central Asia is mostly dry. About 70 percent of Turk-menistan is covered by the Kara-Kum (kar a KUM) Desert.

Melting snow in the eastern mountains feeds rivers and lakes throughout Central Asia. The mighty Syr Dar'ya (sir der ya h) and Amu Dar'ya (ah moo der ya h) rivers flow west from the mountains. Water from these rivers runs into the Aral Sea between Kazakhstan and Uzbekistan. Rainfall is scarce, so this mountain <u>source</u> of water is important to Central Asia.

source, *n.,* the place from which something comes

Reading Check What is a major desert found in Turkmenistan?

Climate and Land Use

The climate of Central Asia is very different from that of the Caucasus. Land use, as a result, is also different in these two regions.

Dry Central Asia Most of Central Asia has an arid or semiarid climate. The weather is hot during the summer. Agriculture is a challenge in this dry, desert climate. Farmers take water from the Amu Dar'ya and Syr Dar'ya to **irrigate**, that is, to supply water to, their crops.

In Central Asia, northern Kazakhstan and the mountain valleys of Kyrgyzstan and Tajikistan have a climate that is somewhat cooler and wetter. Farming is easier here. Kazakhstan exports the wheat grown on its vast plains.

Raising livestock is also important in Central Asia. Herders have long grazed their flocks on the steppes. In mountain areas, herders bring their animals to graze in high mountain meadows in the summer when there is no snow. They return to the lower plains in the winter.

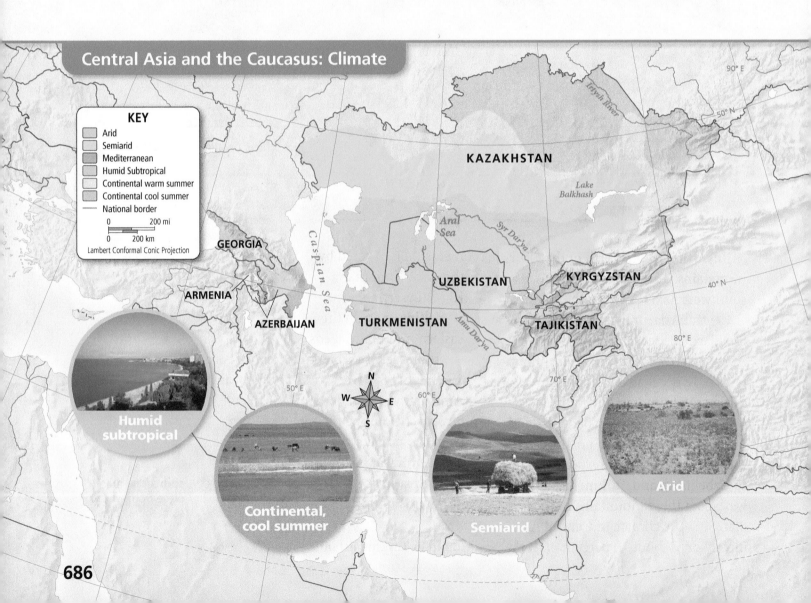

Central Asia and the Caucasus: Climate

KEY
- Arid
- Semiarid
- Mediterranean
- Humid Subtropical
- Continental warm summer
- Continental cool summer
- National border

0   200 mi
0   200 km
Lambert Conformal Conic Projection

Irtysh River

KAZAKHSTAN

Lake Balkhash

Aral Sea

Syr Dar'ya

GEORGIA

Caspian Sea

ARMENIA

AZERBAIJAN

UZBEKISTAN

KYRGYZSTAN

TURKMENISTAN

Amu Dar'ya

TAJIKISTAN

90° E
50° N
40° N
80° E
70° E
60° E
50° E

N
W   E
S

Humid subtropical

Continental, cool summer

Semiarid

Arid

This protects the grassland and prevents **overgrazing,** or so much grazing that the plants are killed.

The Mild Caucasus In the Caucasus, the mountains shape the climate of the region. The mountains block cold winter winds from the north, making the climate more **temperate,** or more mild and less extreme. The mountains also leave a rain shadow to their east. Georgia receives the most rain. The land becomes drier as you move eastward toward Azerbaijan.

The valleys and plains in the Caucasus have fertile soils for agriculture. People have mainly settled in these areas. The local climate dictates the kind of crops grown. A humid climate allows Georgians to plant fruits and vegetables which are grown for export. People grow cotton, grains, and tobacco in Azerbaijan's arid climate. In addition to these crops, rich natural resources are important to the economies in the region.

Reading Check Where are fertile soils found in the Caucasus?

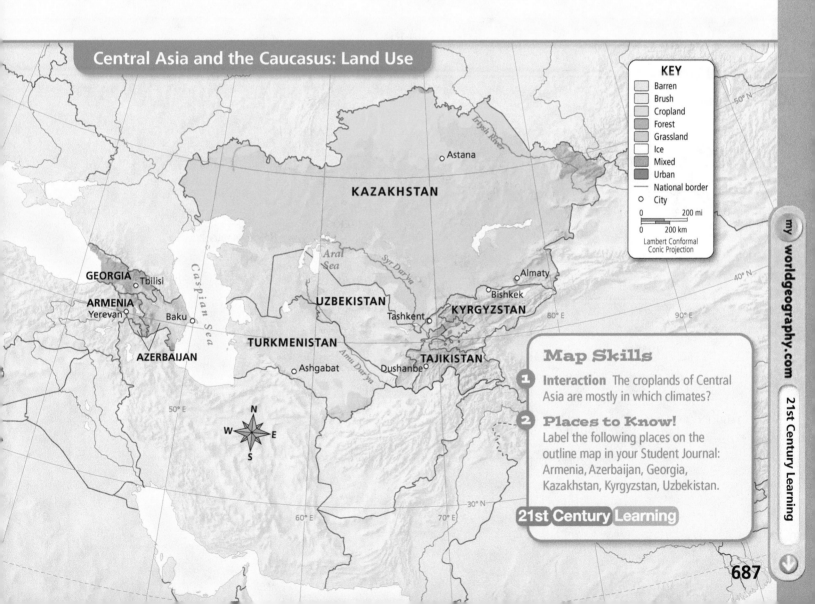

Central Asia and the Caucasus: Land Use

KEY
- Barren
- Brush
- Cropland
- Forest
- Grassland
- Ice
- Mixed
- Urban
- National border
- ○ City

0 200 mi
0 200 km
Lambert Conformal Conic Projection

KAZAKHSTAN
Astana ○
Irtysh River
50° N
40° N
90° E
80° E

Aral Sea
Syr Darya
Almaty ○
Bishkek ○
GEORGIA
Tbilisi ○
ARMENIA
Yerevan ○
Baku ○
Caspian Sea
UZBEKISTAN
Tashkent ○
KYRGYZSTAN
TURKMENISTAN
Amu Darya
TAJIKISTAN
AZERBAIJAN
Ashgabat ○
Dushanbe ○
50° E
60° E
70° E
30° N

N W E S

Map Skills

1 **Interaction** The croplands of Central Asia are mostly in which climates?

2 **Places to Know!** Label the following places on the outline map in your Student Journal: Armenia, Azerbaijan, Georgia, Kazakhstan, Kyrgyzstan, Uzbekistan.

21st Century Learning

Natural Resources

These regions have many resources, including minerals, oil, and natural gas. These natural resources are not evenly distributed. Uzbekistan and Turkmenistan produce the most natural gas. Azerbaijan and Kazakhstan produce the most oil.

Oil and Minerals Several countries in the region are rich in oil. The medieval Italian explorer Marco Polo described an oil seep probably in what is now Azerbaijan.

> 66 This oil is not good to use with food, but 'tis good to burn … People come from vast distances to fetch it … 99
>
> —Marco Polo

Oil later became a source of wealth for the region.

These countries also have important mineral deposits. For example, Armenia has copper, lead, and zinc. Gold is mined in Kyrgyzstan. Exporting minerals plays an important role in the economies of all of these countries.

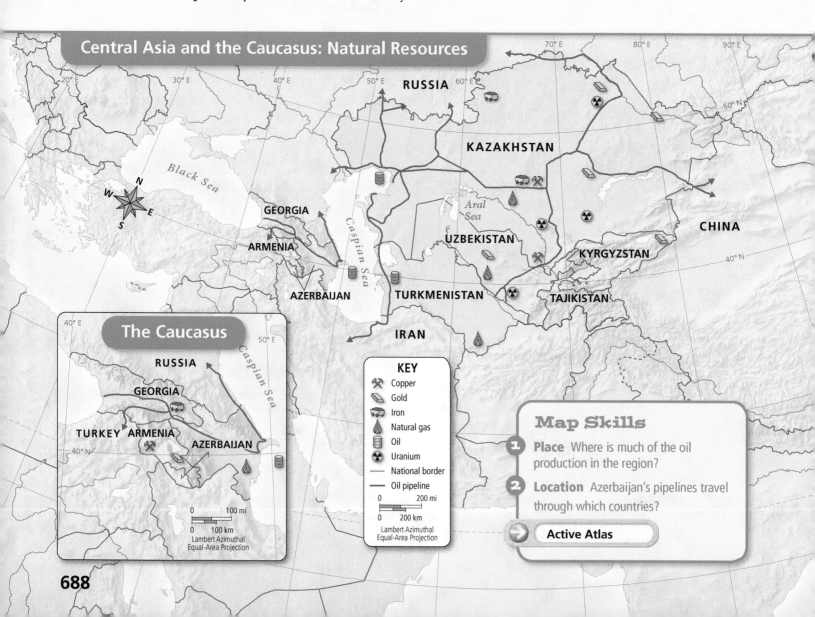

Central Asia and the Caucasus: Natural Resources

The Caucasus

KEY

- ⚒ Copper
- ▱ Gold
- 🚃 Iron
- ⬦ Natural gas
- ⬚ Oil
- ☢ Uranium
- — National border
- — Oil pipeline

0   200 mi
0   200 km
Lambert Azimuthal
Equal-Area Projection

100 mi
100 km
Lambert Azimuthal
Equal-Area Projection

Map Skills

1. **Place** Where is much of the oil production in the region?

2. **Location** Azerbaijan's pipelines travel through which countries?

➤ **Active Atlas**

Transportation Since many of these countries are landlocked, transportation is a major challenge. Oil and gas exports must move through pipelines. One of Azerbaijan's pipelines runs through Georgia, where oil is loaded onto ships in the Black Sea. Another pipeline brings oil to Russia.

Until 2006, all of Kazakhstan's pipelines ran through Russia, which gave Russia great control. Recently, China helped build a pipeline from Kazakhstan into the west of China.

Water Water is also unevenly distributed. This is an important issue, especially in dry Central Asia. Water there comes mainly from the mountains in the east. If countries upstream use too much water, the countries downstream lose out. In 1997, Uzbekistan blocked part of the water flowing into Kazakhstan. Farmers in Kazakhstan feared their crops would die and held a **riot,** a noisy, violent public gathering.

Kyrgyzstan and Tajikistan have built dams along rivers to make electricity. Too many dams could threaten the water flow to their neighbors. Water shortages of Uzbekistan and Turkmenistan could become worse. The countries in this region must cooperate to transport and benefit from their resources.

Reading Check **Which two countries in this region produce the most oil?**

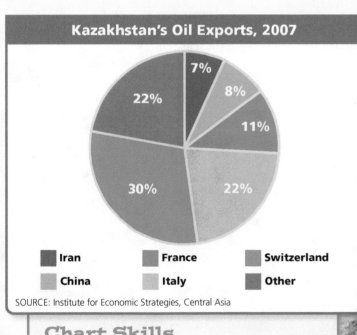

Kazakhstan's Oil Exports, 2007

7%
8%
22%
11%
30%
22%

- Iran
- China
- France
- Italy
- Switzerland
- Other

SOURCE: Institute for Economic Strategies, Central Asia

Chart Skills

Examine the natural resource map on the previous page. How could oil get from Kazakhstan to Italy?

Data Discovery

Workers build an oil pipeline running from Azerbaijan to Georgia.

my worldgeography.com

Data Discovery

**myWorld Activity
One Side of the Coin**

Cultural Diversity

Many groups of traders and invaders have passed through these regions. Each of these groups has left ts mark on local cultures. As a result, these regions are very culturally diverse.

A large number of languages are spoken in the Caucasus. In total, more than 40 different languages are native to the Caucasus. Some of these languages are unique. They are not related to languages anywhere else on Earth.

The reason for this diversity of languages lies partly in the region's geography. People live in small villages separated by mountains. People in these villages were very isolated before there was modern transportation such as cars and buses. Settlers and conquerors brought new languages with them. Earlier local languages also survived in remote mountain valleys.

tension, *n.,* unease, a state of being stressed, not relaxed

All of the countries in this region have many different ethnic groups. These ethnic groups tend to live in clusters. In some cases, a minority group lives mainly in one part of a country. Some of these minorities want their own governments.

Conflict in Georgia Two areas of Georgia, Abkhazia (ab ka h zhuh) and South Ossetia (ah see s huh), have declared independence. The Abkhazians and Ossetians are minority ethnic groups in Georgia. They are the majority in the areas where they live. In 2008, Russian troops invaded to prevent Georgia from regaining control over these areas. Their status remains a source of <u>tension</u> in the Caucasus.

Georgian women cook traditional foods and play traditional music at a culture festival in Tblisi. ▼

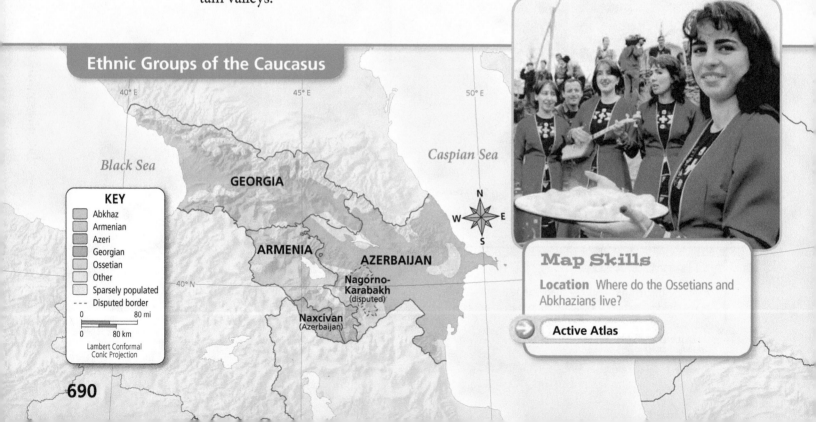

Ethnic Groups of the Caucasus

KEY

- Abkhaz
- Armenian
- Azeri
- Georgian
- Ossetian
- Other
- Sparsely populated
- - - - Disputed border

0   80 mi
0   80 km

Lambert Conformal Conic Projection

Black Sea

GEORGIA

Caspian Sea

ARMENIA

AZERBAIJAN

Nagorno-Karabakh (disputed)

Naxcivan (Azerbaijan)

40° E   45° E   50° E

40° N

N W E S

Map Skills

Location Where do the Ossetians and Abkhazians live?

Active Atlas

690

Nagorno-Karabakh There is a large area of southwestern Azerbaijan, called Nagorno-Karabakh (nuh gor nuh kahr u h bahk). Most people here are Armenian. In 1991, people in this area voted to break away from Azerbaijan.

Azerbaijan opposed this move. The government of Armenia supported the Armenians in Nagorno-Karabakh. In response, Azerbaijan blocked a natural gas pipeline that supplied fuel to Armenia. Azerbaijan also kept food and other supplies from entering Armenia. This hurt the Armenian economy. In this landlocked region, good relations with neighboring countries are important. Armenia and Azerbaijan have stopped fi hting, but the confl ct is unresolved.

Central Asian Crossroads As in the Caucasus, many different ethnic groups have settled in Central Asia. Tajiks are the largest ethnic group in Tajikistan. The Tajiks speak a language that is closely related to Farsi, the language of Iran. The ancestors of the Tajiks were one of the earliest groups to control this region.

Later, Arabs and Turks came to Central Asia. Arabs brought Islam to this region from southwest Asia. Now, most people in Central Asia practice Islam.

The Turks left heir influence on the languages spoken across the region. Most of Central Asia's major ethnic groups, including the Kyrgyz, Uzbeks, Turkmen, and Kazakhs, speak Turkic languages. These groups have different customs, but they are all descended from the many Turkic tribes that came to the region.

The Russians are one of the latest groups to settle in Central Asia. Russia and then the Russian-dominated Soviet Union controlled this region for more than a century. As a result, many Russians made their homes here. During the years of Soviet control, many people, of all ethnic groups, learned to speak Russian. Today, both Central Asia and the Caucasus remain cultural crossroads.

Reading Check What is one reason why many languages are spoken in the Caucasus?

my World
IN NUMBERS

If there were **100** people in the world,

Привет!
Hi!

3 would speak Russian.

Section 1 Assessment

Essential Question
What should governments do?

Key Terms

1. Use the term *landlocked* to describe the location of Central Asia.

2. Use the term *temperate* to describe the climate of the Caucasus.

Key Ideas

3. In Central Asia, where do herders bring their animals to graze during the summer? Where do these animals graze during the winter?

4. Where are most farms in the Caucasus located?

5. What is the main source of water in Central Asia?

Think Critically

6. **Analyze Cause and Effect** What are the effects of the conflict in Nagorno-Karabakh?

7. **Describe** How did Russia come to dominate the region's oil and gas resources?

8. Should the governments of Tajikistan and Kyrgyzstan build hydroelectric dams if the dams will reduce the amount of water that flows to neighboring countries? Go to your Student Journal to record your answer.

History of Central Asia and the Caucasus

<table>
<tr>
<td>Key Ideas</td>
<td>
● Many groups of traders and invaders have influenced the cultures of Central Asia and the Caucasus.
</td>
<td>
● Russian, and then Soviet, control brought great changes to these regions.
</td>
<td>
● The countries in these regions became independent when the Soviet Union collapsed.
</td>
</tr>
</table>

Key Terms • Silk Road • caravan • merchant • sedentary • madrassa

 Visual Glossary

Reading Skill: Summarize Take notes using the graphic organizer in your journal.

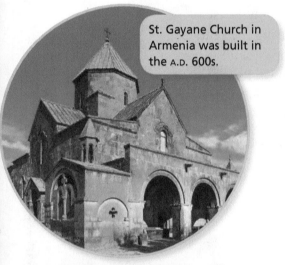
St. Gayane Church in Armenia was built in the A.D. 600s.

Abdul Aziz Khan Madrassa, Bukhara, along the Silk Road

Throughout history, different empires fought to control Central Asia and the Caucasus. Major trade routes crossed these lands. Cities grew along these routes. In the 1800s, the Russian Empire conquered the region. Communists took over Russia in 1917, and Central Asia and the Caucasus became part of the Soviet Union.

Crossroads of the Eastern Hemisphere

Many empires have influenced the culture of this region, which is a crossroads between civilizations. Trade among empires spread ideas and technology across the region.

The Silk Road of Central Asia The **Silk Road,** which was a series of trade routes that crossed Asia, was the most important trade route in the region. The route was named for silk, a highly prized trade good from China. Many other goods traveled the route as well, including spices and fine china.

At the western edge of the Silk Road were civilizations along the Mediterranean Sea and in southwest Asia. The Silk Road connected these civilizations with China in the east. As **caravans,** or groups of people traveling together, made their way along the roads, they carried new ideas. Important technologies, such as papermaking and gunpowder, made their way from Asia to Europe.

Merchants, or traders, relied on the banks, markets, and inns in Central Asian cities. These cities became important fi ancial and cultural centers. For hundreds of years, the fate of these cities was tied to the Silk Road. When trade was brisk, the region prospered.

The Caucasus: Between Two Continents

Many groups traveled across the Caucasus, which was a route between Europe and southwest Asia. In addition, many empires, including the Persian and Roman empires, invaded the Caucasus. These empires introduced new languages, customs, and religions.

Greek-speaking Romans, for example, brought Christianity to the kingdoms of Armenia and Georgia. Armenia soon became the fi st state to adopt Christianity as its official religion.

Islam Spreads Both trade and conquest brought the religion of Islam to these regions. In the early A.D 600s, Islam spread throughout the Arab world. An Arab empire <u>expanded</u> from southwest Asia. This brought Islam to Azerbaijan and parts of Central Asia. Arabs conquered the Silk Road city of Bukhara, for example, in the early A.D 700s.

Islam did not become the dominant religion in most of Armenia and Georgia. Yet by the 1400s, it had become the main religion throughout Central Asia. Traders and traveling scholars brought Islam to the nomads of the steppes.

Reading Check **What were some goods that were traded along the Silk Road?**

expand, v., to increase in size or scope

THE SILK ROAD

Map Skills

Place Why do you think the Silk Road did not follow a straight line from Kashgar to Dunhuang?

Active Atlas

KEY
— Silk Road
— Modern border
○ City

0   600 mi
0   600 km
Miller Cylindrical Projection

Aral Sea
Black Sea
Caspian Sea
Tian Shan
Dunhuang
GOBI
Bukhara
Taklamakan Desert
Merv
Samarqand
Kashgar
Antioch
Tigris R.
Hotan
Huang River
Mediterranean Sea
Euphrates R.
Tehran
Tyre
Baghdad
Xi'an
Persian Gulf
Plateau of Tibet
H I M A L A Y A S

Mechants sell silk in a market in the Silk Road city of Kashgar.

INDIAN OCEAN

Empires Built on Horseback

Great empires also arose on the steppes of Central Asia. The vast grasslands allowed people to keep large herds of horses.

Nomads Emerge from Central Asia

Horses gave the nomads of the steppe a huge military advantage over **sedentary,** or settled, populations to the south. Nomad warriors created great empires that spanned Asia. On horseback, warriors swiftly swept down on their enemies. Armies on foot were no match for these mounted warriors.

The Huns were one early group of nomads from the western steppe. These skilled horsemen conquered the Caucasus and terrorized Europe. Attila the Hun, their most notorious leader, attacked the Roman Empire in the a.d . 400s.

The Huns were likely a Turkic-speaking people. At the time, there were many Turkic tribes in Central Asia. By the A.D. 500s, these tribes <u>dominated</u> much of Central Asia. They controlled an area from Mongolia in the east to the Amu Dar'ya River. Migration and conquest spread Turkic languages. Most of the main ethnic groups in Central Asia today speak Turkic languages.

Mighty Mongols Turkic and Persian states controlled Cenral Asia until the 1200s. At that time, Genghis Khan conquered the region and made it part of the Mongol Empire.

The Mongol warrior Genghis Khan united the Mongol tribes. He died in 1227, but his sons and grandsons continued to expand the Mongol empire. At its height, the Mongols controlled much of Asia and Eastern Europe. Their empire reached east to Korea, west into Russia, and south to northern India. No empire before the Mongol Empire was as large.

Under the Mongols, trade along the Silk Road increased. The Mongols protected caravans from bandits. Merchants moved along the route with few barriers.

Turkic tribes and descendants of the Mongol conquerors would vie for control over Central Asia for centuries until Russia took control over the entire region.

Reading Check **Who was Genghis Khan?**

dominate, v., to rule over, control

A young woman in Kyrgyzstan performs at a festival celebrating the riding culture of the nomads of Central Asia. ▶

Communists Take Control

Russia, and then the communist Soviet Union, took control over Central Asia and the Caucasus. Life changed greatly under the communists.

The Russian Empire Expands During the 1700s and 1800s, the Caucasus region found itself in the middle of a struggle among three great powers: the Ottoman, Persian, and Russian empires. In Central Asia, Great Britain and Russia competed for control. By the close of the 1800s, Russia had won both of these contests. They had conquered the entire region.

Soviet Socialist Republics The communists seized power in Russia in 1917. The communist leaders took control over Central Asia and the Caucasus. They divided the regions into eight soviet republics, or states.

Changes to Culture and Daily Life Under communism, the government made decisions about economic production. Government officials told each republic what to produce. In Central Asia, many nomads were forced to settle and work on government farms. The government often did not manage the economy well. Shortages of basic goods became common.

The leaders of the Soviet Union also wanted to unify the country. They built many new schools. These schools taught in Russian instead of in local languages. The government wanted to control cultural life. It closed churches, mosques, and **madrassas,** that is, schools that teach the Islamic religion. The culture also changed as many Russians moved into both regions.

After years of growing economic problems, the Soviet Union collapsed in 1991. The eight soviet republics of these regions became independent.

Reading Check **What are two ways the Soviet Union changed these regions?**

myWorld Activity
Frozen in Time

Joseph Stalin, one of the Soviet Union's most powerful leaders, was born in Georgia. ▼

Section 2 Assessment

Key Terms

1. What is a madrassa?

2. Use the terms Silk Road, caravan, and merchant to describe trade routes in Central Asia.

Key Ideas

3. Who spread Christianity to the kingdoms of Armenia and Georgia?

4. What is one effect that the Silk Road had on Central Asia?

5. Which empire controlled this region at the end of the 1800s?

Think Critically

6. Summarize Why did nomads have a military advantage over sedentary populations in battle?

7. Draw Inferences Why do you think different empires fought to control these regions?

? Essential Question

What should governments do?

8. Why did the Soviet government encourage the Russian language in these regions? Should the government choose the official language of the country? Go to your Student Journal to record your answers.

Central Asia and the Caucasus Today

Key Ideas
- Some local traditions and religious practices are being revived in this region.
- The governments of Central Asia and the Caucasus face economic, political, and environmental challenges.
- Tensions between different ethnic groups in the Caucasus have caused conflicts.

Key Terms • akyn • election fraud • repressive • demonstration • Rose Revolution

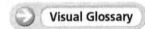 Visual Glossary

 Reading Skill: Identify Main Ideas and Details Take notes using the graphic organizer in your journal.

With the fall of the Soviet Union, the new republics of Central Asia and the Caucasus face many challenges. They must improve their economies and solve serious environmental problems. However, people in the region also are freer to reconnect to local traditions and religions.

Cultural Life of Central Asia and the Caucasus

The Soviet Union encouraged people in these regions to think of themselves as Soviet citizens. Now, people in these eight independent countries have a chance to make national identities based on the unique languages and customs of their countries.

Revival of Religion The Soviet Union did not allow religious freedom. Since independence, people have built new churches, mosques, and madrassas. The Soviets also banned customs and celebrations connected to religion. Now, Christian or Muslim holidays are public holidays in many countries.

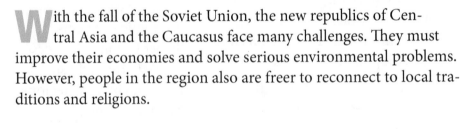

 Culture Close-up

This man is an akyn, a traditional storyteller, from Kyrgyzstan. He memorizes long poems that tell the history of his people.

Local Culture Local languages and customs have also become more important since these countries have become independent. Many schools now teach in local languages, rather than in Russian. Also, people use local languages more often in public life. For example, after independence Islom Karimov, the president of Uzbekistan, began giving speeches in Uzbek rather than Russian. Still, there are large Russian-speaking minorities, especially in Kazakhstan.

Governments and individuals in these regions are acting to revive local arts and traditions. The government of Kyrgyzstan is helping to train traditional storytellers, called **akyn**. These storytellers recite long poems that tell the history and values of the Kyrgyz people. In Georgia and Armenia, churches have trained singers, and governments have supported dance, music, and visual arts.

Still, preserving these cultural traditions is a challenge. Knowledge of local art and literature was lost during the Soviet period. Many people do not have money to attend concerts or time to learn about the arts. Governments have limited budgets. They are trying to preserve traditional culture but also solve the serious problems that the region faces.

New Connections All of these countries now have more contact with countries besides Russia. Movies, music, and sports from the United States, China, and India have become popular in the region. Kazakhstan has also developed its own film industry. People in these regions are both connecting to local customs and sampling the cultures of other countries.

Reading Check Why is there a revival of religion in the region?

my World
IN NUMBERS

There are **27** languages spoken in the Caucasus and **28** languages spoken in Central Asia.

A dancer from Georgia's National Folk Song and Dance Academy performs a traditional dance.

my Story 📷 Photo

Above, the Naryn Mosque in Naryn town, Kyrgyzstan. The mosque was built in 1993.

my worldgeography.com Culture Close-Up

Challenges for New Nations

People in the region must deal with new challenges as well as problems left behind by the Soviet Union.

Respecting Ethnic Diversity Different ethnic groups live side by side in these regions. Before, Russian was a common language. Now, if one group's language is more widely used, other ethnic groups must learn this language. Also, some countries now have more than one official language. Both Kyrgyz and Russian are the official languages of Kyrgyzstan.

Still, minority groups are sometimes treated unfairly. Most of the ancient Central Asian Jewish communities have moved to Israel and America due to harsh treatment. In Uzbekistan, Tajiks have a harder time finding jobs than Uzbeks. Some Tajiks claim to be Uzbek because they fear they will not be treated fairly. While the Uzbek government promotes Uzbek traditions, the Tajik people in Uzbekistan may lose their identity.

Meanwhile, in Georgia and Azerbaijan, ethnic tension has led to armed conflict when minority groups have tried to break away and form separate countries.

Joining the World Economy Before independence, each republic produced goods according to the Soviet Union's economic plan. Now, businesses in these countries must make goods to trade on the global market. Countries such as Azerbaijan and Kazakhstan have had economic success because they have valuable energy resources to trade.

Encouraging economic growth has been difficult. Many people in this region are poor and cannot fi d a job. Some people are frustrated and want the government to improve the economy.

66 The government says that we are independent, but people are going hungry. 99

—Young woman from Tajikistan

Inherited Environmental Problems The Soviet Union often did not manage resources well. They caused water shortages by using too much water to irrigate crops, including cotton. Industrial waste often went directly into lakes and rivers. Pollution of the Caspian Sea has damaged the fishing industry.

Cleaning up the pollution is expensive. Some Central Asian countries still rely on cotton as an important export. Governments must balance protecting the environment with their other responsibilities.

Reading Check What are two environmental problems in this region?

Poverty is a serious problem in many parts of Armenia. ▼

Closer Look

The Shrinking Aral Sea

The Aral Sea, between Kazakhstan and Uzbekistan, was once the fourth-largest lake in the world. The Amu Dar'ya and the Syr Dar'ya rivers fed the lake. The Soviet Union took water from these rivers to irrigate crops, especially cotton. They used so much water that the sea began to shrink. Local farmers still use large amounts of water for their crops. The Aral Sea is still shrinking, as the satellite photos at the right show. Scientists do not know if Kazakhstan and Uzbekistan can act fast enough to save the sea.

THINK CRITICALLY **What are some problems caused by the shrinking Aral Sea?**

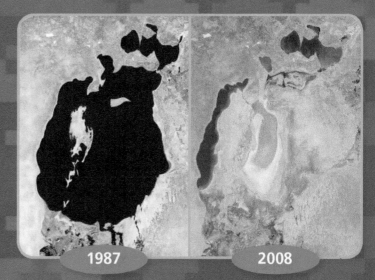
1987   2008

The water became so salty that fish could no longer live in most of the lake. Tens of thousands of people in the fishing industry lost their jobs. ▶

There is a shortage of clean water for people living in the area. ▼

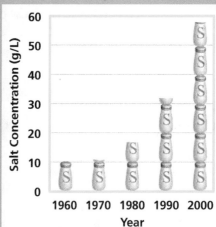

Concentration of Salt in the Aral Sea

Salt Concentration (g/L)

60
50
40
30
20
10
0

1960 1970 1980 1990 2000

Year

SOURCE: Interstate Commission for Water Coordination of Central Asia

This desert used to be the bed of the Aral Sea. Kazakh villagers collect metal parts from boats that were stranded as the waters evaporated. ▼

task, *n.,* something that must be done, duty

Building New Governments

People of these regions face the <u>task</u> of overcoming political challenges. Some governments in these regions are corrupt and undemocratic.

New Governments, Old Leaders When the Soviet Union collapsed, the countries in these regions were left n their own. Often, people from within the Soviet government became leaders in the new countries. For example, both Nursultan Nazarbayev of Kazakhstan and Eduard Shevardnadze of Georgia were officials in the Soviet Union.

The leaders of the newly independent countries wrote new constitutions and laws that seemed to protect peoples' rights. Yet some of these leaders later acted to limit democracy. They have tried to stay in power as long as possible.

Limits on Democracy Elections are held in both regions, but people may not have political freedom. One common problem is **election fraud,** that is, unfair elections in which one group controls the results in order to gain power.

Often, governments have not protected the rights listed in their constitutions. Many leaders have attacked or jailed people who do not support them.

The government of Turkmenistan is one of the most **repressive,** meaning opposed to freedom. It keeps strict control over its citizens. The president holds most of the power. Saparmurat Niyazov, the country's fi st president, was known as Turkemenbashi, "leader of the Turks." He extended his power until his death in 2006. Even now, only one political party is allowed in Turkmenistan, and the press is not free to criticize the president.

In other countries, citizens have successfully protested against bad government. In 2003, many Georgians joined a demonstration against election fraud in a parliamentary election. A **demonstration** is a public display of group opinion, often a rally or march. Many people believed President Shevardnadze rigged the election so that candidates from his party would win.

The protests against this election came to be called the **Rose Revolution** because the demonstrators carried roses as a symbol of peace. Shevardnadze resigned

One of many golden statues of Saparmurat Niyazov, who made himself President for Life of Turkmenistan. ▶

because of these protests, and the country elected a new president.

Across both regions, progress has been uneven. In some countries, protests, like the Rose Revolution, have brought greater democracy. Still, the political systems of most countries are not open and democratic.

The Impact of Corruption Political problems often create problems in the economy. Corruption is a serious problem in most countries of these regions. Government officials often take money meant to build schools and hospitals and help the economy to grow. To improve their economies, many of the countries in these regions need to start by improving their schools, roads, and bridges. To make these improvements, governments will need to fi ht corruption.

Reading Check **What is one political problem in these regions today?**

Standing Up for Democracy

Kyrgyzstan
The government jailed journalist Zamira Sydykova because she reported on government corruption.

Georgia
Students protested election fraud by marching in the Rose Revolution demonstrations.

myWorld Activity
Hot Off the Press

Section 3 Assessment

Essential Question
What should governments do?

Key Terms

1. What are akyn?

2. Use the term election fraud to describe politics in Central Asia and the Caucasus.

Key Ideas

3. Why do many countries in Central Asia and the Caucasus have more than one official language?

4. Why is Turkmenistan considered one of the most repressive countries in Central Asia?

5. What caused the Rose Revolution?

Think Critically

6. **Analyze Cause and Effect** Why has religion revived in Central Asia and the Caucasus since the fall of the Soviet Union?

7. **Compare and Contrast** Have countries in Central Asia and countries in the Caucasus faced similar problems since the fall of the Soviet Union? Explain your answer.

8. Do you think the governments of Central Asia and the Caucasus should try to make farmers and businesses reduce pollution? Explain your answer.

Chapter Assessment

Key Terms and Ideas

1. **Describe** How do the herders of Central Asia prevent **overgrazing**?

2. **Explain** Why are pipelines important to the economies of Central Asia and the Caucasus?

3. **Compare and Contrast** What is the difference between nomads and a **sedentary** population?

4. **Recall** How did Islam spread to Central Asia?

5. **Summarize** How did the people of Georgia protest election fraud in 2003?

6. **Explain** Do you think **irrigating** crops contributes to the water shortage in Central Asia?

7. **Recall** What resource has helped the economies of Azerbaijan and Kazakhstan?

Think Critically

8. **Draw Conclusions** Why have many countries in Central Asia and the Caucasus had undemocratic governments since gaining independence?

9. **Analyze Cause and Effect** How has the geography of the Caucasus affected the cultures of the people living there?

10. **Make Decisions** Do you think Georgia should grant independence to Abkhazia and South Ossetia? Why or why not?

11. **Core Concepts: Conflict and Cooperation** Why did Silk Road trade increase under the Mongols? Why does trade decrease if there is conflict?

Places to Know

For each place, write the letter from the map that shows its location.

12. **Georgia**

13. **Amu Dar'ya River**

14. **Caspian Sea**

15. **Kazakhstan**

16. **Aral Sea**

17. **Syr Dar'ya River**

18. **Estimate** Using the scale bar, estimate the length of the Caspian Sea from northwest to southeast.

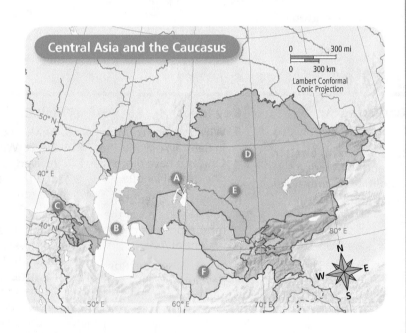

Central Asia and the Caucasus

Essential Question

myWorld Chapter Activity

Money Well Spent Work as a representative of a country from this region to decide how to spend your country's budget. Which problems are the most urgent? In addition, consider whether or not other groups in the country could address some of those problems better than the government.

21st Century Learning

Develop Cultural Awareness

Develop Cultural Awareness Draw a travel poster for a country in either Central Asia or the Caucasus. Research information that a traveler needs to understand the culture of the country. Be sure to show images that deal with the following:

- religion
- language
- the arts
- cuisine

Document-Based Questions

Online at myworldgeography.com

Use your knowledge of Kazakhstan and Documents A and B to answer questions 1–3.

Document A

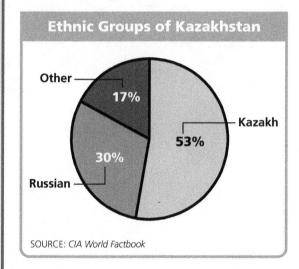

Ethnic Groups of Kazakhstan

Other — 17%

Kazakh — 53%

Russian — 30%

SOURCE: *CIA World Factbook*

Document B

" Under Soviet rule, Russians were not just an ethnic majority, they were also the political, cultural, and social elite. . . Today, the tables have turned. Kazakhs now call the shots from the highest levels of government."

—Jessica P. Hayden, "Who Am I? Russian Identity in post-Soviet Kazakhstan," *Slate*, July 20, 2004

1. What is the largest ethnic group in Kazakhstan?
   A Russian
   B Kazakh
   C Tajik
   D Uzbek

2. What does Document B describe?
   A a change of power in favor of the Kazakhs
   B strong prejudice against Kazaks
   C Kazakhs still under Russian rule
   D Kazakhs sharing power with the Russians

3. **Writing Task** Based on Documents A and B, what has changed in Kazakhstan? Write a paragraph explaining why these changes may have taken place.

my worldgeography.com | Self-Test

Chapter 20

South Asia

Essential Question

What makes a nation?

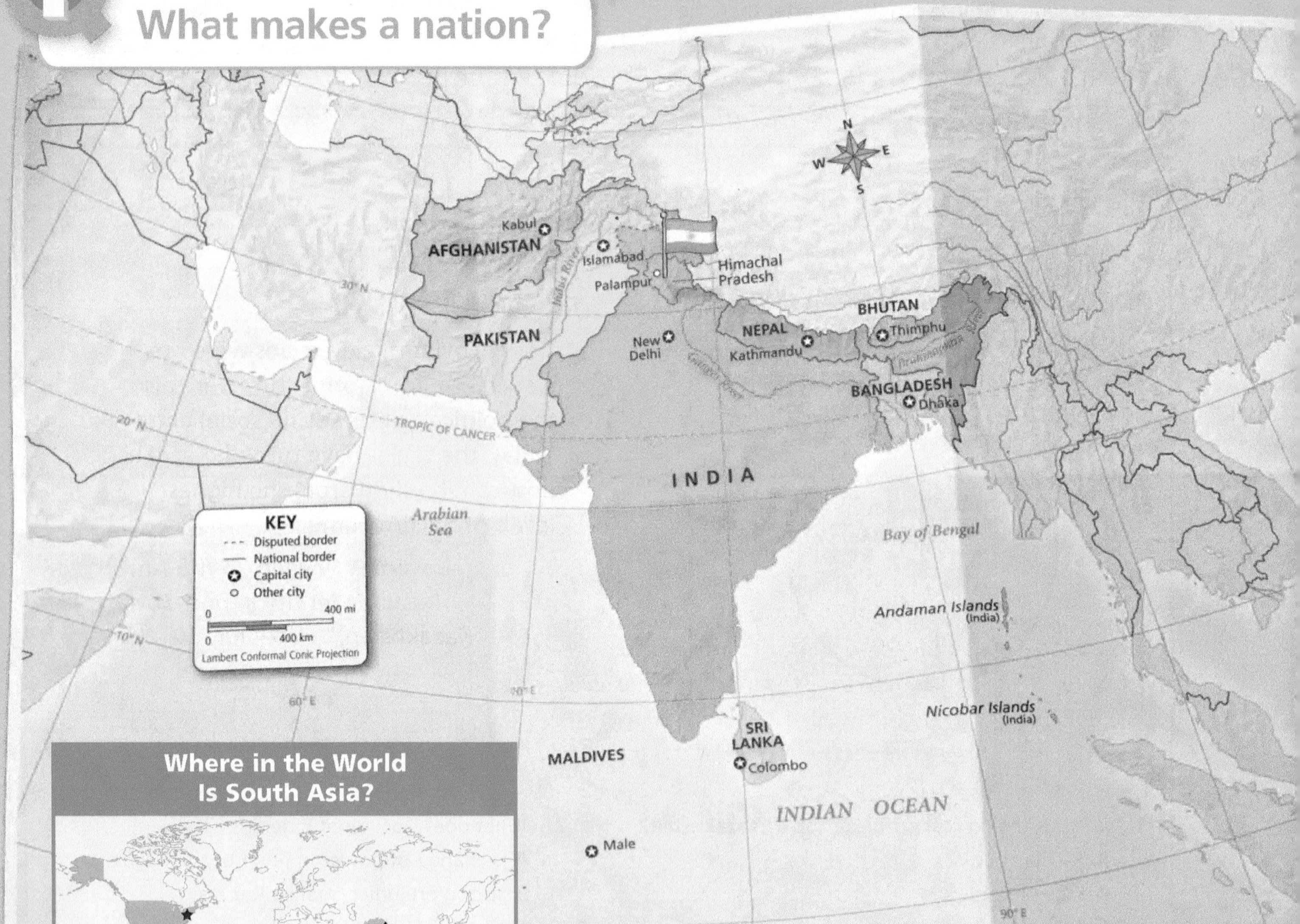

AFGHANISTAN

Kabul

Islamabad

Palampur

Himachal
Pradesh

PAKISTAN

New
Delhi

NEPAL

Kathmandu

BHUTAN

Thimphu

BANGLADESH

Dhaka

Indus River

Ganges River

Brahmaputra River

INDIA

TROPIC OF CANCER

30° N

20° N

10° N

60° E

70° E

80° E

90° E

*Arabian
Sea*

Bay of Bengal

KEY
- - - Disputed border
— National border
✪ Capital city
○ Other city

0   400 mi
0   400 km
Lambert Conformal Conic Projection

Andaman Islands
(India)

Nicobar Islands
(India)

SRI
LANKA

✪ Colombo

MALDIVES

INDIAN OCEAN

✪ Male

Where in the World Is South Asia?

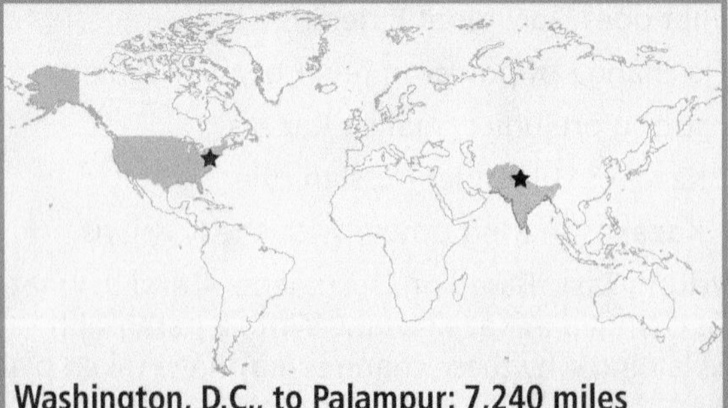

Washington, D.C., to Palampur: 7,240 miles

my Story

Nancy's Fruitful Loan

In this section you'll read about Nancy, a young woman who is helping her mother start a new business in a mountainous region of India. **In what ways does Nancy's work help strengthen her nation?**

Explore the Essential Question
- at my worldgeography.com
- using the myWorld Chapter Activity
- with the Student Journal

Story by Aniruddha Das for myWorld Geography Online

It is a busy time in Nancy's hometown near Palampur, India. Next week there will be a big wedding, but in the meantime there's plenty of other work to do. Nancy already has many daily chores. She gathers food for the cattle, cleans the house, and even helps her grandfather repair her home. Now that she is 18, she has also joined the Samriddhi, a business run by a group of local women. The women of Samriddhi work together to harvest, prepare, and sell pickled fruit products. They have one of the few successful businesses in the area.

Palampur lies within a region known as the Changar belt. This is a dry, rocky area marked by ravines and gullies with a scattering of trees that provide shade and color the hills a dusty green. It is a challenging place to earn a living. The land is difficult to farm, but the women of Samriddhi have found a way to take advantage of local resources. Changar forests are rich with wild fruits. Many of these fruits can be used to make jams and chutney. A chutney is a relish made of fruits mixed with other ingredients such as vinegar and lemon juice.

"We have many different varieties of fruit . . . we have lemon, limes, Indian gooseberry, jackfruit, mango . . . " explains Nancy,

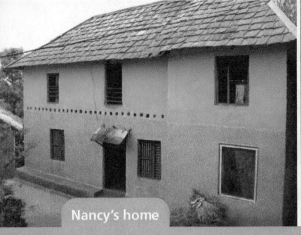
Nancy's home

Nancy cooking at home

Nancy feeding the cows

The landscape around Nancy's home is rocky and dry.

Nancy and her family

gesturing to a range of Samriddhi jams and chutneys. The whole operation is funded by small bank loans, called microcredit loans. Thanks to these low-risk loans the Samriddhi women are able to buy the salt, spices, and sugar needed for pickling. They can also use the money for minor expenses such as renting a truck to transport their products to the Samriddhi office.

Today, Nancy is traveling with her mother and a few other Samriddhi women to the bank to apply for a new microcredit loan. "We need a loan so we can start a plantation. We want to grow some new fruit trees," Nancy explains as we walk along the dusty street to the small local bank. "It will cost us about 80,000 to 90,000 rupees," she adds, which is about $1,800.

The bank has different payment plans for different kinds of microloans. The bank manager explains to Nancy and the group that for a plantation loan, they need to show that they have plans to clear and level the land. They will also

Applying for a loan at the bank

Nancy at work

need to make a down payment of 15 percent of the total cost of the project. The rest of the project will be financed by the bank. Loans for things such as seeds or fertilizer require a 7-percent down payment. The money involved may not seem like much by Western standards, but the average annual income in the region is only about $300 a year.

Nancy is proud to be involved in the process and excited about helping to set up a new plantation. The older women are glad to have Nancy in the group as well. They know she is high-spirited, hardworking, and intelligent.

Later, Nancy and her mother prepare for a week-long sales trip. They fill the sales van with their products and set off. Their first stop is just outside Palampur itself, but they will also travel to several other towns before returning home.

Nancy works hard to sell as much as she can. She knows that the money they make will not only help

pay for the new loan but also provide income for her family. Some of the money will be set aside to educate Nancy and her brother. "Right now I am planning to study computer science," Nancy says. "But if there is a chance for me to join the police then I will do that. I want to serve my country."

The Samriddhi has done more for this village than just make money; it has provided hope for the future. By working together to manage the land and grow a business, the Samriddhi has brought the community together. Sometime soon they hope to see fruit growing on the new plantation that Nancy and the microcredit loan help set up. That will be something for everyone to enjoy!

Meet the Journalist

Name Sachin Singh
Favorite Moment Watching Nancy climb trees to harvest the fruit

myStory Video

Join Nancy as she shows you more about her life.

my worldgeography.com myStory Video

Key Ideas
- Landforms and resources have influenced settlement in South Asia.
- People have adapted to a range of climates in South Asia.
- Physical geography plays a divisive role in South Asia.

Key Terms
- Indian subcontinent
- Green Revolution
- subsistence farming
- flood plain

 Visual Glossary

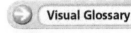 **Reading Skill: Label an Outline Map** Take notes using the outline map in your journal.

The Himalayas

Dancer in Rajasthan, India

Physical Features

Nancy lives in the highlands of Himalchal Pradesh (huh MAHL kul pruh DESH), which are part of the massive mountain range known as the Himalayas (hi muh LAY uz). The land to the south of the Himalayas is called the **Indian subcontinent.** In the distant past, the subcontinent was connected to Africa. Then around 90 million years ago, this huge chunk of land broke away and drifted to the northeast. As the landmass collided with Asia, pressure caused the ground to buckle up. Th s process created the Himalayas—the highest mountains on Earth.

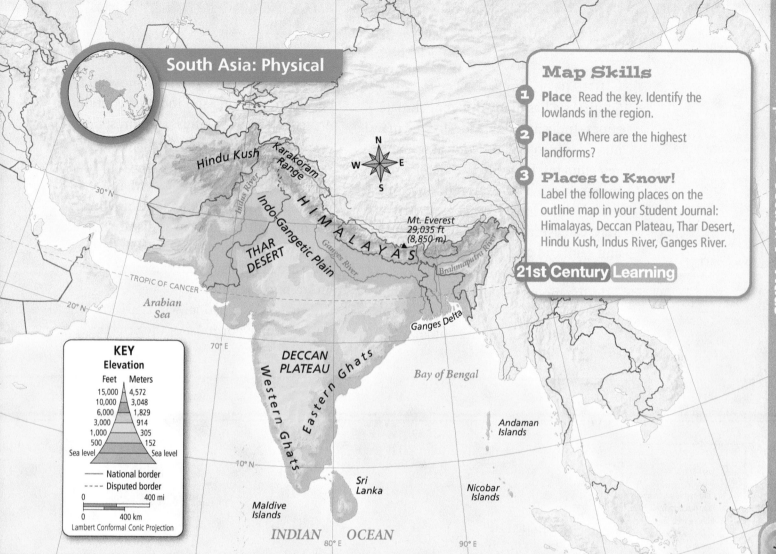

South Asia: Physical

KEY
Elevation

Feet	Meters
15,000	4,572
10,000	3,048
6,000	1,829
3,000	914
1,000	305
500	152
Sea level	Sea level

—— National border
- - - Disputed border

0 ———— 400 mi
0 ———— 400 km
Lambert Conformal Conic Projection

Hindu Kush
Karakoram Range
Indus River
H I M A L A Y A S
Mt. Everest
29,035 ft
(8,850 m)
Indo-Gangetic Plain
THAR DESERT
Ganges River
Brahmaputra River
TROPIC OF CANCER
Arabian Sea
Ganges Delta
DECCAN PLATEAU
Western Ghats
Eastern Ghats
Bay of Bengal
Andaman Islands
Sri Lanka
Nicobar Islands
Maldive Islands
INDIAN OCEAN

30° N
20° N
70° E
10° N
80° E
90° E

Map Skills

1 **Place** Read the key. Identify the lowlands in the region.

2 **Place** Where are the highest landforms?

3 **Places to Know!**
Label the following places on the outline map in your Student Journal: Himalayas, Deccan Plateau, Thar Desert, Hindu Kush, Indus River, Ganges River.

21st Century Learning

The Himalayas form India's northern border. They surround nearly all of Nepal and Bhutan. Smaller ranges, such as the Hindu Kush, extend this wall of mountains into western Pakistan and central Afghanistan.

Large rivers drain the melting snows of the mountains. To the south of the Himalayas, the Ganges (GAN jez) River runs across India's northern plains and meets the Brahmaputra (brah muh POO truh) River in the heart of Bangladesh. In the west, the Indus River flows through the dry plains of Pakistan.

The southern part of South Asia is a peninsula that juts into the Indian Ocean. Much of this peninsula is a fairly flat highland area called the Deccan Plateau. It is bordered by two coastal mountain ranges known as the Western Ghats and the Eastern Ghats.

Off he southern tip of India lies the island nation of Sri Lanka. To the southwest are the Maldives, a chain of 1,190 islands formed from coral.

Reading Check **What physical feature forms the northern border of India?**

Climate

regulate, *v.,* to control

South Asia has many different climate zones. India and Bangladesh have mainly humid subtropical or tropical wet and dry climates. Daytime high temperatures can reach 80°F, even in the coolest months. The most intense heat, in May, can average more than 100°F. Arid and semiarid climates run through the countries of Afghanistan and Pakistan.

In the mountains of the west and far north, the high peaks are covered with snow year-round. Glaciers fill many valleys. But this area is not all snow and ice. The mountains and foothills contain fertile valleys, grasslands, and forests.

The Himalayas help to <u>regulate</u> the region's climate. They block much of the cold, dry air that would otherwise stream into South Asia from the north in winter. The mountains also draw moisture out of the warm, humid summer winds. The moisture falls as snow in the mountains and rain to the south.

South Asia's seasonal winds are known as monsoons. For most of the year the

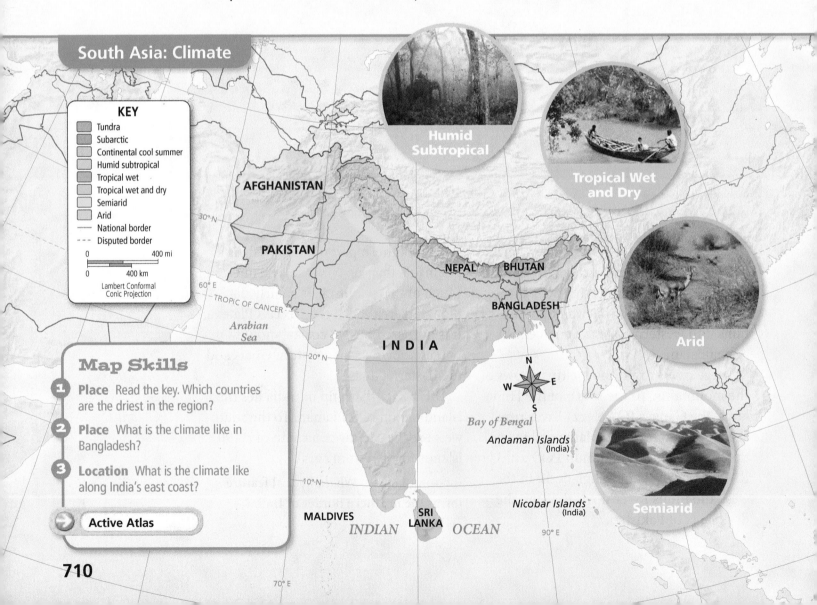

South Asia: Climate

KEY
- Tundra
- Subarctic
- Continental cool summer
- Humid subtropical
- Tropical wet
- Tropical wet and dry
- Semiarid
- Arid
- — National border
- --- Disputed border

0   400 mi
0   400 km

Lambert Conformal Conic Projection

AFGHANISTAN

PAKISTAN

NEPAL   BHUTAN

BANGLADESH

Arabian Sea

INDIA

Bay of Bengal

Andaman Islands (India)

Nicobar Islands (India)

MALDIVES   SRI LANKA

INDIAN OCEAN

30° N
60° E
TROPIC OF CANCER
20° N
10° N
90° E
70° E

Humid Subtropical

Tropical Wet and Dry

Arid

Semiarid

Map Skills

1 Place Read the key. Which countries are the driest in the region?

2 Place What is the climate like in Bangladesh?

3 Location What is the climate like along India's east coast?

Active Atlas

monsoon blows from the northeast and brings dry air. During the wet season, lasting from June to September, the southwest winds bring drenching rain.

The warm wind of the southwest monsoon picks up moisture from the Indian Ocean. It dumps heavy rain on India's western coast, the northern plains, and the northeast. On the west coast of India, the Western Ghats block this moisture, so the land to the east of the Ghats has a semiarid climate.

The southwest monsoon can bring <u>intense</u> storms and fl ods. In 1988, the fl oding of the Ganges and other rivers washed away crops and livestock in Bangladesh and killed some 2,000 people. A quarter of the population was left homeless.

In Afghanistan, much of the land stays dry year-round. The southwest monsoon does not penetrate far into this area.

intense, *adj.,* very strong

Reading Check **How do the mountains affect climate?**

Closer Look

Climate and Culture

People in South Asia have adapted to their environments in many ways. Their houses are well suited to local climates.

THINK CRITICALLY **Where on the climate map might you find each of these buildings? Study each house and read the description for clues.**

This haveli, or mansion, was built for a rich merchant. Its balconies and screens allow breezes to pass through the house—a relief in the hot dry area where it was built.

This stilt house is well adapted to its lowland delta environment. It can easily withstand the seasonal floods, as long as they don't get too high!

Mud brick houses with flat roofs are a common sight in areas that do not get much rain.

In cold climates, farmhouses must shelter people, animals, and grain. In this house, grain and produce are kept in the attic. Farm animals are kept on the ground floor.

711

Land Use and Resources

Most South Asians work in agriculture. Farms tend to be rather small. Their owners engage mainly in **subsistence farming**, which means they use the crops they grow to feed themselves, but have little left ver to send to market.

In the mid-1960s, technology created a **Green Revolution**, an increase in agricultural production. Th s produced more food for growing populations.

However, in some places, farmers overused chemical fertilizers and pesticides. They pumped too much water out of the ground to irrigate crops. Farming practices like these poisoned the soil, fouled rivers, and dried up wells.

The region is also rich in resources. Rivers provide hydroelectric power. Mines in the plateaus and mountains produce iron ore, bauxite, copper, and coal. Petroleum and natural gas are found in the plateaus and mountains, as well as off hore. These resources support manufacturing in India and Pakistan.

Reading Check Why are rivers an important resource?

◄ A farmworker sprays pesticides on his rice fields.

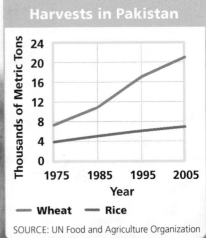

Harvests in Pakistan

Thousands of Metric Tons

24
20
16
12
8
4
0

1975   1985   1995   2005

Year

— Wheat   — Rice

SOURCE: UN Food and Agriculture Organization

Land Use Issues in South Asia

The Green Revolution has helped feed South Asia's growing population. However, new research shows that the use of pesticides is causing medical problems among local people.

Chart Skills

Which crop produces more?

→ **Data Discovery**

Population Explosion

South Asia suffers from two related problems: high population growth and poverty. Nearly half the world's poor live in this region.

The size of South Asia's population is one of the main problems. The region contains three of the ten most populous countries in the world—India, Pakistan, and Bangladesh. Just meeting people's basic needs—food, clothing, and shelter—is a monumental task.

About half of South Asia's population is located on the Indo-Gangetic plain, in the valleys of the Ganges and Brahmaputra rivers. Most of the people of this region live in rural areas.

India, for example, is only 29 percent urban, but its urban population has grown steadily. Much of this increase is made up of rural families moving to cities to improve their lives. Many Indian migrants, however, are forced to live in urban slums or on the streets.

Reading Check **Which countries are the most populous in the region?**

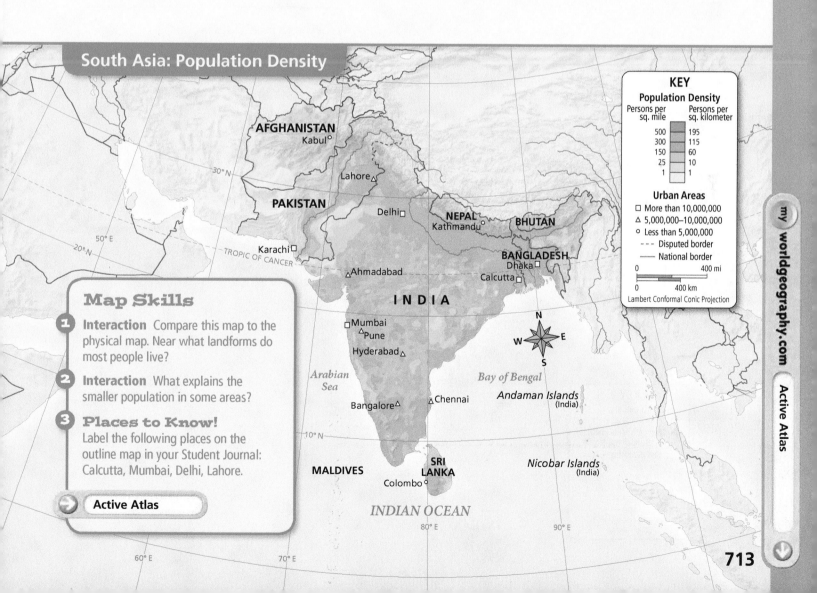

South Asia: Population Density

Map Skills

1. **Interaction** Compare this map to the physical map. Near what landforms do most people live?

2. **Interaction** What explains the smaller population in some areas?

3. **Places to Know!** Label the following places on the outline map in your Student Journal: Calcutta, Mumbai, Delhi, Lahore.

Active Atlas

KEY

Population Density

Persons per sq. mile	Persons per sq. kilometer
500	195
300	115
150	60
25	10
1	1

Urban Areas
□ More than 10,000,000
△ 5,000,000–10,000,000
○ Less than 5,000,000
- - - Disputed border
——— National border

0   400 mi
0   400 km
Lambert Conformal Conic Projection

Geography Shapes History

Since prehistoric times, people have migrated to the rich **flood plains**—the flat lands along the rivers. When snows melt in the mountains, rich soil is washed down onto the lowlands of the Indo-Gangetic plain. Th s fertile plain attracted early settlers. In time, civilization developed and rich cities arose.

The wealth of the cities attracted invaders. Although the Himalayas were too high for armies to cross, newcomers found their way into the subcontinent through mountain gorges such as the famous Khyber Pass.

Other landforms continue to shape the region's history. For example, the mountain landscapes of Afghanistan and Pakistan have always isolated communities. In both countries, fie cely independent tribes have long resisted government interference in their aff irs. Today, governments struggle with rebel forces in these same tribal areas.

Reading Check **How did invaders reach the rich lowlands of India?**

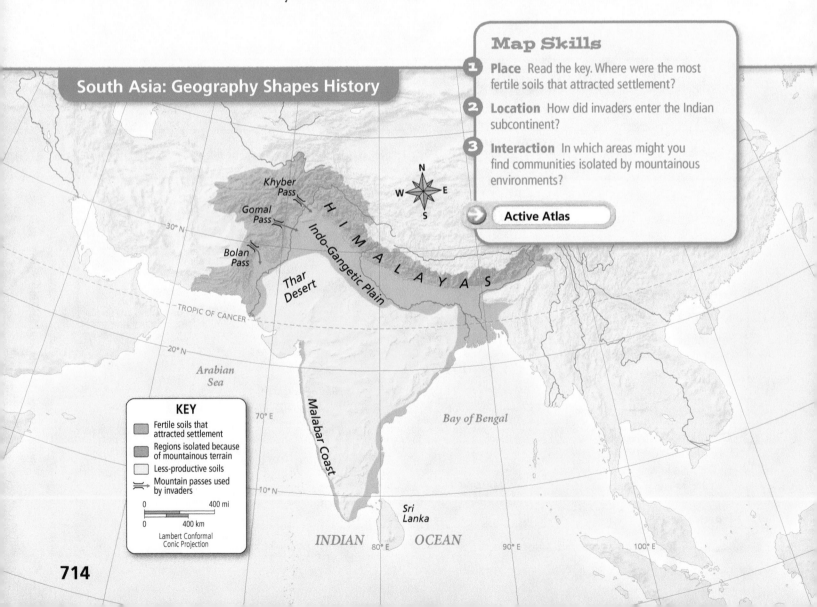

South Asia: Geography Shapes History

Map Skills

1. **Place** Read the key. Where were the most fertile soils that attracted settlement?

2. **Location** How did invaders enter the Indian subcontinent?

3. **Interaction** In which areas might you find communities isolated by mountainous environments?

→ **Active Atlas**

KEY

- Fertile soils that attracted settlement
- Regions isolated because of mountainous terrain
- Less-productive soils
- Mountain passes used by invaders

0   400 mi
0   400 km
Lambert Conformal Conic Projection

Khyber Pass
Gomal Pass
Bolan Pass
HIMALAYAS
Indo-Gangetic Plain
Thar Desert
30° N
TROPIC OF CANCER
20° N
Arabian Sea
Malabar Coast
Bay of Bengal
70° E
10° N
Sri Lanka
INDIAN OCEAN
80° E
90° E
100° E

Crossroads of Culture

While some parts of South Asia were isolated by mountains, other areas have always been in contact with the wider world. Goods and ideas traveled from China to Europe along the Silk Road, which passed through northern Afghanistan. Farther south, India lay at the center of the international sea trade routes.

These trade routes brought immense wealth to the region. Indian cotton, pearls, and pepper from the Malabar coast were in worldwide demand. Sri Lanka exported cinnamon. Ancient Greek traders used the monsoon winds to sail quickly across the Arabian Sea to reach these goods. Merchants from distant lands sometimes settled in the trading ports. Meanwhile, South Asian merchants helped spread the religions and culture of South Asia to China and Southeast Asia.

As you have read, the Himalayas did not stop invaders from entering the region. Some of these invaders came to raid and others to conquer. Each set of newcomers changed the history of the Indian subcontinent. In turn, these newcomers were changed by the regions they invaded. A cultural exchange began that continues today.

The Muslim invasions brought the religion of Islam to South Asia. They also brought cultural influences from Persia and the Arab world.

Despite much peaceful cultural interaction, growing diversity also created tensions. Th s is a region of multiple faiths, ethnic groups, and languages. At times the tension between different groups has led to violence. However, the people of South Asia have also enjoyed periods of religious tolerance and cultural exchange. In the next section you will read how a complex and rich civilization developed in this crossroads of culture.

Reading Check **How did the region become a crossroads of culture?**

my World
IN NUMBERS

If there were
100 people
in the world,

17 would live
in India.

Section 1 Assessment

Essential Question
What makes a nation?

Key Terms

1. Use the following terms to describe the geography of South Asia: Indian subcontinent, subsistence farming, Green Revolution, flood plain.

Key Ideas

2. Identify three roles that the northern mountains play in South Asia's geography.

3. What is the southwest monsoon, and how does it affect South Asia?

4. Where are the most fertile farmlands in South Asia located?

Think Critically

5. **Categorize** Some people categorize South Asia as a hot and humid region. Is that accurate? Explain.

6. **Draw Conclusions** Why are the river valleys among the most densely populated areas of South Asia?

7. How does the geography of a nation help create a common bond among its people and help shape its national identity? Go to your Student Journal to record your answer.

History of South Asia

Key Ideas

- A series of migrations mark the history of South Asia.
- Religious diversity developed early and increased over time.
- Britain slowly gained political control of most of the region.
- After India gained independence, new nations and conflicts emerged.

Key Terms
- cultural hearth
- caste system
- Hinduism
- nirvana
- Buddhism
- partition
- nonalignment

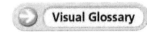 **Visual Glossary**

Reading Skill: Analyze Cause and Effect Take notes using the graphic organizer in your journal.

In ancient times, an advanced civilization developed in the Indus River Valley, in what is now Pakistan. Cities such as Mohenjo Daro and Harappa were amazingly sophisticated and well planned. Brick houses, two to three stories high, lined streets laid out on a grid pattern. The people of these cities had plumbing and clean water. They used a writing system and traded with other parts of the world.

Early History

Indus Valley civilization developed around 2500 b.c. and lasted for almost a thousand years. Its cities were spread over a huge area in the fertile Indus River basin. Here, as in other parts of the world, resources attracted settlement. Farmers in the fertile Indus fl od plain grew wheat, barley, rice, cotton, and other crops. Traders set up networks to exchange goods. Soon Indus Valley products, goods, and ideas reached people in less-advanced areas. In this way, the Indus Valley served as a **cultural hearth**—a place where civilization began and spread.

Around 1900 b.c., the Indus Valley civilization went into a mysterious decline. Some believe that earthquakes or climate change may

◀ A dancing Shiva, Hindu god of creation and destruction

◀ Jain temples on Mount Girnar, a mountain that attracts Jain, Hindu, and Muslim pilgrims

have disrupted the food supply. But even though its cities collapsed and were abandoned, aspects of its culture survived.

A Culture Forms Around 1700 b.c., a massive migration changed the history of the region. Migrants entered the subcontinent through the mountain passes. They spread across the northern plains of the Indus and the Ganges. The newcomers blended with local peoples, forming a group we call Aryans (AYR ee unz). Out of this union came a new culture, religion, and social system.

Social Divisions The Aryan **caste system** divided society into four main groups: priests, warriors, farmers, and laborers. Priests formed the highest caste. Those in the lowest caste were scorned and considered unclean.

Reading Check **What is the caste system?**

New Religions

In South Asia the Aryans' faith merged with local beliefs. The result was **Hinduism,** the religion of most people in India today.

Hindu Beliefs The sacred texts of Hinduism are called the Vedas, a collection of hymns and instructions. The Vedic texts may date to about 1200 B.C. Later, between the years 300 B.C. and A.D 300, great poems, known as epics, were also composed. The *Mahabharata* is the world's longest epic poem. It deals with a confli t between royal cousins.

Hindus believe in one spirit that lives in all things. In Hindu belief, this spirit, called Brahman, also takes the form of

▲ Hindu procession in Mumbai

lesser gods and goddesses. More than thirty gods are mentioned in the Rig Veda hymns.

Another principle of Hinduism is the idea that the human soul is eternal. According to Hindus, when the body dies, the soul passes into a new body. Th s process, known as reincarnation, can occur again and again, in an endless cycle. For believers, reincarnation is also affected by karma, the collection of good and bad deeds of a person's life. Karma determines the kind of life that will follow when the soul has been reborn.

To escape this cycle of rebirth many became ascetics—people who give up the luxuries of the world in order to try to live a spiritual life. The goal of the ascetic was to achieve salvation by uniting the individual soul with the universal soul, the Brahman.

Buddhism The Hindu search for salvation encouraged the development of a new religion. In the 500s b.c., a man named Siddhartha Gautama (sih DAHR uh gow TUH muh) taught that all suffering is caused by desire. In other words, human beings become unhappy when they cannot get what they want. In order to overcome desire, people must follow a code of conduct. According to Gautama, their goal should be to achieve **nirvana,** a state of understanding that releases the soul from the cycle of rebirth.

Gautama became known as the Buddha, or Enlightened One. His teachings developed into a religion known as **Buddhism.** Traders and Buddhist monks spread this new religion throughout Asia.

Another religion, Jainism, also emerged in South Asia. The followers of Jainism, called Jains, believed that the soul can be perfected and purified in this world. One of the ways to reach this perfection is to practice ahimsa, or nonviolence toward all living beings.

Reading Check According to Buddhist teachings, what makes people unhappy?

Early Empires

In 327 b.c., the kingdoms of South Asia were threatened by Greek armies under Alexander the Great.

The Greek Invasion Alexander, king of Macedon, had built a huge empire over Greece and parts of Africa and Asia. His Greek army fought their way into the northern Indus Valley. Alexander's army was exhausted. Faced with a long march across the Ganges plain in monsoon rains, the soldiers forced Alexander to head home.

Shortly after Alexander's retreat, one South Asian state took control of much of the region. That state became known as the Mauryan empire. Its most famous leader was Asoka (uh SOH kuh).

Religious Tolerance Asoka led several campaigns against his enemies in the first dozen years of his reign. But after one especially brutal battle he rejected violence and adopted Buddhist beliefs. Under Asoka, Buddhism spread through the Mauryan empire.

Not long after Asoka's death, the Mauryan empire declined and smaller kingdoms arose once more. Then, around a.d. 320, a state located on the Ganges plain expanded its power to form the Gupta empire. Th s empire ruled territory

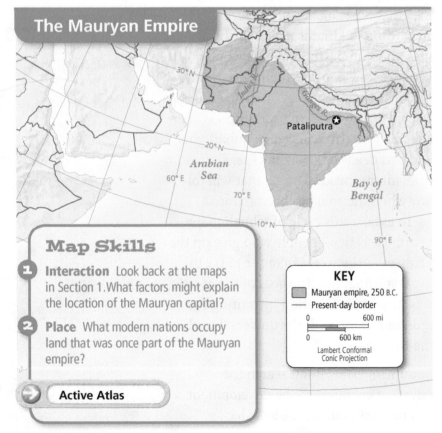

The Mauryan Empire

Pataliputra

Indus R.

Ganges R.

30° N

20° N

10° N

Arabian Sea

60° E

70° E

Bay of Bengal

90° E

Map Skills

1. **Interaction** Look back at the maps in Section 1. What factors might explain the location of the Mauryan capital?

2. **Place** What modern nations occupy land that was once part of the Mauryan empire?

Active Atlas

KEY

Mauryan empire, 250 B.C.
— Present-day border

0   600 mi
0   600 km
Lambert Conformal Conic Projection

from the Himalayas south to the Deccan Plateau. The two centuries of Gupta rule were a golden age of culture. Great advances were also made in science and mathematics. Gupta mathematicians developed the concept of zero. By a.d . 600, Indians were using a system of numbering that uses place value and numerals to represent numbers. Arab traders carried this system to Southwest Asia and Europe. Today, this system, called the Hindu-Arabic system, is used worldwide.

Reading Check **Which South Asian religion did Asoka embrace?**

Islam Arrives

Because India was such an important part of the international trade routes, new ideas and religions were spread by travelers and merchants. Th s is how Islam fi st entered the subcontinent.

Trade and Conquest Islam arrived in India in waves. The fi st came in the early 700s, when Arab traders introduced Islam to South Asia. The new faith spread throughout what is now Pakistan. Then, in the 900s, Turkish Muslim kingdoms began to spread through Afghanistan. Afghan kings launched raids into India to seize the wealth that was stored in the Hindu temples.

In the 1200s, one group of Muslim invaders established the Delhi Sultanate. Th s was a kingdom centered on the city of Delhi and led by a Muslim ruler called a sultan. Muslims would rule much of South Asia for the next 600 years. However, Hindu rajas, or rulers, controlled kingdoms in south India.

The arrival of Islam in a mainly Hindu region changed the history of South Asia. Hindus and Muslims were often rivals. Despite religious differences, there was a great deal of cultural exchange.

As Islam spread in the north, a new religion called Sikhism was born. Most followers of this religion, the Sikhs, live in an area of north India called the Punjab.

The Mughals In 1526, a Muslim from Central Asia named Babur founded the powerful Mughal empire. His grandson, Akbar, was a wise and tolerant ruler. Akbar extended Mughal control over much of South Asia. Akbar included Hindus in his army and government and protected other religions. He supported the arts and learning.

Muslim worshipers at a mosque in Lahore, Pakistan ▼

A grieving Shah Jahan built the Taj Mahal to mark the grave of his wife. ▼

The Mughal Empire

Armor of a Mughal war elephant. War elephants were the tanks of their day. They could easily smash their way through enemy lines.

Starting in the early 1500s, a Muslim dynasty called the Mughals ruled in South Asia. During much of this time the arts flourished, and both Muslims and Hindus helped govern the state.

THINK CRITICALLY Study the timeline. When did Mughal power decline?

Miniature painting showing Akbar welcoming Hindu princes and nobles

1526 Babur founds dynasty.

1628 Shah Jahan begins reign.

1707 Aurangzeb dies.

GOLDEN AGE

DECLINE

1500

1600

1700

1800

1556 Akbar begins reign.

1631 Taj Mahal is begun.

1658 Aurangzeb begins reign.

1858 British exile last Mughal.

720

Akbar's grandson, Shah Jahan, ruled at the height of Mughal power. Following the death of his beloved wife, Mumtaz Mahal, he built the Taj Mahal as a monument to her.

In 1658, Shah Jahan's son Aurangzeb seized power. Aurangzeb ended religious tolerance. He began persecuting Hindus and other non-Muslims, such as the Sikhs. Despite a series of uprisings against him, Aurangzeb continued to expand Mughal territory. However, his military campaigns weakened the empire. After Aurangzeb's death, the empire declined.

Reading Check **What was the Delhi Sultanate?**

The Colonial Period

During the Mughal period, the Portuguese, Dutch, British, and French set up trading ports. They came in search of spices, especially pepper, as well as cotton, silk, and indigo for dyeing cloth.

Trading Ports to Empire The British government sent the powerful East India Company to act as its trading agent in South Asia. By the mid-1700s, the Company had pushed its European rivals off   ost of the subcontinent. To protect its trade, the Company took over some Indian states by force. It also tried unsuccessfully to control Afghanistan.

In 1858, the British government took control of the East India Company's territories. Much of South Asia was now a British colony. It provided Britain with tea, coffee, grain, and raw materials such as cotton. Britain used Indian cotton to make inexpensive cloth in its factories.

India's textile industry <u>collapsed</u>. Its craft people could not compete with British-made cloth. Instead of exporting cloth and other fin shed goods, India became a market for those goods.

Struggle for Independence In the early 1900s, a movement arose to force Britain out of India. Its greatest leader was Mohandas Gandhi (moh HAHN ds GAHN de). Gandhi organized boycotts of British goods and led protest marches. Gandhi urged nonviolent resistance, or peaceful protest.

Gandhi believed that a nation should not be built around only one religion or ethnic group. He called on Hindus and Muslims to unite as one nation.

Reading Check **What tactic did Gandhi use to force Britain out of India?**

collapse, *v.,* to break down

❝ It is my firm conviction that nothing enduring can be built upon violence. ❞
—Mohandas K. Gandhi, 1928

South Asia After Independence

In 1947, Britain withdrew from India. But Muslims in the northwest and northeast feared that they would face discrimination if they remained in Hindu-dominated India. So India was **partitioned**—split into two states, India and Pakistan. At the time, Pakistan was made up of two regions, west and east, with 1,000 miles separating the two.

Partition With partition, a massive migration began. Millions of Hindus moved from Pakistan to India. Millions of Indian Muslims moved to Pakistan.

Many were massacred in an eruption of violence between ethnic and religious communities. In 1948, Gandhi himself was shot and killed by a Hindu extremist.

Ever since partition, relations between India and Pakistan have been <u>tense</u>. Both countries claim the region of Kashmir. In 1947 and again in 1965, India and Pakistan went to war over Kashmir.

India's prime minister during most of this period was Jawaharlal Nehru (juh-WAH hur lahl NAY roo). Nehru sought to modernize India. He also aimed to keep religion out of politics.

In foreign aff irs, Nehru forged a policy of **nonalignment.** Nonalignment means India did not ally itself with either of the superpowers—the United States or the Soviet Union—during the Cold War.

Nehru died in 1964. Two years later his daughter, Indira Gandhi, became prime minister. She oversaw yet another war with Pakistan in 1971.

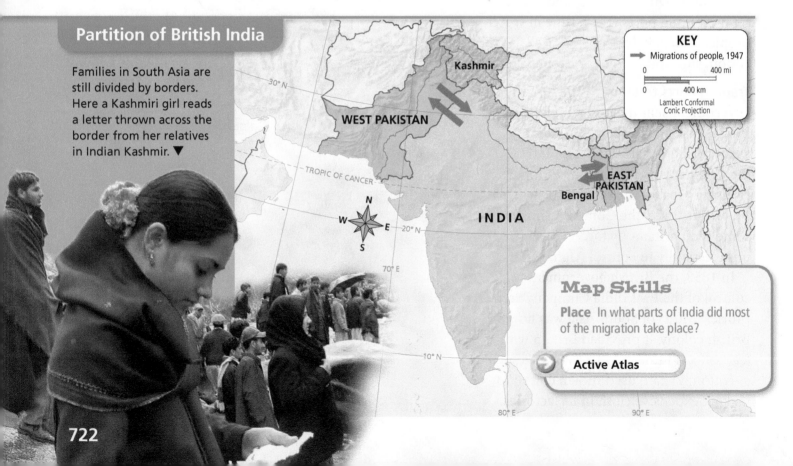

Partition of British India

Families in South Asia are still divided by borders. Here a Kashmiri girl reads a letter thrown across the border from her relatives in Indian Kashmir. ▼

KEY
→ Migrations of people, 1947

0 — 400 mi
0 — 400 km
Lambert Conformal Conic Projection

Kashmir

WEST PAKISTAN

TROPIC OF CANCER

EAST PAKISTAN

Bengal

INDIA

30° N

20° N

70° E

10° N

80° E

90° E

Map Skills

Place In what parts of India did most of the migration take place?

➲ **Active Atlas**

The leading political party in East Pakistan demanded independence. The Pakistani government launched an attack on East Pakistan in March 1971. Some 10 million people, mostly Hindus, fled from East Pakistan into India.

India helped East Pakistan gain independence. In December 1971, East Pakistan became the nation of Bangladesh (BAHNG luh desh).

Other Conflicts Civil war also struck Sri Lanka. In 1983 a group of Hindu Tamils began fi hting for a separate state. The war killed an estimated 70,000 people. In 2009 the government gained control of rebel areas and declared the war over.

In Afghanistan, the king was overthrown in 1973, and the country became a republic. Five years later, a communist political party seized control. In response, rebellions broke out throughout the country. To support the Afghan government, the Soviet Union invaded.

After a decade of fi hting various Muslim rebel groups, the Soviet Union withdrew. One of the groups, the Taliban, took over Afghanistan. The Taliban sheltered and supported Osama bin Laden and al Qaeda, the group that planned and carried out the September 11, 2001, terrorist attacks on the United States. That year, the United States, Britain, and other NATO countries helped Afghans force the Taliban from power.

Reading Check **Why did the partition of India lead to a massive migration?**

Afghan rebels on a captured Soviet helicopter in 1980
▼

Section 2 Assessment

Essential Question

What makes a nation?

Key Terms

1. Use the following terms to describe the history of South Asia: cultural hearth, caste system, Hinduism, nirvana, Buddhism, partition, nonalignment.

Key Ideas

2. How did the Aryans influence the culture of South Asia?

3. How did the colony of India serve the economic needs of Britain?

4. What three present-day countries were formed out of British India?

Think Critically

5. **Synthesize** What might have happened in South Asia if the Mughal empire had not declined?

6. **Compare Viewpoints** Why did many Hindus and Muslims in South Asia migrate during partition?

7. Do you agree or disagree with Gandhi and Nehru's idea of a nation? Explain. Go to your Student Journal to record your answer.

South Asia Today

Key Ideas

- South Asia has a rich mix of cultures.
- Religious and ethnic divisions within countries create tensions in the region.
- Political conflict and border disputes threaten peace in the region.
- Although it has many problems, the region is playing a greater role in the global economy.

Key Terms • epic • Bollywood • secular democracy • outsourcing

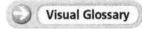 Visual Glossary

Reading Skill: Summarize Take notes using the graphic organizer in your journal.

 Culture Close-up

In India, people throw colored powder as they welcome spring during the festival of Holi. ▼

South Asia today is full of problems and promise. The region includes some of the most populated and poorest countries in the world. These nations suffer from confli ts, political instability, and terrorism. Natural disasters and rising sea levels threaten Bangladesh and the Maldives. India and Pakistan's dispute over Kashmir sometimes brings the two countries close to nuclear war.

Despite the region's troubles, South Asia holds great promise for the future. Democracy thrives in India, a land with pockets of prosperity and a growing middle class. As you have read in myStory, economic programs are helping many people, such as Nancy's family, rise out of poverty. The region's technical and scientific kills are in worldwide demand. South Asia's artistic energies fuel an exciting and influential culture.

South Asian Culture Today

Like Europe, South Asia has always been a well-defi ed cultural area. Many of its languages share a common ancestor. Huge parts of the region were united under Mauryan, Mughal, and British rule. In ancient times, Hinduism was another unifying force through the region. Although its religious diversity has increased, South Asians share many cultural traditions.

The Arts   Ancient Hindu literature is full of stories of gods and heroes. These stories take the form of **epics,** long poems of adventure and confli t. Epics such as *The Ramayana* helped defi e the values of Hindu culture—values such as courage, gentleness, love, and faithfulness.

Today many of these cultural values are expressed in films. India's version of Hollywood is called "**Bollywood,**" because it fi st emerged in Bombay (known today as Mumbai).

Religion   Most people in India and Nepal are Hindu. Muslims form a large minority in India, although in some areas, such as Kashmir, they are in the majority. In Pakistan, Afghanistan, and Bangladesh, Muslims form the largest religious group. Sikhism dominates in the Punjab area of northwest India.

Buddhism was once widespread in South Asia. Today it is strongest in the Himalayan countries of Nepal and Bhutan and on the island of Sri Lanka.

Food   Food is often flavored with a variety of spices, especially in India. A typical meal throughout the region is rice mixed with vegetables and, sometimes, meat. Hindu food rules ban the eating of beef. Islam forbids the eating of pork.

Reading Check   What foods make up a typical meal in South Asia?

my **World** IN NUMBERS
The Indian film industry, known as Bollywood, produces as many as **1,000** films a year.

Closer Look

Bollywood

Bollywood is famous for its dance scenes.

Bollywood is one of the largest film industries in the world. Like Hindu epics, Bollywood films tell tales of heroes, love, and adventure, and are full of music and dancing. Some Bollywood films tell the stories of the Hindu epics.

THINK CRITICALLY In what ways might Bollywood films differ from Hollywood films?

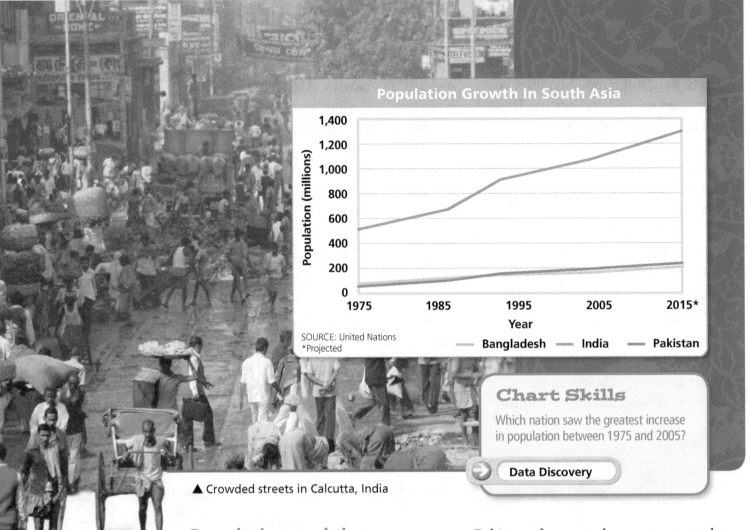

Population Growth In South Asia

Population (millions) vs **Year**

SOURCE: United Nations
*Projected

Bangladesh — India — Pakistan

Chart Skills

Which nation saw the greatest increase in population between 1975 and 2005?

Data Discovery

▲ Crowded streets in Calcutta, India

Population and the Environment

South Asia is home to more than 1.5 billion people. It is a region of dense populations and high birthrates. These factors are associated with poverty and with environmental problems.

Population Growth Today India has some 1.2 billion people. By 2050, India is expected to add 500 million more people and overtake China as the world's most populous country. Th s increase will probably happen even though India's birthrate has <u>dramatically</u> slowed in recent decades.

The populations of other nations in South Asia are also growing rapidly. In Pakistan, for example, a woman can be expected to have an average of four children during her lifetime. Afghanistan's population is growing the fastest. On average nearly seven children are born to each woman.

Search for Resources As in other parts of the world, rising populations are putting pressure on shrinking resources. In Bangladesh, people are moving onto the delta in order to farm. The delta is covered with rich sediment that has washed down from the Himalayas. However, the delta is also prone to cyclones and fl oding.

Th oughout the region, existing farmland may not be able to provide people

dramatically, *adv.,* greatly, strongly

with enough food to eat. In addition, the food that is available may not be very nutritious. In densely populated Bangladesh, some 30 percent of the population is undernourished.

People's health depends on vitamin-rich food and clean water. Clean water is another scarce resource in much of South Asia. Rivers are being dammed and water is being pumped out of the ground to irrigate crops. Such actions reduce the amount of drinking water available for the growing population.

Pollution South Asia's rivers are also polluted. Industries dump chemicals and other waste into them. Cities and villages foul them with raw sewage. For this reason, South Asians face a high risk of waterborne diseases. The Ganges is one of the most heavily polluted rivers in the world. Yet people wash clothes in it, bathe in it, and drink from it.

Much of the air pollution in South Asia comes from factories, power plants, and vehicles. But a signifi ant amount comes from the burning of forests to make way for farms and the burning of wood and coal for cooking and heating.

As a result, a blanket of pollution hovers over South Asia. Some call it the "Asian Brown Cloud." By refl cting sunshine, it cools the land below and warms the air in the mountains. Th s could <u>alter</u> the monsoon to reduce rainfall in the dry northwest. Some scientists believe it is helping speed the melting of Himalayan glaciers by adding to climate change.

Reading Check **What are the main causes of air pollution in South Asia?**

▲ Protest against a dam project in India

Social Problems

South Asia is a mix of the old and the new. It is often caught between traditional ways of life and the demands of the modern world.

Social Issues The caste system is a very ancient feature of society in India. A caste is a social group into which people are born. In the past, it was very difficult to leave one's caste. People were expected to marry within their caste, and their jobs were usually linked to that caste. People in the lower castes, who did forms of labor such as cleaning toilets, were considered unclean. So were those outside the caste system. In the past,

alter, *v.,* to change

my worldgeography.com Data Discovery

these people, or dalits, were forced to live outside town or village boundaries.

Gandhi and other South Asian leaders hoped to create a "casteless society." Toward that end, the constitutions of both India and Pakistan forbid discrimination based on caste. Today, the people who were once called untouchable now call themselves Dalit, meaning oppressed.

India's constitution also bans other common forms of discrimination:

> 66 The State shall not discriminate against any citizen on grounds only of religion, race, caste, sex, place of birth or any of them. 99
>
> —Constitution of India, Part III, Article 15, Clause 1

The legal ban on discrimination has not stopped the practice. Women, for example, still face unequal treatment. Th oughout South Asia, a man is considered the head of the household. In some rural areas, girls are prevented from attending school. Women's social and political roles are limited.

Another social issue in South Asia is unemployment. The region's economies are growing. But they are not growing fast enough to put everyone to work. Unemployment is worst in Afghanistan, where as much as 40 percent of workers do not have paying jobs.

Reading Check **What kinds of discrimination exist in South Asia?**

Closer Look

Women in South Asia

Women enjoy some rights but also endure many restrictions and problems in South Asia. In Pakistan, India, and Bangladesh, women have been elected to powerful leadership positions. However, in many places they suffer from lack of food, poor medical care, and discrimination.

THINK CRITICALLY Read the chart of literacy rates. What might explain the difference between men and women's literacy in the region?

President Patil of India helps lead the region's largest country.

In rural Afghanistan, women who go out in public are expected to cover themselves almost completely. They are often kept from getting an education and may be forced into marriage.

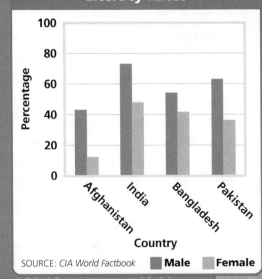

Literacy Rates

Percentage (y-axis: 0, 20, 40, 60, 80, 100)

Country (x-axis): Afghanistan, India, Bangladesh, Pakistan

SOURCE: CIA World Factbook ■ Male ■ Female

Conflicts in South Asia

Political and ethnic confli ts often have a religious aspect in South Asia. In India, rivalry between Hindus and Muslims sometimes explodes into violence. In 2002, Hindu-Muslim violence in India's Gujarat province left ore than 1,000 people dead.

In Afghanistan, the government is under threat from the Taliban, a religious group that follows a fundamentalist form of Islam. In the 1990s, the Taliban ruled the country. Although the United States and its allies forced them from power in 2001, the Taliban fi ht on. An American-led coalition is fi hting Taliban rebels in the south and in the eastern mountains.

But extremist groups like the Taliban can easily cross the Pakistan border to safe havens in the mountainous areas of northwest Pakistan.

Tensions between India and Pakistan often threaten the peace. The main cause of friction is Kashmir, an Indian state with a large Muslim population. In the past, Pakistan's government has backed Kashmiri groups fi hting for independence. These armed rebel forces often clash with Indian troops. Both India and Pakistan possess nuclear weapons. When tensions rise between these two neighbors, the world holds its breath.

Reading Check **Which South Asian countries possess nuclear weapons?**

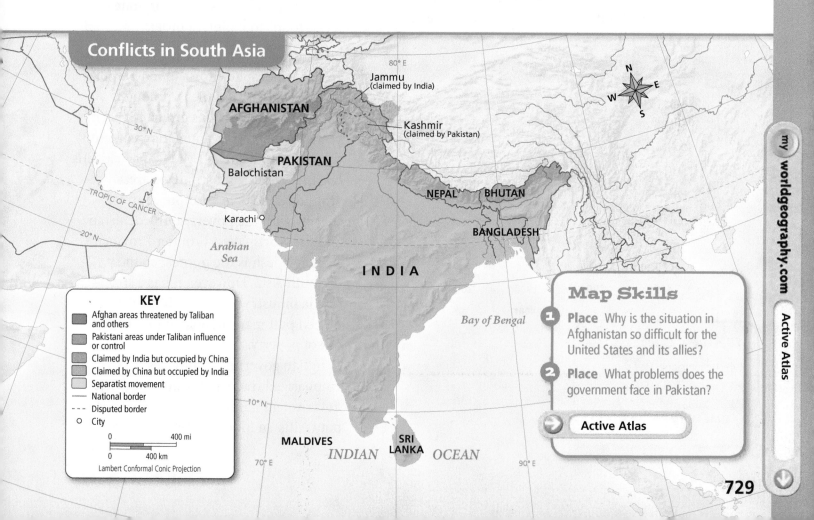

Conflicts in South Asia

KEY

- Afghan areas threatened by Taliban and others
- Pakistani areas under Taliban influence or control
- Claimed by India but occupied by China
- Claimed by China but occupied by India
- Separatist movement
- — National border
- --- Disputed border
- ○ City

0 400 mi
0 400 km
Lambert Conformal Conic Projection

80° E

Jammu (claimed by India)

AFGHANISTAN

30° N

Kashmir (claimed by Pakistan)

PAKISTAN

Balochistan

TROPIC OF CANCER

Karachi ○

NEPAL   BHUTAN

BANGLADESH

20° N

Arabian Sea

I N D I A

Bay of Bengal

10° N

MALDIVES   SRI LANKA
INDIAN   OCEAN

70° E   90° E

Map Skills

1 **Place** Why is the situation in Afghanistan so difficult for the United States and its allies?

2 **Place** What problems does the government face in Pakistan?

Active Atlas

my worldgeography.com   Active Atlas

Governments and Economies

South Asia has a mix of governments. India enjoys a long-lasting parliamentary democracy. However, other South Asian governments have been unstable.

A Variety of Governments India is a representative democracy. People elect nearly all the members of one house of India's parliament, or legislature. One member of parliament is chosen as the prime minister to head the government.

Bangladesh and Sri Lanka have had democratic rule for a long time. But their citizens do not always enjoy the same level of rights and freedoms as citizens do in India. Nepal recently ended its monarchy. It is now a democratic republic. Bhutan also holds democratic elections.

India is a **secular democracy,** which is a democracy not based on religion. In other nations, religion defi es the state. For example, the nations of Pakistan, Afghanistan, and the Maldives are all Islamic republics. In Pakistan, the prime minister must be Muslim.

After a coup by the military in 1999, an army general ran Pakistan for nine years. The courts, the press, and the people all suffered a loss of rights. In 2008, civilians once more gained power.

In Afghanistan, much has changed since the United States helped overthrow the Taliban in 2001. Afghanistan has a constitution and holds elections. However, the central government is weak. The United States and its allies continue to send troops to maintain order.

Economies Much of the region remains very poor, despite efforts to industrialize and diversify economies. Although Pakistan's economy has grown in recent years, its increasing population cuts into these economic gains. Many of its citizens live in poverty. Industrialized areas around Karachi and Lahore contrast sharply with the poverty of Balochistan and the North-West Frontier Province.

Bangladesh is the poorest country in South Asia. However, it has a strong textile industry. Microcredit banks have helped pull many people in that nation out of poverty.

Indian government policies have emphasized trade and technology. The government has lowered trade barriers, but tariffs n food products are high. It

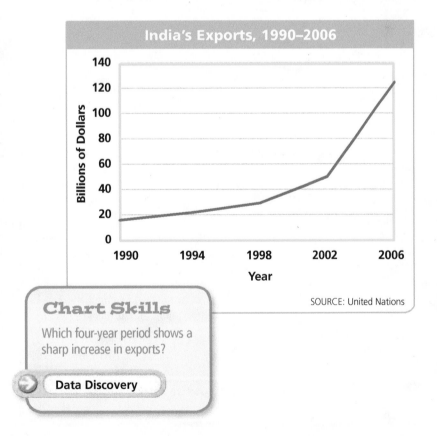

India's Exports, 1990–2006

SOURCE: United Nations

Chart Skills

Which four-year period shows a sharp increase in exports?

Data Discovery

has also signed trade agreements with other countries in South Asia. Trade has helped give India one of the world's fastest-growing economies. Today, about 100 million Indians can afford goods like televisions and washing machines.

In the 1990s, the government began building software technology parks. Here, workers create computer software for worldwide export.

India is also providing software services to companies all over the world. For example, companies in Europe and the United States have found it cheaper to send many computer-related tasks to workers outside the company. Th s practice is called **outsourcing.** India's economy and its skilled workforce have benefited from this practice.

India has put its high-tech skills to work in another area—space. The country has launched many satellites into orbit around Earth for many nations. In 2008,

▲ India has a highly skilled technology workforce.

India successfully landed a space probe on the moon.

Reading Check **In which South Asian country do citizens have the most democratic freedoms?**

my worldgeography.com Data Discovery

Section 3 Assessment

Key Terms

1. Use the following terms to describe life in South Asia today: epic, Bollywood, secular democracy, outsourcing.

Key Ideas

2. What are the two most commonly practiced religions in South Asia?

3. Why is Kashmir one of the main trouble spots in South Asia?

4. What actions by India's government opened up trade with the rest of the world?

Think Critically

5. **Draw Inferences** What is the connection between dense population, poverty, and environmental problems?

6. **Summarize** How is India's economy tied to the world economy?

What makes a nation?

7. What problems threaten the national unity of each nation in South Asia? Go to your Student Journal to record your answer.

Chapter Assessment

Key Terms and Ideas

1. **Recall** What areas in South Asia have good soil and why?

2. **Describe** What benefits has the **Green Revolution** brought to South Asia?

3. **Recall** What religions first emerged in South Asia?

4. **Explain** Why did **partition** take place in India?

5. **Describe** What problems are caused by South Asia's growing population?

6. **Compare and Contrast** What is the difference between the **secular democracy** of India and the Islamic republics of Pakistan and Afghanistan?

7. **Summarize** What are some hopeful signs of economic growth in South Asia?

Think Critically

8. **Draw Conclusions** Why are some areas of South Asia more populated than others?

9. **Synthesize** What factors help slow economic growth in South Asia?

10. **Compare Viewpoints** Why did Gandhi want the British to leave India?

11. **Core Concepts: Human–Environment Interaction** How does South Asia's population growth affect the environment?

Places to Know

For each place, write the letter from the map that shows its location.

12. **Ganges River**

13. **Kabul**

14. **Himalayas**

15. **Lahore**

16. **Indus River**

17. **Sri Lanka**

18. **Estimate** Using the scale, estimate the distance between Kabul and Lahore.

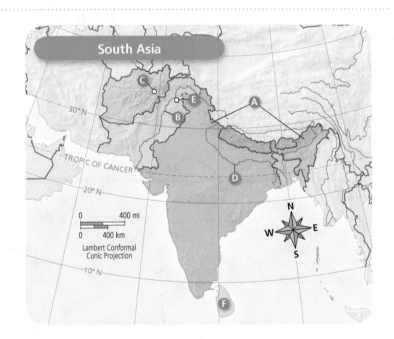

South Asia

30° N

TROPIC OF CANCER

20° N

0   400 mi
0   400 km
Lambert Conformal
Conic Projection

10° N

N
W   E
S

Essential Question

myWorld Chapter Activity

Microloan Assessment Follow your teacher's instructions to study the countries of South Asia in order to recommend a microloan to a group in need. Discuss your findings and decide who should get the loan. Then write a proposal that includes your reasons for granting the loan.

21st Century Learning

Search for Information on the Internet

With a partner, search for sites that give information on the economies of South Asia today. You may want to select three countries before you begin your search. Then do a Web search about each country's trade, manufacturing, exports, and so on.

Document-Based Questions

Success Tracker™
Online at myworldgeography.com

Use your knowledge of South Asia and Documents A and B to answer Questions 1–3.

Document A

Arable Land	
Country	Arable Land
Pakistan	24.44%
India	48.33%
Afghanistan	12.13%

SOURCE: *CIA World Factbook*

Document B

" India has become a key market for many information communication technology products made in the U.S., while the U.S. is an important consumer of Indian [information technology]-enabled services."

—U.S. State Department

1. Which of the following best describes the information about the three countries shown in Document A?

   A Afghanistan has the highest percentage of land that can be farmed.

   B Pakistan has less farmland than Afghanistan.

   C India has the highest percentage of farmland.

   D Afghanistan has more farmland than Pakistan.

2. Which of the following best describes the meaning of the quote in Document B?

   A India buys products made in South Asia.

   B India and the United States have an important economic relationship.

   C The United States does not use Indian products.

   D The United States buys Indian products.

3. **Writing Task** Compare the economic strengths of India and Pakistan, using Documents A and B.

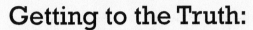

Getting to the Truth:
Fact or *Opinion?*

Your Mission In groups, research Web sites for information on one South or Central Asian nation. As you read, look for examples of facts and opinions and develop a presentation evaluating the Web sites you have visited.

When researching on the Internet, it is important to be able to evaluate the reliability of Web sites. One way to do this is to know how to distinguish between facts and opinions. Facts are claims that can be confirmed by evidence.

Opinions are claims that cannot be confirmed by evidence, even if you agree with them. Your friend may say that basketball is better than baseball, but that claim cannot be confirmed by evidence, as it is merely your friend's opinion.

Web sites can present facts, opinions, or both. When researching, learn to spot the differences by evaluating the evidence that is presented to support any claims.

It's raining.

FACT

If it were raining, I would do better in math class.

OPINION

STEP 1

Break It Down.

First, break down the different elements of your group's task. You will investigate information about your nation in order to make a presentation. As you do so, note where you find information. Then, check another site for the same data and note any discrepancies. For example, India's population figures might differ between two sites. Why might this be? As you research, look for clues to whether or not the Web site is reliable and the data on it are based on fact or based on opinion.

STEP 2

Look for Clues.

Think about the purpose of the Web site. Consider how the site functions. Is it easy to use? Look for the author of the site and how often the site is updated. Also, try to determine if the site has any affiliations. Some sites share content or republish content without reviewing it. Errors may be transferred from site to site in this way. As you read, you should also be aware that Web sites may have certain points of view and are designed to reinforce certain attitudes.

STEP 3

What's the Truth Factor?

Focus your group's presentation on the reliability of the information you found on the sites you visited. As you present your nation's data, discuss what the data mean as well as any conflicting information you discovered. Read aloud at least one quote from each of the news Web sites you visited. Point out specific word clues that led you to believe the quote was fact or opinion. Also, discuss your overall impression of the reliability of the content on these sites.

Regional Overview

East and Southeast Asia

East and Southeast Asia are regions of rugged mountains, vast plains, dense forests, and crowded coastlines. These regions are heavily populated. The largest country in these regions is China, which has more inhabitants than any other country on Earth.

What time is it there?

Washington, D.C.	Wuxi, China
9 A.M. Monday	10 P.M. Monday

60° N

MONGOLIA ✪
Ulaanbaatar

30° N

NORTH KOREA
Beijing ✪   ✪ P'yongyang
CHINA   Seoul ✪ SOUTH KOREA

JAPAN ✪
Tokyo

East China Sea

MYANMAR
Bay of Bengal   LAOS ✪   ✪ Hanoi
Yangon ✪   Vientiane ✪
THAILAND   South China Sea   ✪ Taipei
Bangkok ✪   TAIWAN
CAMBODIA
Phnom Penh ✪   VIETNAM
        ✪ Manila

PHILIPPINES

TROPIC OF CANCER

PACIFIC OCEAN

0°   Kuala Lumpur ✪ MALAYSIA   BRUNEI
Singapore ✪   ✪ Bandar Seri Begawan
SINGAPORE

INDIAN OCEAN

✪ Jakarta

INDONESIA

EQUATOR

EAST TIMOR
✪ Dili

90° E   120° E   150° E   180°

KEY
— National border
✪ Capital city
Orthographic Projection

The Unit Ahead

my worldgeography.com

Plan your trip online by doing a Data Discovery Activity and watching the myStory Videos of the region's teens.

my **Story**

Xiao
Age: 18
Home: Wuxi, China

Chapter 21

my **Story**

Asuka
Age: 18
Home: Yokohama, Japan

Chapter 22

my **Story**

Ridwan
Age: 19
Home: Bukittinggi, Indonesia

Chapter 23

Rice fields in Bali, Indonesia

Regional Overview
Physical Geography

Tian Shan
Taklimakan Desert
Kunlun Shan

Plateau of Tibet
Mt. Everest
29,035 ft (8,850 m)

Himalayas

Gobi

Huang (Yellow) River

North
China Plain

Chang (Yangtze) River

The Himalayas are one of
the many mountain ranges
in East Asia.

Malay Peninsula
Gulf of
Thailand

South China Sea

INDIAN
OCEAN

Java Sea

Active volcanoes lie throughout
the islands of Southeast Asia.

Two deserts shape life in the northern part of this region.

Manchurian Plain

Korean Peninsula

Sea of Japan (East Sea)

Philippine Sea

Mountains give way to plains in China and, on a smaller scale, in Taiwan, the Koreas, and Japan.

PACIFIC OCEAN

Regional Flyover

Beginning your flight in the west, you enter China's airspace high above the Himalayas. Then, you face the high Plateau of Tibet.

To the north of this plateau lie two vast deserts, the Gobi and the Taklimakan. As you fly north over the Gobi Desert, you come to Mongolia, a dry land of deserts, plateaus, and mountains.

Circling south from Mongolia, along the eastern coast of Asia, you see a mountainous peninsula, home to North and South Korea. As you continue south the climate becomes warmer, and soon your eyes glimpse the tropical forests of Vietnam, Laos, Thailand, Cambodia, and the island nations of Malaysia, Singapore, Indonesia, East Timor, Brunei, and the Philippines. As the plane turns north, you pass over the small island nation of Taiwan. When you reach Japan, count the countries you have seen—17!

my worldgeography.com   In-Flight Movie

▶ **In-Flight Movie**

Take flight over East Asia and Southeast Asia and explore the regions from the air.

Regional Overview
Human Geography

Downtown Tokyo is lit up brightly every night.

Where People Live

East and Southeast Asia's physical features have influenced where people in the region live. Many nations in these regions do not have much land that is good for farming or settlement. Not very many people live in the rugged mountains and dry deserts. The dry climate in the north of these regions is particularly challenging. Even in the south, where water is more plentiful, there are many hills and very little land that is flat enough to farm.

As a result, the huge population of these regions is packed into the areas where life is easier—on the plains and along rivers and flat coastal areas. Japan, the Koreas, and many of the nations of Southeast Asia have forested mountains running through their centers, so in those countries people live mainly in valleys and in coastal cities. China and Mongolia both have large plains where people can farm or raise livestock.

This map shows where people live in East and Southeast Asia.

The lights in this satellite photo show electricity use in heavily populated areas of East and Southeast Asia.

my World IN NUMBERS

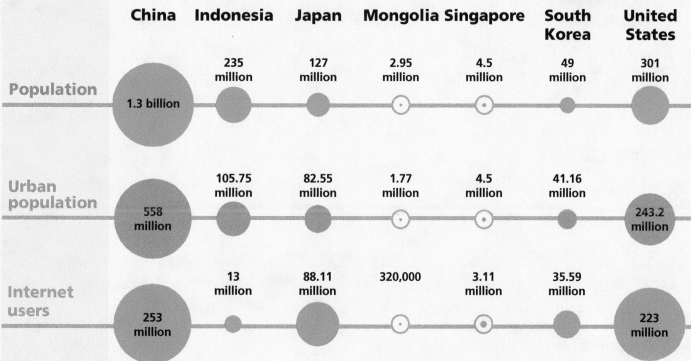

	China	Indonesia	Japan	Mongolia	Singapore	South Korea	United States
Population	1.3 billion	235 million	127 million	2.95 million	4.5 million	49 million	301 million
Urban population	558 million	105.75 million	82.55 million	1.77 million	4.5 million	41.16 million	243.2 million
Internet users	253 million	13 million	88.11 million	320,000	3.11 million	35.59 million	223 million

SOURCE: *CIA World Factbook, Encyclopaedia Britannica*

Put It Together

1. What physical features prevent western China from being heavily settled?

2. Where do many of the rivers in China and Southeast Asia begin?

3. Compare the number of Internet users to the number of urban dwellers. Which country has more Internet users than urban residents?

 Data Discovery

Find your own data to make a regional data table.

Size Comparison

East and Southeast Asia are more than twice as large as the United States but have 7 times the population.

my worldgeography.com Data Discovery

Chapter 21

China and Its Neighbors

How can you measure success?

KEY
- —— National border
- ✪ Capital city
- ○ Other city

0 ___ 400 mi
0 ___ 400 km
Lambert Conformal Conic Projection

Ulaanbaatar ✪

MONGOLIA

Beijing ✪
Tianjin ○

Yellow Sea

CHINA

Wuxi ○ ○ Shanghai
Lake Tai

Wuhan ○

East China Sea

Chongqing ○

Taipei ✪
TAIWAN

Hong Kong ○

South China Sea

TROPIC OF CANCER

Where in the World Are China and Its Neighbors?

Washington, D.C., to Wuxi: 7,440 miles

my Story

Xiao's Lake

In this section you'll read about Xiao, a young man helping to care for his family. He lives in eastern China. What does his story tell you about the challenges China faces?

Explore the Essential Question
- at **my worldgeography.com**
- using the **myWorld Chapter Activity**
- with the **Student Journal**

Story by Megan Shank for myWorld Online

Xiao lives with his father, mother, grandmother, and older brother in a tiny village near Wuxi (woo shee), an ancient city in the east of China. After learning of his father's diabetes diagnosis, 17-year-old Xiao found a full-time job to help support his family.

Xiao (whose name is pronounced show, as in *shower*) and his brother both work at a factory that produces machines that make ice cream. His mother works at a different factory and tends the family's orange and peach orchard. His father is a part-time driver.

Every morning at 7 a.m, Xiao rides his motorcycle to Wuxi. There are many factories in this area. They have easy access to railways and canals that transport goods to large cities, such as Shanghai. Xiao works 10 hours a day, five days a week. Many local youth leave to make their fortunes, but Xiao wants to stay close to his family.

Life has changed as China has become wealthier. Meat used to be too expensive to eat every day. Thirty years ago, few people could afford a television. Now, most families in Xiao's village own one.

Xiao rides home from work.

A street
in Xiao's village

Xiao's mother prepares
dinner in a large wok.

Xiao's family shares
these dishes at dinner.

Xiao's mother applies
pesticides to the
orange trees in the
family orchard.

Unlike his parents' generation, which suffered famine and shortages of many goods, Xiao doesn't remember a time when food was scarce.

He does remember when the waters of Lake Tai were clean and clear. Lake Tai is China's third-largest body of fresh water. It is just a five-minute jaunt from Xiao's house. As a boy, he learned to swim there. He collected snails in the lake and had mud fights with friends.

Walking through the family's fruit orchard, it's hard to imagine this place ever smelled like anything other than sun-ripened oranges. Yet in the summer of 2007 a terrible odor crept from the lake across the orchard and into their home.

An algae bloom covered the lake with green slime. The algae bloom was caused, in part, by pollution and pesticides from the farms and factories around the lake. The algae used up the oxygen in the lake. Suffocated fish floated to the surface, belly up.

"You didn't even want to use the water to bathe, much less to drink," says Xiao.

Thirty million people rely on Lake Tai for drinking water. That summer, families in Xiao's village avoided the lake water. They drew water from local wells or bought bottles of water. Bottled water was rushed to Wuxi during the crisis.

Xiao's family shut the windows and put up with the stench. Flies and mosquitoes swarmed.

A factory by the lake is torn down.

Algae and trash float on this small pond near Xiao's home.

Small ponds where neighbors had once washed their fruit and rinsed their rice filled with algae and muck. People started to throw their garbage into these pools, as well.

"If the environment is better, people behave better," says Xiao. "When there's pollution, people throw their garbage where they shouldn't."

The city of Wuxi has started to solve the problem. They hired people to remove the algae. They have also shut down some factories around the lake to reduce the pollution.

Towns are also being bulldozed. Citizens in the village next to Xiao's village were forced to move when the government claimed the area for a park. Xiao has never lived anywhere else and worries the government will make his family move, too.

He has mixed feelings about his parents' use of pesticides and fertilizers in their orchard. He knows these chemicals run off nto the lake and cause

more harm. He also knows that the factory where he works may be adding to the pollution. Still, Xiao needs his job. He hopes to save money, marry, and start a family—preferably, he says, by the time he's 23— so there are no easy answers.

"How can you choose between your family and your home?"

Meet the Videographer

Name Carl Thelin
Favorite Moment Eating dinner with Xiao's family

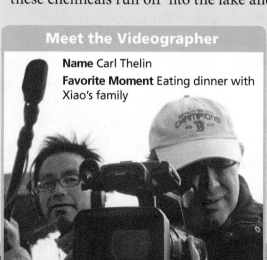

myStory Video

Join Xiao as he shows you more about his life and Lake Tai.

Section 1

Chapter Atlas

Key Ideas
- Most people live on the plains and in the coastal areas of this region.
- Climate, especially rainfall, influences the economic activities in this region.
- Cities have grown rapidly in China in recent years.

Key Terms
- loess
- staple crop
- nomadic herder
- arable land
- one-child policy

 Visual Glossary

 Reading Skill: Label an Outline Map Take notes using the outline map in your journal.

A fisherman uses a cormorant bird to catch fish on the Li River, China.

Physical Features

Travelers who enter China from the west must struggle over a barrier of high mountains. The Himalayas, along China's southwest border, are the highest mountain range in the world.

North of the Himalayas, travelers cross the Tibetan Plateau, the highest and largest plateau in the world. Many rivers begin here. They fl w south and east to many countries, providing drinking water for one third of the world's population.

China's largest rivers—the Chang (or Yangtze) and the Huang (or Yellow)— begin on the Tibetan Plateau. These rivers

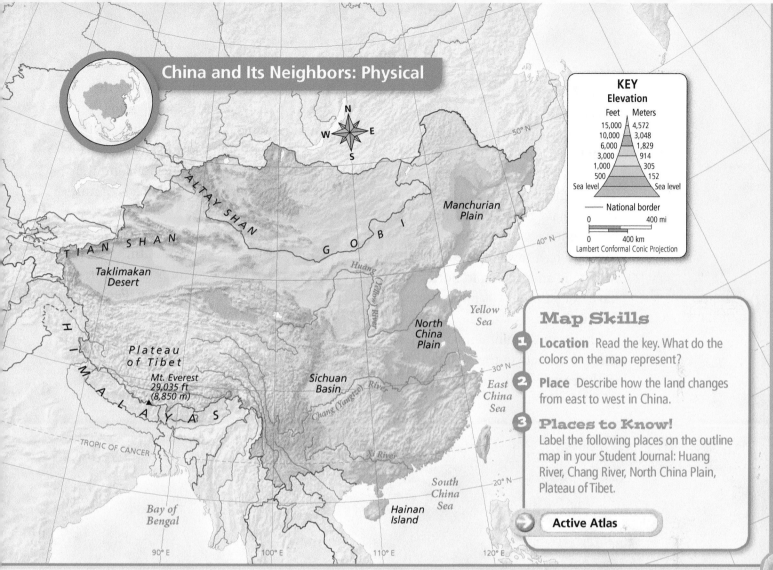

China and Its Neighbors: Physical

ALTAY SHAN

TIAN SHAN

Taklimakan Desert

HIMALAYAS

Plateau of Tibet

Mt. Everest
29,035 ft
(8,850 m)

TROPIC OF CANCER

Bay of Bengal

Sichuan Basin

Chang (Yangtze) River

Xi River

GOBI

Manchurian Plain

Huang (Yellow) River

North China Plain

Yellow Sea

East China Sea

Hainan Island

South China Sea

50° N
40° N
30° N
20° N

90° E   100° E   110° E   120° E

KEY
Elevation

Feet	Meters
15,000	4,572
10,000	3,048
6,000	1,829
3,000	914
1,000	305
500	152
Sea level	Sea level

—— National border

0   400 mi
0   400 km
Lambert Conformal Conic Projection

Map Skills

1 Location Read the key. What do the colors on the map represent?

2 Place Describe how the land changes from east to west in China.

3 Places to Know! Label the following places on the outline map in your Student Journal: Huang River, Chang River, North China Plain, Plateau of Tibet.

Active Atlas

tumble from the highlands down to the plains on the east coast. The island of Taiwan, by contrast, has mountains on the east and <u>fertile</u> plains on the west side.

Mountains and highland plateaus cover much of Mongolia. A huge desert called the Gobi stretches from southern Mongolia toward the Huang River. Winds from the desert carry **loess** (l oh es) into China. Loess is a dustlike material that can form soil. It can pile up more than 100 feet deep. People carve caves into the loess hills and build their homes in them.

The Huang River cuts through these deposits, picking up the loess. Huang

means "yellow" in Chinese. If you hopped on board a boat along the river, you would see that the loess makes it look yellow and muddy. The Huang created the North China Plain by fl oding many times. Each fl od left ehind fertile soil. For thousands of years, Chinese people have farmed the flat lands along the country's rivers.

Landforms, such as rivers, affect where people live. Climate is also important when people decide how to use the land.

Reading Check What physical feature do China and Mongolia share?

fertile, *adj.,* rich in nutrients, capable of growing many plants

Climate and Land Use

Across this region, there are two important climate patterns. The fi st is that the climate is generally colder in the north and warmer in the south. The southern islands of Taiwan and Hainan have hot, humid summers and mild winters. Cities such as Ulaanbaatar (oo lahn bah tawr) in the north of Mongolia and Beijing in northern China have hot summers. Winters there are freezing cold.

The second major climate pattern is that the climate in the west is drier than in the east. Winds blowing from the south carry moisture from the Pacific Ocean to Taiwan and eastern China. Tall mountains block these winds, so the climate of Mongolia and western China is dry. Two great deserts, the Gobi and the Taklimakan, stretch for hundreds of miles across this area.

These climate patterns influence how people use the land. South of the Chang River, crops that need abundant water, such as tea and rice, are grown. People here, such as Xiao's family, generally eat rice with their daily meals. Taiwan's wet western plains grow rice and other tropical crops, such as sugar and bananas.

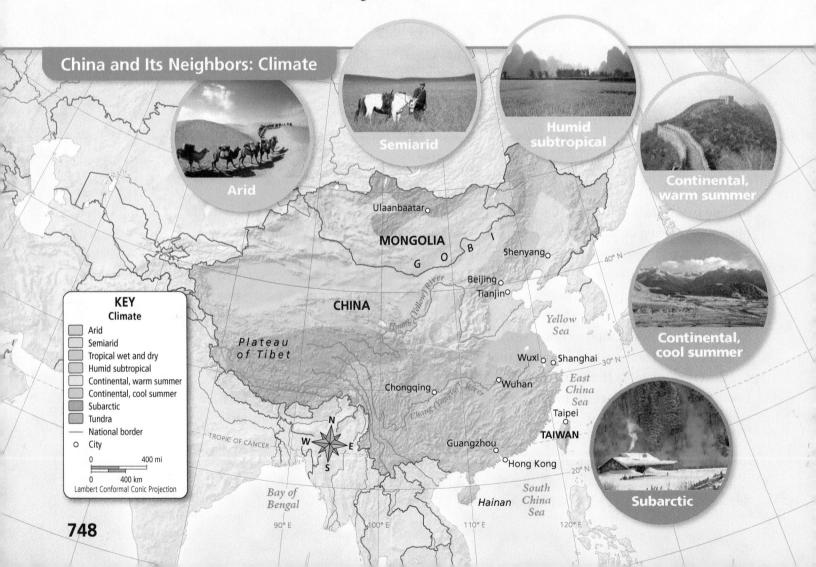

China and Its Neighbors: Climate

Arid

Semiarid

Humid subtropical

Continental, warm summer

Continental, cool summer

Subarctic

Ulaanbaatar

MONGOLIA

G O B I

Shenyang

40° N

Beijing

Tianjin

CHINA

Chang (Yellow) River

Yellow Sea

KEY
Climate

- Arid
- Semiarid
- Tropical wet and dry
- Humid subtropical
- Continental, warm summer
- Continental, cool summer
- Subarctic
- Tundra
— National border
○ City

Plateau of Tibet

Wuxi   Shanghai   30° N

Chongqing

Wuhan

Chang (Yangtze) River

East China Sea

Taipei

TAIWAN

0   400 mi
0   400 km
Lambert Conformal Conic Projection

TROPIC OF CANCER

N
W   E
S

Guangzhou

Hong Kong

20° N

Bay of Bengal

Hainan

South China Sea

90° E   100° E   110° E   120° E

Between the Chang River and the Huang River both rice and wheat are grown. The fertile North China Plain north of the Huang River is too dry for rice. Here, wheat is the **staple crop,** that is, the major crop that is the basis of the diet. Common foods in northern China include steamed bread, dumplings, and noodles made of wheat fl ur.

Still farther north and west, the climate is usually too dry for growing crops. People in these regions have lived mainly as **nomadic herders,** that is, they herd fl cks and do not settle in one place. They must move their herds to fi d sources of water and grassland. Th s nomadic life-style is especially common in Mongolia and Tibet. Like the cowboys of the American West, Mongolian herders become skilled horseback riders at a young age.

In recent years, industry has expanded in China, Taiwan, and Mongolia. More people have moved to the cities to work in offices nd factories, rather than working as farmers or nomadic herders. Large industrial areas have grown around the cities of the region. Peoples' lives across the region are changing.

Reading Check What are the two major climate patterns in this region?

my World IN NUMBERS

China has **10%** of the world's good farmland to feed **20%** of the world's population.

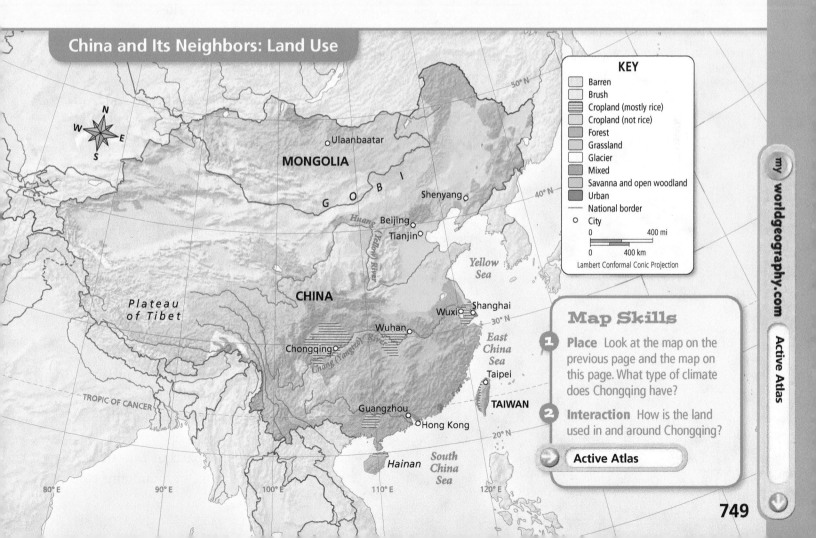

China and Its Neighbors: Land Use

KEY

- Barren
- Brush
- Cropland (mostly rice)
- Cropland (not rice)
- Forest
- Grassland
- Glacier
- Mixed
- Savanna and open woodland
- Urban
- — National border
- ○ City

0 — 400 mi
0 — 400 km
Lambert Conformal Conic Projection

MONGOLIA
Ulaanbaatar
G O B I
Shenyang
Huang (Yellow) River
Beijing
Tianjin
Yellow Sea
CHINA
Plateau of Tibet
Wuxi — Shanghai
Wuhan
East China Sea
Chongqing
Chang (Yangtze) River
Taipei
TROPIC OF CANCER
TAIWAN
Guangzhou
Hong Kong
Hainan
South China Sea
50° N, 40° N, 30° N, 20° N
80° E, 90° E, 100° E, 110° E, 120° E

Map Skills

1 **Place** Look at the map on the previous page and the map on this page. What type of climate does Chongqing have?

2 **Interaction** How is the land used in and around Chongqing?

Active Atlas

my worldgeography.com **Active Atlas**

Growing Cities, Crowded Coasts

People are not evenly spread across the countries in this region. People have settled where it is easiest to make a living. Today, this is a region on the move with millions of people migrating to fi d work.

More people live in China than in any other country. Yet China's resources are limited. Deserts and mountains cover much of the country. Only about 15 percent of China's land is **arable land,** that is, land that can be used to grow crops. Most of the arable land is in the eastern part of the country. More than nine tenths of China's people live in the east, and this area can be very crowded.

The Chinese government realized decades ago that China's large population was a problem. If the population continued to grow quickly, there would not be enough food in the country for everyone.

In the late 1970s, the government started a **one-child policy.** Under this law, many married couples are only allowed to have one child. Couples who have more children are punished. There are some exceptions to this rule. Couples in rural areas may sometimes have more than one child. In the cities the one-child policy has been strictly <u>enforced</u>.

Still, China's cities are large and are growing quickly. Th s is because millions of people are leaving rural areas and moving to the cities to look for work. Many of these workers fi d jobs in factories or on construction sites.

A migrant worker in Chengdu explains why she and her husband moved to the city to work:

> 66 We lived in a village that's surrounded by big mountains. Where we were, you really can't make a cent. . . you raise a little livestock, some crops, but that's really not sufficient [enough]. 99
> —Cai Zisheng, Chinese migrant

Most people in China still live in rural areas. Only about 45 percent of Chinese people live in cities—in the United States almost 80 percent of people live in cities. China's population is much larger than that of the United States, and so many cities in China are very large. China's capital, Beijing, is home to more than 14 million people. Shanghai is the largest city in the country with more than 16 million people.

Like China, some parts of Taiwan are very crowded. A ridge of mountains runs

enforce, *v.,* to make someone follow a rule or law

myWorldActivity
Migration Decisions

In 1990, parts of the Pudong area of Shanghai were covered by farmland (inset). Now, towering skyscapers and even an airport have been built over the fields.

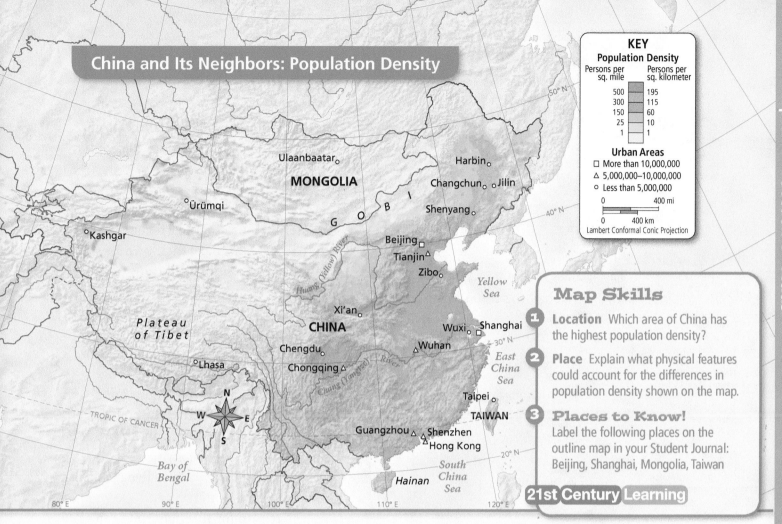

China and Its Neighbors: Population Density

KEY

Population Density

Persons per sq. mile	Persons per sq. kilometer
500	195
300	115
150	60
25	10
1	1

Urban Areas

☐ More than 10,000,000
△ 5,000,000–10,000,000
○ Less than 5,000,000

0 ————— 400 mi
0 ————— 400 km
Lambert Conformal Conic Projection

Map Skills

1 **Location** Which area of China has the highest population density?

2 **Place** Explain what physical features could account for the differences in population density shown on the map.

3 **Places to Know!** Label the following places on the outline map in your Student Journal: Beijing, Shanghai, Mongolia, Taiwan

21st Century Learning

---

along the east coast of the island, so most cities and farms are on the flatter west coast of the island. Almost three quarters of Taiwan's population lives in these coastal cities.

In contrast, Mongolia is a landlocked nation, or a nation without a coastline. About half of all Mongolians are nomadic, moving their homes to follow herds of livestock across the country's grassy plains. The nomads live in tents called gers (gehrz). Most of the rest of the population lives in cities. Almost a third of the population lives in the capital city of Ulaanbaatar.

In Mongolia, cities grow or shrink depending on the weather. When a hard winter strikes, livestock may die from a lack of food. Nomadic herders must go to the cities to fi d work, and the cities grow. During mild winters, some city workers give up their jobs to return to herding. In this region, as in many others, many people move to fi d of work.

Reading Check **Why do many people in both China and Taiwan live along the coast?**

Mongolian nomads often live in gers, which can be easily moved. ▼

⊙ **Culture Close-up**

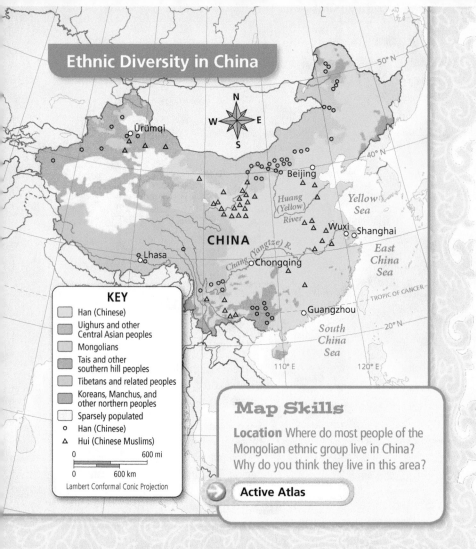

Ethnic Diversity in China

KEY
- Han (Chinese)
- Uighurs and other Central Asian peoples
- Mongolians
- Tais and other southern hill peoples
- Tibetans and related peoples
- Koreans, Manchus, and other northern peoples
- Sparsely populated
- ○ Han (Chinese)
- △ Hui (Chinese Muslims)

0   600 mi
0   600 km
Lambert Conformal Conic Projection

Map Skills

Location Where do most people of the Mongolian ethnic group live in China? Why do you think they live in this area?

Active Atlas

Ethnic Diversity in China

About 92 percent of Chinese people today belong to the Han ethnic group. More than 50 ethnic groups make up the rest of the population.

Some of the larger minority groups are the Uighurs (wee g oorz) of northwestern China and the Tibetans.

These groups have their own languages, traditional clothing, and holidays. Some of these groups are closely identifi d with a religion. For example, many Uighurs are Muslim. Many Tibetans practice a unique form of Buddhism.

China's many ethnic groups are not evenly spread across the country. People of the Han ethnic group live mostly in the east. Many people who belong to minority groups live near the borders of the country.

The reason for this pattern lies in China's history. The Han people built their earliest kingdoms in the east along the Huang River. Later, these kingdoms joined together and created a powerful Chinese empire.

The Chinese emperors conquered new lands. They came to control regions whose people were not Han. These people kept many of their own customs and stayed near their traditional homelands.

People from all ethnic groups have played an important role in China's history. Some emperors were not from the Han ethnic group. Mongolian lead-

Hello! I'm Tibetan. I live in Tibet. I am a Buddhist. Here is what "hello" looks like written in my language:
བཀྲ་ཤིས་བདེ་ལེགས།

Hello! I'm Han Chinese. Most people in China are Han, like me. Here is what "hello" looks like written in my language: 你好

Hello! I'm Korean. I live in the northeast of China. Here is what "hello" looks like written in my language: 안녕 하세 요

Language Lesson

ers ruled China for almost a hundred years. The last emperor and his ancestors belonged to a people called the Manchu.

China's current government has tried to protect the country's rich cultural heritage. For example, the one-child policy only applies to Han Chinese people. Families of other ethnic groups are allowed to have more than one child.

However, the Chinese government has made other rules that control cultural and religious life in China. People cannot freely form groups to practice religion. The government limits the number of churches and religious organizations.

All Chinese people, including the Han, must follow these restrictions. However, these rules make it harder for groups with special religious traditions to preserve their cultures.

Tibetans and Uighurs have protested against the government. Some have called for more autonomy from China. The Chinese government has attacked and imprisoned people who protest against its

policies. The government is trying to improve the economy of borderland areas, but confli t continues because of its rules controlling cultural life.

Reading Check **Why are many minority groups found along China's borders?**

Uighur schoolgirls in China's western province of Xinjiang ▼

Section 1 Assessment

Key Terms

1. Use the following terms to describe land use in this region: loess, staple crop, nomadic herder, arable land.

Key Ideas

2. Why is there little farming in Mongolia?

3. Why did the Chinese government introduce the one-child policy?

4. Where were the early Han kingdoms in China?

Think Critically

5. **Analyze Information** Look at the population density map. Which areas have the highest population density? Why do so many people live in these areas?

6. **Summarize** Why are cities growing in China?

Essential Question

How can you measure success?

7. How can the Chinese government measure whether or not the one-child policy has been successful? Go to your Student Journal to record your answer.

History of China and Its Neighbors

Key Ideas
- For much of its history, China was an advanced, powerful empire.
- Communists created command economies in both China and Mongolia.
- In recent years, Mongolia and China have changed to market economies to increase economic growth.

Key Terms • dynasty • Confucianism • Daoism • command economy • famine

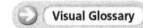
Visual Glossary

Reading Skill: Main Ideas and Details Take notes using the graphic organizer in your journal.

A statue of a warrior from the tomb of Emperor Qin Shi Huangdi ▼

For much of China's long history, it was a successful empire with great achievements in art and technology. The Mongolians also built a huge empire. But for thousands of years, China was the most powerful country in the region. Yet by the 1900s, China had become weak. The Communists promised to make China powerful again when they came to power in 1949.

The Empires of China and Mongolia

The great empires of China and Mongolia were very different. The Chinese empire was based on agriculture. The Mongols' power came from their skill as warriors on horseback.

The Powerful Chinese Empire

China's civilization began when farming villages formed on the North China Plain thousands of years ago. Geographic features

Timeline

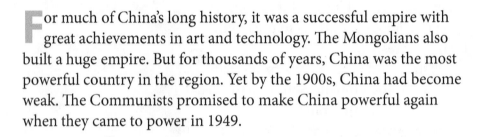

Major Chinese Dynasties			Qin	
Shang	Zhou			Han
1500 B.C.	1000 B.C.	500 B.C.		A.D. 1

■ Period of war or division

isolated China from other early civilizations. High mountains limited communication to the west. By sea, all but a few neighbors were too far to reach. Around 1800 b.c., a series of emperors began to rule China. Usually, emperors were members of a **dynasty,** or a ruling family that held power for many years.

Powerful emperors unified and protected China. The Qin (chin) emperor Shi Huangdi (shur hwahng dee) created a <u>uniform</u> written language for the whole empire. This made communication easier and helped unite the country. It is the basis of China's written language today.

Shi Huangdi also began to connect scattered walls to build the Great Wall, which still stands. The wall was meant to protect farmers from nomadic invaders. Later rulers added to it, extending it more than 4,000 miles.

Chinese Achievements Under the Dynasties The Chinese had many accomplishments during their history. They built roads and canals to make trade and travel easier. The Grand Canal is the longest man-made waterway in the world. It stretches for over a thousand miles from Beijing to Hangzhou. It passes Wuxi where Qian Xiao works.

Chinese inventions include paper, silk, and the magnetic compass. In the Song dynasty, the Chinese developed gunpowder. At first they used it for fireworks. Later, they began to use it in weapons.

A Mongolian Empire Many groups of nomads have lived on the plains north of China. One group, called the Mongols, united under the leadership of Genghis Khan in the 1200s. They were the ancestors of today's Mongolians. They swept over the Great Wall and conquered China. They also rapidly took control of much of Asia. The Mongol empire was the largest empire the world had ever seen, but it was short-lived. In 1368, the Chinese overthrew the Mongols, and the Ming dynasty came to power.

Reading Check **Why did the Chinese build the Great Wall of China?**

uniform, *adj.,* the same, consistent

Today, tourists climb the Great Wall of China. ▼

	Sui			Mongol Rule		Republican Era	Communist Era
	Tang		Song		Ming	Qing	
A.D. 500	A.D. 750		A.D. 1000	A.D. 1250	A.D. 1500	A.D. 1750	A.D. 2000

755

Important Ideas and Beliefs

As dynasties rose and fell, three belief systems strongly influenced this region's culture. **Confucianism** (kuhn fy oo shuh niz um), is based on the ideas of the thinker Confucius. **Daoism** (dow iz um) is a philosophy of seeking the natural way of the universe. The third philosophy, Buddhism, grew from the teachings of Siddhartha Gautama. He taught that people can become free from suffering if they give up selfish desires.

Confucianism Confucius (551–479 B.C.) believed society could be peaceful and harmonious if people acted strictly according to their roles. In the family, the young should respect the old. In government, the ruler should care for his subjects. In return, subjects had a duty to respect and obey the ruler.

Three hundred years after Confucius's death, the influence of his teaching increased. It was then that Emperor Wudi of the Han dynasty began to use Confucianism in government. Dynasties after the Han also supported the ideas of Confucius. Confucianism was taught in schools throughout China. This system of values greatly influenced Chinese culture.

Daoism The ideas of Daoism developed at around the time Confucius was teaching. The word *dao* (dow) means "the

Belief Systems of China

Daoism
Based on the teachings of Laozi, 500s B.C.

Goal To follow the dao. For Daoists, the dao is the rhythm of the universe. They studied nature to harmonize with this rhythm.

Statue of the Buddha meditating. The concentration of meditation helps Buddhists reach enlightenment. ▼

Confucianism
Based on the teachings of Confucius (551–479 B.C.)

Goal To act according to one's role in society. Education teaches values and duties.

Buddhism
Based on the teachings of Siddhartha Gautama, the Buddha, 500s B.C.

Goal To become free from the pain and suffering of the world. This mental state is enlightenment.

◄ Statue of Confucius in a temple in Nanjing, China

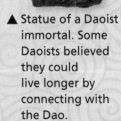

▲ Statue of a Daoist immortal. Some Daoists believed they could live longer by connecting with the Dao.

path" or "the way." Daoists believe people should try to fi d this path. Often, they see evidence of the Dao in natural things, such as water.

> 66 There is nothing in the world more soft and weak than water, and yet for attacking things that are firm and strong, nothing is better than water ... 99
> —Laozi

Water, through patient effort over time, is even stronger than rock. By acting like water, people were following the Dao.

Buddhism Monks and other travelers from India brought Buddhism to China during the Han dynasty. Over time, Buddhism attracted a wide following. Buddhists built monasteries and temples across the country. Buddhism also became popular in Mongolia. Buddhism was much more influential than Daoism and Confucianism on Mongolia's culture.

Reading Check **What did Confucius think people should do to bring order to society?**

The End of the Dynasties

China's last dynasty, the Qing (ching), fell early in the 1900s. New, communist governments took control in both China and Mongolia.

The Qing Dynasty Struggles In 1839, the Qing dynasty fought with Britain over the opium trade. Opium is an addictive drug that Britain had been trading for Chinese tea. The Qing saw the bad effects of the drug and tried to stop the trade. The British sent warships to bombard some Chinese cities. China's weak military could barely put up a fi ht.

The British won. They forced the Chinese to accept the opium trade and foreign domination.

This was just the beginning of the Qing dynasty's troubles. It lost Taiwan to Japan after a brief war in 1895. Taiwan stayed under Japanese control through World War II. The Chinese people were shocked that their country could be defeated by the small island nation of Japan.

Revolution, Civil War, and Invasion Many Chinese people blamed the Qing for the country's weakness. In 1911 and 1912, revolutionaries took power from the Qing dynasty.

The revolutionary leaders hoped to make China a strong, modern nation. Yet, they could not bring peace. China suffered nearly 30 years of almost constant fi hting followed by a Japanese invasion during World War II.

Nationalists under Jiang Jieshi (jahng jeh shur), also know as Chiang Kai-shek, fought Communists led by Mao Zedong (mow dzuh doong) for control of the country. Finally, in 1949, the Communists won the long civil war. They set up a stable government on mainland China.

The Nationalists fled to Taiwan. There, they set up a rival government, which continues to this day.

Mongolia's Revolution The Qing dynasty controlled much of Mongolia. Mongolia's Communist leaders won independence from China in 1921 after the Qing dynasty fell. Mongolia became a new nation.

Reading Check **Why did the Chinese overthrow the Qing dynasty?**

Dr. Sun Yixian served as the first president of China's republic after revolutionaries overthrew the Qing dynasty.

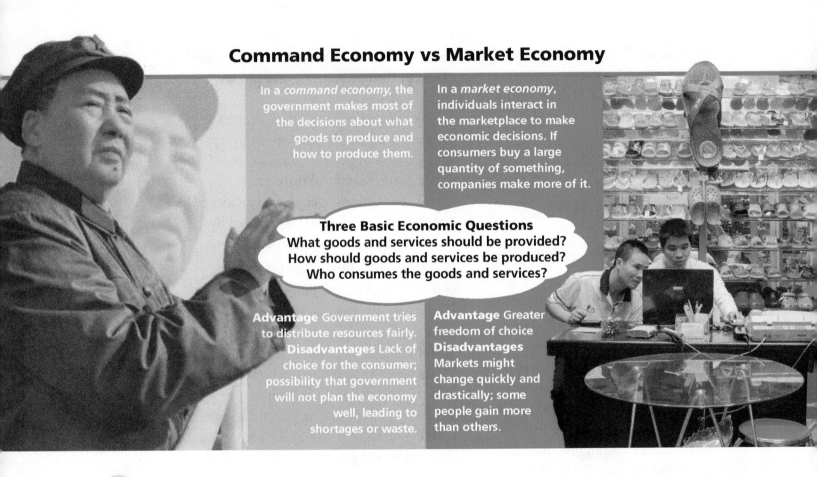

Command Economy vs Market Economy

In a *command economy*, the government makes most of the decisions about what goods to produce and how to produce them.

In a *market economy*, individuals interact in the marketplace to make economic decisions. If consumers buy a large quantity of something, companies make more of it.

Three Basic Economic Questions
What goods and services should be provided?
How should goods and services be produced?
Who consumes the goods and services?

Advantage Government tries to distribute resources fairly.
Disadvantages Lack of choice for the consumer; possibility that government will not plan the economy well, leading to shortages or waste.

Advantage Greater freedom of choice
Disadvantages Markets might change quickly and drastically; some people gain more than others.

myWorldActivity
Command Economy vs. Market Economy

resource, *n.,* something, such as coal, timber, or land, that a country can use

China and Mongolia Under Communism

Communist leaders in China and Mongolia brought great change to their countries. They had little economic success, though, and had to make major changes to their economic systems.

The Command Economy Communism is based on the idea that everyone should share a country's wealth equally. The Communists argued that a society could not reach this goal with a market economy. Instead, the Communists created a **command economy,** an economic system based on government planning and control.

In a command economy, the government owns the land, businesses, and resources of the country. The government makes an economic plan for the country. It decides which goods and services will be produced. People have jobs based on this plan, and the government has great control over the lives of the people. The Communists did not create a democracy. People could not vote. A small number of Communist Party leaders held power.

In both Mongolia and China, the Communists took land, livestock, and businesses away from their owners. Th se <u>resources</u> were supposed to be managed fairly according to the government's economic plan.

These governments also started programs to help people. Doctors, for example, traveled to small villages to provide basic healthcare.

758

Command Economy Problems The command economy often did not work well. When the Mongolian government tried to take livestock away from nomads to create the command economy, many herders decided to kill their animals rather than give them to the government. In part because of this, a **famine,** or severe food shortage, followed.

Poor planning by the Communists in China also led to famine. In 1958, Mao introduced the Great Leap Forward. This policy called for the country to rapidly increase production of steel, as part of an effort to make China's economy more modern.

Making steel took farmers away from their fields. The shift in ocus away from agriculture combined with poor weather created food shortages. Historians believe that as many as 30 million Chinese people may have died of hunger between 1958 and 1962. This tragedy took place because the economic plan ignored the needs of the people.

New Leaders Leave the Command Economy Behind When Mao Zedong died in 1976, a Communist leader named Deng Xiaoping (dung show ping) rose to power. He began reforms that opened China up to international trade.

He also started to move China toward a market economy. New businesses opened. They competed with one another to make the best, cheapest goods. China's economy began to grow rapidly.

At the same time, Deng and other Communist leaders had no intention of allowing political power to slip out of their hands. The Chinese Communist Party's hold on the government stayed as strong as ever.

By contrast, political and economic reforms came at almost the same time in Mongolia. Both the political and economic systems changed in the 1990s. Mongolia became a democracy with a market economy.

Reading Check **How did China change after Deng Xiaoping took power?**

Section 2 Assessment

Key Terms

1. Describe the beliefs of Confucianism and Daosim.

2. What is a command economy?

Key Ideas

3. **Draw Conclusions** Why was China the most powerful country in the region for much of its history?

4. **Cause and Effect** What policies caused famine in China and Mongolia in the 1900s?

Think Critically

5. **Sequence** What was the sequence of events from China's war with Britain to the formation of a new government led by Mao Zedong?

Essential Question

How can you measure success?

6. Do you think the Qing dynasty was unsuccessful? Go to your Student Journal to record your answer.

Section 3

China and Its Neighbors Today

Key Ideas
- The governments of Mongolia and Taiwan have become more democratic, but China's has not.
- Exports have been important to the economies of all three countries.
- China's economy has grown rapidly, but it faces many challenges.

Key Terms • single-party state • wage • life expectancy • illiterate • hydroelectricity

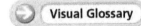 Visual Glossary

○○ Reading Skill: **Compare and Contrast** Take notes using the outline map in your journal.

Protests in Mongolia led to political reform. ▼

In recent years, China, Taiwan, and Mongolia have all experienced great changes. For Taiwan and Mongolia, the changes have been both political and economic. China, by contrast, has seen impressive economic growth with less change in the country's government.

Politics: One Party or Many?

Since the 1980s, Taiwan and Mongolia have changed their governments. In both countries, many parties can compete in elections. People in China, by contrast, do not have the freedom to create new parties. The people of Taiwan and Mongolia also enjoy more freedom in their religious and private lives than the people of China.

The Chinese government used the army to stop protests in Tiananmen Square. ▼

Reforms in Mongolia In 1989, protesters in Mongolia demanded change in the political system. The country's leaders responded and made many reforms. New parties could join free elections. Mongolian leaders also wrote a new constitution. This constitution states that the people directly elect the president and the parliament makes the laws.

The Communist Party is still important in Mongolia. Candidates from this party have won many elections. Now, though, this party competes with other parties for control of the government.

The new constitution also protects certain freedoms, such as religious freedom. In the past, the communists did not allow people to worship freely. Now, many people are again practicing Buddhism and other religions.

Democracy Grows in Taiwan After China's civil war, Jiang Jieshi left hina and set up a government in Taiwan. He created a **single-party state,** that is, a country in which one political party controls the government. Jiang's Nationalist Party controlled the government. In the 1980s, some Taiwanese people began to push the government to become more open.

Finally in 1989, the Nationalists allowed other parties to take part in elections. Like the communists in Mongolia, the Nationalists Party is still important in Taiwan. Now, though, the Taiwanese can choose from more than one party when they vote.

Limited Freedom in China China's leaders have not made major political changes. It continues to be a single-party state. The Chinese Communist Party (CCP) controls the government.

The CCP no longer controls the economy. It does control peoples' lives in other ways. For example, China does not have freedom of the press. That is, journalists are not free to report the news as they see it. The CCP also blocks many Web sites. Chinese people do not have <u>access</u> to all information on the Internet.

Chinese people also do not have freedom of speech. The government may imprison people who say or do things to oppose the government.

In 1989, tens of thousands of people gathered in Tiananmen Square (tyen ahn mun skwehr) in Beijing. They called for more freedom and changes to the government. They refused to leave the square. China's leaders sent in tanks and troops to break up the demonstration. Thousands of people were killed or wounded.

The government refused to make any of the changes that the protesters had demanded. The freedoms of the Chinese people remain very limited.

Reading Check Is Taiwan a single-party state today?

access, *n.,* ability to be used

Political and Economic Systems: China and Its Neighbors

	China	Taiwan	Mongolia
Political Parties	Single-party system	Several parties	Several parties
Elections	Few elections, very limited	Open elections	Open elections
Freedoms	Freedoms limited by government	Religious freedom, freedom of the press	Religious freedom, freedom of the press
Economic System	Market system	Market system	Market system

Chart Skills

How is China different from Taiwan and Mongolia? How are all three countries similar?

→ **Data Discovery**

The skyscaper Taipei 101 towers over Taiwan's capital. ▼

Economic Growth: The Importance of Exports

Trade is important for the economies of all three countries in this region. Taiwan and China have had rapid economic growth. Mongolia struggles to strengthen its economy.

Taiwan: An Asian Tiger Taiwan has been called an "Asian Tiger" because for decades its economy had strong growth. In the mid-1900s, Taiwan began to manufacture more goods. At the time, many people still worked on farms. The country was relatively poor.

People were paid a low **wage,** that is, their pay was low. Factories paid their workers less than factories paid in wealthier countries. As a result, factories in Taiwan could make their products more cheaply. Other countries were happy to buy Taiwan's cheaper goods. Soon, the country was exporting goods. Its economy began to grow quickly.

As money from exports came into the country, Taiwanese people became wealthier and wages increased. The price of making goods in Taiwan went up.

The Taiwanese economy continued to grow even as wages went up. One reason is because the government improved the education system. Better education helped Taiwan to produce new, technologically advanced products, such as chemicals, medicines, and electronics. Taiwan now exports these complex, expensive products. By making this change, the economy continued to grow.

Mongolia's Mineral Resources Early in the 1990s, Mongolia changed to a market economy. Th s change was difficult. In the past, the Soviet Union gave Mongolia economic support. Mongolia struggled without this help.

Wages are not high in Mongolia, but transportation is difficult. Th s increased the cost of making goods in Mongolia. The country is landlocked. Th s means it has no coastline. Moving goods long distances across land is more expensive than shipping them the same distance by sea.

Railroads connect Mongolia to Russia and China. Now, China is one of Mongolia's major trading partners. Mongolia's main exports are its mineral resources. In addition, raising livestock is still important to Mongolia's economy.

With the market economy, Mongolia's economy has grown. More Mongolians now have cellphones and access to the Internet. Still, many people remain poor. The country has not had the strong growth of Taiwan and China.

China's Economic Miracle China's economic reforms began much earlier than Mongolia's. In the late 1970s, the Chinese government told farmers in some areas that they did not have to follow the government's economic plan. The farmers could decide what they wanted to grow. They could sell their harvest and keep the profits. Some farmers figu ed out how to use their land more effici tly than the government plan. They produced more than before.

Because these farmers were successful, the government expanded the policy. Farmers across the country could make their own decisions. The government also let more people start private businesses. Slowly, the government gave up the command economy.

As with Taiwan, trade became important to China's economic growth. Wages in China continue to be relatively low. Companies make their products cheaply and sell them abroad.

The Chinese government also encouraged foreign companies to come to China. These companies had money to build new factories. Most of these factories are along China's long coastline. Here, it is easy for companies to ship their goods around the world. The companies need many workers. People have moved to coastal cities to fi d jobs in these factories. Shenzhen is one coastal city where many factories have been built. In 1980, it was a town of 30,000 people. By 2006 it had become a city of more than 8 million people!

Now, China's economy is one of the largest in the world. Toys, clothing, and many other goods sold in the United States are made in China.

Reading Check Why is trade more difficult for Mongolia?

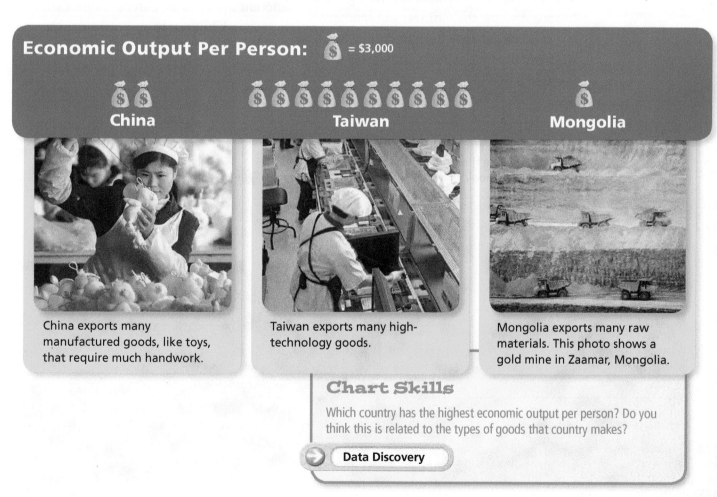

Economic Output Per Person: 💰 = $3,000

China 💰💰

Taiwan 💰💰💰💰💰💰💰💰💰💰💰

Mongolia 💰

China exports many manufactured goods, like toys, that require much handwork.

Taiwan exports many high-technology goods.

Mongolia exports many raw materials. This photo shows a gold mine in Zaamar, Mongolia.

Chart Skills

Which country has the highest economic output per person? Do you think this is related to the types of goods that country makes?

Data Discovery

my worldgeography.com Data Discovery

A More Unequal Society

The economic growth in China has made many people wealthier. Now, more families can afford products such as televisions, refrigerators, and even cars. Still, some people have <u>benefited</u> from this new wealth more than others have.

benefit, *v.,* to help, be of service to

Greater Wealth in the East Trade has helped bring growth to coastal cities. Many factories are located along the south and east coasts. Th s area produces 60% of the nation's industrial output.

Areas in the west and center of China face many of the same challenges as Mongolia. Companies far from the coast fi d it expensive to transport their goods. In recent years, the Chinese government has tried to increase investment in the west and center of China. Still, growth there lags behind eastern China.

Many Rural Areas Struggle Many rural communities have also faced difficulties. Under the command economy, the national government provided some services to rural areas. They sent doctors to rural areas to give everyone basic medical care. The **life expectancy,** that is, the number of years that people live on average, rose rapidly.

Now, individuals or local governments often must pay for these services. Less wealthy areas struggle to pay the costs of basic services. For example, some villages do not have enough money to have their own school. Parents, then, have to pay to send their children to a school in a different town. Some parents cannot afford these fees. Children from rural areas are less likely than those from urban areas to go to college and get higher-paying jobs.

Many villages in rural China cannot afford to have their own school. Five small villages share this primary school. Mr. Dai teaches all classes at the school.

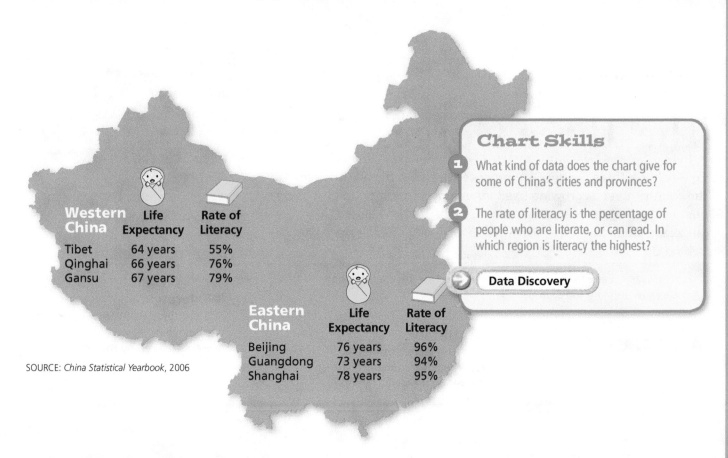

Western China	Life Expectancy	Rate of Literacy
Tibet	64 years	55%
Qinghai	66 years	76%
Gansu	67 years	79%

Eastern China	Life Expectancy	Rate of Literacy
Beijing	76 years	96%
Guangdong	73 years	94%
Shanghai	78 years	95%

SOURCE: *China Statistical Yearbook*, 2006

Chart Skills

1 What kind of data does the chart give for some of China's cities and provinces?

2 The rate of literacy is the percentage of people who are literate, or can read. In which region is literacy the highest?

Data Discovery

The Floating Population Because there are fewer opportunities for education and employment in rural areas, millions of people have been moving to cities.

These migrants are known as the "fl ating population." It is estimated at over 140 million people, or one tenth of China's total population. That is nearly half the population of the United States.

Th s fl ating population is moving illegally. The Chinese government has a rule allowing people to live only where they are registered, usually their birthplace. The government limits new registration in cities. Migrants who work in a city without registration often cannot receive healthcare or other government services. Th s is another challenge for people from rural areas as they try to improve life for their families.

Opportunities for Women Traditionally, couples live with the husband's family. The son takes care of his parents as they grow older. Therefore, many parents want to have at least one son.

The one-child policy changes this situation. If a couple has a daughter, they cannot have a son. They will help their daughter to be as successful as possible. Now, many daughters support their elderly parents.

Still, parents who have more than one child may send their son to school and keep their daughter at home to work. More women than men are **illiterate,** that is, more women than men do not know how to read. Women still do not have equal education and job opportunities.

Reading Check **Why are migrant workers described as a floating population?**

The Three Gorges Dam

China's huge Three Gorges Dam produces clean electricity. This helps the country meet its growing need for energy. In addition to producing energy, the project created thousands of jobs. It also changed the landscape along the Chang River. A 400-mile-long resevoir now extends behind the dam.

THINK CRITICALLY **Examine the diagram below. What are the benefits and drawbacks of building the dam?**

▲ **Relocation**
More than a million people had to move because their homes were covered by the reservoir.

◄ **Lost History**
The rising waters of the reservoir covered many historic sites along the river.

The dam can hold back high waters and help control flooding along the river.

Turbines in the dam produce electricity.

Newly built locks make transport along the river easier.

myWorldActivity
Three Gorges Dam

Environmental Challenges

As the Chinese economy has grown, pollution has become a major problem. China also uses many resources to feed, clothe, and house its large population.

Facing Environmental Problems Chinese cities have some of the worst air pollution in the world. Millions of cars, buses, and coal-burning electricity plants contribute to the smog around Chinese cities.

Water pollution is also a serious problem. Factories and farms dump dangerous chemicals into rivers and lakes near cities. Lake Tai near Xiao's home is one of many lakes affected by this issue.

Drier areas in the north and west are struggling with shortages of water. Factories, farms, and citizens compete to use this limited resource. At times, the Huang River dries up before reaching the sea. The land around Beijing is so dry that sandstorms blow into the city.

China has laws to limit pollution, but local governments do not want to punish polluters too harshly. People would lose their jobs if factories closed down.

Searching for Energy In the past, China could produce all the energy it needed. Now, more energy is needed to run its many new businesses. China has started importing oil. Also, it has been building more coal-burning power plants.

Burning oil and coal makes China's air pollution even worse, so China is looking for cleaner forms of energy. In western China, wind power produces electricity. The Chinese government also built the Th ee Gorges Dam along the Chang River to produces **hydroelectricity** (hy droh ee lek tr ih s uh tee), or electricity made by water power. Building this dam was disruptive and expensive. China's leaders have to balance these costs with the need for new sources of energy.

Reading Check **What kinds of environmental challenges does China face?**

my Story **📷 Photo**

Xiao, like many Chinese people, boils his water to make it safe to drink.

Section 3 Assessment

Key Terms

1. What is a single-party state?

2. What is illiteracy?

Key Ideas

3. Compare and Contrast How has reform been different in China and Mongolia?

4. What is one problem that China faces, and how might China solve it?

Thinking Critically

5. Analyze Cause and Effect What effect does geography have on Mongolia's economic growth?

? Essential Question

How can you measure success?

6. What is one way that China has been successful? Give evidence from the text and from figures to support your point. Go to your Student Journal to record your answer.

Chapter Assessment

Key Terms and Ideas

1. **Discuss** Why are people migrating from villages to cities in China?

2. **Summarize** How has the government of China helped and hurt China's minority groups?

3. **Compare and Contrast** How are men and women treated differently in China?

4. **Explain** What are the important beliefs of Confucianism and Daoism?

5. **Recall** What are some of the main physical features of China?

6. **Compare and Contrast** How do a command economy and a market economy differ?

7. **Describe** How and when did the Mongols conquer China?

Think Critically

8. **Problem Solving** What are some causes of air and water pollution in China? How could you lower pollution in China without forcing many people out of work?

9. **Identify Evidence** What might explain why China's population density is higher than Mongolia's?

10. **Draw Conclusions** Why is it easier for a country to export its goods if wages are low?

11. **Core Concepts: Economics** What three basic questions do economists ask when studying economies? How have the answers to these questions changed for China?

Places to Know

For each place, write the letter from the map that shows its location.

12. **Beijing**

13. **Chang River**

14. **Huang River**

15. **Mongolia**

16. **Shanghai**

17. **Taiwan**

18. **Estimate** Using the scale, estimate the distance between Beijing and Shanghai.

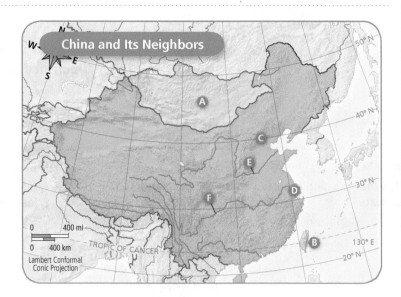

China and Its Neighbors

Essential Question

How can you measure success?

A Changing China: Who Benefits the Most?
Gather data about the changes taking place in China. Answer the question *How do these changes affect different people in different ways?* Organize your findings and write a report to an economic leader.

21st Century Learning

Evaluating Web Sites

Search for three different Web sites that give information on the Three Gorges Dam. Examine each site and answer the following questions. Create a table to record your answers.
- Who is the source of the information?
- How up-to-date is the information?
- Does the information seem accurate?
- Is the information easy to understand?

Document-Based Questions

Success Tracker™
Online at myworldgeography.com

Use your knowledge of the region and Documents A and B to answer Questions 1–3.

Document A

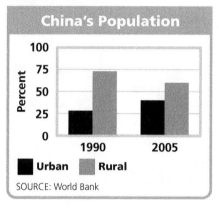

China's Population

SOURCE: World Bank

Document B

" There are no social benefits—all I get is my salary. Hands stop, mouth stops. If I get sick, I just have to keep my eyes open and sit here."

—a migrant worker in urban China

1. Which of the following might explain the change seen in Document A?

   A better health care in rural areas

   B better schools in rural areas

   C better-paying jobs in urban areas

   D natural disasters in urban areas

2. Which of the following best describes the worker quoted in Document B?

   A a member of the "floating population"

   B a person who was born in a big city and has health benefits

   C a government official in a city

   D a farmer in western China

3. **Writing Task** Do you think the situation described in Document B is common? Explain your answer.

Chapter 22

Japan and the Koreas

How much does geography shape a country?

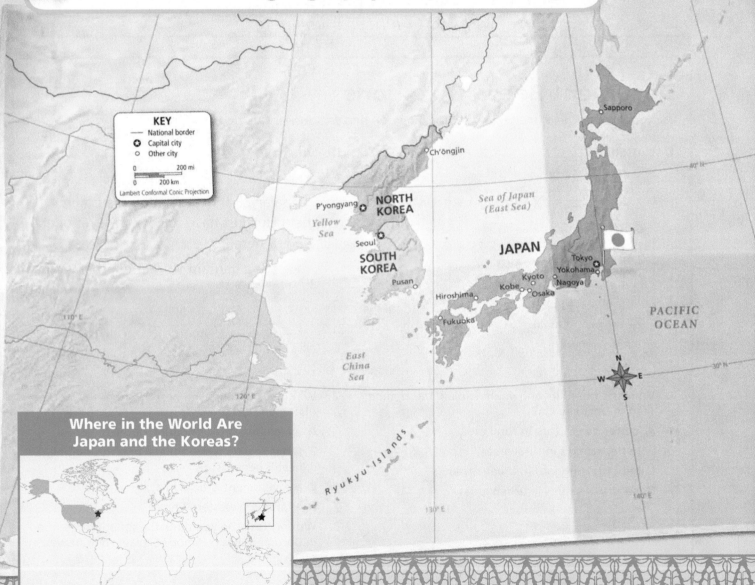

KEY
— National border
⊗ Capital city
○ Other city

0   200 mi
0   200 km
Lambert Conformal Conic Projection

Sapporo

Ch'ŏngjin

P'yongyang   NORTH
              KOREA

Yellow
Sea

Sea of Japan
(East Sea)

Seoul

SOUTH
KOREA

Pusan

JAPAN

Tokyo
Yokohama
Kyoto   Nagoya
Kobe
Osaka

Hiroshima

Fukuoka

East
China
Sea

PACIFIC
OCEAN

Ryukyu Islands

110° E   120° E   130° E   140° E

40° N

30° N

N
W   E
S

**Where in the World Are
Japan and the Koreas?**

Washington, D.C., to Tokyo: 6,770 miles

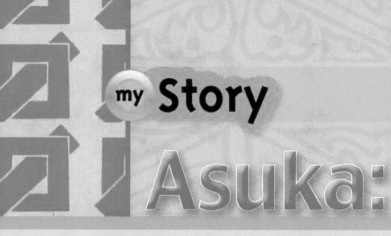

my Story

Asuka: A Girl on the Go

? **Explore the Essential Question**
- at my worldgeography.com
- using the myWorld Chapter Activity
- with the Student Journal

In this section you'll read about Asuka. She is a senior in high school and lives with her family in Yokohama, Japan. Life has not been easy for Asuka, but that has not stopped her from wanting to make the world a better place to live. **What does Asuka's story tell you about the challenges young people face living in Japan?**

Story by Michael Condon for MyWorld Geography Online

In the bamboo- and -concrete-covered hills of Yokohama, a cluster of identical apartment blocks stands out. The drab, box-shaped buildings have numbers stenciled onto the top of their walls to identify them. On the third floor of one of the apartment buildings, in a small apartment no bigger than an average American living room, lives Asuka. The third-year high school student shares the apartment with her father, her grandmother, her 15-year-old brother, the family's pet turtle, and Max, a pet rabbit.

More than 35 million people live in the Greater Tokyo-Yokohama metropolitan area. This is almost twice as many people as live in Greater New York. With so many people needing housing, space is scarce. Most people live in small apartments. About 2,500 people live in this four-block square area of Yokohama. It is very crowded, and the cost of living in Yokohama is high.

my worldgeography.com (On Assignment)

771

Asuka's grandmother serving dinner in a small kitchen

A crowded bedroom and study area

Standing room only on the train to school

For a single-parent family, it can be a struggle to make ends meet. Asuka's family moved to Yokohama after her parents divorced. She was three years old. To support the family, her father took a job as a salesman in the construction industry. With money short, Asuka also helps out by working up to 20 hours a week after school. She gives one third of her wages to the family and uses the rest to pay her other expenses.

Though her family does not have a lot of money, the 18-year-old high school senior considers herself fortunate. Every day she wakes up at 6:30 a .m, grabs the "bento" lunch box her grandmother has prepared, and heads off o school. She attends a high school in the middle of Yokohama, where she studies international affairs. Her curriculum is demanding. It includes courses in world history, politics, economics, Japanese, English, and Korean.

Asuka has developed a keen interest in politics, economics, and history. She plans to major in these subjects when she goes to college. Asuka thinks it is important to study politics and history because they explain how various countries have developed and the way their governments work. With that knowledge, she believes, "We can improve the living conditions of people and make things better."

A Glocally field trip

Class is just about to begin.

Asuka is a high-energy person. In addition to her studies and her job, she takes part in extracurricular activities. These activities range from volunteer work to playing drums in a rock band. Asuka is also the leader of the school's "Glocally" Club. (The club's name is a combination of the words "global" and "locally.") As part of the club's activities, the students go on field trips to observe war ruins. They also learn how wars affect people and look for ways to achieve peace in the modern world.

The teacher in charge of the club has introduced the students to some serious issues that are far from the minds of the average high school student in most developed countries. Asuka is glad he challenges them to think about real-world issues.

Over the last couple of years, Asuka has also taken part in the Yokohama Student Forum. Last year she became a student leader and put together a forum on child labor—an issue that touches the lives of families across Asia.

Asuka appreciates all the opportunities she has had. "I have [led] a privileged life," she says, "while others are suffering elsewhere." After graduating from college, Asuka says she wants to do something to help others less privileged.

Judging by what she has achieved so far, the promising young student will be sure to put her talents to good use in the future.

⊙ **myStory Video**

Join Asuka as she shows you about her life in Yokohama.

Meet the Journalist

Name Heath Cozens
Favorite Moment My favorite memory was Asuka doing karaoke.

my worldgeography.com   myStory Video

Key Ideas

- Mountains cover much of this region.
- A dense population requires careful use of resources.
- People have adapted to sudden natural disasters.

Key Terms • foliage • scarcity • comparative advantage • interdependent

 Visual Glossary

 Reading Skill: Label an Outline Map Take notes using the outline map in your journal.

A hiker at the base of Mt. Fuji in Japan ▼

Physical Features

Japan, at the far eastern edge of Asia, is sometimes called the "land of the rising sun." The Japanese see each day's sunrise before most parts of Asia. North and South Korea lie just to the west of Japan.

Japan is a 1,500-mile-long chain of islands made up of four large islands and about 3,000 smaller islands. The countries of North and South Korea together form the Korean peninsula.

Four tectonic plates are close to Japan and the Koreas. The plates are slowly moving together. The result is

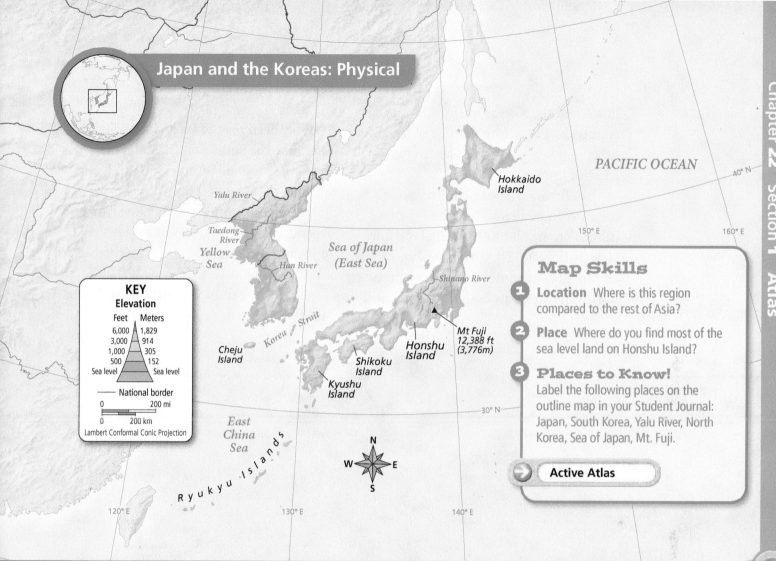

Japan and the Koreas: Physical

PACIFIC OCEAN

40° N

150° E   160° E

Yalu River

Hokkaido
Island

Taedong
River

Yellow
Sea

Han River

Sea of Japan
(East Sea)

Shinano River

KEY
Elevation

Feet	Meters
6,000	1,829
3,000	914
1,000	305
500	152
Sea level	Sea level

National border

0   200 mi

0   200 km

Lambert Conformal Conic Projection

Korea Strait

Cheju
Island

Shikoku
Island

Honshu
Island

Mt Fuji
12,388 ft
(3,776m)

Kyushu
Island

East
China
Sea

Ryukyu Islands

N
W   E
S

30° N

120° E   130° E   140° E

Map Skills

1. **Location** Where is this region compared to the rest of Asia?

2. **Place** Where do you find most of the sea level land on Honshu Island?

3. **Places to Know!** Label the following places on the outline map in your Student Journal: Japan, South Korea, Yalu River, North Korea, Sea of Japan, Mt. Fuji.

Active Atlas

great pressure that causes earthquakes. Earthquakes that <u>occur</u> under the sea can make huge waves that slam into the towns along the shore. As the Pacific Plate sinks beneath Japan, it melts and is called molten rock. The molten rock then rises to Earth's surface, creating volcanic eruptions. Japan has 108 active volcanoes.

Both North Korea and South Korea are mountainous countries. In both countries, there are a wide coastal plain in the west and smaller plains in the east. South Korea has more flat land suitable for farming than North Korea.

Japan is more rugged than the Koreas. Mountains and hills cover about 70 percent of the country's surface. In Japan and the Koreas, most people live in the valleys and coastal plains. In Japan, the largest level area is on Honshu Island.

The mountains in these countries are popular sites for hiking. Mount Fuji, the highest peak in Japan, is particularly popular. The mountain is a volcano, but it has not erupted for centuries. Thousands of people climb Mount Fuji every year.

Reading Check Why are there earthquakes and volcanoes in Japan and the Koreas?

occur, *v.,* to take place; to happen

my worldgeography.com   Active Atlas

Climate

Japan and the Koreas are mid-latitude countries. The seasonal range of temperatures in this region is similar to the east coast of the United States.

The climate of the northern parts of the Korean peninsula and the Japanese islands are similar to New England and New York State. They have cool summers and long, cold winters. In the fall, Japan's northern forests are bright with red and yellow foliage. **Foliage** is the leaves on the trees.

The southern part of Japan has a climate more like the southeast coastal region of the United States. Winters are mild, and summers are hot and humid.

During the winter, winds blow from central Asia into Korea and across the Sea of Japan. These cold winds are very dry, especially in North Korea.

About three fi hs of North Korea's rain falls from June to September. By contrast,

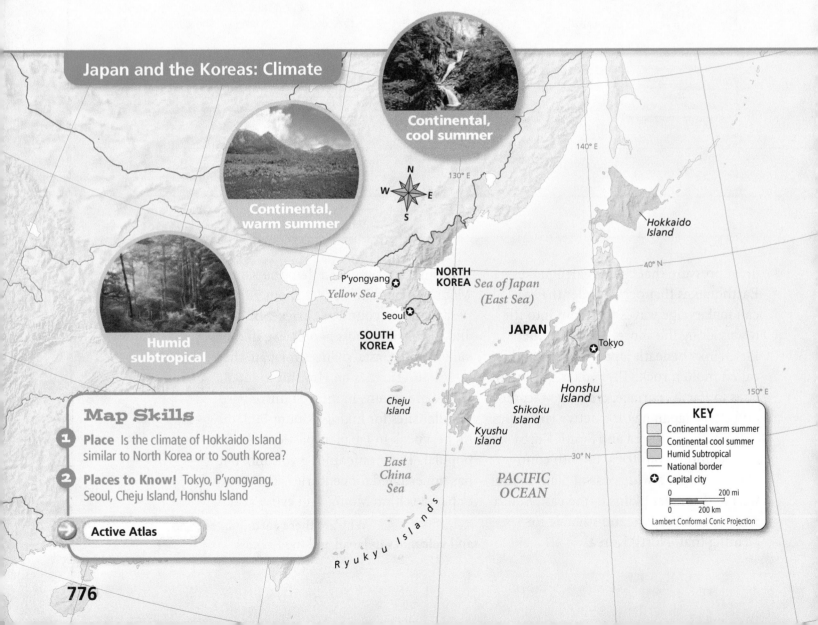

Japan and the Koreas: Climate

Continental, cool summer

Continental, warm summer

Humid subtropical

140° E

130° E

P'yongyang

Yellow Sea

NORTH KOREA

Sea of Japan (East Sea)

Hokkaido Island

40° N

Seoul

SOUTH KOREA

JAPAN

Tokyo

Cheju Island

Honshu Island

Shikoku Island

Kyushu Island

150° E

East China Sea

PACIFIC OCEAN

30° N

Ryukyu Islands

KEY
- Continental warm summer
- Continental cool summer
- Humid Subtropical
- — National border
- ⊛ Capital city

0   200 mi
0   200 km

Lambert Conformal Conic Projection

Map Skills

1. **Place** Is the climate of Hokkaido Island similar to North Korea or to South Korea?

2. **Places to Know!** Tokyo, P'yongyang, Seoul, Cheju Island, Honshu Island

Active Atlas

the sea brings some moisture all year to South Korea and Japan.

Summer seasonal winds, or monsoons, can drop as much as 80 inches of rainfall a year. They sometimes bring powerful tropical cyclones or hurricanes. In this part of the world, these storms are referred to as typhoons. Because of the warm, moist air, summers are humid in this region.

After a dry winter, the Koreas may experience a spring drought. The heavy summer rains that follow these droughts can cause fl oding and mudslides. When this happens, houses are buried, and farmers may lose their crops.

Summer monsoon rainfall supports lush forests. As a result, most of the uplands of Japan and the Koreas are wooded. Particularly in Japan, people have worked hard to preserve their forests. It is one of the few industrialized countries that is heavily forested.

Reading Check **Why are wind patterns important to climate in this region?**

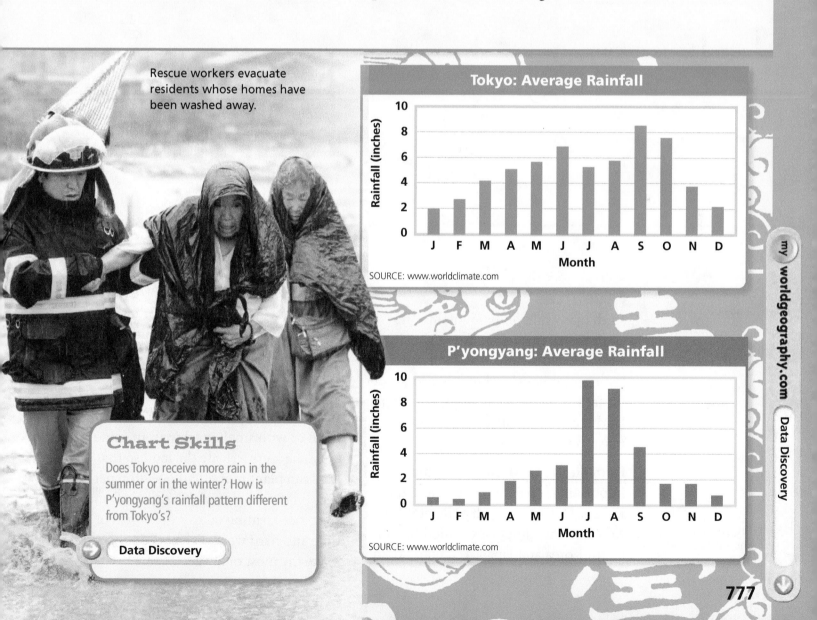

Rescue workers evacuate residents whose homes have been washed away.

Tokyo: Average Rainfall

SOURCE: www.worldclimate.com

P'yongyang: Average Rainfall

SOURCE: www.worldclimate.com

Chart Skills

Does Tokyo receive more rain in the summer or in the winter? How is P'yongyang's rainfall pattern different from Tokyo's?

Data Discovery

my worldgeography.com   Data Discovery

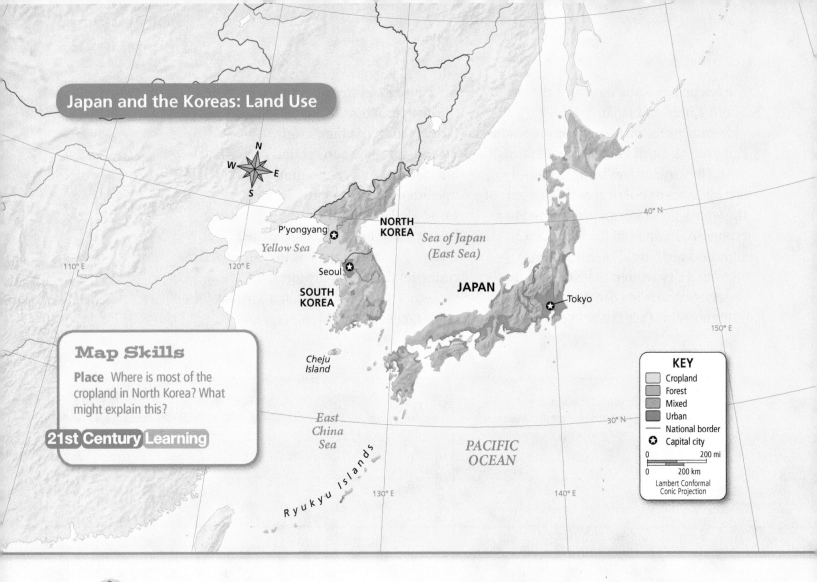

Japan and the Koreas: Land Use

NORTH KOREA

P'yongyang

Yellow Sea

Seoul

SOUTH KOREA

Sea of Japan (East Sea)

JAPAN

Tokyo

Cheju Island

East China Sea

PACIFIC OCEAN

Ryukyu Islands

40° N

150° E

30° N

110° E

120° E

130° E

140° E

Map Skills

Place Where is most of the cropland in North Korea? What might explain this?

21st Century Learning

KEY

Cropland
Forest
Mixed
Urban
— National border
⊛ Capital city

0   200 mi
0   200 km

Lambert Conformal
Conic Projection

myWorld Activity
Trade Off

output, *n,* the amount of something produced

Land Use and Natural Resources

With many hills and mountains, the countries of this region face a **scarcity,** or shortage, of flat land. Th s land is the best location for housing, but it is also needed for farming and industry. As a result, flat land is crowded. Japanese and Koreans must use their land carefully.

Farming the Land Rice is the most important crop in both Japan and the Koreas. With its cool, dry climate, North Korea's farm <u>output</u> lags behind that of South Korea and Japan. Yet, both South

Korea and Japan are highly urbanized. Large cities in these two countries take up space. Less land is available for farming. Farmers often must work on difficult, hilly land. Terraces are used to create flat fi lds on sloping ground. Large tractors are too big to plow the narrow terraces. Instead, rice is planted and harvested by hand or with small machines. In some areas, farmers irrigate the land so that they can plant more than one crop per year on the same land. Th s type of small-scale rice farming takes a great deal of time and hard work. Farmers do this to make the most of limited land.

Food Imports and Exports Many other countries can produce farm goods more cheaply than Japan and the Koreas. These other countries have a comparative advantage over Japan and the Koreas in agriculture. **Comparative advantage** is the ability to produce goods at a lower cost than your competitors.

Because farming is costly in Japan and the Koreas, these countries import food. Still, people in this region continue to farm so that they will not be dependent on other countries for all their food.

The sea is also an important resource. Fish products are an important export for North Korea. The ocean currents near Japan create an environment that is good for many kinds of fish. Fish is also an important export for Japan as well as an important part of the Japanese diet.

Scarce Resources Mineral resources are not evenly spread across this region. Both Japan and South Korea have few mineral resources. North Korea, by contrast, is rich in mineral resources including coal, lead, iron ore, copper, gold, and salt.

Scarcity makes countries **interdependent,** which means they depend on each other. Japan and South Korea trade with each other to acquire some of the raw materials they need for industry.

In addition, all three countries need energy resources. Hydroelectricity is one source of energy. Because of the hilly land, there are many fast fl wing rivers. These rivers are good for hydroelectric dams because the falling waters carry large amounts of energy that can be used to create electricity.

To meet their energy needs, South Korea and Japan have built nuclear power plants and also produce small amounts oil. Still, it is not enough. These countries must import oil and other resources to meet their energy needs.

Reading Check Which country is richest in mineral resources?

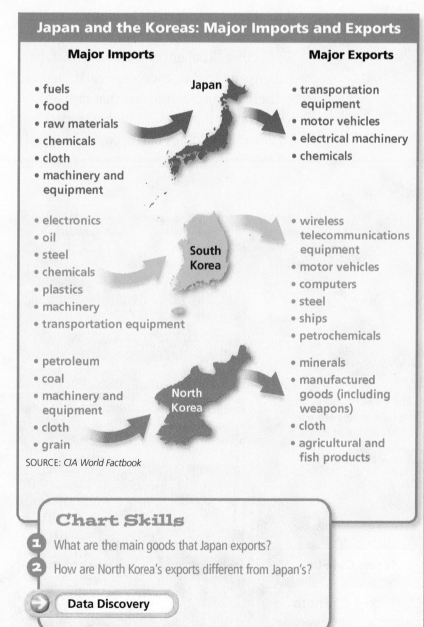

Japan and the Koreas: Major Imports and Exports

Major Imports

Japan
- fuels
- food
- raw materials
- chemicals
- cloth
- machinery and equipment

South Korea
- electronics
- oil
- steel
- chemicals
- plastics
- machinery
- transportation equipment

North Korea
- petroleum
- coal
- machinery and equipment
- cloth
- grain

Major Exports

Japan
- transportation equipment
- motor vehicles
- electrical machinery
- chemicals

South Korea
- wireless telecommunications equipment
- motor vehicles
- computers
- steel
- ships
- petrochemicals

North Korea
- minerals
- manufactured goods (including weapons)
- cloth
- agricultural and fish products

SOURCE: *CIA World Factbook*

Chart Skills

1 What are the main goods that Japan exports?

2 How are North Korea's exports different from Japan's?

Data Discovery

IN NUMBERS

About
10 typhoons
pass over Japan
each year.
Japan's typhoon
season is
6 months long.

Adapting to Challenges

The people of the region have learned to live in a challenging environment. In the past, most buildings in Japan and the Koreas were made of wood. Fires, earthquakes, and fl ods might destroy them, but these wooden structures could be quickly rebuilt.

Today, the people of Japan and the Koreas use modern technology to build structures that can withstand the forces of nature. Rubber pads under skyscrapers dampen the shock waves of earthquakes. There are also computers that move weights in the base of the skyscrapers to keep the buildings balanced.

Safety Alerts Early warning systems also help people to take safety measures during earthquakes. One system developed in Japan can give people as much as 30 seconds warning. Th s might not seem like very much time. But every extra second is important when an earthquake is about to hit.

> 66 School children will be able to take shelter under their desks in classrooms if they have five seconds. In fact . . . if we have 10 seconds to prepare for major tremors, we can reduce the number of deaths caused by quakes significantly. 99
>
> —Yoshinori Sugihara

The small rooms at capsule hotels are an efficient use of space.

716

Tight Spaces

Japan's population density is the third-highest in the world. Skyscrapers fill Japanese cities and underground shopping centers extend for multiple stories underground. Japanese people have found other ways to use space creatively.

Smaller furniture helps save space at home. ▶

Oshiya or "pushers" pack commuters on to a Tokyo subway train.

→ **Culture Close-Up**

my **Story** 📷 **Photo**

Environmental Threats Managing resources is another challenge. With so many people crowded together, it is easy to use limited resources too quickly.

North Korea and South Korea have lost much of their forest land by cutting trees faster than they can grow back. Without tree cover, rain water washes quickly into rivers and streams and fl oding becomes worse. As a result, soil needed for farming is washed away.

Overfishing is also a problem in the region. Near Japan, fish were taken from coastal waters too quickly. Now, ships must go far out to sea to fi d fish.

Intensive use of the land has resulted in serious pollution in all three countries. Factories, cars, and farms create air and water pollution.

While much remains to be done, the people in South Korea and Japan have pushed their governments to make changes. Their governments are working to reduce air and water pollution, fi d cleaner fuels, and recycle more waste.

The North Korean government has made less progress addressing these problems. The shortage of clean water for drinking and bathing is still a problem in that country.

Reading Check **What are two ways people in Japan and the Koreas have adapted to their environment?**

Overfishing threatens to drive the tuna fish into extinction. ▼

Section 1 Assessment

Key Terms

1. What is foliage?

2. What does scarcity mean?

3. Use the term *comparative advantage* to describe the products that Japan imports.

Key Ideas

4. How do physical features affect land use in this region?

5. How have Japan and the Koreas used technology to adapt to the forces of nature?

6. What environmental problems have Japan and the Koreas faced?

Think Critically

7. **Analyze Cause and Effect** How does scarcity make countries interdependent?

8. **Compare and Contrast** Why does North Korea have less agricultural production than Japan and South Korea?

Essential Question

How much does geography shape a country?

9. How much does geography affect the problems that countries in this region face? Are there other factors that influence pollution in these countries? Go to your Student Journal and record your answer.

Section 2

History of Japan and the Koreas

Key Ideas

- Japan and the Koreas all have long histories.

- Japan built an empire early in the 1900s but lost this empire at the end of World War II.

- Korea was divided into two countries, North Korea and South Korea, after the Korean War.

- Japan's economy grew rapidly after World War II.

Key Terms • shogun • samurai • Meiji Restoration • Korean War
• constitutional monarchy

 Visual Glossary

 Reading Skill: Identify Main Ideas and Details Take notes using the graphic organizer in your journal.

The imperial palace in Seoul, South Korea ▼

The people of Japan and the Koreas have adapted to their environment by building skyscrapers that survive the tremors of earthquakes. These nations have also needed to survive political and cultural tremors, such as wars and invasions. Japan and the Koreas have changed since their beginnings, but they are still standing.

Historical Roots

People have lived in this region for about 30,000 years. Powerful kingdoms have influenced the history of these countries, but each has charted its own course.

Korean Dynasties For thousands of years, kingdoms rose and fell on the Korean peninsula. At times, Chinese empires controlled parts of the peninsula. Ideas from China, especially Confucianism and Buddhism, influenced the Korean kingdoms.

In A.D 668, the kingdom of Silla conquered the other Korean kingdoms. They pushed the Chinese empire off he peninsula and created a strong government. Th s dynasty, rulers in the same family, lasted until A.D 935. After that, a series of dynasties kept the peninsula united for centuries.

Korean Achievements Under the various emperors, a unique society developed. Emperor Sejong called for a new writing system to be created in the 1400s. The system, called Hangul, is still used today. The Koreans also invented moveable metal type. This made printing easier. Korean potters also made delicate porcelain that is valued throughout the world.

Emperors and Shoguns in Japan

Around the time of the Silla dynasty in Korea, Japan became a unified country under an emperor. People believed the emperor was descended from a goddess.

For much of Japan's history, however, the emperors were not strong. Powerful military leaders called **shoguns** controlled Japan's government.

At times, neither the emperor nor the shoguns had complete control over all of the country. Some powerful landowners had their own armies. They granted land to **samurai**, or warrior lords, who supported them. These landowners fought each other to gain power. This created a lot of conflict in Japanese society.

grant, *v.,* to give

In 1603, a shogun called Tokugawa Ieyasu (toh koo GAH wah ee yay AH soo) came to power. Ieyasu and the Tokugawa shoguns that followed him tried to bring peace to Japan. The Tokugawa brought the powerful landowners under the shogun's control.

The Tokugawa closed the country off from contact with most other countries. They wanted to keep outside forces from disrupting Japanese society.

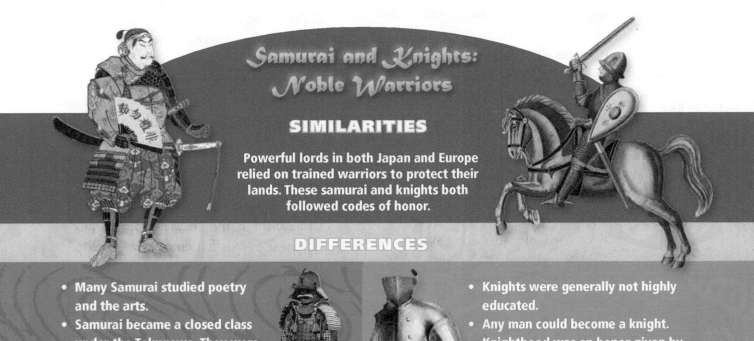

Samurai and Knights: Noble Warriors

SIMILARITIES

Powerful lords in both Japan and Europe relied on trained warriors to protect their lands. These samurai and knights both followed codes of honor.

DIFFERENCES

- Many Samurai studied poetry and the arts.
- Samurai became a closed class under the Tokugawa. They were born into their position.
- Many women of the samurai class learned martial arts.

- Knights were generally not highly educated.
- Any man could become a knight. Knighthood was an honor given by a lord.
- Some women became knights or received training in martial arts.

▲ A dinner at the palace of Emperor Meiji. Western-style clothing became popular in the Meiji court.

myWorld Activity
Best of the Best

The Tokugawa created strict divisions between nobles and commoners. People were not allowed to move between these two groups. The nobles were mostly the large landowners and the samurai. The large landowners had the highest status. The highest-ranking commoners were peasants (or small farmers). Below them were craft people and merchants. Peasants made up 80 percent of the population.

Before the Tokugawa, Japan had close ties with other countries, particularly China and Korea. Buddhism had spread from Korea into Japan. Many Japanese studied Chinese literature and art. The Japanese writing system was based mainly on the Chinese writing system.

New forms of art developed during the Tokugawa period. The country was prosperous. Wealthy nobles and merchants supported artists who created new styles of theater and painting.

Reading Check How did The Tokugawa try to bring stability to Japanese society?

International Conflicts and Connections

Early in the 1800s, both Japan and Korea were largely cut off rom the rest of the world. By the beginning of the 1900s, both nations had been pulled into international confli ts and trade networks.

Early Contact with Europeans Ships from Europe fi st arrived in Japan and Korea around 1600. Both kingdoms had decided to keep Western merchants and missionaries away. Korea allowed only Chinese and Japanese traders. It attacked American and French ships trying to enter its ports. Th s isolation, or lack of contact, continued until the mid-1800s in Japan and even longer in Korea.

Changes Come to Japan In 1854, the American commander Matthew C. Perry sailed into a Japanese port despite the Tokugawa ban on foreigners. The Japanese knew that Perry's ship carried powerful weapons. So they accepted the trade agreement that Perry brought from the United States. Soon other nations pushed Japan to sign similar treaties.

Many Japanese people thought that these trade agreements were unfair to Japan. They blamed the Tokugawa shogun for signing these treaties. Many Japanese people felt change was needed to make Japan a more powerful country.

In 1868, new leaders arose and pushed out the Tokugawa shogun. They brought back the emperor, but they told him what to do. Th s time in Japanese history is called **Meiji Restoration.** It marks the return to power of Emperor Meiji.

The Rise of Japan Japan's new leaders expanded its industry and military. They also increased its power in the region.

In 1910, the Japanese took control over Korea. It was a difficult time for Koreans. They were forced to do hard work in new Japanese industries. They had to learn to speak Japanese, and many were forced to take Japanese sounding names. Japanese control of Korea was harmful to both the Korean people and culture.

Later Japan also invaded other countries. It took over large areas in the north of China as well as Formosa or Taiwan.

When World War II broke out, Japan joined on the side of Germany. Japan soon invaded Southeast Asia. The United States and Japan grew further apart. In 1941, Japan attacked the United States Navy at Pearl Harbor, Hawaii. As a result, the United States entered World War II.

In 1945, the United States dropped atomic bombs on the Japanese cities of Hiroshima and Nagasaki. The resulting casualtes were huge, and Japan surrendered. It lost all the lands it had invaded, including Korea.

Reading Check **How did Japan's empire grow and then shrink?**

A Japanese fighter plane called a "Zero" ▼

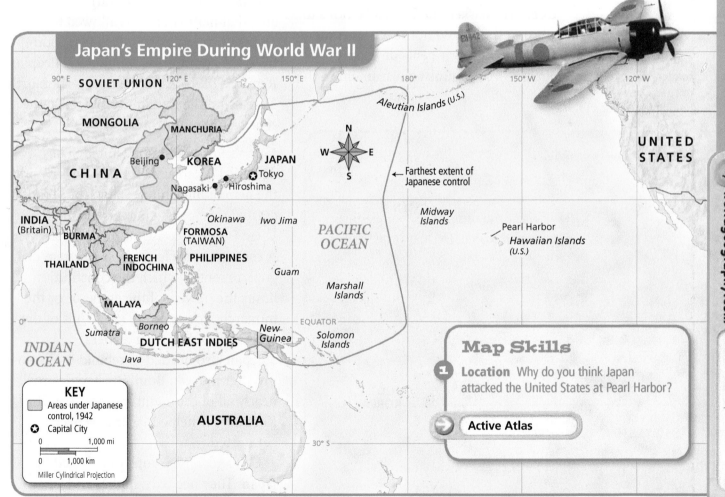

Japan's Empire During World War II

KEY
Areas under Japanese control, 1942
⊙ Capital City
0   1,000 mi
0   1,000 km
Miller Cylindrical Projection

Map Skills

1 **Location** Why do you think Japan attacked the United States at Pearl Harbor?

Active Atlas

my worldgeography.com   Active Atlas

Japan and the Koreas Since World War II

After World War II, Japan focused on rebuilding its government and its economy. In Korea, confli t quickly resumed. Th s confli t would divide a country that had been united for centuries.

The Korean War Japan's control of Korea ended after Japan surrendered at the end of World War II. At that time, the United States occupied the southern part of Korea. The Soviet Union occupied the northern part of the country. The United States and the Soviet Union disagreed about how to unite the two parts of Korea. They asked the United Nations to help, but they could not reach agreement.

Two new governments developed. One was a communist government in the north, which the Soviet Union supported. The other was a democratic government in the south, which the United States supported. Both governments claimed to rule Korea.

North Korea invaded South Korea in 1950. Th s marked the beginning of the **Korean War**. Hoping to limit the spread of communism, the United States led United Nations troops sent to defend South Korea. The Soviet Union and China aided North Korea.

Neither side won. Instead, they agreed to stop fi hting in 1953. The two sides drew a new border. A strip along the border was declared a demilitarized zone, an area that neither army is allowed to enter. The peninsula was split into two countries: the communist Democratic People's Republic of Korea in the north—or North Korea, and the Republic of Korea in the south—or South Korea.

Japan's Recovery The United States occupied Japan after World War II. With the help of the United States, the Japanese created a new system of government. Japan is now a constitutional monarchy. A **constitutional monarchy** is a system of government in which the constitution limits the powers of the emperor or the monarch. Power lies in the hands of the voters, who elect their leaders.

Japan also needed to rebuild its economy after the war. Bombing had destroyed nearly all of the country's industry. The Korean War helped Japan's recovery to get started.

U.S. and U.N. troops were based in Japan. They needed supplies and labor.

occupy, *v.,* to take over, control

South Korean soldiers patrol the border along the demilitarized zone. ▼

Two Koreas

CHINA

NORTH KOREA

P'yongyang

Demilitarized Zone

Seoul

SOUTH KOREA

125° E

130° E

35° N

Korea Strait

N
W   E
S

0   100 mi
0   100 km
Lambert Conformal Conic Projection

The Japanese people went to work to meet those needs.

The Japanese built new factories to replace the ones destroyed during the war. These factories had the most modern technology. They produced goods better and cheaper than the old factories.

The Japanese government supported education and job training. It also encouraged people to work hard and save their money. Banks used these savings to make loans to businesses. Th s helped the economy to grow.

Japan had a well-educated workforce and modern equipment in its factories. Japan produced and exported well-made products such as cars, electronics, and cameras. Those products attracted buyers in many parts of the world. Exports helped Japan's economy grow very quickly for the following 30 years, and the Japanese people grew wealthier.

Reading Check **How did the Korean War affect Japan?**

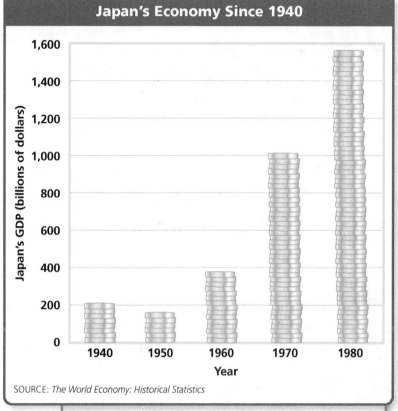

Japan's Economy Since 1940

SOURCE: *The World Economy: Historical Statistics*

Chart Skills

In which decade did Japan's economy grow the most?

Data Discovery

Section 2 Assessment

Essential Question

Key Terms

1. Who were the shogun and the samurai?
2. What happened during the Meiji Restoration?
3. What is a constitutional monarchy?

Key Ideas

4. How did China influence the culture of Japan and Korea?
5. How did the Tokugawa change Japanese society?
6. Why was Korea divided after World War II?

Think Critically

7. **Draw Inferences** Why might the Koreans have wanted to create their own writing system rather than continuing to use the Chinese system?
8. **Analyze Cause and Effect** What factors helped the Japanese rebuild their economy after World War II?

How much does geography shape a country?

9. Both Japan and Korea chose to limit contact with outsiders at certain times during their histories. How do you think their geography helped them to do that? Go to your Student Journal and record your answers.

Japan and the Koreas Today

Key Ideas
- South Korea's economy has grown, and its democracy has become stronger.
- North Korea is a communist dictatorship.
- North Korea's nuclear program is a source of conflict in the region.
- Japan has struggled with economic problems in recent years.

Key Terms
- limited government
- unlimited government
- dictator
- recession
- Shinto

Visual Glossary

Reading Skill: Set a Purpose for Reading Take notes using the graphic organizer in your journal.

◀ 63 Building, the tallest building in Seoul, South Korea

Japan and the Koreas have faced challenges in recent years. Yet, the people of South Korea and Japan have a good standard of living. These countries have become more influential in the world. By contrast, North Korea is largely isolated. Its people have suffered severe hardship.

Prosperity and Democracy in South Korea

South Korea has become more democratic over the years. It has also become a world economic power.

Growing Democracy The leaders of South Korea approved a constitution in 1948 and began building a new government. They created a **limited government**, that is, a government with powers that are limited by law. However, the constitution also stated that leaders did not have to follow those limits or protect individual rights if the country faced serious problems.

As a result, South Korea's political system was not always democratic. More than once, the military took over the country. Freedom of speech and freedom of the press was not always protected. In 1987, people began to call for change. Many South Koreans joined huge political protests. That year, the leaders changed the constitution.

Under the new constitution, the government cannot take away freedoms even when there are political or economic troubles. Citizens have more rights. The military is less powerful. It has not taken over the government since those reforms.

Economic Boom After the Korean War, the leaders of South Korea focused on producing industrial goods for export to other countries. The government supported a number of large companies. It helped them get the money and equipment they needed to make more products. The government also improved the education system.

Now, South Korea exports many high-technology goods, such as cell phones and computers. Its economy is one of the largest in the world. People now live more comfortably and have more belongings.

Still, the growth of South Korea's economy has not been stable. The government borrowed large sums of money from abroad. In the late 1990s, the country had too much debt. Th s hurt the economy. The economy improved, but the government will have to work to avoid this problem in the future.

Daily Life and Culture As the economy has grown, daily life for the people of South Korea has changed. In the past, most Koreans were farmers. Now, most people live in cities. In addition, South Korea now has contact with many countries. Th s has changed Korean culture. It has also introduced Korean culture to people throughout the world.

For example, the popular Korean sport of tae kwon do has become very popular outside the country. Tae kwon do became an offi al Olympic sport in 2000. At the same time, the Koreans have become fans of many sports from abroad. Soccer, in particular, is very popular. Almost every town has its own team. Other sports such

▲ Winner of a gold medal in tae kwon do, South Korea's Hwang Kyungseon (left) at the Beijing Olympics in 2008

as baseball, basketball, and volleyball have a wide following.

Religious life in South Korea has also changed. Christianity spread rapidly through the country after the Korean War. About one quarter of South Korea's population is Christian. In addition, about one quarter of the population is Buddhist. The Buddha's birthday is a national holiday in South Korea. More than ten thousand Buddhist temples dot the landscape. Both foreign visitors and Koreans study Buddhism at these colorful temples. South Koreans enjoy complete religious freedom.

Reading Check How has the South Korean government changed since the 1980s?

STANDARD OF LIVING: NORTH AND SOUTH KOREA

	North Korea	South Korea
Ecomonic output per person	$1,800	$27,100
Number of phone lines	1.2 million	24 million
Number of cell phones	0	43.5 million
Undernourished people	36%	1.6%
Life expectancy	64 years	79 years

SOURCE: *CIA World Factbook*, 2008, UN Common Database, 2001

A standard of living measures the health of a country by the goods and services its people can buy.

Chart Skills

From the information in this table, which country has a higher standard of living?

➡ Data Discovery

Repression and Hardship in North Korea

North Korea is very different from South Korea. North Korea is one of the most isolated countries in the world. The people of North Korea face a hard life with little political freedom.

Dictatorship and Isolation North Korea is not a democracy. Its government is an example of an **unlimited government,** which is a government that, by law, may take any action it wants. Kim Jong-il is the country's leader. Kim is a dictator. A **dictator** has total control over the government. Kim Jong-il came to power when his father, Kim Il-sung, died in 1994.

Kim Il-sung rose to power in 1948. He was the leader of the Communist Party. Other parties were not allowed. Communist Party leaders tightly controlled the North Korean people. Like his father, Kim Jong-il is also a Communist and has kept this system.

The government controls the information reported by newspapers, radio, and television. The news supports Kim's policies. In addition, the leadership limits information from the outside world. Very few North Koreans have cell phones or Internet access.

People are not free to express their opinions. People who disagree with the leadership are punished. The North Korean government may have jailed up to 200,000 people for their political actions.

The North Korean government controls cultural and religious life. People cannot worship freely. Only a few churches and temples are allowed in the country.

The government promotes Korean culture by funding museums and the arts. Still, it controls the work of these writers, dancers, and musicians. It can ban any art that goes against the ideas of the leaders. North Koreans have few of the freedoms that South Koreans now enjoy.

▲ Kim Jong-il

Dancers in North Korea perform at a ceremony for the 95th anniversary of Kim Il-sung's birth.

A Crippled Economy North Korea is a communist country with a command economy. The government controls much of the economy and decides what goods are made. Often, it has not managed the economy well. As a result, the economy has not grown.

The leadership has focused on building a strong military. As a result, it does not spend enough to update machines on farms or in factories. Food production has fallen because of shortages of tractors, fertilizer, and fuel.

Natural disasters have added to these problems. Starting early in the 1990s, frequent fl ods and droughts damaged crops. More than two million people died of starvation in the late 1990s.

Foreign counties have given food <u>aid</u> to help North Koreans survive. Still, the population suffers. The government has focused on keeping control rather than solving its serious economic problems.

A Tense Border Many people in North and South Korea hope the Koreas can be reunited. In recent years, South Korea has given aid, in the form of food, to North Korea. In addition, leaders from North and South Korea have met and agreed to try to improve relations.

However, despite earlier promises not to develop nuclear weapons, North Korea has continued to build them. Th s has hurt North Korea's relationship with South Korea and many other countries around the world.

World leaders have met with North Koreans and tried to persuade the government to stop developing nuclear weapons. The United States and other countries have pressured North Korea to give up these weapons, but its leaders refuse. Peace and prosperity seem far away for North Korea.

Reading Check **Who is the leader of North Korea?**

aid, *n.,* help, assistance

my **worldgeography.com** **Data Discovery**

Challenges and Changes in Japan

Japan's growth in the decades after World War II made it an important economic power. Japan builds many high-technology goods, such as computers and video games. Today, Japan faces new challenges, including slower economic growth and an aging population.

Economic Woes Japan has one of the largest economies in the world. Still, the country's economy has not grown as quickly in recent years.

After the World War II, the Japanese sold more goods abroad. They invested the money they earned to make more advanced products. The Japanese people became wealthier.

At the start of the 1980s, the Japanese economy was doing very well. Each year stock prices went higher and higher. Then in the early 1990s, the Japanese economy started heading downward.

Due to bad bank practices, Japan's economy entered a **recession**, a time when the economy becomes weaker and does not grow. Businesses produced less. They laid off any workers. In 2003, Japan's economy began to improve. In 2008, however, it fell back into recession. Japan continues to face challenges that may make future economic growth difficult.

An Aging Population One of these challenges is supporting a large population of retired people. Japanese people, on average, live longer than people in any other country. They have healthy eating habits and a good healthcare system.

In addition, couples in Japan have fewer children now. As a result, there are

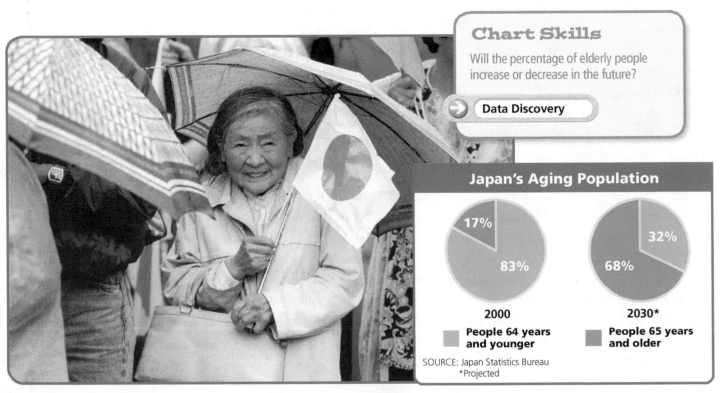

Chart Skills

Will the percentage of elderly people increase or decrease in the future?

Data Discovery

Japan's Aging Population

17%

83%

2000

32%

68%

2030*

People 64 years and younger

People 65 years and older

SOURCE: Japan Statistics Bureau
*Projected

fewer young people to support the elderly population. With fewer young people entering the workforce, Japan may not be able to produce as many goods. Its economy may remain weak.

Some companies in Japan are building new kinds of robots as one way to avoid a possible shortage of future workers. By taking over jobs that people currently do, robots may help keep Japan's economic production high. They can even care for the elderly:

> 66 There are robots [in Japan] serving as receptionists, vacuuming office corridors, spoon-feeding the elderly. They serve tea, greet company guests, and chatter away at public technology displays. 99
> —Associated Press

Changing Family Life Most Japanese people now live in cities. People are more likely to live in small family groups than with their extended families.

When the economy was growing quickly, many companies could provide excellent pay and benefits. Often only the husband worked. Wives generally stayed at home to care for children and older family members. Children were expected to study hard to get into college.

These family roles have changed in many families. During the recession, more women found jobs to help support their families. Also, some companies started hiring women as their older employees retired. These companies also encourage women to return to work after having children rather than becoming stay-at-home mothers.

Now, women have more job opportunities, but they still may not be treated equally to men. For example, women may fi d it difficult to be hired for the highest levels of management in a company.

School life has also changed in Japan. Many schools had classes six days a week to prepare students for difficult college entrance exams. Now, most schools have classes just five days a week.

Yet, the competition to get into the best colleges is as tough as ever. Many students attend extra classes during weekends and evenings in hopes of getting into one of Japan's best universities.

Reading Check How did economic problems change Japanese family life?

In an emergency, this security guard robot can put out a fire. *How might society change if robots could do many jobs that people now do?* ▼

JAPAN'S POPULAR CULTURE

Japan's entertainment industry grew after World War II. People had more time and money for entertainment, such as movies and video games. Japan now has the largest comic book industry in the world, and entertainment is one of Japan's major exports.

CRITICAL THINKING: Why do you think Japanese entertainment has become popular in other countries?

▲ Video games that started in Japan, such as the dancing game above, have become popular across the world.

Manga, or Japanese comics, are reaching a wider audience in the United States. ▼

Sales of Manga in the United States

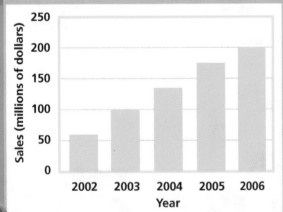

SOURCE: Anime News Network

▲ An anime, or cartoon, character from the Japanese video game Dragon Ball Z

This character is from the famous anime series Yu Gi Oh! The show is popular in Japan and also Australia, Germany, and Britain. ▶

Shoppers in Tokyo browse manga. ▼

myWorld Activity
Political Manga

A Rich Cultural Life

Most people in Japan belong to the same ethnic group and speak Japanese. There are not many immigrants. Yet, like South Korea, Japan is not cut off rom the world. It influences and has been influenced by the cultures of many countries.

Spiritual Beliefs More than 80 percent of all Japanese people practice a combination of Buddhism and Shinto. **Shinto** is a traditional Japanese religion. In Shinto, kami are worshiped. Kami are gods or spirits that may live on earth in animals, trees, rocks, or other natural objects.

Today, many Japanese people practice both Buddhism and Shinto. For example, many Japanese people may have a Shinto marriage ceremony. Yet they will choose a Buddhist funeral.

Many traditions and holidays in Japan are connected to one of these two religions. At New Year's celebrations, Japanese people traditionally visit a Shinto shrine to pray to kami for a good harvest in the coming year.

Recent Cultural Borrowing In recent years, Japan has borrowed from the culture of many countries. Cultural imports, such as baseball and soccer, have been popular for many years in Japan.

At the same time, cultures around the world have borrowed from Japanese culture. Japanese martial arts, such as karate, are now popular around the world. So are Japanese foods such as sushi, or raw fish served with rice. Japanese artists have influenced artists in Europe, the United States, and other countries.

Japan has also had a big impact on the world of entertainment. It has had a large video-game industry for decades. Also, Japanese movies and television programs have a wide audience, especially in Asia.

More recently, Japanese anime—or cartoons—and manga—or comics—have attracted more and more fans throughout the world. Japan has added these products to its long list of successful exports.

Reading Check **How have Shinto and Buddhism influenced Japanese culture?**

Section 3 Assessment

Essential Question

How much does geography shape a country?

Key Terms

1. What is Shinto?
2. What is a limited government?
3. Is Kim Jong-il a dictator? Explain.

Key Ideas

4. Why has North Korea's nuclear program created conflict in the region?
5. How did Japan's economy change beginning in the 1990s?
6. Why is Japan's aging population causing economic problems?

Think Critically

7. **Draw Inferences** Why does the North Korean government limit access to outside information?
8. **Analyze Cause and Effect** What caused South Korea's political system to become more democratic in recent years?

9. How important is geography to the differences between North Korea and South Korea? Go to your Student Journal and record your answers.

Chapter Assessment

Key Terms and Ideas

1. **Explain** During what season do Japan and the Koreas get the most rain? Why is rain heaviest in this season?

2. **Recall** What are some of Japan's and the Koreas important natural resources?

3. **Summarize** What were some of the cultural achievements of the Koreans?

4. **Discuss** What was the Meiji restoration? What changes took place in Japan after this event?

5. **Compare and Contrast** How are the governments of North Korea and South Korea different?

6. **Recall** What were some of the effects of the recession in Japan during the 1990s?

7. **Summarize** What are examples of Japanese culture that have become popular in other countries?

Think Critically

8. **Solve Problems** How has Japan attempted to prepare for earthquakes?

9. **Making Inferences** Under Tokugawa rule, farmers had a higher social status than merchants. Why do you think farming was so highly valued?

10. **Comparing Viewpoints** How does North Korea view culture and the arts? How is this different from Japan?

11. **Core Concepts: Land Use** How does this region's geography create challenges for land use?

Places to Know

For each place, write the letter from the map that shows its location.

12. **Japan**

13. **North Korea**

14. **South Korea**

15. **P'yongyang**

16. **Seoul**

17. **Mt. Fuji**

18. **Estimate** Using the scale, estimate the length of the border between North Korea and South Korea.

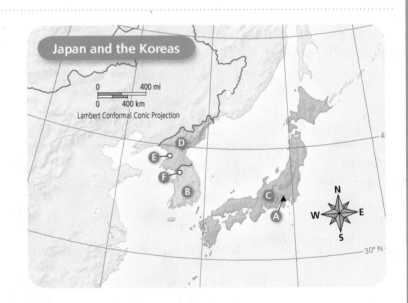

Japan and the Koreas

0   400 mi
0   400 km
Lambert Conformal Conic Projection

Essential Question

How much does geography shape a country?

Demonstrate Understanding Plan a multimedia presenstation that shows how Japan and the Koreas have adapted to and changed their environment. Make recommendations to the United Nations Environment Programme to help these countries solve environmental problems.

21st Century Learning

Search for Information on the Internet

Search for information on the culture of Japan, North Korea, or South Korea. Then write a report about that country's culture. Include pictures with your report. Be sure to include information on:
- religion
- the arts
- recreation
- food

Document-Based Questions

Success Tracker™
Online at myworldgeography.com

Use your knowledge of Japan and Documents A and B to answer the questions below.

Document A

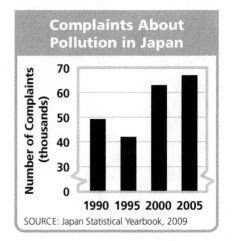

Complaints About Pollution in Japan

Number of Complaints (thousands)

70 60 50 40 30 0

1990 1995 2000 2005

SOURCE: Japan Statistical Yearbook, 2009

Document B

" Japan's greenhouse gas emissions [releases] surged [increased rapidly] last year . . . Emissions of carbon dioxide and other greenhouse gases blamed for global warming spiked 2.3 percent to 1.37 billion tons in the 2007 . . ."

—CBS News, November 12, 2008

1. In Document A, which of the following years shows a drop in complaints about pollution?

A 1990
B 1995
C 2000
D 2005

2. Which of the following BEST describes the information presented in Document B?

A Pollution decreased in 2007, which was encouraging.

B Pollution stayed about the same in 2007.

C Pollution increased a small amount in 2007, which is cause for some concern.

D Pollution increased sharply in 2007, which is cause for alarm.

3. Writing Task Based on Document A and B, did Japan handle its pollution better in the 1990s or in the 2000s? Explain your answer.

Southeast Asia

What are the challenges of diversity?

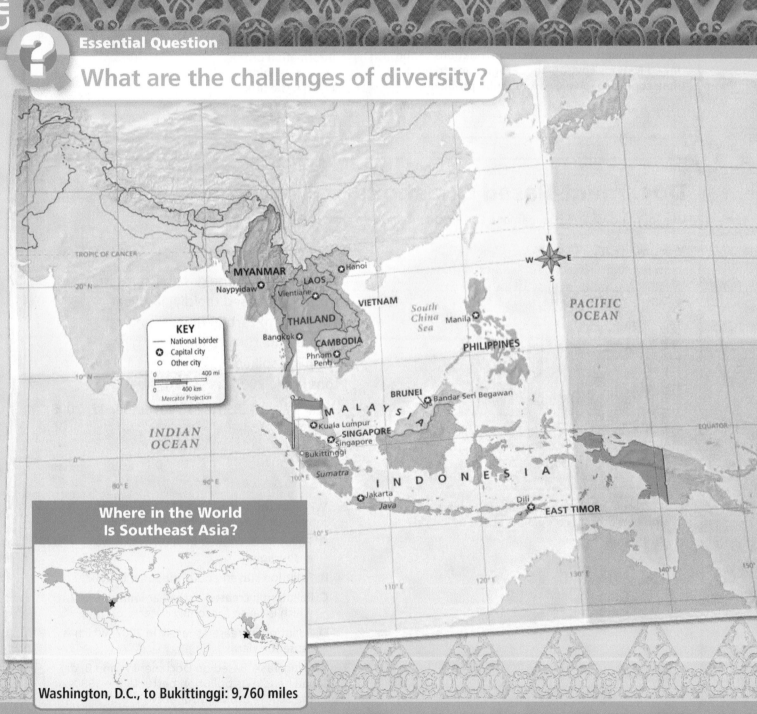

MYANMAR
Naypyidaw ✪
LAOS
Vientiane ✪
○ Hanoi
VIETNAM
THAILAND
Bangkok ○
CAMBODIA
Phnom ✪
Penh
South China Sea
Manila ○
PHILIPPINES
PACIFIC OCEAN
BRUNEI
○ Bandar Seri Begawan
MALAYSIA
✪ Kuala Lumpur
SINGAPORE
✪ Singapore
○ Bukittinggi
INDONESIA
Sumatra
INDIAN OCEAN
Jakarta ✪
Java
Dili ○
EAST TIMOR
TROPIC OF CANCER
20° N
10° N
0°
10° S
EQUATOR
80° E
90° E
100° E
110° E
120° E
130° E
140° E
150° E

KEY
— National border
✪ Capital city
○ Other city

0 ___ 400 mi
0 ___ 400 km
Mercator Projection

Where in the World Is Southeast Asia?

Washington, D.C., to Bukittinggi: 9,760 miles

my Story

A Minangkabau Wedding

In this section you will read about Ridwan, a young man helping his family and friends prepare for his cousin's wedding on the island of Sumatra in Indonesia. **What does Ridwan's story tell you about the culture of Southeast Asia?**

Explore the Essential Question
- at my **worldgeography.com**
- using the **myWorld Chapter Activity**
- with the **Student Journal**

Story by Millie Phuah for myWorld Geography Online

Laughing voices drift hrough the cool air as nineteen-year-old Ridwan works with the men. They are busily moving furniture and cleaning the house where a wedding ceremony will take place. Meanwhile, in the kitchen, dozens of women are preparing chili peppers, onions, garlic, ginger, and a host of other spices. The spices will go into the meat and vegetable dishes of the day-long wedding feast. Although it is still early in the morning, there is not a moment to lose. Soon hundreds of relatives, friends, and neighbors will start arriving to honor the happy couple getting married today.

Ridwan looks out over the rice fields and the sea that surround this village called Bukittinggi, a name meaning "high hill." He can't wait to see his cousin, Nentis, who is the bride, begin her life with Al, her groom.

"Weddings are happy and important events that everyone looks forward to because it's a time for relatives

Preparing the wedding feast

Bride and groom in one pair of wedding costumes. The photo on the facing page shows them wearing another set of costumes.

and friends to get together. Today is especially meaningful to me, not only because my cousin is getting married, but it's also the first time I've attended a Minangkabau wedding," says Ridwan. (The Minangkabau are the main ethnic group in West Sumatra.) "And according to Minangkabau practice, Al is moving into Nentis' home, which belongs to the bride's grandmother."

Minangkabau culture is unique. Minangkabau houses often have upward-curved roofs that look like the horns of a water buffalo. The resemblance is not a coincidence. For centuries the Minangkabau depended on the buffalo for food and to help them plow the rice fields. In fact, the name *Minangkabau* means "winning buffalo." The Minangkabau are also one of the few ethnic groups in the world in which family homes are passed down from mothers to daughters, instead of from fathers to sons.

Nentis starts dressing early, because her wedding costume consists of layers of silk and other fabric woven with gold thread, gold jewelry, and a glittering Minangkabau headdress. Meanwhile, Al dons his suit. He looks like an Indian raja, or king, as he slips on a kris, an ornamental dagger. Such costumes reveal the Chinese and Indian influences that have helped shape Minangkabau culture.

Some wedding guests visit the buffet outside.

Musicians entertain the guests.

Later in the day, as a band plays, the couple moves to the wedding dais, or platform. Everyone lines up to congratulate the smiling pair. It is a long day for the couple as they rise repeatedly to greet new arrivals. During the feast, long-separated relatives laugh and exchange news. Many have traveled from distant parts of Indonesia to be here today.

Traveling and moving away from home are common among the Minangkabau. In fact, Ridwan's parents left ukittinggi years ago to run a textile shop in East Java. Ridwan helps at his family's textile business and lives in his maternal grandmother's house. The house will one day be passed down to Ridwan's mother and aunt, and then to his sister. When the time comes for Ridwan and his brothers to marry, they will move into their wives' homes. It is the Minangkabau way.

"This is part of Minangkabau culture and I totally accept it, just as all the other men do. It just makes me work harder at my vocation," says Ridwan. "I'd like to further my studies in the Indonesian language and be a theatre performer. My father, of course, hopes I'll take over his business one day, but I think I'll deal with that later," he smiles shyly.

Ridwan returns to his video camera, using modern technology to record an ancient tradition and the scenes that his family will enjoy throughout their lives.

myStory Video

Join Ridwan as he shows you more about his life.

Meet the Journalist

Name Millie Phuah
Favorite Moment Talking to Ridwan's grandmother

Chapter Atlas

Key Ideas

- Southeast Asia is a region of varied landforms.
- Location and climate affect both agricultural production and natural resources.
- Geography has influenced Southeast Asian history and settlement patterns.

Key Terms • peninsula • archipelago • tsunami • monsoon • typhoon

 Visual Glossary

 Reading Skill: Label an Outline Map Take notes using the outline map in your journal.

Mount Mayon erupts in the Philippines.

Balinese dancers from Indonesia

Physical Features

Ridwan's cousin's wedding took place on the island of Sumatra in Indonesia. Indonesia is one of the 11 nations that make up Southeast Asia. The region has two parts: a mainland and an island area, part of which lies on the Equator.

The mainland of Southeast Asia is a **peninsula**—a land area almost surrounded by water. It extends from the Shan Plateau down to the narrow Malay peninsula. Among the major rivers are the Mekong, the Irrawaddy, and the Red River. These rivers carry rich soil to fertilize the deltas before they empty into the sea.

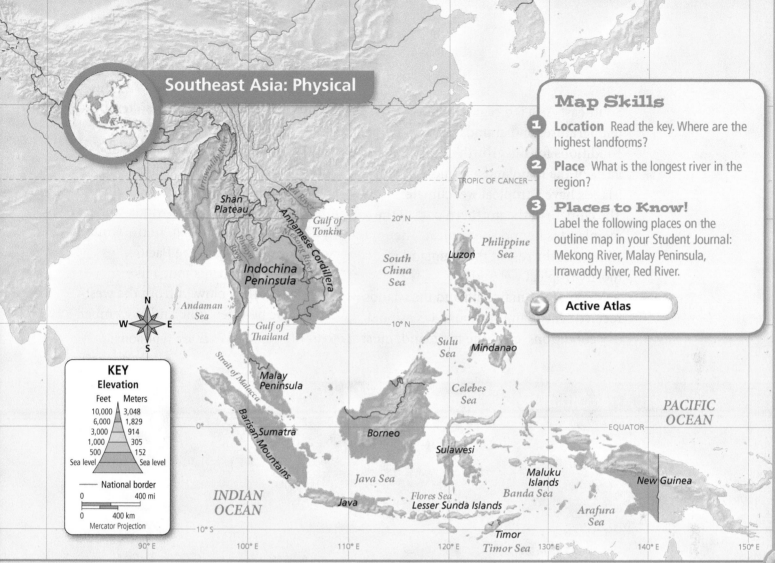

Southeast Asia: Physical

Irrawaddy River
Shan Plateau
Chao Phraya River
Annamese Cordillera
Red River
Mekong River
Gulf of Tonkin
Indochina Peninsula
TROPIC OF CANCER
20° N
South China Sea
Philippine Sea
Luzon
Andaman Sea
Gulf of Thailand
10° N
Sulu Sea
Mindanao
Strait of Malacca
Malay Peninsula
Celebes Sea
PACIFIC OCEAN
Barisan Mountains
Sumatra
0°
Borneo
EQUATOR
Sulawesi
Java Sea
Maluku Islands
New Guinea
INDIAN OCEAN
Java
Flores Sea
Lesser Sunda Islands
Banda Sea
Arafura Sea
10° S
Timor
Timor Sea
90° E   100° E   110° E   120° E   130° E   140° E   150° E

Map Skills

1. **Location** Read the key. Where are the highest landforms?

2. **Place** What is the longest river in the region?

3. **Places to Know!** Label the following places on the outline map in your Student Journal: Mekong River, Malay Peninsula, Irrawaddy River, Red River.

Active Atlas

KEY
Elevation

Feet	Meters
10,000	3,048
6,000	1,829
3,000	914
1,000	305
500	152
Sea level	Sea level

— National border

| 0 | 400 mi |
| 0 | 400 km |

Mercator Projection

The rest of the region is made up of **archipelagoes,** or groups of islands. The sizes of the islands vary greatly, from huge Borneo to tiny islands that may not even appear on some maps. Many island landscapes are breathtaking. Beyond beautiful sandy beaches, mountains and volcanoes tower over narrow coastal plains. Short, fast-flowing rivers run through rain forests filled with great biodiversity, or variety of living things.

Many islands in Indonesia and the Philippines are part of the Ring of Fire, a string of active volcanoes that encircles the Pacific Ocean.

Most of Southeast Asia is part of the Eurasian Plate, which is colliding with the Indo-Australian Plate. When these plates shift eep underground, destructive earthquakes can occur. In December 2004, an earthquake just 150 miles west of the island of Sumatra created a huge **tsunami,** or tidal wave. This tsunami killed more than 230,000 people living around the Indian Ocean. An early warning system has been launched to try to prevent such a disaster from happening again.

launch, *v.,* to set in operation

Reading Check What are the two main parts of Southeast Asia?

Climate

Southeast Asia is a region of hot temperatures and abundant rain—perfect conditions for the growth of rain forests. Parts of the mainland and most of the islands have a tropical wet climate. The climate in the northern part of the mainland is humid subtropical. The climate in the rest of the mainland is mostly tropical wet and dry.

Much of the mainland and the islands receive heavy rain. Although occasional dry conditions affect the mainland, most of the islands have no dry season. The islands are near the Equator, so temperatures are hot everywhere.

Every year **monsoons,** or seasonal winds, blow through the region. The summer monsoons carry heavy rain and cause flooding. These winds come in from the Indian Ocean. In the winter, monsoons blow from the Pacific.

Typhoons are storms much like hurricanes. They blow in from the western Pacific between June and November.

Reading Check **What are typhoons?**

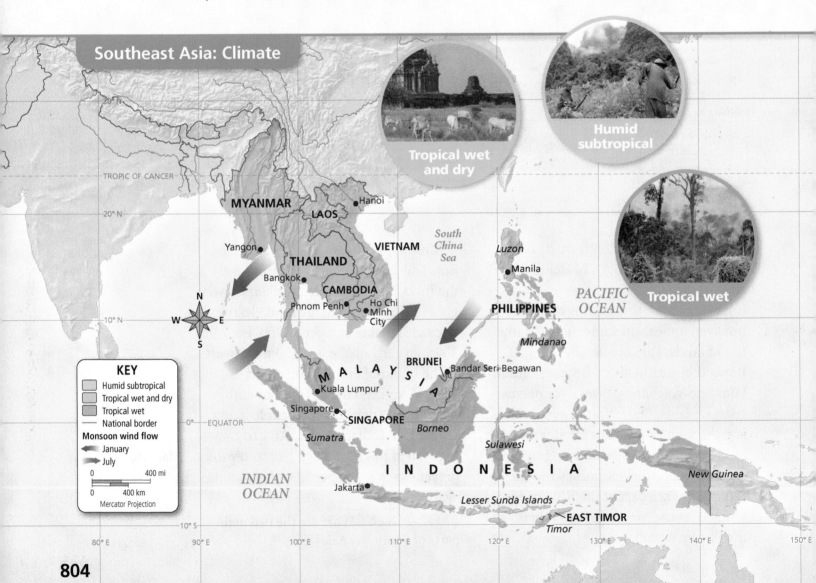

Southeast Asia: Climate

Tropical wet and dry

Humid subtropical

Tropical wet

TROPIC OF CANCER

30° N

MYANMAR
Hanoi
LAOS
20° N
Yangon
VIETNAM
South China Sea
Luzon
THAILAND
Manila
Bangkok
CAMBODIA
Phnom Penh
Ho Chi Minh City
PHILIPPINES
PACIFIC OCEAN
10° N
Mindanao
BRUNEI
Bandar Seri Begawan
MALAYSIA
Kuala Lumpur
Singapore
SINGAPORE
Borneo
0° EQUATOR
Sumatra
Sulawesi
INDONESIA
New Guinea
INDIAN OCEAN
Jakarta
Lesser Sunda Islands
10° S
EAST TIMOR
Timor

80° E   90° E   100° E   110° E   120° E   130° E   140° E   150° E

KEY
Humid subtropical
Tropical wet and dry
Tropical wet
National border
Monsoon wind flow
January
July
0   400 mi
0   400 km
Mercator Projection

People and Geography

Geography has shaped the history and culture of Southeast Asia. In the north, mountains separated mainland Southeast Asia from the rest of Asia. Within the region itself, north-south cordilleras, or parallel mountain ranges, isolated early societies. Later, the cordilleras helped defi e national borders. The rivers that carried rich sediment to the deltas also played an important role, for it was in the <u>fertile</u> river valleys that the fi st civilizations emerged.

The mostly gentle seas of Southeast Asia allowed trade, much of which traveled through the narrow Malacca Strait. For centuries pirates and kings fought to control the riches of this waterway. Another rich prize lay to the east in the Maluku Islands. Here, in the volcanic soil, grew rare spices such as nutmeg and cloves. At one time, these spices could be found nowhere else on Earth. The spice trade attracted Europeans—who came fi st to trade and then to colonize.

Reading Check   Where did spices grow?

fertile, *adj.,* rich, fruitful

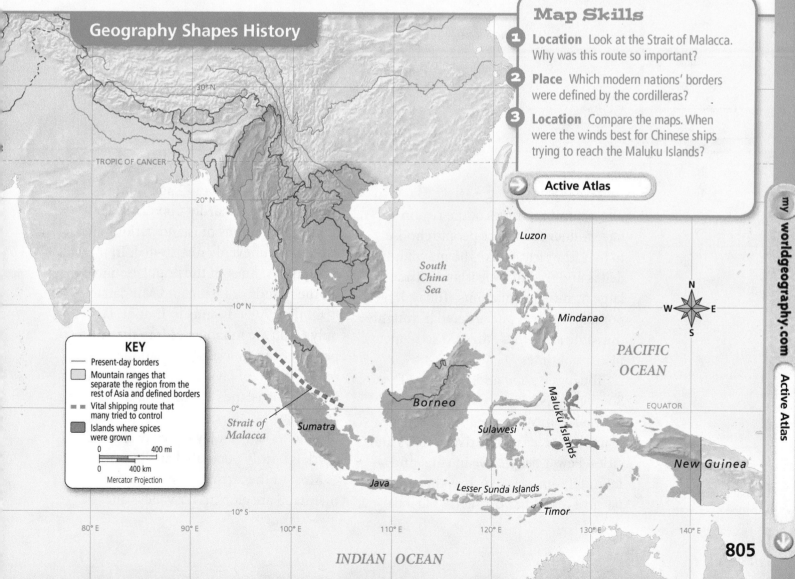

Geography Shapes History

Map Skills

1. **Location** Look at the Strait of Malacca. Why was this route so important?
2. **Place** Which modern nations' borders were defined by the cordilleras?
3. **Location** Compare the maps. When were the winds best for Chinese ships trying to reach the Maluku Islands?

Active Atlas

KEY
- Present-day borders
- Mountain ranges that separate the region from the rest of Asia and defined borders
- Vital shipping route that many tried to control
- Islands where spices were grown

0   400 mi
0   400 km
Mercator Projection

my worldgeography.com Active Atlas

805

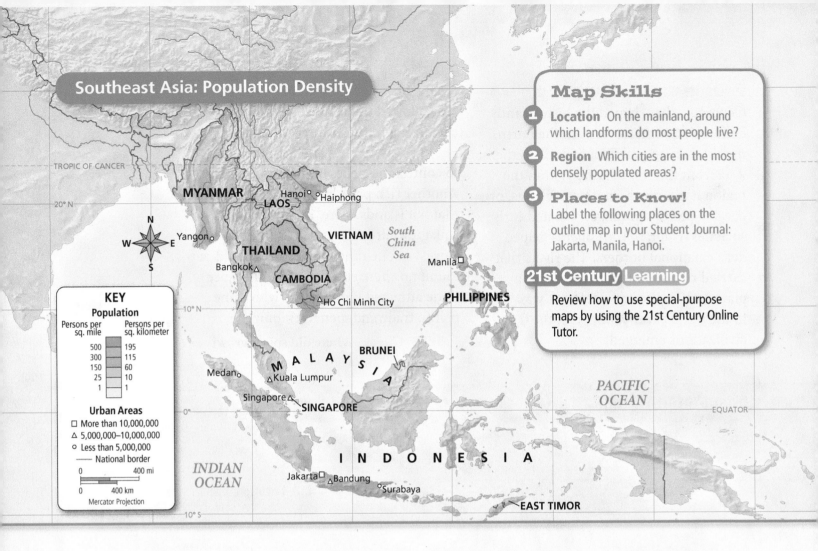

Southeast Asia: Population Density

Map Skills

1 **Location** On the mainland, around which landforms do most people live?

2 **Region** Which cities are in the most densely populated areas?

3 **Places to Know!** Label the following places on the outline map in your Student Journal: Jakarta, Manila, Hanoi.

21st Century Learning

Review how to use special-purpose maps by using the 21st Century Online Tutor.

KEY

Population

Persons per sq. mile	Persons per sq. kilometer
500	195
300	115
150	60
25	10
1	1

Urban Areas

☐ More than 10,000,000
△ 5,000,000–10,000,000
○ Less than 5,000,000
— National border

0   400 mi
0   400 km
Mercator Projection

Settlement and Land Use

The natural resources of the region have influenced where people choose to live. The rich soils of the mainland deltas and the volcanic islands attracted large farming populations. Today, large populations are concentrated in roughly the same areas that attracted settlement in ancient times.

Today the population density of Southeast Asia is very uneven. On the mainland, most people live on coastal plains and deltas, or in river valleys and cities. Fewer people live in rural and mountainous areas, such as the northern parts of Myanmar (formerly Burma),

Thailand, Vietnam, and Laos. Some areas of rain forest are hardly populated at all.

The populations of island nations are even more unevenly distributed. In the Philippines, most of the population live on the islands of Luzon and Mindanao.

Of the 17,000 islands in Indonesia, only 6,000 are inhabited. More than 60 percent of Indonesia's population resides on the island of Java. Nearly all the rest lives on the islands of Sumatra, Borneo, and Sulawesi. The easternmost province of Indonesia, Irian Jaya (IRH æ ahn JAH yuh), is hardly populated at all.

Most of the farming areas on the mainland are along river valleys and

myWorld Activity
Why Settle in Southeast Asia?

deltas where plentiful water and good soil allow people to grow rice. Thailand's rice is some of the best in the world. Because Southeast Asia has very little land that is level enough for farming, the peoples of this mountainous region have cleverly altered their landscape to meet their needs. By sculpting the hillsides into steps, or terraces, they have turned mountain slopes into farmland for rice crops. On the higher slopes, cool temperatures provide the perfect conditions for growing tea.

Southeast Asian forests are a great natural resource. Exported lumber from the rain forests is a major source of income for some nations. The lumber is exported mainly to Japan and the United States.

Reading Check **Why did large populations develop in the deltas?**

Urban Problems

Even though there are many large cities, the region as a whole is mainly rural. However, more people are moving to urban areas in search of jobs and higher living standards. This migration has turned Jakarta, Bangkok, Manila, and Phnom Penh into huge cities with growing urban problems.

The increase in population places great strains on the cities' infrastructures, such as water supplies, electricity, and sewage facilities. Housing, healthcare, and other services also suffer. There are many environmental problems, such as air pollution and traffic congestion. The monsoon rains bring floods that cause sewage overflow and water contamination.

Reading Check **What urban problems can be traced to population increases?**

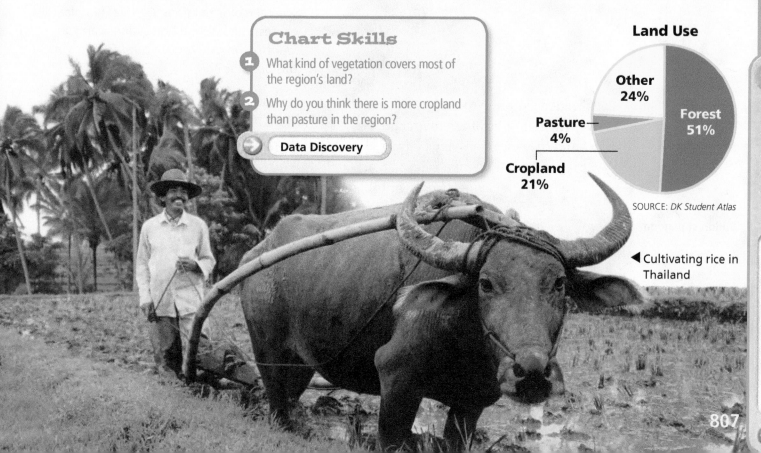

Chart Skills

1. What kind of vegetation covers most of the region's land?

2. Why do you think there is more cropland than pasture in the region?

→ **Data Discovery**

Land Use

Other 24%

Pasture 4%

Forest 51%

Cropland 21%

SOURCE: *DK Student Atlas*

◀ Cultivating rice in Thailand

A History of Diversity

Southeast Asia has a history of cultural and religious diversity. Waves of migrations from the north have brought Burmese, Thai, and Lao peoples onto the mainland. Other ancient migrations brought settlers to the region by sea. Today, Chinese, Indians, Malays, Burmese, Indonesians, Vietnamese, Filipinos, Thai, Khmer, and Hmong all call the region home. In addition, there are indigenous peoples who live in remote, isolated rain forest communities.

There has always been a strong Chinese presence in Southeast Asia. In ancient times, China was ruling parts of what is now Vietnam by 100 B.C. This started a long history of Chinese involvement in Vietnam.

Today, Chinese communities thrive in every country in the region. Many Chinese immigrated into the region in the 1800s when demand for labor was high. The Chinese population ranges from less than 1 percent in East Timor to 77 percent in Singapore. There are also large Indian communities in Malaysia and Myanmar.

Cultural Borrowing

Southeast Asia's location on the international trade routes has created a lively cultural exchange. In Vietnam the Cao Dai religion mixes elements of several major religions. Cao Dai temples express this cultural borrowing. *Can you identify the different cultural features in this building?*

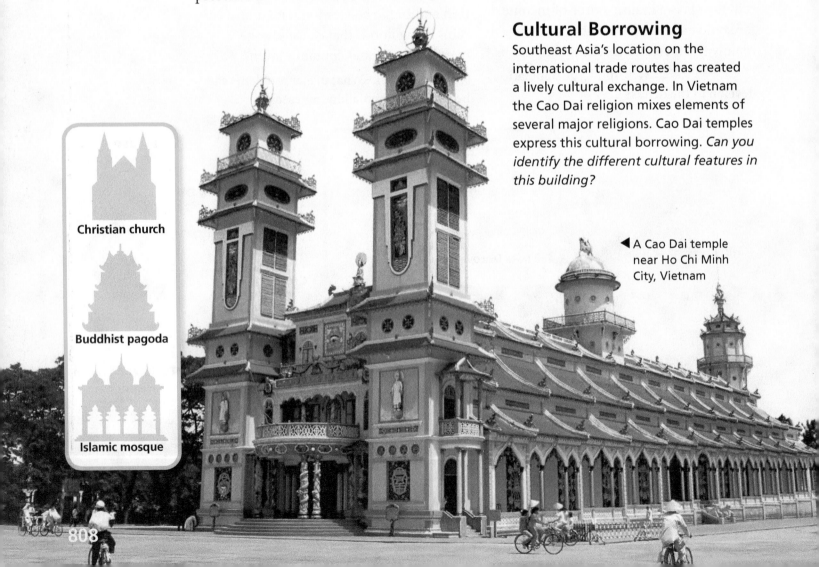

◀ A Cao Dai temple near Ho Chi Minh City, Vietnam

Christian church

Buddhist pagoda

Islamic mosque

In a region of such ethnic diversity, it is not surprising that there is much religious diversity as well. Most of mainland Southeast Asia was influenced by two different forms of Buddhism that spread from India and China.

Islam became the major religion in large parts of island Southeast Asia. On most of the islands it replaced Buddhism and Hinduism. However, islands such as Bali remained Hindu. Today Bali is part of Indonesia, a country that has the largest Muslim population in the world.

While most people of the islands are Muslim, the majority of people in the Philippines are Roman Catholic due to Spanish colonization in the 1500s. However, there are Muslims in the Philippines as well, especially on the two islands of Mindanao and Palawan.

Many religious communities blend customs and traditions from more than one faith. This cultural mixing is a feature of Southeast Asian life. Ridwan's Minangkabau are a good example of this cultural openness, which began in ancient times. From their homeland in the mountains of Sumatra, the Minangkabau traveled downriver to trade. In time they became merchants and travelers, pursuing the knowledge and wealth of the wider world. Along the way they absorbed Indian, Chinese, and Western customs and beliefs. They married their old traditions to the new ways of Islam that they embraced. Later, they enthusiastically adopted the educational system of the Dutch. Their openness to other cultures has served them well. Today the Minangkabau are among the wealthiest, most educated, and most powerful groups in Indonesia.

Southeast Asia's location, which attracted international trade, helped the Minangkabau achieve economic success. In the next section you will see how the story of the Minangkabau connects with Southeast Asia's history of economic trade and cultural exchange.

Reading Check Why is Southeast Asia populated with such a great diversity of ethnic groups?

my World IN NUMBERS

If there were **100** people in the world,

4 would come from Indonesia.

Section 1 Assessment

? **Essential Question**
What are the challenges of diversity?

Key Terms

1. Use the following terms to describe the geography and climate of Southeast Asia: peninsula, archipelago, tsunami, monsoon, typhoon.

Key Ideas

2. What are some differences between the landscapes of the mainland and the islands?

3. Where do most Southeast Asians live?

4. How have Southeast Asians adapted the landscape to meet their needs?

Think Critically

5. **Synthesize** Compare the population density map with the physical map. What patterns do you see?

6. **Draw Conclusions** Why might the coastal areas and islands have had more contact with the outside world?

7. Why did the geography of the region help create such a diverse population? Go to your Student Journal to record your answer.

History of Southeast Asia

Key Ideas
- Southeast Asia's location encouraged trade and cultural and ethnic diversity.
- Europeans transformed the cultural geography of the region.
- Wars of independence were followed by civil wars on mainland Southeast Asia.

Key Terms • reservoir • surplus • maritime • exploit

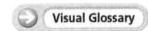
Visual Glossary

Reading Skill: Sequence Take notes using the graphic organizer in your journal.

If the history of Southeast Asia were a video, it would show you a story of migrations and trade. First you would see people living on the volcanic island of Java tens of thousands of years ago. Running the video forward would show newcomers migrating to the region by land and sea. Soon you would notice Indonesian boats carrying the earliest trade goods between India and China.

Ancient Southeast Asia

As the video reached 500 B.C., you would see fields of rice growing in the lowlands of Cambodia and Vietnam. Everywhere you would notice populations increasing because of plentiful harvests. Soon you would see villages specializing in particular crafts nd trading goods with one another as societies became more complex.

More than 2000 years ago, civilizations grew up in the river valleys, where rice crops kept the populations well fed. In the north of what is now Vietnam, the city of Co Loa grew rich. Its wealth attracted the Chinese, who conquered the city by 100 B.C. In the south, port cities bustled with foreign merchants, traders, and traveling priests. The famous ethnic diversity of Southeast Asian cities had emerged.

Reading Check Why did populations increase in ancient times?

◄ A strangler fig tree creeps over the ruins of Angkor Thom, Cambodia.

Culture Close-up

810

The Great Kingdoms

Between A.D 500 and 1500 kingdoms grew and trade expanded. Southeast Asians blended foreign influences into their own culture.

Controlling the Strait The region's location on international trade routes led to contact with India and China. Local kingdoms adopted religions from India, such as Hinduism and Buddhism.

Commerce created such wealth that coastal states fought to control trade. One of the busiest trade routes went through the Strait of Malacca. Srivijaya, a Hindu-Buddhist kingdom on Sumatra, controlled the strait from A.D. 600 to 1300.

Agricultural Empires On the mainland, a civilization rose in what is now Cambodia. The Khmers (kuh MEHRZ) used the landscape to meet their needs.

They built **reservoirs,** or storage pools, of rainwater to irrigate rice fields. This produced huge harvests. They grew rich by selling their extra, or **surplus,** food.

The Khmer empire was a kind of "seed culture" from which many Southeast Asian traditions grew. The Khmers had a strong influence on the culture of Cambodia and Thailand.

As the Khmer empire declined, fierce <u>invaders</u> entered the region. In 1287 the Mongols destroyed the Burmese empire of Bagan (Pagan). But the invaders suffered from the tropical heat and rains. They were also startled by Southeast Asian war elephants, which hurled enemy soldiers into the air with their trunks! During their invasion of Java, the Mongols lost three thousand men.

Reading Check **Which civilizations influenced culture in Southeast Asia?**

invader, *n.,* person who enters a place by force

Ancient Trade Routes

In ancient times, goods from the Mediterranean, China, India, and Southeast Asia were exchanged along the trade routes. Southeast Asia occupied an important position on these routes.

Map Skills

1. **Interaction** Why would traders have wanted to travel such great distances?

2. **Interaction** Why did ancient trade routes hug the coast?

3. **Interaction** Where might you have seen the busiest shipping lanes in ancient times?

Active Atlas

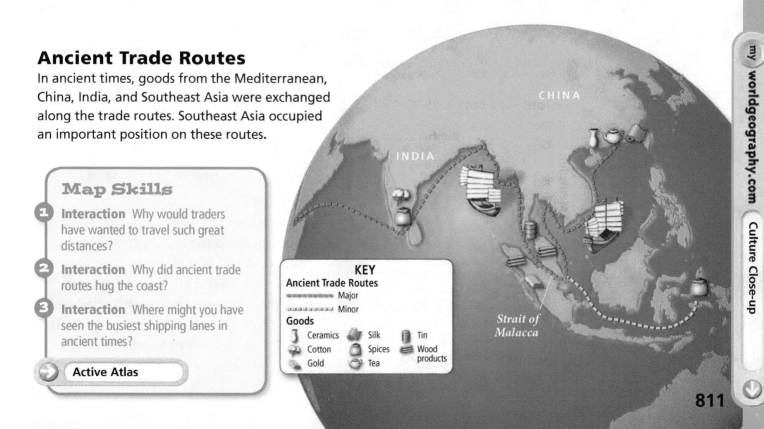

CHINA

INDIA

KEY
Ancient Trade Routes
━━━━━━━ Major
▪▪▪▪▪▪▪▪ Minor
Goods
Ceramics   Silk   Tin
Cotton   Spices   Wood products
Gold   Tea

Strait of Malacca

Closer Look

EFFECTS OF COLONIZATION

Between the 1850s and the 1950s, Southeast Asia was colonized first by Western nations and then occupied by Japan. During that hundred-year period the region changed forever. Large plantations replaced small farms. The demand for cheap labor attracted workers from India and China.

THINK CRITICALLY *Study the graph. Which export increased dramatically around 1910?*

The Dutch built plantations like this one in Indonesia. ▼

▲ Western governments introduced export crops such as rubber and coffee. The region still exports these goods.

Colonial Exports, 1900–1930

Rubber from British Malaya

Coffee from Dutch Indonesia

Thousands of Metric Tons: 500, 450, 400, 350, 300, 250, 200, 150, 100, 50, 0

Year: 1900, 1910, 1920, 1930

SOURCE: *International Historical Statistics*

The Age of Commerce

By the 1400s, the old agricultural empires of Bagan and the Khmer had declined. New regional powers had emerged, based on **maritime,** or sea, trade. Meanwhile, the religion of Islam was spreading along the trade routes, carried by Muslim merchants. After the ruler of the rich port of Malacca converted to Islam in 1414, the religion spread through the islands. Ridwan's Minangkabau ancestors were some of the people who converted to the faith.

The famous wealth of Malacca and its control of the spice trade excited the envy of Europeans. For centuries, Europeans had been trying to gain control of the trade in spices, many of which grew on the Maluku Islands. Then, in 1511, the Portuguese conquered Malacca.

During the following centuries, Western powers tightened their grip on Southeast Asia and **exploited,** or took advantage of, the region's resources. The Spanish, Dutch, British, French, and Americans all founded colonies there. Only Thailand managed to resist colonization.

Reading Check **How did Western powers change Southeast Asia?**

Independence, War, and Recovery

During the early 1900s, independence movements in the region grew. Then, during World War II, Japan took control of most of Southeast Asia. After Japan lost the war, European powers tried and failed to regain control of the region. By 1957 the countries of Southeast Asia had won independence.

Mainland Conflicts For some nations, the fi ht for independence was long and bloody. In Vietnam, communist forces under Ho Chi Minh fought the French. War lasted until 1954, when France gave up control. Vietnam was divided into two republics: a communist north and a non-communist south.

However, fi hting soon developed between north and south. The United States first sent advisers and then troops to South Vietnam to stop the spread of communism. The fi hting spread to neighboring nations. This war dragged on until 1975, when the country was united under communist rule, following the departure of United States troops from the area.

Cambodia, which gained independence in 1953, also suffered confl ct. As the Vietnam War heated up, Cambodia was dragged into the fi ht. This led to years of suffering. Under the brutal communist government of the Khmer Rouge, people who lived in the cities were forced into the countryside, where millions of them were murdered.

Southeast Asia Recovers The 1900s had been a violent century for Southeast Asia. The communist nations of Vietnam, Laos, and Cambodia all suffered terribly from the wars of the mainland. In addition, some communist economic policies had been disastrous. In the late 1980s Vietnam, Laos, and Cambodia adopted some capitalist practices that fi ally turned their economies around. However, today the communist countries of Southeast Asia remain the poorest nations in the region.

The capitalist countries such as Indonesia and Malaysia approached the new century in better shape. They marketed their <u>resources</u> and varied their economies. Rather than relying on agricultural exports, these economies now include manufacturing. Some Southeast Asian nations, like Singapore, were so successful that by the 1990s they were called "Asian Tigers." In the next section, you will read more about Southeast Asia today.

Reading Check What changes did World War II bring to Southeast Asia?

resource, *n.,* something that a country can use to its advantage

myWorld Activity
Historical Cartoon

Section 2 Assessment

Key Terms

1. Use the following terms to describe the history of Southeast Asia: reservoir, surplus, maritime, exploit.

Key Ideas

2. Why was there so much trade in Southeast Asia?

3. How did Europeans transform Southeast Asia?

4. How did Southeast Asians gain independence?

Think Critically

5. **Draw Conclusions** Why did different states want to control the Strait of Malacca?

6. **Make Inferences** Why are the communist countries the poorest in the region?

Essential Question

What are the challenges of diversity?

7. How did Southeast Asians react to contact with many different religions? Go to your Student Journal to record your answer.

Southeast Asia Today

Key Ideas

- Southeast Asia is a culturally diverse region.

- Southeast Asian countries have differing political goals, human rights records, and economies.

- Population and environmental issues affect economies throughout the region.

Key Terms • secular • military junta • insurgency • separatist group • ASEAN

Reading Skill: Identify Main Idea and Details Take notes using the graphic organizer in your journal.

Southeast Asia is one of the world's most diverse regions. Its wide range of governments and income levels sets it apart from other places in the world. Its varied geography is home to many cultures and ethnic groups, such as Ridwan's Minangkabau. Today this diverse region is developing new industries and has an important role to play in international trade.

Southeast Asian Culture Today

Southeast Asia's culture was formed by geography and history. The region's location on international trade routes attracted merchants and immigrants, new customs, and new religions. Southeast Asia's unique culture astonished a famous Indian poet during his visit to Indonesia. He observed,

66 I see India everywhere, but I do not recognize it. 99

—Rabindranath Tagore

Today, the culture of Southeast Asia is still being shaped by a diversity of peoples and the environment they share.

Religion

Over the centuries, Indian traders from the East brought Hinduism and Buddhism from India and Sri Lanka. From China to the north, Mahayana Buddhism and Confucian thought entered Vietnam. These religions and ideas mixed with the local beliefs in spirits.

◀ The Petronas Towers, Kuala Lumpur, Malaysia

Later, Arab and Indian traders brought Islam, which took root in Malaysia and most of Indonesia. As the region came under European influence, Christianity gained <u>converts</u>, especially in the Philippines and Vietnam.

Religious traditions are woven through Southeast Asian culture. On most of the mainland, Buddhism is the main religion. However, Islam dominates on most of the islands and on the Malay Peninsula. In Malaysia, there are two systems of justice. One system is **secular,** or nonreligious, and the other is Islamic. Some Malaysian Muslims prefer to seek justice in courts that use Islamic, or Sharia, law.

Indonesia has the world's largest Muslim population. However, its mixed population of Muslims, Buddhists, Hindus and Christians has created a tolerant society. Through the region there is also much cultural blending, as customs and ideas from different religions are fused.

convert, *n.,* a person who changes from one religion to another

Reading Check **What religion is most popular on the mainland of Southeast Asia?**

Closer Look

LAND AND CULTURE

The environment shapes the culture of Southeast Asia in many ways. In a region of monsoon flooding and long coastlines, water plays a central role in people's lives.

THINK CRITICALLY How have people adapted to the environment of Southeast Asia?

Floating markets are a common sight in the watery lowlands. ▶

Many religious rituals, such as the Buddhist festival of Phaung Daw U in Myanmar, take place on water.

Water puppets entertain children in Hanoi, Vietnam.

815

Governments and Citizens

The governments of Southeast Asia are as diverse as the region's population and religions. Citizens' rights also vary.

Types of Governments Republics such as Indonesia, the Philippines, Singapore, and East Timor have constitutions that provide citizens with some protections and freedoms. Like the United States, these countries have legislative, executive, and judicial branches of government. In Indonesia, democracy has been growing stronger ever since the fall of the dictator Suharto in 1998.

Malaysia, Cambodia, the kingdom of Thailand, and the sultanate of Brunei are all constitutional monarchies in which one person rules as head of state. Yet, there is a <u>considerable</u> degree of democracy in some of these nations.

In other nations governments allow much less democracy. The Communist nations of Laos and Vietnam are one-party states ruled by an oligarchy, or a small group of people. Myanmar is ruled by a brutal **military junta,** a committee of military leaders. The junta punishes its critics and has placed the political leader Aung San Suu Kyi under house arrest. In 2008 the junta blocked disaster relief intended for victims of a cyclone.

Political Tensions In Myanmar, political frustration sometimes erupts into demonstrations. However, political tensions afflict every nation in the region.

In the Philippines, the government is fi hting an **insurgency,** or rebellion, from a Muslim **separatist group** on islands in the south and east. A separatist group is a group of people who want to establish an independent state.

In Thailand, the Constitutional Court brought down the government in 2008, after months of anti-government protests.

Even in more democratic countries, such as Malaysia and Indonesia, disputes rage over economic issues, corruption, election fraud, and crime rates. In this ethnically diverse region, there are also constant concerns over income inequalities between ethnic groups.

Reading Check **Which nations are one-party states?**

considerable, *adj.,* large

Chinese festival in Singapore ▼

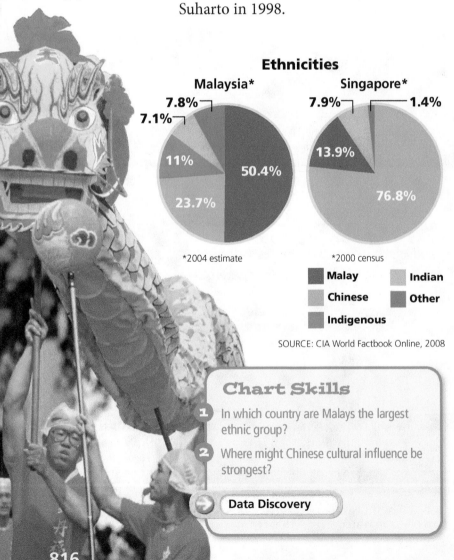

Ethnicities

Malaysia*

7.8%
7.1%
11%
23.7%
50.4%

*2004 estimate

Singapore*

7.9% 1.4%
13.9%
76.8%

*2000 census

- ■ Malay
- ■ Chinese
- ■ Indigenous
- ■ Indian
- ■ Other

SOURCE: CIA World Factbook Online, 2008

Chart Skills

1. In which country are Malays the largest ethnic group?
2. Where might Chinese cultural influence be strongest?

→ **Data Discovery**

Air Pollution

In 1997 an environmental disaster struck Southeast Asia as fires meant to clear land burned out of control. The fires created a huge cloud of smoke that threatened economies and public health. The fires were stopped by a certain Southeast Asian weather pattern. *Can you identify the weather pattern?*

◀ People in cities like Jakarta and Bangkok wore breathing masks.

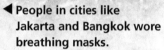

▲ The fires of 1997 destroyed millions of acres of forest.

Population and Environment

Some environmental problems in Southeast Asia have emerged when there are too many people living in an area for its resources to support.

Population Issues Countries with higher rates of population growth must worry about feeding a growing population. Countries with low population growth are also concerned about the future. If there are not enough younger people in the work force, who will pay the taxes that support social security and medical benefits for the elderly? Singapore's population is hardly growing at all. To encourage growth, the government has offered citizens tax rebates of thousands of dollars for every child that is born.

In contrast, Indonesia is dealing with overcrowding on the island of Java, where 60 percent of Indonesians live. Overpopulation strains resources. It also damages the environment.

The government of Indonesia encourages families to migrate to the outer islands such as Sulawesi by providing money and land. However, there are no jobs or social services on the islands. The land must be cleared and the soil is poor.

The Environment Today Because of the global demand for wood products, Southeast Asian forests are disappearing. Countries such as Indonesia are having difficulty stopping this destruction. A weak central government has been unable to enforce regulations.

Reading Check **What are some environmental problems in Southeast Asia?**

my worldgeography.com Data Discovery

Diverse Economies

Southeast Asia includes some of the richest and poorest nations in the world. There are many factors that can hinder economic growth. As you have read, the poorer nations all suffered wars in recent times.

Uneven Development A successful economy depends on certain conditions. There must be a stable government, natural resources, skilled workers, banks, and transportation and communication systems. Singapore and Brunei meet these conditions and are the most successful countries economically. More than half of Brunei's income comes from oil and natural gas production. Singapore's economy is based on exports of consumer electronics and information technology.

The economies of Southeast Asia are as diverse as other aspects of the region. Although international trade is bringing changes to countries such as Indonesia, nations such as Myanmar and Cambodia continue to resist globalization.

Countries without transportation networks, stable government, or freedom for their citizens—such as Myanmar—have difficulty in attracting foreign investments. Nations with oil and natural gas such as Indonesia are more attractive to investors.

Southeast Asian Economies
This graph shows the gross domestic product (GDP) for most countries in Southeast Asia.

Below: Searching through trash in Phnom Penh, Cambodia
Lower right: The modern skyline of wealthy Singapore

Chart Skills
1 Which country has the highest GDP in the region?

2 Which countries have the lowest?

Data Discovery

GDP per Capita of Selected Southeast Asian Nations

Country	GDP
Brunei	$51,000
Singapore	$49,700
Malaysia	$13,300
Thailand	$7,900
Indonesia	$3,700
Philippines	$3,400
Vietnam	$2,600
East Timor	$2,500
Laos	$2,100
Myanmar	$1,900
Cambodia	$1,800
United States (for comparison)	$45,800

SOURCE: CIA World Factbook Online, 2008

Southeast Asia and the World Today Southeast Asia is once again a center of international trade. The Strait of Malacca is a major global shipping lane. The ports of Singapore, Malaysia, and Indonesia benefit greatly from such traffic. But there are also enormous dangers along the strait. Modern-day pirates have attacked merchant ships. And since the al-Qaeda attack on September 11 and later attacks in Indonesia, there is a new fear. Attacks by militant groups on shipping could endanger the world's oil supply. In the words of one writer,

> 66 With 60,000 vessels transiting through the Strait each year, carrying half of the world's oil supplies and a third of its trade, the stakes are high in maintaining stability along these sea lanes. 99
>
> —Chietigj Bajpaee

All the countries in the region have the potential for economic growth. Tourism is an important source of income in all of Southeast Asia. Malaysia is developing a high-technology complex near its capital, Kuala Lumpur. This complex is called the Multimedia Super Corridor. Thailand is attempting to develop high-technology industries, but the lack of skilled labor may be an obstacle.

ASEAN, the Association of Southeast Asian Nations, is a trade group working to promote growth and social progress. The organization has reduced regional tariffs and has created a free-trade area.

Today Southeast Asia's problems and strengths are tied to its geography and history. Many of its people, such as the Minangkabau, continue to welcome foreign culture and new ideas. With its ancient traditions of cultural diversity and international trade, Southeast Asia is well positioned to play an important role in the modern world.

Reading Check **Why is the Strait of Malacca so important to the world's economy?**

my World IN NUMBERS

In 2007, Thailand had a labor force of about **37** million people. In 2008, this figure rose to about **38** million.

myWorld Activity
Facing Challenges

Section **3** Assessment

Key Terms

1. Use the following terms to describe Southeast Asia today: secular, military junta, insurgency, separatist group.

Key Ideas

2. What role does Southeast Asia play in the world economy?

3. What kinds of governments exist in Southeast Asia?

4. Why are Southeast Asian rain forests under threat?

Think Critically

5. **Draw Conclusions** Why is religious tolerance valued in Indonesia, where there are so many religious faiths?

6. **Synthesize** Why is it so difficult for Southeast Asian nations to solve environmental problems?

Essential Question

What are the challenges of diversity?

7. Why has "Unity in Diversity" become the motto of Indonesia? Go to your Student Journal to record your answer.

Chapter Assessment

Key Terms and Ideas

1. **Discuss** How did physical geography determine where people settled in Southeast Asia?

2. **Explain** What kinds of weather conditions do the summer **monsoons** create?

3. **Recall** Which civilizations influenced Southeast Asia?

4. **Explain** How did the ancient Khmer create a food **surplus**?

5. **Summarize** What were the causes and effects of Western colonialism in the region?

6. **Recall** What is the goal of the **insurgency** in the Philippines?

7. **Explain** Why is the Strait of Malacca so important today?

8. **Describe** Which are the richest and the poorest countries in Southeast Asia?

Think Critically

9. **Draw Conclusions** How have the people of Southeast Asia used the environment to meet their needs?

10. **Synthesize** How did geography contribute to the diversity of the region?

11. **Make Inferences** Why did Islam spread through the islands?

12. **Core Concepts: Culture and Geography** How has the environment shaped culture in Southeast Asia?

Places to Know

For each place, write the letter from the map that shows its location.

13. **Mekong River**

14. **Singapore**

15. **Strait of Malacca**

16. **Bangkok**

17. **The Philippines**

18. **South China Sea**

19. **Estimate** Using the scale, estimate the distance between Bangkok and the Philippines.

Essential Question

myWorld Chapter Activity

Gaining Wealth Through History
Follow your teacher's instructions to investigate the geographical factors that have contributed to the economic success of each historical character. Then rank the characters on an economic assessment scale and explain the reasons for your assessment.

21st Century Learning

Develop Cultural Awareness

Look back over the chapter and make a list of features that make Southeast Asian culture unique. Then consider why each feature might have developed—was it because of geography, climate, or history? Create a table that lists each feature and your theory about its origin.

Document-Based Questions

Success Tracker™
Online at myworldgeography.com

Use your knowledge of Southeast Asia and Documents A and B to answer Questions 1–3.

Document A

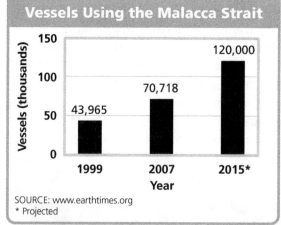

Vessels Using the Malacca Strait

Vessels (thousands)

- 1999: 43,965
- 2007: 70,718
- 2015*: 120,000

Year

SOURCE: www.earthtimes.org
* Projected

Document B

" He who is lord of Malacca has his hand on the throat of Venice."

—Duarte Barbosa describing world trade in the 1400s and 1500s

1. What does Document A tell you about shipping in the Strait of Malacca?

   A The number of vessels is decreasing every decade.

   B The number of vessels peaked in the 1990s and then declined.

   C The projected number of vessels will have nearly tripled in a 16-year span.

   D The projected number of vessels will decline sharply by 2015.

2. Which of the following best describes the meaning of Document B?

   A The European trading city of Venice depends on goods traveling through the Malacca Strait.

   B The trading city of Venice is being attacked by the lord of Malacca.

   C The cities of Venice and Malacca have little contact with each other.

   D Venice defeated Malacca after a long war.

3. **Writing Task** Use Documents A and B to write a short paragraph explaining the role of the Malacca Strait in world trade.

my worldgeography.com Self-Test

Plan the City of Tomorrow

Your Mission Study the effects of population change on a city in East or Southeast Asia. Then present a plan for how to manage more growth in your city, including predictions for its future needs.

The skyline of Kuala Lumpur, the capital of Malaysia, is dominated by the twin spires of the Petronas Towers (left). Architects and urban planners designed the building to be a destination for both workers and their families. North of Kuala Lumpur, across the Gulf of Thailand, lies Ho Chi Minh City, the economic center of Vietnam. Historic and elegant, Ho Chi Minh City boasts some 300,000 businesses and contributes as much as 20 percent to the nation's total revenue.

Neither of these cities was planned as an urban success story, yet each is successful for different reasons. Very few cities are planned. Most cities evolve as history, governments, and populations change. As you investigate cities in this activity, consider how their characteristics might be useful when planning the city of tomorrow.

CITY OF TOMORROW

CITY LIMITS

STEP 1

What's in a Name?

The name of the city you are researching may have changed over the years. City names can change, for example, if the country was once a colony that later declared independence. When this happens, large groups of people may move in or out of a region. Investigate the history of your city's name and begin your presentation with this brief overview—it will engage your listeners right from the start.

STEP 2

What's Your Plan?

Your main goal is to improve life for the people of your city. But you need a solid plan. Gather facts and figures about population trends. Identify areas where your city functions well and areas that need improvement. Remember that you are offering a solution for the future and that you can't always predict what will happen. Thus, your plan should offer reasonable expectations for implementing your ideas.

STEP 3

The Big Finale

An effective presentation ends with a summary of what you have already said. If you have any final arguments, make them with confidence. Avoid arrogance. Chances are that your audience will agree with your proposals—after all, they live in this city!—but they may be concerned with the costs associated with your plan. Keep in mind that planning the city of tomorrow begins with understanding cities of today.

Australia and the Pacific

Australia, New Zealand, and tens of thousands of other Pacific islands are spread across a vast area of ocean to the south and east of Asia. The people of these islands are as diverse as their geography, which includes high mountains, arid deserts, and icy glaciers.

What time is it there?

Washington, D.C.	Auckland, New Zealand
9 A.M. Monday	2 A.M. Tuesday

TROPIC OF CANCER

Philippine Sea

PALAU

FEDERATED STATES OF MICRONESIA

MARSHALL ISLANDS

INDONESIA

PAPUA NEW GUINEA
⊛ Port Moresby

NAURU

Arafura Sea

EAST TIMOR

SOLOMON ISLANDS

KIRIBATI

Coral Sea

PACIFIC OCEAN

VANUATU

TUVALU

TOKELAU (New Zealand)

AUSTRALIA

NEW CALEDONIA (France)

WALLIS AND FUTUNA (France)

EQUATOR

SAMOA

FIJI

AMERICAN SAMOA (United States)

⊛ Canberra

TONGA

NIUE (New Zealand)

Tasman Sea

0°

INDIAN OCEAN

COOK ISLANDS (New Zealand)

TROPIC OF CAPRICORN

30° S

FRENCH POLYNESIA (France)

KEY
— National border
⊛ Capital city
Orthographic Projection

NEW ZEALAND
⊛ Wellington

150° E

180°

150° W

The Unit Ahead

➡ **Chapter 24** Australia and the Pacific

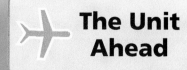

my worldgeography.com

Plan your trip online by doing a Data Discovery Activity and watching the myStory Video of the region's teen.

Jack
Age: 17
Home: Auckland, New Zealand

Chapter 24

New Zealand's South Island has many mountains and thick forests.

Regional Overview
Physical Geography

Most of Australia is very dry. Australians use the continent's dry plains for mining and raising livestock.

Melanesia has many high volcanic islands with fertile soil and mineral resources.

Mount Wilhelm
14,790 ft (4,509 m)

*Arafura
Sea*

*Gulf of
Carpentaria*

Cape York
Peninsula

Coral Sea

Great Barrier Reef

Timor Sea

Great Dividing Range

*INDIAN
OCEAN*

Kimberley
Plateau

Simpson
Desert

Great
Artesian
Basin

Great Sandy Desert

Darling River

Gibson
Desert

Mt. Kosciuszko
7,310 ft (2,228 m)

Great Victoria Desert

Murray River

Nullarbor Plain

Bass Strait

Great Australian Bight

Tasmania

Darling Range

Many Pacific islands are low-lying atolls, islands formed by coral reefs.

PACIFIC OCEAN

North Island

Cook Strait

Southern Alps

Aoraki (Mt. Cook) 12,316 ft (3,754 m)

South Island

New Zealand's Southern Alps are home to more than 20 mountains higher than 10,000 feet.

Regional Flyover

You begin your flight at Easter Island, the easternmost settlement in Polynesia. From here you fly west across the Pacific Ocean, traveling over the thousands of high volcanic islands and low coral atolls that form the Pacific islands. These islands are spread out over 116 million square miles of ocean.

Flying low over the ocean, your airplane reaches Papua New Guinea, a nation on the eastern half of the island of New Guinea. Although it is just south of the Equator, Papua New Guinea has peaks high enough to receive snow. As your plane circles back to the southeast, you fly over New Zealand's icy glaciers, tall mountains, and thick rain forests.

Then you travel west across the Tasman Sea to Australia, following the 1,250-mile-long Great Barrier Reef along Australia's northeast coast. Finally you circle south, landing on the deserts of central Australia. Here you find Uluru, or Ayers Rock, an enormous sandstone rock rising about 1,100 feet above the surrounding land.

In-Flight Movie

Take flight over Australia and the Pacific and explore the region from the air.

my worldgeography.com | In-Flight Movie

Regional Overview
Human Geography

People, Land, and Resources

The Pacific region's physical features have shaped where people in the region live. Most Australians and New Zealanders live in dense urban areas near the ocean. Few people live in Australia's dry deserts or in New Zealand's rugged mountains. The population of the smaller Pacific islands is generally more rural. Most people live in small villages.

Some countries in the region have many natural resources. Others are less fortunate. Australia and New Zealand's many resources have led to strong industrial economies. However, the economies of the smaller islands are generally limited by a lack of resources. Most smaller islands have developing economies, and many islanders fish or farm.

Australia and the Pacific: Population Density

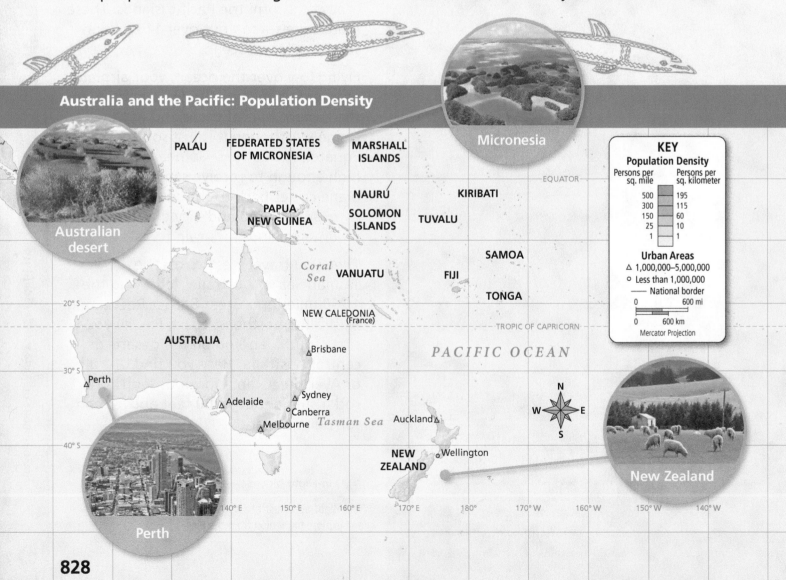

Micronesia

PALAU
FEDERATED STATES OF MICRONESIA
MARSHALL ISLANDS

EQUATOR

NAURU
KIRIBATI

PAPUA NEW GUINEA
SOLOMON ISLANDS
TUVALU

Australian desert

SAMOA

Coral Sea
VANUATU
FIJI

TONGA

20° S

NEW CALEDONIA (France)

TROPIC OF CAPRICORN

AUSTRALIA
△ Brisbane
PACIFIC OCEAN

30° S
△ Perth

△ Sydney
△ Adelaide
○ Canberra
△ Melbourne
Tasman Sea
Auckland △

40° S

NEW ZEALAND
○ Wellington

Perth

New Zealand

KEY

Population Density

Persons per sq. mile	Persons per sq. kilometer
500	195
300	115
150	60
25	10
1	1

Urban Areas
△ 1,000,000–5,000,000
○ Less than 1,000,000
— National border

0   600 mi
0   600 km

Mercator Projection

N
W   E
S

140° E   150° E   160° E   170° E   180°   170° W   160° W   150° W   140° W

my World IN NUMBERS

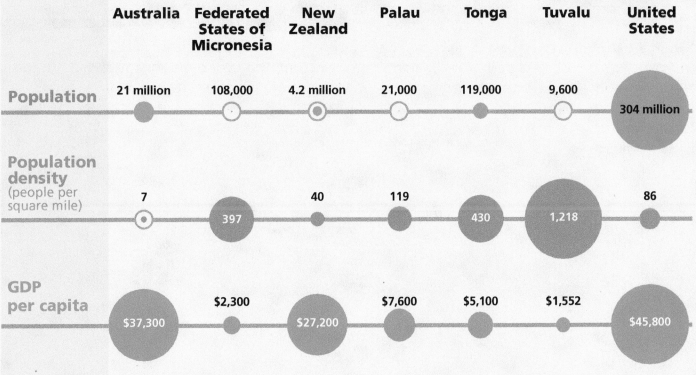

	Australia	Federated States of Micronesia	New Zealand	Palau	Tonga	Tuvalu	United States
Population	21 million	108,000	4.2 million	21,000	119,000	9,600	304 million
Population density (people per square mile)	7	397	40	119	430	1,218	86
GDP per capita	$37,300	$2,300	$27,200	$7,600	$5,100	$1,552	$45,800

SOURCE: *CIA World Factbook, Encyclopaedia Britannica*

Put It Together

1. What might be the advantages and disadvantages of living on a small Pacific island?

2. Remember that GDP per capita is the total economic output per person in a country. What geographic factors might influence the numbers for this region?

3. What seems to be the relationship between land and population? Between land and economy?

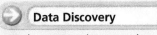

Data Discovery

Find your own data to make a regional data table.

Size Comparison

Australia is slightly smaller than the 48 contiguous states of the United States.

my worldgeography.com Data Discovery

Australia and the Pacific

? Essential Question

What makes a nation?

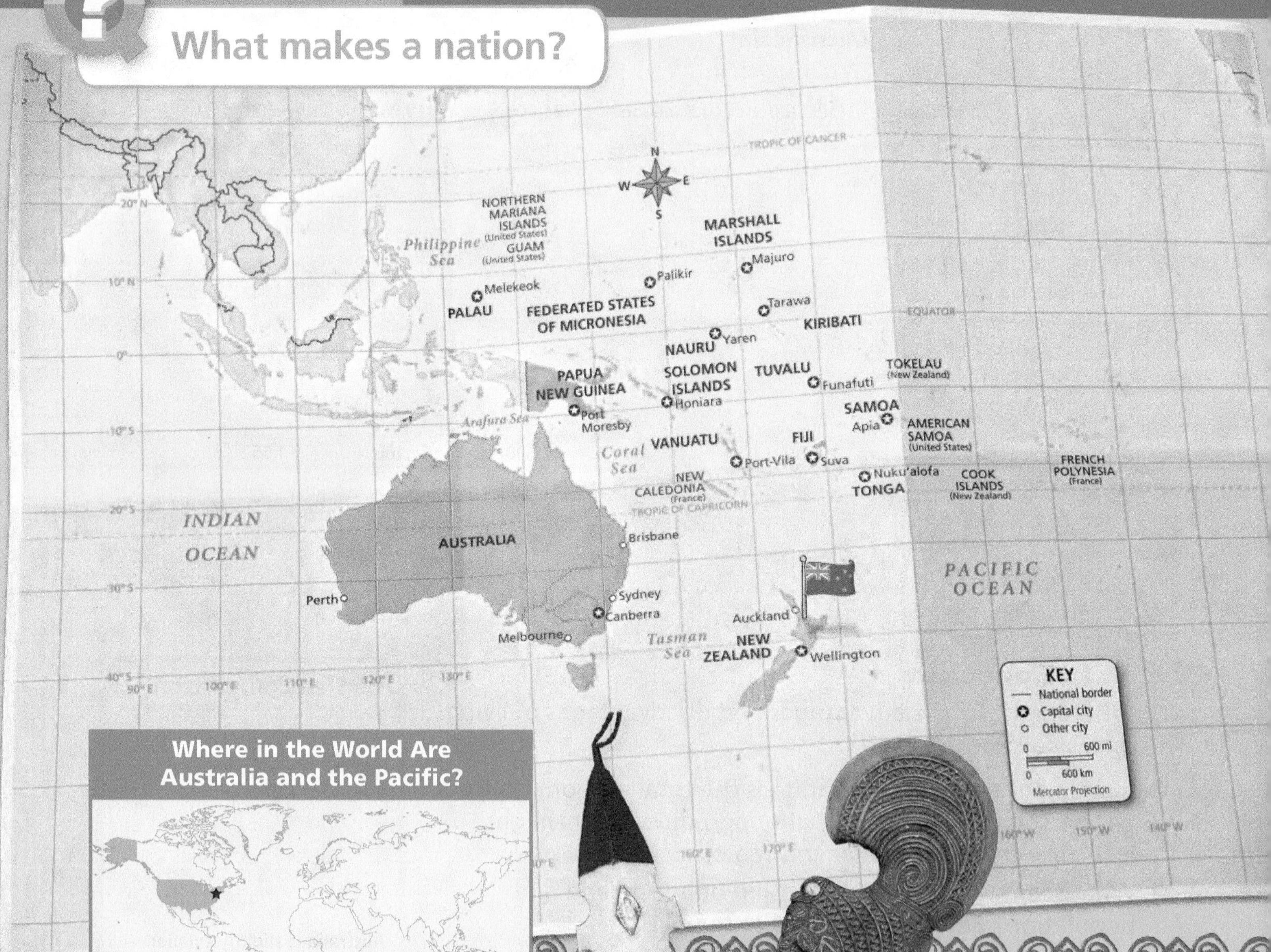

Where in the World Are Australia and the Pacific?

Washington, D.C., to Auckland: 8,620 miles

KEY
— National border
⊗ Capital city
○ Other city

0   600 mi
0   600 km
Mercator Projection

my Story

Jack Connects to His Culture

In this section, you'll read about Jack, a young man from New Zealand trying to keep in touch with his Maori culture. *What does Jack's story tell you about life in Australia and the Pacific?*

Story by Tui Ruwhiu for myWorld Geography Online

It is early one weekday morning, and 17-year-old Jack is busy getting ready for another day at school. Jack lives in Auckland, New Zealand's largest city. By 7:30, Jack is on the bus for the 50-minute ride to his school, Avondale College.

Jack lives with his two younger brothers and his mother, father, and grandmother. Jack's father is a television actor and comedian. His mother manages the household and works in a television production company.

Jack is part Maori (ma ow ree), descended from the original inhabitants of New Zealand. The Maori migrated to New Zealand—which they call Aotearoa (ao w tee ar roh uh)—from other parts of the Pacific region about 1,000 years ago.

Explore the Essential Question

- at my worldgeography.com
- using the myWorld Chapter Activity
- with the Student Journal

Facial expressions like Jack's were often used by Maori to frighten enemies before battle. Today, Maori people make this expression as part of a traditional greeting on important occasions. ▶

my worldgeography.com On Assignment

Jack and his brothers

Maori students make up about 8 percent of the 2,600 students at Avondale College. They have their own wharenui (meeting house) and wharekai (dining hall) at school. At breaks, lunchtimes, and after school, Maori students gather at the wharekai to talk and share food with friends.

But Maori people like Jack and his friends once faced many obstacles in New Zealand. During the 1800s, British colonization of New Zealand led to a series of wars with the Maori. Eventually, the British defeated the Maori. Many Maori moved to cities and lost touch with their culture.

Interest in Maori culture has grown since the mid-1900s. Today, many Maori study their language, history, and customs. Jack feels a strong connection to his culture and to his homeland on New Zealand's North Island. "I know the blood of my ancestors is in that soil," he says quietly, "because they gave their lives fighting for that land."

Jack takes a Maori language class at school every day. He hopes to become a skilled Maori speaker like his father, who grew up speaking Maori.

Jack and his horse

Jack's class practices kapa haka.

Jack's waka ama team

Although Jack went to a Maori-language day care center as a child, his parents decided to send him to English-language schools. English is the language most commonly spoken in New Zealand. At home, the family speaks English.

Jack stays connected to Maori culture in other ways. He is one of the leaders of his school's kapa haka team. Kapa haka is a performance art that combines singing and dancing. It uses parts of traditional Maori songs, dances, and combat techniques.

Each year, New Zealand holds a national competition for high school students of kapa haka. This competition is part of Polyfest, a celebration of Polynesian culture and dance. To prepare for the competition, Jack's kapa haka team practices each day at lunchtime and after school. It also practices for at least one full day each weekend.

Jack is also a member of his school's waka ama team. Waka ama are Maori canoes designed for use on the open ocean. Avondale has male, female, and mixed waka ama teams. Students of all ethnic backgrounds take part in the sport.

Jack plans to continue studying the Maori language and participating in kapa haka after he finishes school. He hopes to increase his understanding of his culture. "If you're interested, it's a lot easier to learn," Jack says. "There are a lot of people out there who have the knowledge. You've just got to be willing to go out and grab it."

myStory Video

Join Jack as he shows you more about his life in New Zealand.

Meet the Journalist

Name Tui Ruwhiu
Favorite Moment Watching Jack's kapa haka team practice

Section 1

Chapter Atlas

Key Ideas

- The physical geography of Australia and the Pacific region is diverse and unusual.

- The Pacific Ocean includes thousands of islands with different sizes, climates, and resources.

- Climate, location, and resources have affected where and how people live.

Key Terms • Outback   • coral reef   • atoll   • plate tectonics

 Visual Glossary

 Reading Skill: Label an Outline Map Take notes using the outline map in your journal.

Children in Papua New Guinea play in an outrigger canoe designed for ocean travel. ▼

Physical Features

The physical geography of Australia and the Pacific region is diverse. The region has tens of thousands of islands of varying sizes. Each has different resources, climates, and ecosystems. The great distance between these islands and other land areas has helped make them unique.

Australia lies at the southwest edge of the Pacific Ocean between Southeast Asia and Antarctica. It is the largest country in the huge Pacific region. The Pacific region also includes three separate subregions of islands: Melanesia, Micronesia, and Polynesia.

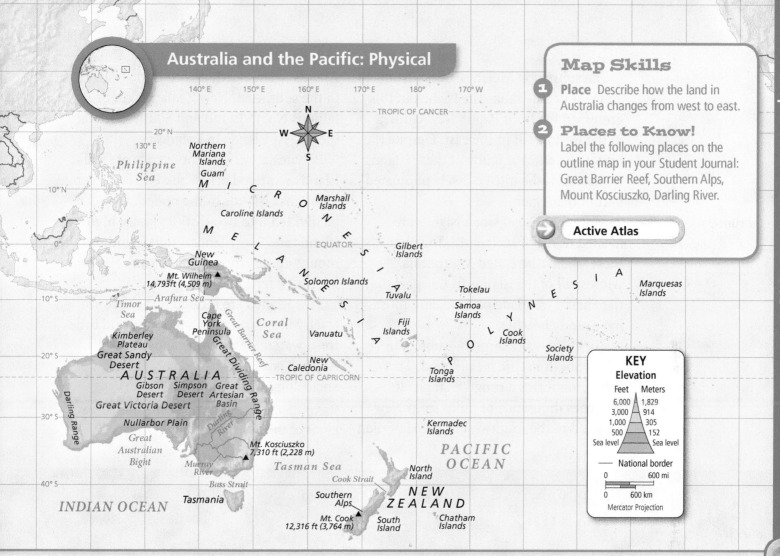

Australia and the Pacific: Physical

Map Skills

1 Place Describe how the land in Australia changes from west to east.

2 Places to Know! Label the following places on the outline map in your Student Journal: Great Barrier Reef, Southern Alps, Mount Kosciuszko, Darling River.

Active Atlas

KEY
Elevation

Feet	Meters
6,000	1,829
3,000	914
1,000	305
500	152
Sea level	Sea level

— National border

0   600 mi
0   600 km
Mercator Projection

Australia is completely surrounded by water, just like an island. But because of its large size, it is considered a continent. It is Earth's smallest continent.

Australia has wide, flat stretches of dry land, especially in its central and western portions. The interior of Australia is known as the **Outback,** a sparsely inhabited region with low plateaus and plains. The Outback is home to a large rock formation known as Uluru, or Ayers Rock. Central and western Australia include three large deserts—the Great Victoria Desert, the Great Sandy Desert, and the Simpson Desert. Eastern Australia, on the other hand, is covered by low mountains, valleys, and a large river system. Australia's coasts also include fertile plains.

Australia's dramatic physical features are not limited to land. The Great Barrier Reef, located off ustralia's northeast coast, is the world's largest grouping of coral reefs. A **coral reef** is a formation of rock-like material made up of the skeletons of tiny sea creatures. The Great Barrier Reef is more than 1,250 miles (2,000 kilometers) long. It is home to many different underwater plants and animals. It is also a popular place for surfi g and scuba diving.

The subregion Melanesia lies just north and east of Australia. The islands in this group stretch from Papua New Guinea in the west to Fiji in the east. Despite the remote location of many of these islands, Melanesia is the most densely populated part of the region.

distinct, adj., different

More than 2,000 small islands are located north of Melanesia. Together, these islands are called Micronesia. Almost all of the islands in this part of the Pacific re made of coral, and most have sandy beaches.

The third—and largest—subregion in the South Pacific s Polynesia. Th s subregion forms a rough triangle. It stretches thousands of miles from New Zealand in the southwest to the Hawaiian Islands in the north and to Easter Island in the southeast. New Zealand's mountainous North Island and South Island are the largest islands in Polynesia.

Polynesia includes thousands of small islands scattered across the Pacific cean. Like other islands in the region, they can be divided into two <u>distinct</u> types: high islands and low islands. High islands are mountainous, rocky, and volcanic. They have very fertile soil.

Low islands are located just above sea level. Most have poor, sandy soil and little fresh water. Many low islands are atolls. An **atoll** is a ring-shaped coral island enclosing a body of water.

Reading Check What are the three subregions of the Pacific region?

Atoll Formation

The diagram below shows how an atoll (right) is formed. **1** An atoll begins as a coral reef around a volcanic island. **2** The coral builds as the island wears away over time. **3** Finally, only a ring of coral remains.

Plate Tectonics

Plate tectonics helps us understand the forces that have shaped Australia and the Pacific. **Plate tectonics** is the theory that explains how huge blocks of Earth's crust called "plates" move. Hundreds of millions of years ago, the region was part of a giant continent. This ancient continent also included the land that now makes up South America, Africa, and India. Over time, Earth's plates separated. The giant continent slowly broke apart.

Australia and the Pacific include the Indo-Australian and Pacific Plates. These two plates move toward each other at a rate of a few inches per year. Although this movement is slow, it has important effects on the region. As the plates <u>collide</u>, they push the ocean floor up above sea level. This creates many islands and volcanoes along the plate boundaries.

Plate movement and volcanic action have formed the two main islands of New Zealand. North Island has a series of high volcanic peaks that tower over green valleys below. South Island's Southern Alps are even higher mountains running along the island's western edge.

The movement of tectonic plates also helps explain the region's unique plant and animal populations. After the region broke away from other areas millions of years ago, its plants and animals were cut off from the rest of the world.

collide, *v.*, to come together

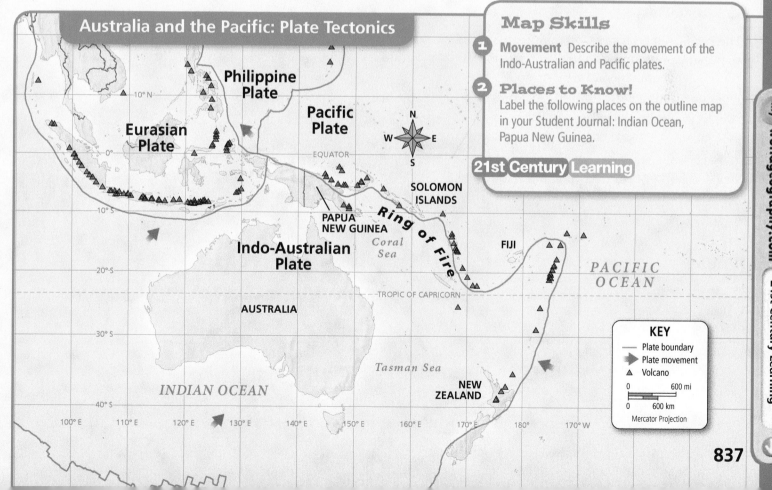

Australia and the Pacific: Plate Tectonics

Philippine Plate

Pacific Plate

Eurasian Plate

Indo-Australian Plate

EQUATOR

10° N

0°

10° S

20° S

30° S

40° S

100° E   110° E   120° E   130° E   140° E   150° E   160° E   170° E   180°   170° W

N
W   E
S

SOLOMON ISLANDS

PAPUA NEW GUINEA

Ring of Fire

Coral Sea

FIJI

PACIFIC OCEAN

TROPIC OF CAPRICORN

AUSTRALIA

Tasman Sea

INDIAN OCEAN

NEW ZEALAND

Map Skills

1. **Movement** Describe the movement of the Indo-Australian and Pacific plates.

2. **Places to Know!** Label the following places on the outline map in your Student Journal: Indian Ocean, Papua New Guinea.

21st Century Learning

KEY
— Plate boundary
➤ Plate movement
▲ Volcano

0   600 mi
0   600 km
Mercator Projection

Over time, small changes have occurred naturally in the region's plants and animals. Because of the area's isolation, these changes have not spread to other places. As a result, Australia and the Pacific Islands have many plant and animal species that cannot be found anywhere else in the world.

However, people have brought new plants and animals to the region. In some areas, the spread of nonnative species such as rabbits, snakes, and wild pigs has harmed the region's ecosystems.

Reading Check **How has plate movement affected the region?**

Climate

Weather and climate patterns vary widely across the Pacific region. Even opposite sides of the same island can have very different weather patterns due to differences in elevation, wind, and ocean currents.

Australia   Australia's climate changes dramatically from one area to another. Its southeast and southwest coasts have temperate climates. The eastern coast has plentiful rainfall. In far northern Australia, heavy monsoon rains are common in the summer months. A winter dry season follows this wet season. However, most

Pacific Ecosystems

The Pacific region is so far from other places that many of its animals and plants are not found anywhere else on Earth. At right, a boab, a tree found only in Australia.

Koalas sleep for about 19 hours a day.

The platypus is a mammal that lays eggs.

A baby kangaroo lives in its mother's pouch.

of central Australia has arid and semiarid climates. Th s region has warm temperatures and little rain year-round.

New Zealand and the Pacific Islands

New Zealand has a mild and wet maritime climate. It is cooler than Australia. Most other Pacific slands are located in the tropics. They tend to have tropical wet climates, with heavy precipitation and high temperatures year-round. On some mountainous islands, such as New Guinea, precipitation and temperature vary with elevation. Places at higher elevations usually have less rain and lower temperatures.

Water and Wildfires

Although many of the Pacific slands receive heavy rainfall, some places still do not have enough fresh water for drinking or other human use. Low-lying atolls and low, sandy islands can collect very little rainwater.

Wildfi es are a serious challenge in dry parts of the region. In Australia, fi es can spread rapidly across the countryside during the winter dry season. These destructive fi es are made worse by the grasses that grow during the summer wet weather and dry out during the winter.

Reading Check How do climates vary within Australia?

myWorld Activity
Traveling Tips

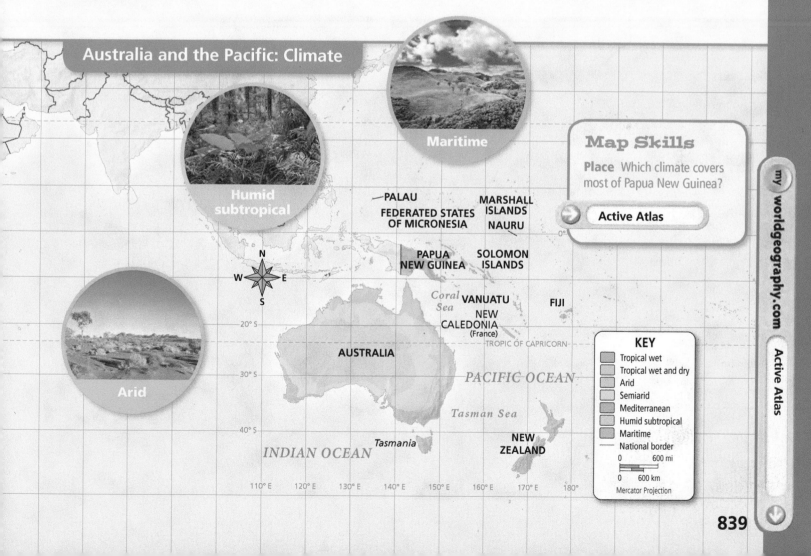

Australia and the Pacific: Climate

Maritime

Humid subtropical

Arid

PALAU
FEDERATED STATES
OF MICRONESIA

MARSHALL
ISLANDS
NAURU

PAPUA
NEW GUINEA

SOLOMON
ISLANDS

Coral Sea VANUATU

FIJI

NEW
CALEDONIA
(France)

AUSTRALIA

PACIFIC OCEAN

20° S

TROPIC OF CAPRICORN

30° S

Tasman Sea

40° S

Tasmania

NEW
ZEALAND

INDIAN OCEAN

110° E   120° E   130° E   140° E   150° E   160° E   170° E   180°

Map Skills

Place Which climate covers most of Papua New Guinea?

Active Atlas

KEY
	Tropical wet
	Tropical wet and dry
	Arid
	Semiarid
	Mediterranean
	Humid subtropical
	Maritime
—	National border

0   600 mi
0   600 km
Mercator Projection

my worldgeography.com   Active Atlas

People and Resources

The region's population patterns vary widely. The availability of natural resources also differs from place to place.

Australia and New Zealand Most Australians and New Zealanders live in urban areas. Most Australians live on the country's mild east coast. Nearly 90 percent of the country's 22 million people live in coastal cities such as Sydney and Melbourne. The hot, dry central area of Australia has fewer people.

Most of New Zealand's 4 million people live on North Island. Th s island includes Auckland and other cities.

Australia is rich in natural resources, including bauxite, iron, and diamonds. It also has energy resources such as coal and natural gas. New Zealand, however, has relatively few mineral resources.

Both Australia and New Zealand have many large farms and ranches. Australia produces cotton, wheat, and sheep, although lack of water is a big challenge

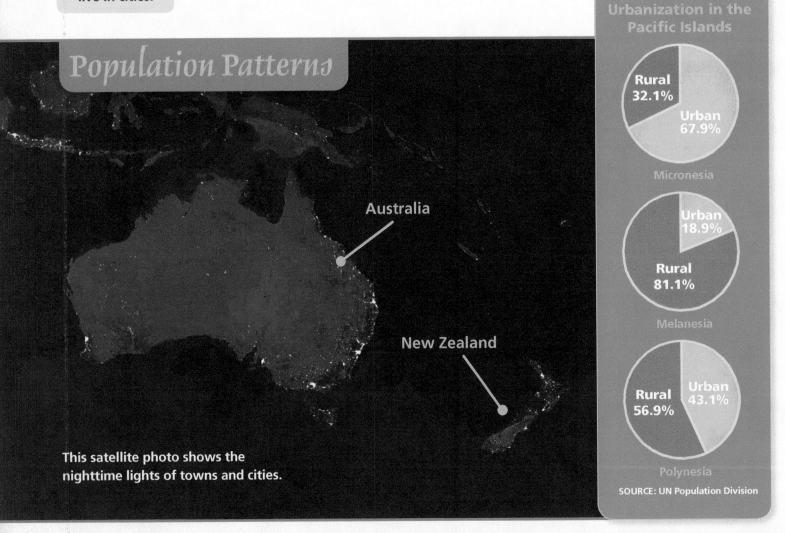

Population Patterns

Australia

New Zealand

This satellite photo shows the nighttime lights of towns and cities.

Urbanization in the Pacific Islands

Rural 32.1%
Urban 67.9%
Micronesia

Urban 18.9%
Rural 81.1%
Melanesia

Rural 56.9%
Urban 43.1%
Polynesia

SOURCE: UN Population Division

for farmers and ranchers. Much of central Australia is too dry for agriculture or grazing. Irrigation is very important.

New Zealand's fertile farmland and supplies of fresh water support its successful agriculture. Wool production is important.

Pacific Islands The population of the Pacific slands is generally less urban than that of Australia and New Zealand. Many people live in small villages in hilly regions or on coastlines.

The availability of natural resources varies. Most of the low islands have poor soil, little vegetation, and few mineral or energy resources. As a result, the low islands have relatively small populations.

High islands have fertile soil and many natural resources. Their farms produce bananas, cacao, and other crops. Some high islands also have resources such as gold, copper, and petroleum.

Reading Check How does the availability of resources affect population in the region?

▲ Many Pacific economies rely on natural resources. Above, oil workers drill in Papua New Guinea.

Section 1 Assessment

Key Terms

1. How has the movement of tectonic plates affected the region?

2. Describe Australia's Outback region.

Key Ideas

3. How have Australia's geography and climate influenced where people live?

4. How do high islands differ from low islands?

5. How does the geography of the region vary from one place to another?

Think Critically

6. Compare and Contrast How do population and resources vary in different parts of the region?

7. Draw Conclusions Why are many Pacific species found nowhere else on Earth?

Essential Question

What makes a nation?

8. How have climate, location, and resources affected the development of Australia, New Zealand, and the Pacific islands?

History of Australia and the Pacific

Key Ideas
- The Pacific region was one of the last places on Earth settled by people.
- By the late 1800s, Australia and the Pacific were under the control of European and other colonial powers.
- Colonization transformed the region.

Key Terms • Aborigines • Maori • assimilation • ethnocentrism • missionary 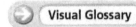 Visual Glossary

Reading Skill: Sequence Take notes using the graphic organizer in your journal.

This Maori woman's chin is marked with the traditional Maori tattoos known as moko. ▼

The Pacific region was one of the last areas on Earth to be settled by people. When European settlers arrived in large numbers in the 1800s, they made the region's native peoples change their ways of life.

Migration and Settlement

People settled the region in three waves of migration, shown on the map in this section. Around 60,000 years ago, the fi st people settled Australia and New Guinea. By 1,000 years ago, people had sailed across the ocean to New Zealand and other Pacific slands.

Australia The original inhabitants of Australia are known as **Aborigines.** Aborigines lived throughout the continent, but most lived in the temperate southeast part of Australia. Early Aborigines were nomadic. They moved together in small groups, hunting animals and gathering plants. Aborigines had a complex society without chiefs or other formal leaders. They had strong religious convictions about nature, believing that it was their responsibility to care for the land.

The Pacific Islands In Melanesia, the great number of islands led to the development of isolated cultural groups over thousands of years. Most island people relied on the ocean for fishing, but Melanesians also developed agriculture about 10,000 years ago. In Polynesia, kingdoms extended over entire groups of islands.

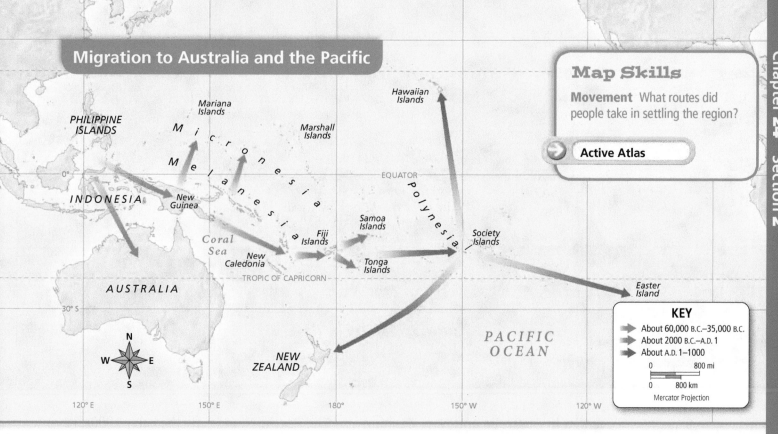

Migration to Australia and the Pacific

PHILIPPINE ISLANDS

Mariana Islands

Marshall Islands

Hawaiian Islands

Micronesia

Melanesia

INDONESIA

New Guinea

EQUATOR

Polynesia

Coral Sea

New Caledonia

Fiji Islands

Samoa Islands

Society Islands

TROPIC OF CAPRICORN

Tonga Islands

AUSTRALIA

30° S

Easter Island

PACIFIC OCEAN

NEW ZEALAND

120° E   150° E   180°   150° W   120° W

Map Skills

Movement What routes did people take in settling the region?

Active Atlas

KEY

About 60,000 B.C.–35,000 B.C.

About 2000 B.C.–A.D. 1

About A.D. 1–1000

0   800 mi

0   800 km

Mercator Projection

Frequent confli t led people to live in protected settlements. Polynesians often went on long-distance ocean trips.

Like other Polynesians, the Maori lived in small settlements. The **Maori** are the original inhabitants of New Zealand and the Cook Islands. The Maori fished, hunted, and farmed. Chiefs were at the top of Maori society. At the bottom of society were slaves, usually captured during warfare.

The center of Maori society is a marae, an enclosed area of land that includes a meeting house and other buildings. Art is an important part of Maori culture. The Maori carve decorations into their buildings, canoes, weapons, and other objects.

Reading Check **How did people settle Australia and the Pacific region?**

Exploration and Colonization

In the late 1700s, British explorer James Cook claimed Australia and New Zealand for Great Britain. Cook's expeditions increased European interest in the region.

f In this Extensive Country it can never be doubted but what most sorts of Grain, Fruits, Roots … of every kind would flourish … and here [is food] for more Cattle at all seasons of the year than ever can be brought into this Country. ™

—James Cook, journal entry, 1770

Colonization Begins British settlement of Australia began in 1788. Many early settlers were convicted criminals who had been <u>exiled</u> to Australia. Colonists farmed and ranched. In 1851, colonists discovered gold, and the British population soared.

exile, *v.,* to force out of one's own home

A Changing Region

Lieutenant James Cook was an early British explorer of the region.

British colonization led to conflict with native peoples.

strategic, *adj.,* important to military or action plans

Conflict in Australia and New Zealand

As British colonists forced Aborigines off heir lands, fi hting broke out. In addition, many Aborigines died from European diseases.

The British also practiced forced assimilation. **Assimilation** is the process by which one group takes on the cultural traits of another. British ethnocentrism led settlers to force Aborigines to adopt British customs. **Ethnocentrism** is the attitude that one's own social or cultural group is better than all others. British colonists took Aboriginal children away from their families and forced them to live in institutions or with white families. Th s practice continued into the 1960s.

British settlers began to arrive in New Zealand in the early 1800s. They were attracted by New Zealand's harbors and fertile soil. Confli t with the Maori led to a series of wars eventually won by Britain.

The Pacific Islands

By the early 1900s, the United States, France, Great Britain, and Japan controlled most of the Pacific islands. Colonizers claimed some islands because of their natural resources. Other islands were taken for their location. For example, the Micronesian islands served as a strategic midpoint between the United States and Japan.

Britain ruled its colonies with colonial governors. Other countries controlled their colonies with military forces or through commercial companies.

Colonizers brought many new ideas and customs. For example, colonizers introduced the concept of owning land instead of using land collectively. Some colonizers were **missionaries,** or people sent to another country by a church to spread its religious beliefs.

Reading Check How did the British treat the region's native people?

844

Left, Aborigines were forced to adopt British ways.
Above, Aborigines protest government policies.

myWorld Activity
Before and After

Independence

Australia and New Zealand gained their independence peacefully in the early 1900s. Today, both belong to the British Commonwealth of Nations, which includes many former British colonies.

Most Pacific slands won independence peacefully in the second half of the 1900s. Independence movements played a role on some islands. In Western Samoa (now Samoa), the nonviolent Mau movement worked for independence, which Samoa won in 1962. Still, not all of the Pacific region has been decolonized. The United States, France, and New Zealand still control some Pacific slands.

Reading Check **How did the region win independence from colonizers?**

Section 2 Assessment

Essential Question

Key Terms

1. How did the British policy of forced assimilation affect Aborigines?

2. What did missionaries to the region seek to do?

Key Ideas

3. Why did countries seek to colonize the region?

4. How did people first settle the region?

5. How did the British colonization of Australia and New Zealand affect native peoples there?

Think Critically

6. **Compare and Contrast** How were the region's people alike and different before British colonization began?

7. **Sequence** In what order were Australia and the three subgroups of Pacific islands settled?

What makes a nation?

8. Does the history of colonization explain the formation of present-day nations in this region? Explain.

Section 3

Australia and the Pacific Today

Key Ideas

- The region has a great deal of cultural diversity.

- Countries in the region have different forms of government and different levels of economic development.

- Protecting the environment is a major concern for the region's people.

Key Terms
- indigenous • coup • secondary industry • primary industry
- drought • climate change • nuclear weapon

 Visual Glossary

Reading Skill: Identify Main Ideas and Details
Take notes using the graphic organizer in your journal.

Most Australians, such as the man below, are descended from British settlers. ▼

Australia and the Pacific region are home to many cultures and ethnic groups, such as Jack's Maori people in New Zealand. A shared history and a blend of different cultures and traditions have shaped life in the region. Today, Australia and New Zealand are wealthy, highly developed nations with modern industrial economies. The smaller Pacific Islands are less developed, with economies based largely on tourism and the use of natural resources.

People and Culture

Australia, New Zealand, and the Pacific Islands include people from many different ethnic groups and cultures. As a result, the population of the region is diverse.

Australia and New Zealand Most Australians and New Zealanders have British ancestors. Since the 1970s, growing numbers of Asians and Pacific Islanders have moved to these two countries.

Smaller numbers of Australians and New Zealanders are descended from **indigenous** people, or people native to the region. Only about 1 percent of Australia's 22 million people are Aboriginal. As you learned in Section 2, British settlers and the Australian government mistreated Aborigines for many years. In 2008, the Australian government offi ally apologized for this unjust treatment of Aborigines.

Culture Close-up

846

One Region, Many Cultures

Australia and the Pacific region are home to people from many different cultures. These cultures developed independently because of the great distances separating them.

Language Lesson

An Aboriginal girl from Australia

A man from Papua New Guinea takes part in a traditional celebration.

Samoan girls wearing woven grass dresses and beaded headbands

Jack, who is from New Zealand, is part Maori.

my Story **Photo**

New Zealand has a larger population of indigenous people: about 8 percent of New Zealand's 4 million people are Maori. Like the Aborigines, the Maori were forced to adopt many British ways of life. Still, Maori culture has survived. In recent years, Maori people have gained more political power. Since the 1970s, the New Zealand government has paid hundreds of millions of dollars to Maori groups to <u>compensate</u> them for having taken Maori land in the past.

In general, Australians and New Zealanders are healthy and well educated, with long average life expectancies. However, many Aborigines and Maori have lower standards of living and levels of education than other Australians and New Zealanders. Government leaders are working to improve the political and economic status of indigenous peoples.

Pacific Islands Over time, Pacific islanders developed many different languages, religions, and customs. European colonization reduced this cultural diversity. For example, Pacific people once practiced hundreds of different religions. Today, most are Christian. Still, most Pacific islanders are indigenous people.

Although modern culture has spread throughout the region, some islanders have kept traditional customs. For example, many Pacific islanders practice traditional forms of art, dance, and music.

Reading Check What is the name of New Zealand's indigenous people?

compensate, *v.,* pay

my **worldgeography.com** Culture Close-up

Government

Australia and New Zealand were once British colonies. As a result, both have governments that are similar to the British system of government.

Australia and New Zealand Australia and New Zealand are parliamentary democracies. In these systems, citizens elect representatives to a parliament, or legislature. The parliament then chooses a prime minister as the head of the government. The prime minister and the parliament govern the country.

Australia has six states. As in the United States, these states have a great deal of power to govern themselves. They also have their own legislatures and court systems. New Zealand does not have any provinces or states, but it does have local and regional governments.

Citizens of Australia and New Zealand have rights and responsibilities similar to those of U.S. citizens. For example, Australians have freedom of religion and freedom of speech. There are also differences. Australians who are registered to vote can be fined for failing to vote, for example.

Pacific Islands The Pacific slands have a variety of governments, although most are democratic. A few of these countries have suffered from political <u>corruption</u> or unstable governments. For example, Fiji's military has led four coups since 1987. A **coup** is the sudden, violent overthrow of a government, often by the military.

Reading Check **How does Australia select leaders and establish laws?**

corruption, *n.,* improper use of power

Queen Elizabeth II of the United Kingdom is the official head of state of Australia, New Zealand, and several other former British colonies. She has little real power, however. ▼

Pacific Governments

Many of the region's countries are parliamentary democracies. Above, a Papua New Guinea man waits to vote in a national election. Left, Australia's Parliament

Economy

The region's levels of economic development vary greatly. While Australia and New Zealand have highly developed market economies, most smaller Pacific islands have developing economies.

Australia and New Zealand Australia's major industries are agriculture, mining, tourism, and manufacturing. Although Australia exports natural resources to many countries in Asia, many Australian businesses are secondary industries. A **secondary industry** involves the use of resources to create new products, as occurs in manufacturing. Australia's highly educated population and advanced technology have helped its industries modernize and succeed. As a result, Australia has a wealthy economy with a high economic output per person.

New Zealand's economy is similar to Australia's, although it is smaller. Services, industry, and tourism are the most valuable elements of New Zealand's economy. New Zealand farmers raise cows and sheep for meat, dairy, and wool products.

Pacific Islands Many island economies rely on primary industries such as fishing. A **primary industry** involves the collection of resources from nature. Agriculture and fishing are important primary industries.

Many islands have joined together in trade and business groups, such as the Pacific Islands Forum. By working together, islanders hope that they can attract international business and tourism to their islands, improving their economies and standards of living.

Reading Check Which countries in the region are wealthiest?

my World IN NUMBERS

The region's countries catch about **1.4** million fish per year—less than **1%** of the world's total fish catch.

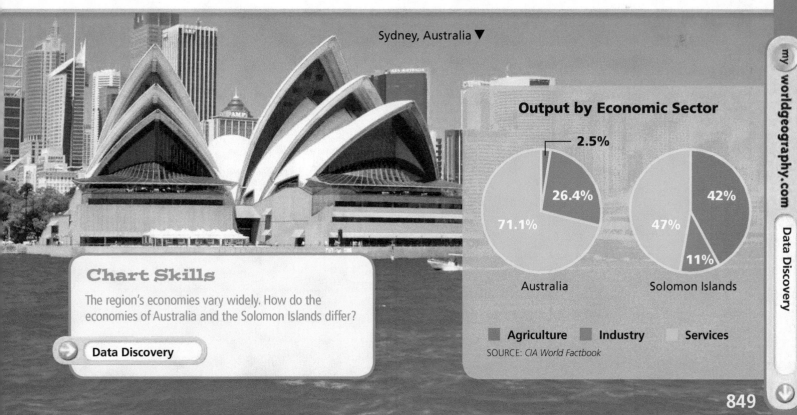

Sydney, Australia ▼

Output by Economic Sector

Australia
- 71.1%
- 26.4%
- 2.5%

Solomon Islands
- 47%
- 42%
- 11%

■ Agriculture ■ Industry ■ Services

SOURCE: *CIA World Factbook*

Chart Skills

The region's economies vary widely. How do the economies of Australia and the Solomon Islands differ?

→ **Data Discovery**

my worldgeography.com Data Discovery

Disappearing Islands

A melting Antarctic glacier ▼

In recent years, higher global temperatures have led to the melting of glaciers. Also, as water warms, it expands. Melting ice and expanding water have raised global sea levels. In the Pacific region, many people live close to sea level. For example, Tuvalu is a group of nine tiny islands about 2,500 miles (4,000 kilometers) northeast of Australia. Its highest point is only 15 feet (4.5 meters) above sea level, and most land is just a few feet above the water. As global sea level rises, Tuvalu—with its 9,600 residents—is slowly sinking below the ocean.

THINK CRITICALLY How is the sea level rise affecting Tuvalu?

Effects on Tuvalu

- High tides regularly flood Tuvalu.
- Waves from strong storms can wash completely over Fongafale, Tuvalu's largest island.
- Rising levels of salt water kill Tuvalu's crops and threaten livestock.
- Some residents are making plans to migrate to Australia or other countries in order to flee the rising seas.

Fongafale, Tuvalu

KEY
- Island
- Reef
- Deep Water
- ○ Village

0   1 mi
0   1 km
Lambert Azimuthal Equal-Area Projection

Lagoon

Fongafale

Vaiaku ○

PACIFIC OCEAN

Today

Lagoon

Fongafale

Vaiaku ○

PACIFIC OCEAN

About 2100

▲ Parts of Tuvalu flood often, forcing people and animals to adapt.

Environment

Pacific economies often depend on the environment. For example, tourism relies on the region's sandy beaches and clear blue water. Agriculture and fishing involve the use of natural resources. Today, people are working to protect the environment and use resources carefully. But the Pacifi region still faces environmental challenges.

Drought Australia is the driest inhabited continent. In recent years, many areas of the country have been affected by drought. A **drought** is a long period of extremely dry weather. Drought has caused Australia's farms to produce fewer and smaller harvests.

Climate Change Climate change is another major environmental problem. **Climate change** is a long-term, signifi ant change to a region's average weather. Natural processes can cause climate change. However, many scientists believe that human activity—such as air pollution—is a major factor.

Perhaps the most important effect of climate change in the Pacific egion is a rise in sea level. Th s rise is caused by the melting of glaciers and the warming and expansion of water due to higher global temperatures. Many scientists believe that the sea level will continue to rise in coming years, perhaps by as much as two feet or more by 2100.

Since many of the people in the Pacific region live near sea level, the sea level rise is a serious concern. Even a small rise can affect low-lying areas. Storms can push higher water farther onto land, causing widespread erosion.

Other Issues Some economic activities can cause environmental harm. For example, mining can cause water and soil pollution. In addition, the United States, France, and the United Kingdom tested nuclear weapons in the region from the 1940s to the 1990s. A **nuclear weapon** is a powerful explosive device that can cause widespread destruction. Th s testing may have harmful long-term effects on the region's people and ecosystems.

Reading Check **How is sea level rise affecting the Pacific region?**

Section 3 Assessment

Essential Question

What makes a nation?

Key Terms

1. How is climate change affecting Australia and the Pacific region?

2. What are primary and secondary industries?

Key Ideas

3. Why are the region's people concerned about the environment?

4. Describe the region's economies.

5. Why does the region have such a wide variety of cultures?

Think Critically

6. **Summarize** Summarize the present-day conditions of Australia's indigenous people.

7. **Draw Conclusions** Why might people who live on an island be able to preserve their culture for a long time without change?

8. How do governments and economies vary among the region's nations?

Antarctica

Key Ideas

- Antarctica is the most remote and least populated continent on Earth.
- Antarctica has a harsh climate.
- People first ventured to Antarctica to claim land and resources, but now the continent is set aside for science.

Key Terms • ice sheet • glacier • iceberg • pack ice • Antarctic Treaty • ozone layer

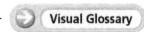 Visual Glossary

Reading Skill: Summarize Take notes using the graphic organizer in your journal.

▲ Adelie penguins on an iceberg off Antarctica

Physical Geography

Covered by a glittering sheet of ice and surrounded by stormy seas, Antarctica is Earth's least populated continent. It is located directly south of Australia, Africa, and South America. It is the coldest and windiest region on Earth.

An Icy Landscape Antarctica is a place unlike anywhere else on Earth. A thick **ice sheet**—a large mass of compressed ice—covers 98 percent of the continent. Th s ice sheet holds most of the world's fresh water. **Glaciers,** or slow-moving bodies of ice, form in Antarctica's valleys

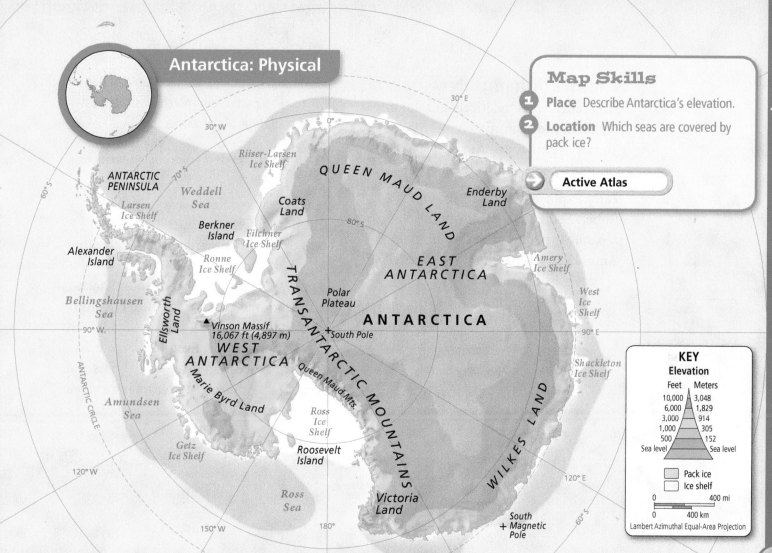

Antarctica: Physical
30° W
0°
30° E
Riiser-Larsen Ice Shelf
QUEEN MAUD LAND
ANTARCTIC PENINSULA
70° S
Weddell Sea
Coats Land
Enderby Land
Larsen Ice Shelf
Berkner Island
Filchner Ice Shelf
80° S
60° S
Alexander Island
Ronne Ice Shelf
EAST ANTARCTICA
Amery Ice Shelf
TRANSANTARCTIC MOUNTAINS
Polar Plateau
West Ice Shelf
Bellingshausen Sea
Ellsworth Land
ANTARCTICA
90° W
Vinson Massif 16,067 ft (4,897 m)
South Pole
90° E
WEST ANTARCTICA
Queen Maud Mts.
Shackleton Ice Shelf
Marie Byrd Land
ANTARCTIC CIRCLE
Amundsen Sea
Ross Ice Shelf
WILKES LAND
Getz Ice Shelf
Roosevelt Island
120° W
120° E
Ross Sea
Victoria Land
150° W
180°
South Magnetic Pole
60° S
KEY
Elevation
Feet Meters
10,000 3,048
6,000 1,829
3,000 914
1,000 305
500 152
Sea level Sea level
Pack ice
Ice shelf
0 400 mi
0 400 km
Lambert Azimuthal Equal-Area Projection

Map Skills

1. **Place** Describe Antarctica's elevation.
2. **Location** Which seas are covered by pack ice?

Active Atlas

and fl w toward the coast. When glaciers reach the sea, the ice breaks off i to **icebergs,** or large fl ating masses of ice.

In winter, the surface of the sea around Antarctica freezes, forming pack ice. **Pack ice** is seasonal ice that fl ats on the water rather than being attached to land.

The Transantarctic Mountains divide Antarctica into two regions, a large, flat area called East Antarctica and a smaller region called West Antarctica. At the tip of West Antarctica, the Antarctic Peninsula extends toward South America. The Transantarctic Mountains have glaciers and dry valleys free of snow and ice.

Climate, Life, and Resources Antarctica's interior is a high, dry plateau. It receives little precipitation, less than two inches per year. The snow that does fall does not melt. Instead, it piles up year after year, eventually turning into glacial ice.

Antarctica's mineral resources include coal and iron ore. Its harsh climate limits vegetation to simple plants such as algae and mosses. Penguins, seals, and other animals spend much of their time in the ocean. The seas are home to a variety of fish, whales, and other marine life.

Reading Check **How do Antarctica's climate and landscape affect life there?**

my worldgeography.com Active Atlas

Exploration and Research

Antarctica was a relatively unknown region at the beginning of the 1900s. Today, scientists use Antarctica as a giant laboratory to examine the natural world.

Early Explorers In 1910, explorers Robert Scott and Roald Amundsen began separate expeditions to the South Pole. Amundsen reached it in December 1911. He described part of the journey:

66 Our walk across this frozen lake was not pleasant. The ground under our feet was evidently hollow, and it sounded as if we were walking on empty barrels. First a man fell through, then a couple of dogs … This part of our march was the most unpleasant of the whole trip. 99

–Captain Roald Amundsen, *The South Pole: An Account of the Norwegian Antarctic Expedition in the* Fram, *1910–1912*

Scott reached the Pole a month after Amundsen. On the return trip, Scott's team died in a blizzard. Still, their studies helped advance Antarctic science.

In 1915, British explorer Ernest Shackleton set out to cross Antarctica. His ship was destroyed by pack ice, forcing his team to live on an ice floe. Eventually, the men crossed the ocean in three small boats and found help. Amazingly, everyone survived.

The Frozen Continent

Early explorers mapped Antarctica by foot and dogsled. At left, Robert Scott (standing) and Edward Wilson at the South Pole in 1912.

myWorld Activity
Dear Antarctica

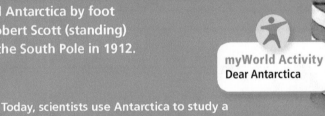

Today, scientists use Antarctica to study a range of topics. Below, a group of biologists. Right, a marker near the South Pole

A shelter used by Antarctic explorer Ernest Shackleton in 1907

Antarctica and Science Early explorers often claimed land in Antarctica. By the 1940s, these competing land claims led to international confli t. In 1959, twelve countries signed the **Antarctic Treaty,** an agreement that preserves Antarctica for peaceful and scientific se. Other protections were adopted in later years.

Today, Antarctica has no permanent human settlement. It does have several scientific esearch stations scattered across the continent. Scientists from a number of countries study topics such as oceans, glaciers, and climate.

Climate and the Ozone Layer To study climate, scientists drill deep into the ice sheet to gather ice samples. By examining the samples, they can learn more about the climate at the time when the ice was formed. By studying past climates, scientists hope to understand more about how climate might change in the future.

Scientists in Antarctica also study the ozone layer. The **ozone layer** is a layer of the atmosphere that filters out most of

the sun's harmful ultraviolet rays. Over time, the ozone layer over Antarctica has grown thinner. Th s area of reduced ozone, called the ozone hole, allows more ultraviolet radiation to reach Earth. A major cause of the hole in the ozone layer has been certain human-made chemical <u>compounds</u>. Today, most uses of these compounds have been banned. Scientists predict that the ozone layer will eventually recover if this ban is maintained.

compound, *n.,* something formed by two or more parts

Reading Check **How do people use Antarctica today?**

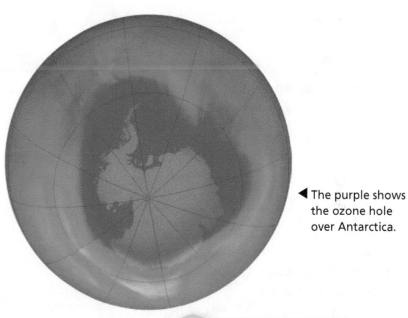

◀ The purple shows the ozone hole over Antarctica.

Section 4 Assessment

Key Terms

1. How does the Antarctic Treaty affect Antarctica?

2. Give short definitions of each of the following terms: ice sheet, glacier, iceberg, and pack ice.

Key Ideas

3. Why is Antarctica the least populated continent?

4. How does Antarctica's climate affect its environment?

5. Why are scientists interested in studying Antarctica?

Think Critically

6. Draw Conclusions How might its geography explain why Antarctica was not explored or settled until relatively recently?

7. Synthesize What challenges might Antarctica face in the future?

8. Why have no nations formed in Antarctica?

Chapter Assessment

Key Terms and Ideas

1. **Describe** How does **plate tectonics** explain the creation of volcanic islands in the Pacific?

2. **Recall** How did people settle the Pacific region?

3. **Summarize** What environmental issues does the region face?

4. **Compare and Contrast** Describe population density in Australia, New Zealand, and the Pacific islands.

5. **Paraphrase** Explain **ethnocentrism** in your own words.

6. **Summarize** What do **Aborigines** and the **Maori** have in common?

7. **Recall** How does the **Antarctic Treaty** protect Antarctica?

Think Critically

8. **Draw Inferences** How do you think Australia and New Zealand would be different today if British colonization had never taken place?

9. **Draw Conclusions** How might early explorers' experiences have helped to inspire the Antarctic Treaty?

10. **Synthesize** If drought continues in Australia, how might its population and economy change?

11. **Core Concepts: Climates and Ecosystems** How do you think the introduction of nonnative plant species has affected the Pacific region's ecosystem? What do you think can be done to better protect native species?

Places to Know

For each place, write the letter from the map that shows its location.

12. **Great Barrier Reef**

13. **Papua New Guinea**

14. **Mount Kosciuszko**

15. **Darling River**

16. **Southern Alps**

17. **Indian Ocean**

18. **Estimate** Using the scale, estimate the distance between the northwest tip of Papua New Guinea and the Southern Alps.

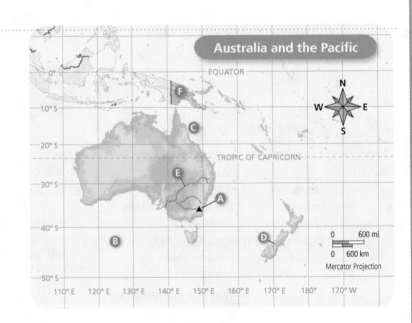

Australia and the Pacific

Essential Question

What makes a nation?

Reporting Back: A Voyage to the Pacific Follow your teacher's instructions to investigate geographic features of Australia and New Zealand as a member of explorer James Cook's crew. Work with your team members to collect and organize information on your field of expertise. Then prepare a multimedia presentation on the region to present to the British king.

21st Century Learning

Search for Information on the Internet

Imagine that you work at a U.S. zoo planning an exhibit on Antarctic penguins, leopard seals, and other animals. Use the Internet to research how to create an accurate exhibit. Then use this information to write a brief report. Remember to consider the following:
- Antarctica's climate and landscape
- Antarctica's land and sea temperatures
- the needs of Antarctic animals

Document-Based Questions

Success Tracker™
Online at myworldgeography.com

Use your knowledge of Australia and the Pacific and Documents A and B to answer Questions 1–3.

Document A

Internet Users	
Country	**Users per 100 People**
Australia	75.1
New Zealand	78.8
Papua New Guinea	1.8
Tonga	3.0
Vanuatu	3.5

SOURCE: United Nations Statistics Division

Document B

" I was definitely not told that I was Aboriginal. What [they] told us was that we had to be white. It was drummed into our heads that we were white … We were prisoners from [the moment] we were born."

—John, an Aboriginal man who was taken away from his family as a child in the 1940s

1. Examine Document A. What can you conclude about Pacific economies based on these data?

 A Australia and New Zealand are less developed than other countries in the region.

 B Australia and New Zealand are more developed than other countries in the region.

 C Countries in the region are equally developed.

 D Smaller countries are more developed than larger countries.

2. Read Document B. What does the quotation describe?

 A climate change

 B forced assimilation

 C migration

 D missionaries

3. **Writing Task** Do you think the situation described in Document B was common? Explain your answer.

my worldgeography.com Self-Test

Meet the Islanders

Your Mission Working in groups, you will research the indigenous peoples of Australia, New Zealand, and the Pacific islands. Then you will choose a person from one of those groups, research his or her life, and develop a multimedia biography.

One memorable moment of the 2000 Olympic Games in Sydney, Australia, came when Cathy Freeman won the 400-meter race. She was the first person of Aboriginal descent to win an Olympic medal. She took her victory lap proudly waving both the Australian and Aboriginal flags.

Many indigenous groups are found in Australia, New Zealand, and the Pacific islands. The indigenous people of Australia are known as Aborigines. The Maori are the indigenous people of New Zealand. The Pacific islands have a variety of indigenous cultures.

STEP **1**

Choose a Subject.

Assign each person in your group to research one of these groups: Aborigines, Maori, and indigenous Pacific islanders. As you learn about these peoples, make a list of well-known or prominent individuals with that heritage. Try to include people from the arts, politics, sports, entertainment, science, and other fields. Share your findings and, as a group, choose one person to be the subject of your multimedia biography.

STEP **2**

Research the Subject.

Do additional research on your subject's life and achievements. Divide up the tasks of finding out about the subject's family and childhood, adult life and achievements, historical events from his or her lifetime, and the customs and heritage of his or her ethnic group. Try to find lively details to enhance your presentation. Share your research with your group, and together decide what you will include in the biography.

STEP **3**

Make a Presentation.

Plan and present a multimedia biography about your subject. Consider using written materials, photographs, videos, music, and other elements. Your biography should be thorough and focused. It should include interesting details as well as accurate facts. Your presentation to the class may take the form of a multimedia slideshow, a podcast, a radio broadcast, a documentary, or an interactive Web site.

The World: Political

ARCTIC OCEAN

GREENLAND
(Denmark)

ALASKA
(U.S.)

ARCTIC CIRCLE

60° N

Reykjavík ✪
ICELAND

CANADA

NORTH

AMERICA

Ottawa ✪

40° N

UNITED STATES

Washington, D.C. ✪

ATLANTIC

OCEAN

Rabat ✪
MOROCCO

TROPIC OF CANCER

WESTERN SAHARA
(Morocco)

20° N

HAWAII
(U.S.)

MEXICO

Mexico ✪
City

CENTRAL AMERICA
AND THE CARIBBEAN
For detail, see map
North and South
America: Political.

WEST AFRICA
For detail, see map
Africa: Political

PACIFIC

OCEAN

Caracas ✪

Georgetown
Paramaribo

VENEZUELA

Bogotá ✪
COLOMBIA

FRENCH GUIANA
(France)

N

Quito ✪
ECUADOR

GUYANA
SURINAME

W   E

0°   EQUATOR

GALÁPAGOS
ISLANDS
(Ecuador)

S

SOUTH

SAMOA ✪

PERU

AMERICA

ATLANTIC

Apia ✪

COOK ISLANDS
(New Zealand)

Lima ✪

OCEAN

20° S

FRENCH POLYNESIA
(France)

La Paz ✪ Brasília ✪

Nuku'alofa ✪

BOLIVIA

BRAZIL

TONGA

Sucre ✪

TROPIC OF CAPRICORN

PITCAIRN ISLAND
(U.K.)

PARAGUAY

Asunción ✪

CHILE

KEY

Buenos
Aires ✪
URUGUAY

- - - Disputed border

Santiago ✪

Montevideo ✪

—— National border

ARGENTINA

✪ Capital city

40° S

FALKLAND ISLANDS
(U.K.)

SOUTH GEORGIA
(U.K.)

160° W   140° W   120° W   100° W   80° W   60° W   40° W   20° W

60° S

SOUTHERN OCEAN

80° S

ANTARCTICA

860

20° E 40° E 60° E 80° E 100° E 120° E 140° E 160° E

SVALBARD
(Norway)

80° N

ARCTIC OCEAN

EUROPE AND SOUTHWEST ASIA
detail, see maps Europe: Political
and Asia: Political.

ARCTIC CIRCLE

RUSSIA

60° N

Moscow

ASIA

EUROPE

Astana

KAZAKHSTAN
Ulaanbaatar
MONGOLIA

Tashkent Bishkek
UZBEKISTAN KYRGYZSTAN
TURKMENISTAN TAJIKISTAN
Ashgabat Dushanbe
Tehran Kabul
IRAQ
Baghdad Islamabad
IRAN AFGHANISTAN
Kuwait Kathmandu
KUWAIT PAKISTAN NEPAL BHUTAN
BAHRAIN Manama New Thimphu
QATAR Doha Delhi Dhaka
Riyadh Abu Dhabi
Muscat INDIA
SAUDI
ARABIA OMAN

NORTH
KOREA
P'yongyang
Beijing Seoul JAPAN
SOUTH
KOREA Tokyo

CHINA

40° N

PACIFIC
OCEAN

Tunis
TUNISIA
Tripoli

Cairo

LIBYA EGYPT

Taipei
MYANMAR Hanoi TAIWAN
BANGLADESH LAOS
Yangon Vientiane
THAILAND VIETNAM
Bangkok CAMBODIA
Phnom Penh

TROPIC OF CANCER

20° N

AFRICA
NIGER CHAD
Khartoum ERITREA
N'Djamena Asmara
SUDAN
CENTRAL
AFRICAN
GERIA REPUBLIC
AMEROON Bangui
REPUBLIC
OF THE
CONGO

Sanaa
YEMEN
Djibouti
DJIBOUTI
Addis Ababa
ETHIOPIA

UNITED
ARAB
EMIRATES

SRI
LANKA

Manila

MARSHALL
ISLANDS
Majuro

Colombo

SOMALIA
Kampala
UGANDA
Kigali KENYA
RWANDA Nairobi
azzaville Bujumbura BURUNDI
NDA DEMOCRATIC
ngola) REPUBLIC
Luanda OF THE
CONGO Dodoma

Male
MALDIVES

Mogadishu

Kuala Lumpur

PHILIPPINES
BRUNEI

PALAU
Melekeok

Palikir
FEDERATED STATES
OF MICRONESIA

KIRIBATI
Tarawa

MALAYSIA
Bandar Seri Begawan
Singapore SINGAPORE

SEYCHELLES
Victoria

EQUATOR

NAURU Yaren 0°

INDONESIA

Dar es Salaam
TANZANIA

PAPUA NEW
GUINEA

SOLOMON
ISLANDS

TUVALU

ANGOLA
ZAMBIA
Lusaka
MALAWI
Lilongwe

COMOROS
Moroni

Jakarta

Dili
EAST TIMOR

Port
Moresby

Honiara

Funafuti

INDIAN
OCEAN

FIJI

Harare
ZIMBABWE
NAMIBIA
Windhoek BOTSWANA
Gaborone
Pretoria Maputo
Bloemfontein Mbabane
SWAZILAND
SOUTH
AFRICA LESOTHO
Cape Town Maseru

Antananarivo

MAURITIUS
Port Louis

RÉUNION
(France)

20° S

MOZAMBIQUE
MADAGASCAR

VANUATU
Port-Vila

NEW
CALEDONIA
(France)

Suva

AUSTRALIA

0 2,000 mi
0 2,000 km
Robinson Projection

Canberra

NEW
ZEALAND

40° S

Wellington

20° E 40° E 60° E 80° E 100° E 120° E 140° E 160° E

60° S

SOUTHERN OCEAN

ANTARCTIC CIRCLE

ANTARCTICA

80° S

The World: Physical

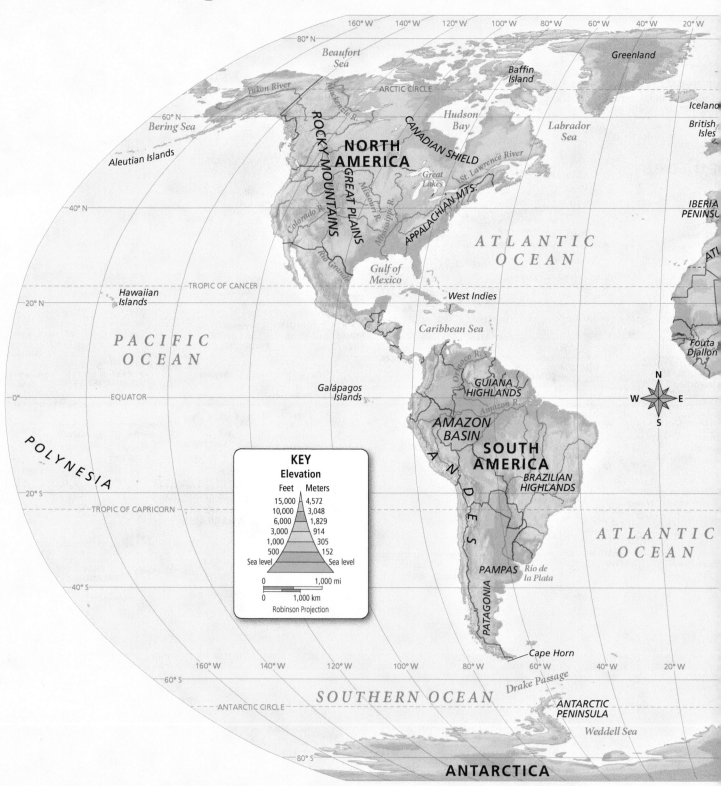

160° W 140° W 120° W 100° W 80° W 60° W 40° W 20° W

80° N

Beaufort Sea

Greenland

Baffin Island

Iceland

ARCTIC CIRCLE

Yukon River

60° N

Bering Sea

Hudson Bay

Labrador Sea

British Isles

Mackenzie R.

CANADIAN SHIELD

ROCKY MOUNTAINS

NORTH AMERICA

Aleutian Islands

Great Lakes

St. Lawrence River

GREAT PLAINS

Missouri R.

Mississippi R.

APPALACHIAN MTS.

40° N

Colorado R.

ATLANTIC OCEAN

IBERIA PENINSU

Rio Grande

Gulf of Mexico

TROPIC OF CANCER

Hawaiian Islands

20° N

West Indies

Caribbean Sea

ATL

PACIFIC OCEAN

Fouta Djallon

Galápagos Islands

Orinoco R.

GUIANA HIGHLANDS

N

0°

EQUATOR

Amazon R.

W   E

AMAZON BASIN

S

SOUTH AMERICA

POLYNESIA

BRAZILIAN HIGHLANDS

20° S

TROPIC OF CAPRICORN

KEY
Elevation

Feet   Meters

15,000   4,572
10,000   3,048
6,000   1,829
3,000   914
1,000   305
500   152
Sea level   Sea level

A
N
D
E
S

ATLANTIC OCEAN

PAMPAS

Río de la Plata

0   1,000 mi

PATAGONIA

0   1,000 km

Robinson Projection

40° S

Cape Horn

160° W 140° W 120° W 100° W 80° W 60° W 40° W 20° W

60° S

Drake Passage

SOUTHERN OCEAN

ANTARCTIC PENINSULA

ANTARCTIC CIRCLE

Weddell Sea

80° S

ANTARCTICA

ARCTIC OCEAN

SCANDINAVIA

Kara
Sea

URAL MOUNTAINS

S I B E R I A

CHERSKIY RANGE

ARCTIC CIRCLE

80° N

60° N

Baltic
Sea

Ob River

Yenisey River

Lena River

NORTH EUROPEAN PLAIN

Volga River

ASIA

ALTAY SHAN

Lake
Baikal

Amur River

Sea of
Okhotsk

ALPS EUROPE

CAUCASUS
MTS.

Aral
Sea

TIAN SHAN

GOBI

Sea of
Japan
(East
Sea)

Hokkaido

40° N

Black Sea

Caspian
Sea

HINDU
KUSH

KUNLUN SHAN

NORTH
CHINA
PLAIN

Honshu

TS.

Mediterranean Sea

IRANIAN
PLATEAU

PLATEAU
OF TIBET

Huang R.

Yellow
Sea

East
China
Sea

PACIFIC
OCEAN

HIMALAYAS

Persian
Gulf

Chang R.

A H A R A

Red Sea

ARABIAN
PENINSULA

DECCAN
PLATEAU

Taiwan

TROPIC OF CANCER

20° N

S A H E L

Nile R.

Arabian
Sea

Bay of
Bengal

INDOCHINA
PENINSULA

South
China
Sea

Philippine
Sea

40° N

AFRICA

ETHIOPIAN
HIGHLANDS

Sri
Lanka

Philippine
Islands

M I C R O N E S I A

CONGO
BASIN

Congo

Lake
Victoria

Malay
Peninsula

Serengeti
Plain

Borneo

Sumatra

Sulawesi

New
Guinea

0°

M E L A N E S I A

Java Sea

Zambezi

Java

Lesser Sunda
Islands

Arafura Sea

INDIAN
OCEAN

Madagascar

Coral Sea

KALAHARI
DESERT

AUSTRALIA

20° S

Great Sandy
Desert

TROPIC OF CAPRICORN

Great Victoria
Desert

GREAT DIVIDING RANGE

Tasman
Sea

Cape of
Good Hope

New
Zealand

40° S

Tasmania

SOUTHERN OCEAN

60° S

ANTARCTIC CIRCLE

ANTARCTICA

80° S

20° E 40° E 60° E 80° E 100° E 120° E 140° E 160° E

North and South America: Political

North and South America: Physical

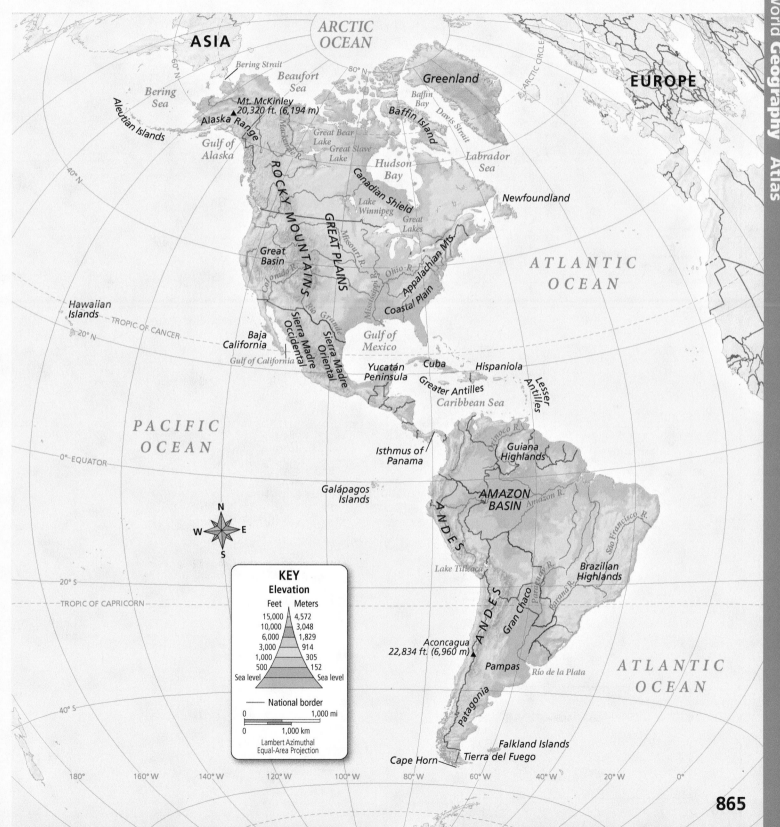

ASIA

ARCTIC OCEAN

Bering Strait

Beaufort Sea

Bering Sea

Greenland

ARCTIC CIRCLE

80° N

Baffin Bay

EUROPE

Mt. McKinley 20,320 ft. (6,194 m)

Alaska Range

Baffin Island

Davis Strait

Aleutian Islands

Gulf of Alaska

60° N

Great Bear Lake

Great Slave Lake

Labrador Sea

40° N

Mackenzie R.

Hudson Bay

Canadian Shield

Newfoundland

ROCKY MOUNTAINS

Lake Winnipeg

Great Lakes

ATLANTIC OCEAN

Great Basin

GREAT PLAINS

Missouri R.

Ohio R.

Appalachian Mts.

Hawaiian Islands

Colorado R.

Mississippi R.

Coastal Plain

TROPIC OF CANCER

20° N

Baja California

Sierra Madre Occidental

Rio Grande

Sierra Madre Oriental

Gulf of Mexico

Gulf of California

Yucatán Peninsula

Cuba

Hispaniola

Lesser Antilles

PACIFIC OCEAN

Greater Antilles

Caribbean Sea

Galápagos Islands

Isthmus of Panama

Orinoco R.

Guiana Highlands

0°-EQUATOR

AMAZON BASIN

Amazon R.

ANDES

N

W · E

S

Lake Titicaca

São Francisco R.

Brazilian Highlands

20° S

TROPIC OF CAPRICORN

Gran Chaco

Pucuguay R.

Paraná R.

Aconcagua 22,834 ft. (6,960 m)

ANDES

Pampas

Río de la Plata

ATLANTIC OCEAN

KEY
Elevation

Feet	Meters
15,000	4,572
10,000	3,048
6,000	1,829
3,000	914
1,000	305
500	152
Sea level	Sea level

— National border

0 ——— 1,000 mi

0 ——— 1,000 km

Lambert Azimuthal Equal-Area Projection

40° S

Patagonia

Falkland Islands

Cape Horn

Tierra del Fuego

180°   160° W   140° W   120° W   100° W   80° W   60° W   40° W   20° W   0°

United States: Political

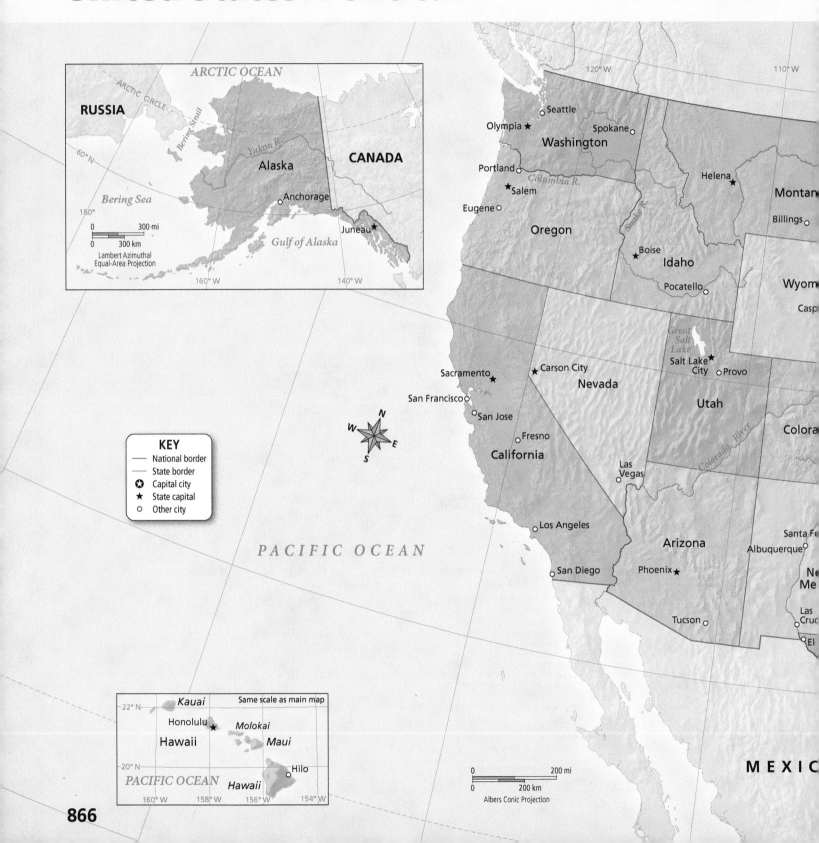

ARCTIC OCEAN

ARCTIC CIRCLE

RUSSIA

Bering Strait

Yukon R.

Alaska

CANADA

60° N

Bering Sea

180°

○ Anchorage

Gulf of Alaska

Juneau ★

0   300 mi
0   300 km

Lambert Azimuthal
Equal-Area Projection

160° W   140° W

120° W   110° W

Seattle ○

Olympia ★   Spokane ○

Washington

Portland ○

Helena ★

Salem ★   *Columbia R.*

Mont

Eugene ○

Billings ○

Oregon

Boise ★

Idaho

Snake R.

Wyom

Pocatello ○

Great Salt Lake

Casp

Salt Lake ★
City

Carson City ★   ○ Provo

Sacramento ★

Nevada

San Francisco ○

Utah

Colora

○ San Jose

Colorado River

○ Fresno

California

Las ○
Vegas

Los Angeles ○

Arizona

Santa Fe

Albuquerque ○

PACIFIC OCEAN

San Diego ○

Phoenix ★

N
Me

Las
Cruc

○ El

Tucson ○

KEY

— National border
— State border
⊛ Capital city
★ State capital
○ Other city

N
W   E
S

22° N   *Kauai*   Same scale as main map

Honolulu ★   *Molokai*

Hawaii   *Maui*

20° N

○ Hilo

PACIFIC OCEAN   *Hawaii*

160° W   158° W   156° W   154° W

0   200 mi
0   200 km

Albers Conic Projection

MEXIC

CANADA

Missouri River

North Dakota
Bismarck★   Fargo○

Minnesota

Lake Superior

South Dakota
Pierre★   ○St. Paul   Green Bay○   *Lake Huron*
○Sioux Falls   Minneapolis○   Wisconsin   Michigan   *Lake Ontario*   Maine
                                                                                    Augusta★
Platte River   Iowa   ○Cedar Rapids   Madison★   Grand Rapids○   Vermont   ○Portland
Nebraska   Des○★ Moines   ★Milwaukee   Lansing★   Montpelier★   New   Concord★   Boston
Cheyenne   ○Omaha   Chicago○   Detroit○   New   Albany★   Massachusetts
Lincoln★★   ○Lansing   Fort   Cleveland○   York   Rochester○   ★Providence
                          Wayne   Ohio   Pittsburgh○   Buffalo○   Hartford★★   Rhode Island

Lake Michigan

nver   Illinois   Indiana   Columbus○   Pennsylvania   Connecticut
olorado   Springfield★   Indianapolis★   Dayton○   Harrisburg★   New York City★
orings   Topeka ★   ○Kansas   ○St. Louis   Cincinnati○   Philadelphia○   New Jersey
                     City   Frankfort★   West   Baltimore○   ○Dover★
Kansas   Jefferson★   Ohio River   Louisville○   Virginia   Washington,⊕★Delaware
Wichita○   City   Kentucky   ★Charleston   Richmond   D.C. Annapolis Maryland
         Arkansas River   Missouri   Nashville★   Knoxville○   ★   Norfolk○
Oklahoma   ○Tulsa   Tennessee   North Carolina   Raleigh★
City★   ○Fort Smith   Memphis○   *Tennessee R.*   Charlotte○
Oklahoma   Arkansas   Birmingham○   Atlanta   South Carolina
         Little Rock★   Mississippi   Alabama   Augusta★   Columbia○   ○Charleston
Red River   ○Shreveport   Jackson★   Montgomery★   Georgia   Savannah○
Fort○○Dallas   Louisiana   Mobile○   Columbus○   ATLANTIC
Worth   Baton○★   Gulfport○   OCEAN
Texas   Rouge   ○New Orleans   Tallahassee★   ○Jacksonville
Austin★   Houston○
San○   *Rio Grande*   Orlando○   Florida
Antonio   Tampa○

Gulf of Mexico   ○Miami

867

Europe: Political

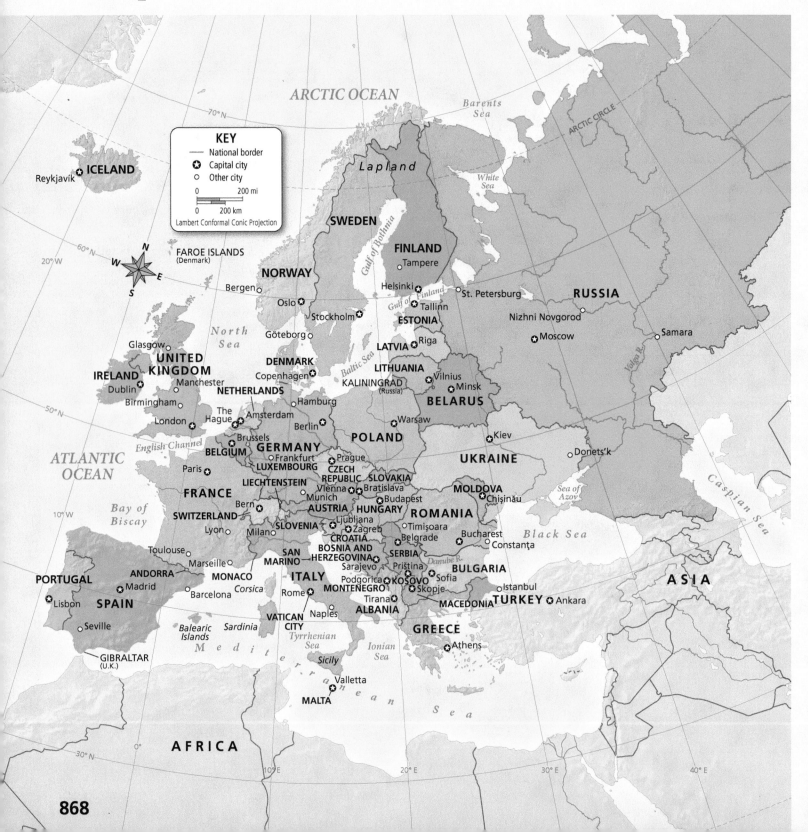

ARCTIC OCEAN

Barents Sea

70° N

ARCTIC CIRCLE

White Sea

Lapland

KEY
— National border
⊛ Capital city
○ Other city
0 ___ 200 mi
0 ___ 200 km
Lambert Conformal Conic Projection

ICELAND
Reykjavík

FAROE ISLANDS
(Denmark)

60° N

20° W

SWEDEN

FINLAND
○ Tampere

NORWAY
Bergen ○
Helsinki ⊛

Gulf of Bothnia

St. Petersburg ○

RUSSIA

Oslo ⊛
Stockholm ⊛
Göteborg ○

Gulf of Finland
Tallinn ⊛

ESTONIA

Nizhni Novgorod ○

Samara ○

Moscow ⊛

Glasgow ○

UNITED
KINGDOM

DENMARK
Copenhagen ⊛

LATVIA
Riga ⊛

LITHUANIA
Vilnius ⊛

KALININGRAD
(Russia)

Minsk ⊛

North Sea

IRELAND
Dublin ⊛
Birmingham ○
Manchester ○
London ⊛

NETHERLANDS
The Hague ⊛
Amsterdam ⊛
Hamburg ○
Berlin ⊛

Baltic Sea

Warsaw ⊛

BELARUS

50° N

English Channel

Brussels ⊛
BELGIUM
GERMANY
LUXEMBOURG
Frankfurt ○
Prague ⊛

POLAND

Kiev ⊛

UKRAINE

Donets'k ○

ATLANTIC
OCEAN

Paris ⊛

FRANCE

LIECHTENSTEIN
CZECH
REPUBLIC
Vienna ⊛
Munich ○
SLOVAKIA
Bratislava ⊛

Budapest ⊛

MOLDOVA
Chișinău ⊛

Sea of Azov

10° W

Bern ⊛
SWITZERLAND
Lyon ○

Bay of Biscay

AUSTRIA HUNGARY

Ljubljana ⊛

SLOVENIA
Milan ○

ROMANIA

Black Sea

Caspian Sea

Toulouse ○

Marseille ○

CROATIA
Zagreb ⊛

Timișoara ○

Belgrade ⊛

Bucharest ⊛
Constanța ○

Volga R.

PORTUGAL

ANDORRA
Madrid ⊛

MONACO
Corsica

SAN
MARINO
BOSNIA AND
HERZEGOVINA
Sarajevo ⊛

SERBIA

Podgorica ⊛
Priština ○
KOSOVO

BULGARIA
Sofia ⊛

ASIA

Barcelona ○

SPAIN

ITALY
Rome ⊛

MONTENEGRO
Tirana ⊛

Skopje ⊛
Istanbul ○
MACEDONIA TURKEY
Ankara ⊛

Lisbon ⊛

Naples ○

ALBANIA

Seville ○

VATICAN
CITY

Balearic Islands
Sardinia

GREECE

GIBRALTAR
(U.K.)

Mediterranean

Tyrrhenian Sea
Sicily
Ionian Sea

Athens ⊛

Danube R.

MALTA
Valletta ⊛

Sea

AFRICA

30° N

0°

10° E

20° E

30° E

40° E

Europe: Physical

ARCTIC OCEAN

Barents Sea

Kola Peninsula

Iceland

ARCTIC CIRCLE

White Sea

Norwegian Sea

URAL MOUNTAINS

Faroe Islands

Kjølen Mountains

SCANDINAVIAN PENINSULA

Northern Dvina R.

Shetland Islands

Gulf of Bothnia

Lake Ludoga

Volga River

Lake Vänern

Gulf of Finland

North Sea

Gotland

Baltic Sea

Jutland

Central Russian Upland

Sjælland

Ireland

Great Britain

Elbe R.

N O R T H   E U R O P E A N   P L A I N

Thames R.

Oder R.

Vistula R.

English Channel

Dnieper River

Volga River

Seine R.

Rhine R.

Dniester R.

Don River

ATLANTIC OCEAN

Loire R.

Danube R.

Carpathian Mountains

Sea of Azov

Crimea

CAUCASUS MTS.

Caspian Sea

Bay of Biscay

Garonne R.

Massif Central

A L P S

▲Mont Blanc 15,781 ft (4,810 m)

Po River

Rhône R.

Transylvanian Alps

▲Mount Elbrus 18,510 ft (5,642 m)

Pyrenees

Apennines

Adriatic Sea

Dinaric Alps

Danube River

Black Sea

ASIA

Douro R.

Ebro R.

Meseta

IBERIAN PENINSULA

Tagus R.

Corsica

ITALIAN PENINSULA

Balkan Mts.

BALKAN PENINSULA

Bosporus

Dardanelles

Sardinia

Balearic Islands

Pindus Mts.

Aegean Sea

Guadalquivir R.

Tyrrhenian Sea

Sicily

Ionian Sea

Peloponnisos

M e d i t e r r a n e a n

Maltese Islands

Crete

S e a

AFRICA

70° N

60° N

50° N

20° W

10° W

0°

10° E

20° E

30° E

40° E

30° N

N W E S

KEY
Elevation

Feet	Meters
10,000	3,048
6,000	1,829
3,000	914
1,000	305
500	152
Sea level	Sea level

0   200 mi

0   200 km

Lambert Conformal Conic Projection

Africa: Political

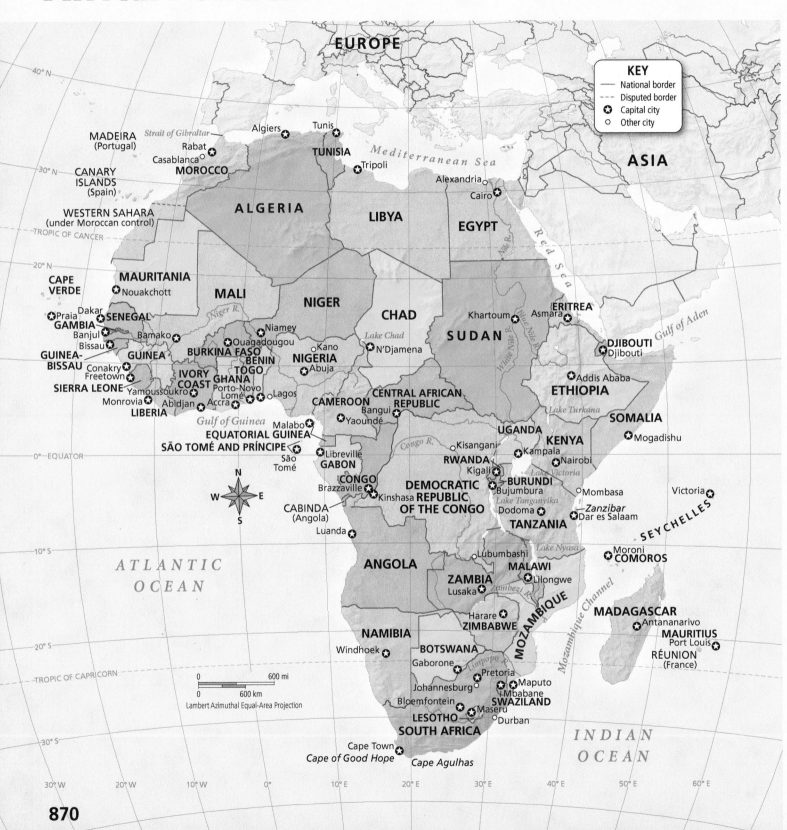

EUROPE

MADEIRA
(Portugal)

Strait of Gibraltar

Algiers ✪   Tunis ○

Rabat ✪   TUNISIA

Casablanca ○   *Mediterranean Sea*

CANARY
ISLANDS
(Spain)   MOROCCO   Tripoli ○

Alexandria ○

Cairo ✪

ASIA

WESTERN SAHARA
(under Moroccan control)

ALGERIA   LIBYA   EGYPT

TROPIC OF CANCER

CAPE
VERDE   MAURITANIA

Nouakchott ✪   MALI   NIGER

CHAD   *Nile R.*

Khartoum ✪   Asmara ✪   ERITREA

Red Sea   *Gulf of Aden*

Praia ✪   Dakar ○   *Niger R.*

GAMBIA   SENEGAL

Banjul ✪   Bamako ✪   Niamey ✪

Bissau ○   Ouagadougou ✪   Kano ○

Lake Chad   N'Djamena ✪

SUDAN   *Blue Nile R.*   *White Nile R.*

DJIBOUTI ✪
Djibouti ○

GUINEA-
BISSAU   GUINEA   BURKINA FASO

BENIN   NIGERIA

Conakry ✪   IVORY   TOGO   Abuja ✪

Freetown ✪   COAST   GHANA

Addis Ababa ✪

SIERRA LEONE   Yamoussoukro ✪   Porto-Novo ✪

ETHIOPIA

Monrovia ✪   Abidjan ○   Accra ✪   Lomé ✪

Lagos ○   CENTRAL AFRICAN
REPUBLIC

LIBERIA   *Gulf of Guinea*   CAMEROON   Bangui ✪

Lake Turkana

SOMALIA

Malabo ✪   Yaoundé ✪   UGANDA   KENYA

EQUATORIAL GUINEA   Kisangani ○   Mogadishu ○

SÃO TOMÉ AND PRÍNCIPE   *Congo R.*   Kampala ✪

São
Tomé   Libreville ✪   RWANDA   Nairobi ○

GABON   Kigali ✪   *Lake Victoria*   Mombasa ○

EQUATOR   CONGO   BURUNDI   Victoria ✪

Brazzaville ✪   DEMOCRATIC   Bujumbura ✪

CABINDA
(Angola)   Kinshasa ✪   REPUBLIC
OF THE CONGO   Dodoma ✪   Zanzibar ○   SEYCHELLES

Lake Tanganyika   Dar es Salaam ○

Luanda ✪   TANZANIA

Moroni ✪
COMOROS

Lubumbashi ○   *Lake Nyasa*

ATLANTIC
OCEAN   ANGOLA   MALAWI

Lilongwe ✪

ZAMBIA   *Zambezi R.*   MADAGASCAR

Lusaka ✪   Antananarivo ✪

Harare ✪   MAURITIUS
Port Louis ✪

NAMIBIA   ZIMBABWE   *Mozambique Channel*

MOZAMBIQUE   RÉUNION
(France)

Windhoek ✪   BOTSWANA

Gaborone ✪   *Limpopo R.*

Pretoria ✪

Johannesburg ○   Maputo ✪

Bloemfontein ○   Mbabane ✪
SWAZILAND

Maseru ✪

LESOTHO   Durban ○

SOUTH AFRICA

Cape Town ○

Cape of Good Hope   *Cape Agulhas*

INDIAN
OCEAN

TROPIC OF CAPRICORN

0   600 mi
0   600 km
Lambert Azimuthal Equal-Area Projection

KEY
— National border
-- Disputed border
✪ Capital city
○ Other city

40° N   30° N   20° N   10° N   0° EQUATOR   10° S   20° S   30° S

30° W   20° W   10° W   0°   10° E   20° E   30° E   40° E   50° E   60° E

870

Africa: Physical

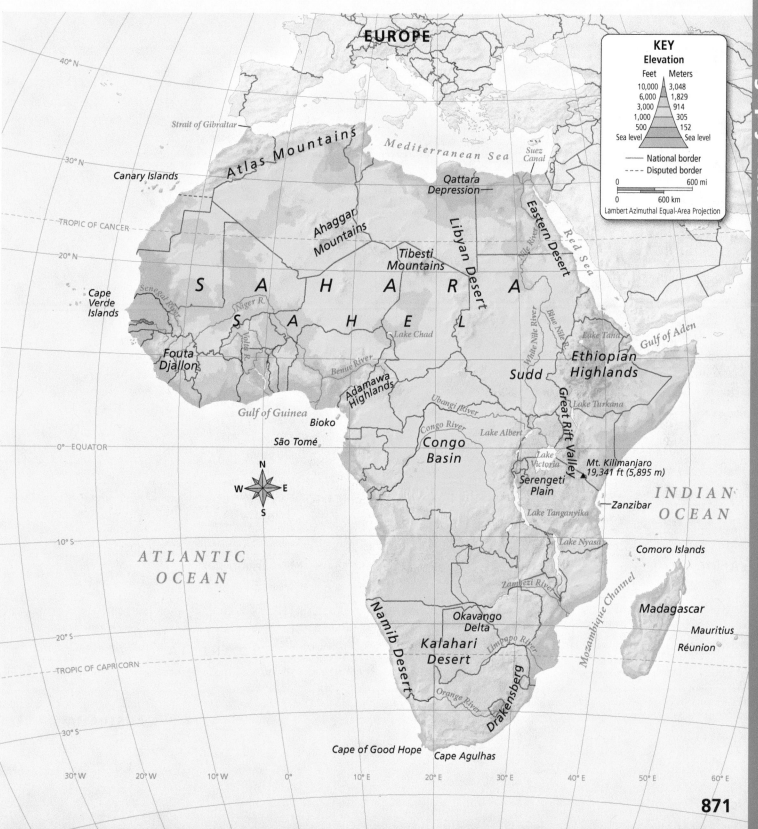

EUROPE

KEY
Elevation

Feet	Meters
10,000	3,048
6,000	1,829
3,000	914
1,000	305
500	152
Sea level	Sea level

—— National border
----- Disputed border

0   600 mi
0   600 km
Lambert Azimuthal Equal-Area Projection

Strait of Gibraltar
Canary Islands
Atlas Mountains
Mediterranean Sea
Suez Canal
TROPIC OF CANCER
Qattara Depression
Ahaggar Mountains
Tibesti Mountains
Libyan Desert
Eastern Desert
Nile River
Red Sea
20° N
S A H A R A
Cape Verde Islands
Senegal River
Niger R.
S A H E L
Lake Chad
White Nile River
Blue Nile
Lake Tana
Gulf of Aden
Fouta Djallon
Volta R.
Benue River
Ethiopian Highlands
Sudd
Gulf of Guinea
Adamawa Highlands
Bioko
São Tomé
Ubangi River
Congo River
Lake Albert
Lake Turkana
0° EQUATOR
Congo Basin
Lake Victoria
Great Rift Valley
Mt. Kilimanjaro
19,341 ft (5,895 m)
N
W   E
S
Serengeti Plain
Zanzibar
INDIAN OCEAN
Lake Tanganyika
10° S
ATLANTIC OCEAN
Lake Nyasa
Comoro Islands
Zambezi River
Mozambique Channel
Madagascar
Namib Desert
Okavango Delta
Mauritius
Kalahari Desert
Limpopo River
Réunion
20° S
TROPIC OF CAPRICORN
Drakensberg
Orange River
30° S
Cape of Good Hope
Cape Agulhas

30° W   20° W   10° W   0°   10° E   20° E   30° E   40° E   50° E   60° E

40° N
30° N
30° N
10° N

Asia: Political

EUROPE

ARCTIC OCEAN

Barents Sea
Kara Sea
Laptev Sea
East Siberian Sea
Bering Sea

St. Petersburg
Moscow
Nizhni Novgorod
Perm'
Yekaterinburg
Samara
Omsk
Novosibirsk
Astana

RUSSIA

ARCTIC CIRCLE

Ob R.
Yenisey R.
Lena R.
Amur R.

Sea of Okhotsk
Sakhalin Island
Kuril Islands
Vladivostok

PACIFIC OCEAN

Istanbul
Ankara
TURKEY
CYPRUS
Nicosia
LEBANON
Beirut
Jerusalem
ISRAEL
Amman
JORDAN

GEORGIA
Tbilisi
ARMENIA
Yerevan
AZERBAIJAN
Baku
SYRIA
Damascus

Black Sea
Caspian Sea
Aral Sea

KAZAKHSTAN
Lake Balkhash

MONGOLIA
Ulaanbaatar
Lake Baikal

JAPAN
Tokyo
Osaka

NORTH KOREA
P'yongyang
Beijing
Tianjin
Seoul
SOUTH KOREA

Mediterranean Sea

UZBEKISTAN
Bishkek
Tashkent
Almaty
KYRGYZSTAN
TAJIKISTAN
Dushanbe

TURKMENISTAN
Ashgabat
Tehran
Mashhad

Yellow Sea
Shanghai

Baghdad
IRAQ
IRAN
Kuwait
KUWAIT

AFGHANISTAN
Kabul
Islamabad

CHINA

Chang R.
Wuhan
East China Sea
Ryukyu Islands

SAUDI ARABIA
BAHRAIN
Manama
QATAR
Doha
Abu Dhabi
Mecca
Riyadh

Huang R.
Chongqing
Taipei
TAIWAN

PAKISTAN
New Delhi
Karachi

NEPAL
Kathmandu
BHUTAN
Thimphu

Guangzhou
Hong Kong

UNITED ARAB EMIRATES
Muscat
OMAN
YEMEN
Sanaa

BANGLADESH
Dhaka
Hanoi

Red Sea
Gulf of Aden

Arabian Sea

INDIA
Calcutta (Kolkata)

MYANMAR (BURMA)
LAOS

Philippine Sea

South China Sea

Manila

AFRICA

SOCOTRA (Yemen)
Mumbai (Bombay)

Chennai (Madras)

Ganges R.

Yangon
THAILAND
Bangkok
Phnom Penh
VIETNAM
Ho Chi Minh City
CAMBODIA

PHILIPPINES

Bay of Bengal

Andaman Sea

BRUNEI
Bandar Seri Begawan

SRI LANKA
Colombo
Male
MALDIVES

Kuala Lumpur
MALAYSIA
Singapore
SINGAPORE
Borneo

New Guinea

INDONESIA
Sumatra
Sulawesi
Dili
EAST TIMOR
Timor

EQUATOR

INDIAN OCEAN

Jakarta
Java
Surabaya

AUSTRALIA

KEY
- - - - Disputed border
———— National border
✪ Capital city
○ Other city

TROPIC OF CANCER

N
W E
S

1,000 mi
1,000 km

Lambert Azimuthal
Equal-Area Projection

160° W
170° W
180°
170° E
160° E
150° E
140° E
130° E

60° N
50° N
40° N
30° N
20° N
10° N
10° S
20° S

50° E
60° E
70° E
80° E
90° E
100° E
110° E
120° E

Asia: Physical

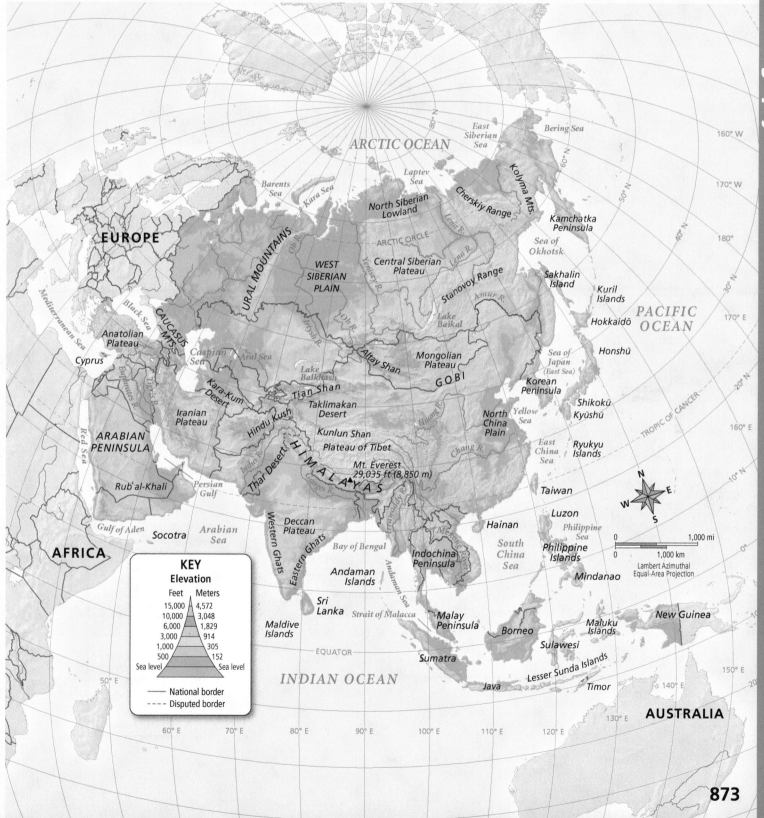

ARCTIC OCEAN

East Siberian Sea

Bering Sea

160° W

170° W

180°

50° N

60° N

40° N

30° N

170° E

160° E

Barents Sea

Kara Sea

Laptev Sea

Cherskiy Range

Kolyma Mts.

North Siberian Lowland

Lena R.

Kamchatka Peninsula

Sea of Okhotsk

ARCTIC CIRCLE

Lena R.

WEST SIBERIAN PLAIN

Ob R.

Central Siberian Plateau

Yenisey R.

Stanovoy Range

Sakhalin Island

Kuril Islands

PACIFIC OCEAN

EUROPE

URAL MOUNTAINS

Ob R.

Amur R.

Hokkaidō

Irtysh R.

Lake Baikal

Honshū

Mediterranean Sea

Black Sea

CAUCASUS MTS.

Anatolian Plateau

Cyprus

Caspian Sea

Aral Sea

Lake Balkhash

Altay Shan

Mongolian Plateau

GOBI

Sea of Japan (East Sea)

Korean Peninsula

Shikokū

Kyūshū

TROPIC OF CANCER

Euphrates R.

Tigris R.

Kara-Kum Desert

Tian Shan

Taklimakan Desert

North China Plain

Yellow Sea

Ryukyu Islands

Iranian Plateau

Hindu Kush

Kunlun Shan

Huang R.

ARABIAN PENINSULA

Red Sea

Indus R.

Thar Desert

H I M A L A Y A S

Plateau of Tibet

Mt. Everest 29,035 ft (8,850 m)

Chang R.

East China Sea

20° N

10° N

0°

Rub' al-Khali

Persian Gulf

Ganges R.

Taiwan

Gulf of Aden

Socotra

Arabian Sea

Deccan Plateau

Western Ghats

Eastern Ghats

Bay of Bengal

Irrawaddy R.

Luzon

Hainan

Philippine Sea

South China Sea

AFRICA

Andaman Islands

Indochina Peninsula

Andaman Sea

Philippine Islands

Mindanao

N
E
S
W

Sri Lanka

Strait of Malacca

Malay Peninsula

Borneo

Maluku Islands

New Guinea

Maldive Islands

Sumatra

Sulawesi

Lesser Sunda Islands

Mekong R.

EQUATOR

Java

Timor

140° E

150° E

INDIAN OCEAN

AUSTRALIA

130° E

50° E

60° E

70° E

80° E

90° E

100° E

110° E

120° E

0   1,000 mi

0   1,000 km

Lambert Azimuthal Equal-Area Projection

KEY
Elevation

Feet	Meters
15,000	4,572
10,000	3,048
6,000	1,829
3,000	914
1,000	305
500	152
Sea level	Sea level

—— National border

- - - Disputed border

Australia and the Pacific

Philippine Sea

NORTHERN MARIANA ISLANDS (U.S.)

GUAM (U.S.)

MARSHALL ISLANDS

⊛ Melekeok   Caroline Islands   ⊛ Palikir   ⊛ Majuro

PALAU   FEDERATED STATES OF MICRONESIA   ⊛ Tarawa

EQUATOR

NAURU ⊛ Yaren   K I R I B A T I

PAPUA NEW GUINEA   SOLOMON ISLANDS   TUVALU   TOKELAU (New Zealand)

Timor Sea   Arafura Sea   ⊛ Port Moresby   ⊛ Honiara   ⊛ Funafuti

Cape York Peninsula   Coral Sea   SAMOA

Kimberley Plateau   VANUATU   FIJI   Apia ⊛   AMERICAN SAMOA (U.S.)

Great Sandy Desert   Great Barrier Reef   ⊛ Port-Vila   ⊛ Suva   NIUE (New Zealand)

AUSTRALIA   NEW CALEDONIA (France)   ⊛ Nuku'alofa   COOK ISLANDS (New Zealand)

TROPIC OF CAPRICORN   TONGA

Gibson Desert   Simpson Desert   Great Artesian Basin   PACIFIC OCEAN

Great Victoria Desert

Nullarbor Plain   Darling River

Darling Range   Great Australian Bight   ⊛ Brisbane

Perth ○   Adelaide ○   ○ Sydney   Auckland ○   North Island

Murray River   ⊛ Canberra   Tasman Sea

○ Melbourne   Cook Strait

Bass Strait   NEW ZEALAND   ⊛ Wellington

Tasmania   South Island   ○ Christchurch

INDIAN OCEAN   ○ Hobart   ○ Dunedin

KEY
Elevation

Feet	Meters
6,000	1,829
3,000	914
1,000	305
500	152
Sea level	Sea level

— National border
⊛ Capital city
○ Other city

0 ——— 600 mi
0 ——— 600 km

Mercator Projection

The Arctic

150° E
120° E
ARCTIC CIRCLE
90° E
60° E
30° E

ASIA

EUROPE

Cherskiy Range

Lena R.

Kara Sea

Kola Peninsula

Laptev Sea

Severnaya Zemlya

Novaya Zemlya

Barents Sea

Baltic Sea

Kolyma Range

New Siberian Islands

Franz Josef Land

Scandinavian Peninsula

PACIFIC OCEAN

East Siberian Sea

North Cape

Svalbard

Norwegian Sea

180°

Wrangel Island

Chukchi Peninsula

Chukchi Sea

ARCTIC OCEAN

North Pole

Greenland Sea

70° N

Iceland

Bering Sea

Aleutian Islands

St. Lawrence Island

Bering Strait

North Magnetic Pole

Denmark Strait

Nunivak Island

Beaufort Sea

Ellesmere Island

Greenland

Alaska Peninsula

Brooks Range

Yukon R.

Banks Island

Queen Elizabeth Islands

Baffin Bay

30° W

Kodiak Island

Alaska Range

ROCKY MOUNTAINS

Mackenzie R.

Victoria Island

Baffin Island

Davis Strait

60° N

Gulf of Alaska

NORTH AMERICA

150° W

120° W

90° W

60° W

KEY
Elevation

Feet	Meters
15,000	4,572
10,000	3,048
6,000	1,829
3,000	914
1,000	305
500	152
Sea level	Sea level

Ice pack
National border

0   600 mi
0   600 km

Lambert Azimuthal Equal-Area Projection

Antarctica

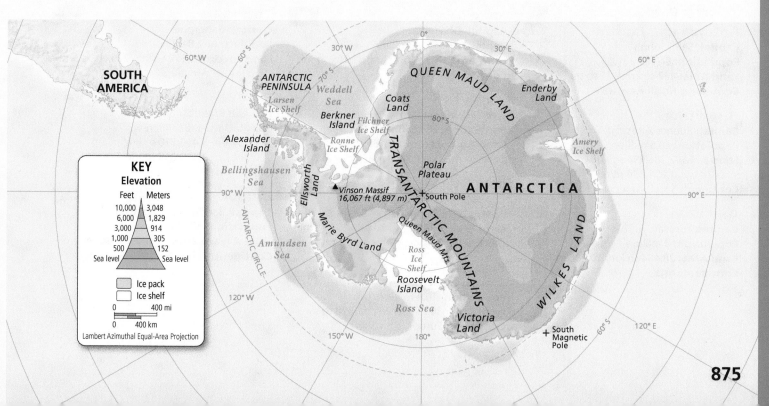

60° W
30° W
0°
30° E
60° E

SOUTH AMERICA

60° S

70° S

ANTARCTIC PENINSULA

Weddell Sea

QUEEN MAUD LAND

Enderby Land

Larsen Ice Shelf

Coats Land

Berkner Island

Filchner Ice Shelf

80° S

Amery Ice Shelf

Alexander Island

Ronne Ice Shelf

TRANSANTARCTIC MOUNTAINS

Bellingshausen Sea

Ellsworth Land

Polar Plateau

ANTARCTICA

90° E

90° W

▲ Vinson Massif
16,067 ft (4,897 m)

South Pole

ANTARCTIC CIRCLE

Amundsen Sea

Marie Byrd Land

Queen Maud Mts.

WILKES LAND

120° W

Ross Ice Shelf

Roosevelt Island

Ross Sea

Victoria Land

South Magnetic Pole

60° S

150° W

180°

120° E

KEY
Elevation

Feet	Meters
10,000	3,048
6,000	1,829
3,000	914
1,000	305
500	152
Sea level	Sea level

Ice pack
Ice shelf

0   400 mi
0   400 km

Lambert Azimuthal Equal-Area Projection

Country Databank

Afghanistan

Capital: Kabul
Population: 32.7 million
Land Area: 647,500 sq km; 250,000 sq mi
Continent: Asia

Albania

Capital: Tirana
Population: 3.6 million
Land Area: 27,398 sq km; 10,578 sq mi
Continent: Europe

Algeria

Capital: Algiers
Population: 33.8 million
Land Area: 2,381,740 sq km;
    919,590 sq mi
Continent: Africa

Andorra

Capital: Andorra la Vella
Population: 82,627
Land Area: 468 sq km; 181 sq mi
Continent: Europe

Angola

Capital: Luanda
Population: 12.5 million
Land Area: 1,246,700 sq km;
    481, 551 sq mi
Continent: Africa

Antigua and Barbuda

Capital: Saint John's
Population: 84,522
Land Area: 442 sq km; 171 sq mi
Continent: North America

Argentina

Capital: Buenos Aires
Population: 40.5 million
Land Area: 2,736,690 sq km;
    1,056,636 sq mi
Continent: South America

Armenia

Capital: Yerevan
Population: 3 million
Land Area: 28,454 sq km; 10,986 sq mi
Continent: Asia

Australia
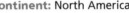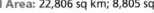
Capital: Canberra
Population: 21 million
Land Area: 7,617,930 sq km;
    2,941,283 sq mi
Continent: Australia and Oceania

Austria
Capital: Vienna
Population: 8.2 million
Land Area: 82,444 sq km; 31,832 sq mi
Continent: Europe

Azerbaijan
Capital: Baku
Population: 8.2 million
Land Area: 86,100 sq km; 33,243 sq mi
Continent: Asia

Bahamas
Capital: Nassau
Population: 307,541
Land Area: 10,070 sq km; 3,888 sq mi
Continent: North America

Bahrain
Capital: Manama
Population: 718,306
Land Area: 665 sq km; 257 sq mi
Continent: Asia

Bangladesh
Capital: Dhaka
Population: 153.5 million
Land Area: 133,910 sq km; 51,705 sq mi
Continent: Asia

Barbados
Capital: Bridgetown
Population: 281,968
Land Area: 431 sq km; 166 sq mi
Continent: North America

Belarus
Capital: Minsk
Population: 9.7 million
Land Area: 207,600 sq km; 80,154 sq mi
Continent: Europe

Belgium
Capital: Brussels
Population: 10.4 million
Land Area: 30,278 sq km; 11,690 sq mi
Continent: Europe

Belize

Capital: Belmopan
Population: 301,270
Land Area: 22,806 sq km; 8,805 sq mi
Continent: North America

Benin

Capital: Porto-Novo
Population: 8.5 million
Land Area: 110,620 sq km; 42,710 sq mi
Continent: Africa

Bhutan

Capital: Thimphu
Population: 682,321
Land Area: 47,000 sq km; 18,147 sq mi
Continent: Asia

Bolivia

Capitals: La Paz and Sucre
Population: 9.2 million
Land Area: 1,084,390 sq km;
    418,683 sq mi
Continent: South America

Bosnia and Herzegovina

Capital: Sarajevo
Population: 4.6 million
Land Area: 51,197 sq km; 19,767 sq mi
Continent: Europe

Botswana

Capital: Gaborone
Population: 1.8 million
Land Area: 585,370 sq km; 226,011 sq mi
Continent: Africa

Brazil

Capital: Brasília
Population: 196 million
Land Area: 8,456,510 sq km;
    3,265,059 sq mi
Continent: South America

Brunei

Capital: Bandar Seri Begawan
Population: 381,371
Land Area: 5,270 sq km; 2,035 sq mi
Continent: Asia

Bulgaria
Capital: Sofía
Population: 7.3 million
Land Area: 110,550 sq km; 42,683 sq mi
Continent: Europe

Burkina Faso

Capital: Ouagadougou
Population: 15.3 million
Land Area: 273,800 sq km; 105,714 sq mi
Continent: Africa

Burundi
Capital: Bujumbura
Population: 8.7 million
Land Area: 25,650 sq km; 9,903 sq mi
Continent: Africa

Cambodia
Capital: Phnom Penh
Population: 14.2 million
Land Area: 176,520 sq km; 68,154 sq mi
Continent: Asia

Cameroon
Capital: Yaoundé
Population: 18.5 million
Land Area: 469,440 sq km; 181,251 sq mi
Continent: Africa

Canada
Capital: Ottawa
Population: 33.2 million
Land Area: 9,093,507 sq km;
3,511,009 sq mi
Continent: North America

Cape Verde
Capital: Praia
Population: 426,998
Land Area: 4,033 sq km; 1,557 sq mi
Continent: Africa

Central African Republic
Capital: Bangui
Population: 4.4 million
Land Area: 622,984 sq km; 240,534 sq mi
Continent: Africa

Chad
Capital: N'Djamena
Population: 10.1 million
Land Area: 1,259,200 sq km;
486,177 sq mi
Continent: Africa

Chile
Capital: Santiago
Population: 16.5 million
Land Area: 748,800 sq km; 289,112 sq mi
Continent: South America

China
Capital: Beijing
Population: 1.33 billion
Land Area: 9,326,410 sq km;
3,600,927 sq mi
Continent: Asia

Colombia
Capital: Bogotá
Population: 45 million
Land Area: 1,038,700 sq km;
401,042 sq mi
Continent: South America

Comoros
Capital: Moroni
Population: 731,775
Land Area: 2,170 sq km; 838 sq mi
Continent: Africa

Congo, Democratic Republic of the
Capital: Kinshasa
Population: 66.5 million
Land Area: 2,267,600 sq km;
875,520 sq mi
Continent: Africa

Congo, Republic of the
Capital: Brazzaville
Population: 3.9 million
Land Area: 341,500 sq km; 131,853 sq mi
Continent: Africa

Costa Rica
Capital: San José
Population: 4.2 million
Land Area: 50,660 sq km; 19,560 sq mi
Continent: North America

Croatia

Capital: Zagreb
Population: 4.5 million
Land Area: 56,414 km; 21,781 sq mi
Continent: Europe

Cuba

Capital: Havana
Population: 11.4 million
Land Area: 110,860 sq km; 42,803 sq mi
Continent: North America

Cyprus

Capital: Nicosia
Population: 792,604
Land Area: 9,240 sq km; 3,568 sq mi
Continent: Europe

Czech Republic

Capital: Prague
Population: 10.2 million
Land Area: 77,276 sq km; 29,836 sq mi
Continent: Europe

Denmark

Capital: Copenhagen
Population: 5.5 million
Land Area: 42,394 sq km; 16,368 sq mi
Continent: Europe

Djibouti

Capital: Djibouti
Population: 506,221
Land Area: 22,980 sq km; 8,873 sq mi
Continent: Africa

Dominica

Capital: Roseau
Population: 72,514
Land Area: 754 sq km; 291 sq mi
Continent: North America

Dominican Republic

Capital: Santo Domingo
Population: 9.5 million
Land Area: 48,380 sq km; 18,679 sq mi
Continent: North America

Ecuador

Capital: Quito
Population: 13.9 million
Land Area: 276,840 sq km; 106,888 sq mi
Continent: South America

Country Databank (continued)

Egypt
Capital: Cairo
Population: 81.7 million
Land Area: 995,450 sq km; 384,343 sq mi
Continent: Africa

El Salvador
Capital: San Salvador
Population: 7.1 million
Land Area: 20,720 sq km; 8,000 sq mi
Continent: North America

Equatorial Guinea
Capital: Malabo
Population: 616,459
Land Area: 28,051 sq km; 10,831 sq mi
Continent: Africa

Eritrea
Capital: Asmara
Population: 5.5 million
Land Area: 121,320 sq km; 46,842 sq mi
Continent: Africa

Estonia
Capital: Tallinn
Population: 1.3 million
Land Area: 43,211 sq km; 16,684 sq mi
Continent: Europe

Ethiopia
Capital: Addis Ababa
Population: 82.5 million
Land Area: 1,119,683 sq km;
           432,310 sq mi
Continent: Africa

Fiji
Capital: Suva
Population: 931,741
Land Area: 18,270 sq km; 7,054 sq mi
Continent: Australia and Oceania

Finland
Capital: Helsinki
Population: 5.2 million
Land Area: 304,473 sq km; 117,557 sq mi
Continent: Europe

France
Capital: Paris
Population: 64 million
Land Area: 545,630 sq km; 310,668 sq mi
Continent: Europe

Gabon
Capital: Libreville
Population: 1.5 million
Land Area: 257,667 sq km; 99,489 sq mi
Continent: Africa

The Gambia
Capital: Banjul
Population: 1.7 million
Land Area: 10,000 sq km; 3,861 sq mi
Continent: Africa

Georgia
Capital: T'bilisi
Population: 4.6 million
Land Area: 69,700 sq km; 26,911 sq mi
Continent: Asia

Germany
Capital: Berlin
Population: 82.4 million
Land Area: 349,223 sq km; 134,835 sq mi
Continent: Europe

Ghana
Capital: Accra
Population: 23.4 million
Land Area: 230,940 sq km; 89,166 sq mi
Continent: Africa

Greece
Capital: Athens
Population: 10.7 million
Land Area: 130,800 sq km; 50,502 sq mi
Continent: Europe

Grenada
Capital: Saint George's
Population: 90,343
Land Area: 344 sq km; 133 sq mi
Continent: North America

Guatemala
Capital: Guatemala City
Population: 13 million
Land Area: 108,430 sq km; 41,865 sq mi
Continent: North America

Guinea
Capital: Conakry
Population: 9.8 million
Land Area: 245,857 sq km; 94,925 sq mi
Continent: Africa

Guinea-Bissau
Capital: Bissau
Population: 1.5 million
Land Area: 28,000 sq km; 10,811 sq mi
Continent: Africa

Guyana
Capital: Georgetown
Population: 770,794
Land Area: 196,850 sq km; 76,004 sq mi
Continent: South America

Haiti
Capital: Port-au-Prince
Population: 8.9 million
Land Area: 27,560 sq km; 10,641 sq mi
Continent: North America

Holy See (Vatican City)
Capital: Vatican City
Population: 824
Land Area: 0.44 sq km; 0.17 sq mi
Continent: Europe

Honduras
Capital: Tegucigalpa
Population: 7.6 million
Land Area: 111,890 sq km; 43,201 sq mi
Continent: North America

Hungary
Capital: Budapest
Population: 9.9 million
Land Area: 92,340 sq km; 35,652 sq mi
Continent: Europe

Iceland
Capital: Reykjavík
Population: 304,367
Land Area: 100,250 sq km; 38,707 sq mi
Continent: Europe

India
Capital: New Delhi
Population: 1.15 billion
Land Area: 2,973,190 sq km;
           1,147,949 sq mi
Continent: Asia

Indonesia
Capital: Jakarta
Population: 237.5 million
Land Area: 1,826,440 sq km;
           705,188 sq mi
Continent: Asia

Iran
Capital: Tehran
Population: 65.9 million
Land Area: 1,636,000 sq km;
631,660 sq mi
Continent: Asia

Iraq
Capital: Baghdad
Population: 28.2 million
Land Area: 432,162 sq km; 166,858 sq mi
Continent: Asia

Ireland
Capital: Dublin
Population: 4.2 million
Land Area: 68,890 sq km; 26,598 sq mi
Continent: Europe

Israel
Capital: Jerusalem
Population: 7.1 million
Land Area: 20,330 sq km; 7,849 sq mi
Continent: Asia

Italy
Capital: Rome
Population: 58.2 million
Land Area: 294,020 sq km; 113,521 sq mi
Continent: Europe

Ivory Coast
Capital: Yamoussoukro
Population: 20.2 million
Land Area: 318,000 sq km; 122,780 sq mi
Continent: Africa

Jamaica
Capital: Kingston
Population: 2.8 million
Land Area: 10,831 sq km; 4,182 sq mi
Continent: North America

Japan
Capital: Tokyo
Population: 127.3 million
Land Area: 374,744 sq km; 144,689 sq mi
Continent: Asia

Jordan
Capital: Amman
Population: 6.2 million
Land Area: 91,971 sq km; 35,510 sq mi
Continent: Asia

Kazakhstan
Capital: Astana
Population: 15.3 million
Land Area: 2,669,800 sq km;
1,030,810 sq mi
Continent: Asia

Kenya
Capital: Nairobi
Population: 38 million
Land Area: 569,250 sq km; 219,787 sq mi
Continent: Africa

Kiribati
Capital: Bairiki (Tarawa Atoll)
Population: 110,356
Land Area: 811 sq km; 313 sq mi
Continent: Australia and Oceania

Korea, North
Capital: Pyongyang
Population: 23.5 million
Land Area: 120,410 sq km; 46,490 sq mi
Continent: Asia

Korea, South
Capital: Seoul
Population: 48.4 million
Land Area: 98,190 sq km; 37,911 sq mi
Continent: Asia

Kosovo
Capital: Pristina
Population: 2.1 million
Land Area: 10,887 sq km; 4,203 sq mi
Continent: Europe

Kuwait
Capital: Kuwait City
Population: 2.6 million
Land Area: 17,820 sq km; 6,880 sq mi
Continent: Asia

Kyrgyzstan
Capital: Bishkek
Population: 5.4 million
Land Area: 191,300 sq km; 73,861sq mi
Continent: Asia

Laos
Capital: Vientiane
Population: 6.7 million
Land Area: 230,800 sq km; 89,112 sq mi
Continent: Asia

Latvia
Capital: Riga
Population: 2.3 million
Land Area: 63,589 sq km; 24,552 sq mi
Continent: Europe

Lebanon
Capital: Beirut
Population: 4 million
Land Area: 10,230 sq km; 3,950 sq mi
Continent: Asia

Lesotho
Capital: Maseru
Population: 2.1 million
Land Area: 30,355 sq km; 11,720 sq mi
Continent: Africa

Liberia
Capital: Monrovia
Population: 3.3 million
Land Area: 96,320 sq km; 37,189 sq mi
Continent: Africa

Libya
Capital: Tripoli
Population: 6.2 million
Land Area: 1,759,540 sq km;
679,358 sq mi
Continent: Africa

Liechtenstein
Capital: Vaduz
Population: 34,498
Land Area: 160 sq km; 62 sq mi
Continent: Europe

Lithuania
Capital: Vilnius
Population: 3.6 million
Land Area: 65,300 sq km; 25,212 sq mi
Continent: Europe

Luxembourg
Capital: Luxembourg
Population: 486,006
Land Area: 2,586 sq km; 998 sq mi
Continent: Europe

Macedonia
Capital: Skopje
Population: 2.1 million
Land Area: 24,856 sq km; 9,597 sq mi
Continent: Europe

Country Databank (continued)

Madagascar
Capital: Antananarivo
Population: 20 million
Land Area: 581,540 sq km; 224,533 sq mi
Continent: Africa

Malawi

Capital: Lilongwe
Population: 13.9 million
Land Area: 94,080 sq km; 36,324 sq mi
Continent: Africa

Malaysia
Capital: Kuala Lumpur
Population: 25.3 million
Land Area: 328,550 sq km; 126,853 sq mi
Continent: Asia

Maldives
Capital: Malé
Population: 385,925
Land Area: 300 sq km; 116 sq mi
Continent: Asia

Mali
Capital: Bamako
Population: 12.3 million
Land Area: 1,220,000 sq km;
        471,042 sq mi
Continent: Africa

Malta
Capital: Valletta
Population: 403,532
Land Area: 316 sq km; 122 sq mi
Continent: Europe

Marshall Islands
Capital: Majuro
Population: 63,174
Land Area: 181.3 sq km; 70 sq mi
Continent: Australia and Oceania

Mauritania
Capital: Nouakchott
Population: 3.4 million
Land Area: 1,030,400 sq km;
        397,837 sq mi
Continent: Africa

Mauritius
Capital: Port Louis
Population: 1.3 million
Land Area: 2,030 sq km; 784 sq mi
Continent: Africa

Mexico
Capital: Mexico City
Population: 110 million
Land Area: 1,923,040 sq km;
        742,486 sq mi
Continent: North America

Micronesia, Federated States of
Capital: Palikir (Pohnpei Island)
Population: 107,665
Land Area: 702 sq km; 271 sq mi
Continent: Australia and Oceania

Moldova
Capital: Chisinau
Population: 4.3 million
Land Area: 33,371 sq km; 12,885 sq mi
Continent: Europe

Monaco
Capital: Monaco
Population: 32,796
Land Area: 1.95 sq km; 0.75 sq mi
Continent: Europe

Mongolia
Capital: Ulaanbaatar
Population: 3.0 million
Land Area: 1,554,731 sq km;
        600,283 sq mi
Continent: Asia

Montenegro
Capital: Podgorica
Population: 678,177
Land Area: 13,812 sq km; 5,333 sq mi
Continent: Europe

Morocco
Capital: Rabat
Population: 34.3 million
Land Area: 446,300 sq km; 172,316 sq mi
Continent: Africa

Mozambique
Capital: Maputo
Population: 21.3 million
Land Area: 784,090 sq km; 302,737 sq mi
Continent: Africa

Myanmar (Burma)
Capital: Yangon (Rangoon)
Population: 47.8 million
Land Area: 657,740 sq km; 253,953 sq mi
Continent: Asia

Namibia

Capital: Windhoek
Population: 2.1 million
Land Area: 825,418 sq km; 318,694 sq mi
Continent: Africa

Nauru

Capital: Yaren District
Population: 13,770
Land Area: 21 sq km; 8 sq mi
Continent: Australia and Oceania

Nepal

Capital: Kathmandu
Population: 29.5 million
Land Area: 143,181 sq km; 55,282 sq mi
Continent: Asia

Netherlands

Capital: Amsterdam
Population: 16.7 million
Land Area: 33,883 sq km; 13,082 sq mi
Continent: Europe

New Zealand

Capital: Wellington
Population: 4.2 million
Land Area: 268,021 sq km; 103,483 sq mi
Continent: Australia and Oceania

Nicaragua

Capital: Managua
Population: 5.8 million
Land Area: 120,254 sq km; 46,430 sq mi
Continent: North America

Niger
Capital: Niamey
Population: 13.3 million
Land Area: 1,226,700 sq km;
        489,073 sq mi
Continent: Africa

Nigeria
Capital: Abuja
Population: 146.3 million
Land Area: 910,768 sq km; 351,648 sq mi
Continent: Africa

Norway

Capital: Oslo
Population: 4.6 million
Land Area: 307,442 sq km; 118,704 sq mi
Continent: Europe

Oman

Capital: Muscat
Population: 3.3 million
Land Area: 212,460 sq km; 82,030 sq mi
Continent: Asia

Pakistan
Capital: Islamabad
Population: 172.8 million
Land Area: 778,720 sq km; 300,664 sq mi
Continent: Asia

Palau
Capital: Koror
Population: 21,093
Land Area: 458 sq km; 177 sq mi
Continent: Australia and Oceania

Panama
Capital: Panama City
Population: 3.3 million
Land Area: 75,990 sq km; 29,340 sq mi
Continent: North America

Papua New Guinea
Capital: Port Moresby
Population: 5.9 million
Land Area: 452,860 sq km; 174,849 sq mi
Continent: Australia and Oceania

Paraguay
Capital: Asunción
Population: 6.8 million
Land Area: 397,300 sq km; 153,398 sq mi
Continent: South America

Peru
Capital: Lima
Population: 29.2 million
Land Area: 1,280,000 sq km;
            494,208 sq mi
Continent: South America

Philippines
Capital: Manila
Population: 96.1 million
Land Area: 298,170 sq km; 115,123 sq mi
Continent: Asia

Poland
Capital: Warsaw
Population: 38.5 million
Land Area: 304,459 sq km; 117,552 sq mi
Continent: Europe

Portugal
Capital: Lisbon
Population: 10.7 million
Land Area: 91,951 sq km; 35,502 sq mi
Continent: Europe

Qatar

Capital: Doha
Population: 824,789
Land Area: 11,437 sq km; 4,416 sq mi
Continent: Asia

Romania
Capital: Bucharest
Population: 22.3 million
Land Area: 230,340 sq km; 88,934 sq mi
Continent: Europe

Russia
Capital: Moscow
Population: 140.7 million
Land Area: 16,995,800 sq km;
            6,592,100 sq mi
Continent: Europe and Asia

Rwanda

Capital: Kigali
Population: 10.2 million
Land Area: 24,948 sq km; 9,632 sq mi
Continent: Africa

Saint Kitts and Nevis

Capital: Basseterre
Population: 39,817
Land Area: 261 sq km; 101 sq mi
Continent: North America

Saint Lucia
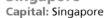
Capital: Castries
Population: 159,585
Land Area: 606 sq km; 234 sq mi
Continent: North America

Saint Vincent and the Grenadines

Capital: Kingstown
Population: 118,432
Land Area: 389 sq km; 150 sq mi
Continent: North America

Samoa
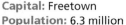
Capital: Apia
Population: 217,083
Land Area: 2,934 sq km; 1,133 sq mi
Continent: Australia and Oceania

San Marino
Capital: San Marino
Population: 29,973
Land Area: 61 sq km; 24 sq mi
Continent: Europe

São Tomé and Príncipe

Capital: São Tomé
Population: 206,178
Land Area: 1,001 sq km; 386 sq mi
Continent: Africa

Saudi Arabia
Capital: Riyadh and Jiddah
Population: 28.2 million
Land Area: 2,149,690 sq km;
            829,997 sq mi
Continent: Asia

Senegal
Capital: Dakar
Population: 12.9 million
Land Area: 192,000 sq km; 74,131 sq mi
Continent: Africa

Serbia

Capital: Belgrade
Population: 10.2 million
Land Area: 77,474 sq km; 29,913 sq mi
Continent: Europe

Seychelles
Capital: Victoria
Population: 82,247
Land Area: 455 sq km; 176 sq mi
Continent: Africa

Sierra Leone
Capital: Freetown
Population: 6.3 million
Land Area: 71,620 sq km; 27,652 sq mi
Continent: Africa

Singapore
Capital: Singapore
Population: 4.6 million
Land Area: 683 sq km; 264 sq mi
Continent: Asia

Slovakia

Capital: Bratislava
Population: 5.5 million
Land Area: 48,800 sq km; 18,842 sq mi
Continent: Europe

Country Databank (continued)

Slovenia
Capital: Ljubljana
Population: 2 million
Land Area: 20,151 sq km; 7,780 sq mi
Continent: Europe

Solomon Islands
Capital: Honiara
Population: 581,318
Land Area: 27,540 sq km; 10,633 sq mi
Continent: Australia and Oceania

Somalia
Capital: Mogadishu
Population: 9.6 million
Land Area: 627,337 sq km; 242,215 sq mi
Continent: Africa

South Africa
Capitals: Cape Town, Pretoria,
and Bloemfontein
Population: 48.8 million
Land Area: 1,219,912 sq km;
471,008 sq mi
Continent: Africa

Spain
Capital: Madrid
Population: 40.5 million
Land Area: 499,542 sq km; 192,873 sq mi
Continent: Europe

Sri Lanka
Capital: Colombo
Population: 21.1 million
Land Area: 64,740 sq km; 24,996 sq mi
Continent: Asia

Sudan
Capital: Khartoum
Population: 40.2 million
Land Area: 2,376,000 sq km;
917,374 sq mi
Continent: Africa

Suriname
Capital: Paramaribo
Population: 475,996
Land Area: 161,470 sq km; 62,344 sq mi
Continent: South America

Swaziland
Capital: Mbabane
Population: 1.1 million
Land Area: 17,203 sq km; 6,642 sq mi
Continent: Africa

Sweden
Capital: Stockholm
Population: 9 million
Land Area: 410,934 sq km; 158,662 sq mi
Continent: Europe

Switzerland
Capital: Bern
Population: 7.6 million
Land Area: 39,770 sq km; 15,355 sq mi
Continent: Europe

Syria
Capital: Damascus
Population: 19.8 million
Land Area: 184,050 sq km; 71,062 sq mi
Continent: Asia

Taiwan
Capital: Taipei
Population: 22.9 million
Land Area: 32,260 sq km; 12,456 sq mi
Continent: Asia

Tajikistan
Capital: Dushanbe
Population: 7.2 million
Land Area: 142,700 sq km; 55,096 sq mi
Continent: Asia

Tanzania
Capitals: Dar es Salaam and Dodoma
Population: 40.2 million
Land Area: 886,037 sq km; 342,099
Continent: Africa

Thailand
Capital: Bangkok
Population: 65.5 million
Land Area: 511,770 sq km; 197,564 sq mi
Continent: Asia

Timor-Leste
Capital: Dili
Population: 1.1 million
Land Area: 15,007 sq km; 5,794 sq mi
Continent: Asia

Togo
Capital: Lomé
Population: 5.9 million
Land Area: 54,385 sq km; 20,998 sq mi
Continent: Africa

Tonga
Capital: Nuku'alofa
Population: 119,009
Land Area: 718 sq km; 277 sq mi
Continent: Australia and Oceania

Trinidad and Tobago
Capital: Port-of-Spain
Population: 1.2 million
Land Area: 5,128 sq km; 1,980 sq mi
Continent: North America

Tunisia
Capital: Tunis
Population: 10.4 million
Land Area: 155,360 sq km; 59,984 sq mi
Continent: Africa

Turkey
Capital: Ankara
Population: 71.9 million
Land Area: 770,760 sq km; 297,590 sq mi
Continent: Asia

Turkmenistan
Capital: Ashgabat
Population: 5.2 million
Land Area: 488,100 sq km; 188,455 sq mi
Continent: Asia

Tuvalu
Capital: Funafuti
Population: 12,177
Land Area: 26 sq km; 10 sq mi
Continent: Australia and Oceania

Uganda
Capital: Kampala
Population: 31.4 million
Land Area: 199,710 sq km; 77,108 sq mi
Continent: Africa

Ukraine
Capital: Kyiv (Kiev)
Population: 46 million
Land Area: 603,700 sq km; 233,090 sq mi
Continent: Europe

United Arab Emirates
Capital: Abu Dhabi
Population: 4.6 million
Land Area: 83,600 sq km; 32,278 sq mi
Continent: Asia

United Kingdom

Capital: London
Population: 60.9 million
Land Area: 241,590 sq km; 93,278 sq mi
Continent: Europe

United States
Capital: Washington, D.C.
Population: 303.8 million
Land Area: 9,161,923 sq km;
              3,537,424 sq mi
Continent: North America

Uruguay
Capital: Montevideo
Population: 3.5 million
Land Area: 173,620 sq km; 67,100 sq mi
Continent: South America

Uzbekistan
Capital: Tashkent
Population: 27.3 million
Land Area: 425,400 sq km; 164,247 sq mi
Continent: Asia

Vanuatu
Capital: Port-Vila
Population: 215,446
Land Area: 12,200 sq km; 4,710 sq mi
Continent: Australia and Oceania

Venezuela
Capital: Caracas
Population: 26.4 million
Land Area: 882,050 sq km; 340,560 sq mi
Continent: South America

Vietnam
Capital: Hanoi
Population: 86.1 million
Land Area: 325,360 sq km; 125,622 sq mi
Continent: Asia

Yemen
Capital: Sanaa
Population: 23 million
Land Area: 527,970 sq km; 203,849 sq mi
Continent: Asia

Zambia

Capital: Lusaka
Population: 11.7 million
Land Area: 740,724 sq km; 285,994 sq mi
Continent: Africa

Zimbabwe
Capital: Harare
Population: 11.4 million
Land Area: 386,670 sq km; 149,293 sq mi
Continent: Africa

SOURCE: *CIA World Factbook Online, 2009*

Landforms and Water Features

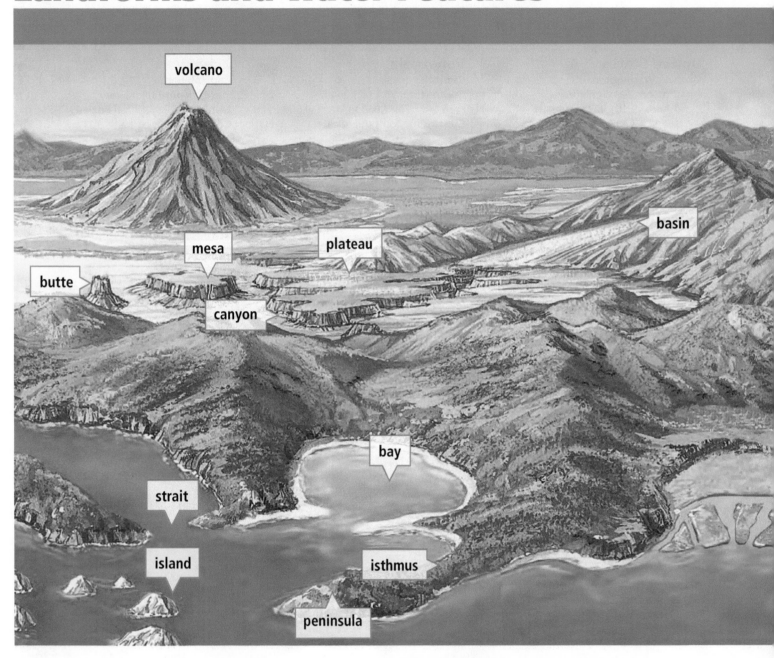

volcano

basin

mesa

plateau

butte

canyon

bay

strait

island

isthmus

peninsula

basin an area that is lower than surrounding land areas; some basins are filled with water

bay a part of a larger body of water that extends into the land

butte a small, high, flat-topped landform with cliff-like sides

canyon a deep, narrow valley with steep sides; often has a stream flowing through it

cataract a large waterfall or steep rapids

delta a plain at the mouth of a river, often triangular in shape, formed when material is deposited by flowing water

flood plain a broad plain on either side of a river, formed when sediment settles during floods

glacier a huge, slow-moving mass of snow and ice

hill an area that rises above surrounding land and has a rounded top; lower and usually less steep than a mountain

island an area of land completely surrounded by water

isthmus a narrow strip of land that connects two larger areas of land

mesa a high, flat-topped landform with cliff-like sides; larger than a butte

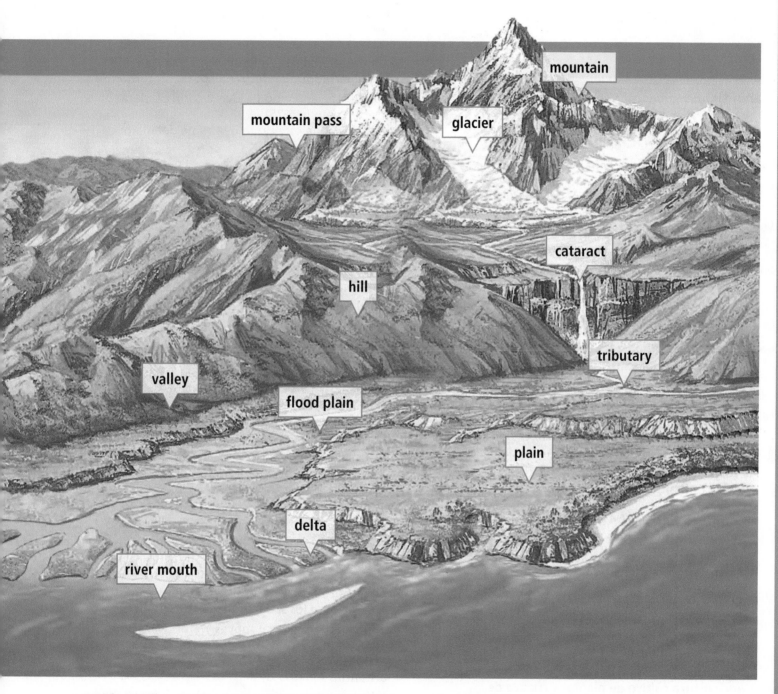

mountain

mountain pass

glacier

cataract

hill

tributary

valley

flood plain

plain

delta

river mouth

mountain a landform that rises steeply at least 2,000 feet (610 meters) above surrounding land; usually wide at the bottom and rising to a narrow peak or ridge

mountain pass a gap between mountains

peninsula an area of land almost completely surrounded by water and connected to the mainland by an isthmus

plain a large area of flat or gently rolling land

plateau a large, flat area that rises above the surrounding land; at least one side has a steep slope

river mouth the point where a river enters a lake or sea

strait a narrow stretch of water that connects two larger bodies of water

tributary a river or stream that flows into a larger river

valley a low stretch of land between mountains or hills; land that is drained by a river

volcano an opening in Earth's surface through which molten rock, ash, and gases from Earth's interior escape

Glossary

A

abolitionist someone who wanted to end slavery (p. 318)
abolicionista dícese de una persona que quiso acabar con la esclavitud

Aborigines the original inhabitants of Australia (p. 842)
aborígenes habitantes indígenas de Australia

absolute location exact position on Earth in terms of longitude and latitude (p. 6)
ubicación absoluta posición exacta en la Tierra según la longitud y la latitud

absolutism centralized and unlimited government power (p. 386)
absolutismo poder ilimitado y centralizado del gobierno

acid rain rain, snow, or mist that is acidic (p. 451)
lluvia ácida lluvia, nieve o neblina con ácidos disueltos

aerial photograph photographic image of Earth's surface taken from the air (p. 8)
fotografía aérea imagen fotográfica de la superficie de la Tierra que se tomó desde el aire

African National Congress South African organization that worked for black civil rights (p. 543)
Congreso Nacional Africano organización sudafricana que laboró por los derechos civiles de los negros

African Union organization formed in 2002 to promote unity among African states and to foster development and end poverty (p. 522)
Unión africana organización que se formó en 2002 para promover la unión entre los estado africanos, fomentar el desarrollo y acabar con la pobreza

agriculture the raising of plants and animals (p. 626)
agricultura cultivo de plantas y crianza de animales

AIDS often-deadly disease that attacks the immune system and is caused by the HIV virus (p. 548)
SIDA enfermedad causada por el virus VIH, y generalmente de carácter mortal, que ataca el sistema inmunológico

akyn traditional storyteller in Kyrgyzstan (p. 697)
akyn narrador de relatos épicos de Kirguistán

Alawite a person who follows a form of Islam similar to Shia Islam (p. 625)
alauí persona que sigue una rama del islam semejante al islam chiita

Altiplano high plateau in Peru and Bolivia (p. 283)
altiplano meseta de gran altitud en Perú y Bolivia

altitude height above sea level (pp. 35, 201)
altitud altura sobre el nivel del mar

Amazon basin all the land drained by the Amazon River (p. 309)
cuenca amazónica área de drenaje del río Amazonas

amend make changes to a constitution (p. 301)
enmendar hacer cambios a una constitución

Antarctic Treaty agreement signed by twelve countries in 1959 that preserves Antarctica for peaceful and scientific use (p. 855)
Tratado Antártico acuerdo firmado en 1959 entre doce países, que designa a la Antártida como un territorio de uso pacífico y científico

anthropology study of humankind in all aspects, especially development and culture (p. 123)
antropología estudio de todos los aspectos de la humanidad, especialmente el desarrollo y la cultura

anti-Semitism discrimination against Jews (p. 632)
antisemitismo discriminación hacia los judíos

apartheid official South African government policy of keeping white and black South Africans apart (p. 542)
apartheid política oficial del gobierno sudafricano que separa a los sudafricanos blancos y negros

aqueduct channel that moves water over a long distance (pp. 207, 351)
acueducto canal que transporta agua por largas distancias

aquifer an underground layer where water collects (p. 622)
acuífero capa subterránea donde se acumula el agua

arable land land that can be used for farming (pp. 508, 750)
tierra fértil terreno que se puede usar para cultivos

archaeology scientific study of ancient cultures through the examination of artifacts and other evidence (p. 123)
arqueología estudio científico de las culturas antiguas a través del análisis de artefactos y otros tipos de evidencia

archipelago group of islands (p. 803)
archipiélago grupo de islas

architect person who designs buildings (p. 94)
arquitecto persona que diseña edificios

architecture the design and construction of buildings (p. 94)
arquitectura diseño y construcción de edificios

arid climate very dry desert climate (p. 41)
clima árido clima desértico muy seco

Armenian Genocide the killing of Armenians in the Ottoman empire in 1915–1918 (p. 660)
genocidio armenio exterminio de armenios que se llevó a cabo desde 1915 hasta 1918 durante el Imperio Otomano

artifact object made by a human being (p. 120)
artefacto objeto hecho por un ser humano

ASEAN Association of Southeast Asian Nations, an organization working to promote growth and social progress in Southeast Asia (p. 819)
Asociación de Naciones del Sureste Asiático (ASEAN, por sus siglas en inglés) organización que promueve el crecimiento y progreso social en el sureste asiático

assimilation process by which one group takes on the cultural traits of another (p. 844)
asimilación proceso en el que un grupo adquiere los rasgos culturales de otro grupo

astronomy the study of the stars and planets (p. 207)
astronomía estudio de las estrellas y los planetas

Ataturk name taken by Mustafa Kemal, the founder of modern Turkey, meaning "Father of the Turks" (p. 660)
Ataturk nombre adoptado por Mustafá Kemal, el fundador de la Turquía moderna, que significa "padre de los turcos"

Atlantic slave trade process by which Europeans brought enslaved Africans to the Americas (p. 514)
comercio de esclavos del Atlántico proceso mediante el cual los europeos trajeron esclavos africanos a las Américas

atmosphere thick layer of gases or air (p. 23)
atmósfera capa gruesa de gases o aire

atoll a ring-shaped coral island enclosing a body of water (p. 836)
atolón isla de coral en forma de anillo que rodea una masa de agua

austerity measure government policies meant to save money (p. 269)
medidas de austeridad políticas gubernamentales con fines de ahorro

authoritarian government in which all power is held by a single person or a small group (p. 107)
autoritario gobierno en el que todo el poder yace en un individuo o grupo pequeño

autocracy a government controlled by one person who has not won a free election (p. 635)
autocracia tipo de gobierno bajo el control de una persona que no participó en elecciones libres

axis imaginary line running through Earth between the North and South Poles (p. 18)
eje línea imaginaria que atraviesa la Tierra y que corre entre los polos Norte y Sur

ayatollah title for high-ranking Shia Muslim leaders in Iran (p. 661)
ayatolá título otorgado a los líderes de alta postura dentro del clero chiita musulman en Irán

B

Berbers indigenous people of western North Africa (p. 567)
bereberes grupo indígena que habita el oeste de África del Norte

Berlin Wall a wall built by the East German government in 1961 to divide East and West Berlin; this wall came to symbolize Cold War divisions (p. 401)
Muro de Berlín muralla construida por el gobierno de la antigua República Democrática Alemana (RDA) en 1961 para dividir las partes este y oeste de Berlín; se convirtió en un símbolo de la divisiva Guerra Fría

bias unfair preference for or dislike of something (p. 121)
prejuicio preferencia injusta o disgusto por algo

biodiversity variety of different kinds of living things in a region or ecosystem (pp. 52, 229)
biodiversidad variedad de clases diferentes de seres vivos de una región o ecosistema

birth rate number of live births per 1,000 people in a year (p. 74)
tasa de natalidad número de nacimientos por cada mil habitantes durante un año

Boers Dutch, French, and other European farmers in colonial South Africa (p. 540)
bóer granjeros europeos de origen holandés y francés, entre otros, que habitaban la Sudáfrica colonial

Bollywood Indian film industry (p. 725)
Bollywood industria del cine indio

Bolsheviks Russian political group that called for worker control (p. 480)
bolcheviques grupo político ruso que defiende el control por parte del proletariado

bond certificate issued by a company or government promising to pay back borrowed money with interest (p. 69)
bono certificado emitido por una compañía o un gobierno que promete pagar el dinero prestado con intereses

boom and bust cycle period of strong economic growth followed by a period of sharp decline (p. 318)
ciclo económico período de gran crecimiento económico seguido de un fuerte declive

brain drain situation when large numbers of educated people migrate out of a country (p. 664)
fuga de cerebros situación en la que un gran número de personas con alta capacitación emigran de un país

brazilwood wood that produces a red dye (p. 317)
madera de brasil tipo de madera que produce un tinte rojo

Buddhism religion that developed out of the teachings of Siddhartha Gautama, the Buddha (p. 718)
budismo religión que se desarrolló a partir de las enseñanzas de Siddhartha Gautama, el Buda

budget plan that shows income and expenses over a period of time (p. 68)
presupuesto plan que muestra los ingresos y los costos para un período de tiempo

C

caliph Muslims' political and religious leader (p. 601)
califa líder religioso y político musulman

canopy the upper leaves of rain forest trees (p. 312)
dosel forestal hojas superiores de los árboles de la selva tropical

capital money or goods that are used to make products (pp. 455, 636)
capital dinero o bienes que se usan para crear productos

caravan group of people traveling together (p. 692)
caravana grupo de personas que viajan juntas

caravel a small, light ship developed by the Portuguese that performed well on long voyages (p. 382)
carabela nave pequeña y ligera diseñada por los portugueses, especialmente efectiva en viajes largos

cardinal directions north, east, south, and west (p. 4)
puntos cardinales norte, sur, este y oeste

carnival religious festival primarily observed by Roman Catholics (p. 238)
carnaval fiesta religiosa que observan principalmente los católicos romanos

cartography the science of making maps and globes (p. 382)
cartografía técnica de trazar mapas y globos terráqueos

cash crop crop grown mainly for export (p. 148)
cultivo comercial cultivo con fines de exportación

caste system system that divides society into groups (p. 717)
sistema de castas sistema que divide a la sociedad en grupos

Catholic Reformation changes made by the Catholic Church to keep Catholicism strong; response to the Reformation (p. 380)
Reforma Católica (o Contrarreforma) cambios que la Iglesia Católica hizo para fortalecer al catolicismo; fue una respuesta a la Reforma Protestante

caudillo chief or dictator (p. 268)
caudillo jefe o dictador

censor to suppress or delete anything considered objectionable (p. 487)
censurar ocultar o borrar cualquier cosa que se considere ofensiva

chronology list of events arranged in the order in which they occurred (p. 118)
cronología lista de sucesos organizados en el orden en que ocurrieron

citizen legal member of a country (p. 112)
ciudadano miembro legal de un país

city-state independent state consisting of a city and its surrounding territory (pp. 106, 341)
ciudad-estado estado independiente que consiste en una ciudad y el territorio aledaño

civic life activities having to do with one's society and community (p. 113)
vida cívica actividades relacionadas con nuestra sociedad o comunidad

civic participation taking part in government (p. 113)
participación cívica tomar parte en asuntos del gobierno

civil rights movement movement for African American equality (p. 151)
movimiento de los derechos civiles movimiento por la igualdad de derechos de los afroamericanos

civilization culture with a written language in which people have many different kinds of jobs (p. 598)
civilización cultura que lleva un lenguaje escrito y en la que las personas desempeñan muchos trabajos diferentes

cleric religious leader (p. 662)
clérigo líder religioso

climate average weather of a place over many years (p. 32)
clima tiempo promedio de un lugar a lo largo de muchos años

climate change long-term significant change to a region's average weather (p. 851)
cambio climático cambio significativo y de largo plazo en el tiempo promedio de una región

Cold War post–World War II period of hostility between the United States and its allies on one side and the Soviet Union and its allies on the other side (p. 400)
Guerra Fría período de hostilidad entre los EE. UU. y la Unión Soviética, más los aliados de ambos, posterior a la Segunda Guerra Mundial

collectivization shift of control to a group, or collective, from an individual or single entity (p. 481)
colectivización cambio del control a un grupo o colectivo de un individuo o entidad individual

colonialism policy by which one country seeks to rule other areas (p. 514)
colonialismo política por medio de la cual un país intenta gobernar otras áreas

colonization movement of new settlers and their culture to an area (p. 51)
colonización mudanza de pobladores nuevos y la cultura de éstos a un área

colony group of people living in a new territory with ties to a distant state (p. 235)
colonia grupo de personas que viven en un territorio nuevo que están ligados a un estado distante

command economy economy in which the central government makes all basic economic decisions (pp. 63, 758)
economía dirigida sistema económico en el que el gobierno central toma todas las decisiones económicas básicas

communism political and economic system in which government owns all property and makes all economic decisions (pp. 107, 397)
comunismo sistema político y económico en el que el Estado posee toda propiedad y toma todas las decisiones económicas

comparative advantage ability of one person or country to produce a good at a lower cost than another (p. 779)
ventaja comparativa capacidad de una persona o país para producir un bien a un costo menor que otra persona o país

compass rose diagram of a compass showing direction (p. 10)
rosa de los vientos diagrama de una brújula que indica la dirección

competition struggle among producers for consumers' money (p. 60)
competencia rivalidad entre los productores por el dinero del consumidor

compromise establishing common ideas that people agree to follow (p. 172)
acordar establecer ideas en común que las personas se comprometen a seguir

Confucianism a belief system based on the ideas of the Chinese thinker Confucius (p. 756)
confucianismo sistema de creencias basadas en la ideología del filósofo chino Confucio

Glossary (continued)

coniferous tree tree that produces cones to carry seeds (p. 42)
árbol conífero árbol que produce frutos en forma de conos que contienen las semillas

conquistador Spanish soldier-explorer (p. 208)
conquistador soldado explorador de origen español

constitution system of basic rules and principles by which a government is organized (p. 105)
constitución sistema de reglas y principios básicos que establece la organización de un gobierno

constitutional monarchy system of government in which the laws in the constitution limit the monarch's or emperor's powers (pp. 179, 422, 786)
monarquía constitucional sistema de gobierno en el que las leyes de la constitución limitan los poderes del monarca o emperador

consumer person or business that buys, or consumes, products (p. 59)
consumidor persona o negocio que compra o consume productos

Copts minority group in Egypt that practices Christianity (p. 571)
coptos grupo minoritario en Egipto que practica el cristianismo

coral reef a formation of rock-like material made up of the skeletons of tiny marine creatures (p. 835)
arrecifes de coral conjunto de material rocoso compuesto de restos de criaturas marinas pequeñas

cordillera chain of mountains (p. 258)
cordillera cadena de montañas

core sphere of very hot metal at the center of Earth (p. 22)
núcleo esfera de metal muy caliente en el centro de la Tierra

corruption use of power for personal gain (p. 519)
corrupción uso del poder para beneficio personal

coup sudden violent overthrow of a government, often by the military (pp. 318, 666, 848)
golpe de estado derrocamiento repentino y violento de un gobierno, generalmente por parte de las fuerzas armadas

cradle-to-grave system system of basic services provided to citizens at every stage of life by Scandinavian governments (p. 425)
sistema "desde la cuna hasta la tumba" sistema de servicios básicos que les ofrecen los gobiernos escandinavos de por vida a sus ciudadanos

credit arrangement in which a buyer can purchase something and pay for it over time (p. 69)
crédito arreglo que permite al consumidor comprar algo y pagarlo durante un plazo de tiempo

criollo person of Spanish descent born in Spain's American colonies (p. 292)
criollo persona de origen español nacida en una colonia española de las Américas

Crusades religious wars in which Christian soldiers from Europe aimed to stop the spread of Islam and to retake control of Palestine, also called the Holy Land (pp. 360, 631)
Cruzadas guerras de índole religiosa en las que los soldados cristianos de Europa buscaban frenar la difusión del islam y retomar el control de Palestina, también conocida como la Tierra Santa

crust thin layer of rocks and minerals that surrounds Earth's mantle (p. 22)
corteza capa fina de rocas y minerales que rodea el manto de la Tierra

cuisine style of food (p. 457)
cocina estilo de comida

cultural borrowing absorbing ideas or customs from other cultures (p. 427)
préstamo cultural absorción de ideas y costumbres de otras culturas

cultural diffusion spread of cultural traits from one culture to another (pp. 96, 435)
difusión cultural diseminación de los rasgos culturales de una cultura a otra

cultural hearth place where cultural traits begin and from which they spread to surrounding cultures and regions (pp. 96, 342, 716)
corazón cultural lugar donde nacen los rasgos culturales y desde donde se difunden hacia las culturas y regiones aledañas

cultural landscape geographic area that has been shaped by people (p. 86)
paisaje cultural área geográfica moldeada por la gente

cultural mosaic place where people from different areas retain their cultural identity (p. 178)
mosaico cultural lugar donde personas de distintos lugares mantienen su identidad cultural

cultural trait idea or way of doing things that is common in a certain culture (p. 86)
rasgo cultural idea o manera de hacer las cosas que es común en una cultura determinada

culture beliefs, customs, practices, and behavior of a particular nation or group of people (p. 86)
cultura creencias, costumbres, prácticas y comportamientos de una nación o un grupo de personas determinado

culture region area in which a single culture or cultural trait is dominant (p. 86)
región cultural área en la que predomina una sola cultura o rasgo cultural

D

Daoism a philosophy of following the Dao, that is, the natural way of the universe (p. 756)
taoísmo filosofía que sigue el Tao, es decir, el orden natural del universo

death rate number of deaths per 1,000 people in a year (p. 74)
tasa de mortalidad número de muertes por cada mil habitantes durante un año

deciduous tree tree that loses its leaves in the fall (p. 42)
árbol de hoja caduca árbol que pierde sus hojas en el otoño

deforestation the loss of forest cover in a region that results from the trees in a forest being destroyed faster than they can grow back (pp. 52, 233, 509)
deforestación destrucción acelerada de los árboles de un bosque que impide su regeneración y resulta en la pérdida de una región boscosa

degree unit that measures angles (p. 4)
grado unidad que se utiliza para medir ángulos

delta a flat plain formed on the seabed where a river deposits material over many years (pp. 25, 557)
delta llanura plana que se forma en el lecho marino donde un río deposita sedimento a través de los años

demand desire for a particular good or service (p. 59)
demanda interés en un bien o servicio determinado

democracy form of government in which citizens hold political power (p. 106)
democracia tipo de gobierno en el que los ciudadanos tienen el poder político

demographer scientist who studies human populations (p. 74)
demógrafo científico que estudia las poblaciones humanas

demonstration a public display of group opinion, often a rally or march (p. 700)
manifestación demostración pública de la opinión de un grupo, generalmente un mitin o una marcha

deportation being sent back to one's home country (p. 439)
deportación acción que consiste en devolver a alguien a su país de origen

deposition process of depositing material eroded and carried by water, ice, or wind (p. 25)
depósito proceso de depositar material que ha sido erosionado y transportado por el agua, hielo o viento

desalination removal of salt from seawater (p. 594)
desalinización proceso de quitar la sal del agua del mar

desertification the change when arable land dries out and becomes desert (p. 509)
desertización transformación de la tierra fértil al secarse y convertirse en desierto

developed country country with a strong economy and a high quality of life (p. 64)
país desarrollado país con una economía fuerte y un alto nivel de vida

developing country country with a less-productive economy and a lower quality of life (p. 64)
país en vías de desarrollo país con una economía menos productiva y un nivel de vida más bajo

development country's economic growth and quality of life (p. 64)
desarrollo el crecimiento económico y la calidad de vida de un país

diaspora spread of people from one place to many others (p. 240)
diáspora dispersión de personas de un lugar a muchos otros lugares

dictator leader with complete control over government (pp. 604, 790)
dictador líder con control total del gobierno

dictatorship government controlled by a single leader (p. 237)
dictadura gobierno bajo el control de un solo líder

diplomacy managing communication and relationships between countries (pp. 111, 156)
diplomacia manejo de las comunicaciones y relaciones entre países

direct democracy government in which citizens take part directly in the day-to-day affairs of government (p. 343)
democracia directa tipo de gobierno en el que los ciudadanos participan directamente en los asuntos diarios del gobierno

disposable income money left after taxes are paid (p. 485)
ingreso disponible dinero restante después de pagar los impuestos

dissenter person whose religious beliefs differ from the state's religion (p. 147)
disidente persona cuyas creencias religiosas son distintas a la religión del estado

distortion loss of accuracy (p. 9)
distorsión pérdida de exactitud

diversified economy economy that depends on a variety of exports or products (p. 299)
economía diversificada economía que depende de exportaciones o productos variados

diversify to add variety (p. 437)
diversificar agregar variedad

diversity cultural variety (p. 97)
diversidad variedad cultural

dominion territory that governs itself but is still tied to its colonizing country (p.176)
dominio territorio sujeto al país colonizador pero que goza de autonomía plena

drought long period of extremely dry weather (p. 851)
sequía largo período de tiempo extremadamente seco

Druze a person who follows a religion related to Islam (p. 625)
druso persona que sigue una religión semejante al islam

dynasty a series of rulers from the same family (p. 755)
dinastía serie de monarcas pertenecientes a la misma familia

E

economic region place where people do particular kinds of work (p. 154)
región económica lugar donde las personas se dedican a ciertos tipos de trabajo

economics study of how people meet their wants and needs (p. 58)
economía estudio de cómo la gente satisface sus deseos y necesidades

ecosystem group of plants and animals that depend on each other and their environment for survival (pp. 43, 261)
ecosistema grupo de plantas y animales cuya sobrevivencia depende de la relación entre sí y con su medio ambiente

ecotourism tourism that focuses on the environment and seeks to minimize environmental impact (pp. 243, 533)
ecoturismo tipo de turismo que se enfoca en el medio ambiente y trata de minimizar el impacto ambiental

El Dorado legendary gold-rich region (p. 266)
El Dorado leyenda sobre una región con grandes reservas de oro

elevation height above sea level (p. 12)
elevación altura sobre el nivel del mar

El Niño warming of ocean water along the west coast of South America (p. 284)
El Niño calentamiento de las aguas oceánicas de la costa oeste de América del Sur

election fraud unfair elections in which one group controls the results to gain power (p. 700)
fraude electoral elecciones injustas en las que un grupo controla los resultados para adueñarse del poder

emigrate to migrate out of a place (pp. 79, 453)
emigrar dejar un lugar

empire state containing several countries or territories (p. 106)
imperio Estado que incluye a varios países o territorios

encomienda legal system to control Native Americans in Spain's American colonies (p. 235)
encomienda sistema legal que se creó para controlar a los indígenas americanos en las colonias españolas en América

English Bill of Rights an act passed in 1689 that limited the power of the English monarch and increased Parliament's power (p. 390)
Declaración de Derechos inglesa ley aprobada en 1689 que limitaba el poder del monarca inglés y aumentaba el poder del Parlamento

Enlightenment a period during the 1600s and 1700s when scholars studied culture and society by applying reason and natural laws (p. 389)
Ilustración período del siglo XVII al siglo XVIII en que los eruditos estudiaron la cultura y la sociedad a partir de la razón y las leyes naturales

entrepreneur person who organizes and manages his or her own business (p. 454)
empresario dícese de la persona que organiza y maneja su propia empresa

entrepreneurship starting a business (p. 608)
espíritu empresarial el establecimiento de un negocio

epic long poem of adventure and conflict (p. 725)
poema épico poema largo que trata de aventuras y conflictos

equinox point at which, everywhere on Earth, days and nights are nearly equal in length (p. 18)
equinoccio momento en el que la duración de los días y las noches es casi la misma en todos los rincones de la Tierra

erosion process in which water, ice, or wind remove rock and soil (p. 24)
erosión proceso en el que el agua, hielo o viento desgasta la roca y tierra

ethanol sugar cane-based fuel (p. 322)
etanol combustible hecho a base de caña de azúcar

ethics beliefs about what is right and wrong (pp. 92, 628)
ética creencias sobre el bien y el mal

ethnic cleansing attempt to create an area with only one ethnic group by removing or attacking other ethnic groups (p. 458)
limpieza étnica intento de crear un área donde sólo habite un grupo étnico por medio del ataque o el traslado de otros grupos étnicos

ethnocentrism attitude that one's own social or cultural group is better than all others (pp. 541, 844)
etnocentrismo tendencia a valorar la cultura o el grupo social propios por encima de otros

European Union economic and political partnership among member nations (p. 403)
Unión Europea asociación económica y política de países miembros

evaporation process in which a liquid changes to a gas (p. 37)
evaporación proceso en el que un líquido se convierte en gas

exploit take advantage of (p. 812)
explotar aprovecharse de algo o alguien

export good or service produced within a country and sold outside the country's borders (pp. 67, 152)
exportación bien o servicio que se produce en un país y se vende fuera de los confines del país

export economy economy based on exports (p. 317)
economía de exportación economía que se basa en exportaciones

extended family family that includes parents, children, and other family members such as grandparents, aunts, uncles, and cousins (p. 88)
familia extensa familia que incluye a los padres, los hijos y otros parientes como los abuelos, los tíos y los primos

F

family two or more people who are closely related by birth, marriage, or adoption (p. 88)
familia dos o más personas que están estrechamente vinculadas por los lazos de sangre, el matrimonio o la adopción

famine a huge food shortage (p. 759)
hambruna gran escasez de comida

fascism a political system that stresses national strength, military might, and the belief that the state is more important than individuals (p. 397)
fascismo sistema político que enfatiza la fuerza nacional, el poderío militar y la creencia de que el estado es más importante que el individuo

fault seam in Earth's crust (p. 26)
falla quiebra en la corteza terrestre

favela Brazilian slum (p. 315)
favela barrio marginal en Brasil

federal system system of government in which power is divided among central, regional, and local governments (p. 108)
sistema federal sistema de gobierno en el que el poder se divide entre los gobiernos centrales, regionales y locales

Fertile Crescent a region with good conditions for growing crops that stretches from the Mediterranean coast east through Mesopotamia (modern Iraq) to the Persian Gulf (p. 619)
Creciente Fértil región con buenas condiciones para cultivos que se extiende desde las áreas de la costa del Mediterráneo hacia el este por Mesopotamia (que hoy se conoce como Iraq) hasta el Golfo Pérsico

feudalism in medieval Europe, a system in which land was owned by lords but held by vassals in return for their loyalty (p. 358)
feudalismo sistema que se practicó en Europa durante la Edad Media en el que la tierra era propiedad de los señores nobles, quienes se la concedían a vasallos a cambio de su lealtad

First Nations native groups who lived south of the Arctic region in Canada (p. 172)
Primeras Naciones grupos indígenas que habitaron la región al sur del Ártico en Canadá

flood plain flat lands along a river (p. 714)
terreno inundable tierras llanas adyacentes a un río

foliage leaves on trees (p. 776)
follaje hojas en árboles

foreign policy set of goals outlining how a country plans to interact with other countries (p. 110)
política exterior conjunto de metas que describe cómo un país planea interactuar con otros

fossil preserved remain of ancient human, animal, or plant (p. 538)
fósil restos conservados de personas, animales o plantas de la antigüedad

fossil fuel nonrenewable resource formed over millions of years from the remains of ancient plants and animals (pp. 49, 592)
combustible fósil recurso no renovable formado durante millones de años de los restos antiguos de plantas y animales

free market economic market in which businesses operate with few governmental restrictions (p. 216)
libre mercado mercado económico en el cual las empresas operan con restricciones mínimas del gobierno

free trade removal of trade barriers (p. 67)
libre comercio eliminación de las barreras comerciales

French Revolution a political movement that removed the French king from power and formed a republic (p. 391)
Revolución Francesa movimiento politico que derrocó al rey francés y estableció una república

fundamentalism belief that holy books should be taken literally, word for word (p. 607)
fundamentalismo idea que sugiere que las escrituras religiosas deben interpretarse literalmente, al pie de la letra

G

genocide attempt to destroy a whole people (p. 546)
genocidio exterminio de todo un grupo social

geographic information system (GIS) computer-based system that stores and uses information linked to geographic locations (p. 8)
sistema de información geográfica (SIG) sistema computarizado que archiva y usa información relacionada con sitios geográficos

geography study of the human and nonhuman features of Earth (p. 4)
geografía estudio de las características humanas y no humanas de la Tierra

glacier slow-moving body of ice (pp. 415, 852)
glaciar gran masa de hielo que se desliza lentamente

government group of people who have the power to make and enforce laws for a country or area (p. 104)
gobierno grupo de personas de un país o área que tiene el poder de crear y hacer cumplir las leyes

Great Depression worldwide economic slump during the 1930s (p. 396)
Gran Depresión crisis económica mundial durante la década de 1930

Great Rift Valley long, unusually flat area of land between areas of higher ground in eastern Africa (p. 530)
Gran Valle del Rift franja de terreno larga y plana ubicada entre terrenos elevados en África oriental

Green Revolution increase in agricultural production created by improved technology (p. 712)
Revolución verde gran aumento en la producción agrícola debido a avances en la tecnología

griot African musician-storyteller who uses music to track heritage and record history as well as entertain (p. 521)
griot músico y narrador de la tradición oral africana; usa la música para entretener y preservar su historia y cultura

gross domestic product (GDP) total value of all goods and services produced in a country in a year (pp. 64, 426, 572)
producto interno bruto (PIB) valor total de todos los bienes y servicios que produce un país durante un año

gross domestic product per capita a country's GDP divided by the number of people who live in the country (p. 572)
producto interno bruto per cápita PIB de un país dividido por la población del país

gross national product (GNP) annual income of a country's companies and residents (p. 431)
producto nacional bruto (PNB) ingreso anual de las empresas y los residentes de un país

guild association of people who have a common interest (p. 364)
gremio asociación de personas que comparten un interés común

H

hacienda huge farm or ranch in Spain's American colonies (p. 236)
hacienda granja o rancho grande en las colonias españolas en las Américas

hemisphere one half of Earth (p. 5)
hemisferio una mitad de la Tierra

hereditary monarch a ruler from a traditional ruling family who is the son, daughter, or younger relative of the last ruler (p. 635)
monarca heredero soberano perteneciente a una familia gobernante tradicional que es hijo, hija o un familiar joven del soberano anterior

hieroglyphics Egyptian system of writing using pictures and other symbols (p. 565)
jeroglíficos sistema de escritura egipcia que utiliza figuras o símbolos

high latitudes areas north of the Arctic Circle and south of the Antarctic Circle; also known as polar zone (p. 34)
latitudes altas áreas al norte del Círculo Polar Ártico y al sur del Círculo Polar Antártico

hijab concealing, baggy garments worn by many Arab women (p. 611)
hiyab prendas de vestir holgadas que muchas mujeres árabes usan para cubrirse

Hinduism religious system of beliefs and practices that emerged in South Asia (p. 717)
Hinduismo sistema de creencias y prácticas religiosas que emergieron del sur asiático

historian person who studies the past (p. 118)
historiador persona que estudia el pasado

historical map special-purpose map that provides information about a place at a certain time in history (p. 125)
mapa histórico mapa con el propósito especial de dar información acerca de un lugar en un momento determinado de la historia

Holocaust the mass murder of Jews by the Nazis during World War II (p. 399)
Holocausto exterminio masivo de judíos por el régimen nazi durante la Segunda Guerra Mundial

human development index a measure of living conditions using factors such as life expectancy, education, and income (p. 573)
índice de desarrollo humano medición de las condiciones de vida basada en factores como la expectativa de vida, la educación y el ingreso económico

human–environment interaction how people affect their environment and how their environment affects them (p. 7)
interacción humanos–medio ambiente manera en la que los seres humanos afectan su medio ambiente y viceversa

humanism the study of secular, or nonreligious, subjects such as history (p. 375)
humanismo estudio de temas laicos, o no religiosos, como la historia

humid subtropical climate climate with year-round precipitation, mild winters, and hot summers (p. 40)
clima subtropical húmedo clima de precipitación continua durante todo el año, inviernos templados y veranos cálidos

hurricane tropical cyclone that forms over the tropical Atlantic Ocean (pp. 39, 228)
huracán ciclón tropical que se forma sobre el Océano Atlántico tropical

hydroelectric power the power produced by water-driven turbines (p. 202)
energía hidroeléctrica poder que producen turbinas impulsadas por agua

hydroelectricity electricity made by water power (p. 767)
hidroelectricidad electricidad producida por la fuerza del agua

I

Iberian Peninsula Spain and Portugal (p. 434)
Península ibérica España y Portugal

ice age time of lower temperatures when much of the land was covered with snow and ice (p. 447)
edad de hielo período de temperaturas bajas donde gran parte de la tierra estaba cubierta de nieve y hielo

iceberg large floating mass of ice (p. 853)
iceberg gran masa de hielo flotante

ice sheet large mass of compressed ice (p. 852)
capa de hielo gran masa de hielo compacto

illiterate not able to read and write (p. 765)
analfabeta que no sabe leer y escribir

immigrate to migrate into a place (p. 79)
inmigrar llegar a un lugar

immunity natural defense against disease (p. 292)
inmunidad defensa natural contra las enfermedades

imperialism process of creating an empire by taking over other areas (p. 514)
imperialismo creación de un imperio por medio del dominio de otras áreas

import good or service sold within a country that is produced in another country (pp. 67, 152)
importación bien o servicio que se vende en un país pero es producido en otro

incentive factor that encourages people to behave in a certain way (p. 59)
incentivo factor que motiva a la gente a actuar de cierta manera

independence right to rule oneself (p. 236)
independencia derecho de gobernarse a sí mismo

Indian subcontinent land to the south of the Himalayas (p. 708)
subcontinente indio territorio al sur de los Himalayas

indigenous native to a region (pp. 544, 846)
indígena nativo de una región

industrialization growth of machine-powered production and manufacturing (p. 51)
industrialización aumento de la producción a máquina y la manufactura

Industrial Revolution a time in which new technologies transformed manufacturing and changed society forever (p. 392)
Revolución Industrial período en el que nuevas tecnologías transformaron la industria manufacturera en particular y la sociedad en general

infant mortality rate number of infant deaths per 1,000 births (p. 75)
tasa de mortalidad infantil número de muertes infantiles por cada mil nacimientos

inflation general increase in prices (p. 61)
inflación alza general de los precios

infrastructure body of public works, such as roads, bridges, and hospitals, that a country needs to support a modern economy (p. 518)
infraestructura conjunto de elementos o servicios públicos como carreteras, puentes y hospitales que un país necesita para mantener una economía moderna

Institutional Revolutionary Party political party that dominated Mexico's government for much of the 1900s (p. 213)
Partido Revolucionario Institucional partido político que dominó el gobierno mexicano por gran parte del siglo XX

insurgency rebellion (p. 816)
insurgencia rebelión

insurgent rebel (p. 274)
insurgente rebelde

interdependent dependent on one another (p. 779)
interdependiente que depende uno de otro

interest price paid for borrowing money (p. 69)
interés precio que se paga por el dinero prestado

interest group group that seeks to influence public policy on certain issues (p. 113)
grupo de interés grupo que busca influir en la política pública en relación a cuestiones particulares

intertropical convergence zone belt of rising air near the Equator (p. 38)
zona de convergencia intertropical cinturón de aire ascendente cerca del ecuador

Intifada a Palestinian campaign of violent resistance against Israeli control (p. 639)
Intifada campaña revolucionaria palestina en contra del control israelí

investing act of using money in the hopes of making a future profit (p. 69)
invertir usar el dinero con la esperanza de obtener ganancias futuras

irrigate to supply water to (pp. 99, 205, 686)
irrigar aportar agua

Islamism belief that politics and society should follow Islamic teachings (p. 607)
islamismo creencia según la cual la política y la sociedad deben seguir las enseñanzas del islam

Israeli settlements places in the West Bank and Gaza Strip where Israelis have settled (p. 638)
asentamientos israelíes áreas de Cisjordania y la franja de Gaza donde se han establecido los israelíes

isthmus strip of land with water on both sides that connects two larger bodies of land (p. 226)
istmo franja de tierra con agua en ambos lados que conecta dos territorios más grandes

J

jihad Arabic word meaning "struggle" (p. 607)
yihad palabra de origen árabe que significa "luchar por la reforma"

K

Kamchatka Peninsula a peninsula in the Russian far east known for its volcanic activity (p. 471)
Península de Kamchatka península del lejano oriente ruso conocida por su estado volcánico

key section of a map that explains the map's symbols and shading (p. 10)
leyenda sección de un mapa que explica el significado de sus símbolos y áreas sombreadas

KGB the Soviet-era secret police (p. 485)
KGB policía secreta de la era soviética

Korean War war between North Korea and South Korea and their allies during the early 1950s (p. 786)
Guerra de Corea guerra entre Corea del Norte y Corea del Sur, más sus aliados, durante los primeros años de la década de 1950

Kremlin a great complex of Russian official buildings, including palaces, state offices, and churches (p. 478)
Kremlin gran recinto de edificios oficiales rusos que incluye palacios, oficinas del Estado e iglesias

L

Lake Baikal a huge lake in Siberia that is more than one mile deep and holds about 20 percent of Earth's fresh water (p. 471)
lago Baikal gran lago localizado en Siberia que tiene más de una milla de hondo y contiene aproximadamente 20 por ciento del agua dulce de la Tierra

landform shapes and types of land (p. 23)
accidente geográfico formas y tipos de terreno

landlocked cut off from direct access to the ocean (p. 684)
sin litoral sin acceso directo al mar

language set of sounds or symbols that make it possible for people to communicate (p. 90); also, the language of a community or a nation
lenguaje conjunto de sonidos y símbolos que hacen posible la comunicación entre las personas
idioma lengua de una comunidad o una nación

Latin America areas of Middle America influenced by the cultures of Spain, France, or Portugal (p. 271)
América Latina regiones de México, América Central y el Caribe y América del Sur con influencia cultural de España, Francia o Portugal

latitude distance north or south of the Equator measured in degrees (p. 4)
latitud distancia en grados que se mide al norte o al sur desde el ecuador

life expectancy the average number of years a person is expected to live (p. 764)
esperanza de vida número promedio de años que se espera que viva una persona

limited government government structure in which government actions are limited by law (pp. 105, 788)
gobierno limitado estructura gubernamental cuyas acciones están limitadas por la ley

literacy ability to read and write (p. 300)
alfabetismo capacidad de leer y escribir

literature written work such as fiction, poetry, or drama (p. 95)
literatura obras escritas como la ficción, la poesía o el drama

Llanos lowland plains in Colombia and Venezuela (p. 259)
Llanos llanuras de tierra baja de Colombia y Venezuela

locator map section of a map that shows a larger area than the main map (p. 10)
mapa localizador sección de un mapa que amplía un área del mismo

loess a dustlike material that can form soil (pp. 416, 747)
loes material polvoroso que puede formar tierra

longitude distance east or west of the Prime Meridian measured in degrees (p. 5)
longitud distancia en grados que se mide al este o al oeste desde el Primer meridiano

lords in medieval Europe, noblemen who gave land to other noblemen in return for services (p. 358)
señores en la Europa medieval, señores nobles que cedían terrenos a otros señores nobles a cambio de sus servicios

low latitudes areas between the Tropic of Cancer and the Tropic of Capricorn; also known as tropics (p. 34)
latitudes bajas áreas entre el Trópico de Cáncer y el Trópico de Capricornio; también se le llama trópico

M

madrassa school that teaches the Islamic religion (p. 695)
madraza escuela que enseña la religión islámica

magma stream of soft, nearly molten rock (p. 26)
magma flujo de roca blanda y casi fundida

Magna Carta document that limited the English king's power (p. 365)
Carta Magna documento que limitaba el poder del rey de Inglaterra

maize corn (p. 206)
maíz choclo

Majlis Iranian legislature (p. 662)
Majlis asamblea legislativa de Irán

majority more than half (p. 596)
mayoría más de la mitad

malaria life-threatening disease spread by mosquitoes and caused by parasites (p. 511)
malaria enfermedad grave causada por parásitos y propagada por mosquitos

Manifest Destiny idea that the United States should expand across the North American continent (p. 149)
Destino manifiesto mentalidad que propone la expansión territorial de los Estados Unidos por todo el continente norteamericano

manorialism in medieval Europe, the economic relationship between a lord and the peasants who worked for him (p. 359)
señorío en la Europa medieval, relación económica entre un señor y sus trabajadores campesinos

mantle thick, rocky layer around Earth's core (p. 22)
manto capa rocosa gruesa alrededor del núcleo de la Tierra

Maori the original inhabitants of New Zealand and the Cook Islands (p. 843)
maorí habitantes nativos de Nueva Zelanda y las islas Cook

maritime having to do with navigation or shipping on the sea (p. 812)
marítimo pertinente a la náutica o la navegación por mar

maritime climate climate that is wet year-round, with mild winters and cool summers (p. 40)
clima marítimo clima que es húmedo todo el año, con inviernos templados y veranos frescos

market organized way for producers and consumers to trade goods and services (p. 60)
mercado intercambio organizado de bienes y servicios entre productores y consumidores

market economy economy in which individual consumers and producers make all economic decisions (pp. 62, 152, 324)
economía de mercado economía en la que los consumidores y los productores toman todas las decisiones económicas

Marshall Plan an economic program initiated by the United States to help Europe recover from World War II (p. 400)
Plan Marshall programa económico iniciado por los EE. UU. para la reconstrucción europea tras la Segunda Guerra Mundial

Mau Mau Kenyan independence movement during the 1950s (p. 542)
Mau Mau movimiento por la independencia de Kenya durante la década de 1950

Maya Native American society living in Central America (p. 234)
Maya sociedad indígena americana que habita en Centroamérica

mechanized farming farming with machines (p. 449)
mecanización agrícola uso de maquinaria en la industria agrícola

Meiji Restoration time period when Japan's Emperor Meiji was returned to power (p. 784)
Restauración Meiji período en el cual el emperador japonés Meiji retomó el poder

mercantilism economic system in which colonies sent raw materials to the mother country; in return, colonists were expected to buy products from the country (p. 293)
mercantilismo sistema económico en el que las colonias enviaban materias primas a la madre patria; a cambio, se esperaba que los colonos compraran los productos del país

merchant trader (p. 693)
comerciante negociante

MERCOSUR trading bloc of the South American countries Brazil, Argentina, Uruguay, and Paraguay, formed in 1991 (p. 299)
MERCOSUR tratado de comercio elaborado en 1991 entre los países sudamericanos de Brasil, Argentina, Uruguay y Paraguay

messiah a leader chosen by God who would restore the Jewish nation and help create God's kingdom in the world (p. 629)
mesías líder enviado de Dios que restauraría el pueblo judío y ayudaría a establecer el reino de Dios en la Tierra

mestizo person of mixed Spanish and Native American ancestry (p. 292)
mestizo persona con ascendencia española e indígena americana

Mexican Revolution armed rebellion in which the Mexican people fought for political and social reform (p. 210)
Revolución mexicana rebelión armada en la que el pueblo mexicano luchó por establecer reformas políticas y sociales

microcredit small loan (pp. 242, 523)
microcrédito préstamo pequeño

middle latitudes areas between the high and low latitudes; also known as temperate zone (p. 34)
latitudes medias (zona templada) áreas entre las latitudes altas y bajas

middle passage voyage across the Atlantic from Africa to the Americas that formed the middle leg of the triangular trade among Europe, American colonies, and Africa (p. 514)
paso central viaje a través del océano Atlántico desde África hasta las Américas que constituía el trayecto medio del comercio triangular entre Europa, las colonias americanas y África

migration movement of people from one place to another (pp. 78, 142)
migración desplazamiento de personas de un lugar a otro

military junta committee of military leaders (p. 816)
junta militar comité de líderes militares

millet self-governing religious community in the Ottoman Empire (p. 659)
millet comunidad religiosa del Imperio Otomano de índole autónoma

minority group making up less than half of a population (p. 603)
minoría grupo que constituye menos de la mitad de una población

missionary a person sent to another country by a church to spread its religious beliefs (p. 844)
misionero persona enviada a otro país por una iglesia con el propósito de diseminar sus creencias religiosas

mixed economy economy that combines elements of traditional, market, and command economic systems (p. 63)
economía mixta economía que combina elementos de los sistemas económicos tradicional, de mercado y dirigida

mixing zone an area where warm and cool water combine and stir nutrients from the ocean floor; fish feed on these nutrients (p. 169)
zona de mezcla área donde la combinación de agua cálida y agua fría revuelve los nutrientes del suelo marino; los peces se alimentan de estos nutrientes

monarchy form of government in which the state is ruled by a monarch (p. 107)
monarquía tipo de gobierno en el que el Estado está regido por un monarca

monotheism the belief in a single God (p. 600)
monoteísmo creencia en un solo dios

monsoon seasonal winds (p. 804)
monzón vientos estacionales

mosque Islamic house of worship (p. 603)
mezquita lugar de culto islámico

movement how people, goods, and ideas get from one place to another (p. 7)
movimiento manera en la que las personas, los bienes y las ideas van de un lugar a otro

mummy a body that has been preserved so it will not decompose (p. 566)
momia cadáver preservado sin descomponerse

music art form that uses sound, usually produced by instruments or voices (p. 95)
música arte que usa sonidos, normalmente producidos por instrumentos o voces

Muslim Brotherhood an Islamist party that opposes the Egyptian government (p. 574)
Hermandad Musulmana partido Islamista que se opone al gobierno egipcio

N

National Action Party Mexican political party that took power in the 2000 presidential election (p. 213)
Partido Acción Nacional (PAN) partido político mexicano que tomó el poder en las elecciones presidenciales del 2000

nationalize government taking ownership of a company (p. 269)
nacionalizar situación en la cual el gobierno toma posesión de una empresa

nation-state state that is independent of other states (p. 107)
estado-nación Estado que es independiente de otros

natural resource useful material found in the environment (p. 48)
recurso natural material útil que se encuentra en el medio ambiente

New France French colony in what is now eastern Canada (p. 173)
Nueva Francia colonia francesa ubicada en lo que hoy se conoce como Canadá oriental

nirvana in Hinduism, a state of understanding that releases the soul from the cycle of rebirth (p. 718)
nirvana según el hinduismo, estado de claridad que libera el alma del ciclo de renacimiento

nomad person who moves from place to place without a permanent home (p. 558)
nómada persona que se desplaza de un lugar a otro sin un hogar permanente

nomadic herder a person who raises livestock for a living and has no settled home but moves from place to place (p. 749)
pastor nómada persona cuyo oficio es criar ganado y que se desplaza de un lugar a otro sin un hogar permanente

nonalignment not becoming an ally of either the United States or the Soviet Union during the Cold War (p. 722)
sin alineación no tener alianzas ni con los Estados Unidos ni con la Unión Soviética durante la Guerra Fría

nongovernmental organization (NGO) group that operates with private funding (p. 549)
organización no gubernamental (ONG) grupo que funciona gracias al financiamiento privado

nonrenewable resource resource that cannot be replaced in a relatively short period of time (p. 49)
recurso no renovable recurso que no se puede reemplazar en un período de tiempo relativamente corto

norm behavior that is considered normal in a particular society (p. 86)
norma comportamiento que se considera normal en una sociedad determinada

northwest passage hypothetical North American passage between the Atlantic and Pacific Oceans (p. 384)
Paso del Noroeste ruta marítima hipotética en Norteamérica que conecta los océanos Atlántico y Pacífico

nuclear family family that consists of parents and their children (p. 88)
familia nuclear familia constituida por los padres y sus hijos

nuclear weapon powerful explosive device that can cause widespread destruction (p. 851)
arma nuclear explosivo de alto poder que puede causar gran destrucción

O

oasis place in the desert where water can be found (p. 557)
oasis lugar del desierto donde se halla agua

oligarchy government in which a small group of people rule (pp. 294, 341)
oligarquía tipo de gobierno en el que un grupo pequeño de personas tiene el poder

one-child policy China's family planning policy; under this law, many married couples are only allowed to have one child (p. 750)
política de hijo único política de planeación familiar china; esta ley permite a muchas parejas casadas tener sólo un hijo o una hija

opportunity cost cost of what you have to give up when making a choice (p. 59)
costo de oportunidad costo de lo que se pierde al elegir una opción

oral tradition community's cultural and historical background, passed down in spoken stories and songs (p. 123)
tradición oral trasfondo cultural e histórico de una comunidad, trasmitido por cuentos hablados y canciones

orbit path one object makes as it circles around another (p. 18)
órbita trayectoria que traza un cuerpo al desplazarse alrededor de otro

Outback a sparsely inhabited region of Australia with low plateaus and plains (p. 835)
outback territorio escasamente poblado de Australia que tiene mesetas y llanuras

outsourcing sending tasks to be done by workers outside a company (p. 731)
subcontratación práctica que consiste en enviar trabajo a trabajadores de otra compañia

overgrazing so much grazing that plants are killed (p. 687)
pastoreo excesivo pastoreo a un nivel tan intenso que causa la muerte de las plantas

ozone layer layer of the atmosphere that filters out most of the sun's harmful ultraviolet rays (p. 855)
capa de ozono capa de la atmósfera que bloquea la mayoría de los nocivos rayos ultravioleta del sol

P

pack ice seasonal ice that floats on water rather than being attached to land (p. 853)
banquisa hielo estacional flotante que no está conectado a la tierra

Pan-Africanism political and social movement that sought to unite black Africans across the globe (p. 516)
panafricanismo movimiento sociopolítico que promueve la hermandad de los africanos de raza negra alrededor del mundo

Pan-Arabism idea that all Arabic-speaking countries should cooperate and join together (p. 569)
panarabismo ideología que promueve la cooperación y unión de todos los países de habla árabe

paramilitary unauthorized armed forces (p. 269)
paramilitar se refiere a un grupo civil con estructura de tipo militar

Parliament British legislature (p. 423)
parlamento asamblea legislativa británica

parliamentary democracy a democracy in which parliament chooses the government (p. 634)
democracia parlamentaria democracia en la que el parlamento escoge al gobierno

partition splitting a country into two states (p. 722)
división separación de un país en dos estados

patricians wealthy aristocrats in ancient Rome (p. 349)
patricios aristócratas adinerados de la antigua Roma

Pax Romana period of stability in the Roman empire under Augustus (p. 351)
Paz Romana período de estabilidad del Imperio Romano bajo el mandato de Augusto

peninsula area of land almost completely surrounded by water but connected to the mainland (pp. 414, 802)
península área de tierra rodeada en su mayoría por agua pero conectada a un territorio más extenso

period length of time singled out because of a specific event or development that happened during that time (p. 118)
período lapso de tiempo resaltado debido a un suceso o desarrollo específico que sucedió durante ese tiempo

permafrost permanently frozen soil (pp. 168, 472)
permafrost tierra permanentemente congelada

Glossary (continued)

perspective a technique that allows artists to portray a three-dimensional space on a flat surface (p. 375)
perspectiva técnica que permite al artista crear un espacio tridimensional en una superficie plana

Pharaoh king of ancient Egypt (p. 565)
faraón rey del antiguo Egipto

philosophy general study of knowledge and the world; Greek for "love of wisdom" (p. 345)
filosofía estudio general sobre el conocimiento y el mundo; en griego significa "amor por la sabiduría"

physical map map that shows physical, or natural, features (p. 12)
mapa físico mapa que muestra las características físicas o naturales

place mix of human and nonhuman features at a given location (p. 6)
lugar combinación de características humanas y no humanas en un sitio determinado

plain large area of flat or gently rolling land (pp. 25, 414)
llanura área extensa de terreno ondulado o llano

plantation large commercial farm (pp. 148, 384)
plantación granja grande con fines comerciales

plate block of rock and soil that makes up Earth's crust (pp. 26, 591)
placa bloque de piedra y tierra que forma la corteza de la Tierra

plate tectonics theory that explains how huge blocks of Earth's crust called "plates" move (pp. 26, 837)
tectónica de placas teoría que explica el movimiento de las placas de la corteza terrestre

plateau large, mostly flat area that rises above the surrounding land (p. 25)
meseta gran extensión de terreno, generalmente plano, que se eleva sobre la tierra circundante

plebeians nonpatrician citizens of ancient Rome (p. 349)
plebeyos ciudadanos de la antigua Roma que no se consideraban patricios

plural society society in which distinctive cultural, ethnic, and racial groups are encouraged to maintain their own identities and cultures (p. 182)
sociedad plural sociedad en la que se fomenta la conservación de la identidad cultural de los distintos grupos culturales, étnicos y raciales

poaching illegal hunting (p. 533)
furtivismo caza ilegal

polar zone areas north of the Arctic Circle and south of the Antarctic Circle; also known as high latitudes (p. 34)
zona polar (latitudes altas) área al norte del Círculo Polar Ártico o al sur del Círculo Polar Antártico

polders areas of dry land reclaimed from lake bottoms or the seabed (p. 431)
pólderes áreas de tierra seca ganadas a los lechos laguneros o marinos

political map map that shows political units, such as countries or states (p. 13)
mapa político mapa que muestra las unidades políticas, como países o estados

political party group that supports candidates for public offices (p. 113)
partido político grupo que apoya a los candidatos que postulan a cargos públicos

pollution waste that makes the air, soil, or water less clean (pp. 53, 419)
contaminación desechos que alteran la pureza del aire, el suelo o el agua

population density measure of the number of people per unit of land (pp. 77, 144)
densidad de población medida del número de personas por unidad de territorio

population distribution spreading of people over an area of land (p. 76)
distribución de población dispersión de las personas a lo largo de un área geográfica

precipitation water that falls to the ground as rain, snow, sleet, or hail (pp. 32, 166)
precipitación agua que cae sobre la tierra en forma de lluvia, nieve, aguanieve o granizo

prehistory time before humans invented writing (p. 119)
prehistoria época anterior a la invención de la escritura

primary industry industry involving the collection of resources from nature, such as fishing (p. 849)
sector primario industria relacionada con la recolección de recursos naturales, como la pesca

primary source information that comes directly from a person who experienced an event (p. 120)
fuente primaria información sobre un suceso que proviene directamente de una persona que experimentó el suceso

902

privatization individual and private group ownership of businesses (p. 430)
  privatización situación en la que individuos o grupos privados son los dueños de las empresas

producer person or business that makes and sells products (p. 59)
  productor persona o negocio que fabrica y vende productos

productivity amount of goods and services produced given the amount of resources used (p. 65)
  productividad cantidad de bienes y servicios producidos en relación a la cantidad de recursos empleados

profit money a company has left over after subtracting the costs of doing business (p. 60)
  ganancias dinero que sobra después que una compañía deduce los costos de operar el negocio

projection way to map Earth on a flat surface (p. 9)
  proyección manera de trazar un mapa de la Tierra sobre una superficie plana

prophet a messenger of God (p. 627)
  profeta mensajero de Dios

province territory that is under the control of a larger country (p. 175)
  provincia territorio que se encuentra bajo la administración de un país más grande

pull factor cause of migration that pulls, or attracts, people to new countries (p. 79)
  factor de arrastre causa de la migración que arrastra o atrae a la gente a países nuevos

push factor cause of migration that pushes people to leave their home country (p. 79)
  factor de empuje causa de la migración que empuja a la gente a dejar su país de origen

Q

qanat tunnel that provided water to Persian villages by bringing water from an aquifer (p. 652)
  qanat túnel que transportaba agua de un acuífero a las aldeas persas

Quran holy book of Islam (p. 600)
  Corán libro sagrado del islam

R

rain shadow a dry area that forms behind a highland that captures rainfall and snow (p. 620)
  sombra orográfica área árida que se forma detrás de una zona montañosa donde cae lluvia y nieve

recession decline in economic growth for six or more months in a row (pp. 61, 792)
  recesión declive en el crecimiento económico por un período continuo de seis meses o más

Reconquista reconquering of Spain by Christians beginning in the 1000s (p. 362)
  Reconquista la conquista cristiana de España que comenzó en el siglo XI

referendum vote held to reject or accept a law (p. 301)
  referéndum someter una ley al voto para rechazarla o aceptarla

Reformation a religious movement in which calls for reform led to the emergence of non-Catholic, or Protestant, churches (p. 378)
  Reforma Protestante movimiento religioso cuya convocación de la reforma de la Iglesia Católica conllevó a la creación de iglesias protestantes o no católicas

region area with at least one unifying physical or human feature such as climate, landforms, population, or history (p. 7)
  región área con al menos una característica física o humana que es unificadora, como el clima, los accidentes geográficos, la población o la historia

relative location location of a place relative to another place (p. 6)
  ubicación relativa ubicación de un lugar con respecto a otro

religion people's beliefs and practices about the existence, nature, and worship of a god or gods (p. 92)
  religión creencias y prácticas de los seres humanos acerca de la existencia, la naturaleza y la adoración de un dios o dioses

remittance money sent to another place (p. 217)
  remesa envío de dinero

Renaissance a time of a renewed interest in art and learning in Europe; "rebirth" (p. 374)
  Renacimiento período de renovado interés en el arte y el aprendizaje en Europa; "un nuevo nacimiento"

Glossary (continued)

renewable resource a resource that Earth or people can replace (p. 49)
recurso renovable recurso que la Tierra o las personas pueden reemplazar

representative democracy democracy in which people elect representatives to make the nation's laws (p. 273)
democracia representativa democracia en la que el pueblo elige representantes que redactan las leyes de la nación

repressive opposed to freedom (p. 700)
represivo que se opone a la libertad

reservoir storage pool of water (p. 811)
embalse depósito donde se almacena agua

reunification process of becoming unified again (p. 432)
reunificación proceso para volver a unificar

revenue money earned by selling goods and services (p. 60)
ingresos dinero recaudado de la venta de bienes y servicios

revolution circular journey around the sun (p. 18)
revolución vuelta alrededor del Sol

riot noisy, violent public gathering (p. 689)
motín reunión público de carácter violento y ruidoso

Rose Revolution peaceful protests against the results of the 2003 Georgia election (p. 700)
Revolución de las Rosas protestas pacíficas contra el resultado de las elecciones nacionales de Georgia en 2003

rotation complete turn (p. 20)
rotación vuelta completa

rural settlement in the country (p. 80)
rural poblado del campo

S

Sahel a semiarid area that lies between the Sahara and moister regions to the south in northern Africa. (p. 505)
Sáhel área semiárida ubicada entre el desierto del Sahara y las regiones más húmedas al sur del norte de África

salt trade exchange between West Africans selling gold and Arab traders selling salt, beginning around A.D. 750 (p. 513)
comercio de la sal intercambio comercial del oro de África occidental por la sal de los mercaderes árabes, que comenzó alrededor del A.D. 750

samurai Japanese warrior lord (p. 783)
samurái guerrero japonés miembro de la nobleza

Santeria Cuban religion that combines Catholic and West African beliefs (p. 239)
santería religión cubana que combina el catolicismo y creencias de África occidental

satellite image picture of Earth's surface taken from a satellite in orbit (p. 8)
imagen de satélite fotografía de la superficie de la Tierra que tomó un satélite en órbita

satrap Persian governor (p. 657)
sátrapa gobernador persa

savanna parklike landscape of grasslands with scattered trees that can survive dry spells, found in tropical areas with dry seasons (pp. 42, 309, 506)
sabana pradera con árboles dispersos que pueden sobrevivir periodos de sequía; se encuentra en las áreas tropicales que tienen estaciones secas

saving setting aside money for future use (p. 68)
ahorrar reservar dinero para el uso futuro

scale relative size (p. 8)
escala tamaño relativo

scale bar section of a map that shows how much distance on the map represents a given distance on the land (p. 10)
barra de escala sección de un mapa que muestra la correspondencia entre las distancias del mapa y las distancias reales sobre la Tierra

scarcity having a limited quantity of resources to meet unlimited wants (pp. 58, 778)
escasez tener una cantidad limitada de recursos para satisfacer deseos ilimitados

schism split (p. 355)
cisma división

science active process of acquiring knowledge of the natural world (p. 98)
ciencia proceso activo de obtener conocimientos sobre el mundo natural

904

Scientific Revolution a series of major advances in science during the 1500s and 1600s (p. 388)
Revolución Científica serie de grandes avances científicos durante los siglos XVI y XVII

secede to break away (p. 458)
separarse desprenderse

secondary industry industry involving the use of resources to create new products, such as manufacturing (p. 849)
sector secundario industria relacionada con el uso de recursos para crear nuevos productos, como la industria manufacturera

secondary source information about an event that does not come directly from a person who experienced that event (p. 120)
fuente secundaria información sobre un suceso que no proviene directamente de una persona que experimentó el suceso

secular nonreligious (p. 815)
laico no religioso

secular democracy democracy not based on religion (p. 730)
democracia laica tipo de democracia que no se basa en la religión

secularism idea that government should be separate from religion (p. 574)
laicismo idea que promueve la separación entre el Estado y la religión

sedentary settled (p. 694)
sedentario asentado

semiarid climate dry climate (p. 41)
clima semiárido clima seco

separatist group group of people who want to establish an independent state (p. 816)
grupo separatista grupo de personas que quieren establecer un estado independiente

Serengeti Plain a part of the savanna in Kenya and Tanzania, home to many animals such as elephants and gazelles (p. 532)
Llanura del Serengeti parte de la sabana de Kenya y Tanzania donde habitan animales como elefantes y gacelas

serf a peasant who is legally bound to live and work on land owned by a lord (p. 478)
siervo persona que está legalmente forzada a vivir y trabajar en la tierra de su noble

shah Persian word for king (p. 659)
sah término persa para rey

shamal hot, dry winds that blow across Iran from west to east (p. 651)
shamal viento seco y cálido que atraviesa Irán de oeste a este

Shinto traditional religion that originated in Japan (p. 795)
sintoísmo religión tradicional que se originó en Japón

shogun powerful Japanese military leader who often had more power than the emperor (p. 783)
shogún poderoso líder militar japonés que por lo general tenía más poder que el emperador

Siberia Asiatic Russia (p. 468)
Siberia Rusia asiática

Silk Road series of trade routes that crossed Asia (p. 692)
Ruta de la Seda red de rutas comerciales que atravesaban Asia

single-party state a country in which one political party controls the government (p. 761)
estado de un solo partido país en donde un partido político controla el gobierno

sinkhole depression on the surface of the land caused by the collapse of a cave roof (p. 199)
dolina depresión de la superficie de la tierra causada por el colapso del techo de una cueva

slum poor, overcrowded urban neighborhood (p. 81)
barrio marginal vecindario urbano pobre y sobrepoblado

social class group of people living in simliar economic conditions (p. 89)
clase social grupo de personas que tienen una condición económica similar

social services programs designed to help the poor (p. 325)
servicios sociales programas con el fin de ayudar a los pobres

social structure pattern of organized relationships among groups of people within a society (p. 89)
estructura social patrón de las relaciones organizadas entre los grupos de personas de una sociedad

society group of humans with a shared culture who have organized themselves to meet their basic needs (p. 88)
sociedad grupo de personas con una cultura compartida que se han organizado para satisfacer sus necesidades básicas

solstice point at which days are longest in one hemisphere and shortest in another (p. 18)
solsticio momento en el que la duración de los días es más larga en un hemisferio y más corta en el otro

sovereignty supreme authority (p. 110)
soberanía autoridad suprema

soviet a republic or unit of government under a central communist government (p. 480)
sóviet república o unidad gubernamental bajo un gobierno central comunista

specialization act of concentrating on a limited number of goods or activities (p. 60)
especialización concentrarse en una cantidad limitada de bienes o actividades

special-purpose map map that shows the location or distribution of human or physical features (p. 13)
mapa temático o de propósito particular mapa que muestra la ubicación o distribución de características humanas o físicas

sphere round-shaped body (p. 4)
esfera cuerpo geométrico de forma redonda

spillover an effect on someone or something not involved in an activity (p. 53)
externalidad efecto sobre alguien o algo que no participa en una actividad

standard of living level of comfort enjoyed by a person or society (p. 99)
nivel de vida nivel de comodidad que posee un individuo o una sociedad

staple crop the most important crop produced or consumed in a region (p. 749)
alimento básico el producto alimenticio más importante que se produce o se consume en una región

state region that shares a common government (p. 106)
estado región que tiene un gobierno común

steppes vast areas of grasslands (pp. 471, 685)
estepa territorio extenso de llanuras

stock share of ownership in a country (p. 69)
acción porción de la propiedad de una compañía

strait narrow body of water that cuts through land, connecting two larger bodies of water (p. 649)
estrecho cuerpo de agua angosto que pasa por tierra para conectar a dos cuerpos de agua más grandes

subarctic climate climate with limited precipitation, cool summers, and very cold winters (p. 41)
clima subártico clima de precipitación limitada, veranos frescos e inviernos muy fríos

subduct movement of one part of Earth's crust under another (p. 283)
subducción movimiento de una parte de la corteza terrestre por debajo de otra

subsidence sinking of the ground (p. 272)
hundimiento inmersión de la tierra

subsistence farming farming with little left over to send to market (p. 712)
agricultura de subsistencia tipo de agricultura en el que casi no sobran productos para el mercado

suburb residential area on the edge of a city or large town (p. 51)
suburbio área residencial ubicada en los límites de una ciudad o un pueblo

suburban sprawl spread of suburbs away from the core city (p. 81)
dispersión suburbana extensión de los suburbios lejos del centro de la ciudad

superpower an extremely powerful nation (p. 487)
superpotencia nación sumamente poderosa

supply amount of a good or service that is available for use (p. 59)
oferta cantidad disponible de un bien o servicio

surplus extra (p. 811)
superávit excedente

Swahili Bantu language that has many Arabic elements and words from other languages (p. 545)
swahili lengua bantú que contiene muchos elementos del idioma árabe y palabras de otras lenguas

T

taiga thick forest of coniferous trees (p. 417)
taiga denso bosque de árboles coníferos

tariff tax on imports (p. 67)
arancel impuesto a las importaciones

technology practical application of knowledge to accomplish a task (p. 65)
tecnología aplicación práctica del saber para ejecutar una tarea

temperate moderate in terms of temperature (pp. 140, 687)
templado de temperatura moderada

temperate zone areas between the high and low latitudes; also known as middle latitudes (p. 34)
zona templada área entre las latitudes altas y bajas; también se le llama latitudes medias

temperature measure of how hot or cold the air is (p. 32)
temperatura medida de cuán caliente o fría se encuentra la atmósfera

terraced farming sculpting the hillsides into different levels for crops (p. 264)
cultivo en terrazas laderas que han sido esculpidas para crear superficies de cultivo niveladas o escalonadas

terrorism use of violence to create fear for political reasons (p. 607)
terrorismo actos violentos destinados a crear un clima de temor para fines políticos

theocracy a government run by religious power (p. 565)
teocracia gobierno en el que rige el poder religioso

timeline line marked off with a series of events and their dates (p. 118)
línea cronológica línea marcada con una serie de sucesos y sus fechas

time zones areas sharing the same time (p. 20)
husos horarios áreas que comparten la misma hora

tornado swirling funnel of wind that can reach 200 miles (320 km) per hour (p. 39)
tornado túnel de aire giratorio que puede alcanzar una velocidad de 200 millas (320 km) por hora

tourism business of providing food, places to stay, and other services to visitors from other places (p. 231)
turismo industria que facilita comida, hospedaje y otros servicios a visitantes de otros lugares

trade exchange of goods and services in a market (p. 66)
comercio intercambio de bienes y servicios en un mercado

trade barrier something that keeps goods and services from entering a country (p. 67)
barrera comercial obstáculos para la entrada de bienes y servicios a un país

traditional economy economy in which people make economic decisions based on their customs and habits (p. 62)
economía tradicional economía en la que la gente toma decisiones económicas de acuerdo a sus costumbres y hábitos

treaty formal agreement between two or more countries (p. 111)
tratado acuerdo formal entre dos o más países

triangular trade three-stage trade pattern that carried goods and enslaved people among Europe, Africa, and the Americas (p. 386)
comercio triangular sistema comercial de tres partes que transportó bienes y personas esclavizadas entre Europa, África y las Américas

tribunes representatives of plebeians in ancient Rome (p. 349)
tribuno representante de los plebeyos de la antigua Roma

Trinity the three persons, or forms, of God according to Christian belief: God the Father, God the Son, and the Holy Spirit (p. 630)
Trinidad dícese de las tres personas o formas de Dios de acuerdo con las creencias cristianas: Dios padre, Dios hijo y Espíritu Santo

tropical cyclone intense rainstorm with strong winds that forms over oceans in the tropics (p. 39)
ciclón tropical aguacero intenso con vientos fuertes que se forma sobre el océano en los trópicos

tropical wet and dry climate climate with a wet season in summer and a dry season in winter (p. 40)
clima tropical húmedo y seco clima de temporada húmeda durante el verano y temporada seca en el invierno

tropical wet climate climate with hot temperatures and heavy rainfall year-round (p. 40)
clima tropical húmedo clima de temperaturas cálidas y lluvia abundante durante todo el año

tropic areas between the Tropic of Cancer and the Tropic of Capricorn; also known as low latitudes (p. 34)
trópico área comprendida entre el Trópico de Cáncer y el Trópico de Capricornio (latitudes bajas)

tsar ruler of imperial Russia; a term used by Byzantine rulers, derived from the Latin *caesar*, or king (p. 478)
zar gobernador del Imperio Ruso; término derivado del latín *césar* o rey, que usaban los gobernadores del Imperio Bizantino

Glossary (continued)

tsunami tidal wave (p. 803)
   maremoto ola sísmica

tundra area with limited vegetation, such as moss and shrubs (pp. 167, 416)
   tundra área con vegetación limitada, como musgos y arbustos

tundra climate climate with cool summers and bitterly cold, dry winters (p. 41)
   clima de tundra clima de veranos frescos e inviernos gélidos y secos

typhoon storm much like a hurricane (p. 804)
   tifón tormenta parecida a un huracán

tyranny unjust use of power (p. 105)
   tiranía uso injusto del poder

U

unitary system system of government in which a central government has the authority to make laws for the entire country (p. 108)
   sistema unitario sistema de gobierno en el que un gobierno central tiene la autoridad de hacer leyes para todo el país

universal theme subject or theme that relates to the entire world (p. 94)
   tema universal materia o tema que se relaciona con todo el mundo

unlimited government government structure in which there are no effective limits on government actions (pp. 105, 790)
   gobierno ilimitado tipo de gobierno en el que no existen límites sobre las acciones del gobierno

Ural Mountains low-lying mountains that separate European Russia from Asiatic Russia (p. 469)
   Montes Urales cadena montañosa de poca elevación que separa a Rusia europea de Rusia asiática

urban located in cities (p. 80)
   urbano localizado en la ciudad

urbanization movement of people from rural to urban areas (pp. 80, 559)
   urbanización desplazamiento de personas de las áreas rurales a las áreas urbanas

urban planning the planning of a city (p. 322)
   planeación urbana planeación de una ciudad

urbanized place where most people live in cities (p. 595)
   urbanizado lugar donde la mayoría de las personas viven en la ciudad

V

valley stretch of low land between mountains or hills (p. 25)
   valle extensión de terreno bajo ubicado entre montañas o colinas

vassals in medieval Europe, noblemen who received land from other noblemen in return for their services (p. 358)
   vasallos en la Europa medieval, señores nobles que recibían terrenos de otros señores nobles a cambio de sus servicios

vertical climate zones climate zones in a region that change according to elevation (p. 285)
   zonas climáticas verticales zonas climáticas de una región que cambian de acuerdo a la altura

visual arts art forms such as painting, sculpture, and photography (p. 94)
   artes visuales expresiones artísticas como la pintura, la escultura y la fotografía

W

wage money paid to an employee (p. 762)
   sueldo dinero que se le paga a un empleado

water cycle the movement of water from Earth's surface into the atmosphere and back (p. 37)
   ciclo del agua movimiento del agua desde la superficie de la Tierra hacia la atmósfera y viceversa

weather condition of the air and sky at a certain time (p. 32)
   tiempo condiciones del aire y el cielo en un momento determinado

weathering process that breaks rocks down into tiny pieces (p. 24)
   meteorización proceso que rompe la roca en pedazos muy pequeños

World War I 1914–1918, sometimes called the Great War, the first truly global conflict (p. 394)
   Primera Guerra Mundial 1914 a 1918, a veces llamada La Gran Guerra, fue el primer verdadero conflicto global

World War II 1939–1945, second major global conflict (p. 398)
  Segunda Guerra Mundial 1939 a 1945, segundo gran conflicto global

Z

Zionism a movement to create a Jewish state in Jews' historic homeland in Palestine (p. 632)
  sionismo movimiento que busca la creación de un estado judío en el la patria histórica en Palestina de los judíos

Zoroastrianism an Iranian religion that dates back to ancient times (p. 655)
  zoroastrismo religión iraní que data de tiempos antiguos

Index

The letters after some page numbers refer to the following: c = chart; g = graph; m = map; p = picture; q = quotation.

Index (continued)

Index (continued)

Index (continued)

Index (continued)

Acknowledgments

The people who made up the **myWorld Geography** team—representing composition services; core design, digital, and multimedia production services; digital product development; editorial; editorial services; materials management; and production management—are listed below.

Leann Davis Alspaugh, Sarah Aubry, Deanna Babikian, Paul Blankman, Alyssa Boehm, Peter Brooks, Susan Brorein, Megan Burnett, Todd Christy, Neville Cole, Bob Craton, Michael Di Maria, Glenn Diedrich, Frederick Fellows, Jorgensen Fernandez, Thomas Ferreira, Patricia Fromkin, Andrea Golden, Mary Ann Gundersen, Christopher Harris, Susan Hersch, Paul Hughes, Judie Jozokos, Lynne Kalkanajian, John Kingston, Kate Koch, Stephanie Krol, Karen Lepri, Ann-Michelle Levangie, Salena LiBritz, Courtney Markham, Constance J. McCarty, Anne McLaughlin, Rich McMahon, Mark O'Malley, Alison Muff, Jen Paley, Gabriela Perez Fiato, Judith Pinkham, Paul Ramos, Charlene Rimsa, Marcy Rose, Rashid Ross, Alexandra Sherman, Owen Shows, Melissa Shustyk, Jewel Simmons, Ted Smykal, Emily Soltanoff, Frank Tangredi, Simon Tuchman, Elizabeth Tustian, Merle Uuesoo, Alwyn Velásquez, Andrew White, Heather Wright

Maps
XNR Productions, Inc.

Illustration
Kerry Cashman, Marcos Chin, Dave Cockburn, Jeremy Mohler

Photography
FRONT MATTER Pages vi–xxix, Bkgrnd sky, Image Source/Getty Images; **vi–vii,** Image Source/Getty Images; **vii, T,** ZZ/Alamy; **viii, L,** Jim Sugar/Corbis; **R,** GoGo Images Corporation/Alamy; **viii–ix,** Image Source/Getty Images; **ix,** Superstock/age Fotostock; **x,** Jeff Greenberg/PhotoEdit; **xii–xxiii, All,** Pearson Education Inc.; **xxx, Bkgrnd,** Michele Falzone/JAI/Corbis; **LT,** Pearson Education, Inc.; **TM,** Pearson Education, Inc.; **RT,** Pearson Education, Inc.; **xxxi, RM,** iStockphoto.com.

CORE CONCEPTS Pages xxxii–1, Bkgrnd sky, Image Source/Getty Images; **xxxii, L,** Shutterstock; **LM,** Jim Sugar/Corbis; **M,** Fabian Gonzales/Alamy; **RM, All** Canada Photos/Alamy; **R,** Gavin Hellier/Getty Images; **1, L,** Reed Kaestner/Corbis/JupiterImages; **LM,** Gavin Hellier/Getty Images; **RM,** Todd Gipstein/Corbis; **R,** Digital Vision/Getty Images; **2, LT,** Shutterstock; **RT,** Photo courtesy of Jason Young; **B,** Beth Wald/Aurora/Getty Images; **LB,** Harley Couper/Alamy; **3, LT,** Photo courtesy of Jason Young; **RT,** Photo courtesy of Jason Young; **4, LM,** Mike Agliolo/Corbis; **6,** Saul Loeb/AFP/Getty Images; **8, RT,** Silver Burdett Ginn; **LM,** Bill Curtsinger/National Geographic Stock; **16, RT,** Jim Sugar/Corbis; **LT,** Shutterstock; **M,** Jerry Driendl/Getty Images; **17, RT,** Stephen Alvarez/Getty Images; **Inset,** Courtesy of Tamsen Buriak; **LT,** Hyogo Prefectural Government/epa/Corbis; **24,** Goodshoot/Corbis; **25, RT,** Shutterstock, Inc.; **RM,** Digital Vision/Alamy; **26, L,** Jim Sugar/Corbis; **27, RM,** Hyogo Prefectural Government/epa/Corbis; **RB,** AP Photo/Ric Francis; **30, RT,** NOAA; **M,** David J. Phillip/AP Images; **LT,** NASA/Corbis; **31, RT,** Photo courtesy of Airin McGhee; **LT,** Alex Brandon/Newhouse News Service/Landov; **TM,** Smiley N. Pool/Dallas Morning News/Corbis; **32, LB,** Paul Zahl/National Geographic/Getty Images; **33, LT,** M. Spencer Green/AP Photo; **RB,** Indranil Mukherjee/AFP/Getty Images; **39, B,** Wave RF/Photolibrary; **40,** Francisco González/age Fotostock; **41, RT,** B. & C. Alexander/Photo Researchers, Inc.; **RB,** James L. Stanfield/National Geographic Stock; **42, T,** Fabian Gonzales/Alamy; **LM,** Joseph Sohm-Visions of America/Getty Images; **TM,** John Glover/Getty Images; **LB,** Jake Rajs/Getty Images; **M,** David Ball/Getty Images; **42–43, B,** Macduff Everton/Corbis; **43, TM,** Radius Images/Photolibrary; **M,** Mike Tittel/Getty Images; **T,** Ruth Tomlinson/Getty Images; **LM,** Ron Sanford/Photo Researchers; **RB,** Bill Curtsinger/National Geographic Stock; **46, LT,** Jon Holloway/Stock Connection; **RT,** Marilyn Humphries/The Image Works; **M,** Ashley Cooper/Picimpact/Corbis; **47, RT,** Photo courtesy of Lauren Hexilon; **TM,** Frank Perry/AFP/Getty Images; **LT,** Atlantide Phototravel/Corbis; **48, LM,** Melanie Stetson Freeman/The Christian Science Monitor/Getty Images; **B,** vario images GmbH & Co.KG/Alamy; **50–51, All,** Pearson Education, Inc.; **52, B,** Paul Hanna/Reuters/Corbis; **53, RT,** All Canada Photos/Alamy; **56, RT,** San Rostro/age Fotostock; **LT,** Alexey U/Shutterstock; **B,** Jim Russi/age Fotostock; **57, RT,** Photo courtesy of Chris Krestner; **TM,** Imagebroker/Alamy; **LT,** J.R. Bale/Alamy;

TM, James A. Isbell/Shutterstock; **58, LB,** LWA/Getty Images; **BM,** Ariel Skelley/Blend Images/Corbis; **BM,** fotog/Getty Images; **RB,** Getty Images; **59, RT,** Brigitte Sporrer/zefa/Corbis; **62, B,** Dennis MacDonald/PhotoEdit; **M,** Bruno Morandi/age Fotostock; **63, T,** Reuters/KNS Korean News Agency; **64, LB,** Gavin Hellier/Getty Images; **RB,** Mike Cohen/Shutterstock; **66, B,** SuperStock/age Fotostock; **67, LB,** The Seattle Times/Newscom; **RB,** Photo by Wang Kai/ChinaFotoPress/Newscom; **68, LB,** Ed Kashi/Corbis; **69, RT,** Hou Jun/Newscom; **72, M,** Reed Kaestner/Corbis/JupiterImages; **LT,** DDCoral/Shutterstock; **RT,** Mark Gabrenya/Shutterstock; **73, RT,** Photo courtesy of Ludwig Barragan; **TM,** Pearson Education, Inc.; **LT,** Steven Senne/AP Images; **74–75, B,** Shutterstock; **75, RT,** ©2008 by Ira Lippke/Newscom; **LB,** Thony Belizaire/AFP/Getty Images; **76, B,** Travelpix Ltd/Getty Images; **77, B,** PCL/Alamy; **78, LT,** Private Collection/The Bridgeman Art Library; **B,** Bettmann/Corbis; **79, RT,** Jack Kurtz/Newscom; **80, LT,** Paul Almasy/Corbis; **LB,** iStockphoto.com; **81, RT,** Bettmann/Corbis; **RB,** Fly Fernandez/zefa/Corbis; **84, B,** Interfoto/Alamy; **RT,** Sylvain Grandadam/age Fotostock; **LT,** Sergei Bachlakov/Shutterstock, Inc.; **85, TM,** Photo courtesy of Joanna Baca; **RT,** David Muench/Corbis; **RT,** Photo courtesy of Joanna Baca; **86, LT,** Gavin Hellier/Getty Images; **LB,** Pearson Education, Inc.; **BM,** Pearson Education, Inc.; **RB,** Pearson Education, Inc.; **87, All,** Pearson Education, Inc.; **88, LM,** Glenda M. Powers/Shutterstock; **B,** GoGo Images Corporation/Alamy; **89, RB,** Rubberball/Getty Images; **RM,** Kuzma/Shutterstock; **RT,** Silver Burdett Ginn; **TM,** Kokhanchikov/Shutterstock; **TM,** Lebedinski Vladislav/Shutterstock; **M,** George Doyle & Ciaran Griffin/Getty Images; **M,** Pearson Education, Inc.; **TM,** Cecile Treal and Jean-Michel Ruiz/Dorling Kindersley; **90, LT,** Pearson Education, Inc.; **LT,** Pearson Education, Inc.; **LM,** Pearson Education, Inc.; **LM,** Pearson Education, Inc.; **LB,** Pearson Education, Inc.; **B,** dbimages/Alamy; **91, RT,** Pearson Education, Inc.; **RT,** Pearson Education, Inc.; **RM,** Rubberball/age Fotostock; **RM,** Jaime Mota/age Fotostock; **RB,** Pearson Education, Inc.; **RB,** Pearson Education, Inc.; **94, LT,** Carp (1848). Woodcut by Taito/The Granger Collection, New York; **B,** Jarno Gonzalez Zarraonandia/Shutterstock; **95, BM,** Hellestad Rune/Corbis Sygma; **T,** Bob Krist/eStock Photo; **96,** Stephane De Sakutin/AFP/Getty Images; **97, TM,** Dmitry Kosterev/Shutterstock; **RT,** Dave King/Dorling Kindersley; **RM,** Luchschen/Shutterstock; **RB,** Dorling Kindersley; **BM,** Owen Franken/Corbis; **RB,** James Marshall/Corbis; **98, L,** Alistair Duncan/Dorling Kindersley; **LB,** Michael Holford/Dorling Kindersley; **RB,** Bruce Forster/Dorling Kindersley/Courtesy of the National Historic Oregon Trail Interpretive Center; **99, LB,** Swim Ink 2, LLC/Corbis; **RB,** Matthew Ward/Dorling Kindersley; **102, RT,** Kim Sayer/Dorling Kindersley; **B,** Tom Sliter/The Stennis Center for Public Service Leadership; **RT,** Phil Sandlin/AP Images; **103, LT,** Reuters/Hans Deryk; **RT,** Photo courtesy of Anne Marie Sutherland; **104, LB,** Art Resource/Musée du Louvre; **RB,** Spc Katherine M. Roth/HO/epa/Corbis. All Rights Reserved; **105, L,** Todd Gipstein/Corbis; **R,** Imaginechina via AP Images; **106, R,** Pool/Anwar Hussein Collection/Getty Images; **L,** Karel Prinsloo/AP Images; **107,** John Leicester/AP Images; **108, T,** Kim Sayer/Dorling Kindersley; **M,** L. Clarke/Corbis; **B,** AP Photo/Douglas Healey; **109, M,** White House Photo Office; **T,** Wally McNamee/Corbis; **B,** The Collection of the Supreme Court of the United States; **110,** Alan Gignoux/age fotostock; **111, B,** Kote Rodrigo/EFE/Corbis; **T,** Karel Prinsloo/AP Images; **112, B,** Jeff Greenberg/PhotoEdit; **T,** William Whitehurst/Corbis; **113, RB,** Wally McNamee/Corbis; **116, RT,** Jim Zuckerman/Corbis; **LT,** Digital Vision/Getty Images; **B,** El Comercio Newspaper, Dante Piaggio/AP Images; **117, RT,** Photo courtesy of Brian McCray; **LT,** Ira Block/National Geographic/Getty Images; **TM,** University of Oregon/AP Images; **118, LB,** The British Museum/Dorling Kindersley; **LB,** O. Louis Mazzatenta/National Geographic Stock; **RB,** Ivonne Wierink/Shutterstock; **M,** Giles Stokoe/Felix deWeldon/Dorling Kindersley; **119, RB,** Dagli Orti/Picture Desk, Inc./Kobal Collection; **M,** Andy Crawford/Dorling Kindersley, Courtesy of the University Museum of Archaeology and Anthropology, Cambridge; **RB,** Getty Images/De Agostini Editore Picture Library; **120, LB,** Bettmann/Corbis; **LM,** Bettmann/Corbis; **121, RB,** Hulton Archive/Getty Images; **L,** The Granger Collection, New York; **122, LT,** Sean Hunter/Dorling Kindersley; **B,** Martin Gray/National Geographic Stock; **R,** Robert F. Sisson/National Geographic Society; **123, LB,** O. Louis Mazzatenta/National Geographic Stock; **LB,** Anders Ryman/Corbis.

UNIT 1: Pages 128–133, T, Bkgrnd sky, Image Source/Getty Images; **129, L,** Pearson Education, Inc.; **R,** Pearson Education, Inc.; **Bkgrnd,** Ray Juno/Corbis;

130, LB, Jupiter Unlimited; 131, LT, Life in Frames Photography/Shutterstock; LB, iStockphoto.com; M, gary718/Shutterstock; 132, L, Archive Holdings Inc./Getty Images; R, Dragan Trifunovic/Shutterstock; 133, T, Pearson Education, Inc.; T, Pearson Education, Inc.

CHAPTER 1: Pages 135–137, All, Pearson Education, Inc.; 138, LB, Karl Weatherly/Getty Images; LB, John Shaw/Photo Researchers, Inc.; 140, RB, Pearson Education, Inc.; RM, Mark Karrass/Corbis; RM, LeCajun/Shutterstock; RM, Gavin Hellier/JAI/Corbis; LB, Shutterstock; 142, LB, Robert Llewellyn/age Fotostock; RB, PCL/Alamy; 143, LB, Gregory Wrona/Alamy; RB, Rudi Von Briel/PhotoEdit; 145, Spencer Grant/Photo Researchers, Inc.; 146, LB, Dynamic Graphics/age Fotostock; 147, RT, Bettmann/Corbis; RM, Corbis; RB, Corbis; 150, LB, Corbis; LM, Corbis; LB, AP/Wide World Photo; 152, LB, Pearson Education, Inc.; 153, B, Shutterstock; RT, Michael Rosa/Shutterstock Inc.; RM, Laurence Gough/Shutterstock Inc.; RB, Gai Mooney/Corbis; RB, Flashon Studio/Shutterstock; 155, LB, moodboard/Corbis; BM, Wally McNamee/Corbis; RB, Robert Galbraith/Reuters; 157, Stefan Rousseau/PA Wire URN:5867212 (Press Association via AP Images).

CHAPTER 2: Pages 160–163, All, Pearson Education, Inc.; 164, LB, Randy Faris/Corbis; Bkgrnd, Rudy Sulgan/age Fotostock; 166, LB, Kurt Werby/Photolibrary; LM, Alaska Stock/age Fotostock; RM, John E Marriott/Getty Images; RM, Oleksiy Maksymenko/Alamy; 168, LT, Alaska Stock/age Fotostock; RT, Michael Kline/Alamy; 170, LT, Volkmar K. Wentzel/National Geographic Stock; 171, RT, Ulga/Shutterstock; LM, Nathan Benn/Alamy; 173, RB, Stock Montage/Getty Images; 174, LB, Colored gravure reproduction, 1894, of a painting by Augustus Tholey. The Granger Collection, New York; 175, RB, Austin Andrews/Zuma Press/Newscom; LB, Library and Archives Canada/Charles Walter Simpson collection/C-013945; 176, B, Illustrated London News Ltd/Mary Evans/Everett Collection; 177, RT, Library and Archives Canada/C. J. Patterson, Lawson and Jones Limited/C-029568; 178, LB, Reuters/Andy Clark AC/SV/Corbis; 180, LB, Corbis/Bettmann; 181, UN Photo; 182, LM, Chris Cheadle/Photolibrary; LB, Peter Mintz/age Fotostock; LB, Gunter Marx Photography/Corbis; LT, Pete Ryan/National Geographic Stock; 183, Pearson Education, Inc.

UNIT 1 CLOSER: Page 186, Bkgrnd, Stacey Lynn Payne/Shutterstock; 187, B, Péter Gudella/Shutterstock.

UNIT 2: Pages 188–193, T, Bkgrnd sky, Image Source/Getty Images; 189, LM, Pearson Education, Inc.; RM, Pearson Education, Inc.; Bkgrnd, Gary718/Shutterstock; 190, LB, Michael Boyny/age Fotostock; LT, Robert Francis/Photolibrary; RB, Dreamtours/Photolibrary; 191, LT, Sébastien Boisse/Photononstop/Photolibrary; 192, LM, Susana Gonzalez/Newsmakers/Getty Images; LB, Brian Bailey/Getty Images; RM, Richard Bickel/Corbis; RB, Andoni Canela/Photolibrary; 193, L, Pearson Education, Inc.; R, Pearson Education, Inc.

CHAPTER 3: Pages 194–197, All, Pearson Education, Inc.; 198, Bkgrnd, Travel Ink/Alamy; B, Robert Fried/Alamy; 200, LT, Scott S. Warren/National Geographic Stock; LB, Ales Liska/Shutterstock; RB, LOOK Die Bildagentur der Fotografen GmbH/Alamy; RT, Radius Images/Alamy; 201, RT, Didier Dorval/Radius Images/JupiterImages; RB, urosr/Shutterstock; LB, Geoff Dann/Dorling Kindersley; RM, Rusty Dodson/Shutterstock; 203, RM, Richard Melloul/Sygma/Corbis; 205, R, AFP Photo/Jorge Uzon/Newscom; 206, LB, The Trustees of The British Museum/Art Resource, NY; 207, T, Demetrio Carrasco/Conaculta-Inah-Mex. Authorized reproduction by the Instituto Nacional de Antropologia e Historia/Dorling Kindersley; M, The Granger Collection, New York; B, The Granger Collection, New York; 208, The Art Archive/National Palace Mexico City/Gianni Dagli Orti; R, The Art Archive/National Palace Mexico City/Gianni Dagli Ort; 209, L, The Art Archive/National Palace Mexico City/Alfredo Dagli Orti; 210, Schalkwijk/Art Resource, NY; 211, L, The Art Archive/National Palace Mexico City/Gianni Dagli Orti; R, Schalkwijk/Art Resource, NY; 212, Jeff Topping/Reuters; 213, LB, Library of Congress; BM, AFP/Getty Images; RB, Jorge Silva/Reuters; RM, Holger Mette/Shutterstock; 214, LB, L. Zacharie/Alamy; RB, Danny Lehman/Corbis; 214–215, Peregrina /iStockphoto.com; 215, LB, Robert Harding Picture Library/age Fotostock; RB, Andy Mead/Icon SMI/Newscom; 216, L, Linda Whitwam/Dorling Kindersley; 217, AP Photo/Carlos Osorio; 218, LB, Paul E. Rodriguez/Newscom; BM, Keith Dannemiller/Alamy; LT, Ivan Vdovin/age Fotostock; RT, Ivan Vdovin/age Fotostock.

CHAPTER 4: Pages 222–225, All, Pearson Education, Inc.; 226, RB, Frans Lemmens/zefa/Corbis; Bkgrnd, P. Narayan/age Fotostock; 228, LT, Jeff Grabert/Shutterstock, Inc.; RT, Demetrio Carrasco/JAI/Corbis; RM, Stephen Frink/Corbis;

RB, Radius Images/Alamy; 229, Jeff Greenberg/PhotoEdit; 231, John Miller/Robert Harding World Imagery/Corbis; 232, B, Enrique de la Osa/Reuters; 233, Lynn M. Stone/Nature Picture Library; 234, L, Jim Clare/Nature Picture Library; LB, The Art Archive/Archaeological Museum, Tikal, Guatemala/Gianni Dagli Orti; 235, RT, The Granger Collection, New York; RB, The Art Archive; 236, Time & Life Pictures/Getty Images; 237, AP/Wide World Photo; 238, Laurent Grandadam/age Fotostock; 239, L, Owen Franken/Corbis; LM, www.imagesource.com/Newscom; R, Pearson Education, Inc.; RM, Holly Wilmeth/Aurora Photos/Corbis; RT, AP Images; T, Sharon Hudson/Corbis; 240, Mark Edwards/Still Pictures/Peter Arnold, Inc.; 241, Didi/Alamy; 242, T, Pearson Education, Inc.; 243, RB, Pearson Education, Inc.

UNIT 2 CLOSER: Page 246, iStockphoto.com; 247, Pearson Education, Inc.

UNIT 3: Pages 248–253, T, Bkgrnd sky, Image Source/Getty Images; 249, LT, Pearson Education, Inc.; RT, Pearson Education, Inc.; TM, Pearson Education, Inc.; Bkgrnd, Wildlife/Peter Arnold Inc.; 250, T, Martin Harvey/Corbis; B, Blickwinkel/Alamy; 251, LT, Paul Harris/Photolibrary; 253, RT, Pearson Education, Inc.

CHAPTER 5: Pages 254–257, All, Pearson Education, Inc.; 258, Bkgrnd, James Sparshatt/Corbis; B, Reuters/Jorge Silva; 260, M, Patricio Robles Gil/naturepl.com; RB, Demetrio Carrasco/JAI/Corbis; BM, Ann Johansson/Corbis; LB, Neil Beer/Corbis; 261, LB, Pete Oxford/Minden Pictures; B, Frank Greenaway/Dorling Kindersley; RB, Imagebroker/Alamy; 262, Danita Delimont/Alamy; 263, L, Charles Bowman/age Fotostock; R, Jody Amiet/AFP/Getty Images; 264, All, Pearson Education, Inc.; 266, The Art Archive/Museo del Oro Bogotá/Dagli Orti/Picture Desk; 267, R, Illustration from Howard Pyle's Book of Pirates/National Maritime Museum, Greenwich, London; M, Tina Chambers/British Museum/Dorling Kindersley; 268, Photoshot Holdings Ltd/Bruce Coleman; 270, Pearson Education, Inc.; 271, RM, Doug Benc/Getty Images; RB, Suraj N. Sharma/Dinodia Picture Agency; L, Philippe Giraud/Goodlook/Corbis; 272, Neil Beer/Getty Images; 273, LT, Fernando Ruiz/AFP/Getty Images/Newscom; LT, Martin Bernetti/Agence France Presse/Getty Images; TM, Roslan RahmanAFP/Getty Images; RT, Timothy A. Clary/AFP/Getty Images/Newscom; RT, Pascal Le Segretain/Getty Images; 274, LM, Juan Barreto/AFP/Getty Images/Newscom; LB, Juan Barreto/AFP/Getty Images/Newscom; 275, ESA/AP Images.

CHAPTER 6: Pages 278–281, All, Pearson Education, Inc.; 282, Bkgrnd, Gordon Wiltsie/Getty Images; 284, RM, Andoni Canela/age Fotostock; BM, Javier Etcheverry/Alamy; LB, Cephas Picture Library/Alamy; LB, Tui De Roy/Minden Pictures; 286, RM, Paul Harrison/Photolibrary; RB, Diego Giudice/Corbis; 287, Frans Lanting/Corbis; 289, Jeremy Hoare/Alamy; 290, Travel Ink/Getty Images; 291, B, Pete Oxford/naturepl.com; RB, The Art Archive/Stephanie Colasanti; 292, Museo Municipal, Quito, Ecuador/The Bridgeman Art Library; 294, B, AP Images; 295, Private Collection/Archives Charmet/The Bridgeman Art Library; 296, Pearson Education, Inc.; 297, BM, WIN-Initiative/Getty Images; RB, Superstock/age Fotostock; 298, BM, Claudio Frias Beyer/Newscom; RB, MIXA Co., Ltd./Alamy; 299, LB, Steve Allen/Getty Images; LB, AFP/Getty Images; 301, Ricardo Mazalan/AP Images.

CHAPTER 7: Pages 304–307, All, Pearson Education, Inc.; 308, Bkgrnd, Michael David/age Fotostock; LB, Reuters/Christian Veron; 310, RM, Jacques Jangoux /Alamy; RM, Digital Vision /Alamy; RB, Ricardo Junqueira /Alamy; RB, Berndt Fischer /age Fotostock; 312, B, Shutterstock; 313, RB, Pearson Education, Inc. Education; RM, OSF/Wothe, Konrad/Animals Animals/Earth Scenes; LM, Dorling Kindersley; BM, iStockphoto.com; LB, Todd Pusser/naturepl.com; M, iStockphoto.com; 314, LT, NASA; L, David R. Frazier/Photolibrary/Alamy; 315, B, Paulo Fridman/Corbis; 316, LB, Michel Renaudeau/age Fotostock; 318, LB, The Art Archive/Bibliothèque des Arts Décoratifs Paris/Gianni Dagli Orti; LB, Guilherme Gaensly; 319, Reuters/Jamil Bittar; 320, Pearson Education, Inc.; 321, RM, Sergio Moraes /Reuters; RB, Sergio Moraes/Reuters; 322, M-Sat Ltd/Photo Researchers, Inc.; RB, Paulo Fridman/Corbis; 323, B, Marcelo Rudini/Alamy; M, Carlos Cazalis/Corbis; LM, Collart Herve/Corbis Sygma; RM, Marcelo Rudini/Alamy.

UNIT 3 CLOSER: Page 328, LB, Shutterstock; Bkgrnd, iStockphoto.com; BM, Barnabas Kindersley/Dorling Kindersley; RB, PeterK/Shutterstock; 329, L, GlowImages/Alamy; R, Insadco Photography/Alamy.

UNIT 4: Pages 330–335, T, Bkgrnd sky, Image Source/Getty Images; 331, All, Pearson Education, Inc.; Bkgrnd, Vidler Vidler/Photolibrary; 332, TM, Robert

Acknowledgments (continued)

Zywucki/Shutterstock; **LT,** Roy Rainford/Robert Harding World Imagery; **333, M,** Pichugin Dmitry/Shutterstock; **334, T,** Hulton Archive/Getty Images; **B,** Jose Fuste Raga/Photolibrary; **335, All,** Pearson Education, Inc.

CHAPTER 8: Pages 336–339, All, Pearson Education, Inc.; **340, LB,** HO/AFP/Getty Images/Newscom; **342–343, RB,** Jonothan Potter/Dorling Kindersley; **343, RB,** Peter Hayman/The British Museum/Dorling Kindersley; **RB,** Paul Harris/Dorling Kindersley; **344, M,** The Art Archive/Agora Museum Athens/Gianni Dagli Orti; **RT,** The Art Archive/Agora Museum Athens/Gianni Dagli Orti; **345, RT,** Nick Nicholls/The British Museum/Dorling Kindersley; **346, LM,** Hoberman Collection/Corbis; **348, L,** Réunion des Musées Nationaux/Art Resource, NY; **350, LT,** John Heseltine/Dorling Kindersley; **351, B,** Franck Guiziou/Hemis/Corbis; **353, RT,** PoodlesRock/Corbis; **354, LB,** Cameraphoto Arte, Venice/Art Resource, NY; **355, RB,** Museum of History of Sofia, Sofia, Bulgaria/Archives Charmet/Bridgeman Art Library; **357, RT,** Gianni Dagli Orti/Corbis. All Rights Reserved; **359, RT,** Réunion des Musées Nationaux/Art Resource, NY; **360, LB,** Geoff Dann/Dorling Kindersley; **361, RT,** Werner Forman/Art Resource, NY; **363, RB,** SIME s.a.s/eStock Photo; **364, L,** Bridgeman Art Library; **LB,** Bettmann/Corbis; **365, RB,** Snark/Art Resource, NY; **366, M,** Bettmann/Corbis; **LB,** *The Dance Macabre* (detail, 1485), Artist unknown, Fresco. L'Oratorio dei Disciplini/SuperStock; **LT,** Frank Greenaway/Dorling Kindersley; **L,** maxstockphoto/Shutterstock.

CHAPTER 9: Pages 370–373, All, Pearson Education, Inc.; **374,** Philip Gatward/Dorling Kindersley; **375, RM,** *The Last Supper* (1495–1498), Leonardo da Vinci (1452–1519). Fresco. Santa Maria delle Grazie, Milan/A.K.G., Berlin/SuperStock; **RB,** Dorling Kindersley; **376, LT,** Ellen Howdon/Dorling Kindersley, Courtesy of Glasgow Museum; **T,** FPG/Getty Images; **RT,** Pearson Education, Inc.; **377, M,** Dorling Kindersley; **RB,** Adrea Pistolesi/Getty Images; **380, BM,** *Portrait of Henry VIII* (16th century), Hans Holbein the Younger, Oil on canvas. Belvoir Castle, Leicestershire. The Bridgeman Art Library Ltd.; **LB,** Portrait of Catherine of Aragon (1485–1536), 1st Queen of Henry VIII (1825), from "Memoirs of the Court of Queen Elizabeth," watercolor and gouache on paper. Private Collection/The Bridgeman Art Library; **382, Bkgrnd,** Joel W. Rogers/Corbis; **383, RT,** Reuters New Media Inc./Corbis; **BM,** James Stevenson/Dorling Kindersley, Courtesy of the National Maritime Museum, London; **RB,** Clive Streeter/Dorling Kindersley, Courtesy of The Science Museum, London; **LT,** Dorling Kindersley; **384, LB,** *Padshahnama: Europeans Bring Gifts to the Shah Jahan.* The Royal Collection, Her Majesty Queen Elizabeth II; **385, RT,** Chas Howson/The British Museum/Dorling Kindersley; **386, LB,** Erich Lessing/Art Resource, NY; **387, RM,** *Louis XIV, King of France* (1701), Hyacinthe Rigaud. Oil on canvas, 277 x 194 cm. Louvre, Paris, France. Photo: Herve Lewandowski. Louvre, Paris, France. Réunion des Musées Nationaux/Art Resource, NY; **388, LB,** Martin Jones/Corbis; **389, LT,** The Granger Collection, New York; **T,** Shutterstock; **391, RB,** Reduced model of a guillotine (18th century), French School, wood and metal. Musée de la Ville de Paris, Musée Carnavalet, Paris, France, Giraudon/Bridgeman Art Library; **RT,** Getty Images/De Agostini Editore Picture Library; **BM,** Musée de la Révolution Française, Vizille, France/The Bridgeman Art Library; **392, TM,** Lebrecht Music & Arts Photo Library; **RT,** The Francis Frith Collection/Corbis; **393, RT,** Underwood & Underwood/Corbis; **LT,** Musée National de l'Education, Rouen, France/The Bridgeman Art Library; **394, B,** Bettmann/Corbis; **396, LB,** Hulton-Deutsch Collection/Corbis; **397, RB,** Dorling Kindersley; **398, LT,** Andy Crawford/Dorling Kindersley/Imperial War Museum, London; **399,** PhotoDisc/Getty Images; **400, B,** Bettmann/Corbis; **401, RT,** U. S. Navy/Photo Researchers; **402, RB,** AP Images; **B,** Bettmann/Corbis; **404, BM,** Bettmann/Corbis; **LB,** Bettmann/Corbis; **405, L,** The Punch Cartoon Library; **R,** Str Old/Reuters; **406, T,** Peter Dejong/AP Images; **LT,** Peter Dench/Corbis; **407, T,** Dorling Kindersley.

CHAPTER 10: Pages 410–413, All, Pearson Education, Inc.; **414, Bkgrnd,** Sylvain Grandadam/age Fotostock; **B,** J. D. Heaton/age Fotostock; **416, RM,** iStockphoto.com; **M,** Dhoxax/Shutterstock; **T,** Pierre Jacques/Hemis/Corbis; **M,** Bo Zaunders/Corbis; **RB,** Rick Price/Corbis; **RB,** Gavin Hellier/Robert Harding World; **419, B,** Lawson Wood/Corbis; **RM,** Simon Fraser /Photo Researchers; **422,** Dallas and John Heaton/Stock Connection; **425, M,** Pearson Education, Inc.; **RB,** Erik Svensson and Jeppe Wikstrom/Dorling Kindersley; **R,** David Lomax/Robert Harding/Getty Images; **426,** Annie Griffiths Belt/Corbis; **427,** Ken Straiton/Corbis; **428, LB,** Patrick Müller © Centre des monuments nationaux, Paris; **429, T,** Britta Jaschinski/Dorling Kindersley; **B,** Prentice Hall School; **RB,** Le Segretain Pascal/Corbis Sygma; **RM,** Perrush/Shutterstock; **430,** AP Photo/Cristophe Ena; **431,** Bjorn Svensson/Photolibrary; **432,** George Hammerstein/Solus-Veer/Corbis;

433, Fancy/Veer/Corbis; **434,** Dorling Kindersley; **435,** Pearson Education, Inc.; **RM,** Bob Sacha/Corbis; **RB,** iStockphoto.com; **436,** massimo Borchi/Corbis; **438, RB,** Reuters/Susana Vera (SPAIN); **439,** George Christakis/epa/Corbis.

CHAPTER 11: Pages 442–445, All, Pearson Education, Inc.; **446, Bkgrnd,** Erich Lessing/Magnum Photos; **LB,** Stefano Pensotti/age Fotostock; **448, LB,** Per Karlsson—BKWine.com/Alamy; **LB,** Jaroslaw Grudzinski/Shutterstock; **449, M,** Dean Conger/Corbis; **B,** AFP/Getty Images; **450, RB,** Zaichiki/Alamy; **RB,** Reuters/Vasily Fedosenko; **RM,** AP Photo/CTK, David Veis; **LM,** iStockphoto.com; **LB,** Photoshot Holdings Ltd./Alamy; **451,** Stan Kujawa/Alamy; **453, TM,** Idealink Photography/Alamy; **RT,** ziontek/Dabrowski-KPA/Zuma Press, © 2004 by Wziontek/Dabrowski-KPA (Newscom TagID: zumaphotos661194) [Photo via Newscom]; **LT,** AP Photo/Hidajet Delic; **LT,** Martin Bureau/AFP/Getty Images; **454, LB,** Steven May/Alamy; **455, RB,** imagebroker/Alamy; **456, B,** Petr Josek Snr/Reuters; **457, B,** Carlos Nieto/age Fotostock; **459, B,** Getty Images/De Agostini Editore Picture Library; **460, RT,** Viktor Drachev/AFP/Getty Images; **461, LT,** East News/Getty Images; **RT,** AFP Photo/Daniel Mihailescu/Newscom.

CHAPTER 12: Pages 464–467, All, Pearson Education, Inc.; **468, Bkgrnd,** Sergey Yakovlev/Shutterstock; **LB,** David Turnley/Corbis; **470, R,** isoft/iStockphoto.com; **M,** Dean Conger/Corbis; **L,** Superstock; **471,** Gerd Ludwig/Corbis; **472,** Sovfoto/Eastfoto; **475, R,** Gideon Mendel/Corbis; **L,** Pearson Education, Inc.; **476, L,** Werner Forman/Art Resource, NY; **R,** Erich Lessing/Art Resource, NY; **477, L,** Jeremy Horner/Corbis; **R,** *Ivan the Terrible* (20th century), English School, Gouache on paper. Private Collection/© Look and Learn/The Bridgeman Art Library; **478, L,** The Art Archive/Russian Historical Museum Moscow/Alfredo Dagli Orti; **R,** The Granger Collection, New York; **479, LB,** David South/Alamy; **LT,** The Gallery Collection/Corbis; **RB,** Réunion des Musées Nationaux/Art Resource, NY; **480,** Photos 12/Alamy; **481,** Charles & Josette Lenars/Corbis; **482, L,** Gianni Giansanti/Sygma/Corbis; **R,** Peter Turnley/Corbis; **484,** Iain Masterton/Alamy Images; **485, L,** Peter Turnley/Corbis; **R,** David Young-Wolff/PhotoEdit; **486,** Vasily Fedosenko/Reuters/Corbis; **487,** Lystseva Marina/ITAR-TASS Photo/Corbis; **489,** Gleb Garanich/Reuters/Corbis.

UNIT 4 CLOSER: Page 492, B, Shutterstock; **LB,** Shutterstock; **RT,** Shutterstock; **RT,** Shutterstock; **492–493, Bkgrnd,** Shutterstock; **493, R,** European Communities, 1995–2009; **R,** Shutterstock.

UNIT 5: Pages 494–499, T, Bkgrnd sky, Image Source/Getty Images; **495, LT,** Pearson Education, Inc.; **TM,** Pearson Education, Inc.; **RT,** Pearson Education, Inc.; **B,** Stellapictures/JupiterImages; **496, T,** Radius Images/JupiterImages; **B,** Matthew Septimus/Getty Images; **497, T,** Gavin Hellier/Photolibrary; **B,** Roger De La Harpe/Photolibrary; **M,** Eric Isselée/Shutterstock; **498,** Hugh Sitton/zefa/Corbis; **499, All** Pearson Education, Inc.

CHAPTER 13: Pages 500–503, All, Pearson Education, Inc.; **504,** Bruno Morandi/Getty Images; **506,** Bruno Morandi/Getty Images; **507, LM,** Pearson Education, Inc.; **L,** Nigel Bean/naturepl.com; **RM,** Atlantide Phototravel/Corbis; **R,** Bruno Fert/Corbis; **509, Inset,** Bruce Dale/National Geographic/Getty Images; **Bkgrnd,** George Steinmetz/Corbis; **510,** Martin Dohrn/Photo Researchers, Inc.; **512,** Frans Lemmens/zefa/Corbis; **513, L,** John Webb/The Art Archive; **R,** Joan Pollock/Alamy; **514,** Courtesy of the Wilberforce House Museum, Hull/Dorling Kindersley; **515, T,** National Archives Image Library, UK/Dorling Kindersley; **B,** Popperfoto/Getty Images; **516, L,** Bettmann/Corbis; **R,** AFP/Getty Images; **517,** AP Images; **518,** Gideon Mendel/ActionAid/Corbis; **519,** Jacob Silberberg/Getty Images; **520, L,** AFP/Getty Images; **R,** George Osodi/AP Images; **521, Cloth,** Dorling Kindersley; **LT,** Comstock Images/Jupiter Unlimited; **RT,** Paul Almasy/Corbis; **LB,** Studio Patellani/Corbis; **RB,** Philippe Lissac/Godong/Corbis; **523,** Pearson Education, Inc.

CHAPTER 14: Pages 526–257, Ksenia Khamkova/iStockphoto.com; **526, B,** Pearson Education, Inc.; **527, T,** Pearson Education, Inc.; **B,** Pearson Education, Inc.; **528–529, All,** Pearson Education, Inc.; **530, Bkgrnd,** SuperStock; **B,** Steve Outram/Mira.com; **533, L,** Tim Laman/Getty Images, Inc.; **L Inset,** Mitsuaki Iwago/Minden Pictures; **M Inset,** Beckman/Dorling Kindersley; **R Inset,** Mitsuaki Iwago/Minden Pictures; **R,** Image Source/Photolibrary; **534, L,** Ian Murphy/Getty Images; **M,** Charles O'Rear/Corbis; **R,** Kulka/zefa/Corbis; **535, Bkgrnd,** franco pizzochero/age Fotostock; **B,** F.A.O. Food and Agriculture Organization of the United Nations; **536, T,** Reza/Webistan/Getty Images; **TM,** Peter Martell/AFP/Getty Images; **BM,** Andrew Holt/Getty Images; **B,** Jenny Matthews/Alamy; **537,** Liba Taylor/Corbis; **538, T,** Ric Ergenbright/Corbis; **B,** Gallo Images/Corbis;

942

539, B, Peter Groenendijk/age Fotostock; **T,** Yadid Levy/age Fotostock; **541, RT,** The Granger Collection, New York; **LT,** The Granger Collection, New York; **B,** Bettmann/Corbis; **542,** Bettmann/Corbis; **543,** David Turnley/Corbis; **544,** PCN Photography/PCN/Corbis; **545, T,** Patrick Robert/Sygma/Corbis; **B,** Lindsay Hebberd/Corbis; **546,** Alfred De Montesquiou/AP Images; **548, B,** AFP Photo/HO/U.S. Navy/Jason R. Zalasky/Newscom; **T,** epa/Corbis; **549,** Wolfgang Schmidt/Peter Arnold, Inc.

CHAPTER 15: Pages 553–555, All, Pearson Education, Inc.; **556, Bkgrnd,** Franck Guiziou/Hemis/Corbis; **B,** Hugh Sitton/zefa/Corbis; **558,** Jacques Descloitres, MODIS Land Science Team/NASA; **559, LB,** Tony Craddock/zefa/Corbis; **RB,** Sylvain Grandadam/age Fotostock; **LT,** Aristidis Vafeiadakis/Alamy; **RT,** R. Matina/age Fotostock; **560, B,** Otto Lang/Corbis; **T,** Otto Lang/Corbis; **561,** Cecile Treal and Jean-Michel Ruiz/Dorling Kindersley; **564,** Roger Wood/Corbis; **565, T,** Bojan Brecelj/Corbis; **M,** Peter Hayman/The British Museum/Dorling Kindersley; **B,** The Gallery Collection/Corbis; **Bkgrnd,** Yanta/Shutterstock; **566, LB,** Peter Hayman/The British Museum/Dorling Kindersley; **BM,** John Hepver/The British Museum/Dorling Kindersley; **Bkgrnd,** Hydromet /Shutterstock; **LT,** Peter Hayman/The British Museum/Dorling Kindersley; **RB,** Kazuyoshi Nomachi/Corbis; **RT,** Pearson Education, Inc.; **567, R,** Gavin Hellier/Robert Harding World/Corbis; **L,** The Gallery Collection/Corbis; **M,** Pearson Education, Inc.; **568,** Interpress/Interpress/Kipa/Corbis; **569,** Bettmann/Corbis; **570,** Brakefield Photo/Brand X/Corbis; **571, T,** Claudia Wiens/Das Fotoarchiv/Peter Arnold; **B,** Hekimian Julien/Corbis; **M,** Franck Guiziou/Hemis/Corbis; **573, R,** Olivier Martel/Corbis; **L,** Alan Hills/Dorling Kindersley; **574,** Mona Sharaf/Reuters/Corbis; **575,** John Chiasson/Liaison/Getty Images.

UNIT 5 CLOSER: Page 578, RT, Shutterstock; **B,** iStockphoto.com; **578–579, B,** Pearson Education, Inc.; **579, LM,** Shutterstock; **RM,** Christian Musat/Shutterstock; **RT,** Pearson Education, Inc.; **Bkgrnd,** iStockphoto.com; **LT,** Shutterstock; **M,** Shutterstock.

UNIT 6: Pages 580–585, T, Bkgrnd sky, Image Source/Getty Images; **581, B,** Polly Wreford/Photolibrary; **LT,** Pearson Education, Inc.; **RM,** Pearson Education, Inc.; **LM,** Pearson Education, Inc.; **RT,** Pearson Education, Inc.; **582,** Yvan Travert/Photononstop/Photolibrary; **583, T,** Nik Wheeler/Corbis; **B,** Ray Ellis/Photo Researchers; **584, L,** Christian Kober/Photolibrary; **M,** Ahmad Al-Rubaye/AFP/Getty Images/Newscom; **R,** Mark Hannaford/Photolibrary; **585, L,** Pearson Education, Inc.; **RM,** Pearson Education, Inc.; **LM,** Pearson Education, Inc.; **R,** Pearson Education, Inc.

CHAPTER 16: Pages 586–589, All, Pearson Education, Inc.; **590, Bkgrnd,** John Warburton-Lee Photography/Photolibrary; **B,** Patrick Robert/Sygma/Corbis; **593,** Essam Al-Sudani/AFP/Getty Images; **594, T,** Homer Sykes Archive/Alamy; **B,** Ed Kashi/Aurora Photos; **596, T,** Thaier Al-Sudani/Reuters/Corbis; **B,** Marwan Ibrahim/AFP/Getty Images; **M,** David Turnley/Corbis; **598, Bkgrnd,** Georg Gerster/Photo Researchers; **L,** Jane Sweeney/lonelyplanetimages.com; **M,** The London Art Archive/Alamy; **R,** Accounts Table with cuneiform script, (about 2400 B.C.), Mesopotamia, Terracotta. Louvre, Paris, France/The Bridgeman Art Library; **599,** Erich Lessing/Art Resource, NY; **600,** Picture Partners/Alamy; **601, T,** Sucheta Das/Reuters/Corbis; **TM,** World Religions Photo Library/Alamy; **BM,** Akhtar Soomro/epa/Corbis; **B,** Hassan Ammar/AFP/Getty Images; **603, L,** Jane Sweeney/Art Directors.co.uk/Ark Religion.com; **RB,** Turkish School/Getty Images; **RT,** General Photographic Agency/Getty Images; **604, R,** Bettmann/Corbis; **L,** AP Photo; **605, LT,** Jacques Langevin/Sygma/Corbis; **606,** Jose Fuste Raga/Corbis; **607,** JTB Photo/Photolibrary; **608, L,** Karim Sahib/AFP/Getty Images; **R,** AFP/Getty Images; **610, RB,** Photopqr/La Voix Du Nord/karine Delmas/Newscom; **T,** Khaled Desouki/AFP/Getty Images; **LB,** Safin Hamed/AFP/Getty Images; **611,** Pearson Education, Inc.

CHAPTER 17: Pages 614–617, All, Pearson Education, Inc.; **618, Bkgrnd,** Grapheast/Photolibrary; **B,** Ali Kabas/Alamy; **620, B,** Josef F. Stuefer/Shutterstock; **M,** Sami Sarkis Travel/Alamy; **T,** Israel images/Alamy; **623,** Mike Abrahams/Alamy; **624, T,** Rosebud Pictures/Getty Images; **B,** Chris Hondros/Getty Images; **M,** Anwar Amro/Getty Images; **626,** Ancient Art & Architecture/DanitaDelimont.com; **627,** The Art Archive/University Library Istanbul/Dagli Orti; **628, L,** Image Asset Management Ltd./SuperStock; **R,** Menahem Kahana/AFP/Getty Images; **629,** Bridgeman-Giraudon/Art Resource, NY; **630,** Megapress/Alamy; **631,** Magnus Rew/Dorling Kindersley; **633,** Rolls Press/Popperfoto/Getty Images; **634,** David Silverman/Getty Images; **635, L,** Hussein Malla/AP Photo; **M,** Julian Herbert/Getty Images; **R,** AFP PHOTO/Louai Beshara/Newscom; **636,**

R, Alan Keohane/Photolibrary; **L,** Salah Malkawi/Getty Images; **637, T,** Israel images/Alamy; **M,** AFP/Getty Images; **B,** An Qi/Alamy; **639,** Alexandra Boulat/VII/AP Images; **640, L,** Ricki Rosen/Corbis; **R,** Shawn Baldwin/Corbis; **641,** Pearson Education, Inc.

CHAPTER 18: Page 644, Bkgrnd, Ebru Baraz/iStockphoto.com; **B,** Pearson Education, Inc.; **644–645,** Sufi70/iStockphoto.com; **645, RT,** Pearson Education, Inc.; **RB,** Pearson Education, Inc.; **LT,** Cokeker/Shutterstock; **646–647, All,** Pearson Education, Inc.; **648, Bkgrnd,** Alistair Duncan/Dorling Kindersley; **B,** Chris Rout/Alamy; **650, L,** Kate Clow, Terry Richardson, Dominic Whiting/Dorling Kindersley; **R,** David Poole/Robert Harding Word Imagery; **M,** Rainer Jahns/Alamy; **651,** Ryan Pyle/Corbis; **653, B,** Arthur Thèvenart/Corbis; **T,** Raheb Homavandi CJF/KS/Reuters; **654, R,** Superstock/age Fotostock; **L,** Peter Guttman/Corbis; **655,** Robert Preston Photography/Alamy; **656, L,** The Art Archive/Dagli Orti; **R,** The Gallery Collection/Corbis; **657,** The Granger Collection, New York; **659, B,** Reinhard Dirscherl/Alamy; **T,** Hanan Isachar/Corbis; **Bkgrnd,** Can Balcioglu/Shutterstock; **660, R,** Mary Evans Picture Library/Alamy; **L,** Tolga Bozoglu/epa/Corbis; **661,** Bettmann/Corbis; **662,** Raheb Homavandi/Reuters/Corbis; **663,** AFP/Getty Images; **664,** Behrouz Mehri/AFP/Getty Images; **665, T,** Sygma/Corbis; **LB,** Michele Falzone/JAI/Corbis; **RB,** Charles & Josette Lenars/Corbis; **Bkgrnd,** javarman/Shutterstock; **666, L,** Pearson Education, Inc.; **R,** Harvey Lloyd/Getty Images; **667, R,** The Image Bank/Getty Images; **L,** Image Bank/Getty Images; **668,** Phyllis Picardi/Photolibrary; **669,** David Rubinger/Time Life Pictures/Getty Images.

UNIT 6 CLOSER: Page 672, R, Shutterstock; **RB,** Vladimir Wrangel/Shutterstock; **673, R,** Tom Stoddart Archive/Getty Images.

UNIT 7: Pages 674–679, T, Bkgrnd sky, Image Source/Getty Images; **675, L,** Pearson Education, Inc.; **Bkgrnd,** Michele Falzone/Photolibrary; **R,** Pearson Education, Inc.; **676, T,** PCL/Alamy; **B,** Jerry Kobalenko/Getty Images; **677, T,** Marco Simoni/JupiterImages; **B,** Frans Lemmens/Alamy; **678, T,** Eric Feferberg/AFP/Getty Images; **LB,** Am Panthaky/AFP/Getty Images; **RB,** Dennis Meyer/Photolibrary; **679, LT,** Pearson Education, Inc.; **RT,** Pearson Education, Inc.

CHAPTER 19: Pages 681–683, All, Pearson Education, Inc.; **684,** dbimages/Alamy; **686, LM,** Wolfgang Kaehler/Corbis; **L,** Sylvia Cordaiy Photo Library Ltd/Alamy; **RM,** Christopher and Sally Gable/Dorling Kindersley; **R,** Robert Harding Picture Library Ltd/Alamy; **689,** Jeremy Nicholl/Alamy; **690,** Sakinform/Newscom; **692, B,** Michele Falzone/JAI/Corbis; **T,** De Agostini Editore Picture Library/Getty Images; **693, L,** Jamie Marshall/Dorling Kindersley; **R,** Ron Yue/Alamy; **694,** Igor Kovalenko/AP Images; **695,** National Portrait Gallery, Smithsonian Institution/Art Resource, NY; **696,** Janet Wishnetsky/Corbis; **697, R,** Pearson Education, Inc.; **L,** Brooks Kraft/Corbis; **698,** Mangasaryan/Patker/DasFotoarchiv/Peter Arnold; **699, LT,** Courtesy of USGS; **RT,** Jeff Schmaltz MODIS Land Rapid Response Team, NASA GSFC; **RB,** Shamil Zhumatov/Reuters; **LB,** David Turnley/Corbis; **700,** Tim Brakemeier/dpa/Corbis; **701, T,** The Embassy of the Kyrgyz Republic to the United States and Canada; **B,** Shakh Aivazov/AP Images.

CHAPTER 20: Pages 705–707, All, Pearson Education, Inc.; **708, Bkgrnd,** Michele Falzone/Alamy; **B,** Theo Allofs/Corbis; **710, M,** Studio Carlo Dani/Animals Animals/Earth Scenes; **B,** Jon Arnold Images Ltd/Alamy; **RT,** CuboImages srl/Alamy; **LT,** WorldFoto/Alamy; **711, LT,** Petr Svarc/Alamy; **RB,** Raimund Franken/Peter Arnold; **RT,** Juli Etchart/Peter Arnold; **LB,** Shaul Schwarz/Corbis; **712,** Robb Kendrick/Aurora Photos; **716, T,** Burstein Collection/Corbis; **B,** Robert Harding World Imagery/Corbis; **717,** Frédéric Soltan/Sygma/Corbis; **719,** V1/Alamy; **720, L,** Erich Lessing/Art Resource, NY; **M,** Jim Zuckerman/Corbis; **R,** Victoria & Albert Museum, London/Art Resource, NY; **721,** Bettmann/Corbis; **722,** AP Photo/Roshan Mughal; **723,** Alain DeJean/Sygma/Corbis; **724,** Reuters/Corbis; **R,** PhotosIndia.com LLC/Alamy; **725,** Monopole-Pathé/Photofest; **726,** James Strachan/Robert Harding World Imagery/Corbis; **727,** Kapoor Baldev/Sygma/Corbis; **728, R,** Desmon Boylan/Reuters/Corbis; **L,** Harish Tyagi/epa/Corbis; **731,** S. Forster/Alamy.

UNIT 7 CLOSER: Page 734, LB, Jupiter Unlimited; **RB,** Shutterstock; **734–735, Bkgrnd,** Shutterstock; **735, T,** Miodrag Gajic/Shutterstock.

UNIT 8: Pages 736–741, T, Bkgrnd sky, Image Source/Getty Images; **737, Bkgrnd,** Michele Falzone/JAI/Corbis; **LT,** Pearson Education, Inc.; **TM,** Pearson Education, Inc.; **RT,** Pearson Education, Inc.; **738, T,** China Tourism Press/Getty Images; **B,** Diehm/Getty Images; **739, T,** Robert Harding Picture Library Ltd/Alamy; **B,** Kazuyoshi Nomachi/Corbis; **740, L,** Ken Straiton/Corbis; **R,** Planetary Visions Limited; **741, All,** Pearson Education, Inc.

Acknowledgments (continued)

CHAPTER 21: Pages 743–745, All, Pearson Education, Inc.; **746, Bkgrnd,** PanStock RF/Newscom; **B,** Angelo Cavalli/Getty Images; **748, B,** Panorama Media (Beijing) Ltd./Alamy; **RM,** Nigel Hicks/Alamy; **LM,** Hiroji Kubota/Magnum; **LT,** Robert Harding Picture Library Ltd/Alamy; **RT,** Liu Liqun/Corbis; **M,** Kazuyoshi Nomachi/Corbis; **750, T,** Robin Moyer/Onasia.com; **B,** Tim Graham/Getty Images; **751,** Bruno Morandi/Robert Harding World Imagery/Getty Images; **752, R,** Picture Finders Ltd./eStock Photo; **M,** John Slater/Corbis; **L,** Craig Lovell/Corbis; **753,** Gordon Wiltsie/National Geographic Stock; **754, L,** O. Louis Mazzatenta/National Geographic Stock; **754–755,** Peter Gridley/Getty Images; **756, R,** Alan Hills/The British Museum/Dorling Kindersley; **M,** Danny Lehman/Corbis; **L,** Linda Whitwam/Dorling Kindersley; **757,** Bettmann/Corbis; **758, L,** Bettman/Corbis; **R,** Mark Leong/Redux Pictures; **760, L,** Peter Charlesworth/Onasia.com; **R,** AP Photo/Jeff Widener; **762,** Simon Kwong/Reuters/Corbis; **763, R,** Elizabeth Dalziel/AP Images; **M,** David Hartung/Onasia.com; **L,** Gao feng-Imaginechina/AP Images; **764,** Yin Hai/epa/Corbis; **766, R,** Bob Sacha/Corbis; **L,** Keren Su/Corbis; **767,** Pearson Education, Inc.

CHAPTER 22: Pages 771–773, All, Pearson Education, Inc.; **774, Bkgrnd,** Jon Arnold Images Ltd/Alamy; **B,** Kazuko Kimizuka/Getty Images; **776, M,** Robert Harding Picture Library Ltd/Alamy; **R,** TongRo Image Stock/Alamy; **L,** Radius Images/JupiterImages; **777, L,** AP Photo/Yonhap, Yu Hyung-je; **780, L,** Daisuke Akita/amanaimages/Corbis; **M,** Pearson Education, Inc.; **R,** Chad Ehlers/Alamy; **781,** Stringer/AFP/Getty Images; **782,** dbimages/Alamy; **783, LT,** *Portrait of Izumi Tadahira (d. 1189) with a poem,* from "Famous Generals of Japan," (about 1858), Yoshitora, color wood block print. School of Oriental and African Studies Library, University of London/The Bridgeman Art Library; **RT,** Stapleton Collection/Corbis; **RB,** Geoff Dann/Courtesy of the Wallace Collection, London/Dorling Kindersley; **LB,** The Metropolitan Museum of Art/Art Resource, NY; **784,** Asian Art & Archaeology/Corbis; **785,** Museum of Flight/Corbis; **786,** Gary Knight/VII/AP Images; **788,** ImageGap/Alamy; **789,** AP Photo/Matt Dunham; **790, L,** Paul Gadd/Corbis; **R,** Paul Souders/Corbis; **791, R,** AFP/Getty Images; **L,** AP Photo/Korea News Service; **792,** Peter Turnley/Corbis; **793,** Issei Kato/Reuters/Corbis; **794, LB,** Laurence Mouton/PhotoLibrary; **LT,** Yoshikazu Tsuno/AFP/Getty Images; **RB,** Courtesy of Warner Bros/Bureau L.A. Collection/Corbis; **RT,** Photos 12/Alamy.

CHAPTER 23: Pages 799–801, All, Pearson Education, Inc.; **802, B,** PCL/Alamy; **Bkgrnd,** Reuters/Corbis; **804, R,** © Frans Lanting/Corbis; **L,** Ingo Jezierski/Corbis; **M,** Thierry Falise/OnAsia; **807,** Peter Horree/Alamy; **808,** Mickael David/age Fotostock; **810,** David Halbakken/Alamy; **812, R,** Roger Viollet/Getty Images; **L,** Eightfish/Alamy; **814,** International Photobank/Alamy; **815, Bkgrnd,** Jon Arnold Images Ltd/Alamy; **R,** Free Agents Limited/Corbis; **L,** Michael Freeman/Corbis; **816,** Chad Ehlers/Photolibrary; **817, Bkgrnd,** AP Photo/Jonathan Head; **Inset,** Viviane Moos/Corbis; **818, L,** Paula Bronstein/Getty Images; **R,** Travelpix Ltd/Getty Images.

UNIT 8 CLOSER: Pages 822–823, All, Shutterstock.

UNIT 9: Pages 824–829, T, Bkgrnd sky, Image Source/Getty Images; **825, M,** Pearson Education, Inc.; **Bkgrnd,** Peter Bush/Dorling Kindersley; **826, R,** Ross Armstrong/Alamy; **L,** Martin Horsky/Shutterstock; **827, T,** Chad Ehlers/Getty Images; **B,** Ian Cumming/Getty Images; **828, RT,** Stephen Alvarez/Getty Images; **LB,** David Messent/Photolibrary; **RB,** Paul Nevin/Photolibrary; **LT,** Ted Mead/Photolibrary; **829,** Pearson Education, Inc.

CHAPTER 24: Pages 830–833, All, Pearson Education, Inc.; **834, Inset,** Rob Howard/Corbis; **Bkgrnd,** Craig Tuttle/Corbis; **836,** George Steinmetz/Corbis; **838, L,** Liv Falvey/Shutterstock; **R,** Tap10/Shutterstock; **Bkgrnd,** Thomas Schmitt/Getty Images; **M,** Dave Watts/naturepl.com; **839, L,** David Messent/Photolibrary; **R,** Peter Wey/Shutterstock; **M,** Ralph Loesche/Shutterstock; **840,** Craig Mayhew (GSFC/NASA) and Robert Simmon (GSFC/NASA); **841,** George Steinmetz/Corbis; **842,** Alexander Turnbull Library, Wellington, N.Z. Ref. G-516; **844, L,** *Portrait of Captain Cook,* c. 1800 (copy of portrait in the National Maritime Museum, Greenwich, England), after Sir Nathaniel Dance-Holland. National Library of Australia, Canberra, Australia/The Bridgeman Art Library; Bkgrnd, Erich Lessing/Art Resource, NY; **Bkgrnd,** Erich Lessing/Art Resource, NY; **R,** *The Harbour at Anamooka* (about 1820s–1830s), plate 82 from *Le Costume Ancien et Moderne,* by Jules Ferrario. Color lithograph. Private Collection/The Stapleton Collection/The Bridgeman Art Library International; **845, L,** Cannon Collection/Australian Picture Library/Corbis; **Bkgrnd,** Lawrence Manning/Corbis; **R,** Mark Baker/AP Photo; **846,** Barry Lewis/Corbis; **847, R,** Pearson Education, Inc.; **LM,** Bob Krist/Corbis; **RM,** James Davis Photography/Alamy; **L,** Penny Tweedie/Corbis; **848, LT,** Rob Griffith/epa/Corbis; **RB,** AP Photo/Palani Mohan/SMH; **LB,** Jonathan Marks/Corbis; **849,** Bruce Martin/Alamy; **850, RB,** Ashley Cooper/Corbis; **LB,** Richard Vogel/AP Photo; **T,** Seth Resnick/Science Faction/Corbis; **M,** Ashley Cooper/Corbis; **852,** Sea World of California/Corbis; **854, RT,** Courtesy: Anthony Gibson/National Science Foundation; **LB,** Galen Rowell/Corbis; **LT,** Bettmann/Corbis; **RB,** Galen Rowell/Corbis; **855,** NASA.

UNIT 9 CLOSER: Page 858, L, R McKown/Shutterstock; **858–859, Bkgrnd,** Shutterstock; **B,** Shutterstock.

Text Acknowledgments

Grateful acknowledgment is made to the following for copyrighted material:

Page 404 Address at the Institute of Contemporary Arts, London; quoted in *The Independent,* March 22, 1990.

Page 750 Excerpt from "Migrant Couple Struggles to Earn in New China" from NPR, May 20, 2008. Copyright © NPR.

Page 769 Excerpt from "Voices from Modern China: Fu Ansi, Migrant Worker" from bbc.com. Copyright © BBC.

Note: Every effort has been made to locate the copyright owner of material reproduced in this publication. Omissions brought to our attention will be corrected in subsequent editions.